This book provides an alternate foundation for the measurement of the production of nations, and applies it to the U.S. economy for the postwar period. The patterns that result are significantly different from those derived within conventional systems of national accounts.

Conventional national accounts seriously distort basic economic aggregates because they classify military, bureaucratic, and financial activities as creation of new wealth. In fact, these authors argue, such aggregates should be classified as forms of social consumption which, like personal consumption, actually use up social wealth in the performance of their functions.

The difference between the two approaches has an impact not only on basic aggregate economic measures, but also on the very understanding of the observed patterns of growth and stagnation. In a world of burgeoning militaries, bureaucracies, and sales forces, such matters can assume great significance at the levels of both theory and policy.

MEASURING THE WEALTH OF NATIONS

# Measuring the wealth of nations
## The political economy of national accounts

ANWAR M. SHAIKH
*New School for Social Research*

E. AHMET TONAK
*Simon's Rock College of Bard*

CAMBRIDGE
UNIVERSITY PRESS

Published by the Press Syndicate of the University of Cambridge
The Pitt Building, Trumpington Street, Cambridge CB2 1RP
40 West 20th Street, New York, NY 10011-4211, USA
10 Stamford Road, Oakleigh, Melbourne 3166, Australia

© Cambridge University Press 1994

First published 1994

Printed in the United States of America

*Library of Congress Cataloging-in-Publication Data*
Shaikh, Anwar.
Measuring the wealth of nations : the political economy of
national accounts / Anwar M. Shaikh, E. Ahmet Tonak.
p.   cm.
Includes bibliographical references and index.
ISBN 0-521-41424-5
1. National income – Accounting.   2. Gross national product.
3. National income – United States – Accounting.   4. Gross national
product – United States.   5. Wealth – United States.   I. Tonak,
Ertuğrul Ahmet.   II. Title.
HB141.5.S52     1994
339.3'1 – dc20                                                93-37399
                                                                  CIP

A catalog record for this book is available from the British Library.

ISBN 0-521-41424-5 hardback

# CONTENTS

v

# FIGURES

TABLES

# PREFACE

This book has been a long time in the making. The interest in providing an empirical framework that would correspond to Marxian categories dates back to 1972–73, when Anwar Shaikh first discovered Shane Mage's pathbreaking work and developed an alternate schema and an alternate set of estimates based on Mage's own data.

In 1974 Shaikh came across Edward Wolff's working paper on input–output-based estimates of the rate of surplus value in Puerto Rico. This added a new dimension to the problem. Mage's work emphasized the significance of the distinction between productive and unproductive labor, but it was restricted to only the value-added side of national income accounts. On the other hand, whereas Wolff's work was located within the more comprehensive double-entry framework of input–output accounts, it did not distinguish between productive and unproductive labor. This led Shaikh to attempt to develop a comprehensive framework for Marxian categories which made both distinctions simultaneously.

The procedure that emerged in 1975 was essentially the same one used in this book: a mapping between Marxian and input–output categories illustrated by means of a continuing numerical example in which both total price (the sum of purchasers' prices) and the magnitudes of the aggregate value flows (total value and its basic components) were held constant, while the associated money forms became ever more complex as more concrete factors were considered. This allowed one to verify, at each stage of the argument, that the overall mapping was correct.

For a short time in the mid-1970s Wolff and Shaikh joined forces, but their paths soon diverged. By 1978 Shaikh had produced a final draft of a paper that systematically built up a mapping between Marxian and national income account categories, provided measures of the rate of surplus value in the United States, and made some preliminary estimates (for three sample years) of the size and direction of the net transfer between workers and the state (i.e., of the balance between taxes paid by workers and the social expenditures directed toward them). This paper circulated widely, but was never published (although an extended and somewhat different version appeared in Shaikh 1980b). Instead, Shaikh turned his attention to broadening the framework to encompass input–output accounts and data.

In the late 1970s, Ahmet Tonak also became interested in the estimation of Marxian categories. Using the schema of Shaikh's unpublished paper, he produced one of the first systematic estimates of the rate of surplus value in Turkey, published (in Turkish) in 1979. During the early 1980s, Tonak focused on the United States, extending the sample estimates of the net tax on workers to the whole postwar period, providing his own estimates of variable capital and surplus value, and tracing out the general impact of the net tax on the rate of surplus value. This work became his Ph.D. dissertation in 1984, which was the basis for subsequent extensions by Tonak (1987) and Shaikh and Tonak (1987).

During the early 1980s, our attempts to utilize input–output data were greatly hampered by a lack of computer facilities. Many people were instrumental in helping to overcome these and other related barriers. Michel Juillard, who was at the time working on recasting U.S. input–output and national income account data into a Marxian departmental schema, was of invaluable theoretical and empirical help. So too was Katherine Kazanas, whose work focused on the impact of the distinction between production and nonproduction labor for the measurement of productivity. Julie Graham and Don Shakow provided similarly crucial support in the manipulation of the input–output tables. Ernest Mandel and Dimitri Papadimitriou helped secure funding at various points. With the help of Eduardo Ochoa, Paul Cooney, and Michel Juillard, Ara Khanjian created an input–output database and used the basic framework to measure and compare money and labor value flows in the United States (Khanjian 1989). All provided great moral and intellectual support throughout.

By the mid-1980s, the two of us had begun working together on turning this project into the present book. A first draft was produced in 1985, thanks to a grant provided through the generous support of the Hamburg Institute for Social Studies, and the basic results were made available in the same year at a conference supported by Bard College. A second, substantially revised draft was produced in 1989, which was once again extended and revised in 1992. During much of this period, Dimitri Papadimitriou of Bard College and Bernard Rodgers of Simon's Rock College of Bard provided moral and material assistance for our efforts. We owe them a special debt.

From the mid- to late 1970s onward, the various stages of this project have regularly appeared in Shaikh's lectures on advanced political economy. Many graduate students who have been (willingly and unwillingly) exposed to this material over the years have provided both support and criticism which has helped shape the final result.

In addition to those mentioned previously, we note our debts to Peter Brooks, Etelberto Ortiz, Hector Figueroa, Rebecca Kalmans, and Nezih Güner. Korkut Boratav, Nail Satlıgan, and Sungur Savran provided critical feedback on a version of the manuscript, as did an anonymous referee for this press. Hakan Arslan, Matt Noyes, and Greg Bongen were vital to the production of the many charts which adorn this book. We also thank Russell Miller for his contribution to the construction of the index. Matt Darnell provided superb editorial assistance in rendering the final product.

Most of all, we wish to express our gratitude to our families for their support and forbearance during this long and difficult task. It is to Fadime and Ali, and to Diana, Kirsten and Lia, that we owe the greatest debt.

*A.M.S.*
*E.A.T.*

# 1

# Introduction

## 1.1 Approaches to the measurement of national product

This book aims to provide an alternate foundation for the measurement of the production of nations. The framework developed here is applied to the U.S. economy for the postwar period. The patterns that result are significantly different from those derived within conventional systems of national accounts.

National accounts give systematic empirical form to the structure, patterns, and performance of an economy (Young and Tice 1985). In the modern world, they provide the objective basis for judging the level and progress of the wealth of nations and for identifying the causes of success and failure.

Conventional systems of national accounts include the United Nations System of National Accounts, the United States National Income and Product Accounts, and various forms of input–output accounts. It is our contention that these types of accounts seriously distort the levels and trends of the national product, the surplus product, productivity, and other major aggregate economic variables. Because measurement and analysis are inextricably intertwined, our understanding of intertemporal and international economic development is correspondingly affected.

Criticisms of official national accounts are not new. Debates about their purpose and structure have gone on from the very start (Eisner 1988, p. 1611). In recent times, there has been a renewed flurry of questions about their adequacy. Such criticisms come from a variety of quarters, ranging from official agencies such as the United Nations to a variety of prestigious economists. In Section 2 we address the issues involved.

The measurement of national product lies at the core of all systems of national accounts (Carson and Honsa 1990, pp. 28–9). In this regard, it is

1

interesting to note that most critics of official accounts accept the basic definitions of production embodied in the official accounts, and seek instead to extend and improve their coverage. Issues of coverage are evidently important. But the definition of production is clearly prior, and this is precisely where we differ from orthodox economists. Thus, while our own criticism is part of the general chorus, it is quite different in character from most of the others, and has different implications.

The basic problem arises from the fact that conventional accounts classify many activities as "production," when in fact they should be classified as forms of social consumption. For example, the military, the police, and private guards protect property and social structure. Civil servants and lawyers administer rules and laws. Traders in commodities and paper circulate wealth or titles to it. It is our contention that such activities are actually forms of social consumption, not production.

Consider the basic difference between production and consumption. Production activity uses up wealth to create new wealth (i.e., to achieve a production outcome). Personal consumption uses up wealth to maintain and reproduce the individual (a nonproduction outcome). In like manner, military, police, administrative, and trading activities use up wealth in the pursuit of protection, distribution, and administration (also nonproduction outcomes). The issue is not one of necessity, because all these activities are necessary, in some form or the other, for social reproduction (Beckerman 1968, pp. 27–8). Rather, the issue concerns the nature of the outcome; protection, distribution, and administration are really forms of social consumption, not production.

At the heart of this discussion is a distinction between *outcome* and *output*. Not all outcomes are outputs. This is evidently the case with personal consumption, whose outcome is the maintenance of the individual, not the production of new wealth. It is our contention that the same reasoning applies to the other social activities listed.

It should be emphasized that the distinction being made is between production and nonproduction activities, *not* between goods and services. We shall see that a substantial portion of service activities (transportation, lodging, entertainment, repairs, etc.) will be classified under production, whereas others (wholesale/retail, financial services, legal services, advertising, military, civil service, etc.) will be classified as nonproduction activities. The real distinction is between outcomes and output. All activity results in outcomes. Some outcomes are also outputs, directly adding to social wealth. But others preserve or circulate this wealth, or help maintain and administer the social structure in which it is embedded. One way to formalize these distinctions is to imagine a list (a vector) of properties associated with every commodity. Some of these characteristics, to use

Lancaster's (1968, pp. 113–18) terminology, would be relevant to the commodity as an object of social use, while others would be relevant to it as an object of ownership. Production would enhance one set, distribution another, and so forth. Needless to say, this extension of Lancaster's "characteristics" approach is different from the conventional neoclassical one.

Our general approach is rooted in the classical tradition, parts of which can be found in Smith, Ricardo, Malthus, Mill, Marx, Sismondi, Baudrillart, and Chalmers, among others (Studenski 1958, p. 20). Although its presentation was incomplete and occasionally inconsistent, it was nonetheless part of "the mainstream of economic thought for almost a century" (Kendrick 1968, p. 20). Only when neoclassical economics rose to the fore was the classical distinction between production and nonproduction activities displaced by the notion that *all* socially necessary activities, other than personal consumption, resulted in a product (Bach 1966, p. 45). With this change, lawyers, private guards, and traders of all sorts came to be counted as adding to national wealth. So too did armies, police, and civil servants.

In his monumental work on the history of national accounts, Studenski has labeled the above transition as the switch from the "restricted production" definition of the classicals to the "comprehensive production" definition of the neoclassicals (Studenski 1958, p. 12).[1] But from our point of view, this change is really a retreat from the "comprehensive consumption" approach of the classicals (who treat many activities as forms of social consumption, not production) to the "restricted consumption" definitions of the neoclassicals (who restrict the definition of social consumption to personal consumption alone). Under the neoclassical definition, an activity is considered a production activity if it is deemed socially necessary. This in turn rests on the conclusion that (at least some) people would be willing to pay for it directly (Bach 1966, p. 45). It follows that, within neoclassical economics, *all potentially marketable activities are considered to be production activities.*[2] The ideological convenience of a

---

[1]  Studenski's treatment of the classical and Marxian traditions is quite superficial. He is so attached to the neoclassical "utility based" concepts of production that he is unable to see the fundamental issue at stake in the distinction between production and nonproduction activities: namely, the difference between total production and total (private and social) consumption (Studenski 1958, pp. 18–22, 24–5).

[2]  According to the Bureau of Economic Analysis (BEA), "the basic criterion used for distinguishing an activity as economic production is whether it is reflected in the sales and purchase transactions of a market economy" (cited in Eisner 1988, p. 1612). Eisner (pp. 1616–17) proposes to extend this definition of production to encompass all activities that contribute to economic welfare. Of course, within

definition of production which treats all market activities as productive is obvious.

In spite of its other breaks with neoclassical theory, Keynesian economics did little to change the neoclassical conventions. As a result they are now embodied in all official national accounts of the Western world (although not without challenge, as we shall see).[3]

Although the neoclassical concept of production has dominated the official accounts of the Western world in the twentieth century, until recently quite another concept ruled in (what used to be called) the socialist world: that of the National Material Product. At the heart of this latter approach is the idea that production consists of physical goods alone. From this point of view, the value of the total product consists of what is essentially the final cost of the total physical product: that is, the price charged by the producer plus the costs of repair, transportation, and distribution (UN 1991, p. xxii). The originators of this concept claim to derive it from Marx, but this physicalist notion of the total product is actually rooted in Smith. It is quite explicitly rejected by Marx, as even Studenski concedes (Studenski 1958, p. 22).

The undifferentiated production categories of the neoclassicals and the overly restricted production concept of the modern physicalists form the two poles of official accounting systems (UN 1990, p. vi). But between this Scylla and Charybdis lies another path, one which it is our purpose to develop and apply.

Independent from theoretical and academic discourse is the language and understanding of practical experience. In this regard, it is quite striking that even though the very concept of nonproduction market activities has been abolished from the theoretical lexicon of orthodox economics, the notion continues to thrive in practical discourse. The Prime Minister of Japan was recently quoted as arguing that American resources were "squandered" on financial and trading activities in the 1980s (Sanger 1992). *Fortune* magazine reports that "representatives of the manufacturing sector indict the legal and financial sectors as highly *unproductive*" (Farnham 1989, pp. 16, 65; cited by Chernomas 1991, p. 1; emphasis added). Business economists Summers and Summers (1989, p. 270) report that

> neoclassical economics, the fundamental test of this status is that someone would be willing to pay for the activity – i.e., that the activity is marketable (Bach 1966, p. 45). Hence only those nonmarket activities that are judged to fail this potential marketability test, such as perhaps some portion of government activity, could be deemed unnecessary and hence by definition unproductive. Official accounts do not make such distinctions.

> [3] Extended accounts that fall within the orthodox economics tradition are discussed in Section 1.3. Those falling within the tradition of Marxian economics are discussed in Chapter 6.

"the most frequent complaint about current trends in financial markets is that so much talented human capital is devoted to trading paper assets *rather than to actually creating wealth*" (cited in Chernomas 1991, p. 2; emphasis added).

In like vein, Thurow (1980, p. 88) has argued that while "security guards protect old goods, [they] *do not produce new goods since they add nothing to output*" (emphasis added), and that military activities are "a form of public consumption" which "use up a lot of human and economic resources" (Thurow 1992, p. 20). The *New York Times* has expressed the same sentiment, noting that "[s]ecurity people – or guard labor, as some economists call them – are proliferating . . . [in] a nation trying to protect itself from crime and violence." It goes on to quote Harvard University economist Richard Freeman to the effect that if "'you go to a sneaker outlet in a not-so-poor neighborhood in Boston, there will be three private guards. . . . We are employing many people who *are essentially not producing anything*'" (Uchitelle 1989, emphasis added).

The growth of the military and the bureaucracy is endemic in the postwar world, in developed and developing countries alike. Within many parts of the capitalist world in the 1970s and 1980s, the same was true of financial and trading activities. At present in the American economy, guard labor is one of the most rapidly growing forms of employment. Within an orthodox national accounts framework, all such activities are viewed as resulting in additional output. But within a classical framework, because these same activities are viewed as forms of social consumption, their relative growth is seen as serving to absorb an increased portion of the national product and hence lower the share available for investment and accumulation. The difference between the two approaches has an impact not only on the measures of national production, but also on the very understanding of the observed patterns of growth and stagnation. In a world full of burgeoning militaries, bureaucracies, and sales forces, such matters can assume great significance at the most practical level.

As noted previously, conventional national accounts have been criticized from a variety of viewpoints in recent years. We share many of the expressed concerns about the desirability of extending and improving the coverage of such accounts. But our primary concern is with the very definition of production itself, since this lies at the heart of all systems of accounts. In the next two sections, we will briefly trace the history of national accounts and outline the basic structure of various alternative systems of accounts currently under discussion. Section 4 will summarize the essential differences between our approach and those which fall within the tradition of orthodox economics.

## 1.2 Official national accounts

Modern systems of national accounts are actually a set of inter-related accounts that attempt to cover different aspects of the functionings of market economies. The most fundamental of these are the production accounts (national-income-and-product and input–output accounts), which attempt to measure the creation and use of new national wealth. These in turn may be supplemented by ones that track financial flows in the economy (capital and flow-of-funds accounts) or ones that link production and financial flows to the corresponding stocks (national balance sheets).

At the heart of any set of national accounts lies some common definition of production activities. To construct production accounts, one must first distinguish between production and nonproduction activities, and hence between their corresponding actual or imputed transaction flows.[4] All transactions not associated with production activities are excluded from the measure of national product. Because orthodox economics defines production activities very broadly, its definition of nonproduction activities is correspondingly narrow – limited to transfer payments (such as social security, unemployment payments, etc.) and any nonmarket activities deemed to be socially unnecessary.

Given the actual and imputed transactions that are deemed to correspond to some definition of production activities, the next step is to choose a particular measure of production. At the most general level is the *total product,* which is the sum of all output produced in a given year. This is the basic measure used in input–output accounts. It can in turn be decomposed into two elementary components: the portion which is the equivalent of the inputs used (materials and capital depreciation) in producing the total product; and the remainder, which is the *net product.* It is this latter component which is the focus of national-income-and-product accounts.

Since for every receipt there corresponds a payment by someone, there are two sets of actual or imputed money flows associated with any given measure of national product: production-related receipts of the producers, which are used to measure the money value of output; and associated (nontransfer) payments representing purchases of the product by its various users.[5] These are the basic elements of a double-entry production

---

[4] Because national accounts are built around transactions, it is necessary to impute a money value transaction to any production activity (e.g., production in the home or payments in kind) which is not mediated by actual money flows (Beckerman 1968, p. 9).

[5] Since the object is to measure production, not merely sales, the money revenues of a unit are supplemented by adding to it the excess of production over sales

account. Further detail can then be added by subdividing the output side into different types of producing sectors and by subdividing the use side into different types of users. Individual accounts can then be constructed for business, household, government, and foreign sectors.

Conventional production accounts come in two basic forms: *national-income-and-product* (NIP) accounts and *input–output* (IO) accounts. Since the former are only concerned with the final use of the product,[6] they focus solely on the net product.[7] This is split into personal consumption, government purchases, private investment, and net exports on the use side; and wages, profits, and taxes on the revenue side. Input–output accounts go one step further, in that they keep track of the whole product.[8] By including the portions of the product used as inputs by various industries, they are able to illuminate the structure of interindustrial production relations in addition to capturing the main aggregates of NIP accounts. It is because of their greater coverage that we use them as our theoretical foil in the development of our own accounting framework.

Both NIP and IO accounts focus solely on production-related flows. As such, they leave out two important aspects of the overall economic picture: transactions that are not directly related to production; and stocks of real and financial wealth.

*Financial accounts* attempt to correct for the first limitation by expanding the coverage of financial flows beyond those directly tied to production.

(this item can be negative, of course). To balance the accounts, the same amount is treated as a (positive or negative) payment by the unit to itself, for "unintended inventory investment." This is typically merged into gross investment expenditures.

[6] Because the goal of NIP accounts is to measure the *net* product, they must exclude the portion of total product which is the equivalent of inputs used up in the year's production. To do otherwise would be double counting. But if the goal is to measure the total product, as is the case with input–output accounts, then obviously it would be undercounting to ignore input use. There is nothing sacrosanct about the net product as a measure.

[7] The proper measure of net product within conventional accounts is net national product (NNP). But since depreciation measures are frequently unreliable, production accounts commonly leave depreciation (capital consumption) in the measure of net product (in value added on the revenue side, and in investment on the use side). This gross-of-depreciation measure of net product is called gross national product (GNP) if it refers to the net production of the nationals of a country (including those who live abroad), and is called gross domestic product (GDP) if it refers to net production within a nation.

[8] It is useful to note that the total product is a more general and useful measure than the net product. Two nations with the same net product per unit labor can have different input requirements. Focusing on the net product alone would then be quite misleading when considering national productivity, employment and resource use, etc.

Capital finance accounts such as those associated with the United Nations System of National Accounts (described hereunder) focus on the sources and uses of funds for capital transactions (transactions which affect stocks of financial and real assets). Flow-of-funds (FOF) accounts, which are associated with the U.S. NIP accounts, track the sources and uses of funds for both capital transactions and current transactions (production-related flows as well as transfer payments) (Ruggles 1987, p. 380). They show the financial interrelationships among economic units, and can be viewed "as a direct extension of [NIP accounts] . . . into the financial markets" (Ruggles and Ruggles 1982, p. 10).

*National balance sheets* address the second limitation of production accounts by linking flows to changes in stocks.[9] This allows one to build a comprehensive picture of national wealth encompassing nonreproducible assets (land, natural resources), reproducible assets (business fixed capital and inventory stocks, stocks of consumer durables, stocks of monetary metals), and net external claims on foreign tangible and financial assets (Goldsmith 1968, p. 52).

To be fully useful, the production, financial, and balance sheet accounts should be integrated into one another. Although this has not yet been done for official U.S. accounts, it has been more or less accomplished in the United Nations System of National Accounts (UN/SNA). For this reason, and for the sake of comparability with other nations (almost all of whom use the UN/SNA), the United States is expected to change over to the UN/SNA by the mid-1990s (Carson and Honsa 1990, p. 20).

The UN/SNA are more comprehensive than the U.S. accounts, because they constitute an integrated system that uses consistent definitions and classifications to link together NIP and IO national production accounts, financial accounts, and balance sheets. There are also some notable differences between the classification systems of the two sets of accounts. The UN/SNA focuses on gross domestic product (GDP), not gross national product (GNP). GDP measures net production within a nation while GNP measures net production by nationals of a country (including those who live abroad), and the differences can be significant for some countries. The UN/SNA also distinguishes between government consumption and investment (the latter being the change in nonmilitary government equipment and structures). Under discussion are issues concerning the treatment of research-and-development expenditures and of natural resources and the environment (see the remarks on Eisner and Repetto in Section 1.3). Revisions of the UN/SNA are currently under way, but substantial changes are not expected (Carson and Honsa 1990, pp. 21–30).

---

[9] For instance, positive net investment adds to the stock of fixed capital, and positive household savings adds to the stock of household financial assets.

### 1.3 Extended national accounts for the United States

Although the various official U.S. accounts are not integrated, much work has been done by individual researchers on linking production flows with balance-sheet stocks, and on expanding the coverage of production accounts themselves to encompass both nonmarket and nonlegal activities. In addition, there has been considerable discussion of a more adequate treatment of natural resources and environmental issues.

Ruggles and Ruggles (1982, pp. 1, 17) attempt to extend U.S. NIP accounts by improving their treatment of various individual items and by linking stocks and flows. In the former domain, they split both household and government expenditures into current and capital components (capital expenditures being defined as the net acquisition of durable equipment and structures), list imputed values in separate accounts, and attempt to allocate transactions in a more accurate way (e.g., owner-occupied housing expenses are allocated to the household sector rather than to unincorporated business enterprises).[10] But their main concern is to integrate stock and flow accounts in such a way as to link up with already existing capital stock estimates of the Bureau of Economic Analysis (BEA), which are now broadened to include stocks of household and government durables, and the financial flow-of-funds accounts of the Federal Reserve Board. They end up with larger measures of NNP (net national product) and GNP, because they add in "net imputed income from consumer durables" (which increases both NNP and GNP) and imputed "depreciation allowances" on consumer and government durables (which increases GNP). They also obtain a much larger estimate of national savings and investment, because they count changes in the stocks of consumer and government durables as part of savings and investment. This is a common feature of all extended accounts, as we shall see. Denison (1982, pp. 60, 62–3) argues against such procedures, on the grounds that the resulting adjusted measures of GNP, NNP, and national savings are less meaningful than the conventional NIP measures.

There are several other sets of alternate accounts, the most important of which is from Eisner (1985, 1988). In an important article, Eisner (1988) surveys six proposed extensions of NIP accounts, including his own and that of Ruggles and Ruggles.

Eisner begins by noting how crucial it is to have adequate definitions of production, primary incomes, intermediate and final output, and investment and consumption. On the issue of production, he proposes extending the definition to cover nonmarket production (e.g. in households)

---

[10] Carson and Jaszi (1982, p. 58) note that Ruggles and Ruggles's definition of the household sector includes soldiers, prisoners, people in sanitariums, etc.

and illegal production (drugs, gambling, prostitution), pointing out that it would make international comparisons much more meaningful (Eisner 1988, pp. 1613-14). On the other hand, he rejects the notion that "leisure time" be counted as a production activity, even though most other extended accounts do add a very large imputation for the value of leisure time to their measures of national output. Finally, he points out (p. 1622) that since extensions of the production measure to nonmarket activities require corresponding imputations on the income side (as the two sides must balance), extended accounts tend to give a radically different picture of the distribution of income (real and imputed) between capital and labor, employed and unemployed, and so forth. For instance, in official GNP accounts for 1966, the share of labor income is 82.6% and of capital income 24.3%. In the extended accounts of Jorgenson and Fraumeni (1987), because of imputations for the "services" of household durable goods and for the value of household production and leisure time, the total (real and imputed) income of households is raised over fivefold! Thus in the Jorgenson-Fraumeni accounts the labor share appears as 93% and the property share as a mere 7% (Eisner 1988, p. 1672, table S.4).

On the question of investment, Eisner argues in favor of counting the net changes in consumer and government durables as part of aggregate investment (as do Ruggles and Ruggles). He notes that various researchers also include in investment one or more of the following: changes in the value of land; expenditures for the development and discovery of natural resources; research and development (R & D) expenditures; and expenditures on health, education, training, and information (human capital). As he shows, such adjustments cause enormous changes in the measure of gross investment and national product. Finally, if one accepts the Haig-Simon-Hicks definition of income as that which can be consumed without changing real wealth, then real income, savings, and investment must all include an adjustment for the net monetary revaluations in stocks. This can add a sharply fluctuating component to the measure of national product (Eisner 1988, pp. 1622-5).

From our point of view, one of the most intriguing aspects of Eisner's survey is his discussion of the treatment of police, fire protection, guard, and national defense activities. Recall that we classify all such activities as nonproduction activities. As such, we would exclude them from the total product and hence also from the net product. Eisner argues that they should be treated as intermediate inputs rather than final product, citing Kuznets to the effect that such activities constitute "the mere cost of maintaining the social fabric, a *precondition* for net product rather than the net product itself" (cited in Eisner 1988, p. 1617; see also Beckerman 1968, pp. 11-12, 23-4, 27-8). This means that they would be counted as production activities and would add to the total product, but would not enter into the net product. It is interesting to note that Mage (1963; p. 66) adopts a similar approach.[11]

We would also view these activities as costs of maintaining the social fabric. But we treat them as nonproduction activities instead of as intermediate inputs into production. How then would one decide between the two approaches? To begin with, we note that the normal definition of an input into production is something that enters directly into the production process, such as steel into the production of an automobile. In this sense, an activity such as national defense would surely not qualify as a production input.

The other possibility is to view national defense as an *indirect* input into the total product, on the grounds that it serves to maintain the social fabric. But to say that something is an indirect input is only to claim that it is a necessary part of the overall process of social reproduction: by serving to maintain the social fabric, national defense constitutes what Kuznets calls a "precondition" for other social activities. This does not imply, we would argue, that it is thereby an input into production. First of all, national defense is just as much a precondition for personal consumption as it is for production. To put it the other way, it is just as little an input into production as it is into personal consumption. Second, once we introduce the notion of preconditions, personal consumption is even more important than national defense as a precondition of production.[12] Is personal consumption then also to be treated as an intermediate input into production?[13] To answer in the affirmative would vitiate the very distinction between consumption and production. Conversely, if we are to maintain this distinction then we must be able to say that production and consumption have different (albeit necessary) outcomes, and that the outcome of consumption is not an output. In this same sense, the outcome of national defense is not an output either. This is why we argue that national defense, like personal consumption, is a nonproduction activity.[14] And since, like consumption, it uses up resources in pursuit of a nonproduction goal, we label it as a form of social consumption.

In his survey of conventional extended national accounts,[15] Eisner examines six alternative systems: those of Nordhaus and Tobin (NT), Zolotas

---

[11] Mage (1963, pp. 61–8) argues that nonproduction activities in general should be treated as part of intermediate input (constant capital in the sense of Marx).

[12] Indeed, production is a precondition for personal consumption and national defense.

[13] Eisner (1988, p. 1617) expresses uncertainty on just this issue when he asks "Is eating itself intermediate to the creation and maintenance of human capital?"

[14] It is worth noting that this debate is not new; Marx (1963, pp. 161, 172) remarks on exactly this point.

[15] Eisner makes no mention of the national and international Marxian literature that we survey in Chapter 6.

(Z), Jorgenson and Fraumeni (JF), Kendricks (K), Ruggles and Ruggles (R), and Eisner (E). The latter two have already been discussed in some detail. In what follows, we will focus on the major characteristics of these types of accounts.

In principle, orthodox economics defines production activities as all those that affect the welfare (welfare as utility) of individuals in a nation (Kendrick 1968, p. 24).[16] In practice, however, official accounts are built largely around market activities, supplemented by imputations for the "services" furnished by owner-occupied buildings, services furnished without payment by financial intermediaries, and some small imputations for farm products consumed on farms and food furnished to employees, et cetera (Eisner 1988, p. 1620).[17] Thus one of the central tasks of conventional extended accounts is to revise and expand the measure of production in a manner consistent with the underlying core of economic theory (p. 1616).

The differences among the various accounts arise solely from the specifics of this process. In particular, whereas most authors seek to measure production in terms of activities that contribute to economic welfare, a few "seek explicitly to measure" welfare itself (Eisner 1988, p. 1627, n. 15). Thus Nordhaus and Tobin, as well as Zolotas, reduce the measure of national product by their estimates of "regrettables and disamenities" (Eisner 1988, p. 1670, table 1).

Certain themes are common to almost all accounts. Most would add the imputed value of household activities and of illegal market production to their estimates of the national product, if good data were available (Eisner 1988, p. 1670, table 1).[18] Our own approach would be similar,

---

[16] Eisner (1988, p. 1617) states that "we are looking for all economic activity related to welfare." Tobin remarks that "we do have to admit that there are lots of problems in the utility criterion of welfare that we economists love so well" (cited in Eisner 1988, p. 1619, n. 8).

[17] Orthodox accounts treat owner-occupied housing as a source of utility-generating "services" whose value is estimated by imputing a rental value to such housing. In 1986, this (fictitious) imputed value is listed as $305 billion. In addition, in order to treat financial firms in exactly the same way as other "producers" (as opposed to admitting that they are nonproduction firms), it is necessary to create an imputed flow of "services furnished without payment" by them. This amounts to $71 billion in 1986. The implications and alternate treatments of such issues are discussed in Chapter 3.

[18] Ruggles and Ruggles (1982, p. 5) exclude "housewive's services and do-it-yourself activities" on the grounds of the difficulty of obtaining "accurate and valid measurements." Illegal activities suffer from this problem to an even greater extent. As Carson (1984, p. 33) notes, the relative size of the underground economy varies considerably across countries, and even within any one country. For the United States, for instance, the estimates range from a low of 4% of GNP to a high of 34%.

except that we would distinguish between production and nonproduction activities, and also between capitalist and noncapitalist activities – just as we do in the case of legal market activities (see Chapter 2).

A second common characteristic of extended accounts is that they strive to integrate the treatment of sectoral wealth stocks with corresponding production-flow accounts. However, in attempting to do this, conventional accounts adopt the business sector as their basic model. In business, purchases of plant and equipment are capital investments that yield returns (profits) in subsequent years. On the (false) premise that the salient characteristic of business fixed capital is its durability,[19] extended accounts treat stocks of consumer durables (houses, cars, shoes, clothing, equipment, and furnishings) and government durables (building and equipment) as household and government "capital," respectively (Eisner 1988, p. 1653). Of course, unlike business capital, there is no actual profit – indeed, no revenue at all – attached. It therefore becomes necessary to impute a stream of "services" to household and government durables, and add these imputed amounts to the measure of national product.[20] Official accounts already carry out such imputations for owner-occupied housing, in which private homeowners are treated as unincorporated businesses renting out their homes to themselves for fictitious sums of money (BEA 1980, p. 47). Most extended accounts follow a similar procedure for so-called intangible capital, cumulating health and education expenditures to derive a stock of "human capital" and cumulating business research and development to get a stock of business "intangible" capital (Eisner 1988, p. 1670, table S.1). As a corollary, it becomes necessary to shift all household and government expenditures on durables, health, and education from the category of current expenditures to a newly created category of capital "investment" expenditures.

As far as we are concerned, the conventional treatment conflates two distinct issues. On one hand, they are quite right to stress the importance of keeping track of the stocks of household and consumer wealth, and of integrating the formation of these stocks into corresponding flows of revenue. On the other hand, we would argue that it is wrong to treat mere durable goods as if they were equivalent to business capital, and even worse to impute fictitious profits to such goods. The capital stock of a business is part of a profit-making venture, and comprises not only

---

[19] The reduction of the concept of capital to a merely durable good obscures the difference between a capital good and a consumption good. It is also inadequate as a description of capital itself, since profit in no way depends on the durability of an investment (huge profits are routinely made on short-term financial capital).

[20] Gross imputed services of household and government durable goods are calculated as imputed depreciation on the stock of these goods, plus a gross imputed return on these same stocks (Eisner 1988, p. 1626).

durable items (plant, equipment, and durable financial assets) but also nondurable items (inventories of materials and work in progress as well as short-term financial assets). It is because money is tied up as capital – be it in the form of durable goods or short-term financial assets – that the possibility of profit arises. The substantial profits made in speculation and trade make it clear that the durability of the investment is a completely secondary matter.

The goods of a household, both durable and nondurable, are part of the consumption circuit; those of the government are part of social administration. To reduce business, household, and government stocks to mere durable goods is to negate the differences between capitalist enterprise, personal consumption, and social administration.[21] To impute fictitious gross profits to the latter two only compounds the problem. In a similar vein, while it is perfectly proper to assess the skill and knowledge of the population, and perhaps even to cumulate the total cost of acquiring these attributes, it is not appropriate to treat the resulting measure of imbedded cost as yet another stock of "capital."

Business R & D expenses and exploration costs are a different matter; they *are* a part of the circuit of capital. The question here is whether they should be reclassified as fixed investment expenditures (rather than current costs or circulating investment), and then cumulated to form some stock of intangible business capital. In this regard, it is useful to note that R & D and similar expenses are, after all, exploratory expenditures which may or may not bear fruit. By treating them as current costs, businesses already take account of the expense when it is incurred. And if they do bear fruit at some time in the future, the resulting capital investment is counted when it is made, as are any associated profits if they in turn appear. An artificially constructed stock of intangible R & D capital is therefore redundant.

Eisner lists several other major modifications specific to particular authors. A significant number (NT, Z, JF, K) expand their measures of total output by a large amount representing the estimated output of leisure time; since leisure contributes to utility, it is appropriate within neoclassical economics to view it as a production activity (Eisner 1988, p. 1626).[22]

21  It is interesting to note that even though many other countries count some part of government durables as a stock of capital, military durables are specifically excluded (Ruggles and Ruggles 1982, p. 12). Thus durability per se is evidently not sufficient as a definition of capital.

22  Relative to the official BEA measure of GNP, the estimated additional product attributed to leisure time is very large: 48.7% for Z in 1965 (Eisner 1988, p. 1636, table Z.1), 96.6% for K in 1984 (p. 1646, table K.6), 101.5% for NT (p. 1632, table NT.2), and 115.5% for JF in 1982 (p. 1638, table JF.1, which shows $4,200.7 billion for the JF estimate of the 1982 value of total time spent in household production and leisure, from which the leisure component can be estimated using the Kendrick estimates of the two components in Eisner 1988, p. 1646, table K.6).

A number of authors (JF, R, E) also add a large and volatile component representing the effects of price changes on the value of household, government, and business stocks of wealth, on the grounds that the appropriate "Haig–Hicks–Simon concept of income [is] that which can be consumed while keeping real wealth intact" (p. 1624). Eisner argues in favor of this procedure, even though it entails "a significant conceptual departure from conventional accounts, which focus on the direct output of current productive activity," and even though it creates a large component that exhibits "some sharp year-to-year variations" (p. 1625). Scott (1990, p. 1175) argues against this procedure on both theoretical and practical grounds, noting in passing that if revaluations were counted as part of income and output flows then one would have to conclude "that the U.S. national income was negative during October 1987" (the month of the stock market crash). Finally, as we have already noted, some authors (NT, Z, E) shift police, fire protection, defense, and guard activities from the final product to intermediate input; NT directly subtract other "regrettables and disamenities."[23] Both procedures serve to lower the measure of final product.

Figure 1.1 presents the various estimates of gross final product which flow from the six conventional extended accounts, relative to the official BEA measure of GNP, as summarized by Eisner (1988, p. 1673, table S.5) for the mid-1960s. Also included are our own estimates, as developed in subsequent chapters of this book.

Two things are notable in Figure 1.1. First, all the estimates, including our own (ST), are larger than the official measure of GNP. In the case of the six conventional extended accounts, this is due to the fact that virtually all authors include estimates of the value of housework and of the "services" of household and government durable goods, and that most also include quite large estimates for the value of leisure. As for our own estimates, we find that our basic estimate of market production is smaller than GNP. But when we supplement this with Eisner's estimate of housework, in order to make the coverage somewhat similar to that of other extended accounts,[24] the resulting figure is about 21% larger than GNP.

The second striking feature of the estimates in Figure 1.1 is their great range of variation: from a low of 112% of the official measure of GNP (Ruggles and Ruggles) to a high of 468% (Jorgenson and Fraumeni). In

---

[23] Regrettables include the previously discussed items of national defense, police, etc., as well as costs of commuting to work and road maintenance, all on the grounds that these are instrumental expenditures that do not directly enter utility but are (regrettably) necessary for activities which do. Disamenities represent costs of pollution, litter, congestion, noise, etc. (Eisner 1988, pp. 1627–8).

[24] We have already argued against the notion of adding the "services" of durables or the value of leisure time to the measure of the product.

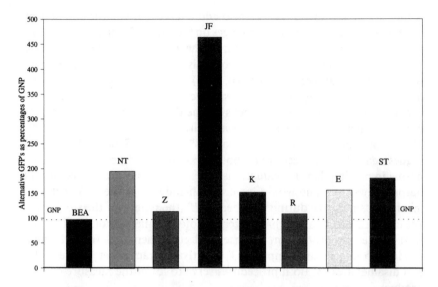

Figure 1.1. Alternate measures of GFP. *Key:* NT = Nordhaus and Tobin for 1965; Z = Zolotas for 1965; JF = Jorgenson and Fraumeni for 1966; K = Kendrick for 1966; R = Ruggles and Ruggles for 1969; E = Eisner for 1966; ST = Shaikh and Tonak for 1966. The ST estimate is from Table 5.4, supplemented by the addition of Eisner's (1985, p. 36) estimate of the value of housework ($267.9 billion in 1966). *Source:* Eisner (1988, p. 1638, table S.5).

the JF case, this is almost entirely due to a particularly large estimate of the value of leisure, and to a huge addition for investment in human capital (Eisner 1988, p. 1638, table JF.1).[25]

Many of these account extensions involve significant changes in the components of the production accounts (Eisner 1988, p. 1626). For instance, the treatment of expenditures on household durables as investment involves shifting their purchases from consumption to (household) investment. Similar effects obtain for government purchases on durables, and for expenditures on health and education (investment in human capital). The net result is to radically alter the size, ratios, and even the meanings of categories such as consumption and investment.

Environmental and resource issues are much less discussed in these extended accounts (Ruggles and Ruggles 1982, p. 5; Eisner 1988, pp. 1622–

[25] JF's estimate of the value of housework and leisure is itself almost 1½ times as large as official GNP, while their measure of investment in human capital is almost 3 times as large as GNP and almost 18½ times as large as the official measure of gross private domestic investment (Eisner 1988, pp. 1637–8, table JF.1).

3). It is well known that official conventions can lead to very inconsistent results. The degradation of the environment is not counted as reduction in income or wealth. If industry cleans up its own mess, the expenditure is counted as an intermediate input and hence output is not affected. But if government cleans it up, this expands the measure of net output because government expenditures are considered to be purchases of final goods and services. Finally, if households incur medical expenses as a consequence of environmental problems, their expenditures raise the measure of consumption and hence of the final product (Repetto et al. 1989, p. 16).

Although such issues are beyond the scope of the present book, it is interesting to note that within our accounting schema the above anomalies would not appear. Neither the cleanup expenditures by industry or government, nor the medical expenditures by consumers, would be counted as production activities. Indeed, like all nonproduction activities, they would use up resources in responding to the environmental problem. As for the environmental degradation itself, this could be counted as a reduction in the stock of (environmental) wealth.

In any case, there exists no consensus on the appropriate treatment of environmental issues within any system of accounts.[26] But it is possible to address the somewhat more manageable issue of resource depletion. Eisner (1988, pp. 1622–3) suggests that the improvement or exhaustion of natural resources be treated on a par with any other investment. Economic activity that increases the value of land or natural resources would be counted as investment, and activity that exhausts them would be counted as depreciation. Repetto et al. (1989, pp. 22–4) propose a similar scheme, in which the change in the physical stock of resources, valued at average prices over the period, is added to net national product (as net investment or disinvestment). Such a procedure would reduce the measured net national product when income is derived essentially from the depletion of resources.[27]

### 1.4 Toward an alternate approach to national accounts

In spite of the complexity and sophistication of the various extended accounts surveyed here, it is important to note that they all share

---

[26] Of the six extended accounts surveyed, only Nordhaus and Tobin attempt to address this issue directly, in the form of their deduction for "regrettables and disamenities." But this is a rather ad hoc treatment, and as Eisner (1988, p. 1627, n. 15) points out, it crosses over the line between the measurement of production (creation of objects of utility) and utility or disutility itself.

[27] Unlike Eisner, Repetto et al. (1989, pp. 23–4) would not count the monetary revaluation (the change in the monetary value of a given physical stock) in the measure of income and product.

certain critical characteristics. First, they are intended to be extensions, not alternatives, to the conventional accounts that form their core (Eisner 1988, p. 1616). Second, like the conventional accounts around which they are built, the "theoretical constructs they are presumed to serve" (p. 1612; Repetto 1989, p. v) are those of neoclassical economics. Third, at the core of all national accounts lie the production accounts (Carson and Honsa 1990, pp. 28-9). Fourth, the neoclassical concept of production embodied in conventional production accounts is a very elastic one, encompassing not only all results of potentially marketable human labor, but also the "services" of durable goods and even the "benefits" of leisure time. At the other extreme we find the restricted concept of production embodied in the National Material Product system of the formerly socialist bloc. Here, the core accounts are focused on the production and distribution of physical goods.

The system we develop falls between these two polar extremes. On one hand, our production encompasses both goods and services. Indeed, the vast bulk of the traditionally defined service sector falls within our definition of production activities. On the other hand, we do not identify all activities as production: trading, military, police, and administrative activities are treated as forms of social consumption, not production. At the heart of the matter is a distinction between outcomes and outputs. The outcomes of nonproduction activities may be socially desirable results, but they are not outputs.

Our system has its roots in the classical tradition. The classical economists were deeply concerned with the factors that regulate the growth of the wealth of nations. Once it was recognized that some activities were actually forms of social consumption, not production, two crucial implications followed. First, an increase in employment need not signal an increase in production; on the contrary, it might signify an increase in social consumption. Second, an increase in the share of social consumption in net output is a decrease in the social savings rate, and this tends to reduce the rate of growth of the system (see Chapter 7).[28]

---

[28] If we write net output as $Y = C' + I$, where $C' =$ personal and social consumption and $I =$ net investment, then the social savings rate is $s' = (Y - C')/Y = 1 - C'/Y$. An increase in the relative share of social consumption is then a decrease in the social savings rate, and hence a direct reduction in the Harrodian warranted rate of growth $g^* = s'/v$, where $v =$ the ratio of capital to normal capacity output. In a depressive situation in which the actual growth rate is below the warranted rate, the two might move in opposite directions. In normal growth, however, the actual growth rate will fluctuate around the warranted rate (i.e., capacity utilization will fluctuate around normal levels), so that a decrease in the social savings rate will lower the latter by lowering the former. See Chapter 7 for further analysis and data.

From this perspective, a deficit-financed increase in (say) military expenditures may indeed stimulate an increase in aggregate demand, output, and employment in the short run. But, insofar as it expands the share of social consumption, it will tend to reduce the rate of growth of the system. The short-run gain will therefore be achieved at the expense of a long-run loss that will eventually outweigh it.[29]

The location of the dividing line between production and nonproduction activities has other implications as well. We will find that it changes the very measures of net product, surplus product, consumption, investment, and productivity. The observed trends of these and many other critical variables are also quite different from those in conventional accounts. As a result, one may achieve a very different understanding about the progress of the U.S. economy and the determinants of its postwar growth.

---

[29] The short-run stimulatory effect may, in the Keynesian sense, raise the level of output. But the decline in the propensity to save will reduce the rate of growth, and eventually the new level of output will be lower than what it would have been at the old rate of growth. See Chapter 7 for further details.

# 2

## Basic theoretical foundations

### 2.1 The distinction between production and nonproduction activities

Marxist national accounts depend crucially on the distinction between labor which is productive of *capital* and that which is not. Because this distinction is so often presented in a confused and contradictory manner, we will not begin from it. Instead, this section will focus on the prior and more general distinction between production and nonproduction activities. The next section will then develop this into more concrete distinctions between labors which are and are not productive of capital. As we shall see, our derivation will enable us to arrive at a definition that corresponds exactly to the one Marx uses. Deriving the definition from first principles, rather than simply beginning with it, allows us to endow it with considerably greater depth.

#### 2.1.1 *Mistaken conceptions of the distinction*

It is useful to begin by emphasizing what the distinction between production and nonproduction labor does *not* refer to. In the first place, it is not a distinction between necessary and unnecessary activities. We intend no connotation that production activities are either more (or less) necessary than nonproduction activities. The dividing line does not rest on either technical or social standards of efficiency, though of course such standards may well be applied to either set of activities. Baran and Sweezy's argument that some labor under capitalism would be unnecessary in a "rationally ordered" (i.e. socialist) economy (Baran 1957, p. 32) is one such efficiency approach. But it is easy to show that they draw the distinction between "productive" and "unproductive" labor in ways that are quite different from those in Marx (Hunt 1979, pp. 304–8), and certainly from those which we will develop.

20

Second, we are not attempting to demarcate between "good" and "bad" activities. One might well argue that certain activities (e.g. nuclear weapons production) are dangerous and destructive and thus bad, or that much of advertising is manipulative and dishonest. These would be moral critiques. But such labels are clearly applicable to both production activities (nuclear weapons) and nonproduction activities (advertising). The production–nonproduction distinction is independent of our evaluation of their social merit.

Third, we are not attempting to construct a political distinction, because production labor is not a designation for the working class, nor nonproduction labor one for the petty bourgeoisie, as Poulantzsas (1975) would have it.[1] Finally, we will not equate production activities with "physical goods" nor nonproduction activities with "services." Such a conflation has its origins in the fact that the classical economists adopt it on practical grounds.[2] Marx certainly rejects any such association at the theoretical level, and explicitly criticizes Adam Smith for confusing the "materialization" of labor in a use value with its embodiment in a physical good (Marx 1963, pp. 171–2).

In sum, the distinction we seek has nothing to do with the efficiency, morality, physicality, or politics of the activities involved. With this in mind, we can turn to the argument itself.

### 2.1.2 *Basic activities of social reproduction*

In analyzing the overall process of social reproduction, we can distinguish four major types of social activities:

*production,* in which the various objects of social use (use values) are utilized in the process of the creation of new such objects;

*distribution,* in which various objects of social use are utilized in order to transfer such objects from their immediate possessors to those who intend to use them;

*social maintenance and reproduction,* in which use values are used up in the private and public administration, maintenance,

---

[1] According to Poulantzas (1975, pp. 20, 212, 216, 221), not only all unproductive laborers but also some productive laborers are new petty bourgeois. Wright (1978) provides an effective critique of this position.

[2] Smith associates productive labor with a physical "vendible commodity." Ricardo (1951, p. 13) refers to Malthus's argument that the most practical distinction is the one that "separates material from immaterial objects," which in turn implies that productive labor - i.e., labor productive of wealth - is that labor which produces material objects (p. 23). Malthus feels this to be the most useful, if not most subtle, classification (Ricardo 1951, p. 23), and Ricardo concurs (p. 15).

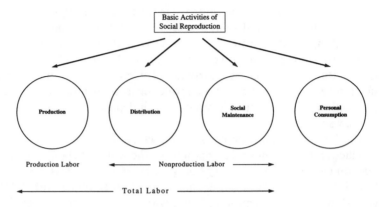

Figure 2.1. Production and nonproduction labor.

and reproduction of the social order by the government, the
legal system, the military, corporate security personnel, etc.;
and

*personal consumption,* in which the objects of social use are
consumed directly by individual consumers.

Of these types of activities, only the first three qualify as labor (since
personal consumption is not labor). But since only the first activity constitutes production, it follows that labor is not synonymous with production.
We must distinguish, in other words, between production labor and nonproduction (distribution and social maintenance) labor. See Figure 2.1.

### 2.1.3 *Production, distribution, and social maintenance*

From the most general point of view, the process of production
involves the creation or transformation of objects of social use by means
of purposeful human activity (Marx 1977, p. 183). This definition is de-
ceptively simple; it appears easy to grasp when we conceive of a useful
object as a *physical* object. But in fact the definition of an object of social
use is more general than that. Broadly speaking, it is a *material thing or
effect,* some of whose properties satisfy human wants.[3] It makes no difference, as Marx puts it, whether these wants "spring from stomach or
fancy" (Marx 1967a, p. 35), or whether they are satisfied directly by the
consumption of this object or indirectly through its use in social reproduction (e.g., distribution or maintenance of the social order).

What we have been calling an object of social use is what Marx calls a
*use value:* a material thing or effect, some of whose objective (i.e. space-

---

[3] The concrete expressions of human wants are, of course, largely socially determined.

time) properties make it an object of social use. As such, these useful objective material properties are quite distinct from the satisfaction we may or may not derive from its actual use.

Let us consider various such objects. In a factory, a set of workers produces a car. This car has objective material properties – shape, color, engine displacement, etc. – which make it an object of our consumption. These properties are the car's useful objective characteristics and serve as the material basis for the subjective satisfaction we may derive from the car, but they are clearly distinct from this satisfaction itself.

Now consider the case of so-called services. A barber uses scissors to transform the shape of someone's hair, thus producing a material effect which is the object of the customer's personal consumption, an effect whose useful objective properties are evident in the mirror, to the touch, and even in a photograph. Similarly, a singer who projects a song into the air produces an object of consumption so material that it can be captured on a record and reproduced electronically. In both cases, the useful objective material properties of this song are very different from the satisfaction one may or may not derive from them (Marx 1963, p. 157).

Even transportation can result in the creation of a use value. Broadly speaking, transportation consists of passenger transport and commodity transport. Each of these encompasses both production and nonproduction activities, depending on more specific considerations. For instance, planes or trains taken as part of vacations and visits bring about a desired change of location which is a direct element of overall consumption. Thus consumption-related passenger transport is part of the production services that enter directly into consumption. Similarly, by shipping oranges from their point of production to their point of consumption, a trucker transforms a useful objective property of these oranges (their location in space) which is crucial to them as objects of consumption. To be consumed, an orange must not merely be an orange somewhere, it must be an orange where the consumer is. Transportation from the orange grove to the consumption region is therefore productive transportation, a completion of the process of the creation of an object of consumption – that is, a completion of the process of production. It is internal to the process of production.[4]

It is important to understand that not all transportation constitutes production activity. Some part of commodity transport may be internal to the distribution process itself. Suppose our oranges are produced in California to be sold in New York, but are stored in New Jersey because of cheaper warehouse facilities. As already noted, the transport from

---

[4] This is precisely why Marx counts transportation as part of the production process (Marx 1963, pp. 152, 412).

California to New York is the productive leg of the journey, because it changes the objective useful properties of the orange. The loop through New Jersey has no (positive) effect on the useful properties of the orange as an object of consumption,[5] but it does improve those properties which affect the orange as an object of distribution. As such, this loop is internal to the distribution system. It therefore constitutes distributive transport of commodities, a nonproduction activity. A similar argument can be made for business-related transport of salespeople, which would be distributive transport of passengers.

In the case of production activities, the labor involved is production labor, which utilizes certain use values in the creation of new use values. As products of this labor, these new use values are quite distinct from either the labor or the materials that went into their own production: a song is not the singer, nor merely the medium of air; cut and shaped hair is neither barber nor scissors, nor uncut hair; an orange in New York is objectively different, as a New Yorker's object of consumption, from the orange that began its journey in California.

It should be evident that the definition of a use value has nothing to do with the conventional distinction between goods and services. Indeed, as we shall see, the very term "services" conflates a vital distinction between production and nonproduction labor. The preceding discussion also allows us to clarify a point of confusion in the literature concerning the difference between the production of a use value and its subsequent use. We begin by considering the various alternative uses of some given set of use values which have just emerged from a production process.

In the first place, use values may re-enter into another production process as material inputs. A truck may be used in transportation, an orange may be used in making food, a coiffure may be part of the performance of a song. In all these cases, they are used up as part of a new production process involving fresh production labor and resulting in new use values. The original use values are destroyed (they are productively consumed, in Marx's terminology), but in the process *new wealth is created*. At the other extreme, the original use values may enter directly into personal consumption, in which case they are used up in the process of reproducing the consumers themselves; they are individually consumed.

Whether an orange is re-used in the further production of food or consumed directly, it must first be produced as an orange. This means that, regardless of the further use to which the orange is put, *the labor which originally produced it remains production labor*. If it is re-used in further

---

[5] To the extent that oranges deteriorate over time, the additional time involved in a distribution loop may actually degrade their useful characteristics.

production, then new production labor must be performed to transform it into a new use value (such as orange juice). On the other hand, if it is consumed then consumption activity (though not labor) is required. In either case, the original labor remains what it was, since its status is not determined by the use to which the fruits of this labor, so to speak, are put.[6]

A second important point can be made even at this level. All economic theory distinguishes between production and consumption, and recognizes that only production results in the creation of new use values or (as classical economists put it) in the creation of new wealth of nations. Even neoclassical economics distinguishes between the production that creates objects of utility (the arguments of utility functions) and the personal consumption that realizes the potential utility of these objects. Thus all economic theory contains an elementary distinction between production and nonproduction activities. What distinguishes the classical/Marxian tradition from the neoclassical/Keynesian one is the location of the dividing line. The former places distribution and social maintenance activities in the sphere of nonproduction activities, whereas the latter places them in production.[7]

The dividing line between production and personal consumption activities is at the same time a dividing line between labor and nonlabor activities. But it was precisely this latter division which the classical economists felt to be inadequate, because it was their contention that not all labor resulted in the creation of new wealth. It was therefore necessary for them to distinguish not merely between production and nonproduction activity, but also between production and nonproduction labor – in other words, between what they called "productive" and "unproductive" labor.

It must be emphasized once again that the classical distinction between production and nonproduction labor is essentially analytical. It is founded on the insight that certain types of labor share a common property with the activity of consumption – namely, that in their performance they use up a portion of existing wealth without directly resulting in the creation of new wealth. To say that these labors indirectly result in the creation of this wealth is only another way of saying that they are necessary. Consumption also indirectly results in production, as production indirectly results in consumption. But this hardly obviates the need for distinguishing between the two.

---

6 This speaks to a certain strand in the literature which conflates the production of a use value with its subsequent use. See, for example, O'Connor (1975).

7 Neoclassical and Keynesian approaches will be discussed in Section 2.3.

We have already seen that, at one extreme, use values emerging from a process of production may be productively consumed (re-entering into another production process as its material inputs); at the other extreme, they may be personally consumed. What we need to examine now is their use in distribution or in maintenance of the social order.

In order to forestall any possible confusion, we should note that we use the term "distribution" to cover only those activities (not necessarily firms) which transfer the use values, titles, or money from one set of individuals to another. We have already argued, for instance, that transportation can be either productive or distributive, depending on its context.[8] By the same token, a particular firm may encompass both distribution activities and production activities (as in the example of advertising that follows).

Generally speaking, distribution involves the utilization of some use values as material inputs in a process that transfers the ownership of (other) use values from their immediate possessors to those who finally intend to use them. As such, the labor involved in this process brings about the circulation or distribution of pre-existing use values by changing their possession. Thus, although distribution activity does transform the use values it circulates, this transformation relates to their properties *as objects of possession and appropriation,* not to the properties which define them *as objects of social use.* A cashier who charges you money is performing a very different activity from the singer who sings the song. The latter activity results in the use value itself, while the former circulates titles to it. A song heard for free is all the more sweet to the listener. But then, of course, the seller hears a different tune altogether.

Advertising and sales activities have the same character, because their aim is to change not the use value itself but rather the knowledge of, and desire for, this use value. They therefore attempt to locate, enhance, and create the effective demand for this use value so as to transfer title to (sell) it on as profitable terms as they can.[9] This in no way precludes

---

[8] Insofar as transportation completes the creation of a use value, such as in the case of the shipping of fruit from its place of production to where the consumer is, then it is productive transportation. But transportation can also be wholly internal to the distributive process, when for example supplies are shipped back and forth between warehouses and retail outlets. In this case, the transportation involved is distributive transportation.

[9] Advertising and sales activity should not be confused with television or radio, which are the *media* for these activities, just as they function as media for the production of use values in the form of the TV or radio shows themselves. The labor that produces such media is production labor. The labor that uses media is production labor (e.g. entertainment) or distribution labor (e.g. advertising), depending on the type of activity in which the labor is involved.

an advertising firm from encompassing production activities such as the production of a commercial. Similarly, since money is the means of circulation, all money-dealing activities also fall into the category of distribution labor. As we have already noted, none of this implies that distribution labor is in any way inferior (or superior) to production labor; it only implies that the two are distinct.[10]

Finally, we have all those activities that revolve around the maintenance and reproduction of the social order. Police, fire departments, courts, and prisons involve the protection of persons, property, and the social relations that surround them. National defense and international affairs do much the same, only on a world scale. General government activities (such as those involving administration, public assistance, pensions, social security, etc.) fall into the same category. But not all such activities are performed in the public sphere. Corporate security personnel and private guards protect persons and their private property. In each case, use values enter as material inputs into activities designed to protect, maintain, administer, and reproduce the social order, and as such they are quite distinct from production labor.

The fact that most of the activities just mentioned are performed by the state should not mislead us into conflating social maintenance and reproduction activities with state activities. Corporate security is a private activity. On the other hand, government-owned electric power plants are part of production, while government agencies that buy and sell grain are engaging in distribution activities. All labor activities can have private and public components.

In the same way, individual people or firms can also encompass more than one type of activity. A manufacturing firm, for instance, will encompass both production and distribution (sales, credit, advertising) activities. Similarly, a given person such as a butcher may both cut meat to a customer's specification and also ring up the purchase. The boundary between production and distribution is in this case crossed by the same person. Nonetheless, the boundary remains a very real one. Should the butcher be so fortunate as to expand into a capitalist enterprise of sufficient scale, then butchers and cashiers will perform different tasks altogether.[11]

---

[10] As noted in Chapter 1, one could formalize this argument in terms of Lancaster's notion of commodities as characteristics (Lancaster 1968, pp. 113–8). Of course, our treatment would nonetheless differ from a neoclassical one (see Section 2.3).

[11] Because all circuits of capital begin and end with money, every firm must engage in at least some distribution activity. We are of course unable to separate empirically the production and distribution components of any single person's activities. But we can (approximately) separate out production and nonproduction workers within each firm or industry. This latter division is by far the most

### 2.1.4 *Personal and social consumption*

We have emphasized that production, distribution, maintenance of the social order, and personal consumption are all part and parcel of the process of social reproduction. The distinctions between them have nothing to do with one being intrinsically more necessary than the others.[12] Each type of activity *uses up* use values as material inputs in order to arrive at its own distinctive outcomes. But only the first activity directly results in the creation of new wealth and hence in a net product over and above what it uses up. The other three facilitate, respectively, the social transfer of this new wealth, the maintenance and reproduction of the social conditions of existence, and the maintenance and reproduction of individuals in the society.[13]

Of the three nonproduction activities, the first two (distribution and social maintenance) involve the performance of labor, while the third (personal consumption) does not.[14] Nonetheless, they have in common the property that they all use up use values in their performance without themselves directly resulting in the creation of new wealth. As such, they must necessarily be supported by existing physical or nonphysical wealth. They are, in other words, similar to personal consumption itself in that their net effect is to consume a portion of the net social product: *nonproduction labor is a form of social consumption.* This is precisely why classical economists insisted on distinguishing between production ("productive") labor and nonproduction ("unproductive") labor. See Figure 2.2.

> important, precisely because capitalist production tends to confine individual workers to distinct activities.
>
> [12] The fact that social reproduction requires all four activities in one form or another need not prevent us from arguing that one existing form is wasteful, dangerous, etc. Thus one could argue, as many radicals do, that some production activities (nuclear weapons), some distribution activities (false and misleading advertising) and some social maintenance activities (subsidies to corporate agribusiness) are undesirable. This superimposes the distinction between desirable and undesirable upon the four analytical categories we have defined, thereby adding another dimension to the analysis.
>
> [13] To say that the latter three "indirectly" result in production is only to say that they are necessary for social reproduction. Thus, consumption indirectly results in production because it reproduces the producers themselves. Conversely, production indirectly results in consumption insofar as it produces the articles of present consumption or the means of future consumption. The concept of indirect production therefore tells us nothing new.
>
> [14] Household labor should not be confused with consumption activity. Activities such as cooking and cleaning are production labor. Consumption activity is quite distinct from this.

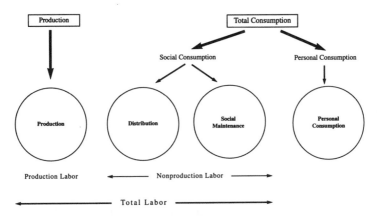

Figure 2.2. Nonproduction labor and social consumption.

## 2.2 Productive labor under capitalism

The preceding definitions of production and nonproduction labor are perfectly general. However, they take on additional content when they are considered in relation to specific social relations under which they might be conducted. Broadly speaking, labor might be conducted for *direct use,* for *sale for income,* and for *sale for profit.* Each of these represents a distinct social relation under which any given labor process is organized and developed. Only the last represents capitalistically employed labor, in which capitalists advance capital value as wages in order to purchase and utilize labor power for a specified period. It follows from this that capitalistically employed labor is not only wage labor but also wage labor whose labor-power is first exchanged against capital (Marx 1977, p. 477). This covers not only production labor but also distribution and social maintenance labors, insofar as they are capitalistically organized.

Now consider each of these activities in turn. All types of production create use values. Insofar as production is organized for direct use, as in household or community production, it produces use values alone. On the other hand, insofar as it is organized for sale for revenue (income), as in petty commodity production, it produces use values that are simultaneously values (materializations of abstract labor time). Finally, insofar as production is for sale for profit, it represents capitalist commodity production that produces not only use values and values but also *surplus value.* This last category is represented by the unshaded sections in Figure 2.3. It represents capitalistically employed labor which is also production labor.

Production Distribution Social Maintenance

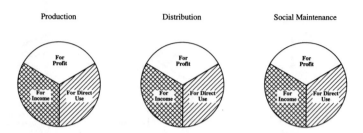

Figure 2.3. Productive and unproductive labor under capital.

The identification of that labor which produces surplus value – in other words, that labor which is productive of capital – immediately allows us to specify its two salient properties:

(a) it is wage labor which is first exchanged against capital (i.e., it is capitalistically employed);

(b) it is labor which creates or transforms use values (i.e., it is production labor).

The definition derived here is identical to the one Marx (1977, p. 644) uses to characterize productive labor. All other labor is thereby unproductive of capital, either because it is production labor that produces direct use values or commodities but not capital, or because it is non-production labor. Thus even capitalistically employed wage labor can be unproductive of capital if it is distribution or social maintenance labor (Marx 1977, p. 1042). It is surprising how often this basic point has been misunderstood in the literature.[15]

The fact that all labor other than capitalistically employed production labor is unproductive of capital does not in any way negate the specificity of the individual components of this labor. Petty commodity production and household labors have very different effects on capitalist reproduction, even though they both produce use values. For instance, suppose that – at a particular stage in economic development – half of the standard of living of the working class is supported out of the use values produced by (unpaid) household labor, and the other half by commodities purchased with the wages of employed workers. If over time the directly produced use values were gradually replaced by the products of petty commodity production, then in order to maintain the same standard of living the purchasing power of workers would have to rise to double its initial level, other things being equal. Thus a given standard of living could correspond

---

[15] See Gough (1972). Even Hunt's careful tracing of Marx's argument stumbles over this issue (Hunt 1979, pp. 313–15).

to very different values of labor power, and hence rates of surplus value, depending on the proportion in which the products of the two types of unproductive labors enter the standard of living. The rate of surplus value depends only on the length of the working day and the unit value of labor power in either case, other things being equal. But this unit value of labor power is not independent of the conditions under which noncapitalist (i.e. unproductive) production labors are performed. These considerations are especially important in the context of the Third World.

In a similar way, even though both salespeople and (say) military people are primarily nonproduction personnel, they do not have the same impact on reproduction. Suppose that the amount of value and surplus value is given, that new sales employment is financed out of current profits, and that new military expenditures are financed directly out of taxes on wages. An increase in sales employment diminishes the amount of surplus value left for aggregate profit (though it may well transfer more surplus value to the firms that increase their sales force). Aggregate profits therefore decline, other things being equal. On the other hand, an increased military employment financed out of taxes on wages need not alter aggregate profit.[16] In both cases, the mass and rate of surplus value are unaltered, but aggregate profit is altered in one case and not the other – even though both types of labor involved are unproductive labor from the standpoint of capital.

It is important to note that all capitalistically employed labor is exploited by capital, whether it is productive labor or unproductive labor. The rate of exploitation of each is their respective ratio of surplus labor time to necessary labor time. Necessary labor time is simply the value of the labor power involved, that is, the labor value of the average annual consumption per worker in the activities in question. Surplus labor time is excess of working time over necessary labor time. In the case of productive workers, their rate of exploitation is also the rate of surplus value, since their surplus labor time results in surplus value. This concept is so practical that we can use it to calculate the separate rates of exploitation of productive and unproductive workers (see Sections 4.2 and 5.6).

The illustrations in this section were designed to emphasize the point that the distinction between productive and unproductive labor is necessary, but not sufficient, for the analysis of reproduction. We need also to know the specific components of unproductive labor and their interaction with the circuits of capital and revenue. This is precisely why we began our analysis with the general distinction between production, distribution, social

---

16 The decreased consumption of taxed workers is assumed to be compensated for by the increased consumption of military employees, so that aggregate demand is unchanged.

maintenance, and personal consumption activities, rather than merely beginning with Marx's definition of productive labor.

### 2.3 Productive labor in orthodox economics

Production, distribution, social maintenance, and personal consumption are all necessary links in the social reproductive process. But their common necessity does not imply similar effects. Indeed, all economic theories recognize that production and personal consumption have polar effects, in that the former creates wealth and the latter uses it up to reproduce individuals. The question is, where do the middle two activities fit?

Both classical and Marxian economics view distribution and social maintenance activities as forms of consumption – they are part of social consumption, as opposed to personal consumption. Orthodox economics takes exactly the opposite tack. It argues that distribution and social maintenance are forms of production. Is not distribution (for instance) just as necessary as production? In fact, is this necessity not manifested precisely in the fact that distribution "transforms" a commodity into a different commodity, and that people are willing to pay for this transformation?

As we have seen, distribution does indeed transform a commodity, by altering its ownership. In doing so it completely transforms the commodity from the point of view of the seller, changing it from a commodity with a price tag to one that has been successfully sold. Thus, if we were to enumerate the vector of "characteristics of the commodity" à la Lancaster (1968), some of these characteristics would now be changed. But from the point of view of the user, the characteristics that define its use value remain just as they were: they are not altered merely because it has been sold. As far as the user is concerned, the sale is only one of many ways of achieving access to the pre-existing use value. This becomes evident when it is "accessed" by being stolen instead of being purchased.

In the eyes of orthodox theory, however, it is sufficient that the use value be somehow transformed, and that someone be willing to pay for it. The former establishes that some change is brought about, the latter that someone finds this change to be necessary. Taken together, they establish that distribution activities produce services – that is, useful effects for which someone is willing to pay. From this point of view, distribution activity is identical to production activity, since both are necessary. The sole distinction then resides in the (unimportant) fact that whereas the former consists entirely of services, only part of the latter does, the rest being made up of (physical) goods. And so, in the end, the orthodox definition of production reduces to that of labor which is deemed to be socially necessary:

> To the economist, production is the creation of any good or service that people are willing to pay for. . . . The agricultural, manufacturing, and marketing services all satisfy human wants; and people are willing to pay for them. . . . Half of what you pay for many products goes for middlemen's services – the retailer, the wholesaler, the banker, the trucker, and many others. Lots of people object violently to this situation. "There are too many middlemen!" they say. Maybe there are. But . . . the real test for all producers is whether they satisfy a consumer demand – not how many pounds of physical stuff they produce. (Bach 1966, p. 45)

The thrust of this logic is clear. Either the definition of production is confined to "physical stuff" (goods), or else it must be broadened to include all "services," the latter being defined to encompass all marketable activity. To the practical economist, one who gathers the actual data and renders these definitions concrete, this leads to the following *operational* criterion: If it is sold, or could be sold, then it is defined as production.[17] Thus – within orthodox accounts – commodity traders, private guards, and even private armies are all deemed to be producers of social output, because someone is paying for their services. So too are all government employees and military personnel, in this case because their employment by the state is usually taken to mean that the society deems them necessary.[18]

When we consider only production and personal consumption, the distinction between them is also a distinction between labor and nonlabor activity. But once we introduce distribution and social maintenance activities, labor need no longer be an undifferentiated category. Since classical and Marxian economics view distribution and social maintenance as nonproduction activities, the corresponding portion of labor becomes nonproduction labor. Orthodox economists view these same activities as production. For them, all labor is production labor, and the distinction between production and consumption becomes synonymous with the distinction between labor and leisure.

At an abstract level, the orthodox argument turns on the notion that marketability is equivalent to production. But at a more concrete level, marketability is only a measure of the ability to attract money, and it rapidly becomes evident that money flows are not synonymous with counterflows

[17] It need not actually be paid for; it is sufficient that it could fetch a price. Many components of actual national income accounts depend heavily on imputed money values.

[18] The application of operation criteria is always circumscribed by social practice. Thus nonmarket government labor has long been included, and its "product" estimated by imputing some money value to it, even when it has been what we designate as nonproduction labor. On the other hand, production labor performed in the household has almost always been ignored in official accounts. Only recently has this latter issue begun to be addressed, albeit unofficially (see Ruggles and Ruggles 1982 and Eisner 1988).

of new wealth. Even orthodox economics then admits that some monetary transactions correspond to transfer payments, which "are simply means of redistributing, among the members of the community, the goods and services produced in the economy" (Beckerman 1968, p. 7). As a practical measure, the theoretical notion of marketability must then be applied in such a way as to exclude transactions involving transfer payments from those involving production, on the grounds that the persons receiving the former do not "render current services" (BEA 1986, p. xi). Yet at the same time, those who *administer* such payments are counted as producing wealth. Thus, in orthodox economics, the flow of unemployment benefits is excluded from the measure of production because it does not correspond to any service rendered by those who receive it. Unemployment benefits are a transfer of wealth. But the civil servants who administer these large and growing transfers of wealth are counted as producing new wealth in the form of administrative services. In Marxian economics, both would be excluded from production.

### 2.4 Production labor, surplus value, and profit

Any concrete capitalist social formation is a mixture of capitalist and noncapitalist relations of production in which the former dominates. But the dominance of capital should not obscure the fact that all spheres participate in the reproduction of the social formation, and that the capitalist sphere is not independent of the others. This gives rise to several new considerations.

The first issue concerns the difference between capitalistically produced wealth and total new wealth. We have already noted that all types of production labor create new wealth. Thus, household and commodity production labor create use values that are bearers of value aimed at earning a revenue; they create simple commodities. Capitalist commodity production labor creates use values that also are bearers of both value and surplus value, and are aimed at making a profit; such labor creates commodity capital (Marx 1963, pp. 156–7). The wealth of capitalist nations generally encompasses all three forms, in proportions that vary over time, space, and stage of capitalist development. But not all are captured in conventional accounts. Commodity production and capitalist commodity production are generally well covered (subject to the usual difficulties of estimating hidden transactions) because the product is sold for money, and much of the nonmarketed product (such as directly consumed farm production, repairs to owner-occupied houses, etc.) is captured by imputing a money value to it. But official national accounts still leave out the imputed value of household production, although all extended accounts now correct for this (see Chapter 1). Because our concern is with an alternative to the official accounts for market activities, we will not deal with nonmarket and illegal activities in this particular work. Such matters are, however, important in any extension of the basic accounts developed here.

The next issue regards the relations between profit and surplus value. It is well known that, at the most abstract level of Marxist theory, aggregate profit is simply the monetary expression of aggregate surplus value. But it is often forgotten that profit can also arise from transfers between the circuit of capital and other spheres of social life. Marx calls this latter form of profit *profit on alienation*, which – unlike profit on surplus value – is fundamentally dependent on some sort of unequal exchange. Its existence enables us to solve the famous puzzle of the difference between the sum of profits and the sum of surplus values brought about by the transformation from values to prices of production (Shaikh 1984, 1992a). More importantly, it allows us to explain how capitalism can derive a profit from noncapitalist spheres without any creation of surplus value. In what follows, we will focus on the latter aspect alone, since the former has been treated in detail elsewhere (Shaikh 1984).

Consider a barter between a noncapitalist tribe and a merchant capitalist. The merchant purchases guns worth £100 in London, barters them for furs from the tribe, and sells the furs back in London for £250. The merchant thus gains £150, which covers both trading costs and merchant profit. Yet there has been no corresponding increase in surplus value. Nor has there been an offsetting loss to the members of the tribe, since (under this idealized version of trade) they have traded one set of goods (furs) for a more desirable set (guns). Aggregate profits have risen by £150, apparently out of thin air. How is that possible?

The answer lies in the fact that different measures of gain have been applied across the two poles of the above transaction. The tribe is operating within the simple commodity circuit C–C', in which one set C of use values is bartered for another useful set C'. The comparison here is in terms of social usefulness. At the other pole, the merchants operate within the capital circuit M–C–C'–M', in which one sum of money (M = £100) is transformed into a larger sum (M' = £250), through the exchange of one set C of use values for a more valuable set C'. Because only one of the poles is assessed in monetary terms, any monetary gain recorded there has no counterpart at the other pole, so that a net monetary gain appears for the system as a whole. If both poles were treated in the same way, then it would be obvious that one side's monetary gain was another side's monetary loss: the tribe would have exchanged assets valued at £250 (furs) for those valued at £100 (guns), for a net change of asset value of −£150; the merchants would correspondingly have recorded a net change in asset value of +£150, which they would then realize as profits of £150 through the sale of the furs.

Similar results can be derived for transfers between capitalist and petty commodity spheres. For example, suppose a petty commodity producer sells a product for $50 to a merchant who then sells it on the open market for $250 (handicrafts are an obvious example). For simplicity of exposition, assume that the final selling price is merely the money equivalent of the commodity's (labor) value.[19] Then, from a global point of view, the merchant has merely succeeded in transferring four-fifths ($200/$250) of the total value of the product to himself, leaving only one-fifth in the hands of the original producers. But whereas a portion of the value transferred in to the merchant will show up as part of aggregate capitalist profit (in the wholesale–retail sector), there will be no corresponding transfer out listed in the petty commodity sector because its product will be valued only at its immediate selling price (producer's price) of $50, rather than its final selling price (purchaser's price) of $250. A portion of the transfer in of value will therefore show up as a net addition to aggregate profit.

Finally, consider transfers within the capitalist sector itself, between the circuit of capital and the circuit of revenue. Suppose an (uninsured) object such as a television set is stolen from a house, sold to an unscrupulous merchant for $50, and then resold on the open market for $250. From the point of view of the society as a whole, the original owner has lost an asset worth $250, a new owner has gained an asset worth $250 but has given up a money sum of exactly the same amount, and the merchant and thief have shared out a net gain of $250. The merchant's profit is then clearly the counterpart of a portion of the original owner's loss. But if we disregard this latter loss, or record it only at partial value, then of course the merchant's profit will seem to spring out of thin air. Section 3.2.2 provides a particularly striking example of this effect.

The preceding examples should make it clear that, even at the most abstract level, aggregate profit encompasses both profit on surplus value and profit on alienation. At a more concrete level, we must also allow for some profit on alienation derived from various transfers between national capitals and other foreign capitals and noncapitals. The issue here is not

---

[19] Thus, if the labor value of the commodity is 125 hours and the value of money is half an hour per dollar, then the commodity's direct money equivalent (direct price) would be $250. If the commodity were to be sold for more or less than $250, then value would be transferred in or out of the combined petty commodity and merchant capital circuit. This additional transfer could then be treated separately, and poses no new problems except those involved in the so-called transformation problem. See Shaikh (1984, 1986, 1992a) for further discussion.

one of money flows of profits, dividends, and interest, but rather of the difference between the sum of such flows and the surplus value that supports them in modern capitalism. Since it is our object to measure the money equivalent of this surplus value, we must be mindful of the fact that our measure will pick up some part of profit on alienation. For the United States, with its highly developed capitalist sphere and its relatively small foreign trade sector, the error in associating aggregate profit with aggregate surplus value appears to be small.[20] But in earlier times, or in less developed capitalist nations, no such a priori identification can be made. It would then be necessary to explicitly separate profit on surplus value from profit on alienation.

---

[20] Khanjian (1989, pp. 108–13) finds that value measures of surplus value differ from corresponding money measures by 6%–9%. He attributes this to transfers of value brought about by price–value deviations within the U.S. economy. Our own estimates of foreign transfers of value indicate that they are quite small (Section 3.4.2).

# 3

## Marxian categories and national accounts: Money value flows

The purpose of this chapter is to develop a mapping between Marxian categories and those of conventional national accounts. The essential points of the argument will be presented here, with all further detail reserved for Appendix A.

National income and product accounts (NIPA) are the traditional base for national accounting. But input–output (IO) tables provide a more general framework in that they encompass both interindustrial flows and national income–product flows. We will therefore use IO tables as our basic theoretical and empirical foils.

Although IO accounts provide a superior description of the economy for our purposes, they suffer from the drawback of being available only for benchmark years (1947, 1958, 1963, 1967, 1972, 1977) for the United States. We will therefore use these tables only to provide comprehensive benchmark estimates, which will then be expanded into annual series using NIPA data.

Our project requires us to distinguish between three different sets of measures, for which we adopt different notation: Marxian labor value measures such as constant capital, variable capital, and surplus value $(C, V, S)$; their money forms $(C^*, V^*, S^*)$; and corresponding IO–NIPA aggregates such as intermediate inputs, wages, and profit-type (unearned) income $(M, W, P)$. Since all accounts in question will be double-entry accounts, each of the revenue-side flows will have use-side counterparts (such as U for the labor value of the inputs used in production, $U^*$ for the corresponding money value, and M for the orthodox measure of intermediate inputs). The letter P taken by itself will refer to profit-type income, but when preceded by another letter or when appearing as a subscript it will refer to production. Thus TP stands for total product, and $P_p$ refers to profits in the production sector.

All results will be summarized both graphically and algebraically. In addition, we illustrate what will become an increasingly complex mapping between Marxian and IO categories by means of a continuing numerical example in which the magnitude of the total product, of the corresponding total (labor) value, and of their respective components are held constant throughout. Thus a given quantity of total value TV* will always be divided into the same amount of constant capital C*, variable capital V*, and surplus value S*. Similarly, total product TP* will always be divided into the same amounts of inputs used up in production U*, necessary product NP* (consumption of production workers), and surplus product SP* (used for capitalist consumption, investment, nonproduction, and state activities). As we move beyond production alone to consider wholesale and retail trade, finance, government, and the external sector, these given amounts of value and product will be subject to progressively more complicated modes of circulation and distribution, and their corresponding forms of appearance within IO tables will become more complex. Nonetheless, precisely because we have the original numerical quantities already in hand, we can immediately verify that our measures of the aggregates are correct.

Sectors (such as production and wholesale/retail trade) which are directly involved in the production and domestic realization of the total commodity product will be called *primary* sectors. Those (such as finance, land rental and sales, and general government) involved in the subsequent recirculation of the value and money streams originating in the primary sectors will be called *secondary* sectors.[1] Such a distinction is rooted in the Marxian approach to capitalist reproduction, and its rationale will become evident as we proceed with the argument. In what follows, we will begin with the analysis of the primary sectors and then move on to the various components of the secondary sectors. The sections on foreign trade and noncapitalist labor activities sectors will round out the argument, to be followed by an overall summary of the relations between Marxian and orthodox national measures. Table 3.1 illustrates the sectoral divisions just outlined; further detail will be developed in the sections that follow.

Finally, it should be noted that we will conduct our argument as if actual input–output tables included fixed capital used up in intermediate inputs (as depreciation) and in intermediate demand (as replacement investment), so that value added and final demand are net measures. We will also proceed as if value added were explicitly divided between wages

---

[1] It should be obvious that primary and secondary, as used here, do not at all mean the same thing as "primary products" (extracted products), etc.

Table 3.1. *Sectoral structure of reproduction*

| |
|---|
| Primary sectors |
|    Production (goods/services, private/public) |
|    Trade (wholesale/retail, building/equipment rentals) |
| Secondary sectors |
|    Finance, ground rent, royalties (private) |
|    General government (public) |
| Foreign trade sectors |
| Noncapitalist labor activities |

and profits, and consumption demand were explicitly divided between workers' consumption and capitalist consumption. Conventional tables lack this level of detail, but could be modified to incorporate it. The mapping between Marxian and IO categories is greatly enhanced by these adjustments. As noted earlier, Appendix A provides further detail on the material developed in this chapter.

### 3.1 Primary flows: Production and trade

This section will deal with primary flows only. We will begin with a consideration of production activities alone, and then move on to analyze production and trade taken together. Before we proceed, it is useful to recall some critical points concerning the definitions of production and trading activities.

Briefly, "production" encompasses those activities that create or transform material objects of social use (use values). As derived in Chapter 2, this definition covers not only goods but also many so-called services such as transportation, entertainment, lodging, cooking, and so forth. Moreover, since the definition depends on the character of the process, not on its formal ownership, it also covers government enterprises insofar as they produce use values (such as electricity).

The definition of "trade," on the other hand, encompasses not only wholesale/retail trade but also the rental of produced commodities such as cars and buildings (since this is merely the piecemeal sale of the product's use value over its functioning lifetime), the activities of government trading enterprises, and any transportation involved in conjunction with these realization activities. Table 3.2 outlines the basic components of the primary (production and trade) sectors. Further detail will be reserved for the empirical analysis in Chapter 5.

Table 3.2. *Production and trade sectors*

| Production | Trade |
|---|---|
| Goods | Wholesale/retail |
| Productive services | Building, equipment, and car rentals |
| Government production | Government trading |
| Productive transportation | Distributive transportation |

### 3.1.1 *National accounts with production sectors alone*

Consider production alone. Suppose that the total product consists of 2000 hours of (labor) value, whose aggregate selling price is any money sum, say 4000 "currency units" (CU). The total labor value of 2000 hours is expressed in 4000 CU of money. But we can always redefine the unit of money to be equal to 2 CUs, name this new unit a "dollar," and say that the total selling price of 2000 hours of value is $2000. While this is merely a notational device, it simplifies our exposition by allowing one magnitude (with differing units) to represent total labor value and also its monetary expression, the total selling price of the product. The term "value" will therefore be used for both labor value and its monetary expression, unless we wish to explicitly distinguish them.

Once we introduce trading activities, we need to distinguish between the producer's price (the price at which the product is sold by the producer to the wholesaler/retailer), and the final selling price charged by the wholesaler/retailer (which includes their markup). As long as the markup is positive, there will be a transfer of value from the producing sector to the trading sector. This was discussed in Section 2.4.

None of the results we derive depend significantly on whether or not producer prices or final selling prices of individual commodities deviate from their corresponding labor values. Regardless of any such deviations, the sum of individual producer prices defines an aggregate producer price, and the sum of individual final selling prices defines an aggregate final selling price of the total product; this is all we need to know at present. The issue of individual price–value deviations and their impact is taken up in Sections 4.1 and 5.10.

Throughout this chapter, we will assume that the $2000 selling price of the total product is composed of $400 in production costs, $200 in production worker wages, and $1400 in profits (profit-type income) and other expenses. In order to track the *use* of this same aggregate product, we will assume that production costs represent the costs of inputs used in

Table 3.3. *Value and use of the product*

| Value of product | Use of product | Amount |
|---|---|---|
| Production costs = Inputs used | | = $ 400 |
| Worker wages | = Workers' consumption | = $ 200 |
| Profits | = { Capitalist consumption ($700) / Total investment ($700) } | = $1400 |
| Total price | = Total use | = $2000 |

Table 3.4. *Marxian and IO measures: Revenue side*

| Marxian name | IO name | Amount |
|---|---|---|
| Constant capital C* | = Intermediate input M | = $ 400 |
| Variable capital V* | = Wages W | = $ 200 |
| Surplus value S* | = Profits P | = $1400 |
| Total value TV* | = Gross output GO | = $2000 |
| C* + V* + S* | = M + W + P | = $2000 |

production, that workers' consumption is equal to their wages, that capitalist consumption is equal in magnitude to one half of profits, and that the sum of (intended) business investment in plant, equipment, inventories, and "unintended inventory investment" (i.e. unsold or oversold goods) will be equal to the other half of profits. This latter assumption does not imply that sectoral or aggregate supply and demand balance. Rather, it is simply a standard accounting device in which the difference between supply and demand is added to the "total investment" on the use side as "unintended inventory change" so as to make the revenue and use sides balance ex post. Table 3.3 provides a numerical illustration of these basic principles.

Table 3.4 compares the Marxian and IO representations of the flows portrayed in Table 3.3. Precisely because we are considering production alone, the correspondence is straightforward: Constant capital C* is the same as intermediate input M, variable capital V* the same as wages W, surplus value S* the same as profits (profit-type income), and total value TV* the same as gross output GO. The relation between Marxian and IO measures of the use side is equally transparent, at this level of abstraction. The Marxian measure of the amount of product used as inputs U* will be the same as the corresponding IO measure of intermediate demand M;

Table 3.5. *Marxian and IO measures: Use side*

| Marxian name | IO name | Amount |
|---|---|---|
| Production input U* | = Intermediate demand M | = $ 400 |
| Necessary product NP* | = Workers' consumption CONW | = $ 200 |
| Surplus product SP* | = $\begin{cases} \text{Capitalist consumption CONC (\$700)} \\ \text{Total investment I (\$700)} \end{cases}$ | = $1400 |
| Total product TP* | = Gross product GP | = $2000 |
| U* + NP* + SP* | = M + CONW + (CONC + I) | = $2000 |

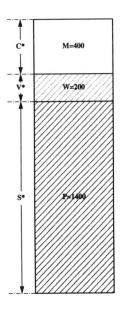

Figure 3.1. Division of value: Production alone.

the Marxian measure of necessary product (the consumption of production workers) NP* the same as the IO measure of workers' consumption CONW; and the surplus product SP* the same as the sum of capitalist consumption CONC and total investment I. See Table 3.5.

The numerical outcomes in Tables 3.4 and 3.5 are illustrated graphically in Figures 3.1 and 3.2. Within their respective figures, Marxian total value TV* and total product TP* are enclosed in solid lines, Marxian value added (VA* = V* + S* = 1600) and final product (FP* = NP* + SP* = 1600) in

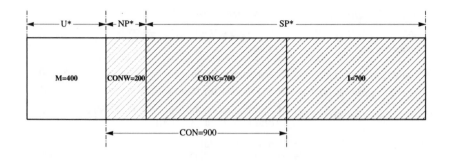

Total Product =2000

Figure 3.2. Use of product: Production alone.

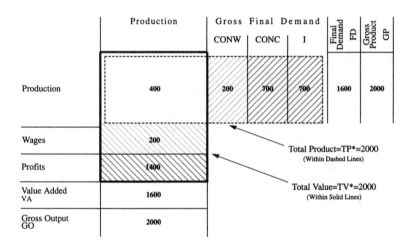

Figure 3.3. IO accounts and Marxian categories: Production alone.

hatched areas, and surplus value and surplus product in shaded hatched areas. We will use these conventions in all subsequent figures.

Finally, we can map the relations expressed in Figures 3.1 and 3.2 onto the (rudimentary) input–output table in Figure 3.3. At this level of abstraction, the input–output table is merely a concatenation of the two sides depicted in Figures 3.1 and 3.2. In the resulting table, Marxian total value TV* and total product TP* are enclosed within the solid and dashed areas, respectively, while the various hatched areas within each represent Marxian value added VA* and final product FP*, respectively.

Figures 3.1–3.3 establish that when all activities are assumed to be production activities, Marxian measures are identical to their orthodox counterparts, at least at this level of abstraction.[2] But *this direct and simple correspondence is quite deceptive.* It disappears as soon as we consider nonproduction activities.

### 3.1.2 *National accounts with production and trade sectors*

We now broaden our inquiry to include wholesale/retail trade (other trading activities will be considered later). Production and its elements are the same as before, but the circulation of this given total value and product is now explicitly mediated by trading activities.

Suppose that the previously considered output worth $2000 is now realized in two distinct steps. First, it is sold by the producing sector p to the trading sector t, for a *producer's price* of $1000.[3] Second, this very same product is then sold by the trading sector to individuals for use in personal consumption, to firms for use as materials and fixed capital, or is retained as unsold goods in inventories.[4] The sum of these dispositions, which equals the final selling price of the product, is called the *purchaser's price* of the product. The $1000 difference between the producer's price and purchaser's price is known as the *trading margin* TM of the trade sector.[5] The trading sector thereby converts an aggregate product worth $2000 into money and unsold goods totaling $2000, keeping $1000 of the proceeds for itself.

The present two-stage realization process distributes the previously given total value of $2000 in a new manner. The intermediate input and wage bill of the production sector are unchanged ($M_p + W_p = 400 + 200 = 600$), but since its total revenue is now only $1000, its profit $P_p$ is reduced to $400 (from $1400). At the same time, the $1000 which is lost to the producing sector is captured by the trading sector in the form of its trading margin, which in turn is allocated among its own inputs $M_t$, wages $W_t$, and profits $P_t$. From the Marxian point of view, nothing has changed in the production process, so that constant capital $C^*$, variable capital $V^*$, and surplus value $S^*$ are unchanged. But whereas the total surplus value $S^* = \$1400$ previously accrued entirely to the production sector as profits, it is now divided between the profits of the

---

[2] This assumes that profits are measured accurately – i.e., that allowance is made for the extent to which profits may be disguised as fictitious costs and expenses.

[3] We may think of the producing and trading sectors as production and sales divisions of the same company.

[4] National accounts trace the disposition of the actual product. Thus if some of it is unsold, the unsold portion is counted as a (positive) "investment" in inventories. If more is sold than is produced, then the excess of sales over production is treated as a negative investment (a "disinvestment") in inventories. Either way, the sum total in question is made equal to the current annual product.

[5] Since we have assumed that depreciation is listed as part of the input costs in our examples, the trading margin is net of depreciation.

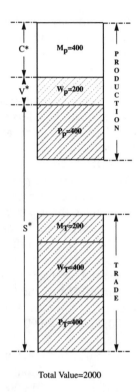

Total Value=2000

Figure 3.4. Division of value: Production and trade.

production sector ($P_p = \$400$) and the trading margin of the trade sector ($TM = M_t + W_t + P_t = \$1000$).

To derive the use-value side, we follow our previous conventions: For each sector, intermediate use of the product is the same as its materials inputs on the revenue side ($U_p = M_p = \$400$, $U_t = M_t = \$200$); workers' consumption is equal to their wages ($CONW_p = W_p = \$200$, $CONW_t = W_t = \$400$); capitalist consumption is half of sectoral profits ($CONC_p = \$200$, $CONC_t = \$200$); and total investment (including unintended inventory change) is equal in magnitude to the other half of profits ($I_p = \$200$, $I_t = \$200$).

From a Marxian point of view, the productive input use $C^*$, the necessary product $NP^*$, and the surplus product $SP^*$ are unchanged by their more complex mode of circulation. This means that $C^* = M_p = \$400$, $NP^* = CONW_p = \$200$, and $SP^* = \$1400$, as before. But the disposition of the surplus product is now different, since it is absorbed not only by capitalist consumption and investment in the production sectors but also by *all* uses of the trading sector. Thus

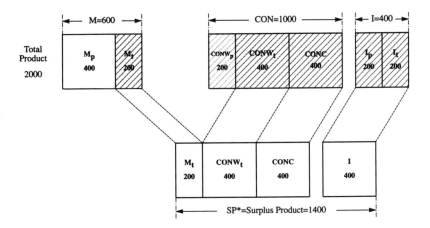

Figure 3.5. Use of product: Production and trade.

$$SP^* = (CONC_p + I_p) + (M_t + CONW_t + CONC_t + I_t)$$
$$= (\$200 + \$200) + (\$200 + \$400 + \$200 + \$200) = \$1400.$$

Figures 3.4 and 3.5 depict these new divisions of value and use value.

The last step is to assemble all the preceding information into a mapping between input–output and Marxian accounts. To accomplish this, we need to delve further into the conventions of IO tables.

We begin by noting that whereas commodities are sold to their final users at purchasers' prices, most input–output tables are cast in terms of producers' prices. Thus the total revenue listed for any given activity (gross output and gross product, in IO terminology) is its estimated producer's price, not its actual sales revenue (purchaser's price). By the same token, the total revenue of the trading sector (its "producers' price") is the sum of the trading margins on all activities that pass through this sector.[6] But such a procedure immediately creates a problem in the valuation of purchases of inputs and of elements of final demand, since these items are acquired at purchasers' prices. Conventional IO tables get around this by treating any single commodity purchase as two separate but simultaneous transactions, one from the producing sector in an amount equal to the producer's price of the commodity input, and one from the trading sector in an amount equal to the trading margin on the same bundle of commodities. In this way

---

[6] In this context, the term "producers' price" means the total revenue generated from the activity minus any wholesale/retail margins. Since all revenue-generating activities are treated as production activities in orthodox economics, even the trading sector has a producers' price.

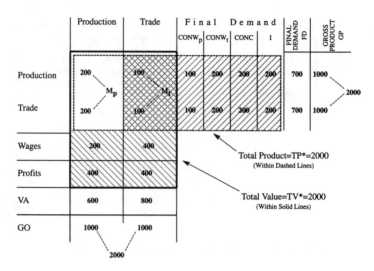

Figure 3.6. IO accounts and Marxian categories: Production and trade.

the final purchaser's price of any input is decomposed into its producer's price and its trading margin, and the two components are recorded separately as "goods" purchased from the producing sector and "trading services" purchased from the trading sector (BEA 1980, pp. 19–20).

In our numerical example, the total value of the aggregate product is split between producer's price and gross trading margin in the proportions $1000:1000 = 1:1$. For simplicity in constructing our IO table, we will assume that the same split holds for each individual component of the total product. On this assumption, each commodity purchase (M, CONW, CONC, and I) appearing in Figures 3.4 and 3.5 will be recorded as two equal "purchases" from the production and trade sectors, respectively. The row sum of all these commodity trade margins is the "gross product" of the trade sector in input–output terminology, and this of course is the same as the corresponding column sum of its input costs, wages, and profits (its total revenue or "gross output"). The resulting IO table is depicted in Figure 3.6, with our usual conventions for representing the various Marxian measures.

The translation from the Marxian value and use-value flows depicted in Figures 3.4 and 3.5 to the conventional input–output mappings in Figure 3.6 brings out the difference between the two theoretical bases. A glossary of terms is provided next, and Table 3.6 summarizes the algebraic and numerical relations between the two sets of measures as derived from Figure 3.6.

| Marxian measures | Input–output measures |
|---|---|
| $TV^* = C^* + V^* + S^*$ <br> $= $ total value | $GO = M + W + P$ <br> $= $ gross output |
| $VA^* = V^* + S^*$ <br> $= $ value added | $VA = W + P$ <br> $= $ final demand |
| $TP^* = U^* + FP^*$ <br> $= $ total product | $GP = M + FD$ <br> $= $ gross product |
| $FP^* = NP^* + SP^*$ <br> $= $ final product | $FD = CON + I = CONW + CONC + I$ <br> $= $ final demand |
| $L_p = $ productive employment | (no direct counterpart) |
| $L_u = $ unproductive employment | (no direct counterpart) |
| $L = $ total employment <br> $= L_p + L_u$ | $L = $ total employment |

Table 3.6 (p. 50) makes it clear that once we distinguish between productive and unproductive activities, Marxian and IO–NIPA categories no longer correspond directly. Since the revenue sides are more similar across frameworks than are the use-value sides (there being no input–output equivalents of necessary and surplus product), we will focus our explanation on the former. Even at this level of abstraction we can identify several general patterns.

Production and trade are the sectors through which the commodity product is produced and realized. Their combined total revenue therefore represents the total price of the product $TV^*$. In input–output tables, this combined total revenue will show up as the sum of the gross outputs of the production and trade sectors $GO_p$ and $GO_t$. It will not include the revenues ("gross output") of any secondary sectors ($GO_s$) because such revenues originate in transfers of portions of the value flows of the primary sectors, and all such source flows have already been counted in the sector of their origin. Thus we will always find that total value $TV^* = GO_p + GO_t$, constant capital $C^* = M_p$, variable capital $V^* = W_p$, and productive employment equals the employment of capitalistically employed production workers $L_p$ alone. For this same reason, in general each of these Marxian categories will always be less than their orthodox counterparts GO, M, W, and L, respectively, precisely because these latter measures count trade, ground rent, finance, and a host of other non-production activities as forms of production.[7]

Other patterns in Table 3.6 will not necessarily carry over to the general case. For instance, the present equality of Marxian total value $TV^*$ and

---

[7] If we use the subscript s to denote secondary sector variables, then conventional gross output $GO = GO_p + GO_t + GO_s$, intermediate input $M = M_p + M_t + M_s$, total wages $W = W_p + W_t + W_s$, and total employment $L = L_p + L_t + L_s$, respectively.

Table 3.6. *Marxian and IO measures: Production and trade*

| Marxian | | Input–output |
|---|---|---|
| **A. Revenue side** | | |
| $TV^* = GO_p + GO_t = 2000$ | $=$ | $GO = GO_p + GO_t = 2000$ |
| $= 1000 + 1000$ | | $= 1000 + 1000$ |
| $C^* = M_p = 400$ | $<$ | $M = M_p + M_t = 400 + 200 = 600$ |
| $VA^* = TV^* - C^* = 1600$ | $>$ | $VA = GO - M = 1400$ |
| $= VA_p + GO_t = 600 + 1000$ | | $= VA_p + VA_t = 600 + 800$ |
| $V^* = W_p = 200$ | $<$ | $W = W_p + W_t = 200 + 400 = 600$ |
| $S^* = VA^* - V^* = 1400$ | $>$ | $P = P_p + P_t = 400 + 400 = 800$ |
| $= P_p + GO_t$ | | |
| $= P_p + P_t + (W_t + M_t)$ | | |
| $= 400 + 400 + (400 + 200)$ | | |
| $S^*/V^* =$ rate of surplus value | $\gg$ | $P/W =$ profit/wage ratio |
| $= 1400/200 = 700\%$ | | $= 800/600 = 133\%$ |
| $= [P_p + P_t + (W_t + M_t)]/W_p$ | | $= (P_p + P_t)/(W_p + W_t)$ |
| **B. Use side** | | |
| $TP^* = GP_p + GP_t = 2000$ | $=$ | $GP = GP_p + GP_t = 2000$ |
| $U^* = M_p = 400$ | $<$ | $M = M_p + M_t = 400 + 200 = 600$ |
| $FP^* = TP^* - U^* = 1600$ | $>$ | $FD = GP - M = 1400$ |
| $= M_t + CON + I$ | | $= CON + I$ |
| $= 200 + 1000 + 400$ | | $= 1000 + 400$ |
| $NP^* = CONW_p = 200$ | | (no direct counterpart) |
| $SP^* = FP^* - NP^* = 1400$ | | (no direct counterpart) |
| $= M_t + CON + I - CONW_p$ | | |
| $= M_t + CONW_t + CONC + I$ | | |
| $= 200 + 400 + 400 + 400$ | | |
| $SP^*/NP^* =$ rate of exploitation | | (no direct counterpart) |
| $= 1400/200 = 700\%$ | | |
| $= (M_t + CONW_t + CONC + I)/CONW_p$ | | |

input–output gross output GO does not hold in general, for the reasons discussed previously. More importantly, although we will be able to derive the precise relations between Marxian value added VA* and orthodox value added VA, and between Marxian surplus value S* and aggregate profits P (which at this level of abstraction is the same as "profit-type income" P′, i.e. the sum of profits, rents, and interest), it turns out that at a more general level the relative magnitudes of the two sets cannot be determined a priori. Indeed, the empirical evidence in Chapter 5 indicates that whereas S* continues to be greater than P' and P, the present finding that VA* > VA (see Table 3.5) is actually reversed at a more concrete level. Table 3.12 will summarize these and other general patterns in our findings.

### 3.1.3 *Further types of trading activities*

We indicated in Table 3.1 that the definition of trading activities encompasses not only private wholesale/retail trade but also any trading done by government enterprises, as well as distributive transport and the rental of buildings and equipment. Because input–output accounts place specific government enterprises in the same industries as their private counterparts (BEA 1980, p. 45), we can assume that government trading enterprises are already part of the overall trade sector.

The treatment of transportation is similar to that of trade in IO accounts (see Section 3.1.2). That is to say, only transportation *margins* enter into the transportation sector's gross output and product, and the individual margins are all "unbundled and shifted forward" (BEA 1980, p. 20). Thus, if we were able to estimate the portion of transportation which qualifies as distributive transport, we could in principle merge this directly into the trade sector. But in practice the necessary information is lacking, so that our empirical estimates are based on the assumption that all transportation is productive transport.

The identification of building and equipment rentals is more complex. To begin with, the overall real estate and rental sector in conventional accounts is comprised of three disparate activities. The first is a fictitious (imputed) component known as "owner-occupied rentals," arising from the fact that IO–NIPA accounts treat homeowners who live in their own houses as if they were businesses renting out their homes to themselves. This must be discarded altogether. Second is the rental and sale of land, which we will shift to the secondary sector (along with finance) since such activities really amount to the recirculation of revenues, titles, and claims to revenues. The third activity is the sale and rental of buildings, which involves either the direct or piecemeal sale of a produced commodity and must therefore be merged into the overall trade sector.

Furthermore, IO accounts treat building and equipment rentals as production activities, whereas we need to treat them as trading activities; this means that when we merge building/equipment rentals (br) into the trade sector, we must ensure that only the rental margins enter into gross output and product and that the individual rental margins (the low elements of the sector) are unbundled and shifted forward. Figure 3.7 summarizes the overall treatment of the primary flows. All further detail is reserved for Appendix A.

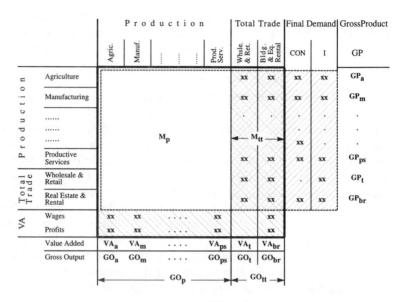

Figure 3.7. IO accounts and Marxian categories: Primary flows.

## 3.2 Secondary flows

Production and trade activities derive their revenues directly from the sale of the commodity product. These primary flows in turn give rise to a series of secondary flows, such as payments for ground rent,[8] finance charges, fees, royalties, and taxes.

*Secondary sectors* are therefore defined by the fact that they derive their revenues from the recirculation of the money flows generated by the primary sectors, or from the circulation of socially validated claims upon portions of these primary flows, or both. Thus, (pure) ground rent[9] (as opposed to building and equipment rental, which we have already analyzed) is a royalty paid for access to land, interest a royalty paid for access to money and credit, and a patent or other fee a royalty paid for access to a particular process of some sort. The sale of land, of financial instruments, and of patent rights then circulates the claims to these royalties. A similar conclusion applies to taxes, which are (quite literally) royalty payments made to a sovereign social power.

[8] The term "ground rent" refers to the rental of land, mines, etc.

[9] Capitalist ground rent, as Marx notes, is part of surplus value that accrues to landowners because of their "ownership of certain portions of our planet" (Marx 1967b, p. 634).

The transfers between the primary and secondary sectors can take place directly when the former pay royalties (ground rent, interest, etc.) to the latter. Or they can take place indirectly, when (say) the households who derive their revenues from the primary sectors (as wages, dividends, interest payments, etc.) in turn pay over some portion of these revenues to the royalties sector. In either case, since the original sources of these secondary-sector revenues are already captured in the accounts of the primary sectors, we cannot count them again in the measure of total value. By the same token, since the total product is produced and realized in the primary sector, we cannot count the revenues received by secondary sectors as measures of some additional production emanating from these sectors. Thus we cannot count them in the measure of total product. *Secondary flows are part of total transactions, but not part of total value or total product.*

Note that this does not mean that we ignore the actual use of the product by the secondary sector or by households whose incomes derive from it. Royalty payments are deductions from the purchasing power of the primary sector and its associated households. Their receipt by the secondary sector enhances that sector's purchasing power and that of its associated households. What the former sector loses, the latter gains. In this way the redistribution of value brought about through transfers between the primary and secondary sectors leads to a changed use of the product.

A.  PRIVATE SECONDARY FLOWS: GROUND RENT, FINANCE, ROYALTIES

3.2.1 *General implications of royalty payments*

In what follows, we will use the term "royalty payments" to designate secondary flows in general. As we have already noted, transfers between the primary and secondary sectors do not change the basic Marxian measures.[10] But because IO–NIPA accounts treat these transfers as purchases of the royalties-sector "product," they do change the corresponding orthodox measures. Hence the consideration of royalty payments adds a new element to the mapping between the Marxian and orthodox accounts. We next analyze the cumulative effects of these changes on measures of total output and product, on value added and net product, and on total profit-type income.

Since orthodox accounts treat the receipts of the royalties sector as a measure of its so-called product, they increase the measures of economy-wide gross output GO by adding a column for royalties-sector revenues,

[10] Royalty payments that come out of the wage of productive workers can lower their true wage and hence raise surplus value. We address this issue in Section 3.3.

and increase the measure of total gross product GP by adding a row of disbursements to the royalties sector from all other sectors. From our point of view, these are merely records of transfers, and must be left out of our measures of total value TV* and total product TP*. Thus, as before, $TV^* = GO_p + GO_t$ and $TP^* = GP_p + GP_t$. We will see shortly that the same principles apply to the general government sector.

The effects on orthodox measures of value added and profit are a bit more complex. There are three possibilities, depending on whether royalty payments are treated as costs or disbursements.

First, primary sectors' accounts treat some particular type of royalties $(RY_p + RY_t)$ paid to the secondary sectors as *costs* and hence record them among intermediate inputs (by adding them to intermediate inputs and then subtracting them from value added by creating a matching negative entry for "imputed interest received"). This is the case with ground rent paid to the real estate sector and net interest paid to the financial sector,[11] so that the measured level of the value added of the primary sectors is reduced by this amount. At the same time, the receipt of these payments shows up as the total revenue $(GO_{ry} = RY_p + RY_t)$ of the royalties sector. But since some of this is absorbed by the intermediate inputs $(M_{ry})$ of the royalties sector, the amount that re-appears as the value added of the royalties sector is less than the amount that was lost to the value added of the primary sectors on the original transfer. Thus the IO–NIPA measure of aggregate value added VA falls below its Marxian counterpart VA* (see Section B.2.2). The reduction in the orthodox measure of aggregate profit-type income (profits, rents, and interest) relative to aggregate surplus value is even greater, because a portion of the value added of the secondary sector is also absorbed in its wage bill. Finally, to the extent that rents and (some) interest payments are treated as costs, aggregate profit will be even smaller.

Second, some types of royalties are treated as *disbursements* from value added $(RY_p' + RY_t')$. These comprise net interest and dividends paid to households, foreigners, and the government, as well as indirect business taxes.[12] Such payments leave the conventional measure of the primary sectors' total value added unchanged (although they may change the division between profits and royalties). Since these disbursements are not made directly to the secondary sectors, total business revenues are also

---

[11] Businesses actually list net interest paid as part of disbursements from value added, but IO–NIPA accounts treat the interest paid to the finance sector as a cost and shift it to intermediate inputs. However, interest paid to consumers, government, and foreigners is left in value added. See Section B.2.

[12] As noted previously, orthodox accounts treat net interest paid by business to the finance sector as business costs, and record them in intermediate input.

unchanged. Thus transfers of this sort leave unchanged the relation between Marxian value added VA* and orthodox value added VA. The same can be said for disbursements from profit-type income (the sum of profits, rents, interest, and taxes), though obviously aggregate profits themselves may be reduced by the amount of royalties paid out as net interest and indirect taxes.

Finally, the households, government, and foreigners supported out of primary-sector revenues may pay a portion $(RY_c + RY_g + RY_{x-m})$ of their incomes over to the secondary sectors as ground rent, net interest, and so forth. Because such transfers take place "downstream" of the primary sectors' gross output, value added, and profits, the originating flows will not be affected. Of course, the receipt of these payments will increase revenues of the secondary sector, and orthodox accounts will register this increased revenue as an increase in gross output. On the use side, orthodox accounts record the transfers in question as purchases of secondary sector output, to be listed in the household-, government-, and foreign-sector columns of final demand; this raises the aggregate measure of final demand. Since none of the primary-sector measures are affected, and all of the secondary-sector measures are raised, the aggregate orthodox measures are all raised relative to the corresponding Marxian measures. The same argument applies to profit-type income relative to surplus value. This latter result gives rise to the possibility that profit can actually be greater than surplus value, owing solely to the manner of circulation of the product. We will examine this new and striking result in more detail in Section 3.2.2.

In summary, royalty flows increase the orthodox measures of gross output GO and gross product GP relative to their Marxian counterparts total value TV* and total product TP*. But the effect on the magnitude of conventional value added VA and final demand FD relative to Marxian value added VA* and final product FP* is not similarly determinate. Royalty payments by primary sectors to the secondary sectors decrease orthodox measures relative to Marxian ones, but royalty payments from the primary sectors to households, government, and foreigners have no effect on the relative positions of Marxian and orthodox measure. And royalty payments made by households, government, and foreigners to the secondary sectors increase orthodox measures relative to their Marxian counterparts. The same can be said for measures of aggregate profit-type income (the sum of profits and royalties) relative to aggregate surplus value. Thus the overall effect of royalty flows on orthodox measures of value added, final demand, and aggregate profit, relative to their Marxian counterparts, is indeterminate. A more detailed derivation of these results is provided in Appendix B.

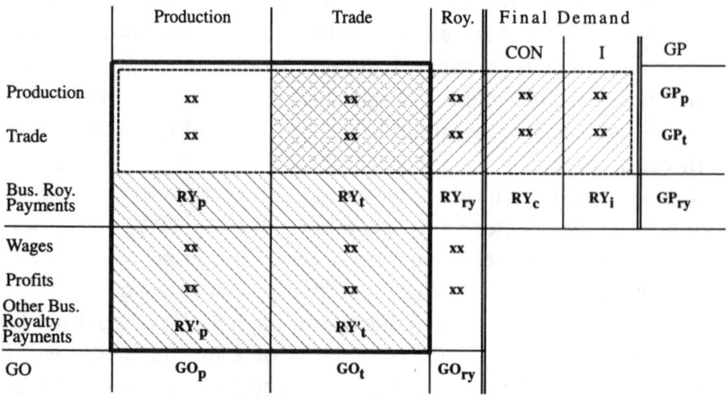

| | Production | Trade | Roy. | Final Demand CON | I | GP |
|---|---|---|---|---|---|---|
| Production | xx | xx | xx | xx | xx | $GP_p$ |
| Trade | xx | xx | xx | xx | xx | $GP_t$ |
| Bus. Roy. Payments | $RY_p$ | $RY_t$ | $RY_{ry}$ | $RY_c$ | $RY_i$ | $GP_{ry}$ |
| Wages | xx | xx | xx | | | |
| Profits | xx | xx | xx | | | |
| Other Bus. Royalty Payments | $RY'_p$ | $RY'_t$ | | | | |
| GO | $GO_p$ | $GO_t$ | $GO_{ry}$ | | | |

Figure 3.8. IO accounts and Marxian categories: Private royalties payments.

Figure 3.8 depicts the overall effects of royalty flows on the mapping between Marxian and IO categories. Some royalty payments $(RY_p + RY_t)$ made by the primary sectors (production and trade) are listed as costs and hence recorded in the intermediate inputs of these sectors. Others $(RY'_p + RY'_t)$ are shown as disbursement from the value added in these sectors. Finally, transfers out of household income and other final expenditures are listed as purchases $(RY_C, RY_I)$ in the final demand column.

Table 3.7 provides the corresponding algebraic summary. Note that in light of the discussion concerning the effects of transfers of value, no general pattern between VA* and VA, or between S* and P, has been presumed to hold. But the rate of surplus value S*/V* is shown as being larger than the measure of the profit/wage ratio because this general empirical pattern is rooted in the fact that V* < W.

### 3.2.2 *Profit-type income can exceed surplus value*

We have seen that whereas royalty payments by primary sectors to secondary sectors tend to reduce the measure of profit-type income relative to surplus value, similar transfers originating in household, government, or foreign sectors (i.e., in nonbusiness sectors) tend to make profit-type income larger relative to surplus value. At an empirical level, the profit-reducing effect of transfers of value swamps the profit-increasing effect. But the very fact that two such opposing effects exist implies that we cannot say a priori whether or not surplus value will be greater than total profit. This only serves to emphasize the theoretical point that aggregate profit is the sum of realized surplus value *and* the net transfer of value between circuits of capital and circuits of revenue (see Section 2.4).

Table 3.7. *Marxian and IO measures: Private royalties payments*

| Marxian | | Input–output |
|---|---|---|
| *A. Revenue side* | | |
| $TV^* = GO_p + GO_t$ | $<$ | $GO = GO_p + GO_t + GO_{ry}$ |
| $C^* = M_p$ | $<$ | $M = (M_p + RY_p) + (M_t + RY_t)$ $+ (M_{ry} + RY_{ry})$ |
| $VA^* = TV^* - C^*$ | | $VA = GO - M$ |
| $\quad = RY_p + VA_p + (GO_t)$ | | $\quad = VA_p + VA_t + VA_{ry}$ |
| $\quad = VA_p + VA_t + (M_t + RY_p + RY_t)$ | | |
| $V^* = W_p$ | $<$ | $W = W_p + W_t + W_{ry}$ |
| $S^* = VA^* - V^*$ | | $P = P_p + P_t + P_{ry}$ |
| $\quad = VA_p + VA_t + (M_t + RY_p + RY_t)$ | | |
| $\quad - W_p$ | | |
| $\quad = P_p + P_t + RY'_p + RY'_t$ | | |
| $\quad + (M_t + W_t + RY_p + RY_t)$ | | |
| $S^*/V^* = [P_p + P_t + (M_t + W_t + RY_p$ | $\gg$ | $P/W = (P_p + P_t + P_{ry})/(W_p + W_t + W_{ry})$ |
| $\quad + RY'_p + RY_t + RY'_t)]/W_p$ | | |
| *B. Use side* | | |
| $TP^* = GP_p + GP_t$ | $<$ | $GP = GP_p + GP_t + GP_{ry}$ |
| $U^* = M_p$ | $<$ | $M = M_p + M_t + M_{ry}$ |
| $FP^* = TP^* - U^*$ | | $FD = GP - U$ |
| $\quad = M_t + M_{ry} + (CON - RY_C)$ | | $\quad = CON + I$ |
| $\quad + (I - RY_I)$ | | |
| $\quad = M_t + M_{ry} + CON^* + I^*$ | | |
| $NP^* = CONW_p$ | | (no corresponding category) |
| $SP^* = FP^* - NP^*$ | | (no corresponding category) |
| $\quad = M_t + M_{ry} + CON^* + I^* - CONW_p$ | | |

*Note:* $CON^* = CON - RY_C$ and $I^* = I - RY_I$ (see Figure 3.8).

To obtain an insight into the profit-enhancing effect of transfers of value, it is useful to consider the simple case of household royalty payments in conjunction with the production sector alone. With production alone and no household royalty payments, aggregate profit is equal to aggregate surplus value ($1400 as in Section 3.1.1). According to our convention, this aggregate profit is also the income of the capitalist class. Suppose that the capitalists in turn pay $450 of this personal revenue over to the royalties sector as net interest and ground rent. The royalties sector will then have a total business revenue of $450, split into (say) $300 in costs and $100 in profits. Aggregate business profits will now equal the profits of the production sector ($1400) plus the profits of the royalties

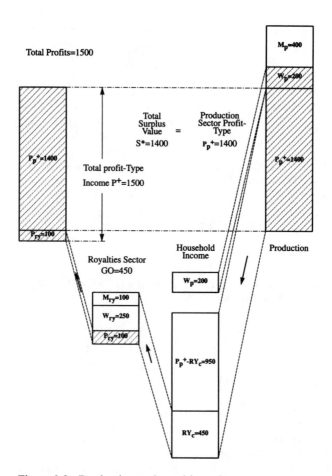

Figure 3.9. Production and royalties only.

sector ($100), for a total of $1500. Yet aggregate surplus value is $1400. *Total profit exceeds total surplus value.* Figure 3.9 illustrates these flows, with total profits and total surplus value explicitly mapped out.[13]

This result is a variant of the one that has always bedeviled the discussion of the transformation problem. In both cases, the mystery is solved once we recall that monetary profit is the sum of surplus value and any

[13] The upper limit to this effect is when all profits of the production sector flow back to the royalties sector (profits are used solely to pay royalties) *and* all of this flow shows up as royalties-sector profits (there being no input or wage costs in the royalties sector). In this case, aggregate profits would be twice as large as surplus value!

(positive or negative) transfers of value between the (flow) circuit of capital and all other circuits (see Section 2.4). In the present case, the disbursement of dividends out of the profits of the production sector is recorded as a sharing out of profits, not as a deduction from it (unlike payments of ground rent or net interest, which are recorded as costs of business and hence as deductions from production profits). Because dividend payments are not treated as deductions from profits, there is no recorded *transfer-out* of value from the circuit of capital. But when capitalists in turn pay a portion of this dividend income back to the business sector, the corresponding business receipt constitutes a recorded *transfer-in* of value into the circuit of capital, a portion of which then shows up as additional recorded profit. It is the particularity of profit–loss accounting that gives rise to this effect, not some mysterious creation or negation of value in circulation.

Another way to look at this outcome is to recognize that although surplus value is the foundation of modern capitalist profit, some components of total profit-type income are not derived from surplus value. The profit-type income of the primary sector is always part of aggregate surplus value (see Figure 3.7 and Table 3.6); however, the profit-type income of the secondary sector is not included in surplus value, precisely because its sources are already contained within other parts of total value (captured in the accounts of primary sectors). This is clearest in the simple case in which there are only production and royalties sectors (Figure 3.9). Here, while the profit-type income of the production sector is equal to surplus value, total profit-type income is greater because of secondary-sector profits.

In actual empirical estimates for the United States, the abstract possibility pictured here does not predominate. Indeed, aggregate profit-type income $P^+$ is roughly 60% of total surplus value, and aggregate profit P is 40%. Moreover, since variable capital $V^* \equiv W_p$ is roughly 40% of total wages W, the rate of surplus value $S^*/V^*$ is generally five times greater than the profit/wage ratio P/W (see Section 5.4).

### B. Public secondary flows: General government activities

The state sector as a whole encompasses two types of activities. First, there are government *enterprises.* Depending on the particular type of activity in which they engage, such enterprises appear in IO–NIPA accounts as part of the production, trade, or private royalties sectors (BEA 1980, pp. 27–8), and are treated in the same way as are private enterprises in those sectors.[14] Second, government *agencies* oversee the maintenance

---

[14] We treat government enterprises in the United States as essentially capitalist enterprises. This need not be the case in other countries.

and reproduction of the social order: police, fire departments, courts and prisons, defense and international affairs, and general administration. All of these are nonproduction activities.

Within conventional national accounts, government receipts consist of taxes (business and personal, net of subsidies and transfers), fees and fines, rents and royalties, and personal and employer contributions for social insurance. Government disbursements consist of the purchases of goods and services (including payments to unproductive sectors and government employees), transfer payments to persons, net interest paid to persons and foreigners,[15] and net subsidies to government enterprises, minus dividends received by government. The government surplus or deficit is the difference between receipts and disbursements (BEA 1986, pp. ix–xii).

Input–output accounts only partially capture the flows associated with general government. On the revenue side, they only pick up business payments (taxes, fees, net interest paid) to government. Household payments to government, like those to the royalties sector, do not explicitly show up here. On the use side, transfer payments to persons and business are excluded (having been netted out of taxes and fees received by government).

This leaves only two major elements: government purchases of goods and services G' (which include royalty payments such as ground rent and finance charges); and purchases of labor power, the wages $W_G$ paid to government employees. Input–output accounts treat these two components in quite different ways. Government expenditures G' are treated as part of the final use of the product, and therefore appear under final demand. In keeping with the orthodox treatment of royalties, expenditures on net interest and ground rent are treated as purchases of the output of the royalties sector.

Treating G' as part of final use, rather than as an intermediate input into some government production activity, is an implicit admission that general government activities are nonproduction activities. To be consistent, one would also have to similarly treat the government purchase of labor power $W_G$ as part of the same nonproduction activity – but this is not done. On the contrary, IO–NIPA accounts treat government purchases of labor power as purchases of a service which is the sole constituent of a government net product (and hence of government value added). Since these wages do not appear anywhere in the accounts, a dummy "government industry" is added to the IO table: its row contains

15 In keeping with the treatment of net interest in IO–NIPA accounts, the net interest paid to businesses is redefined as a purchase of a financial service. It is therefore part of the government disbursements on goods and services.

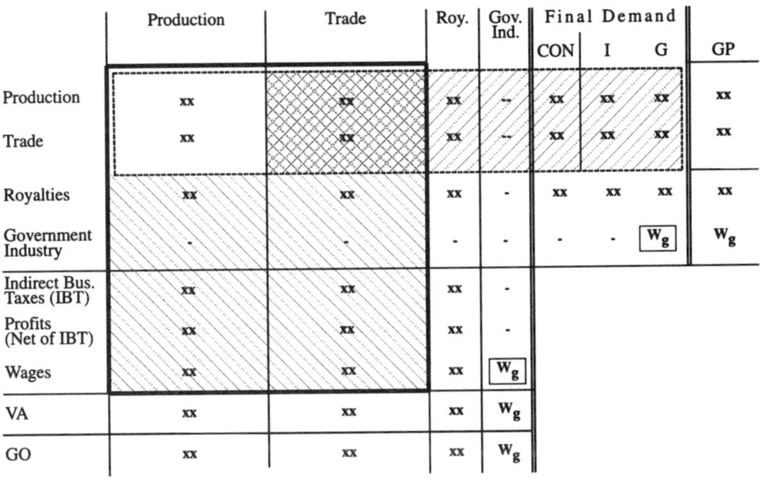

| | Production | Trade | Roy. | Gov. Ind. | Final Demand CON | I | G | GP |
|---|---|---|---|---|---|---|---|---|
| Production | xx | xx | xx | -- | xx | xx | xx | xx |
| Trade | xx | xx | xx | -- | xx | xx | xx | xx |
| Royalties | xx | xx | xx | - | xx | xx | xx | xx |
| Government Industry | - | - | - | - | - | - | $W_g$ | $W_g$ |
| Indirect Bus. Taxes (IBT) | xx | xx | xx | - | | | | |
| Profits (Net of IBT) | xx | xx | xx | - | | | | |
| Wages | xx | xx | xx | $W_g$ | | | | |
| VA | xx | xx | xx | $W_g$ | | | | |
| GO | xx | xx | xx | $W_g$ | | | | |

Figure 3.10. IO accounts and Marxian categories: General government.

only one entry ($W_G$) under the government column (representing the government's purchase of the government industry's net product), and its column contains only one element ($W_G$) in its value-added row (representing the value added of the government industry). Through this device, orthodox measures of gross and net product are each expanded by $W_G$.

From our point of view, the payments made by businesses and households to general government are simply a form of royalty payments. As such, the basic principles governing the treatment of royalties also apply here. Thus, since the accounts of primary sectors already include the original sources of government receipts, we cannot now count them twice. In our view, neither government commodity purchases $G'$ nor purchases of labor power $W_G$ enter into a production activity; we must exclude not only the former (as IO–NIPA accounts do) but also the latter (which they do not). As indicated in Figure 3.10, this means excluding the dummy government industry from aggregate measures of output and product. As before, the basic Marxian measures are contained within the primary-sector blocks.

Note that exclusion of the government dummy industry does not imply that we ignore either the government use of actual product (which shows up in the government final-demand column of the production row) or the personal consumption of government workers (which shows up in the consumption column of the production row). Both of these items are *genuine uses* of the existing total product. By excluding the dummy government industry, we simply exclude any *expansion of the measure* of this product.

Because business payments to government (net interest paid and taxes net of subsidies) are recorded in value added, their introduction changes the distribution but not the magnitude of business value added. But since the subsequent payment of government wages out of these same revenues is recorded as the creation of a government net product, the conventional aggregate measures of gross and net product are expanded by $W_G$.

Business payments to government leave the measure of business value added unchanged, so they also leave the measure of business profit-type income unchanged (where profit-type income is defined as value added plus royalties paid minus wages). There being no profit-type income for government, it follows that aggregate profit-type income is unchanged by the inclusion of general government. On the other hand, since net interest paid and indirect business taxes reduce the portion of business value added which goes to profit, and since profit taxes reduce the portion of profit which firms get to keep, the inclusion of general government reduces the aggregate measures of pre- and post-tax profit.

Finally, to the extent that the government transfers some of its revenues back to the royalties sector as (say) ground rent or finance charges, this would expand the revenues of the royalties sector. Measured gross output, value added, and even profits of the royalties sector would rise, and with this so too would the corresponding aggregate measures (since, as we have already seen, the payment of taxes etc. does not reduce the measured gross or net output of the business sector). This result is the same as the one derived earlier from household payments to the royalties sector, and includes the possibility that measured profit-type income could exceed surplus value.

In summary, royalty payments by primary sectors to the government already show up in the value added of the originating sectors and cannot therefore be counted again if they happen to be transferred to some other sector or group. But orthodox accounts do count (a portion of) such transfers, precisely because they view them as measures of the government's output; thus they inflate the measures of total value and total product by the sum of these transfers. Specifically, they count any wages paid by government to its nonproduction employees as a measure of additional government product (recorded through the creation of a dummy government industry), and count any transfer from the government to the royalties sector as a measure of the additional product created by the royalties sector. By restricting ourselves to the sum of the gross output

Table 3.8. *Public secondary flows: General government activities*

| Marxian | Input–output |
|---|---|
| *A. Revenue side* | |
| $TV^* = GO_p + GO_t$ | $< \quad GO = GO_p + GO_t + W_G$ |
| $C^* = M_p$ | $< \quad M = M_p + M_t$ |
| $VA^* = TV^* - C^*$ | $VA = GO - M$ |
| $\quad = VA_p + GO_t$ | $\quad = VA_p + VA_t + W_G$ |
| $\quad = (W + P^+)_p + (M + W + P^+)_t$ | |
| $V^* = W_p$ | $< \quad W = W_p + W_t + W_G$ |
| $S^* = VA^* - V^*$ | $< \quad P^+ \equiv VA - W = P + IBT$ |
| $\quad = (P_p^+ + P_t^+) + (W_t + M_t)$ | |
| $\quad = P + IBT + (W_t + M_t)$ | |
| $S^*/V^* = [P + IBT + (W_t + M_t)]/W_p$ | $\gg P/W = P/(W_p + W_t)$ |
| *B. Use side* | |
| $TP^* = GP_p + GP_t$ | $< \quad GP = GP_p + GP_t + W_G$ |
| $U^* = M_p$ | $< \quad U = M_p + M_t$ |
| $FP^* = TP^* - U^*$ | $FD = GP - U$ |
| $\quad = CON + I + G' + M_t$ | $\quad = CON + I + G' + W_G$ |
| $NP^* = CONW_p$ | (no corresponding category) |
| $SP^* = FP^* - NP^*$ | (no corresponding category) |
| $\quad = I + G' + (CONW_t + M_t)$ | |

*Notes:*
IBT = indirect business taxes;
$\quad$ P = profit-type income, net of indirect business taxes;
$\quad$ $P^+$ = profit-type income, gross of indirect business taxes.

and gross product of the primary sectors, we avoid these spurious over-statements of total measured product.

Table 3.8 summarizes the treatment of public secondary flows (except for the issue of net taxes on productive worker wages, which is addressed in Section 3.3). We abstract from private royalty flows here.

### 3.3 Net transfers from wages, the social wage, and the adjusted rate of surplus value

Whereas royalty payments from primary to secondary sectors do not change the basic Marxian measures, those which come out of the wage of productive workers are different. The true measure of variable capital is the nominal wage of productive workers minus any net royalty payments made by them. Thus, in order to estimate true variable capital, we should deduct net interest, net ground rent, and net taxes (net of social benefit expenditures received) paid by production workers from our apparent measure of variable capital.

At a conceptual level, the calculation of net interest and net ground-rent payments is relatively straightforward. But the estimation of net taxes paid requires a comparison between the gross taxes paid by production workers and the corresponding transfers and other social welfare expenditures (for health, education, roads, parks, etc.) directed back toward them. These further details are taken up in Section 5.9 and Appendix N.

Once the sum of net royalty paid by production workers $NRY_{wp}$ has been estimated, it must be subtracted from production worker wages and added to surplus value in order to obtain the true measures of each. The measure of surplus value will then be correspondingly larger, as will the adjusted rate of surplus value. Using primes to denote these adjusted measures, we have on the revenue side:

$$V^{*\prime} = W_p - NRY_{wp} = V^* - NRY_{wp};$$

$$S^{*\prime} = S^* + NRY_{wp};$$

adjusted rate of surplus value

$$= S^{*\prime}/V^{*\prime} = (S^* + NRY_{wp})/(V^* - NRY_{wp})$$
$$> \text{apparent rate of surplus value} = S^*/V^*.$$

On the use side, the corresponding adjustment comes in the measure of the necessary and surplus products, as follows:

$$NP^{*\prime} = CONW_p - NRY_{wp} = NP^* - NRY_{wp}$$

$$SP^{*\prime} = FP^* - NP^{*\prime}$$
$$= M_t + CON^* + I^* + NRY_{wp} - CONW_p;$$
$$= SP^* + NRY_{wp}$$

adjusted rate of exploitation

$$= SP^{*\prime}/NP^{*\prime} = (SP^* + NRY_{wp})/(NP^* - NRY_{wp})$$
$$> \text{apparent rate exploitation} = SP^*/NP^*$$

All actual calculations appear in Section 5.9 and Appendix N. There, we confine ourselves to the net tax on variable capital $NT_{wp}$. The estimation of this net tax (which may be negative, insofar as social expenditures on workers exceed the taxes they pay) is part of a much larger issue involving the debate that concerns the welfare state and the so-called social wage or citizen wage (Bowles and Gintis 1982; Shaikh and Tonak 1987). It should be noted that our analysis of state-induced transfers deals with actual empirical flows - that is, with the observed incidence of taxes - corresponding to what Ursula Hicks (1946) has called the "social accounting approach." The further analysis of tax incidence based on some assumed pattern of tax shifting, which would involve a comparison between the actual flows and some hypothetical alternative set of flows deemed to hold in the imagined absence of some taxes, is beyond the scope of this book.

### 3.4 Foreign trade

We have tracked down the various forms taken by produced value as it is absorbed by the trade, royalties, and state sectors by means of a complex series of value transfers. But this was for a closed economy. The question now is: How are these results modified for an open economy?

In the case of an open economy, our object is to distinguish between domestically *produced* value and domestically *realized* value. The difference between the two arises from transfers of value which cut across national boundaries. There are three basic causes of these international transfers: foreign trading margins on exports and imports, which transfer value between nations; deviations between purchasers' prices and values, which do the same thing; and international flows of wages and salaries, dividends, interest, et cetera, which transfer value directly in the form of money. The first two issues will be addressed in the treatment of international commodity trade (merchandise trade accounts) and the third in that of international payments for "factor services" (rest-of-world accounts). Before we proceed, however, we need to specify what we mean by national economic boundaries.

The precise distinction between domestic and foreign economic activities depends on the purpose of the analysis. For instance, we can define "domestic" in two basic ways; in terms of the national boundaries of the country involved; or in terms of the nationality of the person or organization in question. We will adopt the former, because our purpose is to measure the production of value within a given nation. This use of national boundaries to define domestic activities implies that location takes precedence over nationality. Thus foreign workers or corporations located within the United States are counted as part of the domestic sector.

Transportation activity involves a further consideration. A cargo loaded onto a domestic carrier can cross over to foreign territory before it is unloaded at its foreign destination. Along the way, it may cut across the territory of some third nation, or cross neutral space such as the ocean. Alternately, the domestic carrier may hand over its cargo to a foreign carrier at some point before the foreign port of call. The complications arising from all of these instances can be handled by extending the definition of the national economic boundary to encompass domestic carriers. On this basis, we will count an import as entering the United States either when it is unloaded at a U.S. port or when it is transferred onto a U.S. carrier. Similarly, an export will be counted as leaving the United States either when it is loaded onto a foreign carrier or when it is unloaded at a foreign port of call.

### 3.4.1 *GDP, GNP, and the rest-of-world (ROW) accounts*

Orthodox national accounts distinguish between gross domestic product (GDP), which seeks to measure "the output of goods and services produced by labor and property located in the United States," and gross national product (GNP), which corresponds to "the goods and services produced by U.S. residents" (Tice and Moczar 1986, p. 28). The first measure is based on the location, the second on the nationality, of the corporations or persons involved.

The GNP measure of national product is derived from the GDP measure by adding the rest-of-world (ROW) accounts, because ROW flows are designed to represent the difference between the two concepts of national product. GDP counts the wages and salaries, dividend and interest earnings, and retained earnings of foreign persons and corporations located in the United States. On the other hand, it excludes the same earnings of U.S. nationals and U.S. corporations located abroad. GNP, which is structured according to nationality, excludes the first set and includes the second. The ROW accounts are simply the difference between the second and first sets, so that adding them to GDP produces GNP (BEA 1980, pp. 29–32).

For our purposes, it is the GDP concept which is the relevant starting point. Since sectoral accounts in both NIPA and IO tables are structured according to the GDP concept, we can work directly with them and ignore the ROW accounts altogether. With this out of the way, we proceed to the analysis of transfers of value brought about by foreign trading margins on exports and imports, even when commodities sell at final (purchasers') prices proportional to values. We then extend the analysis to cover purchaser price–value deviations, ending up with a general summary of the transfers of value induced by international trade. This will help us separate out domestically produced value from the realized values that are recorded in conventional accounts.

### 3.4.2 *Transfers of value in international trade*

Within one nation, the production sector transfers a portion of the value of its product to the trading sector by selling it at a (producer's)

Table 3.9. *Domestically produced and used
commodities*

| | |
|---|---|
| Producer's price:<br>  Manufacturer's price: $70<br>  Transport margin: $10 | $ 80 |
| Trade margin: | $ 20 |
| Purchaser's price: | $100 |

price below its value. The difference between the two sets of sales is the revenue of the domestic trade sector (the total trading margin on all goods sold). This holds even when commodities are sold to their final users at (purchasers') prices proportional to their values.

Exactly the same thing occurs when a domestic producer exports a commodity. In this case, however, the value transferred to the trade sector may be split up between domestic and foreign trading capitals, so that only a portion of the total value is retained within the country. Exports therefore transfer value *out of* a nation, ceteris paribus, in an amount equal to the trade margin of the foreign trading capital. The opposite holds for imports. The domestic trading capital captures a portion of foreign value by acquiring a commodity below its final selling price (which by assumption is equal to its value). Imports transfer value *into* a country, other things being equal.

Tables 3.9–3.11 illustrate these arguments. In Table 3.9, we see that in the case of a domestically produced and used commodity (say steel), the total value of the product (equal to its purchaser's price of $100) is split up between the production sector ($70), the domestic transportation sector ($10), and the domestic trade sector ($20). On the assumption that the transportation in question is productive transport, a total value of $100 is created by the production sectors (steel producers and transporters), of which $20 is transferred to the domestic trade sector by virtue of the fact that the total producers' price ($80 = $70 + $10) is less than the total value.

The same basic principle applies to exports and imports, with the difference that the connection between producers, transporters, and traders now cuts across national boundaries and thus gives rise to international transfers of value. Keep in mind that our definition of a nation's economic boundary encompasses any transport by national carriers.

Table 3.10 applies this rule to the case of an export. The *domestic export price* – the price received by domestic producers, transporters, and traders – is defined as the domestic port price plus any cost of international

Table 3.10. *Exports*

| | |
|---|---|
| X* = domestic export price = value retained: | $ 70 |
| = domestic port price ($55) <br> + international transport by domestic carriers ($15) | |
| Foreign margins = value transferred abroad: | $ 30 |
| = international transport by foreign carriers ($5) <br> + foreign importer's duties ($3) <br> + foreign importer's insurance ($2) <br> + transport within foreign country ($13) <br> + trade within foreign country ($7) | |
| X⁺ = foreign purchaser's price: | $100 |

Table 3.11. *Imports*

| | |
|---|---|
| IM* = domestic import price = value paid for: | $ 60 |
| = foreign port price ($50) <br> + international transport by foreign carriers ($10) | |
| Domestic margins = value transferred in <br> = value received − value paid <br> = $100 − $60: | $ 40 |
| = international transport by domestic carriers ($5) <br> + domestic import duties ($7) <br> + domestic importer's insurance ($3) <br> + domestic transport of imported goods ($15) <br> + domestic trade in imported goods ($10) | |
| IM⁺ = domestic purchaser's price: | $100 |

transport by domestic carriers.[16] This represents that portion of the total value of the commodity which is retained within the country. The remainder of the export's final selling price (its foreign purchaser's price), which for the moment is assumed to be equal to the commodity's value, represents the value which is transferred abroad.

Table 3.11 examines the case of imports. Here, the outcome is reversed since it is the foreigners who retain only a portion of the value produced in their country, with the rest being captured by domestic importers, transporters, and traders. The *domestic import price* is therefore the foreign

---

[16] The structure of merchandise trade accounts is described in BEA (1980, pp. 4, 20, 22-4).

port price plus any costs of international transport by foreign carriers. This total is, of course, the same as the value retained by the foreign country.

It follows that value can be transferred between nations – even when all final selling prices are equal to values – depending on the balance between the value transferred in through imports and the value transferred out through exports. This is a systematic effect whose direction is tied to the location of the commodity within foreign trade (as export or import), quite different from the indeterminate direction of transfers associated with purchaser price–value deviations. *Relative* producer prices, including domestic export and import prices, are relative prices of production whose deviation from relative values depends on the relative organic capitals of the sectors and the relative efficiency of the capitals within a given sector (Shaikh 1980a). But all producer prices are less than purchaser prices because of the intervening domestic and foreign trading margins. Thus the transfers of value due to trading margins are unidirectional, from producers to traders. On the other hand, purchaser price–value deviations are the synthesis of factors causing relative producer prices to deviate from relative values and factors causing absolute producer prices to be less than purchaser prices.

For the analysis of international transfers of value, the trading-margin transfers are clearly more fundamental than those arising from purchaser price–value deviations. The latter are easily introduced into the analysis. Any (positive or negative) deviation between purchaser prices and direct prices (prices proportional to values) must be added to the previously analyzed deviations between domestic import and export prices and the corresponding purchaser prices. As shown in what follows, the overall transfer can be derived directly by substituting direct prices for purchaser prices in Tables 3.10 and 3.11. But it is more useful to show the two sets of deviations separately, since they are determined differently. The measures $T_x$, $T_{im}$, and T are constructed so that a transfer in is positive and a transfer out is negative:

$X^*$, $IM^*$ = domestic prices of total exports and imports;

$X^+$, $IM^+$ = purchaser prices of total exports and imports;

$X^v$, $IM^v$ = direct prices (values) of total exports and imports.

$T_x$ = transfer of value on exports

= transfer out on foreign margins

+ transfer on price–value deviations of exports

= (domestic export price − foreign purchaser price)

+ (foreign purchaser price − direct price)

$$= \text{domestic export price} - \text{direct price of exports}$$
$$= (X^* - X^+) + (X^+ - X^v) = X^* - X^v.$$

$T_{im} = \text{transfer of value on imports}$
$\quad = \text{transfer in on domestic margins on imported goods}$
$\quad\quad + \text{transfer on price-value deviations of imports}$
$\quad = (\text{domestic import price} - \text{domestic purchaser price})$
$\quad\quad + (\text{domestic purchaser price} - \text{direct price of imports})$
$\quad = \text{domestic import price} - \text{direct price of imports}$
$\quad = (IM^* - IM^+) + (IM^+ - IM^v) = IM^* - IM^v.$

$T = \text{Net transfer of value through foreign trade} = T_x - T_{im}$
$\quad = (X^* - IM^*) - (X^v - IM^v).$

The net transfer of value T (expressed in its money equivalent) is therefore the difference between the conventional realized-value measure of the balance of trade $(X^* - IM^*)$[17] and the corresponding labor value measure $(X^v - IM^v)$. This means that adding T to the revenue and use sides of conventional accounts will replace the realized values recorded there with the corresponding produced values. The resulting total value and total product will then correctly measure produced, rather than realized, magnitudes.

In estimating the net international transfer of value T, it is useful to express it in a somewhat different form. Let

$d_x \equiv (X^* - X^v)/X^* = $ the percentage deviation of basic export
$\qquad\qquad\qquad\qquad$ prices from direct export prices (values),
$\qquad\qquad\qquad\qquad$ and let

$d_{im} \equiv (IM^* - IM^v)/IM^* = $ the percentage deviation of basic
$\qquad\qquad\qquad\qquad\qquad$ import prices from direct import
$\qquad\qquad\qquad\qquad\qquad$ prices (values); then

$T = d_x \cdot X^* - d_{im} \cdot IM^*.$

The last expression is the most convenient one for the empirical estimation of net transfers. Note that if trade is balanced $(X^* = IM^*)$ then the

---

[17] In actual practice, NIPA measures differ slightly from the domestic export and import prices defined here. Exports are valued in orthodox accounts at their domestic port price alone, which makes their valuation smaller than our definition of the domestic export price by the cost of their shipping on domestic carriers. On the other hand, noncomparable imports are similarly undervalued relative to our measure, since orthodox accounts leave out the cost of shipping by foreign carriers. The net difference between the orthodox trade balance measure $(X - IM)$ and our measure of net realized trade balance $(X^* - IM^*)$ is quite small; we therefore ignore it in what follows.

transfer of value depends solely on the difference in export and import price–value deviations and on the level of trade: $T = (d_x - d_{im}) \cdot X^*$. Conversely, if the price–value deviations are the same for exports and imports $(d_x = d_{im} = d)$ then the net transfer depends solely on the level of this average deviation and on the balance of trade: $T = d \cdot (X^* - IM^*)$. If we estimate d at 12% (see Section 5.10) then T is quite small relative to $S^*$ and can safely be neglected.

In summary, the production accounts within any one country will record only domestically realized values. To correct for this, it is necessary to adjust surplus value on the revenue side, and the recorded trade balance $X^* - IM^*$ on the use side, by subtracting the amount of the net transfer of value T. This replaces realized surplus value and the realized trade balance $X^* - IM^*$ with produced surplus value and the produced trade balance $X^v - IM^v$. The resultant measures of total value and total product will then reflect domestic production alone.

### 3.5 Noncapitalist activities and illegal activities

In principle, noncapitalist activities should be distinguished from capitalist ones. But in the official accounts of an advanced capitalist economy such as the United States, such activities are either merged into the corresponding capitalist sectors (e.g., self-employed mechanics are treated as unincorporated enterprises within the automobile repair industry) or they are left out altogether (most notably in the case of the household sector). We are unable to transcend these limitations in the data, although we do provide estimates of the impact of unpaid household activities. As we saw in Chapter 1, unofficial extended accounts do address such issues.

The one case in which noncapitalist activities are explicitly treated is a dummy industry designed to capture the output of paid household labor such as that of "maids, chauffeurs, and baby sitters" (BEA 1980, p. 28). As in the case of the government industry sector, the household industry dummy sector has only one entry in each row and column, in each case representing the estimated wages of the workers involved. Even assuming that such labor is mostly production labor, it is generally not capitalist production labor.[18] The cost of this labor power therefore cannot be included in variable capital. The household industry sector, like the government industry sector, must be excluded from our measures of total value and total capitalistic product. Both are unproductive of capital,

---

[18] To the extent that the household workers in question are employed by a capitalist enterprise (e.g., a capitalist housecleaning service), their labor in the household is simply the application of labor power that has first been exchanged against capital (when they were hired by the housecleaning firm). It is therefore productive labor, not merely production labor; but then it shows up under productive services.

albeit for different reasons: the government industry is a nonproduction sector, and the household industry is a noncapitalist production sector.

## 3.6 Summary of the relation between Marxian and conventional national accounts

### 3.6.1 *Overall summary*

In a closed economy, the total value produced within a country is realized in the sales of the primary (i.e., production and trade) sectors, whose combined revenue represents the total price (money equivalent) of the output created in the production sector. Production involves the creation or transformation of the useful properties of material objects of social use (use values). It includes goods created in agriculture, mining, construction, public utilities, manufacturing, and government production enterprises, in addition to services such as productive transport and a host of other productive services (e.g., hotels, haircutting salons, repair services, entertainment, health and educational services, and household production labor).

Trade circulates use values, redistributing them from seller to buyer in return for a counterflow of money. Trade encompasses wholesale/retail trade, building and equipment rentals (piecemeal sales), distributive transportation, and government trading enterprises. Two steps are required to derive an estimate of the building and equipment rental sector. First, the fictitious components of the real estate and rental sector, which consist of imputed wages and profits of private homeowners (who are treated as businesses renting their own homes to themselves), must be excised from the accounts on both revenue and use sides (Section 3.1.3 and Figure 3.7). Second, the remaining nonimputed real estate and rental flows must be split into building and equipment rental (which is included in total trade) and land rental and sales (which becomes a part of the royalties sector).

The value which is realized in the primary sectors can be further recirculated through a series of transfers (which we call royalty payments) between the primary sector and various secondary sectors. These secondary flows involve the payment of net interest, finance charges, ground rent, fees, royalties, and taxes. The sectors receiving these can be grouped into the (private) royalties sector (finance, insurance, ground rent, etc.) and the general government sector. The two are treated as separate parts of the royalties sector.

Because the original sources of the revenues of the secondary sectors are already counted in the revenues of the primary sectors, we cannot count them again in the measure of the total product and its total value. Secondary flows are part of total transactions, but *not* part of total product. In the case of the royalties sector, this means leaving out the royalties-sector column on the revenue side; and leaving out royalty payments from the consumption, investment, government, and net-trade columns on the use side, since these are transfer payments, not purchases of use values (Figure 3.8).

The same principle applies to the general government sector (government enterprises are treated as part of other sectors, according to the activity in which they engage). As a royalties-receiving sector, its revenues (taxes and fees) derive from the already counted flows in the primary sector, and thus cannot be counted again in the measure of the total product (although these revenues may add powerfully to total transactions). In IO tables, this means excluding the government industry dummy sector from the revenue side, as well as the corresponding row entry in the final-demand government column on the use side (Figure 3.10).

The next step is to extend the analysis to the case of an open economy. Since our purpose is to measure domestically produced value and surplus value, the GDP concept (which measures output produced within the nation) is preferable to the GNP concept (which measures output produced by U.S. persons or corporations anywhere in the world). We therefore exclude the rest-of-world industry column and row from our coverage of production and trade, because this is merely the balancing item between the GDP and the GNP concepts. In addition, since foreign trade induces transfers of value, the value realized within the primary sectors reflects not only the value produced within the country but also any (negative or positive) international transfers of value. We would therefore have to adjust for these transfers in order to recover the magnitude of produced value. This could be done by adding the net international transfer of value $T$ to realized surplus value on the revenue side, and to the realized trade balance $X^* - IM^*$ on the use side, once the basic Marxian totals have been derived.

Finally, input–output tables list a dummy industry called the household industry; it is designed to represent the output of the domestic services of maids, chauffeurs, and baby-sitters. The money value of this output is taken to be equal to wages alone, since the activities in question are noncapitalist. The only entries associated with this dummy industry appear in the value-added row of the household column and in the household row of the consumption column, both equal to the wages of domestic workers. We exclude this sector from our coverage of total value and product, on the grounds that paid domestic labor is largely noncapitalist activity.

Adjusting conventional IO tables in the ways just indicated (except for the transfer of value $T$), we can map out the overall relation between IO accounts and Marxian categories as depicted in Figure 3.11. A dash in a cell indicates that it is empty by construction (as in the case of most of

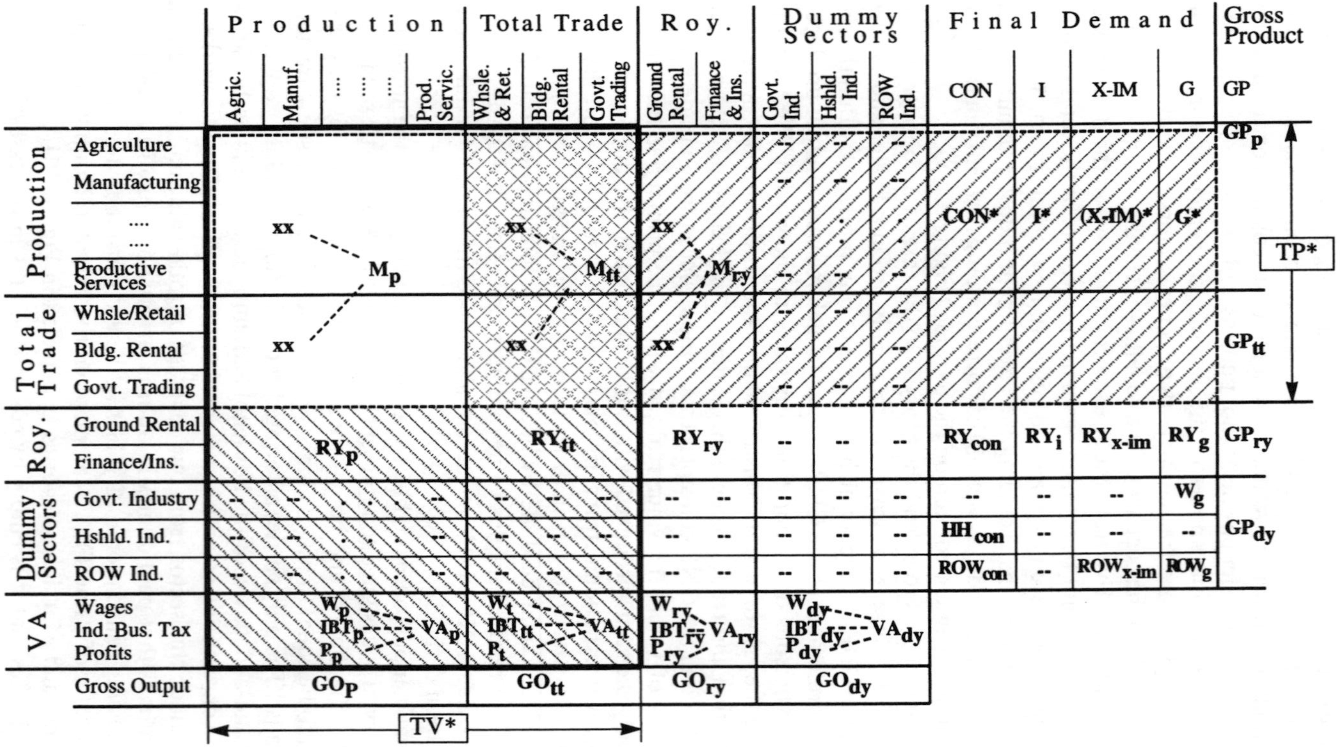

Figure 3.11. IO accounts and Marxian categories: Overall summary.

those associated with dummy sectors). Blank cells, or those with xx in them, contain (or could contain) entries; dots in cells indicate continuation of the existing pattern. The Marxian revenue-side flows are indicated by the area within the bold rectangle, and the corresponding use flows by that within the dotted rectangle. Value added is broken down here into wages W (employee compensation), indirect business taxes IBT, and profits P (property-type income), as in actual IO tables. For reasons discussed previously, neither the royalties sector nor the dummy government and household industry sectors appear in the measure of total value.

Table 3.12 provides the corresponding algebraic summary. As always, the subscripts p, tt, and ry refer to the production, total trade, and royalties sectors, respectively. The subscript dy has been added to refer to the overall dummy sector, while g, hh, and row refer to the government, household, and rest-of-world dummy industries, respectively. None of the dummy industries have any intermediate inputs, but the ROW industry does include property income. Table 3.12 also summarizes those patterns which can be said to hold in general, either theoretically or empirically. By and large, the Marxian measures of gross and net product are smaller than the corresponding orthodox measures, since the latter include many transactions that we would exclude from measures of production. We show surplus value as larger than the orthodox measures of profit-type income because this is empirically true, even though surplus value can in principle be larger (see Section 3.2.2).

### 3.6.2 The balance between the two sides of the Marxian accounts

In order to establish the balance between the revenue and use sides of the Marxian accounts, it is helpful to recall that input–output accounts are constructed in such a way that row sums equal column sums for all industries. Three such identities are particularly useful (cf. Figure 3.11):

(a) $GO \equiv GO_p + GO_{tt} + GO_{ry} + GO_{dy}$
$= GP \equiv (M_p + M_{tt} + M_{ry}) + (RY_p + RY_{tt} + RY_{ry}) + CON$
$+ I + (X - IM) + G;$

(b) $GO_{ry} = GP_{ry} \equiv RY_p + RY_{tt} + RY_{ry} + RY_{con} + RY_i + RY_{x-im} + RY_g;$

(c) $GO_{dy} = GP_{dy} \equiv GP_g + GP_h + GP_{row}$
$= W_g + HH_{con} + (ROW_{con} + ROW_{x-im} + ROW_g).$

We will show that the equality of TV* and TP* is predicated on these identities. Looking once again at Figure 3.11, TV* = TP* implies that

(d) $TV^* \equiv GO_p + GO_{tt}$
$= TP^* \equiv (M_p + M_{tt} + M_{ry})$
$+ (CON - RY_{con} - HH_{con} - ROW_{con})$
$+ (I - RY_i) + [(X - IM) - RY_{x-im} - ROW_{x-im}]$
$+ (G - RY_g - W_g - ROW_g).$

Table 3.12. *Marxian and IO measures: Overall summary*

| Marxian | Input–output |
|---|---|

**A. Revenue side**

$TV^* = GO_p + GO_{tt}$  $<$  $GO = GO_p + GO_{tt} + GO_{ry} + GO_{dy}$

$C^* = M_p$  $<$  $M = (M_p + RY_p) + (M_{tt} + RY_{tt})$
$+ (M_{ry} + RY_{ry}) + (M_{dy} + RY_{dy})$

$VA^* = TV^* - C^* = GO_p + GO_{tt} - M_p$  $VA = GO - M$
$= (M_p + RY_p + VA_p)$  $= VA_p + VA_{tt} + (VA_{ry} + VA_{dy})$
$+ (M_{tt} + RY_{tt} + VA_{tt}) - M_p$
$= VA_p + VA_{tt}$
$+ (RY_p + RY_{tt} + M_{tt})$

$V^* = W_p$  $<$  $W = W_p + W_{tt} + W_{ry} + W_{dy}$

$S^* = VA^* - V^*$  $P^+ \equiv$ profit-type income[a]
$= (P_p + P_{tt}) + (IBT_p + IBT_{tt})$  $= VA - W = P + IBT$
$+ (RY_p + RY_{tt}) + (W_{tt} + M_{tt})$  $= (P_p + P_{tt} + P_{ry} + P_{dy})$
$+ (IBT_p + IBT_{tt} + IBT_{ry} + IBT_{dy})$

$S^*/V^* = (IBT_p + IBT_{tt} + P_p + P_{tt} + W_{tt}$  $> P/W = (P_p + P_{tt} + P_{ry} + P_{dy})/(W_p + W_{tt} + W_{ry} + W_{dy})$
$+ RY_p + RY_{tt} + M_{tt})/W_p$

**B. Use side**

$TP^* = GP_p + GP_{tt}$  $<$  $GP = GP_p + GP_{tt} + GP_{ry} + GP_{dy}$
$= (M_p + M_{tt} + M_{ry}) + CON^*$  $= (M_p + M_{tt} + M_{ry}) + (RY_p + RY_{tt} + RY_{ry})$
$+ I^* + (X^* - IM^*) + G^*$  $+ CON + I + (X - IM) + G$

$U^* = M_p$  $<$  $U = M = M_p + (M_{tt} + M_{ry}) + (RY_p + RY_{tt} + RY_{ry})$

$FP^* = TP^* - U^*$  $FD = GP - U$
$= CON^* + I^* + (X^* - IM^*)$  $= CON + I + (X - IM) + G$
$+ (M_{tt} + M_{ry})$

$NP^* = CONW_p = W_p$  (no corresponding category)

$SP^* = FP^* - NP^*$  (no corresponding category)
$= (CONW_{np} + CONC)^b + I^*$
$+ (X^* - IM^*) + G^* + (M_{tt} + M_{ry})$

*Notes:*
$CON^* = (CON - RY_{con} - HH_{con} - ROW_{con});$[c]
$I^* = (I - RY_i);$
$X^* - IM^* = [(X - IM) - RY_{x-im} - ROW_{x-im}];$
$G^* = (G - RY_g - W_g - ROW_g).$

[a] A naive measure of surplus value would be the sum of all profits, rents, interest, and taxes: $S^{*\prime} = VA + (RY_p + RY_{tt} + RY_{ry}) - W = P + IBT + (RY_p + RY_{tt} + RY_{ry})$. We make use of this in our technique for approximating the rate of surplus value in Section 5.12.

[b] Total consumption $CON = CONW_p + CONW_{np} + CONC$, where $CONW_p =$ consumption of productive workers, $CONW_{np} =$ consumption of all other workers, and $CONC =$ consumption of capitalists. Thus $CON - CONW_p = CONW_{np} + CONC$.

[c] As is evident from the discussion in the text, the Marxian measure of consumption $CON^*$ excludes the transfer payments $RY_{con}$, $HH_{con}$, and $ROW_{con}$, while the conventional measure of consumption CON includes them. Thus $CON^* = CON - RY_{con} - HH_{con} - ROW_{con}$. The expressions for $I^*$, $(X - IM)^*$, and $G^*$ are derived in the same way.

In expression (a) we can move the term $(GO_{ry} + GO_{dy})$ to the right-hand side and expand it by means of expressions (b) and (c) to obtain

$$GO_p + GO_{tt} \equiv (M_p + M_{tt} + M_{ry}) + (RY_p + RY_{tt} + RY_{ry} - GO_{ry}) + CON + I$$
$$+ (X - IM) + G - GO_{dy}$$
$$= (M_p + M_{tt} + M_{ry}) + (CON - RY_{con} - HH_{con} - ROW_{con})$$
$$+ (I - RY_i) + [(X - IM) - RY_{x-im} - ROW_{x-im}]$$
$$+ (G - RY_g - W_g - ROW_g)$$

But the preceding expression is simply the equality $TV^* = TP^*$, as can be seen by comparing it with expression (d). It follows that $VA^* = FD^*$ and $S^* = SP^*$, since these latter two relations are derived by subtracting equal elements from $TV^*$ and $TP^*$, respectively.

# 4

## Marxian categories and national accounts: Labor value calculations

The previously derived mappings describe the relation between input–output accounts and the *money value* form of Marxian categories, on both the revenue and use sides of the accounts. We now turn to the corresponding calculation of the *labor value* form of these same categories. In what follows, we will outline a procedure first developed in Shaikh (1975) and extended and applied by Khanjian (1989). Only the basic elements will be presented here, since a fuller development is beyond the scope of this book.

### 4.1 Calculating labor value magnitudes

Let us begin by recalling our money value mapping previously summarized in Figure 3.11 and Table 3.12. Figure 4.1 is a simplified version of Figure 3.11. In it, we have explicitly labeled elements of the production and trade rows so as to facilitate later discussion. Thus the (purchaser) price of the total intermediate input of the productive sectors $M_p = (M_p)_p + (M_p)_t$, where $(M_p)_p$ represents the total producer price of the commodities used as intermediate input in the productive sectors[1] and $(M_p)_t$ represents the trading margin on these same goods. The same breakdown holds for all input and final-demand elements. In addition, final demand has been considered into two main categories: the consumption of productive workers $CONW_p$; and surplus demand SD, which is the remainder of final demand (equal to the sum of the consumption of unproductive workers and capitalists, investment, net exports, and government expenditures). As always, constant capital in money form $C^* = M_p$, and Marxian value added $VA^*$ and final product $FP^*$ are shown in cross-hatched areas.

---

[1] We recall that, at a theoretical level, depreciation is part of intermediate inputs.

| | Production | Trade | Royalties | Final Demand CONW$_p$ | SD* | GP |
|---|---|---|---|---|---|---|
| Production | $(M_p)_p$ $M_p$ | $(M_t)_p$ $M_t$ | $(M_{ry})_p$ $M_{ry}$ | $(CONW_p)_p$ $CONW_p$ | $SD_p$ | $GP_p$ |
| Trade | $(M_p)_t$ | $(M_t)_t$ | $(M_{ry})_t$ | $(CONW_p)_t$ | $SD_t$ | $GP_t$ |
| Royalty Payments | $RY_p$ | $RY_t$ | $RY_{ry}$ | $(RY)$ $conw_p$ | $RY_{sd}$ | $GP_{ry}$ |
| VA | $VA_p$ | $VA_t$ | $VA_{ry}$ | | | |
| GO | $GO_p$ | $GO_t$ | $GO_{ry}$ | | | |

\* "Surplus Demand"= $(CON)_{wu} + CON_c + (X-IM) + G$

Figure 4.1. IO accounts and Marxian categories: Condensed form.

It should be noted that Figure 4.1 collapses all the productive industries into one sector. For aggregate money value calculations, this is adequate because we are only interested in the sum of money values. But for labor value calculations, we generally need to know the individual elements of the productive sectors. Therefore we may also think of the production-row elements in Figure 4.1 as *matrices* representing corresponding partitions of the matrix pictured in Figure 3.11. We will use the notation $(M_p)_p, M_p, \ldots$ for the sum of money values, and $(\mathbf{M}_p)_p, \mathbf{M}_p, \ldots$ to represent corresponding matrices.

The numerical examples in our text are constructed on the assumption that selling (i.e. purchaser) prices are equal in magnitude to labor values.[2] Indeed, all these examples were predicated on the same physical and revenue flows: a total product whose labor value $TV = 2000$ hours and total selling price $TV^* = \$2000$, composed of 400 in production inputs ($C = 400$ hr, $C^* = \$400$) and 1600 in value added (of which 200 represents the wages and consumption of production workers and the rest surplus value, so that $V = 200$ hr, $V^* = \$200$ and $S = 1400$ hr, $S^* = \$1400$). The purpose of all of this was to allow us to check that the various elements add up to the correct totals, no matter how complicated the transfers of value. It also ensured that any discrepancies that arose between individual Marxian categories and their orthodox counterparts were due solely to differences in their concepts, not to price–value deviations.

For the money form of Marxian categories, we need to estimate the purchaser price of various commodity bundles, because these are the final selling prices. Since input–output tables are constructed in terms of

---

[2] We assumed that purchaser prices were proportional to labor values, and also that the constant of proportionality was \$1/hr (see Section 3.1.1).

producer prices, this means that we must take the sum of the producer price and the trading margin of the commodity bundle in question. Thus the purchaser price of productive inputs $M_p = (M_p)_p + (M_p)_t$. Similarly, the purchaser price of the total product (the total sum of prices) is $TP^* = GO_p + GO_t$ – that is, the sum of the producer price of productive sectors $GO_p$ and the total revenue of the trading sector $GO_t$ (which is the trading margin on the total output).

It is important to note that while there is enough information in standard (i.e. producer-price) input–output tables to calculate the purchaser price of aggregate inputs, outputs, and final demand components, there is *not* enough to calculate the purchaser price of individual commodities. For instance, the $j$th column of an input–output matrix lists the producer price of various individual intermediate inputs $[(M)_p]_{ij}$, but only lists their combined trade margin $[(M)_t]_j$ in that trade row of that column. Similarly, the gross outputs $[GO_p]_j$ of various productive sectors are the producer prices of their products, while the gross output of the trading sector $GO_t$ is the combined trading margin on all productive sector outputs. Because the trade margins are always combined ones, we lack the information required to estimate individual purchaser prices.

For labor value measures, we need to calculate the labor value of various commodity bundles. Since individual commodities in actual input–output tables are listed in producer prices, we can calculate their labor values by multiplying the $j$th commodity by its labor-value/producer-price ratio $\lambda_j^*$. The first task, then, is to calculate these $\lambda_j^*$s. The second step is to apply these solely to the producer price components of various commodity flows.

If input–output tables recorded actual quantity flows (rather than money flows), we could calculate labor values $\lambda_j$ by adding the hours of productive labor[3] worked to the labor value of the inputs used in production. For the production sector $j$, let:

$\lambda_j$ = labor value per unit output;

$hp_j$ = hours of productive labor per unit output;

$app_{ij}$ = quantity of the $i$th production input used per unit output = $[(M_p)_p]_{ij}/X_j$;

$X_j$ = quantity of output.

Then unit labor values must satisfy the relation

$$\lambda_j = hp_j + \Sigma_i \lambda_i \cdot app_{ij}.$$

---

[3] Ideally, one should adjust labor time flows for skill differences. If sectoral wage-rate differences are correlated with skill differences, then we could use wage rates as a first approximation. But this can cause problems (see the discussion of Wolff (1975, 1977) in Section 6.1.2).

If we define row vectors $\lambda$ and **hp**, with elements $\lambda_j$ and $hp_j$, respectively, as well as an input–output coefficients matrix of (productive) inputs **app** with elements $app_{ij}$, then we may equivalently write:

$$\lambda = \mathbf{hp} + \lambda \cdot \mathbf{app};$$
$$\lambda = \mathbf{hp} \cdot (I - \mathbf{app})^{-1}.$$

All this would apply if input–output tables were in quantity terms. But actual input–output tables are constructed in terms of money flows evaluated in producer prices, not quantity flows. This means that instead of input quantity coefficients $a_{ij}$ we actually have input money value coefficients $app_{ij}^* = p_i \cdot app_{ij}/p_j$, where $p_i$, $p_j$ represent producer prices. The corresponding labor coefficients are $hp_j^* = hp_j/p_j$. Our empirical equation for labor values now reads:

$$\lambda^* = \mathbf{hp}^* + \lambda^* \cdot \mathbf{app}^*;$$
$$\lambda^* = \mathbf{hp}^* \cdot (I - \mathbf{app}^*)^{-1},$$

where the estimated unit values $\lambda_j^*$ now represent labor-value/producer-price ratios (Shaikh 1984, apx. B). We have:

$\lambda^* = $ the row vector of labor-value/producer-price ratios;
$$\lambda_j^* = \lambda_j/p_j,$$

where

$\lambda_j = $ unit labor values;
$p_j = $ unit producer prices.

Since the $\lambda_j^*$s are ratios of labor values to producer prices, we must be careful to apply them only to the producer-price components of commodity flows. Thus the labor value of productive inputs C is derived by multiplying the *producer* price of the $i$th input by the labor-value/producer-price ratio $\lambda_j^*$. In terms of Figure 4.1, this means that the labor value of constant capital is calculated by multiplying only the matrix of elements $(\mathbf{M_p})_p$ by $\lambda^*$. Yet the corresponding money value of constant capital C*, which is the purchaser price of productive inputs, is equal to their producer price $(\mathbf{M_p})_p$ *plus* the trading margin on these same inputs $(\mathbf{M_p})_t$. In our previous examples, in which purchaser prices are equal to labor values, the two magnitudes C and C* will be equal under this calculation procedure. The difference in their mode of calculation is due solely to the fact that input–output tables are cast in terms of producer prices.

The same issue arises in the calculation of the labor value of productive labor power V. Given some estimate of the consumption basket of production workers $\mathbf{CONW_p}$, the labor value of this is the labor-value/producer-price ratio vector $\lambda^*$ multiplied only by the producer price component $(\mathbf{CONW_p})_p$ (see Figure 4.1). On the other hand, the money value equivalent V* is the sum of both the producer-price elements $(\mathbf{CONW_p})_p$

Table 4.1. *Labor value and money value measures*

| Money value measures | Labor value measures |
|---|---|
| *A. Revenue side* | |
| $C^* = M_p = (M_p)_p + (M_t)_p$ | $C = \lambda^* \cdot (M_p)_p$ |
| $VA^* = VA_p + VA_t + RY_p + RY_t$ $+ (M_p)_t + (M_t)_t$ | $VA = H_p = $ total hours of productive labor in the economy as a whole |
| $V^* = W_p = CONW_p$ $= (CONW_p)_p + (CONW_p)_t$ | $V = \lambda^* \cdot (CONW_p)_p$ |
| $S^* = VA^* - V^*$ | $S = H_p - V$ |
| *B. Use side* | |
| $U^* = M_p = (M_p)_p + (M_t)_p$ | $U = \lambda^* \cdot (M_p)_p$ |
| $FP^* = (M_t)_p + (M_t)_t + (M_{ry})_p$ $+ (M_{ry})_t + (CONW_p)_p$ $+ (CONW_p)_t + SD_p + SD_t$ | $FP = \lambda^* \cdot [(M_t)_p + (M_{ry})_p$ $+ (CONW_p)_p + SD_p]$ |
| $NP^* = V^* = CONW_p$ $= (CONW_p)_p + (CONW_p)_t$ | $NP = V = \lambda^* \cdot (CONW_p)_p$ |
| $SP^* = FD^* - V^*$ | $SP = FP - NP$ |

and the corresponding trade margin $(CONW_t)_p$. Similarly, the labor value of the total product TP is the sum of the labor value of constant capital C and the value of labor power V (whose calculation was discussed previously) and the labor value of the surplus product (calculated as the product of the vector $\lambda^*$ and the matrix of the producer prices of surplus demand components $SD_p$ in Figure 4.1). Table 4.1 summarizes these results. Khanjian (1988) provides many detailed numerical illustrations of the consistency of this procedure, based on an unpublished schema set out by Shaikh in 1975, so we will not pursue the issue any further here.

We may illustrate the procedures outlined here by using our basic numerical example. Figure 4.2 is a numerical example of the basic flows in Figure 4.1, with the value-added row broken down into wages and profits, and with the associated labor flows for each sector shown explicitly below the main table.[4] This example is particularly simple because it contains only one productive sector, but all procedures we illustrate generalize readily to the general case of $n$ productive sectors. Figure 4.3 represents the resulting input–output coefficients matrix $a^*$ and corresponding labor coefficients vector $h^*$ (derived by dividing production, trade and

[4] By construction, in all numerical examples the aggregate labor value added is $H_p = V + S = 1600$ hr, while the aggregate wages of production workers are $W_p = \$200$. This implies an hourly wage rate of $\$\frac{1}{8}$. The labor flows in Figure 4.2 are derived by dividing the sectoral wage bills by this wage rate.

| | Production | Trade | Royalties | Final Demand: $CONW_p$ | Final Demand: SD* | GP |
|---|---|---|---|---|---|---|
| Production | 200 ($M_p$) | 100 ($M_t$) | 25 ($M_{ry}$) | 100 ($CONW_p$) | 575 | 1000 |
| Trade | 200 ($M_p$) | 100 ($M_t$) | 25 ($M_{ry}$) | 100 ($CONW_p$) | 575 | 1000 |
| Royalty Payments | 100 | 150 | -- | -- | -- | 250 |
| WAGES | 200 | 400 | 100 | | | |
| PROFITS | 300 | 250 | 100 | | | |
| GO | 1000 | 1000 | 250 | | | |
| LABOR FLOWS ($H_p$) | 1600 | 3200 | 800 | | | |

* "Surplus Demand"= $(CON)_{wu}+CON_c+(X-IM)+G$

Figure 4.2. Production, trade, and royalties sectors.

$$\mathbf{a}^* = \begin{bmatrix} \boxed{1/5} & 1/10 & 1/10 \\ 1/5 & 1/10 & 1/9 \\ 1/10 & 3/20 & 0 \end{bmatrix}$$

$$\mathbf{h}^* = \begin{bmatrix} \boxed{8/5} & 16/5 & 16/5 \end{bmatrix}$$

Figure 4.3. Input–output coefficients matrix and labor coefficients vector.

royalties sectors' column entries, and their labor flow by their respective gross outputs). Neither the value-added and gross-output rows, nor the final-demand and gross-product columns, enter into **a***.

In Figure 4.3, the producer-price element app* of productive sector inputs, and the productive labor coefficient hp*, are each outlined in a rectangle. We will write these as (one-element) matrices and vectors, so as to illustrate the general procedure. Thus

$$\mathbf{app}^* = [1/5] \quad [\$/\$];$$

$$\mathbf{hp}^* = (8/5) \quad [\text{hr}/\$];$$

$$\lambda^* = \mathbf{hp}^* \cdot [\mathrm{I} - \mathbf{app}^*]^{-1} = (8/5)[1-1/5]^{-1} = 2 \quad [\text{hr}/\$].$$

Table 4.2. *Calculations of labor value flows:*
*Numerical example*

---

*Value side*

$C = \lambda^* \cdot (\mathbf{M_p})_p = 2 \cdot 200 = 400$

$VA = H_p = 1600$

$V = \lambda^* \cdot (\mathbf{CONW_p})_p = 2 \cdot 100 = 200$

$S = VA - V = 1600 - 200 = 1400$

$TV = C + V + S = 2000$

*Use side*

$U = \lambda^* \cdot (\mathbf{M_p})_p = 400$

$FP = \lambda^* \cdot [(\mathbf{M_t})_p + (\mathbf{M_{ry}})_p + (\mathbf{CONW_p})_p + \mathbf{SD_p}]$
$\quad = 2 \cdot (100 + 25 + 100 + 575) = 1600$

$NP = V = 200$

$SP = FP - NP = 1600 - 200 = 1400$

$TP = U + NP + SP = 2000$

---

Because there is only one productive sector, the calculated $\lambda^* = 2$ hr/$ should represent the ratio of the labor value of the total product TV to its producer price $GO_p$ (the input–output gross product of the productive sector). This is clearly the case, because by construction $TV = 2000$ hr and $GO_p = \$1000$. Applying the formulas in Table 4.1 to the numbers in Figure 4.2, we correctly recover the labor value flows (in hours of abstract socially necessary labor time) which underly the money flows depicted. Table 4.2 displays the results.

The mappings shown in Tables 4.1 and 4.2 are *consistent,* in the sense that they give the same magnitudes in value terms and in price terms when unit purchaser prices are equal to unit values (compare the value measures of Marxian measure flows in Table 4.2 to their money value counterparts in Table 4.1). In this way, when prices deviate from values, the resulting discrepancies between value magnitudes and their price forms are due solely to the price–value deviations themselves. In actual input–output tables, where purchasers' prices generally do differ from values, we can then interpret the deviations between value and money magnitudes as a measure of the aggregate effects of price–value deviations. This effect is generally small. For instance, using the procedure outlined here, Khanjian (1988, p. 109, table 19) finds that the money rate of surplus value $S^*/V^*$ and the labor value rate $S/V$ differ by only 6%–9% in all the years studied. He also finds that the former is consistently lower than the latter. Further details may be found in Section 5.10.

Table 4.3. *An inconsistent (symmetric) mapping between Marxian and IO categories: Use side*

| Money value measures | Labor value measures |
|---|---|
| $U^{*\prime}=C^{*\prime}=(M_p)_p=200$ (\$) | $U=C=\lambda^*\cdot(M_p)_p=400$ (hr) |
| $NP^{*\prime}=V^*=(CONW_p)_p=100$ | $NP=V=\lambda^*\cdot(CONW_p)_p=200$ |
| $FP^{*\prime}=(M_t)_p+(M_{ry})_p+(CONW_p)_p$ $+SD_p$ $=100+25+100+575=800$ | $FP=\lambda^*\cdot[(M_t)_p+(M_{ry})_p+(CONW_p)_p$ $+SD_p]$ $=2\cdot(100+25+100+575)=1600$ |
| $SP^{*\prime}=FD^{*\prime}-V^{*\prime}=700$ | $SP=FP^\prime-NP^\prime=1400$ |

However, observed differences in money and labor value ratios will be indicators of price–value deviations only if the mapping involved is consistent in the sense just described. If it is not, then the two sets of magnitudes would differ even when purchaser prices are equal to labor values, simply because the calculation procedure is inconsistent.

It is easy to see how an inconsistent procedure might evolve. As indicated in Tables 4.1 and 4.2, only the producer-price components enter into the value calculations, whereas both the producer price and the trading margin enter into the money calculation. For instance, the necessary product in value terms is $NP=V=\lambda^*\cdot(CONW_p)_p$, whereas in price terms it is $NP^*=CONW_p=(CONW_p)_p+(CONW_p)_t$. If one has not derived the detailed representation of the money form, as we have attempted to do, then it is tempting to make the price form symmetric with the value form. As we can see from Figure 4.1, this would mean leaving out all the trade row and column elements from the revenue- and product-side calculation of the money forms – in effect, treating the trade sector as a royalties sector on the grounds that both are "unproductive." This false symmetry would then yield estimated money magnitudes that would be *smaller* than corresponding value ones, even when prices were equal to values. The procedure would be inconsistent, and the levels of money magnitudes would be underestimated. Table 4.3 illustrates such a symmetric – and hence inconsistent – procedure, using the (more complex) product side of the accounts. The revenue side will of course yield the same discrepancy.

Note that, in our numerical example, the inconsistent procedure biases each money magnitude downward (relative to its correct level) by the amount of the trading margin on that bundle of commodities, that being the element which such a procedure leaves out. In this particular example, the *ratios* of the inconsistent money measures still match the ratios of (correct) labor value measures (i.e., $SP^{*\prime}/NP^{*\prime} = 700/100 = SP/NP = 1600/200$), but this is solely because our numbers embody the convenient assumption that the percentage trading margins are the same for all bundles of commodities. In actual IO tables this is definitely not the case, so that the ratios of money magnitudes could be biased in either direction depending on the relative trading markups. For example, the inconsistent estimate of the necessary product $NP^{*\prime}$ is lower than the true estimate by the amount of the trading margin on productive workers' consumption goods, whereas the inconsistent estimate of the surplus product $SP^{*\prime}$ is lower by the amount of the average trading margin on the mix of consumer, investment, net export, and government purchases in the surplus product. Since consumer goods pass through both wholesale and retail channels, they tend to have higher overall margins than goods purchased for investment or government (Khanjian 1988, pp. 109–13). Leaving out trading margins therefore imparts a relatively greater downward bias to the necessary product than to the surplus product. Thus, an inconsistent procedure in which the calculations of the money forms is made symmetric with that of the value forms will tend to yield money rates of surplus value that are higher than the corresponding value rates, all other things being equal.[5]

The false symmetry described here is not merely hypothetical. As we shall see in Section 6.2.3, the only other attempt to provide a complete mapping between input–output accounts and Marxian categories comes from Wolff (1977a,b, 1987), and it suffers from precisely this defect: Wolff treats money and labor value calculations symmetrically, which makes the former inconsistent with the latter. Indeed, as expected on theoretical grounds, Wolff's estimates of money rates of surplus value are uniformly higher than his labor value estimates by about 4%–8% (Wolff 1977b, p. 103, table 3, ll. 1, 3). On the other hand, Khanjian's (1988) estimates are consistent, and they indicate that $S^*/V^*$ is uniformly lower than $S/V$ by about 6%–8% (Khanjian 1988, p. 109, table 19). This allows us to estimate that an inconsistent procedure biases the money rate of surplus value $S^*/V^*$ upward by 12%–15% (the sum of the two sets of differences in years common to both Khanjian and Wolff). Our discussion of the actual empirical techniques is located in Sections 5.10 and 6.2.3.

### 4.2 Rates of exploitation of productive and unproductive workers

The calculation of labor-value/producer-price ratios $\lambda_j^*$ also enables us to distinguish the rate of exploitation from the rate of surplus

[5] Assuming that revenue- and product-side estimates are defined correctly, they will be equal. Thus, an inconsistent procedure will yield biased estimates of the money rates of surplus value from either side of the money accounts.

Table 4.4. *Calculating rates of exploitation*

| Productive labor | Unproductive labor |
|---|---|
| $V_p = \lambda^* \cdot (\mathbf{CONW_p})_p = V$ | $V_u = \lambda^* \cdot (\mathbf{CONW_u})_p$ |
| $e_p = (H_p - V)/V = S/V$ | $e_u = (H_u - V_u)/V_u$ |

*Notes:*

$e_p, e_u$ = rates of exploitation of productive and unproductive workers;
$V_p, V_u$ = values of productive and unproductive labor powers;
$H_p, H_u$ = total working time of productive and unproductive workers;
$(\mathbf{CONW_p})_p, (\mathbf{CONW_u})_p$ = producer price components of the consumption
vectors of productive and unproductive workers.

value. The rate of exploitation is the ratio of surplus labor time to necessary labor time. This concept applies to all capitalistically employed wage
labor, whether it is productive or unproductive (Shaikh 1978b, p. 21).
Necessary labor time is simply the value of the labor power involved, that
is, the labor value of the average annual consumption per worker in the
activities in question. Surplus labor time is excess of working time over
necessary labor time. For productive workers, their rate of exploitation is
also the rate of surplus value, since their surplus labor time results in surplus value. Table 4.4 summarizes the calculation of rates of exploitation.

The expressions in Table 4.4 give rise to a powerful approximation
technique, which we will use in Section 5.10. The two rates of exploitation can be written as

$$\frac{1+e_u}{1+e_p} = \frac{H_u/V_u}{H_p/V_p} = \frac{H_u/H_p}{V_u/V_p} = \frac{H_u/H_p}{[\lambda^* \cdot (\mathbf{CONW_u})_p]/[\lambda^* \cdot (\mathbf{CONW_p})_p]}.$$

The denominator of the last fraction is itself a ratio in which the vector
$\lambda^*$ appears in both numerator and denominator. If the consumption proportions of productive and unproductive workers are relatively similar,
which is quite plausible, then the vector product ratio $[\lambda^* \cdot (\mathbf{CONW_u})_p]/$
$[\lambda^* \cdot (\mathbf{CONW_p})_p]$ will be roughly the same as the scalar ratio $(\mathbf{CONW_u})_p/$
$(\mathbf{CONW_p})_p$, where $(\mathbf{CONW_u})_p$ and $(\mathbf{CONW_p})_p$ refer to the sum of the
producer-price components of unproductive and productive workers' con-
sumption (see Figure 4.1). Thus

$$\frac{1+e_u}{1+e_p} \approx \frac{H_u/H_p}{\mathbf{CONW_u}/\mathbf{CONW_p}}.$$

If the average consumption of workers is roughly equal to their wage
(which is empirically true because the saving of some workers is offset by

the dissaving of others), then the consumption of each type of worker is approximately equal to that worker's wage bill. If we divide the top and bottom of the preceding expression by the employment ratio $L_u/L_p$, then

$$\frac{1+e_u}{1+e_p} \approx \frac{h_u/h_p}{ec_u/ec_p},$$

where

$h_u$, $h_p$ = hours *per* unproductive and productive worker;

$ec_u$, $ec_p$ = employee compensation *per* unproductive and productive worker.

Finally, since the rate of exploitation of productive workers is simply the rate of surplus value, we can directly estimate the rate of exploitation of unproductive workers:

$$e_u = \frac{h_u/h_p}{ec_u/ec_p} \cdot [1+S/V].$$

In effect, the relative rates of exploitation will depend solely on the relative working time and on the relative wage rates. Both these items are easily estimated from annual data. In addition, since the money rate of surplus value is quite close to the value rate of surplus value (as shown in Section 5.10), we can substitute $S^*/V^*$ for $S/V$ in the previous expression. This allows us to directly estimate the annual rate of exploitation of unproductive workers and compare it with that of productive labor. We will see that in the United States the two rates remain within 10% of each other for almost all of the postwar period (see Section 5.6).

# 5

## Empirical estimates of Marxian categories

Our empirical analysis of the U.S. economy will be set out in several sections. Sections 5.1 and 5.2 will utilize suitably modified input–output tables to develop benchmark year estimates of Marxian measures of the total, intermediate, and final product, and then use NIPA data to interpolate between benchmark estimates to create an annual series for each of these measures. Sections 5.3 and 5.4 develop the estimates of annual employment, wages, variable capital $V^*$, surplus value $S^*$, surplus product $SP^*$, and the rate of surplus value $S^*/V^*$, and compare them to the more conventional measures such as profit-type income and the profit/wage ratio. Section 5.5 measures the Marxian rate of profit, and compares it with the average observed rate (net of those parts of surplus value which are absorbed into nonproduction expenses) and the observed corporate rate. Section 5.6 measures the rate of exploitation of unproductive workers, and compares it to that of productive labor; Section 5.7 compares Marxian and conventional measures of productivity. Sections 5.8 and 5.9 examine the impact of the state on accumulation, through its absorption of surplus value and through the effects of taxes and social expenditures on the rate of surplus value. Section 5.10 examines the effects of price–value deviations on aggregate Marxian measures, and Section 5.11 develops a technique that allows us to approximate the rate of surplus value in a relatively simple manner. Section 5.12 provides an overall summary and some conclusions. The basic methodology for each section is described in the text, with all further details reserved for the appendixes.

### 5.1 Primary Marxian measures in benchmark years

Input–output tables for the United States are available only in select (benchmark) years: 1947, 1958, 1963, 1967, 1972, 1977. The theoretical

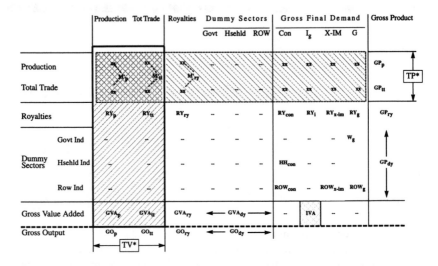

Figure 5.1. IO accounts and Marxian categories: Summary mapping.

relations between Marxian and orthodox categories in any one such table were summarized in Figure 3.11 and Table 3.12.

Figure 5.1 provides a condensed version of this same mapping. Production, total trade, and royalties are each aggregated into single sectors, so as to highlight the structural patterns of the mapping. Value added (and hence profit) are shown as gross of depreciation, while final demand (and hence investment) are shown as gross of retirements, as in actual input–output tables. Intermediate inputs of the various sectors therefore do not include fixed capital used up, which is why we label them as $M'_p, \ldots$ rather than $M_p, \ldots$ as in Figure 3.11 previously. The inventory valuation adjustment (IVA) row is merged into gross value added (GVA), and the corresponding IVA column into gross investment ($I_G$) on the final-demand side.[1] The cross-hatching around IVA indicates that it is included in the Marxian measures of both gross value added GVA* and gross final product GFP*.

Finally, the total trade sector consists of private and public wholesale/retail trading activities, plus an estimate of the building and equipment rentals sector (see Appendix B). Distributive transport was not estimated

---

[1] The IVA dummy industry has only one entry, in the intersection of its own row and column. When the row is merged into GVA and the column into $I_G$, this one entry is shifted to the GVA row of the $I_G$ column.

| 1972 | Production | Tot Trade | Royalties | Dummy Sectors | | | Gross Final Demand | | | | Gross Product |
|---|---|---|---|---|---|---|---|---|---|---|---|
| | | | | Govt | Hsehld | ROW | Con | $I_g$ | X-IM | G | |
| Production | 619148.1 | 54809.2 | 22725.3 | -- | -- | -- | 468702.7 | 127993.8 | -22509.0 | 101767.3 | 1372637.4 |
| Total Trade | 78676.1 | 22853.4 | 9696.4 | -- | -- | -- | 181973.3 | 10837.9 | 7046.5 | 2982.2 | 314065.8 |
| Royalties | 54094.4 | 17524.9 | 28891.4 | -- | -- | -- | 50171.5 | 249.3 | 1411.4 | 10872.7 | 163215.6 |
| Dummy Sectors  Govt Ind | -- | -- | -- | -- | -- | -- | -- | -- | -- | 137400.0 | 137400.0 |
| Hsehld Ind | -- | -- | -- | -- | -- | -- | 5349.0 | -- | -- | -- | 5349.0 |
| Row Ind | -- | -- | -- | -- | -- | -- | -3524.4 | -- | 10645.8 | -203.3 | 6918.1 |
| Gross Value Added | 620718.3 | 218878.0 | 101902.4 | 137400.0 | 5349.0 | 6918.1 | -- | -15182.0 | -- | -- | 1075984.7 |
| Gross Output | 1372637.9 | 314065.5 | 163215.4 | 137400.0 | 5349.0 | 6918.1 | 702672.1 | 123899.0 | -3405.3 | 252819.0 | 1999585.9 |

Figure 5.2. 1972 IO table.

because of its relatively small impact[2] and because of a paucity of data on the subject. Estimated building and equipment rental was merged into the total trade sector, but was neither unbundled nor adjusted for the amortization of building and equipment rented out (ABR). As noted in Appendix B.1, a failure to unbundle has no effect on the major Marxian totals, though it does somewhat overstate the total trade sector relative to the production sector. When we move to the annual NIPA-based estimates in Section 5.2, we do incorporate an ABR adjustment.[3]

Figure 5.2 presents an actual summary input–output table for 1972. Like other similar tables (shown in Appendix C), this was derived in two steps from benchmark tables published by the Bureau of Economic Analysis (BEA). First, a consistent set of 82-order (82 × 88) tables were produced, after making various adjustments to the published tables so as to render the classification of industries and treatment of secondary products and

---

[2] In 1972, the gross output of the transportation and warehousing sector (BEA 1979, pp. 65–7; see second half of 1972 IO table) came to roughly 3.5% of total gross output. Of this, a large part is passenger transportation and the rest business-related (most of which is productive transport). If we estimate business-related transportation to be 50% of the total, and distributive transport to be 25% of this, the latter amounts to only 0.5% of the economywide gross output.

[3] Figure B.3 makes it clear that an ABR adjustment without unbundling would be inconsistent at the IO level (compare GO and GP of the production sector). But aggregate GO = 2000 and aggregate GP = 2000 are unaffected.

comparable imports consistent across years. Second, these $82 \times 88$ tables were aggregated into $8 \times 11$ summary tables constructed in the form of Figure 5.1 above. Details are in Appendix A.

As indicated in Figure 5.2, total value TV* is simply the sum of the gross outputs of the production and total trade sectors (the sum of the elements in the bold rectangle). Materials used up in production $C_m^*$ and intermediate productive use $U_m^*$, both net of depreciation, are simply equal to $M_p'$, the sum of the first two entries in the top left-hand corner of Figure 5.2. Marxian gross value added $GVA^* \equiv TV^* - C_m^*$ is the sum of the downward hatched elements (including $M_{tt}'$) within the dashed rectangle. Finally, the commodity uses CON*, $I_G^*$, $X^* - IM^*$, and G* are calculated directly from those elements of consumption CON, gross investment $I_G$, net exports $X - IM$, and government expenditures G which lie within the Marxian final-use dashed rectangle.

By way of contrast, the IO measure of total gross product GP, which is really the sum of all transactions, is the sum of all intermediate inputs (including royalty payments) and all final demand GFD (shown as the column sums of the elements within the gross final-demand block). GP appears as the lower right-hand element of the IO table, and GFD appears directly above it.

Comparisons between the elements of corresponding Marxian and orthodox measures make it clear that TV* will always be less than GO (since the former is a subset of the latter), but that GVA* may be less than, equal to, or greater than GFD (because GVA* excludes some elements in GVA and includes others which are not in GVA). Similar remarks apply to use-side comparisons.

Table 5.1 summarizes the calculations of Marxian and IO measures for 1972, in millions of dollars, as derived from Figure 5.2. Table 5.2 repeats these calculations for each of the benchmark years in which input–output tables are available. Note that the orthodox measure GP (the sum of all input–output transactions) is consistently larger than the Marxian measure of total product TP*. On the other hand, the orthodox and Marxian measures of gross value added (GFD and GFP*, respectively) are surprisingly close: roughly equal in 1947 and roughly 11% apart by 1987.

### 5.2 Annual series for primary measures, based on NIPA data

Our previous IO benchmark estimates in Table 5.2 can be converted into annual series by making use of National Income and Product Accounts (NIPA) data. Such a conversion is complicated by two factors. First of all, NIPA data cover only gross value added and gross final demand, and even here there is insufficient detail. In terms of Figures 5.1

Table 5.1. *Primary Marxian and IO measures, 1972*

*Marxian measures*

$TV^* = GO_p + GO_{tt} = 1,372,637.4 + 314,065.8 = 1,686,703.2$

$C_m^* = M_p' = 619,148.1 + 78,676.1 = 697,824.2$

$GVA^* = TP^* - C_m^* = 988,879.0$

$$TP^* = M_p' + M_{tt}' + M_{ry}' + CON^* + I^* + (X - IM)^* + G^*$$
$$= 697,824.2 + (544,809.2 + 22,853.4) + (22,725.3 + 9,696.4)$$
$$+ (468,702.7 + 181,973.3) + (127,993.8 + 10,837.9)$$
$$+ (-22,509.0 + 7,046.5) + (101,767.3 + 2,982.2)$$
$$= 1,686,703.2$$

$U_m^* = M_p' = 697,824.2$

$GFP^*$ (with IVA) $= TP^* - U_m^* = 988,879.0$

$M_{tt}' + M_{ry}' = (54,809.2 + 22,853.4) + (22,725.3 + 9,696.4) = 110,084.3$

$CON^* = (468,702.7 + 181,973.3) = 650,676.0$

$I^*$ (with IVA) $= (127,993.8 + 10,837.9 - 15,182) = 123,649.7$

$(X - IM)^* = (-22,509.0 + 7,046.5) = -15,462.4$

$G^* = (101,767.3 + 2,982.2) = 104,747.5$

*Comparisons with selected IO measures*

$$GP = M_p' + M_{tt} + M_{ry}' + RY_p + RY_{tt} + RY_{ry}$$
$$+ CON + I + X - IM + G = 1,999,586.0 > TP^* = 1,686,703.2$$

$M = M_p' + M_{tt}' + M_{ry}' + RY_p + RY_{tt} + RY_{ry} = 908,419.2 > C_m^* = M_p' = 697,824.2$

$GFD$ (with IVA) $= CON + I + X - IM + G = 1,075,984.2 > GFP^* = 988,879.0$

$CON = 702,672.1 > CON^* = 650,676.0$

$I = 123,899.0 > I^* = 123,649.7$

$X - IM = -3,405.3 > (X - IM)^* = -15,462.4$

$G = 252,819.0 \gg G^* = 104,747.5$

and 5.2, this means that we have annual data only on the elements of the gross value-added row, and on certain elements of the gross final-demand block (such as the column sums CON, I, etc., and the dummy industry entries $HH_{con}$, $W_g$). Intermediate inputs $M'$ and RY are not covered at all in NIPA data, while others such as the elements of the ROW industry are only partially covered (NIPA only lists the total). Second, even where the two data sets overlap, their estimates generally differ. Individual sectors are defined differently in NIPA than in IO accounts, so that sectoral GVAs do not match (BEA 1980, p. 8). Even total GVA and GNP, which are constructed so as to be the same in the two sets of accounts, do not

Table 5.2. *Primary Marxian and IO measures, benchmark years (millions of dollars)*

| Variables | 1947 | 1958 | 1963 | 1967 | 1972 | 1977 |
|---|---|---|---|---|---|---|
| *Marxian measures* | | | | | | |
| TV* | 398,680 | 699,168 | 892,319 | 1,163,717 | 1,686,703 | 2,917,921 |
| C*'=M'$_p$ | 178,823 | 306,471 | 384,414 | 489,379 | 697,824 | 1,308,609 |
| GVA* | 219,858 | 392,697 | 507,905 | 674,338 | 988,879 | 1,609,312 |
| TP* | 398,680 | 699,168 | 892,320 | 1,163,716 | 1,686,703 | 2,918,488 |
| U*'=M'$_p$ | 178,823 | 306,471 | 384,414 | 489,379 | 697,824 | 1,308,609 |
| GFP* (with IVA) | 219,858 | 392,697 | 507,906 | 674,377 | 988,879 | 1,609,879 |
| M'$_{tt}$+M'$_{ry}$ | 23,964 | 43,094 | 54,511 | 74,946 | 110,084 | 195,907 |
| CON* | 152,894 | 258,600 | 332,101 | 418,315 | 650,676 | 1,059,878 |
| IG* | 23,512 | 40,253 | 58,043 | 94,253 | 138,832 | 236,438 |
| X*−IM* | 9,883 | −1,579 | 139 | −3,064 | −15,462 | −39,213 |
| G* | 9,604 | 52,330 | 63,111 | 89,888 | 104,750 | 156,869 |
| *Selected IO measures* | | | | | | |
| GP | 435,986 | 792,424 | 1,022,054 | 1,356,514 | 1,999,586 | 3,481,690 |
| M | 214,736 | 381,104 | 479,271 | 625,709 | 908,419 | 1,688,870 |
| GFD (with IVA) | 219,723 | 410,697 | 541,779 | 727,120 | 1,075,985 | 1,794,842 |
| CON | 160,246 | 274,997 | 355,611 | 452,094 | 702,672 | 1,139,024 |
| IG (with IVA) | 22,030 | 39,734 | 57,159 | 90,775 | 123,899 | 238,981 |
| X−IM | 11,528 | 2,206 | 5,812 | 5,132 | −3,405 | −3,981 |
| G | 25,918 | 93,760 | 123,198 | 179,119 | 252,819 | 420,817 |

generally match, because the totals for a given input–output table are benchmarked on NIPA estimates available when that particular table was created whereas currently available NIPA data incorporate many revisions of earlier estimates.

For all of these reasons, one cannot simply use NIPA data to fill in observations between IO benchmark years. Instead, we use NIPA data directly for components such as $GVA_p$ or CON (containing the latest available revisions) and indirectly to interpolate between benchmark estimates of other components such as $M'_p$ or $RY_{con}$.

Consider the estimation of the total value TV*. By definition, we can write this as (see Figure 5.1):

$$TV^* = GO_p + GO_{tt} = \text{total value},$$

where
$$GO_p = M'_p + RY_p + \{GVA_p\}, \text{ and}$$
$$GO_{tt} = M'_{tt} + RY_{tt} + \{GVA_{tt}\}.$$

We have:

$C_m^* = M_p' =$ materials inputs into production;

$C_d^* = \{D_p\} =$ depreciation of productive fixed capital;

$C^* = M_p' + D_p =$ constant capital used up (flow);

$GVA^* \equiv TV^* - C_m^* =$ Marxian gross value added;

$VA^* \equiv TV^* - C^* = GVA^* - C_d^* =$ Marxian (net) value added.

Our estimation procedure then consists of three steps:
  (i) The three items in braces $\{GVA_p, GVA_{tt}, D_p\}$ are calculated directly from NIPA, by aggregating individual NIPA industries into production and total trade sectors in much the same way that we aggregated input–output sectors earlier.
  (ii) The four components $M_p'$, $RY_p$, $M_{tt}'$, and $RY_{tt}$ are interpolated between benchmark years in a manner to be described shortly.
  (iii) The GVAs, Ms, and RYs are used to form $GO_p$ and $GO_{tt}$, and their sums give us $TV^*$. $D_p$ and $M_p'$ give us $C_d^*$ and $C_m^*$, respectively, which in turn allow us to calculate $GVA^*$ and $VA^*$.

The calculation of $TP^*$ follows the same general procedure. For instance, from Figure 5.1 we can write

$$TP^* = M_p' + M_{tt}' + M_{ry}' + CON^* + I_G^* + (X - IM)^* + G^*.$$

Figure 5.1 also makes it clear that the Marxian final-use categories such as $CON^*, I^*, \ldots$ can be derived by reducing the corresponding NIPA measures $CON, I, \ldots$ by those items which are excluded from the Marxian measure (i.e., which fall outside the dashed hatched rectangle and the cross-hatched section around IVA in Figure 5.1), as well as by those items already excluded from our benchmark tables (e.g., the imputed rental component $GVA_{ir}$ in consumption, as shown in Appendix B.1 and Figure B.1). We have:

$$CON^* = \{CON\} - GVA_{ir} - RY_{con} - \{HH_{con}\} - ROW_{con};$$

$$I_G^* = \{I_G\} - RY_i;[4]$$

$$(X - IM)^* = \{X - IM\} - RY_{x-im} - ROW_{x-im};$$

$$G^* = \{G\} - \{W_G\} - ROW_G.$$

Once again we proceed in three steps.

---

[4] As noted earlier, the inventory valuation adjustment IVA was merged into value added on the revenue side, and hence into $I_G^*$ on the use side.

(i) The items in braces $\{CON, I_G, X-IM, G, W_G\}$ are taken directly from NIPA.

(ii) The Ms, RYs, and ROWs are interpolated between input–output benchmark years, as described in what follows.

(iii) The remaining components of TP* are then calculated and assembled together to yield an estimate of the total.

The Ms, RYs, and ROWs that enter into TV* and TP* do not appear in NIPA at all. They must therefore be carried over from the benchmark years in which we have input–output tables, and interpolated to create annual series for each variable. This is accomplished in the following manner.

(a) In each input–output year, we calculate the ratio of the component to either its using or its receiving industry's gross value added. For material inputs M' (and depreciation D later on) we utilize the using industry's GVA. Thus for $M'_p$ we create the ratio $x_p \equiv (M'_p/GVA_p)_{IO}$, where the subscript IO refers to the fact that both variables are from input–output tables. For royalties RY we use the receiving industry's GVA (i.e. $GVA_{ry}$) as the numeraire, as in $x_i \equiv (RY_i/GVA_{ry})_{IO}$. This is done because some royalties such as $RY_i$ and $RY_{x-im}$ appear as components of highly unstable final-demand totals like I or X−IM (see Figure 5.1). Benchmark coefficients created by dividing these royalties by unstable totals are not very useful. The same reasoning applies to rest-of-world (ROW) entries in Figure 5.1, which are divided by total ROW in order to form coefficients for extrapolation, as in $x_{row_g} \equiv ROW_g/ROW$.

(b) All coefficients created as described in (a) are linearly interpolated between benchmark (IO) years. The result is an annual series for each coefficient, derived entirely from input–output data.

(c) The annual observation for each coefficient is multiplied by the NIPA measure of the relevant gross value added (or ROW in the case of rest-of-world coefficients) so as to create a NIPA-based estimate of the original IO variable. Thus

$$(M'_p)_{NIPA} \equiv x_p \cdot (GVA_p)_{NIPA}, \qquad (RY_i)_{NIPA} \equiv x_i \cdot (GVA_{ry})_{NIPA},$$

and

$$(ROW_g)_{NIPA} \equiv x_{row_g} \cdot (ROW)_{NIPA}.$$

The resulting annual estimates are then used in all subsequent calculations.

Details of the interpolation procedure are in Appendix D, and of the annual estimates of the primary Marxian measures in Appendix E.

Table 5.3 presents the NIPA-based estimates for the benchmark years only. Since the IO-based measures in Table 5.2 do not include an ABR adjustment (see Section 5.1, para. 3), our present NIPA-based estimates also omit this adjustment (although it is incorporated into the full annual series in Table 5.4). Note that current estimates differ slightly from those in Table 5.2, as indicated by the ratios of NIPA-based estimates to IO-based ones. This is a reflection of the previously noted differences between IO and NIPA measures.[5] It is nonetheless striking that the totals are fairly close, although individual components such as investment and net exports differ substantially. In any case, the stability of almost all ratios at the bottom of Table 5.3 indicates that the trends are the same in both data sets.

Table 5.4 extends coverage to the full period 1947-87, this time with the ABR adjustment. The previous patterns are now fully borne out. Figures 5.3 and 5.4 compare Marxian real total product (real TP*) and its orthodox equivalent (real GNP). The striking thing in Figure 5.4 is that their ratio falls consistently, except for a brief reversal from 1972 to 1977. The ratios TP*/GP (Marxian total product to NIPA-based IO gross product), GFP*/GNP (Marxian gross final product to NIPA gross national product), and the corresponding net ratio FP*/NNP also fall steadily until 1972 and then essentially level out. The much larger reversal in the total-product/GNP ratio is probably explained by the oil-price rise in 1973, since the ratio of production inputs to GNP (C*'/GNP) rises by 17% over this interval while the ratio of Marxian gross final product to GNP (GFP*/GNP) is roughly constant.

Figure 5.5 looks at the major components of total value $TV^* = GO_p + GO_{tt}$; Figure 5.6 looks at those of TP*, broken down in this case into total intermediate use $M' = M'_p + M'_{tt} + M_{ry}$ and gross final use $GFU^* = CON^* + IG^* + (X - IM)^* + G^*$ (see Figure 5.1). In both cases, the respective component shares are remarkably constant. Throughout the postwar period, the gross trading margin $GO_{tt}/TV^*$ holds steady at about 18%, while the input use share $M'/TP^*$ holds steady at about 50% of the total product. A similar constancy holds for the productive inputs share $M'_p/TP^*$ (calculated from Table 5.4), which hovers around 43% throughout, rising slightly during the oil shock and then coming back down to normal levels. In Marxian terms, this translates into the proposition that the flow of constant capital used as materials $C^*_m \equiv M'_p$ is a stable proportion of total value $TV^*$ ($= TP^*$). This constant-flow/flow ratio does not say anything, however, about the ratio of fixed constant

---

[5] The difference in investment measures seems to stem from the fact that the IO measure excludes residential investment, which is included in the NIPA measure.

Table 5.3. *Primary Marxian and NIPA measures, benchmark years (NIPA based; billions of dollars)*

| Sources | Variables | 1947 | 1958 | 1963 | 1967 | 1972 | 1977 |
|---|---|---|---|---|---|---|---|
| *Marxian measures* | | | | | | | |
| Table E.1 | TV* | 395.60 | 711.79 | 914.05 | 1200.79 | 1728.88 | 3054.58 |
| Table D.2 | $C_m^* = M_p'$ | 173.22 | 308.00 | 389.68 | 500.66 | 714.33 | 1367.27 |
| Table E.1 | GVA* | 222.00 | 403.79 | 524.38 | 700.13 | 1014.55 | 1687.31 |
| Table E.2 | TP* | 395.09 | 711.67 | 913.42 | 1199.81 | 1728.41 | 3058.10 |
| | $U^{*\prime} = M_p'$ | 173.22 | 308.00 | 389.68 | 500.66 | 714.33 | 1367.27 |
| | $GFP^* = TP^* - U^{*\prime}$ | 223.33 | 403.67 | 523.74 | 699.15 | 1014.08 | 1690.83 |
| Table D.2 | $M_{tt} + M_{ry}'$ | 24.15 | 43.93 | 55.95 | 75.99 | 108.05 | 196.66 |
| Table E.2 | CON* | 147.10 | 251.64 | 319.67 | 421.33 | 637.77 | 1068.01 |
| Table E.2 | IG* | 32.47 | 58.40 | 86.80 | 117.28 | 187.77 | 318.62 |
| Table E.2 | (X − IM)* | 9.53 | −2.03 | −0.20 | −3.33 | −15.55 | −35.29 |
| Table E.2 | G* | 8.62 | 51.73 | 61.52 | 87.90 | 96.04 | 142.84 |
| *Selected NIPA–IO measures* | | | | | | | |
| | GP = M + GFD | 445.20 | 845.30 | 1099.77 | 1462.58 | 2143.39 | 3750.53 |
| | $M = M_p' + M_{tt}' + M_{ry}' + RY_p + RY_{tt} + RY_{ry}$ | 210.00 | 388.40 | 492.97 | 646.08 | 930.59 | 1760.03 |
| | GFD = GNP | 235.20 | 456.90 | 606.80 | 816.50 | 1212.80 | 1990.50 |
| Table E.2 | CON | 161.90 | 294.60 | 381.70 | 503.60 | 757.60 | 1257.20 |
| Table E.2 | IG | 35.00 | 63.60 | 93.10 | 125.70 | 202.00 | 344.10 |
| Table E.2 | (X − IM) | 11.90 | 3.30 | 8.20 | 7.40 | 3.20 | 1.90 |
| Table E.2 | G | 26.40 | 95.40 | 123.80 | 179.80 | 250.00 | 387.30 |

*Comparisons of IO and NIPA-based estimates*

| | | | | | | |
|---|---|---|---|---|---|---|
| $TV^*_{IO}/TV^*_{NIPA}$ | 1.01 | 0.98 | 0.98 | 0.97 | 0.98 | 0.96 |
| $(M'_p)_{IO}/(M'_p)_{NIPA}$ | 1.03 | 1.00 | 0.99 | 0.98 | 0.98 | 0.96 |
| $GVA^*_{IO}/GVA^*_{NIPA}$ | 0.99 | 0.97 | 0.97 | 0.96 | 0.97 | 0.95 |
| $TP^*_{IO}/TP^*_{NIPA}$ | 1.01 | 0.98 | 0.98 | 0.97 | 0.98 | 0.95 |
| $(M'_{tt} + M'_{ry})_{IO}/(M'_{tt} + M'_{ry})_{NIPA}$ | 0.99 | 0.98 | 0.97 | 0.99 | 1.02 | 1.00 |
| $CON^*_{IO}/CON^*_{NIPA}$ | 1.04 | 1.03 | 1.04 | 0.99 | 1.02 | 0.99 |
| $IG^*_{IO}/IG^*_{NIPA}$ | 0.78 | 0.75 | 0.72 | 0.86 | 0.80 | 0.81 |
| $(X - IM)^*_{IO}/(X - IM)^*_{NIPA}$ | 1.04 | 0.78 | -0.70 | 0.92 | 0.99 | 1.11 |
| $G^*_{IO}/G^*_{NIPA}$ | 1.11 | 1.01 | 1.03 | 1.02 | 1.09 | 1.10 |

Table 5.4. *Primary Marxian and NIPA measures, 1948–89 (NIPA based; billions of dollars)*

| Sources | Variables | 1948 | 1949 | 1950 | 1951 | 1952 |
|---|---|---|---|---|---|---|
| *Marxian measures* | | | | | | |
| Table E.1 | $TV^*$ | 446.25 | 432.02 | 481.79 | 551.61 | 573.67 |
| Table D.2 | $C_m^* = M_p'$ | 198.47 | 189.06 | 212.56 | 244.59 | 254.35 |
| Table E.1 | $GVA^*$ | 247.78 | 242.95 | 269.23 | 307.02 | 319.32 |
| Table E.1 | $VA^* = GVA^* - C_d^*$ | 238.35 | 233.66 | 258.42 | 294.17 | 305.52 |
| Table E.1 | $C_d^*$ | 9.42 | 9.29 | 10.81 | 12.85 | 13.80 |
| Table E.2 | $TP^*$ | 446.21 | 431.96 | 481.62 | 551.62 | 573.95 |
| | $U^{*'} = M_p'$ | 198.47 | 189.06 | 212.56 | 244.59 | 254.35 |
| | $GFP^* = TP^* - U^{*'}$ | 247.74 | 242.90 | 269.06 | 307.03 | 319.61 |
| Table D.2 | $M_{tt}' + M_{ry}'$ | 26.54 | 26.67 | 28.60 | 31.26 | 32.67 |
| Table E.2 | $CON^*$ | 158.46 | 160.16 | 171.79 | 185.65 | 194.14 |
| Table E.2 | $IG^*$ | 44.27 | 33.55 | 51.96 | 56.94 | 49.73 |
| Table E.2 | $(X - IM)^*$ | 4.06 | 3.76 | −0.71 | 0.67 | −0.98 |
| Table E.2 | $G^*$ | 14.40 | 18.76 | 17.42 | 32.50 | 44.06 |
| | $GFU^* = GFP^* - (M_{tt}' + M_{ry}')$ | 221.20 | 216.23 | 240.45 | 275.76 | 286.94 |
| | $FP^* = GFP^* - C_d^*$ | 238.32 | 233.60 | 258.25 | 294.18 | 305.81 |
| | $TP_{real}^*$ | 1890.71 | 1838.13 | 2015.13 | 2197.70 | 2250.80 |
| | $GFP_{real}^*$ | 1049.74 | 1033.61 | 1125.76 | 1223.22 | 1253.36 |
| | $GNP_{real}$ | 1108.47 | 1107.66 | 1205.86 | 1328.69 | 1378.82 |
| 101 1[a] | $GNP$ | 261.60 | 260.30 | 288.20 | 333.50 | 351.60 |
| 705 1[a] | $GNP$ deflator | 23.60 | 23.50 | 23.90 | 25.10 | 25.50 |
| | $TP^*/GNP$ | 1.71 | 1.66 | 1.67 | 1.65 | 1.63 |
| Table E.1 | $GO_p/TV^*$ | 0.82 | 0.81 | 0.82 | 0.83 | 0.83 |
| Table E.1 | $GO_{tt}/TV^*$ | 0.18 | 0.18 | 0.18 | 0.17 | 0.17 |
| | $M'/TP^{*\,b}$ | 0.50 | 0.50 | 0.50 | 0.50 | 0.50 |
| | $GFU^*/TP^*$ | 0.50 | 0.50 | 0.50 | 0.50 | 0.50 |
| *Selected NIPA–IO measures* | | | | | | |
| | $GP = M + GFD$ | 501.09 | 491.85 | 546.81 | 628.80 | 660.15 |
| | $M^c$ | 239.49 | 231.55 | 258.61 | 295.30 | 308.55 |
| | $GFD = GNP$ | 261.60 | 260.30 | 288.20 | 333.50 | 351.60 |
| Table E.2 | $CON$ | 174.9 | 178.3 | 192.1 | 208.1 | 219.1 |
| Table E.2 | $IG$ | 47.1 | 36.5 | 55.1 | 60.5 | 53.5 |
| Table E.2 | $(X - IM)$ | 7.0 | 6.5 | 2.2 | 4.5 | 3.2 |
| Table E.2 | $G$ | 32.6 | 39.0 | 38.8 | 60.4 | 75.8 |
| Table H.1 | $NNP$ | 241.20 | 238.40 | 264.60 | 306.20 | 322.50 |
| *Comparisons* | | | | | | |
| | $TP^*/GP$ | 0.89 | 0.88 | 0.88 | 0.88 | 0.87 |
| | $GFP^*/GNP$ | 0.95 | 0.93 | 0.93 | 0.92 | 0.91 |
| | $FP^*/NNP$ | 0.99 | 0.98 | 0.98 | 0.96 | 0.95 |

[a] From NIPA (e.g. BEA 1986), where the first three digits denote the relevant table number and subsequent digits the line numbers within those tables.
[b] $M'/TP^* = (M_p' + M_{tt}' + M_{ry}')/TP^*$    [c] $M = M_p' + M_{tt}' + M_{ry}' + RY_p + RY_{tt} + RY_{ry}$.

| 1953 | 1954 | 1955 | 1956 | 1957 | 1958 | 1959 | 1960 | 1961 |
|---|---|---|---|---|---|---|---|---|
| 605.61 | 596.59 | 653.31 | 687.44 | 717.68 | 711.79 | 774.37 | 796.20 | 812.01 |
| 268.66 | 261.36 | 287.18 | 303.11 | 314.63 | 308.00 | 334.93 | 343.72 | 347.54 |
| 336.95 | 335.23 | 366.14 | 384.33 | 403.05 | 403.79 | 439.44 | 452.48 | 464.47 |
| 321.91 | 320.15 | 349.07 | 365.79 | 383.25 | 383.87 | 417.99 | 430.69 | 442.67 |
| 15.04 | 15.08 | 17.07 | 18.54 | 19.79 | 19.92 | 21.44 | 21.78 | 21.80 |
| 605.37 | 596.63 | 652.91 | 687.21 | 717.30 | 711.67 | 774.29 | 795.67 | 811.42 |
| 268.66 | 261.36 | 287.18 | 303.11 | 314.63 | 308.00 | 334.93 | 343.72 | 347.54 |
| 336.71 | 335.26 | 365.74 | 384.10 | 402.67 | 403.67 | 439.36 | 451.95 | 463.88 |
| 34.07 | 35.16 | 37.96 | 40.31 | 42.56 | 43.93 | 47.60 | 49.10 | 50.66 |
| 204.41 | 209.09 | 224.27 | 234.18 | 246.03 | 251.64 | 269.19 | 279.74 | 286.69 |
| 50.96 | 49.97 | 65.31 | 67.95 | 66.06 | 58.40 | 74.79 | 72.55 | 71.27 |
| -2.69 | -1.55 | -1.85 | -0.24 | 1.09 | -2.03 | -4.14 | -0.37 | 0.48 |
| 49.96 | 42.59 | 40.05 | 41.89 | 46.93 | 51.73 | 51.92 | 50.93 | 54.77 |
| 302.64 | 300.10 | 327.78 | 343.79 | 360.11 | 359.74 | 391.75 | 402.85 | 413.22 |
| 321.68 | 320.18 | 348.67 | 365.56 | 382.88 | 383.75 | 417.91 | 430.16 | 442.08 |
| 2337.35 | 2268.55 | 2400.42 | 2445.57 | 2464.96 | 2396.20 | 2547.01 | 2574.98 | 2600.71 |
| 1300.05 | 1274.76 | 1344.63 | 1366.90 | 1383.76 | 1359.16 | 1445.26 | 1462.61 | 1486.80 |
| 1434.36 | 1416.35 | 1492.28 | 1523.84 | 1549.83 | 1538.38 | 1631.25 | 1667.96 | 1710.90 |
| 371.50 | 372.50 | 405.90 | 428.20 | 451.00 | 456.90 | 495.90 | 515.40 | 533.80 |
| 25.90 | 26.30 | 27.20 | 28.10 | 29.10 | 29.70 | 30.40 | 30.90 | 31.20 |
| 1.63 | 1.60 | 1.61 | 1.60 | 1.59 | 1.56 | 1.56 | 1.54 | 1.52 |
| 0.83 | 0.82 | 0.83 | 0.83 | 0.83 | 0.82 | 0.82 | 0.82 | 0.82 |
| 0.17 | 0.17 | 0.17 | 0.17 | 0.17 | 0.18 | 0.18 | 0.18 | 0.18 |
| 0.50 | 0.50 | 0.50 | 0.50 | 0.50 | 0.49 | 0.49 | 0.49 | 0.49 |
| 0.50 | 0.50 | 0.50 | 0.50 | 0.50 | 0.51 | 0.51 | 0.51 | 0.51 |
| 698.29 | 695.08 | 759.29 | 802.66 | 841.93 | 845.30 | 918.12 | 949.79 | 975.53 |
| 326.79 | 322.58 | 353.39 | 374.46 | 390.93 | 388.40 | 422.22 | 434.39 | 441.73 |
| 371.50 | 372.50 | 405.90 | 428.20 | 451.00 | 456.90 | 495.90 | 515.40 | 533.80 |
| 232.6 | 239.8 | 257.9 | 270.6 | 285.3 | 294.6 | 316.3 | 330.7 | 341.1 |
| 54.9 | 54.1 | 69.7 | 72.7 | 71.1 | 63.6 | 80.2 | 78.2 | 77.1 |
| 1.3 | 2.6 | 3.0 | 5.3 | 7.3 | 3.3 | 1.5 | 5.9 | 7.2 |
| 82.7 | 76.0 | 75.3 | 79.6 | 87.3 | 95.4 | 97.9 | 100.6 | 108.4 |
| 340.70 | 340.00 | 371.50 | 390.10 | 409.90 | 414.00 | 451.20 | 468.90 | 486.10 |
| 0.87 | 0.86 | 0.86 | 0.86 | 0.85 | 0.84 | 0.84 | 0.84 | 0.83 |
| 0.91 | 0.90 | 0.90 | 0.90 | 0.89 | 0.88 | 0.89 | 0.88 | 0.87 |
| 0.94 | 0.94 | 0.94 | 0.94 | 0.93 | 0.93 | 0.93 | 0.92 | 0.91 |

*(more)*

Table 5.4 *(cont.)*

| Sources | Variables | 1962 | 1963 | 1964 | 1965 | 1966 |
|---|---|---|---|---|---|---|
| *Marxian measures* | | | | | | |
| Table E.1 | TV* | 870.18 | 914.05 | 973.89 | 1057.74 | 1150.25 |
| Table D.2 | $C_m^* = M_p'$ | 371.40 | 389.68 | 412.31 | 447.41 | 483.74 |
| Table E.1 | GVA* | 498.78 | 524.38 | 561.59 | 610.33 | 666.51 |
| Table E.1 | $VA^* = GVA^* - C_d^*$ | 475.73 | 500.46 | 536.54 | 583.42 | 637.72 |
| Table E.1 | $C_d^*$ | 23.05 | 23.91 | 25.05 | 26.91 | 28.79 |
| Table E.2 | TP* | 869.52 | 913.42 | 973.35 | 1057.19 | 1149.69 |
| | $U^{*'} = M_p'$ | 371.40 | 389.68 | 412.31 | 447.41 | 483.74 |
| | $GFP^* = TP^* - U^{*'}$ | 498.12 | 523.74 | 561.05 | 609.78 | 665.94 |
| Table D.2 | $M_{tt}' + M_{ry}'$ | 53.59 | 55.95 | 60.52 | 65.06 | 70.54 |
| Table E.2 | CON* | 303.64 | 319.67 | 343.59 | 370.24 | 400.85 |
| Table E.2 | IG* | 81.54 | 86.80 | 92.94 | 109.07 | 120.83 |
| Table E.2 | (X − IM)* | −0.92 | −0.20 | 1.59 | −0.39 | −2.41 |
| Table E.2 | G* | 60.26 | 61.52 | 62.41 | 65.80 | 76.14 |
| | $GFU^* = GFP^* - (M_{tt}' + M_{ry}')$ | 444.53 | 467.79 | 500.53 | 544.71 | 595.40 |
| | $FP^* = GFP^* - C_d^*$ | 475.07 | 499.83 | 536.00 | 582.87 | 637.16 |
| | $TP_{real}^*$ | 2725.78 | 2819.18 | 2958.52 | 3127.77 | 3284.82 |
| | $GFP_{real}^*$ | 1561.50 | 1616.48 | 1705.31 | 1804.07 | 1902.69 |
| | $GNP_{real}$ | 1800.94 | 1872.84 | 1975.08 | 2086.39 | 2205.71 |
| 101 1 | GNP | 574.50 | 606.80 | 649.80 | 705.20 | 772.00 |
| 705 1 | GNP deflator | 31.90 | 32.40 | 32.90 | 33.80 | 35.00 |
| | TP*/GNP | 1.51 | 1.51 | 1.50 | 1.50 | 1.49 |
| Table E.1 | $GO_p / TV^*$ | 0.82 | 0.82 | 0.82 | 0.82 | 0.82 |
| Table E.1 | $GO_{tt} / TV^*$ | 0.18 | 0.18 | 0.18 | 0.18 | 0.18 |
| | M′/TP* | 0.49 | 0.49 | 0.49 | 0.48 | 0.48 |
| | GFU*/TP* | 0.51 | 0.51 | 0.51 | 0.52 | 0.52 |
| *Selected NIPA-IO measures* | | | | | | |
| | GP = M + GFD | 1044.76 | 1099.77 | 1173.84 | 1273.88 | 1389.06 |
| | M | 470.26 | 492.97 | 524.04 | 568.68 | 617.06 |
| | GFD = GNP | 574.50 | 606.80 | 649.80 | 705.20 | 772.00 |
| Table E.2 | CON | 361.9 | 381.7 | 409.3 | 440.7 | 477.3 |
| Table E.2 | IG | 87.6 | 93.1 | 99.6 | 116.2 | 128.6 |
| Table E.2 | (X − IM) | 6.9 | 8.2 | 10.9 | 9.7 | 7.5 |
| Table E.2 | G | 118.1 | 123.8 | 130.0 | 138.6 | 158.6 |
| Table H.1 | NNP | 525.20 | 555.50 | 595.90 | 647.70 | 709.90 |
| *Comparisons* | | | | | | |
| | TP*/GP | 0.83 | 0.83 | 0.83 | 0.83 | 0.83 |
| | GFP*/GNP | 0.87 | 0.86 | 0.86 | 0.86 | 0.86 |
| | FP*/NNP | 0.90 | 0.90 | 0.90 | 0.90 | 0.90 |

| 1967 | 1968 | 1969 | 1970 | 1971 | 1972 | 1973 | 1974 | 1975 |
|---|---|---|---|---|---|---|---|---|
| 1200.79 | 1307.97 | 1406.84 | 1457.17 | 1568.48 | 1728.88 | 1980.04 | 2161.80 | 2366.72 |
| 500.66 | 545.14 | 586.54 | 602.47 | 644.70 | 714.33 | 837.40 | 926.56 | 1023.78 |
| 700.13 | 762.83 | 820.30 | 854.70 | 923.78 | 1014.55 | 1142.64 | 1235.25 | 1342.95 |
| 670.66 | 730.40 | 785.04 | 818.11 | 884.22 | 970.28 | 1090.24 | 1176.75 | 1277.77 |
| 29.48 | 32.43 | 35.26 | 36.59 | 39.56 | 44.27 | 52.40 | 58.50 | 65.17 |
| 1199.81 | 1307.46 | 1406.26 | 1456.35 | 1567.82 | 1728.41 | 1979.91 | 2162.38 | 2368.48 |
| 500.66 | 545.14 | 586.54 | 602.47 | 644.70 | 714.33 | 837.40 | 926.56 | 1023.78 |
| 699.15 | 762.32 | 819.72 | 853.88 | 923.12 | 1014.08 | 1142.52 | 1235.82 | 1344.71 |
| 75.99 | 82.18 | 88.39 | 92.71 | 99.94 | 108.05 | 122.49 | 135.35 | 151.11 |
| 421.33 | 464.47 | 502.02 | 537.49 | 580.57 | 637.77 | 708.07 | 776.70 | 860.42 |
| 117.28 | 127.76 | 142.73 | 137.31 | 159.69 | 187.77 | 222.71 | 222.26 | 198.56 |
| −3.33 | −6.51 | −6.39 | −4.25 | −9.56 | −15.55 | −9.23 | −14.12 | 4.02 |
| 87.90 | 94.42 | 92.96 | 90.63 | 92.46 | 96.04 | 98.47 | 115.63 | 130.59 |
| 623.17 | 680.14 | 731.33 | 761.18 | 823.17 | 906.03 | 1020.02 | 1100.47 | 1193.60 |
| 669.68 | 729.89 | 784.46 | 817.30 | 883.56 | 969.81 | 1090.12 | 1177.33 | 1279.53 |
| 3342.09 | 3468.05 | 3533.32 | 3467.51 | 3531.12 | 3717.01 | 3999.83 | 4004.40 | 3994.07 |
| 1947.50 | 2022.06 | 2059.60 | 2033.06 | 2079.09 | 2180.82 | 2308.11 | 2288.56 | 2267.64 |
| 2274.37 | 2367.90 | 2422.11 | 2417.86 | 2483.56 | 2608.17 | 2746.06 | 2727.22 | 2695.78 |
| 816.50 | 892.70 | 964.00 | 1015.50 | 1102.70 | 1212.80 | 1359.30 | 1472.70 | 1598.60 |
| 35.90 | 37.70 | 39.80 | 42.00 | 44.40 | 46.50 | 49.50 | 54.00 | 59.30 |
| 1.47 | 1.46 | 1.46 | 1.43 | 1.42 | 1.43 | 1.46 | 1.47 | 1.48 |
| 0.82 | 0.82 | 0.82 | 0.81 | 0.81 | 0.81 | 0.82 | 0.82 | 0.82 |
| 0.18 | 0.18 | 0.18 | 0.19 | 0.19 | 0.19 | 0.18 | 0.18 | 0.18 |
| 0.48 | 0.48 | 0.48 | 0.48 | 0.47 | 0.48 | 0.48 | 0.49 | 0.50 |
| 0.52 | 0.52 | 0.52 | 0.52 | 0.53 | 0.52 | 0.52 | 0.51 | 0.50 |
| | | | | | | | | |
| 1462.58 | 1595.80 | 1722.72 | 1800.78 | 1945.90 | 2143.39 | 2440.00 | 2667.47 | 2919.00 |
| 646.08 | 703.10 | 758.72 | 785.28 | 843.20 | 930.59 | 1080.70 | 1194.77 | 1320.40 |
| 816.50 | 892.70 | 964.00 | 1015.50 | 1102.70 | 1212.80 | 1359.30 | 1472.70 | 1598.60 |
| 503.6 | 552.5 | 597.9 | 640.0 | 691.6 | 757.6 | 837.2 | 916.5 | 1012.8 |
| 125.7 | 137.0 | 153.2 | 148.8 | 172.5 | 202.0 | 238.8 | 240.8 | 219.6 |
| 7.4 | 5.5 | 5.6 | 8.5 | 6.3 | 3.2 | 16.8 | 16.3 | 31.1 |
| 179.8 | 197.7 | 207.3 | 218.2 | 232.3 | 250.0 | 266.5 | 299.1 | 335.1 |
| 749.00 | 818.70 | 882.50 | 926.60 | 1005.10 | 1104.80 | 1241.20 | 1335.40 | 1436.60 |
| | | | | | | | | |
| 0.82 | 0.82 | 0.82 | 0.81 | 0.81 | 0.81 | 0.81 | 0.81 | 0.81 |
| 0.86 | 0.85 | 0.85 | 0.84 | 0.84 | 0.84 | 0.84 | 0.84 | 0.84 |
| 0.89 | 0.89 | 0.89 | 0.88 | 0.88 | 0.88 | 0.88 | 0.88 | 0.89 |

*(more)*

Table 5.4 *(cont.)*

| Sources | Variables | 1976 | 1977 | 1978 | 1979 | 1980 |
|---|---|---|---|---|---|---|
| *Marxian measures* | | | | | | |
| Table E.1 | TV* | 2691.95 | 3054.58 | 3456.06 | 3832.06 | 4140.14 |
| Table D.2 | $C_m^* = M_p'$ | 1187.33 | 1367.27 | 1545.89 | 1710.49 | 1851.27 |
| Table E.1 | GVA* | 1504.62 | 1687.31 | 1910.17 | 2121.56 | 2288.87 |
| Table E.1 | VA* = GVA* − $C_d^*$ | 1428.45 | 1598.95 | 1810.27 | 2011.02 | 2169.23 |
| Table E.1 | $C_d^*$ | 76.18 | 88.36 | 99.90 | 110.54 | 119.64 |
| Table E.2 | TP* | 2694.39 | 3058.10 | 3456.76 | 3833.25 | 4141.10 |
| | $U^{*\prime} = M_p'$ | 1187.33 | 1367.27 | 1545.89 | 1710.49 | 1851.27 |
| | GFP* = TP* − $U^{*\prime}$ | 1507.06 | 1690.83 | 1910.87 | 2122.76 | 2289.84 |
| Table D.2 | $M_{tt}' + M_{ry}'$ | 170.35 | 196.66 | 221.85 | 248.44 | 266.86 |
| Table E.2 | CON* | 961.28 | 1068.01 | 1185.13 | 1321.81 | 1454.98 |
| Table E.2 | IG* | 254.84 | 318.62 | 387.90 | 421.18 | 398.22 |
| Table E.2 | (X − IM)* | −12.91 | −35.29 | −40.48 | −44.04 | −36.36 |
| Table E.2 | G* | 133.49 | 142.84 | 156.47 | 175.38 | 206.13 |
| | GFU* = GFP* − $(M_{tt}' + M_{ry}')$ | 1336.70 | 1494.17 | 1689.02 | 1874.32 | 2022.98 |
| | FP* = GFP* − $C_d^*$ | 1430.88 | 1602.47 | 1810.97 | 2012.22 | 2170.20 |
| | $TP_{real}^*$ | 4270.03 | 4543.98 | 4787.75 | 4876.91 | 4832.09 |
| | $GFP_{real}^*$ | 2388.36 | 2512.38 | 2646.64 | 2700.71 | 2671.92 |
| | $GNP_{real}$ | 2825.20 | 2957.65 | 3115.79 | 3191.09 | 3197.98 |
| 101 1 | GNP | 1782.70 | 1990.50 | 2249.60 | 2508.20 | 2732.10 |
| 705 1 | GNP deflator | 63.10 | 67.30 | 72.20 | 78.60 | 85.70 |
| | TP*/GNP | 1.51 | 1.54 | 1.54 | 1.53 | 1.52 |
| Table E.1 | $GO_p$/TV* | 0.82 | 0.82 | 0.83 | 0.82 | 0.83 |
| Table E.1 | $GO_{tt}$/TV* | 0.18 | 0.18 | 0.18 | 0.18 | 0.17 |
| | M'/TP* | 0.50 | 0.51 | 0.51 | 0.51 | 0.51 |
| | GFU*/TP* | 0.50 | 0.49 | 0.49 | 0.49 | 0.49 |
| *Selected NIPA–IO measures* | | | | | | |
| | GP = M + GFD | 3305.49 | 3750.53 | 4248.52 | 4731.53 | 5146.84 |
| | M | 1522.79 | 1760.03 | 1998.92 | 2223.33 | 2414.74 |
| | GFD = GNP | 1782.70 | 1990.50 | 2249.60 | 2508.20 | 2732.10 |
| Table E.2 | CON | 1129.3 | 1257.2 | 1403.5 | 1566.8 | 1732.6 |
| Table E.2 | IG | 277.7 | 344.1 | 416.8 | 454.8 | 437.0 |
| Table E.2 | (X − IM) | 18.8 | 1.9 | 4.1 | 18.8 | 32.1 |
| Table E.2 | G | 356.9 | 387.3 | 425.2 | 467.8 | 530.4 |
| Table H.1 | NNP | 1603.60 | 1789.00 | 2019.80 | 2242.40 | 2428.10 |
| *Comparisons* | | | | | | |
| | TP*/GP | 0.82 | 0.82 | 0.81 | 0.81 | 0.80 |
| | GFP*/GNP | 0.85 | 0.85 | 0.85 | 0.85 | 0.84 |
| | FP*/NNP | 0.89 | 0.90 | 0.90 | 0.90 | 0.89 |

| 1981 | 1982 | 1983 | 1984 | 1985 | 1986 | 1987 | 1988 | 1989 |
|---|---|---|---|---|---|---|---|---|
| 4653.19 | 4762.47 | 5085.62 | 5689.10 | 6014.56 | 6236.33 | 6614.45 | 7223.85 | 7639.86 |
| 2078.34 | 2114.61 | 2235.61 | 2497.25 | 2618.65 | 2664.48 | 2808.66 | 3122.99 | 3278.25 |
| 2574.85 | 2647.86 | 2850.01 | 3191.85 | 3395.91 | 3571.85 | 3805.79 | 4100.86 | 4361.61 |
| 2440.54 | 2511.20 | 2705.53 | 3030.46 | 3226.68 | 3399.66 | 3624.28 | 3899.03 | 4149.75 |
| 134.31 | 136.66 | 144.48 | 161.39 | 169.23 | 172.19 | 181.51 | 201.83 | 211.86 |
| 4654.40 | 4763.86 | 5086.97 | 5691.02 | 6014.18 | 6224.47 | 6606.59 | 7226.22 | 7641.82 |
| 2078.34 | 2114.61 | 2235.61 | 2497.25 | 2618.65 | 2664.48 | 2808.66 | 3122.99 | 3278.25 |
| 2576.06 | 2649.25 | 2851.36 | 3193.77 | 3395.53 | 3559.99 | 3797.93 | 4103.23 | 4363.57 |
| 301.66 | 317.07 | 352.37 | 394.43 | 436.73 | 472.79 | 511.57 | 553.24 | 597.13 |
| 1599.86 | 1710.89 | 1853.81 | 2013.39 | 2161.53 | 2275.73 | 2434.73 | 2619.76 | 2777.29 |
| 485.10 | 414.52 | 466.85 | 626.53 | 601.72 | 614.64 | 651.16 | 694.94 | 714.89 |
| −41.22 | −47.94 | −79.65 | −129.87 | −141.28 | −156.38 | −164.96 | −131.34 | −110.05 |
| 230.67 | 254.71 | 257.99 | 289.29 | 336.83 | 353.20 | 365.44 | 366.63 | 384.31 |
| 2274.41 | 2332.19 | 2499.00 | 2799.34 | 2958.81 | 3087.20 | 3286.36 | 3549.99 | 3766.45 |
| 2441.75 | 2512.59 | 2706.88 | 3032.38 | 3226.30 | 3387.80 | 3616.42 | 3901.40 | 4151.71 |
| 4951.49 | 4763.86 | 4896.03 | 5284.14 | 5374.60 | 5417.29 | 5547.09 | 5957.31 | 6050.53 |
| 2740.49 | 2649.25 | 2744.33 | 2965.43 | 3034.44 | 3098.34 | 3188.86 | 3382.71 | 3454.93 |
| 3247.45 | 3166.00 | 3277.86 | 3502.60 | 3587.94 | 3682.86 | 3791.44 | 4017.89 | 4117.82 |
| 3052.60 | 3166.00 | 3405.70 | 3772.30 | 4014.90 | 4231.60 | 4515.60 | 4873.70 | 5200.80 |
| 94.00 | 100.00 | 103.90 | 107.70 | 111.90 | 114.90 | 119.10 | 121.30 | 126.30 |
| 1.52 | 1.50 | 1.49 | 1.51 | 1.50 | 1.47 | 1.46 | 1.48 | 1.47 |
| 0.83 | 0.82 | 0.82 | 0.82 | 0.81 | 0.81 | 0.81 | 0.82 | 0.81 |
| 0.17 | 0.18 | 0.18 | 0.18 | 0.19 | 0.19 | 0.19 | 0.19 | 0.19 |
| 0.51 | 0.51 | 0.51 | 0.51 | 0.51 | 0.50 | 0.50 | 0.51 | 0.51 |
| 0.49 | 0.49 | 0.49 | 0.49 | 0.49 | 0.50 | 0.50 | 0.49 | 0.49 |
| | | | | | | | | |
| 5768.06 | 5951.66 | 6407.16 | 7119.72 | 7594.93 | 7974.71 | 8510.87 | 9198.45 | 9789.83 |
| 2715.46 | 2785.66 | 3001.46 | 3347.42 | 3580.03 | 3743.11 | 3995.27 | 4324.75 | 4589.02 |
| 3052.60 | 3166.00 | 3405.70 | 3772.30 | 4014.90 | 4231.60 | 4515.60 | 4873.70 | 5200.80 |
| 1915.1 | 2050.7 | 2234.5 | 2430.5 | 2629.0 | 2797.4 | 3009.4 | 3238.2 | 3450.1 |
| 515.5 | 447.3 | 502.3 | 664.8 | 643.1 | 659.4 | 699.5 | 747.1 | 771.2 |
| 33.9 | 26.3 | −6.1 | −58.9 | −78.0 | −97.4 | −114.7 | −74.1 | −46.1 |
| 588.1 | 641.7 | 675.0 | 735.9 | 820.8 | 872.2 | 921.4 | 962.5 | 1025.6 |
| 2704.80 | 2782.80 | 3009.10 | 3356.80 | 3577.60 | 3771.50 | 4028.60 | 4359.40 | 4646.40 |
| | | | | | | | | |
| 0.81 | 0.80 | 0.79 | 0.80 | 0.79 | 0.78 | 0.78 | 0.79 | 0.78 |
| 0.84 | 0.84 | 0.84 | 0.85 | 0.85 | 0.84 | 0.84 | 0.84 | 0.84 |
| 0.90 | 0.90 | 0.90 | 0.90 | 0.90 | 0.90 | 0.90 | 0.89 | 0.89 |

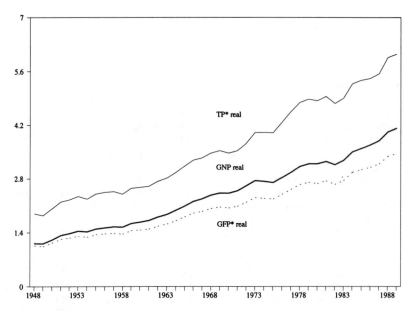

Figure 5.3. Real total and final product, and real GNP (billions of 1982 dollars). *Source:* Table 5.4.

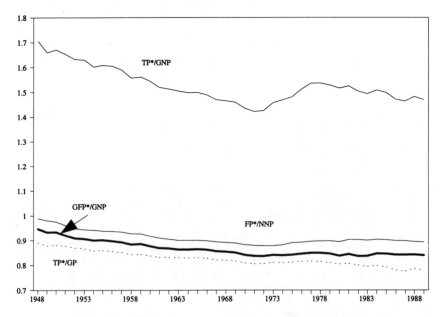

Figure 5.4. Ratios of real product measures. *Source:* Table 5.4.

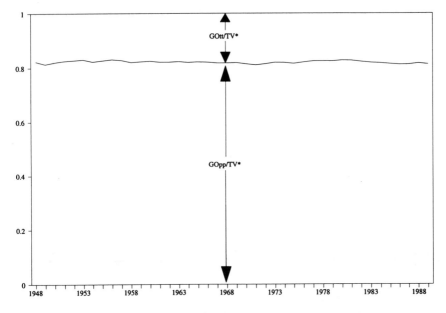

Figure 5.5. Components of total value. *Source:* Table 5.4.

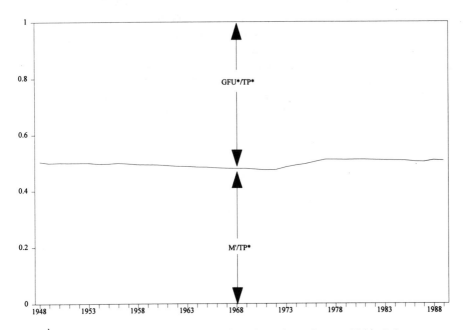

Figure 5.6. Components of total product. *Source:* Table 5.4.

capital to total value or to value added. For information on the latter, see Shaikh (1987, 1992b). Finally, it is worth noting that the relative stability of the proportion between productive and total trade sectors in Figure 5.5 does not carry over to the proportion between productive and unproductive labor in Figure 5.9, which rises dramatically over the postwar period.

### 5.3  Employment, wages, and variable capital

The transition from input–output tables to a NIPA-based data set allows us to take advantage of the employment and wage data available in NIPA and in related sources such as the Bureau of Labor Statistics (BLS). Our primary database for employment and wages is from NIPA. For total employment L we use "persons engaged in production" (PEP), since this includes both employees and self-employed persons; for wages we use "employee compensation" (EC), which includes wages and salaries of employees as well as employer contributions to social security. Employee compensation is the appropriate measure upon which to base our estimates of variable capital, since it represents the total cost of labor power to the capitalist.

NIPA data make no distinction between production and nonproduction workers, unlike BLS data.[6] We therefore use the latter to calculate the ratios of production labor to total labor in each production sector. These ratios are then applied to relevant NIPA employment totals in order to split them into comparable components. A combination of BLS and NIPA data is also used to estimate the wage per production worker, which is then applied to the previous estimate of the number of productive workers to derive the total wage bill of productive labor (variable capital). The wage bill of unproductive workers is derived as the difference between total NIPA wages and our estimate of total variable capital. These procedures allow us to retain NIPA estimates of total employment and total wages – which are tied to the value-added and final-demand estimates used to create our primary measures – while still making use of important information available only from the BLS. The basic steps involved are outlined next.

*Total labor and productive labor:* Productive labor is the production labor employed in capitalist production sectors: agriculture, mining, con-

---

[6] The *Employment and Training Report of the President* (BLS 1981) lists two types of employment for each sector: total employment, and production and nonsupervisory workers. In production sectors we take the latter to be a good estimate of the number of production workers.

struction, transportation and public utilities, manufacturing, and productive services (defined as all services except business services, legal services, miscellaneous professional services and private households, as in Table E.1 and Table F.1, note 3). It thereby excludes nonproduction labor (sales etc.) employed in the production sectors; it also excludes all labor in nonproduction sectors such as trade or finance. Thus total productive labor is the sum of the production workers in each production sector. Total unproductive labor is the sum of the nonproduction workers in the production sectors and all the workers in the nonproduction sectors.[7] Listing the production sectors as $j = 1, \ldots, k$ and the nonproduction sectors as $j = k+1, \ldots, n$, we calculate

$L_j$ = total employment in the $j$th sector (from NIPA)[8]

    = "persons engaged in production" (PEP)

    = full-time equivalent employees (FEE)

      + self-employed persons (SEP);[9]

$L = \sum L_j$ = total labor;

$(L_p/L)'_j$ = ratio of production/total workers

      in the $j$th production sector,    $j = 1, \ldots, k$ (BLS);

$(L_p)_j = (L_p/L)'_j \cdot (L_j)$

    = estimated production worker

      employment in the $j$th production sector,    $j = 1, \ldots, k$;

$L_p = \sum (L_p)_j$ = total productive labor;

$L_u = L - L_p$ = total unproductive labor.

---

[7] We should in principle attempt to separate out production from nonproduction activities in the nonproduction sectors, just as we do for production sectors, but the data for this is lacking. Also, there is a genuine asymmetry between production and nonproduction sectors. All capitalist enterprises must devote a certain amount of their activities to buying and selling and to finance; thus, even productive sectors will contain a significant amount of nonproduction activities. But nonproduction sectors have no such systematic reason for incorporating production activities.

[8] To estimate the labor in the productive service sectors, we take the ratio of the GNP of the productive service sectors to the GNP of total services, and apply that to the total employment in services (Table E.1 and F.1).

[9] Persons engaged in production (PEP) is a standard NIPA series. The inclusion of self-employed persons alongside full-time equivalent employees suggests that the former are also largely full-time.

Table 5.5. *Total labor and productive employment, 1948–89 (thousands)*

| Variables | 1948 | 1949 | 1950 | 1951 | 1952 | 1953 | 1954 |
|---|---|---|---|---|---|---|---|
| $L$ | 58,301 | 56,919 | 58,600 | 62,366 | 63,457 | 64,247 | 62,324 |
| $L_p$ | 32,994 | 31,201 | 32,226 | 33,123 | 32,768 | 33,043 | 31,230 |
| $L_u = L - L_p$ | 25,307 | 25,718 | 26,374 | 29,243 | 30.689 | 31,204 | 31,094 |
| $L_p/L_u$ | 1.30 | 1.21 | 1.22 | 1.13 | 1.07 | 1.06 | 1.00 |
| $L_p/L$ | 0.57 | 0.55 | 0.55 | 0.53 | 0.52 | 0.51 | 0.50 |

| Variables | 1955 | 1956 | 1957 | 1958 | 1959 | 1960 | 1961 |
|---|---|---|---|---|---|---|---|
| $L$ | 63,366 | 64,522 | 64,779 | 62,765 | 64,099 | 64,989 | 64,740 |
| $L_p$ | 31,714 | 31,864 | 31,433 | 29,349 | 30,020 | 30,047 | 29,363 |
| $L_u = L - L_p$ | 31,652 | 32,658 | 33,346 | 33,416 | 34,079 | 34,942 | 35,377 |
| $L_p/L_u$ | 1.00 | 0.98 | 0.94 | 0.88 | 0.88 | 0.86 | 0.83 |
| $L_p/L$ | 0.50 | 0.49 | 0.49 | 0.47 | 0.47 | 0.46 | 0.45 |

| Variables | 1962 | 1963 | 1964 | 1965 | 1966 | 1967 | 1968 |
|---|---|---|---|---|---|---|---|
| $L$ | 66,091 | 66,655 | 67,874 | 70,128 | 73,301 | 75,137 | 76,929 |
| $L_p$ | 29,937 | 30,013 | 30,280 | 31,365 | 32,566 | 32,856 | 33,445 |
| $L_u = L - L_p$ | 36,154 | 36,642 | 37,594 | 38,763 | 40,735 | 42,281 | 43,484 |
| $L_p/L_u$ | 0.83 | 0.82 | 0.81 | 0.81 | 0.80 | 0.78 | 0.77 |
| $L_p/L$ | 0.45 | 0.45 | 0.45 | 0.45 | 0.44 | 0.44 | 0.43 |

| Variables | 1969 | 1970 | 1971 | 1972 | 1973 | 1974 | 1975 |
|---|---|---|---|---|---|---|---|
| $L$ | 78,875 | 78,275 | 77,937 | 79,856 | 83,299 | 84,612 | 82,827 |
| $L_p$ | 34,125 | 33,247 | 32,727 | 33,896 | 35,462 | 35,657 | 33,615 |
| $L_u = L - L_p$ | 44,750 | 45,028 | 45,210 | 45,960 | 47,837 | 48,955 | 49,212 |
| $L_p/L_u$ | 0.76 | 0.74 | 0.72 | 0.74 | 0.74 | 0.73 | 0.68 |
| $L_p/L$ | 0.43 | 0.42 | 0.42 | 0.42 | 0.43 | 0.42 | 0.41 |

| Variables | 1976 | 1977 | 1978 | 1979 | 1980 | 1981 | 1982 |
|---|---|---|---|---|---|---|---|
| $L$ | 85,151 | 88,116 | 92,539 | 95,525 | 95,734 | 96,582 | 94,990 |
| $L_p$ | 34,677 | 35,798 | 37,610 | 38,598 | 37,863 | 37,738 | 36,203 |
| $L_u = L - L_p$ | 50,474 | 52,318 | 54,929 | 56,927 | 57,871 | 58,844 | 58,787 |
| $L_p/L_u$ | 0.69 | 0.68 | 0.68 | 0.68 | 0.65 | 0.64 | 0.62 |
| $L_p/L$ | 0.41 | 0.41 | 0.41 | 0.40 | 0.40 | 0.39 | 0.38 |

| Variables | 1983 | 1984 | 1985 | 1986 | 1987 | 1988 | 1989 |
|---|---|---|---|---|---|---|---|
| $L$ | 95,952 | 100,607 | 103,031 | 104,831 | 107,891 | 110,962 | 113,511 |
| $L_p$ | 36,088 | 37,872 | 38,229 | 38,312 | 39,344 | 40,538 | 41,148 |
| $L_u = L - L_p$ | 59,864 | 62,735 | 64,802 | 66,519 | 68,547 | 70,424 | 72,363 |
| $L_p/L_u$ | 0.60 | 0.60 | 0.59 | 0.58 | 0.57 | 0.58 | 0.57 |
| $L_p/L$ | 0.38 | 0.38 | 0.37 | 0.37 | 0.36 | 0.37 | 0.36 |

*Source:* Appendix F.

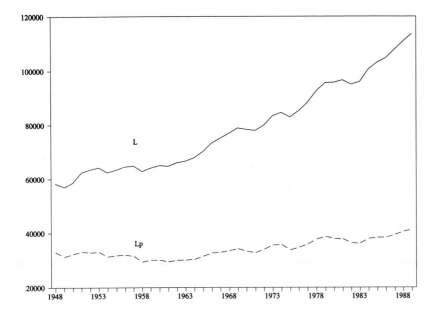

Figure 5.7. Total labor and productive labor (hours). *Source:* Table 5.5.

Appendix F gives the details of the calculations. Table 5.5 and Figure 5.7 present the estimates for L, $L_p$, $L_u$, and $L_p/L$ for the years 1948–89. Note that productive employment rises much more slowly than total employment, so that their ratio in Figure 5.9 declines by more than 37% over the postwar period. The same trend is depicted in Figure 5.11, where we see that the ratio of unproductive to productive labor $L_u/L_p$ rises sharply, by almost 138%, over the same period.

*Total wages and variable capital:* As noted earlier, we want our basic measure of wages to include supplements to wages such as employer contributions to social security and other pension funds, since these are part of the total cost of hiring labor power. The NIPA measure of employee compensation (EC) is therefore the appropriate starting point,[10] but we must make two adjustments to it. First, since EC covers only employees whereas total employment L includes both employees and self-employed persons, we need to make some estimate of the wage equivalent of self-

---

[10] Employee compensation EC includes the salaries of corporate officers (COS) and supplements to these salaries. Mage (1963) excludes these on the grounds that they are really part of capitalist income, not wages. We do essentially the same thing (see Appendix G).

employed persons.[11] Second, we must split the resulting measure of total wages into wages of productive and unproductive workers. Let:

$EC_j$ = total employee compensation in the $j$th sector (NIPA);

$FEE_j$ = total full-time equivalent employees in the $j$th sector (NIPA);

$ec_j \equiv (EC/FEE)_j$ = employee compensation per full-time equivalent employee;

$W_j \equiv ec_j \cdot L_j$ = estimated wage equivalent of employees and self-employed persons in the $j$th sector; and

$W = \sum W_j$ = total wage and wage equivalent.

This extends the coverage of employee compensation to include the wage equivalent of self-employed persons. We must now divide total wages into those of productive and unproductive workers. Given our previous data on the numbers of productive and unproductive workers ($L_p, L_u$), and on the total wage bill of all workers ($W$), an estimate of the unit employee compensation of productive workers ($ec_p$) would be sufficient to derive the wage bill of unproductive workers ($W_p \equiv ec_p \cdot L_p$) and also that of unproductive workers ($W_u = W - W_p$).

The BLS provides data on the unit wages of production workers in various sectors, excluding the service sector. But unlike our desired measure of employee compensation, BLS wage data do not include employer contributions to social security and other pension plans.[12] It is therefore adjusted upward by the ratio of employee compensation to wages and salaries taken from NIPA data. For the service sector, we use the employee compensation per full-time equivalent employee ($ec_{serv}$) as our measure of

---

[11] In NIPA, the value added of proprietorships and partnerships is not broken down into wages and profits. Ignoring the wage equivalent of self-employed persons (proprietors and partners) amounts to treating *all* of the value added as profit-type income. We have chosen instead to impute a wage equivalent to the labor of self-employed persons, and treat the rest of value added as profit-type income (which may be negative in the case of losses). As Mandel (1976, p. 945) notes, Marx includes "engineers, technologists and even managers" under the category of collective labor. Of course, only those involved in capitalist production would count as productive workers.

[12] The BLS wage data differ also in reflecting wage per employed worker, whereas our NIPA-based unit compensation ec is per full-time equivalent worker. By using the former, we are implicitly assuming that the wage of the average production worker is fairly close to that of the average full-time production worker. Since the latter is probably higher than the former, we somewhat underestimate variable capital.

the employee compensation of workers in productive services (see Table G.1). We have:

$(w_p)'_j$ = unit wage of production workers in the $j$th production sector,

$\quad j = 1, \ldots, k$ (from BLS), except services, for which $(w_p)_{serv} = ec_{serv}$;

$x_j \equiv (EC/WS)_j$

$\quad$ = ratio of employee compensation EC to wages and salaries W, in the $j$th production sector, $j = 1, \ldots, k$ (from NIPA);

$(ec_p)_j \equiv (w_p)'_j \cdot (x_j)$

$\quad$ = estimated employee compensation of production workers in the $j$th production sector;[13]

$V_j \equiv ec_j \cdot (L_p)_j \equiv (W_p)_j$ = variable capital in the $j$th production sector;

$V^* \equiv W_p = \Sigma(W_p)_j$ = total variable capital;

$W_u \equiv W - V^*$ = total wages of unproductive workers in all sectors;

$ec_p \equiv W_p/L_p$ = average wage of productive workers;

$ec_u \equiv W_u/L_u$ = average wage of unproductive workers.

Appendix G provides the details of the calculations. Table 5.6 and Figures 5.8–5.11 present the estimates W, V, $W_u$, $ec_p$, and $ec_u$ for the entire interval 1948–89. Figure 5.8 contrasts the levels of real variable capital and of the total real wage bill. Their absolute growth is greater than that of the corresponding labor totals in Figure 5.7 because the wage measures also incorporate the effects of growing real wages. But the relative movements of wage and employment measures is virtually the same, as is evident in Figure 5.9. $V^*/W$ declines by 34%, while $L_p/L$ declines by 37%. Figures 5.10 and 5.11 make quite explicit that the unit wages of productive and unproductive workers change only slightly, whereas their relative employments change drastically. We can therefore unambiguously conclude that the relative decline in productive to total wages $W_p/W$ ($\equiv V^*/W$) is almost entirely due to the relative decline in productive to total employment $L_p/L$.

### 5.4 Surplus value and surplus product

The estimates of variable capital in the previous section allow us to calculate surplus value and surplus product. By definition,

---

[13] This procedure implicitly assumes that the ratio supplements to wages is the same for both production and nonproduction workers. Our estimates in Appendix G justify this assumption.

S* = VA* − V* = surplus value (in money form);

S*/V* = rate of surplus value;

NP* = the necessary product (consumption of productive workers) = V*;

SP* = FP* − NP* = surplus product.

It is instructive to compare these Marxian measures with their orthodox counterparts, since naive readings of Marx have tended to confuse the two sets (see Section 6.1). Let

$(P^+) = NNP − EC$ = profit-type income (gross of all business taxes)[14]

and

$$P = (P^+) − IBT = NNP − IBT − EC = \text{profit (gross of profit tax)},$$

where

NNP = net national product in NIPA = VA = value added;
    EC = total employee compensation;
    IBT = indirect business tax;
$(P^+)/EC$ = ratio of profit-type income to wages; and
    P/EC = profit/wage ratio.

Appendix H gives further details. Table 5.7 and Figures 5.12–5.15 present the key Marxian ratios and their orthodox counterparts for 1948–89. Figure 5.12 compares real surplus value and real profits (defined here as real P). Both rise strongly, but not equally so; real surplus value rises about 16% relative to real profits. This latter movement is a reflection of the corresponding decline in productive to total wages, because $S^* \equiv VA^* − W_p = VA^* − EC_p$ and $(P^+) \equiv NNP − EC = VA − EC$, and the two measures of value added remain fairly close (see Figure 5.4).[15] Incidentally, it is useful to recall that only production and trading profits appear within total surplus value (see Section 3.6.1), so that the connection between S* and $(P^+)$ is not direct.

Figure 5.13 is the pièce de résistance. It compares the rate of surplus value S*/V* (which is the rate of exploitation of productive workers) with its "naive" equivalent $(P^+)/EC$. At midperiod, the former is almost four times as large as the latter. It also rises by over 40% during the postwar

---

[14] The profit measure defined here includes indirect business taxes because our aim is to simulate a "naive" estimation of surplus value.

[15] For U.S. data, the orthodox measure VA = P + EC remains within 10% of the Marxian measure $VA^* = V^* + S^*$, so the difference between P/EC and S*/V* is largely due to the fact that $V^* \equiv W_p \ll EC$. But we cannot assume that the rough equality that holds for the United States between the two value-added measures is a universal phenomenon.

Table 5.6. *Total wages and variable capital, 1948–89*

| Variables | Units | 1948 | 1949 | 1950 | 1951 | 1952 | 1953 | 1954 |
|---|---|---|---|---|---|---|---|---|
| W | billions of \$ | 164.76 | 164.75 | 178.76 | 206.23 | 222.10 | 236.85 | 235.67 |
| V* | billions of \$ | 88.41 | 85.02 | 93.16 | 105.91 | 111.01 | 117.39 | 111.95 |
| V*/W | | 0.54 | 0.52 | 0.52 | 0.51 | 0.50 | 0.50 | 0.48 |
| $W_u = W - V^*$ | billions of \$ | 76.35 | 79.73 | 85.60 | 100.32 | 111.08 | 119.46 | 123.72 |
| $W_{real} = W/pc^a$ | billions of 1982 \$ | 641.10 | 643.57 | 682.30 | 741.84 | 782.03 | 816.71 | 809.86 |
| $V^*_{real} = V^*/pc$ | billions of 1982 \$ | 344.01 | 332.12 | 355.58 | 380.98 | 390.89 | 404.79 | 384.71 |
| $(W_u)_{real} = W_u/pc$ | billions of 1982 \$ | 297.09 | 311.45 | 326.72 | 360.86 | 391.14 | 411.92 | 425.15 |
| pc | | 25.70 | 25.60 | 26.20 | 27.80 | 28.40 | 29.00 | 29.10 |
| $ec_p = V^*/L_p = W_p/L_p$ | \$/prod. worker/year | 2,679.59 | 2,724.93 | 2,890.85 | 3,197.52 | 3,387.82 | 3,552.62 | 3,584.71 |
| $ec_u = W_u/L_u$ | \$/unpr. worker/year | 3,017.07 | 3,100.28 | 3,245.65 | 3,430.59 | 3,619.70 | 3,828.25 | 3,978.90 |
| $L_u/L_p$ | | 0.77 | 0.82 | 0.82 | 0.88 | 0.94 | 0.94 | 1.00 |
| $ec_u/ec_p$ | | 1.13 | 1.14 | 1.12 | 1.07 | 1.07 | 1.08 | 1.11 |
| $L_p/L$ | | 0.57 | 0.55 | 0.55 | 0.53 | 0.52 | 0.51 | 0.50 |

| Variables | Units | 1955 | 1956 | 1957 | 1958 | 1959 | 1960 | 1961 |
|---|---|---|---|---|---|---|---|---|
| W | billions of \$ | 252.73 | 272.67 | 286.75 | 289.27 | 311.71 | 328.35 | 338.08 |
| V* | billions of \$ | 120.52 | 128.82 | 133.00 | 127.72 | 139.57 | 144.23 | 146.13 |
| V*/W | | 0.48 | 0.47 | 0.46 | 0.44 | 0.45 | 0.44 | 0.43 |
| $W_u = W - V^*$ | billions of \$ | 132.21 | 143.85 | 153.75 | 161.55 | 172.14 | 184.12 | 191.95 |
| $W_{real} = W/pc^a$ | billions of 1982 \$ | 856.71 | 905.88 | 925.00 | 915.41 | 965.05 | 998.03 | 1,015.24 |
| $V^*_{real} = V^*/pc$ | billions of 1982 \$ | 408.53 | 427.99 | 429.03 | 404.17 | 432.11 | 438.39 | 438.83 |
| $(W_u)_{real} = W_u/pc$ | billions of 1982 \$ | 448.18 | 477.90 | 495.97 | 511.24 | 532.95 | 559.64 | 576.41 |
| pc | | 29.50 | 30.10 | 31.00 | 31.60 | 32.30 | 32.90 | 33.30 |
| $ec_p = V^*/L_p = W_p/L_p$ | \$/prod. worker/year | 3,800.09 | 4,042.90 | 4,231.17 | 4,351.67 | 4,649.18 | 4,800.21 | 4,976.64 |
| $ec_u = W_u/L_u$ | \$/unpr. worker/year | 4,177.14 | 4,404.69 | 4,610.83 | 4,834.57 | 5,051.31 | 5,269.27 | 5,425.74 |
| $L_u/L_p$ | | 1.00 | 1.02 | 1.06 | 1.14 | 1.14 | 1.16 | 1.20 |
| $ec_u/ec_p$ | | 1.10 | 1.09 | 1.09 | 1.11 | 1.09 | 1.10 | 1.09 |
| $L_p/L$ | | 0.50 | 0.49 | 0.49 | 0.47 | 0.47 | 0.46 | 0.45 |

115

Table 5.6 (cont.)

| Variables | Units | 1962 | 1963 | 1964 | 1965 | 1966 | 1967 | 1968 |
|---|---|---|---|---|---|---|---|---|
| W | billions of $ | 360.89 | 379.43 | 406.66 | 436.64 | 480.94 | 515.03 | 566.66 |
| V* | billions of $ | 155.54 | 162.76 | 172.00 | 188.43 | 207.07 | 216.26 | 236.77 |
| V*/W | | 0.43 | 0.43 | 0.42 | 0.43 | 0.43 | 0.42 | 0.42 |
| $W_u = W - V*$ | billions of $ | 205.35 | 216.67 | 234.66 | 248.21 | 273.87 | 298.78 | 329.89 |
| $W_{real} = W/pc^a$ | billions of 1982 $ | 1,064.56 | 1,103.00 | 1,161.89 | 1,226.50 | 1,310.46 | 1,369.77 | 1,441.89 |
| $V*_{real} = V*/pc$ | billions of 1982 $ | 458.81 | 473.13 | 491.42 | 529.29 | 564.22 | 575.15 | 602.47 |
| $(W_u)_{real} = W_u/pc$ | billions of 1982 $ | 605.75 | 629.86 | 670.47 | 697.22 | 746.24 | 794.62 | 839.42 |
| pc | | 33.90 | 34.40 | 35.00 | 35.60 | 36.70 | 37.60 | 39.30 |
| $ec_p = V*/L_p = W_p/L_p$ | $/prod. worker/year | 5,195.52 | 5,442.92 | 5,680.27 | 6,007.47 | 6,358.51 | 6,581.91 | 7,079.28 |
| $ec_u = W_u/L_u$ | $/unpr. worker/year | 5,679.79 | 5,913.26 | 6,242.06 | 6,403.30 | 6,723.18 | 7,066.52 | 7,586.58 |
| $L_u/L_p$ | | 1.21 | 1.22 | 1.24 | 1.24 | 1.25 | 1.29 | 1.30 |
| $ec_u/ec_p$ | | 1.09 | 1.09 | 1.10 | 1.07 | 1.06 | 1.07 | 1.07 |
| $L_p/L$ | | 0.45 | 0.45 | 0.45 | 0.45 | 0.44 | 0.44 | 0.43 |

| Variables | Units | 1969 | 1970 | 1971 | 1972 | 1973 | 1974 | 1975 |
|---|---|---|---|---|---|---|---|---|
| W | billions of $ | 624.70 | 667.55 | 712.25 | 783.12 | 875.19 | 961.23 | 1,024.74 |
| V* | billions of $ | 261.22 | 270.43 | 287.53 | 324.30 | 370.49 | 398.50 | 410.75 |
| V*/W | | 0.42 | 0.41 | 0.40 | 0.41 | 0.42 | 0.41 | 0.40 |
| $W_u = W - V*$ | billions of $ | 363.48 | 397.12 | 424.72 | 458.82 | 504.70 | 562.72 | 613.99 |
| $W_{real} = W/pc^a$ | billions of 1982 $ | 1,523.65 | 1,556.06 | 1,586.30 | 1,676.91 | 1,764.49 | 1,754.06 | 1,730.98 |
| $V*_{real} = V*/pc$ | billions of 1982 $ | 637.11 | 630.38 | 640.37 | 694.44 | 746.95 | 727.20 | 693.83 |
| $(W_u)_{real} = W_u/pc$ | billions of 1982 $ | 886.54 | 925.69 | 945.93 | 982.47 | 1,017.53 | 1,026.86 | 1,037.14 |
| pc | | 41.00 | 42.90 | 44.90 | 46.70 | 49.60 | 54.80 | 59.20 |
| $ec_p = V*/L_p = W_p/L_p$ | $/prod. worker/year | 7,654.58 | 8,133.96 | 8,785.45 | 9,567.50 | 10,447.47 | 11,175.92 | 12,219.18 |
| $ec_u = W_u/L_u$ | $/unpr. worker/year | 8,122.58 | 8,819.44 | 9,394.50 | 9,982.99 | 10,550.34 | 11,494.79 | 12,476.44 |
| $L_u/L_p$ | | 1.31 | 1.35 | 1.38 | 1.36 | 1.35 | 1.37 | 1.46 |
| $ec_u/ec_p$ | | 1.06 | 1.08 | 1.07 | 1.04 | 1.01 | 1.03 | 1.02 |
| $L_p/L$ | | 0.43 | 0.42 | 0.42 | 0.42 | 0.43 | 0.42 | 0.41 |

116

| Variables | Units | 1976 | 1977 | 1978 | 1979 | 1980 | 1981 | 1982 |
|---|---|---|---|---|---|---|---|---|
| $W$ | billions of \$ | 1,140.36 | 1,268.47 | 1,433.64 | 1,610.76 | 1,773.25 | 1,956.87 | 2,071.62 |
| $V^*$ | billions of \$ | 459.63 | 515.81 | 589.20 | 664.78 | 706.53 | 772.35 | 786.53 |
| $V^*/W$ | | 0.40 | 0.41 | 0.41 | 0.41 | 0.40 | 0.39 | 0.38 |
| $W_u = W - V^*$ | billions of \$ | 680.73 | 752.65 | 844.43 | 945.98 | 1,066.73 | 1,184.52 | 1,285.09 |
| $W_{real} = W/pc^a$ | billions of 1982 \$ | 1,821.65 | 1,901.75 | 2,002.29 | 2,059.79 | 2,047.64 | 2,068.57 | 2,071.62 |
| $V^*_{real} = V^*/pc$ | billions of 1982 \$ | 734.23 | 773.34 | 822.91 | 850.11 | 815.85 | 816.44 | 786.53 |
| $(W_u)_{real} = W_u/pc$ | billions of 1982 \$ | 1,087.43 | 1,128.42 | 1,179.38 | 1,209.69 | 1,231.79 | 1,252.13 | 1,285.09 |
| $pc$ | | 62.60 | 66.70 | 71.60 | 78.20 | 86.60 | 94.60 | 100.00 |
| $ec_p = V^*/L_p = W_p/L_p$ | \$/prod. worker/year | 13,254.44 | 14,409.09 | 15,666.28 | 17,223.18 | 18,659.88 | 20,466.34 | 21,725.60 |
| $ec_u = W_u/L_u$ | \$/unpr. worker/year | 13,486.78 | 14,386.11 | 15,373.08 | 16,617.40 | 18,432.98 | 20,129.64 | 21,860.07 |
| $L_u/L_p$ | | 1.46 | 1.46 | 1.46 | 1.47 | 1.53 | 1.56 | 1.62 |
| $ec_u/ec_p$ | | 1.02 | 1.00 | 0.98 | 0.96 | 0.99 | 0.98 | 1.01 |
| $L_p/L$ | | 0.41 | 0.41 | 0.41 | 0.40 | 0.40 | 0.39 | 0.38 |

| Variables | Units | 1983 | 1984 | 1985 | 1986 | 1987 | 1988 | 1989 |
|---|---|---|---|---|---|---|---|---|
| $W$ | billions of \$ | 2,199.81 | 2,404.60 | 2,565.70 | 2,719.89 | 2,913.09 | 3,152.11 | 3,337.04 |
| $V^*$ | billions of \$ | 839.73 | 928.68 | 967.99 | 998.55 | 1,060.90 | 1,146.22 | 1,206.40 |
| $V^*/W$ | | 0.38 | 0.39 | 0.38 | 0.37 | 0.36 | 0.36 | 0.36 |
| $W_u = W - V^*$ | billions of \$ | 1,360.07 | 1,475.92 | 1,597.71 | 1,721.35 | 1,852.19 | 2,005.89 | 2,130.64 |
| $W_{real} = W/pc^a$ | billions of 1982 \$ | 2,113.17 | 2,218.26 | 2,286.72 | 2,358.97 | 2,445.92 | 2,537.93 | 2,568.93 |
| $V^*_{real} = V^*/pc$ | billions of 1982 \$ | 806.66 | 856.72 | 862.74 | 866.04 | 890.76 | 922.88 | 928.71 |
| $(W_u)_{real} = W_u/pc$ | billions of 1982 \$ | 1,306.51 | 1,361.55 | 1,423.98 | 1,492.93 | 1,555.15 | 1,615.05 | 1,640.22 |
| $pc$ | | 104.10 | 108.40 | 112.20 | 115.30 | 119.10 | 124.20 | 129.90 |
| $ec_p = V^*/L_p = W_p/L_p$ | \$/prod. worker/year | 23,269.07 | 24,521.58 | 25,320.89 | 26,063.32 | 26,964.96 | 28,275.23 | 29,318.41 |
| $ec_u = W_u/L_u$ | \$/unpr. worker/year | 22,719.44 | 23,526.17 | 24,655.20 | 25,877.64 | 27,020.58 | 28,483.03 | 29,443.84 |
| $L_u/L_p$ | | 1.66 | 1.66 | 1.70 | 1.74 | 1.74 | 1.74 | 1.76 |
| $ec_u/ec_p$ | | 0.98 | 0.96 | 0.97 | 0.99 | 1.00 | 1.01 | 1.00 |
| $L_p/L$ | | 0.38 | 0.38 | 0.37 | 0.37 | 0.36 | 0.37 | 0.36 |

$^a$ pc = consumer price index.

117

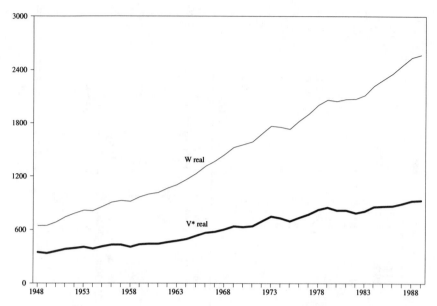

Figure 5.8. Total real wage and variable capital (billions of 1982 dollars). *Source:* Table 5.6.

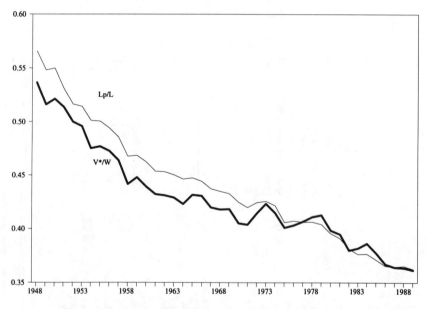

Figure 5.9. Productive employment and wage shares. *Source:* Table 5.6.

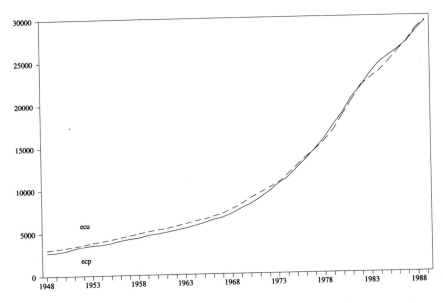

Figure 5.10. Productive and unproductive employment compensation (dollars per worker per year). *Source:* Table 5.6.

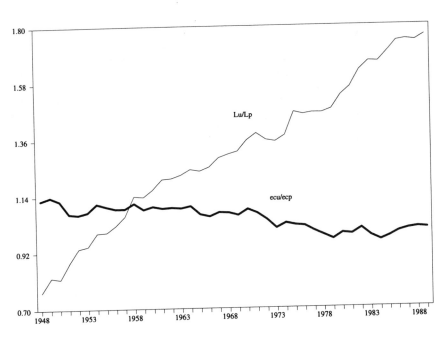

Figure 5.11. Relative rates of employment and compensation. *Source:* Table 5.6.

Table 5.7. *Marxian variables and their orthodox counterparts, 1948–89 (billions of dollars)*

| Variables | 1948 | 1949 | 1950 | 1951 | 1952 | 1953 |
|---|---|---|---|---|---|---|
| $S^*_{real}$ | 635.36 | 632.50 | 691.46 | 750.01 | 762.77 | 789.67 |
| $P^+_{real}$ | 419.97 | 410.22 | 456.83 | 496.43 | 494.71 | 503.01 |
| $S^*/V^*$ | 1.70 | 1.75 | 1.77 | 1.78 | 1.75 | 1.74 |
| $P^+/EC$ | 0.70 | 0.68 | 0.70 | 0.69 | 0.64 | 0.62 |
| $C^*_{real}$ | 880.90 | 844.07 | 934.59 | 1025.69 | 1051.56 | 1095.36 |
| $V^*_{real}$ | 344.01 | 332.12 | 355.58 | 380.98 | 390.89 | 404.79 |
| $C^*/V^{*a}$ | 2.35 | 2.33 | 2.40 | 2.43 | 2.42 | 2.42 |
| $M/EC$ | 1.69 | 1.63 | 1.66 | 1.63 | 1.57 | 1.55 |

| Variables | 1962 | 1963 | 1964 | 1965 | 1966 | 1967 |
|---|---|---|---|---|---|---|
| $S^*_{real}$ | 1003.76 | 1042.30 | 1108.02 | 1168.64 | 1230.43 | 1265.74 |
| $P^+_{real}$ | 619.99 | 648.10 | 683.63 | 733.38 | 762.71 | 761.79 |
| $S^*/V^*$ | 2.06 | 2.07 | 2.12 | 2.10 | 2.08 | 2.10 |
| $P^+/EC$ | 0.60 | 0.61 | 0.61 | 0.62 | 0.60 | 0.58 |
| $C^*_{real}$ | 1236.52 | 1276.51 | 1329.36 | 1403.30 | 1464.38 | 1476.69 |
| $V^*_{real}$ | 458.81 | 473.13 | 491.42 | 529.29 | 564.22 | 575.15 |
| $C^*/V^{*a}$ | 2.54 | 2.54 | 2.54 | 2.52 | 2.48 | 2.45 |
| $M/EC$ | 1.44 | 1.43 | 1.41 | 1.42 | 1.39 | 1.36 |

| Variables | 1976 | 1977 | 1978 | 1979 | 1980 | 1981 |
|---|---|---|---|---|---|---|
| $S^*_{real}$ | 1535.38 | 1609.41 | 1691.23 | 1712.77 | 1706.77 | 1774.67 |
| $P^+_{real}$ | 864.89 | 909.93 | 956.47 | 955.47 | 921.68 | 954.67 |
| $S^*/V^*$ | 2.11 | 2.10 | 2.07 | 2.03 | 2.07 | 2.16 |
| $P^+/EC$ | 0.52 | 0.52 | 0.52 | 0.50 | 0.48 | 0.50 |
| $C^*_{real}$ | 2002.39 | 2162.90 | 2279.49 | 2316.84 | 2299.78 | 2353.89 |
| $V^*_{real}$ | 734.23 | 773.34 | 822.91 | 850.11 | 815.85 | 816.44 |
| $C^*/V^{*a}$ | 2.75 | 2.82 | 2.79 | 2.74 | 2.79 | 2.86 |
| $M/EC$ | 1.44 | 1.50 | 1.50 | 1.49 | 1.47 | 1.50 |

*a* Flow ratio.

period, whereas the latter actually falls by almost 30%. Thus $P^+/EC$ grossly understates the level, and falsifies the trend, of $S^*/V^*$. *The profit/wage ratio is not a good proxy for the rate of surplus value.*

Figure 5.14 pursues the analysis of the central value categories by breaking down real total value into its principal components: $TV^* = C^* + V^* + S^*$, in 1982 constant dollars. By far the biggest component is $C^*$, which is roughly 50% of total value.

| 1954 | 1955 | 1956 | 1957 | 1958 | 1959 | 1960 | 1961 |
|------|------|------|------|------|------|------|------|
| 791.63 | 840.27 | 843.31 | 859.98 | 862.46 | 915.87 | 927.06 | 950.45 |
| 496.70 | 535.24 | 517.30 | 522.82 | 519.34 | 559.07 | 557.40 | 578.65 |
| 1.86 | 1.90 | 1.84 | 1.88 | 2.01 | 1.99 | 1.99 | 2.03 |
| 0.62 | 0.64 | 0.59 | 0.59 | 0.59 | 0.60 | 0.58 | 0.59 |
| 1051.12 | 1118.53 | 1144.64 | 1149.23 | 1104.10 | 1172.29 | 1182.87 | 1183.78 |
| 384.71 | 408.53 | 427.99 | 429.03 | 404.17 | 432.11 | 438.39 | 438.83 |
| 2.47 | 2.52 | 2.50 | 2.51 | 2.57 | 2.55 | 2.53 | 2.53 |
| 1.54 | 1.56 | 1.53 | 1.52 | 1.50 | 1.50 | 1.46 | 1.45 |

| 1968 | 1969 | 1970 | 1971 | 1972 | 1973 | 1974 | 1975 |
|------|------|------|------|------|------|------|------|
| 1309.36 | 1316.15 | 1303.99 | 1343.91 | 1389.20 | 1454.04 | 1441.19 | 1462.10 |
| 779.79 | 764.15 | 734.08 | 778.68 | 814.11 | 865.40 | 822.84 | 822.80 |
| 2.08 | 2.01 | 2.03 | 2.08 | 1.99 | 1.94 | 1.95 | 2.11 |
| 0.56 | 0.53 | 0.50 | 0.52 | 0.52 | 0.53 | 0.50 | 0.51 |
| 1532.02 | 1562.30 | 1521.57 | 1541.12 | 1631.40 | 1797.57 | 1824.17 | 1836.34 |
| 602.47 | 637.11 | 630.38 | 640.37 | 694.44 | 746.95 | 727.20 | 693.83 |
| 2.44 | 2.38 | 2.36 | 2.38 | 2.34 | 2.40 | 2.47 | 2.65 |
| 1.34 | 1.31 | 1.27 | 1.28 | 1.28 | 1.33 | 1.34 | 1.39 |

| 1982 | 1983 | 1984 | 1985 | 1986 | 1987 | 1988 | 1989 |
|------|------|------|------|------|------|------|------|
| 1724.68 | 1795.76 | 1951.51 | 2018.49 | 2089.74 | 2152.29 | 2269.42 | 2330.44 |
| 875.79 | 951.30 | 1061.17 | 1081.37 | 1096.69 | 1124.43 | 1198.93 | 1241.01 |
| 2.19 | 2.22 | 2.26 | 2.33 | 2.40 | 2.42 | 2.40 | 2.44 |
| 0.46 | 0.49 | 0.52 | 0.51 | 0.50 | 0.50 | 0.50 | 0.51 |
| 2251.27 | 2290.75 | 2468.56 | 2491.40 | 2468.82 | 2510.64 | 2740.99 | 2763.35 |
| 786.53 | 806.66 | 856.72 | 862.74 | 866.04 | 890.76 | 922.88 | 928.71 |
| 2.86 | 2.83 | 2.86 | 2.88 | 2.84 | 2.82 | 2.90 | 2.89 |
| 1.46 | 1.49 | 1.51 | 1.51 | 1.49 | 1.49 | 1.49 | 1.49 |

Finally, Figure 5.15 compares the value composition (of the flows) of capital $C^*/V^*$ with its orthodox counterpart, the ratio of intermediate inputs to wages $M/EC$. Once again, we see that the orthodox measure is not a proxy for the Marxian one. $C^*/V^*$ is from 50% to 90% longer than $M/EC$, and during the postwar period rises by 23% while the latter falls by almost 11%. Neither the level nor the trend of the former is captured by that of the latter.

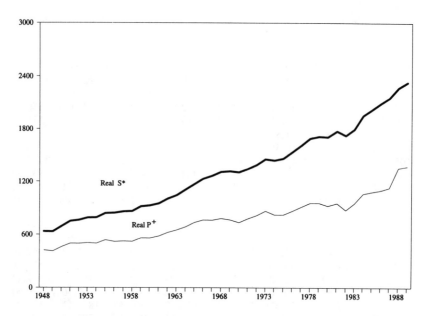

Figure 5.12. Real surplus value S* and profit-type income P⁺ (millions
of 1982 dollars). *Source:* Table 5.7.

### 5.5 Marxian, average, and corporate rates of profit

The production of data on the mass of surplus value S* and profit
P allows us then to estimate and compare three measures of the rate of
profit: the Marxian general rate of profit r*, defined here as the ratio of
surplus value to total fixed capital K;[16] the average rate of profit r, defined
as the ratio of profit-type income to K; and the corporate rate of profit
$r_{corp}$, which is the ratio of the NIPA measure of corporate profit to the
BEA measure of corporate capital. We also estimate the value composition of (fixed) capital $C_f^*/V^* = K/V^*$, as well as the materialized composition of (fixed) capital $C_f^*/(V^*+S^*) = K/(V^*+S^*)$. All variables are in
current dollars, including the capital stock that is measured at current
replacement costs.

Finally, since we are concerned here with the long-term tendencies of
the rates of profit, all measured ratios are adjusted for cyclical fluctuations
by means of a measure of capacity utilization developed in Shaikh (1987,
1992a). The rate of profit may be thought of as responding to long-term
structural changes in the rate of surplus value and the organic composition

---

[16] More properly, one should add the stock of circulating capital to the stock of
fixed capital. But consistent data on the former are not readily available.

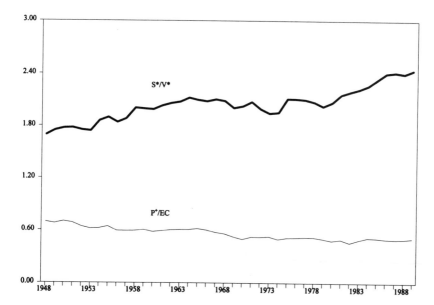

Figure 5.13. Rate of surplus value S*/V* and profit/wage ratio P⁺/EC.
*Source:* Table 5.7.

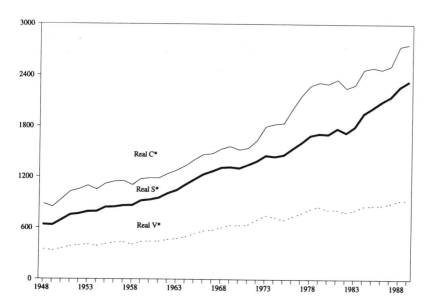

Figure 5.14. Components of real total value (millions of 1982 dollars).
*Source:* Table 5.7.

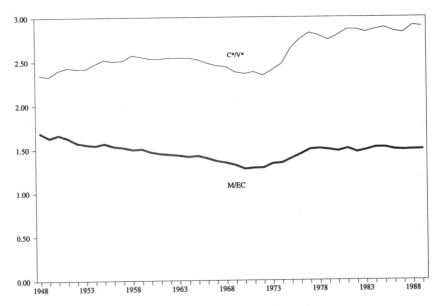

Figure 5.15. Value composition and the input/wage ratio.
*Source:* Table 5.7.

of capital, and to short-term fluctuations arising from cycles and from specific historical events such as wars, droughts, and so on. The latter will be reflected as fluctuations in the rate of utilization of the capital stock, which show up as corresponding fluctuations in the mass of profit. To eliminate this effect, we divide the mass of profit by the rate of capacity utilization, in much the same way as actual output is traditionally divided by capacity utilization to estimate potential output.

Table 5.8 and Figures 5.16 and 5.17 present the basic results. The data are partitioned into two major periods. The main period is from 1948 to 1980, during which the rate of surplus value rises modestly by almost 22%, the adjusted value composition rises by over 77%, and the adjusted materialized composition rises by over 56%. Because the large rise in the value composition overwhelms the modest one in the rate of surplus value, the adjusted Marxian rate of profit falls by almost a third over this period. The NIPA-based average rate of profit r′ falls even faster, by over 48%, and the corporate rate the fastest of all, by over 57%. These more rapid declines can be explained by the relative rise in the proportion of unproductive to productive activities, which absorbs a growing proportion of surplus value and reduces the amount available as profit (see Sections 5.3 and 5.4).

Table 5.8. *Aggregate rates of profit and compositions of capital, 1948–89*

| Sources | Variables | 1948 | 1949 | 1950 | 1951 | 1952 | 1953 | 1954 | 1955 | 1956 | 1957 | 1958 | 1959 |
|---|---|---|---|---|---|---|---|---|---|---|---|---|---|
| | $r^{*\prime}$ = profit rate adjusted for utilization = $r^*/u$ | 0.52 | 0.53 | 0.48 | 0.49 | 0.49 | 0.46 | 0.48 | 0.46 | 0.43 | 0.45 | 0.47 | 0.45 |
| | $r^* = S^*/K^*$ = Marxian general rate of profit | 0.39 | 0.37 | 0.38 | 0.39 | 0.38 | 0.39 | 0.38 | 0.39 | 0.36 | 0.36 | 0.36 | 0.38 |
| Table H.1 | $S^*$ | 149.94 | 148.64 | 165.26 | 188.25 | 194.51 | 204.52 | 208.20 | 228.55 | 236.97 | 250.25 | 256.15 | 278.42 |
| BEA 1987 | $K^* = C_t^*$ = fixed nonresidential gross private capital | 384.30 | 400.20 | 438.70 | 480.80 | 506.20 | 526.60 | 546.20 | 591.20 | 650.30 | 689.70 | 710.90 | 738.00 |
| Shaikh 1992 | $u$ | 0.75 | 0.70 | 0.78 | 0.81 | 0.79 | 0.84 | 0.80 | 0.85 | 0.84 | 0.81 | 0.77 | 0.84 |
| | $r' = r/u$ = NIPA-based general rate of profit | 0.27 | 0.27 | 0.25 | 0.26 | 0.25 | 0.23 | 0.23 | 0.23 | 0.20 | 0.21 | 0.21 | 0.21 |
| | $r = P/K^*$ | 0.21 | 0.19 | 0.20 | 0.21 | 0.19 | 0.19 | 0.18 | 0.19 | 0.17 | 0.17 | 0.16 | 0.17 |
| Table H.1 | $P = VA - EC - IBT = (P^+) - IBT$ | 78.91 | 75.10 | 85.68 | 99.31 | 98.45 | 100.58 | 101.03 | 113.29 | 110.36 | 114.64 | 115.54 | 128.06 |
| B-79[a] | IBT = indirect business tax | 20.20 | 21.30 | 23.50 | 25.30 | 27.70 | 29.70 | 29.60 | 32.30 | 35.00 | 37.50 | 38.70 | 41.90 |
| | $r'_n = r_n/u$ | 0.23 | 0.23 | 0.20 | 0.20 | 0.20 | 0.18 | 0.19 | 0.18 | 0.16 | 0.17 | 0.18 | 0.17 |
| | $r_n = P_n/K^*$ | 0.17 | 0.16 | 0.15 | 0.16 | 0.16 | 0.15 | 0.15 | 0.15 | 0.14 | 0.14 | 0.14 | 0.14 |
| Table H.1 | $P_n = (VA - EC) - IBT - CPT = (P^+) - IBT - CPT = P - CPT$ | 66.51 | 64.90 | 67.78 | 76.71 | 79.05 | 80.28 | 83.43 | 91.29 | 88.36 | 93.24 | 96.54 | 104.46 |
| | $(r)'_{corp} = (r)_{corp}$ adjusted for utilization = $(r)_{corp}/u$ | 0.14 | 0.13 | 0.14 | 0.14 | 0.13 | 0.12 | 0.11 | 0.13 | 0.11 | 0.11 | 0.10 | 0.11 |
| | $(r)_{corp}$ = corporate rate of profit = $P_{corp}/K_{corp}$ | 0.11 | 0.09 | 0.11 | 0.11 | 0.10 | 0.10 | 0.09 | 0.11 | 0.09 | 0.09 | 0.08 | 0.09 |
| B-84[a] | $P_{corp}$ | 30.30 | 28.00 | 34.90 | 39.90 | 37.50 | 37.70 | 36.60 | 47.10 | 45.70 | 45.30 | 40.30 | 51.40 |
| BEA 1987 | $K_{corp}$ | 285.69 | 297.28 | 323.98 | 353.42 | 372.61 | 388.72 | 403.72 | 436.86 | 482.66 | 514.62 | 531.35 | 552.80 |
| Table H.1 | $S^*/V^*$ | 1.70 | 1.75 | 1.77 | 1.78 | 1.75 | 1.74 | 1.86 | 1.90 | 1.84 | 1.88 | 2.01 | 1.99 |
| | $C^*/V^*$ = value composition of fixed capital (adj.) | 3.27 | 3.32 | 3.67 | 3.66 | 3.60 | 3.76 | 3.88 | 4.17 | 4.24 | 4.17 | 4.27 | 4.42 |
| | $C_t^*/(V^* + S^*) = (C_t^*/V^*)/[1 + (S^*/V^*)]$ | 1.21 | 1.21 | 1.32 | 1.32 | 1.31 | 1.37 | 1.36 | 1.44 | 1.49 | 1.45 | 1.42 | 1.48 |

125

Table 5.8 (cont.)

| Variables | 1960 | 1961 | 1962 | 1963 | 1964 | 1965 | 1966 | 1967 | 1968 | 1969 | 1970 | 1971 | 1972 | 1973 | 1974 |
|---|---|---|---|---|---|---|---|---|---|---|---|---|---|---|---|
| $r^{*'}$ | 0.45 | 0.46 | 0.46 | 0.45 | 0.45 | 0.43 | 0.42 | 0.42 | 0.41 | 0.40 | 0.42 | 0.42 | 0.40 | 0.39 | 0.36 |
| $r^*$ | 0.38 | 0.38 | 0.40 | 0.41 | 0.42 | 0.42 | 0.42 | 0.42 | 0.41 | 0.40 | 0.38 | 0.37 | 0.37 | 0.37 | 0.33 |
| $S^*$ | 286.46 | 296.54 | 320.20 | 337.71 | 364.54 | 395.00 | 430.65 | 454.40 | 493.63 | 523.83 | 547.67 | 596.70 | 645.98 | 719.75 | 778.25 |
| $K^*$ | 755.70 | 775.40 | 802.30 | 832.00 | 872.30 | 932.30 | 1014.40 | 1093.00 | 1202.50 | 1320.90 | 1453.40 | 1598.90 | 1737.70 | 1940.30 | 2387.10 |
| u | 0.84 | 0.83 | 0.87 | 0.90 | 0.93 | 0.98 | 1.01 | 0.99 | 0.99 | 0.99 | 0.90 | 0.88 | 0.93 | 0.96 | 0.90 |
| $r'$ | 0.20 | 0.21 | 0.21 | 0.21 | 0.20 | 0.20 | 0.20 | 0.19 | 0.18 | 0.17 | 0.16 | 0.17 | 0.16 | 0.17 | 0.15 |
| $r$ | 0.17 | 0.17 | 0.18 | 0.19 | 0.19 | 0.20 | 0.20 | 0.19 | 0.18 | 0.16 | 0.15 | 0.15 | 0.15 | 0.16 | 0.13 |
| $P$ | 126.74 | 132.44 | 146.08 | 155.28 | 166.11 | 185.18 | 201.55 | 203.08 | 214.98 | 217.53 | 214.01 | 242.13 | 267.16 | 307.37 | 314.82 |
| IBT | 45.50 | 48.10 | 51.70 | 54.70 | 58.80 | 62.70 | 65.40 | 70.40 | 79.00 | 86.60 | 94.30 | 103.60 | 111.40 | 121.00 | 129.30 |
| $r'_n$ | 0.16 | 0.17 | 0.18 | 0.17 | 0.17 | 0.17 | 0.16 | 0.16 | 0.15 | 0.14 | 0.14 | 0.15 | 0.14 | 0.14 | 0.12 |
| $r_n$ | 0.14 | 0.14 | 0.15 | 0.16 | 0.16 | 0.17 | 0.17 | 0.16 | 0.15 | 0.13 | 0.12 | 0.13 | 0.13 | 0.13 | 0.11 |
| $P_n$ | 104.04 | 109.64 | 122.08 | 129.08 | 138.11 | 154.28 | 167.85 | 170.38 | 175.58 | 177.83 | 179.61 | 204.43 | 225.26 | 258.07 | 263.02 |
| $(r)'_{corp}$ | 0.10 | 0.10 | 0.11 | 0.11 | 0.12 | 0.12 | 0.11 | 0.10 | 0.10 | 0.09 | 0.08 | 0.08 | 0.08 | 0.08 | 0.06 |
| $(r)_{corp}$ | 0.09 | 0.09 | 0.10 | 0.10 | 0.11 | 0.12 | 0.11 | 0.10 | 0.10 | 0.09 | 0.07 | 0.07 | 0.08 | 0.08 | 0.06 |
| $P_{corp}$ | 49.50 | 50.30 | 58.30 | 63.60 | 70.70 | 81.30 | 86.60 | 84.10 | 90.70 | 87.40 | 74.70 | 87.10 | 100.70 | 113.30 | 101.70 |
| $K_{corp}$ | 566.86 | 580.86 | 600.02 | 620.82 | 650.51 | 694.93 | 756.52 | 818.63 | 901.62 | 989.13 | 1089.42 | 1195.84 | 1295.64 | 1445.86 | 1789.70 |
| $S^*/V^*$ | 1.99 | 2.03 | 2.06 | 2.07 | 2.12 | 2.10 | 2.08 | 2.10 | 2.08 | 2.01 | 2.03 | 2.08 | 1.99 | 1.94 | 1.95 |
| $C^*/V^*$ | 4.41 | 4.41 | 4.47 | 4.58 | 4.73 | 4.85 | 4.97 | 5.00 | 5.05 | 4.99 | 4.84 | 4.89 | 5.00 | 5.01 | 5.40 |
| $C_f^*/(V^*+S^*)$ | 1.48 | 1.46 | 1.46 | 1.49 | 1.52 | 1.57 | 1.61 | 1.61 | 1.64 | 1.66 | 1.60 | 1.59 | 1.67 | 1.70 | 1.83 |

| Variables | 1975 | 1976 | 1977 | 1978 | 1979 | 1980 | 1981 | 1982 | 1983 | 1984 | 1985 | 1986 | 1987 | 1988 | 1989 |
|---|---|---|---|---|---|---|---|---|---|---|---|---|---|---|---|
| $r^{*'}$ | 0.41 | 0.40 | 0.38 | 0.36 | 0.36 | 0.36 | 0.36 | 0.38 | 0.36 | 0.37 | 0.38 | 0.40 | 0.39 | 0.39 | 0.39 |
| $r^{*}$ | 0.33 | 0.33 | 0.33 | 0.32 | 0.32 | 0.32 | 0.30 | 0.29 | 0.31 | 0.33 | 0.34 | 0.34 | 0.34 | 0.35 | 0.35 |
| $S^{*}$ | 867.02 | 968.82 | 1083.13 | 1221.07 | 1346.70 | 1462.70 | 1668.19 | 1724.68 | 1865.80 | 2101.78 | 2258.68 | 2401.11 | 2563.38 | 2752.81 | 2943.35 |
| $K^{*}$ | 2661.70 | 2920.80 | 3253.50 | 3774.60 | 4225.20 | 4844.40 | 5503.70 | 5859.20 | 6094.71 | 6432.91 | 6706.44 | 7056.52 | 7459.32 | 7895.58 | 8387.49 |
| u | 0.79 | 0.83 | 0.87 | 0.89 | 0.89 | 0.85 | 0.84 | 0.77 | 0.84 | 0.89 | 0.89 | 0.85 | 0.87 | 0.90 | 0.89 |
| $r'$ | 0.17 | 0.16 | 0.16 | 0.15 | 0.15 | 0.14 | 0.14 | 0.14 | 0.14 | 0.15 | 0.15 | 0.15 | 0.15 | 0.15 | 0.15 |
| $r$ | 0.13 | 0.13 | 0.14 | 0.14 | 0.13 | 0.12 | 0.12 | 0.11 | 0.12 | 0.13 | 0.13 | 0.13 | 0.13 | 0.14 | 0.14 |
| P | 347.92 | 394.15 | 446.88 | 512.77 | 562.30 | 577.88 | 648.09 | 619.39 | 708.30 | 833.38 | 880.15 | 914.60 | 974.20 | 1069.00 | 1156.40 |
| IBT | 140.00 | 151.60 | 165.50 | 177.80 | 188.70 | 212.00 | 249.30 | 256.40 | 280.10 | 309.50 | 329.90 | 345.50 | 365.00 | 385.30 | 411.00 |
| $r'_n$ | 0.14 | 0.14 | 0.13 | 0.13 | 0.13 | 0.12 | 0.12 | 0.12 | 0.12 | 0.13 | 0.13 | 0.14 | 0.13 | 0.13 | 0.14 |
| $r_n$ | 0.11 | 0.11 | 0.11 | 0.11 | 0.11 | 0.10 | 0.10 | 0.09 | 0.10 | 0.11 | 0.12 | 0.11 | 0.11 | 0.12 | 0.12 |
| $P_n$ | 297.02 | 329.95 | 373.88 | 429.27 | 474.30 | 493.08 | 566.99 | 556.29 | 631.10 | 739.48 | 783.75 | 808.30 | 847.30 | 932.80 | 1021.30 |
| $(r)'_{corp}$ | 0.07 | 0.08 | 0.08 | 0.08 | 0.07 | 0.06 | 0.05 | 0.05 | 0.05 | 0.06 | 0.06 | 0.06 | 0.06 | 0.07 | 0.06 |
| $(r)_{corp}$ | 0.06 | 0.07 | 0.07 | 0.07 | 0.06 | 0.05 | 0.04 | 0.03 | 0.05 | 0.05 | 0.05 | 0.05 | 0.06 | 0.06 | 0.05 |
| $P_{corp}$ | 117.60 | 145.20 | 174.80 | 197.20 | 200.10 | 177.20 | 188.00 | 150.00 | 213.70 | 264.70 | 280.70 | 271.60 | 319.80 | 365.00 | 351.70 |
| $K_{corp}$ | 2016.46 | 2216.71 | 2469.64 | 2847.30 | 3203.38 | 3681.60 | 4187.64 | 4471.11 | 4631.59 | 4899.36 | 5121.71 | 5416.32 | 5738.57 | 6110.95 | 6502.54 |
| $S^{*}/V^{*}$ | 2.11 | 2.11 | 2.10 | 2.07 | 2.03 | 2.07 | 2.16 | 2.19 | 2.22 | 2.26 | 2.33 | 2.40 | 2.42 | 2.40 | 2.44 |
| $C^{*}/V^{*}$ | 5.11 | 5.27 | 5.47 | 5.72 | 5.67 | 5.80 | 5.95 | 5.74 | 6.11 | 6.19 | 6.19 | 5.98 | 6.12 | 6.17 | 6.20 |
| $C^{*}_f/(V^{*}+S^{*})$ | 1.64 | 1.70 | 1.76 | 1.86 | 1.87 | 1.89 | 1.88 | 1.80 | 1.90 | 1.90 | 1.86 | 1.76 | 1.79 | 1.81 | 1.80 |

*Notes*: Shaikh (1992a) calculates capacity utilization as $u = u_{MHI}/s$ up to 1985, where $u_{MHI}$ is a capacity utilization index based on the McGraw-Hill survey of capital spending, and s is a shift-work index based on Foss (1984). Since the McGraw-Hill survey was discontinued in 1986, the utilization index $u_{MHI}$ was extended to 1989 by means of a regression on the Federal Reserve Capacity Utilization Index ($u_{FRB}$). For the years 1948–58, CEA (1971, table C-66) and CEA (1983, table B-77) were utilized.
[a] Table number from CEA (1991).

127

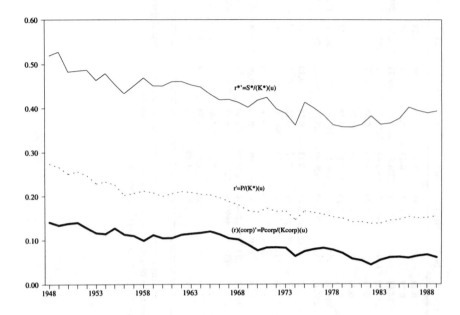

Figure 5.16. Aggregate rates of profit. *Source:* Table 5.8.

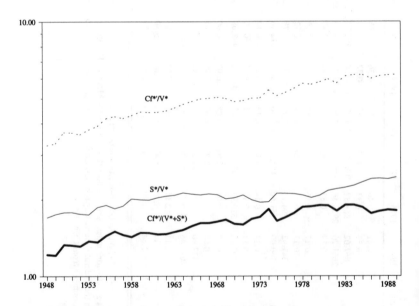

Figure 5.17. Rate of surplus value and composition of capital
(log scale). *Source:* Table 5.8.

Table 5.9. *Changes in profit rates and basic components*

| Variable | Overall change (%) | | Annual trend rate (%) | |
|---|---|---|---|---|
| | 1948–80 | 1980–89 | 1948–80 | 1980–89 |
| $S^*/V^*$ | +21.8 | +17.9 | +0.6 | +1.8 |
| $C_f^*/V^*$ | +77.4 | +6.9 | +1.6 | +0.7 |
| $C_f^*/(V^*+S^*)$ | +56.2 | −4.8 | +1.2 | −0.6 |
| $r^{*\prime}$ (Marxian) | −30.8 | +8.3 | −1.0 | +1.1 |
| $r'$ (average) | −48.4 | +9.9 | −1.8 | +1.2 |
| $r'_{corp}$ (corporate) | −57.1 | +7.0 | −2.2 | +2.6 |

The second period represents the Reagan–Bush era from 1980 to 1989, in which the capitalist class unleashed a systematic assault on workers' living standards and working conditions (see Section 5.9 for further details). The rise in the rate of surplus value accelerates over this interval, its trend rate more than doubling. Moreover, the rates of growth of $C_f^*/V^*$ and $C_f^*/(V^*+S^*)$ slow down in this period, because the rate of profit is still low and accumulation is slow (which in turn slows down the adoption of new, more capital-intensive technologies). The overall effect is to reverse the trends in the three measures of the rate of profit: During this nine-year interval, the Marxian rate of profit recovers about 7% of its initial (1948) value, the NIPA-based average rate about 5%, and the corporate rate a mere 3%. Table 5.9 summarizes these patterns, with trend rates calculated by regressing the logged values of variables against time. Further analysis of the relation between profitability and accumulation in the postwar period can be found in Shaikh (1987).

### 5.6 Rates of exploitation of productive and unproductive workers

The rate of exploitation is the ratio of surplus labor time to necessary labor time. This can be calculated for any capitalistically employed wage labor, be it productive or unproductive. Necessary labor time is simply the value of the labor power involved, that is, the labor value of the average annual consumption per worker in the activities in question. Surplus labor time is excess of working time over necessary labor time. In the case of productive workers, their rate of exploitation is also the rate of surplus value, since their surplus labor time results in surplus value.

The first step is to calculate the relative rates of exploitation of unproductive and productive labor, in the manner derived in Section 4.2:

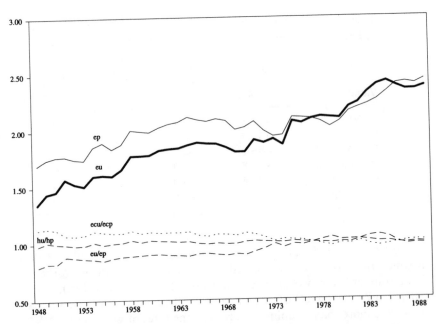

Figure 5.18. Rates of exploitation and related measures.
*Source:* Table I.1.

$$\frac{1+e_u}{1+e_p} \approx \frac{h_u/h_p}{ec_u/ec_p},$$

where

$e_u, e_p$ = rates of exploitation of unproductive and productive workers;
$h_u, h_p$ = hours per unproductive and productive worker;
$ec_u, ec_p$ = employee compensation per unproductive and productive worker.

Because the rate of exploitation of productive workers is simply the rate of surplus value, we can directly estimate the rate of exploitation of unproductive workers. We use the money rate of surplus value $S^*/V^*$ since we already know that it is quite close to the value rate, as shown in Section 4.2:

$$e_u = \frac{h_u/h_p}{ec_u/ec_p} \cdot [1 + S^*/V^*].$$

The detailed calculations are in Appendix I. Figure 5.18 displays the basic results. The relative rates of exploitation $e_u/e_p$ depend on two sets of factors: relative working times $h_u/h_p$, which never vary by more than

2% (as shown on the middle of the three lower curves in Figure 5.18); and relative wage rates $ec_u/ec_p$. At the beginning of the postwar period the wage of unproductive workers is some 11%–12% higher than that of productive workers, but this relative advantage gradually disappears until, by the end of the period, unproductive wages are 3%–4% lower than productive wages (see the highest of the three lower curves). As a result, the relative rates of exploitation move in exactly the opposite fashion (the lowest curve). Looking at the separate rates themselves, we see that the top two curves of Figure 5.18 both rise strongly over the postwar period, with rate of exploitation of unproductive workers starting out below that of productive workers but surpassing it after 1973. For most of the postwar period, the two rates stay within 10% of one another.[17]

### 5.7 Marxian and conventional measures of productivity

Precisely because the Marxian concept of production differs greatly from the orthodox concept, the corresponding measures of productivity are also very different. The logic of these measures is outlined in what follows; all other details are in Appendix J.

In Marxian terms, the appropriate measure of productivity $q*$ is the constant-dollar total product $TP_r$ divided by the total number of productive worker hours $H_p$. The corresponding orthodox measure is y, the ratio of constant-dollar gross domestic product $GDP_r$ divided by total (productive and unproductive) hours worked $H_1$. Two variants of the orthodox measure are shown: real GDP per employee hour y, and nonfarm business real GDP per hour of persons engaged $y_2$ ($y_1$ is the equivalent BLS measure shown in Appendix J, which is only available in index-number form). Finally, because orthodox measures are always based on the final product (GDP) rather than the total product, we also calculate a quasi-Marxian measure $y*$ as the ratio of real Marxian gross final product $GFP_r$ to hours of productive labor $H_p$. This has a much lower level than the true measure $q*$, but has essentially the same trend. Within the limits of the approximation of the Marxian final product added by GDP (see Table 5.4), we can therefore approximate the trend of the true measure by the ratio of real GDP to hours of productive labor $H_p$:

---

[17] Implicit in such a calculation is the notion that the differences in productive and unproductive wage rates do not reflect differences in skill. Insofar as part of such wage differentials do reflect skill differences, the skill-adjusted relative rates of exploitation will be even closer than our unadjusted figures. It should also be borne in mind that the productive and unproductive sectors are aggregates of very many individual sectors, so factors such as gender and race discrimination are likely to be fairly similar across such broad composites.

$q^* \equiv TP_r / H_p =$ Marxian measure of labor productivity;

$y \equiv GDP_r / H =$ conventional measure of labor productivity;

$y^* \equiv GFP_r / H_p =$ quasi-Marxian measure of labor productivity,

where
    $TP_r =$ constant-dollar product $\equiv TP^*/p_y$;
    $p_y =$ GNP deflator from NIPA;[18]
  $GFP_r =$ constant-dollar Marxian gross final product $= GFP^*/p_y$;
    $H_p =$ productive labor;
$GDP_r =$ constant-dollar GDP (real gross domestic product); and
    $H =$ all labor (productive and unproductive).

Appendix J contains detailed calculations of the Marxian and ortho-dox measures of productivity, along with associated measures of hours worked. Table 5.10 and Figures 5.19 and 5.20 present the data. Figure 5.19 compares the two Marxian measures of productivity $q^*$ and $y^*$ with the orthodox measure $y$. Figure 5.20, which is in index number form, also depicts orthodox measures $y_2$ and $y_1$ (BLS). All measures in Figure 5.19 grow steadily throughout the postwar period, and exhibit a slowdown in their growth rate over time (Figure 5.19 is a log graph, so that the slope of a curve is the variable's rate of growth). Yet, as Figure 5.19 shows, the Marxian measure of productivity $q^*$ is between three and four times as large as the conventional measure $y$. Moreover, $q^*$ rises relative to $y$ for significant periods. This is most notable during the post-1972 period, which is exactly when the pernicious and puzzling "productivity slow-down" is supposed to have occurred (Naples 1987). Notice from Figure 5.19 that the growth rate of $q^*$ slows down gradually over the entire post-war period, whereas $y$ shows a marked change in pattern in the critical period from 1972 to 1982. Figure 5.20 shows that the Marxian measures $(q^*, y^*)$ grow substantially faster than the orthodox measures $(y, y_2, y_1)$.

The ratio $y/q^* = (GDP/TP^*)/(L/L_p)$.[19] We have already seen in Figure 5.4 that GNP/TP* falls from 1972 to 1982, most probably because the oil-price shock in 1973 raises TP* relative to GDP. At the same time, the ratio of total employment relative to productive employment rises more rapidly in this period (because of the relatively rapid growth of unpro-ductive employment), as shown in Figures 5.9 and 5.11. *The so-called productivity showdown* exhibited by the conventional measures $(y, y_1, y_2)$ in this critical period *is the result of these two disparate movements.*

[18] We chose the implicit GNP deflator because it allows us to deflate both measures in the same way, so that any differences between $q$ and $y$ only reflect the differ-ences between Marxian and orthodox production measures.

[19] The same deflator was used for both real figures, so their real ratio is the same as their nominal ratio.

Table 5.10. *Marxian and conventional measures of productivity, 1948–89*

| Variables | Units | 1948 | 1949 | 1950 | 1951 | 1952 | 1953 | 1954 |
|---|---|---|---|---|---|---|---|---|
| $q^* = TP_r/H_p$ | $/hr worked, prod. workers | 27.56 | 28.98 | 30.30 | 32.04 | 33.02 | 34.21 | 35.77 |
| $q^*$ (index numbers)[a] | | 100.00 | 105.15 | 109.96 | 116.25 | 119.82 | 124.14 | 129.78 |
| $y^* = GFP_r/H_p$ | $/hr worked, prod. workers | 15.30 | 16.30 | 16.93 | 17.83 | 18.39 | 19.03 | 20.10 |
| $y^*$ (index numbers) | | 100.00 | 106.50 | 110.64 | 116.54 | 120.18 | 124.36 | 131.35 |
| $y = GDP_r/H1$ | $/hr worked, pt & ft workers[b] | 11.11 | 11.51 | 11.98 | 12.14 | 12.34 | 12.68 | 13.02 |
| $y$ (index numbers) | | 100.00 | 103.61 | 107.82 | 109.27 | 111.08 | 114.16 | 117.22 |
| $y_1$ (BLS; 1948=100) | GDP in $/hr worked by PEP | 100.00 | 101.71 | 108.17 | 111.41 | 114.07 | 116.54 | 118.25 |
| $y_2 = GDP2_r/H2$[c] | $/hr by workers & SEP | 9.59 | 10.03 | 10.57 | 10.87 | 11.20 | 11.60 | 11.95 |
| $y_2$ (index numbers) | | 100.00 | 104.57 | 110.16 | 113.27 | 116.71 | 120.92 | 124.50 |

| Variables | Units | 1955 | 1956 | 1957 | 1958 | 1959 | 1960 | 1961 |
|---|---|---|---|---|---|---|---|---|
| $q^* = TP_r/H_p$ | $/hr worked, prod. workers | 36.55 | 37.32 | 38.67 | 40.70 | 41.61 | 42.57 | 43.82 |
| $q^*$ (index numbers)[a] | | 132.63 | 135.41 | 140.32 | 147.69 | 150.97 | 154.46 | 159.02 |
| $y^* = GFP_r/H_p$ | $/hr worked, prod. workers | 20.48 | 20.86 | 21.71 | 23.09 | 23.61 | 24.18 | 25.05 |
| $y^*$ (index numbers) | | 133.82 | 136.32 | 141.88 | 150.88 | 154.30 | 158.02 | 163.74 |
| $y = GDP_r/H1$ | $/hr worked, pt & ft workers[b] | 13.27 | 13.26 | 13.52 | 13.87 | 14.21 | 14.34 | 14.72 |
| $y$ (index numbers) | | 119.51 | 119.39 | 121.72 | 124.89 | 127.97 | 129.07 | 132.57 |
| $y_1$ (BLS; 1948=100) | GDP in $/hr worked by PEP | 121.67 | 122.43 | 124.71 | 127.57 | 131.75 | 133.08 | 137.45 |
| $y_2 = GDP2_r/H2$[c] | $/hr by workers & SEP | 12.29 | 12.39 | 12.63 | 12.81 | 13.33 | 13.41 | 13.79 |
| $y_2$ (index numbers) | | 128.06 | 129.12 | 131.65 | 133.47 | 138.89 | 139.75 | 143.74 |

Table 5.10 *(cont.)*

| Variables | Units | 1962 | 1963 | 1964 | 1965 | 1966 | 1967 | 1968 |
|---|---|---|---|---|---|---|---|---|
| $q^* = TP_r/H_p$ | \$/hr worked, prod. workers | 44.88 | 46.09 | 48.01 | 48.71 | 49.36 | 50.64 | 51.73 |
| $q^*$ (index numbers)[a] | | 162.84 | 167.26 | 174.20 | 176.74 | 179.11 | 183.73 | 187.70 |
| $y^* = GFP_r/H_p$ | \$/hr worked, prod. workers | 25.71 | 26.43 | 27.67 | 28.09 | 28.59 | 29.51 | 30.16 |
| $y^*$ (index numbers) | | 168.02 | 172.73 | 180.85 | 183.61 | 186.86 | 192.84 | 197.11 |
| $y = GDP_r/H1$ | \$/hr worked, pt & ft workers[b] | 15.05 | 15.40 | 15.88 | 16.18 | 16.32 | 16.57 | 16.89 |
| $y$ (index numbers) | | 135.49 | 138.66 | 142.98 | 145.68 | 146.94 | 149.16 | 152.06 |
| $y_1$ (BLS; 1948=100) | GDP in \$/hr worked by PEP | 141.83 | 146.96 | 152.85 | 156.65 | 160.27 | 164.26 | 169.20 |
| $y_2 = GDP2_r/H2$[c] | \$/hr by workers & SEP | 14.16 | 14.56 | 15.08 | 15.36 | 15.51 | 15.83 | 16.18 |
| $y_2$ (index numbers) | | 147.60 | 151.70 | 157.12 | 160.07 | 161.63 | 165.01 | 168.65 |

| Variables | Units | 1969 | 1970 | 1971 | 1972 | 1973 | 1974 | 1975 |
|---|---|---|---|---|---|---|---|---|
| $q^* = TP_r/H_p$ | \$/hr worked, prod. workers | 51.63 | 52.93 | 55.03 | 55.58 | 57.21 | 57.60 | 61.64 |
| $q^*$ (index numbers)[a] | | 187.36 | 192.07 | 199.69 | 201.67 | 207.60 | 208.99 | 223.67 |
| $y^* = GFP_r/H_p$ | \$/hr worked, prod. workers | 30.10 | 31.04 | 32.40 | 32.61 | 33.01 | 32.92 | 35.00 |
| $y^*$ (index numbers) | | 196.71 | 202.83 | 211.76 | 213.12 | 215.77 | 215.13 | 228.72 |
| $y = GDP_r/H1$ | \$/hr worked, pt & ft workers[b] | 16.82 | 17.06 | 17.61 | 17.97 | 18.09 | 17.92 | 18.25 |
| $y$ (index numbers) | | 151.46 | 153.61 | 158.57 | 161.76 | 162.90 | 161.37 | 164.34 |
| $y_1$ (BLS; 1948=100) | GDP in \$/hr worked by PEP | 168.63 | 169.39 | 174.52 | 179.85 | 183.65 | 180.23 | 183.46 |
| $y_2 = GDP2_r/H2$[c] | \$/hr by workers & SEP | 16.04 | 16.07 | 16.49 | 16.80 | 16.74 | 16.58 | 16.93 |
| $y_2$ (index numbers) | | 167.19 | 167.50 | 171.86 | 175.06 | 174.46 | 172.85 | 176.40 |

| Variables | Units | 1976 | 1977 | 1978 | 1979 | 1980 | 1981 | 1982 |
|---|---|---|---|---|---|---|---|---|
| $q^* = TP_r/H_p$ | $/hr worked, prod. workers | 63.70 | 65.61 | 66.02 | 65.55 | 66.99 | 69.13 | 70.28 |
| $q^*$ (index numbers)[a] | | 231.13 | 238.08 | 239.57 | 237.85 | 243.08 | 250.86 | 255.00 |
| $y^* = GFP_r/H_p$ | $/hr worked, prod. workers | 35.63 | 36.28 | 36.50 | 36.30 | 37.04 | 38.26 | 39.08 |
| $y^*$ (index numbers) | | 232.85 | 237.09 | 238.53 | 237.24 | 242.09 | 250.07 | 255.42 |
| $y = GDP_r/H1$ | $/hr worked, pt & ft workers[b] | 18.58 | 18.81 | 18.94 | 18.77 | 18.91 | 19.20 | 19.10 |
| $y$ (index numbers) | | 167.32 | 169.34 | 170.55 | 169.02 | 170.24 | 172.85 | 171.93 |
| $y_1$ (BLS; 1948=100) | GDP in $/hr worked by PEP | 188.40 | 191.83 | 193.54 | 190.49 | 189.92 | 191.83 | 190.11 |
| $y_2 = GDP2_r/H2$[c] | $/hr by workers & SEP | 17.34 | 17.57 | 17.65 | 17.38 | 17.49 | 17.68 | 17.48 |
| $y_2$ (index numbers) | | 180.70 | 183.17 | 183.98 | 181.10 | 182.27 | 184.27 | 182.17 |

| Variables | Units | 1983 | 1984 | 1985 | 1986 | 1987 | 1988 | 1989 |
|---|---|---|---|---|---|---|---|---|
| $q^* = TP_r/H_p$ | $/hr worked, prod. workers | 71.66 | 73.13 | 74.25 | 74.75 | 74.47 | 78.01 | 78.03 |
| $q^*$ (index numbers)[a] | | 260.02 | 265.37 | 269.41 | 271.25 | 270.21 | 283.05 | 283.13 |
| $y^* = GFP_r/H_p$ | $/hr worked, prod. workers | 40.17 | 41.04 | 41.92 | 42.75 | 42.81 | 44.29 | 44.56 |
| $y^*$ (index numbers) | | 262.51 | 268.23 | 273.96 | 279.42 | 279.78 | 289.48 | 291.19 |
| $y = GDP_r/H1$ | $/hr worked, pt & ft workers[b] | 19.56 | 19.90 | 20.01 | 20.45 | 20.54 | 21.07 | 21.15 |
| $y$ (index numbers) | | 176.10 | 179.14 | 180.19 | 184.08 | 184.95 | 189.67 | 190.41 |
| $y_1$ (BLS; 1948=100) | GDP in $/hr worked by PEP | 195.63 | 199.81 | 202.47 | 206.65 | 208.75 | 213.88 | 212.36 |
| $y_2 = GDP2_r/H2$[c] | $/hr by workers & SEP | 17.94 | 18.20 | 18.40 | 19.62 | 19.64 | 19.37 | 19.33 |
| $y_2$ (index numbers) | | 187.00 | 189.72 | 191.73 | 204.44 | 204.71 | 201.84 | 201.47 |

[a] 1948 = 100 for all index numbers.     [b] pt = part-time; ft = full-time.     [c] Nonfarm private business.

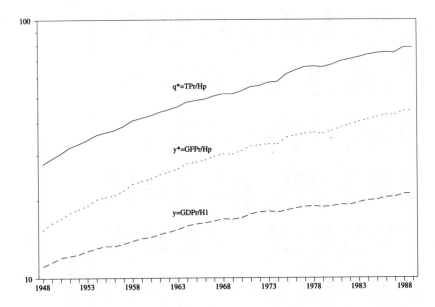

Figure 5.19. Productivity measures (1982 dollars, log scale).
*Source:* Table 5.10.

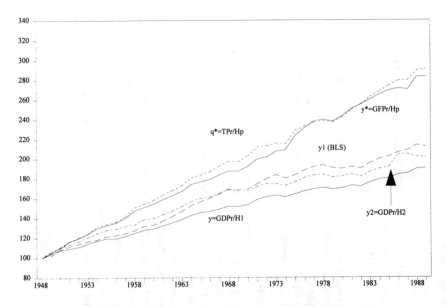

Figure 5.20. Productivity indexes (1982 dollars, 1948 = 100).
*Source:* Table 5.10.

## 5.8 Government absorption of surplus value

Another issue concerns the relation between total surplus value and government purchases of commodities and of labor power. Government purchases of commodities directly absorb a portion of the surplus product, and government administrative employment indirectly absorbs another portion through the consumption expenditures of the government workers (see Section 3.2.B). Thus total government expenditure $G_T^* \equiv G^* + W_G$ is a measure of the total absorption of the surplus product by unproductive government expenditures. Table 5.11 and Figure 5.21 show the progress of $G_T^*$ and $G_T^*/SP^*$ over the postwar period. What is most striking here is the stability of the government share of the surplus product. For most of the postwar period, this share remains around 35%, in spite of the Korean War buildup from 1950 to 1953 (itself following upon the demobilization after World War II) and the Vietnam War buildup from 1965 to 1968.

## 5.9 Net tax on labor and adjusted rate of surplus value

As noted in Section 3.3, the nominal wages of production workers must be adjusted for the net transfers of royalties (ground rent, interest, and taxes) from variable capital. We calculate only the portion of this arising from the net transfer between workers and the state. The methodology and actual estimates are from Shaikh and Tonak (1987) for the United States from 1952 to 1985.[20] Our adjustment procedure involves two steps. First, we estimate the social benefit expenditures directed toward wage and salary earners by the state, the taxes paid by them, and the difference between the two, which is the *net transfer* (a positive number when benefits exceed taxes and negative in the opposite case). The true compensation of wage and salary earners is their apparent compensation plus the net transfer.[21] The tax, benefits, and net transfer rates are also calculated relative to the apparent employee compensation. The next step is to adjust the rate of surplus value for the net transfer from variable capital. The previously derived net transfer rate is applied to apparent variable capital $V^*$ to estimate the net transfer from variable capital, and the resulting sum is added to $V^*$ and subtracted from $S^*$ to obtain the adjusted rate of surplus value.

It is important to note that the taxes we estimate are those flowing directly out of total employee compensation (the purchase price of labor

[20] The necessary data are only available from 1952 onward. See Tonak (1984, chap. 4, and apx. 1-2).

[21] Employee compensation is our starting point because it represents the direct cost incurred by capitalists for hiring labor power; to the individual capitalist this is the same as variable capital. But for the system as a whole, we must adjust for the net transfer between wage and salary workers and the state.

Table 5.11. Government absorption of surplus value, 1948–89 (billions of dollars)

| Sources | Variables | 1948 | 1949 | 1950 | 1951 | 1952 | 1953 | 1954 |
|---|---|---|---|---|---|---|---|---|
| | $G_T^* = G^* + WG$ | 32.50 | 38.86 | 38.62 | 60.20 | 75.56 | 82.36 | 75.59 |
| Table E.2 | $G^*$ | 14.40 | 18.76 | 17.42 | 32.50 | 44.06 | 49.96 | 42.59 |
| Table E.2 | WG | 18.10 | 20.10 | 21.20 | 27.70 | 31.50 | 32.40 | 33.00 |
| Table H.1 | $SP^*$ | 149.91 | 148.58 | 165.09 | 188.26 | 194.79 | 204.29 | 208.23 |
| | $G_T^*/SP^*$ | 0.22 | 0.26 | 0.23 | 0.32 | 0.39 | 0.40 | 0.36 |

| Sources | Variables | 1955 | 1956 | 1957 | 1958 | 1959 | 1960 | 1961 |
|---|---|---|---|---|---|---|---|---|
| | $G_T^* = G^* + WG$ | 74.85 | 79.09 | 86.73 | 94.63 | 96.72 | 99.03 | 106.37 |
| Table E.2 | $G^*$ | 40.05 | 41.89 | 46.93 | 51.73 | 51.92 | 50.93 | 54.77 |
| Table E.2 | WG | 34.80 | 37.20 | 39.80 | 42.90 | 44.80 | 48.10 | 51.60 |
| Table H.1 | $SP^*$ | 228.16 | 236.74 | 249.88 | 256.04 | 278.34 | 285.93 | 295.95 |
| | $G_T^*/SP^*$ | 0.33 | 0.33 | 0.35 | 0.37 | 0.35 | 0.35 | 0.36 |

| Sources | Variables | 1962 | 1963 | 1964 | 1965 | 1966 | 1967 | 1968 |
|---|---|---|---|---|---|---|---|---|
| | $G_T^* = G^* + WG$ | 115.66 | 120.82 | 126.81 | 135.10 | 154.54 | 175.30 | 192.22 |
| Table E.2 | $G^*$ | 60.26 | 61.52 | 62.41 | 65.80 | 76.14 | 87.90 | 94.42 |
| Table E.2 | WG | 55.40 | 59.30 | 64.40 | 69.30 | 78.40 | 87.40 | 97.80 |
| Table H.1 | $SP^*$ | 319.54 | 337.07 | 364.00 | 394.44 | 430.09 | 453.42 | 493.12 |
| | $G_T^*/SP^*$ | 0.36 | 0.36 | 0.35 | 0.34 | 0.36 | 0.39 | 0.39 |

| Sources | Variables | 1969 | 1970 | 1971 | 1972 | 1973 | 1974 | 1975 |
|---|---|---|---|---|---|---|---|---|
| | $G_T^* = G^* + WG$ | 200.46 | 210.13 | 222.76 | 238.64 | 253.47 | 284.33 | 318.29 |
| Table E.2 | $G^*$ | 92.96 | 90.63 | 92.46 | 96.04 | 98.47 | 115.63 | 130.59 |
| Table E.2 | $WG$ | 107.50 | 119.50 | 130.30 | 142.60 | 155.00 | 168.70 | 187.70 |
| Table H.1 | $SP^*$ | 523.25 | 546.86 | 596.04 | 645.51 | 719.63 | 778.82 | 868.78 |
| | $G_T^*/SP^*$ | 0.38 | 0.38 | 0.37 | 0.37 | 0.35 | 0.37 | 0.37 |

| Sources | Variables | 1976 | 1977 | 1978 | 1979 | 1980 | 1981 | 1982 |
|---|---|---|---|---|---|---|---|---|
| | $G_T^* = G^* + WG$ | 337.29 | 363.34 | 396.97 | 435.78 | 494.43 | 547.37 | 598.61 |
| Table E.2 | $G^*$ | 133.49 | 142.84 | 156.47 | 175.38 | 206.13 | 230.67 | 254.71 |
| Table E.2 | $WG$ | 203.80 | 220.50 | 240.50 | 260.40 | 288.30 | 316.70 | 343.90 |
| Table H.1 | $SP^*$ | 971.25 | 1086.66 | 1221.76 | 1347.44 | 1463.67 | 1669.40 | 1726.06 |
| | $G_T^*/SP^*$ | 0.35 | 0.33 | 0.32 | 0.32 | 0.34 | 0.33 | 0.35 |

| Sources | Variables | 1983 | 1984 | 1985 | 1986 | 1987 | 1988 | 1989 |
|---|---|---|---|---|---|---|---|---|
| | $G_T^* = G^* + WG$ | 624.39 | 679.89 | 755.83 | 797.00 | 837.34 | 871.73 | 925.91 |
| Table E.2 | $G^*$ | 257.99 | 289.29 | 336.83 | 353.20 | 365.44 | 366.63 | 384.31 |
| Table E.2 | $WG$ | 366.40 | 390.60 | 419.00 | 443.80 | 471.90 | 505.10 | 541.60 |
| Table H.1 | $SP^*$ | 1867.15 | 2103.70 | 2258.31 | 2389.25 | 2555.52 | 2755.18 | 2945.32 |
| | $G_T^*/SP^*$ | 0.33 | 0.32 | 0.33 | 0.33 | 0.33 | 0.32 | 0.31 |

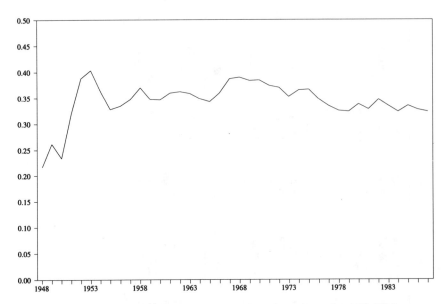

Figure 5.21. Government absorption of surplus value ($G_T^*/SP^*$).
*Source:* Table 5.11.

power to individual capitalists). From a Marxian point of view, we are
concerned with the actual flows of royalties into, and out of, the actual
flow of variable capital. This is what Ursula Hicks (1946) has called the
*statistical* or "social accounting calculation" of taxes:

> We arrive thus at two fundamental concepts in fiscal theory: (i) the so-
> cial accounting calculation of the proportions of people's incomes paid
> over to taxing authorities in a defined period, and (ii) the analysis of all
> the economic adjustments through time and space resulting from a par-
> ticular tax. These two concepts are different in kind . . . . Social account-
> ing is concerned with a *statistical* comparison at a moment of time . . .
> [whereas] the analytical concept is essentially hypothetical. It is a com-
> parison of two complete economic situations, one with a particular tax
> in force, the other without it. One of these setups will normally be imag-
> inary. (U. Hicks 1946, p. 49)

We do not attempt here to estimate the *analytical* or "tax-shifting" incidence of taxes. As Hicks notes, this latter calculation concerns itself with
the comparison between the actual level of some income and the hypothetical alternative level that might exist in the absence of some taxes.
It is a further stage of analysis which requires some plausible model of
the overall impact of taxes on reproduction; such models are beyond the
scope of our present analysis. Thus we concern ourselves only with the

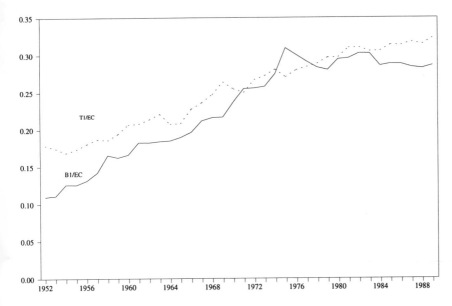

Figure 5.22. Benefit and tax rates relative to total employee compensation. *Source:* Table N.2.

social accounting of taxes and transfers. However, it should be noted that, where such calculations have been made, they greatly strengthen our conclusion that the net balance is strongly against the working population; that is, U.S. workers pay a net tax to the state, rather than receiving a net subsidy from it in the form of some "social wage" (Miller 1989).

Appendix N lists the detailed calculations of our social accounting of taxes and benefits. Figure 5.22 shows the resulting tax and benefit rates (relative to total employee compensation), and Figure 5.23 shows the corresponding net transfer rate for the United States from 1952 to 1985. It is immediately evident that, for most of the postwar period, wage and salary earners *paid more in taxes than they received in social benefit expenditures.* As a result, the true rate of surplus value is generally higher than the apparent one (see Figure 5.24).

### 5.10 Empirical effects of price–value deviations

The previously calculated Marxian measures are the money forms of Marxian categories – the monetary expressions of realized quantities of value. It is therefore of interest to see if these money measures accurately represent the levels and movements of the underlying labor value

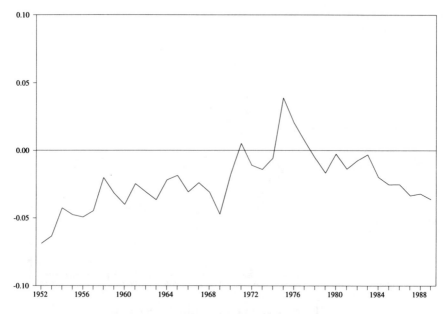

Figure 5.23. Net transfer rate. *Source:* Table N.2.

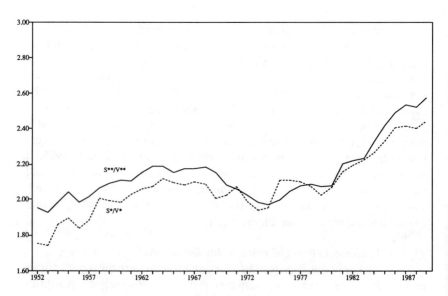

Figure 5.24. Rate of surplus value adjusted for net taxes.
*Source:* Table N.2.

magnitudes. In other words, we now ask: How significant is the impact of price–value deviations on aggregate measures?

The problem can be approached indirectly by looking at the empirical magnitudes of price–value deviations. Shaikh (1984) has argued on mathematical and structural grounds that individual price–value deviations are likely to be modest, and that their effects on aggregate measures are likely to be quite small. He examines a variety of different empirical estimates, and finds that they provide support for the argument. Ochoa (1984, 1988) makes a more detailed and systematic investigation of this issue, estimating labor values for the five available input–output tables between 1947 and 1972 in the United States. He finds that the average absolute deviation of market (producer) prices[22] from labor values is only about 12%, and that the average deviation of the market rate of profit from the corresponding labor value rate of profit is less than 1% (and never exceeds 3.5% in any one year). He also calculates Sraffian prices of production, and finds that on average these too deviate from labor values by only 15%, while the corresponding "uniform" rate of profit deviates from the labor value rate by less than 4% (and never exceeds 5%) (Shaikh 1984; Ochoa 1984b, pp. 128, 143, 151, 162, 214; Ochoa 1988, pp. 420–1, tables 1–3). Similar results have been found by Petrovic (1987) for Yugoslavia.

On the basis of these results, we would expect that estimates of the value rate of surplus value would be quite close to money rate, *provided the method of estimation is consistent* in the sense discussed in Section 4.1. Following the procedure developed by Shaikh in 1975, Khanjian (1989) has made direct estimates of both labor value and money rates of surplus value. His methodology is that outlined in Section 4.1, and his empirical procedures are similar to ours except for the treatment of the wage equivalent of self-employed persons. We split the income of unincorporated enterprises into the wage equivalent WEQ of proprietors, partners, and unpaid family members and a profit-type return, whereas he implicitly treats the whole of unincorporated income as a profit-type return. Thus his measure of surplus value is larger than ours, and his measure of variable capital is smaller. These two effects make his estimates of the rate of surplus value roughly 20% higher than ours.

Because Khanjian's method of estimating the value rate of surplus value is consistent with his estimates of the money rates, the difference between

----

[22] It would be preferable to examine purchaser-price–labor-value deviations, but this is not possible because input–output tables do not contain enough information to estimate purchaser prices of individual commodities (since the trading margins on the individual commodities in a given column are all aggregated into one trading-row entry).

Table 5.12. *Labor value and money rates of surplus value*

|  | 1958 | 1963 | 1967 | 1972 | 1977 |
|---|---|---|---|---|---|
| *Revenue side* | | | | | |
| $e^* \equiv S^*/V^*$ | 2.445 | 2.467 | 2.648 | 2.606 | 2.674 |
| $e \equiv S/V$ | 2.638 | 2.644 | 2.884 | 2.874 | 2.913 |
| $(e-e^*)/e$ | 7.3% | 6.7% | 8.2% | 9.3% | 8.2% |
| *Use side* | | | | | |
| $e^* \equiv S^*/V^*$ | 2.444 | 2.467 | 2.648 | 2.604 | 2.630 |
| $e \equiv S/V$ | 2.605 | 2.617 | 2.858 | 2.849 | 2.890 |
| $(e-e^*)/e$ | 6.2% | 5.7% | 7.3% | 8.6% | 9.0% |

*Source:* Khanjian (1989, table 19).

the two sets of measures is an index of the aggregate impact of purchaser-price–labor-value deviations. Table 5.12 shows that these differences are minor, ranging from 6% to 9%. Note that the value rate of surplus value is always smaller than the money rate (although they have the same trend). This is apparently due to the fact that the prices of consumer goods have higher trading markups than the average bundle of goods in net output (consumer goods pass through both wholesale and retail channels, whereas investment goods do not). By construction, the price of the average commodity is equal to its value.[23] The relatively greater markup of consumer goods tends to make their purchaser prices higher than labor values, leading to a money form of variable capital $V^*$ which is higher than the value of labor power $V$, as well as a money rate of surplus value $S^*/V^*$ which is lower than the value rate $S/V$ (Khanjian 1989, pp. 109–13).

The small and stable differences between the value and money rates of surplus value implies that their trends are virtually identical. Figure 5.25, which plots the use-side measures of the two rates, makes it abundantly clear that *the money rate of surplus value is an excellent index of the value rate of surplus value.*

### 5.11 Approximating the rate of surplus value

Our own calculations of the rate of surplus value have required a large amount of detailed data, ranging from several input–output tables

---

[23] We define direct price (money price proportional to labor value) as the labor value multiplied by the ratio of the sum of total prices $TV^*$ to the sum of total values $TV$. Alternately, one could define the realized value represented by any money price as the money price multiplied by $TV/TV^*$. In either case, the average purchaser price equals the average labor value.

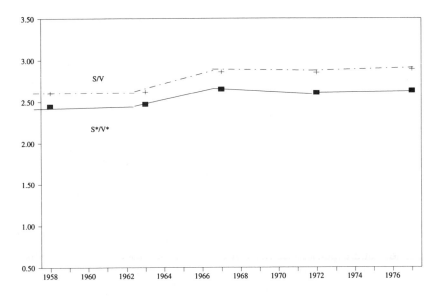

Figure 5.25. Value (S/V) and money (S*/V*) rates of surplus value, use side. *Sources:* Khanjian (1989, table 19); Table 5.7.

to annual NIPA data by major industry and annual BLS data on production and nonproduction workers by major industry. It is of interest, therefore, to ascertain whether a simpler and more intuitive approximation of the rate of surplus value can be constructed. This has particular importance for countries and periods in which the necessary detail for more precise estimates is unavailable.

Variable capital is the employee compensation of production workers in productive sectors. One widely used approximation (see the estimates by Labor Research Association 1948, Eaton 1966, and Papadimitriou 1988 in Section 6.2.2) is to take the total employee compensation (of both production and nonproduction workers) in the productive sectors (agriculture, mining, construction, transportation and public utilities, manufacturing, and productive services). Note that this proposed approximation V*′ would be larger than the actual variable capital V*, because it would include the wages of nonproductive workers in the productive sectors.

A commonly cited definition of Marxian value added is the sum of all wages, profits, taxes, interest, and rents (e.g., Gillman 1958 in Section 6.2.1). In Section 3.2.1 we saw that orthodox NNP is the sum of all sectoral wages, profits, and taxes, plus sectoral net interest paid to households, government, and foreigners. Net interest paid by businesses to the finance sector, as well as business rental payments, are not included in NNP but are rather shifted into intermediate inputs. Therefore, to actually estimate the sum of all wages, profits, rents, and interest paid by business, one would have to shift these items back into value added. This approximation is larger than NNP, and hence larger than Marxian value added.[24]

The approximation to variable capital is $V^{*'}$, the sum of employee compensation in agriculture, mining, construction, transportation and public utilities, manufacturing, and productive services (defined as all services except business services, legal services, miscellaneous professional services, and private households, as in Table E.1 and Table F.1, note 3). To arrive at the Marxian value added approximation $VA^{*'}$, we need only add to NNP estimated business net rental payments and net interest payments to the finance sector. Such information can be derived from business sources, or as Mage (1963) does, from tax information on business revenues and expenses (see Section 6.2.2). In our case, the sum of these latter two items appears in the royalty row of the production, trade, and royalties columns, respectively, in the overall summary IO table of Figure 3.11. Table 5.13 summarizes the calculation procedure and its results.

Both $V^{*'}$ and $VA^{*'}$ considerably overstate the corresponding true measures. Nonetheless, in a ratio the two biases offset each other, thus providing a fairly good overall approximation to the rate of surplus value. Figure 5.26 demonstrates this result.

### 5.12 Summary of empirical results

The purpose of these investigations has been to examine the empirical relation between Marxian and orthodox measures. By and large, we have found them to be very different in size and trend, and to produce a very different picture of capitalist reality. Nowhere is this more striking than in the differences between key Marxian variables and their orthodox counterparts, as in Figures 5.3, 5.9, 5.12, 5.13, 5.15, and 5.19. Table 5.14 summarizes the relative changes in these variables over the postwar period, and – in the case of the productivity measures – over the critical period 1972–82 in which the productivity showdown puzzle is supposed to be lodged.

Not all Marxian variables exhibit different patterns from their orthodox counterparts. The two measures of gross value added, $GVA^*$ and $GVA$, were quite close in size throughout the postwar period. And although the Marxian measure of the rate of profit was substantially higher than a

---

[24] Marxian value added $VA^*$ is empirically smaller than NNP, but this result does not seem to be a logical necessity.

Table 5.13. *Approximation to the rate of surplus value, 1948–89*

| Sources | Variables | 1948 | 1949 | 1950 | 1951 | 1952 | 1953 | 1954 |
|---|---|---|---|---|---|---|---|---|
| Table H.1 | $S^*/V^*$ | 1.70 | 1.75 | 1.77 | 1.78 | 1.75 | 1.74 | 1.86 |
| | Approximation procedure: | | | | | | | |
| | $S^*/V^{*\prime}=(VA^{*\prime}-V^{*\prime})/V^{*\prime}$ | | | | | | | |
| | $VA^{*\prime}=NNP+RY'_{ry}+RY'_p+RY'_{tt}$ | 1.83 | 1.91 | 1.91 | 1.88 | 1.84 | 1.78 | 1.86 |
| 112 1[a] | NNP | 255.71 | 254.24 | 282.06 | 325.64 | 344.03 | 364.75 | 366.03 |
| Table D.2 | | 241.20 | 238.40 | 264.60 | 306.20 | 322.50 | 340.70 | 340.00 |
| | $RY'_{ry}+RY'_p+RY'_{tt}$ | 14.51 | 15.84 | 17.46 | 19.44 | 21.53 | 24.05 | 26.03 |
| | $V^{*\prime}=ec_{prod}+ec_{prserv}$ | 90.22 | 87.44 | 96.99 | 112.88 | 121.21 | 131.40 | 127.93 |
| Table G.1 | $ec_{prod}$ | 80.85 | 77.77 | 86.78 | 101.87 | 109.60 | 118.89 | 114.95 |
| Table G.2 | $ec_{prserv}$ | 9.37 | 9.67 | 10.22 | 11.01 | 11.61 | 12.51 | 12.98 |

| Sources | Variables | 1955 | 1956 | 1957 | 1958 | 1959 | 1960 | 1961 |
|---|---|---|---|---|---|---|---|---|
| Table H.1 | $S^*/V^*$ | 1.90 | 1.84 | 1.88 | 2.01 | 1.99 | 1.99 | 2.03 |
| | Approximation procedure: | | | | | | | |
| | $S^*/V^{*\prime}=(VA^{*\prime}-V^{*\prime})/V^{*\prime}$ | | | | | | | |
| | $VA^{*\prime}=NNP+RY'_{ry}+RY'_p+RY'_{tt}$ | 1.88 | 1.80 | 1.81 | 1.92 | 1.91 | 1.90 | 1.96 |
| 112 1[a] | NNP | 399.72 | 421.09 | 443.57 | 450.39 | 490.75 | 510.31 | 529.46 |
| Table D.2 | | 371.50 | 390.10 | 409.90 | 414.00 | 451.20 | 468.90 | 486.10 |
| | $RY'_{ry}+RY'_p+RY'_{tt}$ | 28.22 | 30.99 | 33.67 | 36.39 | 39.55 | 41.41 | 43.36 |
| | $V^{*\prime}=ec_{prod}+ec_{prserv}$ | 139.00 | 150.63 | 157.66 | 154.30 | 168.53 | 176.20 | 178.71 |
| Table G.1 | $ec_{prod}$ | 124.80 | 135.22 | 141.05 | 136.79 | 149.61 | 155.50 | 156.78 |
| Table G.2 | $ec_{prserv}$ | 14.20 | 15.41 | 16.61 | 17.51 | 18.91 | 20.70 | 21.93 |

Table 5.13 *(cont.)*

| Sources | Variables | 1962 | 1963 | 1964 | 1965 | 1966 | 1967 | 1968 |
|---|---|---|---|---|---|---|---|---|
| Table H.1 | $S^*/V^*$ | 2.06 | 2.07 | 2.12 | 2.10 | 2.08 | 2.10 | 2.08 |
| | Approximation procedure: | | | | | | | |
| | $S^*/V^*=(VA^{*\prime}-V^{*\prime})/V^{*\prime}$ | 1.97 | 2.00 | 2.01 | 2.04 | 2.02 | 2.02 | 2.01 |
| | $VA^{*\prime}=NNP+RY'_{ry}+RY'_{p}+RY'_{tt}$ | 570.28 | 602.63 | 646.90 | 703.68 | 772.44 | 818.21 | 894.25 |
| 112 1[a] | NNP | 525.20 | 555.50 | 595.90 | 647.70 | 709.90 | 749.00 | 818.70 |
| Table D.2 | $RY'_{ry}+RY'_{p}+RY'_{tt}$ | 45.08 | 47.13 | 51.00 | 55.98 | 62.54 | 69.21 | 75.55 |
| | $V^{*\prime}=ec_{prod}+ec_{prserv}$ | 191.77 | 201.01 | 214.89 | 231.65 | 256.16 | 270.94 | 297.46 |
| Table G.1 | $ec_{prod}$ | 168.02 | 175.52 | 187.43 | 201.85 | 223.11 | 234.21 | 256.36 |
| Table G.2 | $ec_{prserv}$ | 23.75 | 25.49 | 27.46 | 29.80 | 33.05 | 36.73 | 41.10 |

| Sources | Variables | 1969 | 1970 | 1971 | 1972 | 1973 | 1974 | 1975 |
|---|---|---|---|---|---|---|---|---|
| Table H.1 | $S^*/V^*$ | 2.01 | 2.03 | 2.08 | 1.99 | 1.94 | 1.95 | 2.11 |
| | Approximation procedure: | | | | | | | |
| | $S^*/V^*=(VA^{*\prime}-V^{*\prime})/V^{*\prime}$ | 1.95 | 1.96 | 2.06 | 2.05 | 2.04 | 1.99 | 2.10 |
| | $VA^{*\prime}=NNP+RY'_{ry}+RY'_{p}+RY'_{tt}$ | 966.06 | 1016.51 | 1103.47 | 1212.86 | 1361.96 | 1468.28 | 1528.21 |
| 112 1[a] | NNP | 882.50 | 926.60 | 1005.10 | 1104.80 | 1241.40 | 1335.40 | 1436.60 |
| Table D.2 | $RY'_{ry}+RY'_{p}+RY'_{tt}$ | 83.56 | 89.91 | 98.37 | 108.06 | 120.76 | 132.88 | 145.61 |
| | $V^{*\prime}=ec_{prod}+ec_{prserv}$ | 327.22 | 342.87 | 360.64 | 397.58 | 448.58 | 491.77 | 511.13 |
| Table G.1 | $ec_{prod}$ | 280.48 | 291.04 | 303.82 | 333.95 | 377.28 | 411.81 | 421.93 |
| Table G.2 | $ec_{prserv}$ | 46.74 | 51.82 | 56.82 | 63.63 | 71.30 | 79.96 | 89.20 |

148

| Sources | Variables | 1976 | 1977 | 1978 | 1979 | 1980 | 1981 | 1982 |
|---|---|---|---|---|---|---|---|---|
| Table H.1 | $S^*/V^*$ | 2.11 | 2.10 | 2.07 | 2.03 | 2.07 | 2.16 | 2.19 |
| | Approximation procedure: | | | | | | | |
| | $S^{*\prime}/V^{*\prime}=(VA^{*\prime}-V^{*\prime})/V^{*\prime}$ | 2.08 | 2.09 | 2.08 | 2.04 | 2.04 | 2.09 | 2.08 |
| | $VA^{*\prime}=NNP+RY'_{ry}+RY'_{p}+RY'_{tt}$ | 1768.91 | 1985.44 | 2251.33 | 2507.18 | 2725.12 | 3040.72 | 3137.27 |
| 112 1[a] | NNP | 1603.60 | 1789.00 | 2019.80 | 2242.40 | 2428.10 | 2704.80 | 2782.80 |
| Table D.2 | $RY'_{ry}+RY'_{p}+RY'_{tt}$ | 165.31 | 196.44 | 231.53 | 264.78 | 297.02 | 335.92 | 354.47 |
| | $V^{*\prime}=ec_{prod}+ec_{prserv}$ | 574.52 | 643.32 | 731.84 | 824.04 | 895.62 | 984.62 | 1017.83 |
| Table G.1 | $ec_{prod}$ | 474.79 | 533.13 | 605.22 | 682.08 | 734.30 | 803.02 | 814.52 |
| Table G.2 | $ec_{prserv}$ | 99.73 | 110.19 | 126.62 | 141.95 | 161.32 | 181.60 | 203.31 |

| Sources | Variables | 1983 | 1984 | 1985 | 1986 | 1987 | 1988 | 1989 |
|---|---|---|---|---|---|---|---|---|
| Table H.1 | $S^*/V^*$ | 2.22 | 2.26 | 2.33 | 2.40 | 2.42 | 2.40 | 2.44 |
| | Approximation procedure: | | | | | | | |
| | $S^{*\prime}/V^{*\prime}=(VA^{*\prime}-V^{*\prime})/V^{*\prime}$ | 2.23 | 2.29 | 2.36 | 2.44 | 2.49 | 2.51 | 2.57 |
| | $VA^{*\prime}=NNP+RY'_{ry}+RY'_{p}+RY'_{tt}$ | 3423.12 | 3813.15 | 4103.64 | 4377.91 | 4703.77 | 5088.97 | 5447.86 |
| 112 1[a] | NNP | 3009.10 | 3356.80 | 3577.60 | 3771.50 | 4028.60 | 4359.40 | 4646.40 |
| Table D.2 | $RY'_{ry}+RY'_{p}+RY'_{tt}$ | 414.02 | 456.35 | 526.04 | 606.41 | 675.17 | 729.57 | 801.46 |
| | $V^{*\prime}=ec_{prod}+ec_{prserv}$ | 1060.52 | 1158.17 | 1222.88 | 1272.37 | 1346.92 | 1451.53 | 1526.37 |
| Table G.1 | $ec_{prod}$ | 839.31 | 919.34 | 963.89 | 994.68 | 1035.67 | 1108.04 | 1152.03 |
| Table G.2 | $ec_{prserv}$ | 221.21 | 238.83 | 258.99 | 277.69 | 311.24 | 343.49 | 374.34 |

[a] From NIPA (e.g. BEA 1986), where the first three digits denote the relevant table number and subsequent digits the line numbers within those tables.

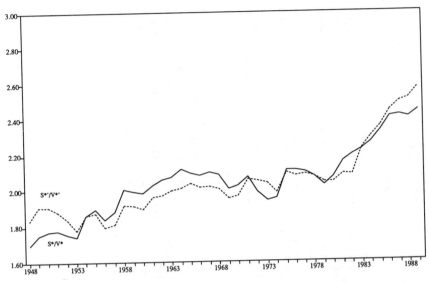

Figure 5.26. Approximation to the rate of surplus value.
*Source:* Table 5.13.

NIPA-based general rate and the observed corporate rate, all three exhibited similar tendencies to decline from 1948 to 1980, and then to reverse themselves slightly thereafter. Finally, we found that it was possible
to construct a good approximation to the rate of surplus value largely
from NIPA data alone. This allows us the possibility of estimating the
rate of surplus value for countries and periods in which the detailed data
we would prefer is unavailable.

There were some surprises in the data, in that several key Marxian
ratios were extremely stable over the entire postwar period. The productive and trade-sector shares of total value, and the intermediate and final-
use shares of the total product, both remained virtually constant over
time, as shown in Figures 5.5 and 5.6. A similar and interesting result
was the close parallelism between the unit wages of productive and unproductive workers in Figures 5.10 and 5.11, and hence between the ratios
$V^*/W$ and $L_p/L$ in Figure 5.9. Finally, there was the surprising stability
of the share of the surplus product absorbed by unproductive government
activities, as depicted in Figure 5.21.

The data also uncovered some strong empirical trends. The rate of surplus value $S^*/V^*$ rose significantly over the postwar period, as did the
value composition of capital $C^*/V^*$ and the productivity of labor $q^*$, as
seen in Figures 5.13, 5.15, and 5.19. respectively. The Marxian rate of

Table 5.14. *Comparison of key Marxian and orthodox measures*

| Variable | Typical relative levels 1967 | Change in relative levels 1948–89 | 1972–82 |
|---|---|---|---|
| TP*/GP | 82% | −12% | |
| TP*/GNP | 147% | −14% | |
| $L_p$/L | 44% | −37% | |
| V*/W | 42% | −33% | |
| S*/P | 224% | +34% | |
| C*/V* | 245% | +23% | |
| M/EC | 136% | −12% | |
| S*/V* | 210% | +44% | |
| $P^+$/EC | 58% | −27% | |
| q*/y | 306% | +49%[a] | +19%[b] |

[a] +1.2% per annum.    [b] +1.9% per annum.

profit fell steadily until 1980, when the Reagan–Bush attack on labor accelerated the growth of the rate of surplus value and reversed the postwar trend of the rate of profit (although it remains much lower than at the beginning of the period). Finally, the ratio of unproductive to productive labor $L_u$/$L_p$ rose dramatically, as is evident in Figure 5.11. The resulting relative absorption of surplus value by unproductive expenses in turn helps explain two facts: Both the NIPA-based average rate of profit and the observed corporate rate of profit declined more rapidly than the Marxian one; and the conventional measure of productivity rises much more slowly than the Marxian one, which is an important clue to the so-called productivity growth slowdown of these years.

All these results confirm our basic premise that the theoretical difference between Marxian and orthodox economic analysis is reflected in a fundamentally different empirical picture of capitalist reality.

# 6

## A critical analysis of previous empirical studies

The classical and Marxian traditions share the distinction between production and nonproduction labor. But Marx was particularly concerned with that portion of production labor which is productive of capital, since only this labor creates surplus value. The rest of labor is unproductive of capital, even though it may be wage labor (in distribution and state activities) or production labor (productive of value or of use value). Marx himself does not imply that productive labor is in any way superior to, or more necessary than, unproductive labor. But as we pointed out in Chapter 2, not all Marxists proceed in the same way. Most notably, Baran (1957, p. 32) redefines productive labor as labor that would be necessary under a "rationally ordered" (socialist) society. Marx's definition of productive labor is thereby replaced with a definition based on necessity,[1] and the concept of surplus value is replaced with the concept of "surplus" – defined as the excess of the total product over essential personal and public consumption.

This chapter will analyze the various attempts to measure Marxian categories. In order to make the account manageable, we restrict ourselves to studies published in English, and to estimates of the rate of surplus value. Sharpe (1982a) covers some of literature available in French, but a comprehensive worldwide survey remains to be done. The Japanese are pioneers in this regard. Izumi's brief survey of Japanese estimates makes it clear that many of the issues taken up in the English language literature were first, and often better, addressed in the sophisticated Japanese discussion. Matsuzaki makes company-level estimates of the rate of surplus

---

[1] It is no coincidence that Baran turns to a criterion of necessity. Neoclassical economics is also based on a criterion of necessity. In their case, the benchmark is a "perfectly competitive market," which perfectly reflects social preferences. Baran retains the necessity criterion, but inverts the benchmark by making a "rationally ordered [socialist] society" the point of reference.

value as early as 1924, Terashima makes industry-level ones by 1935, Shah Riff develops aggregate estimates by 1940, and Okishio pioneers the use of input–output tables to make labor value estimates by 1959. All in all, Izumi lists 56 sets of estimates of the rate of surplus value in Japan from 1924 to 1980 (Izumi n.d.). In our own survey, we will analyze studies by Okishio (1959), Izumi (1980, 1983), and Okishio and Nakatani (1985), because these four have been translated into (or published in) English.

The studies we cover will be grouped according to the manner in which they treat the distinction between production and nonproduction activities. There are three basic categories of studies: those which implicitly or explicitly reject the distinction between productive and unproductive labor, so that they end up treating Marxian categories as equivalent to NIPA categories; those which do base themselves on Marx's distinction between productive and unproductive labor, but differ in the way they implement this distinction; and those which substitute some sort of distinction between necessary and unnecessary activities for the distinction between production and nonproduction, thereby substituting some concept such as Baran and Sweezy's notion of "surplus" (the excess of total product over necessary social use) for Marx's concept of "capitalist surplus product" (the excess of total capitalist product over the consumption of the productive workers). Within each category, we will also distinguish between sectoral and aggregate studies, because systematic transfers of value make the former less reliable than the latter.[2] Aggregate studies will also be distinguished according to whether or not they make labor value estimates of Marxian categories.

The distinction between money and labor value measures gives rise to a further consideration. We have seen that the distinction between productive and unproductive labor implies that the money form of surplus value will generally differ in magnitude from aggregate profit, even if (final selling) prices were proportional to values. On the other hand, even if all labor were productive labor, the deviations of prices from values could make the money measure of surplus value differ from the labor value measure.[3] Of these two theoretically distinct issues, the second is far better

---

[2]   If we abstract from transfers of value between nations, or between capitalist and noncapitalist sectors, then the total surplus value realized in the production sector as a whole will always be less than that produced in it, because of the portion transferred to the trade sector. Price–value deviations may cause further intersectoral and international transfers, which can in principle reverse the outflow from production. See Sections 3.1.2 and 3.4.2.

[3]   Strictly speaking, the comparison is between the money form of surplus value at prices that are not proportional to values (such as market prices and prices of production), and the money form of surplus value at prices proportional to values (which we call "direct prices").

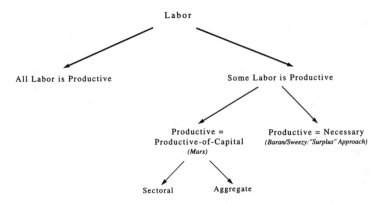

Figure 6.1. Theoretical bases for the type of empirical estimates.

known. But empirical studies typically encompass both issues. For instance, the early studies by Wolff (1975, 1977a) estimate both the labor value magnitudes and their money forms on the assumption that *all* wage labor is productive. This is tantamount to assuming that the money forms of Marxian categories are the equivalent to IO–NIPA categories, because – as we have seen in Section 3.1.1 – the mapping between the two is one-to-one when all labor is treated as productive. On the other hand, later studies by Wolff (1977b, 1979, 1987) and Khanjian (1989) do distinguish between Marxian and IO–NIPA categories, since they incorporate the distinction between productive and unproductive labor in their estimation of value categories and their money forms.

The impact of price–value deviations on the relation between the money and value measures of the rate of surplus value has already been analyzed (in Section 5.10) and shown to be an entirely secondary consideration. Accordingly, in this chapter we will group the studies under review according to the manner in which they treat the distinction between productive and unproductive labor. Thus Wolff's earlier studies are placed in the category of those that fail to distinguish between Marxian and NIPA categories, while his later studies and the one by Khanjian fall into the category of those that do make such a distinction. The issue of price–value deviations will then be addressed as it crops up. Figure 6.1 provides a graphical summary of our schema of categorization.

### 6.1 Studies that fail to distinguish between Marxian and NIPA categories

There exists an entire class of empirical studies that make no real distinction between NIPA categories and Marxian ones. Studies of this type generally assume that the rate of surplus value can be approximated

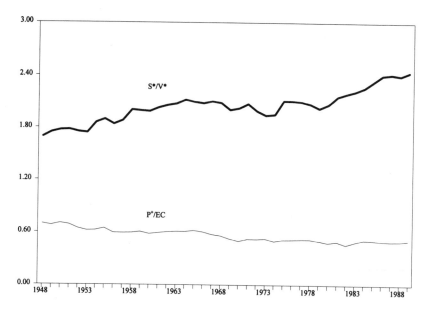

Figure 6.2. Rate of surplus value S*/V* and profit/wage ratio P⁺/EC.
*Source:* Table 5.7.

by some measure of the profit/wage ratio, so that the levels and movements of the former are deduced from those of the latter (except perhaps for any disturbing influence of price–value deviations). Yet, as we have seen, such an association is utterly mistaken, both theoretically and empirically (cf. Section 3.6.1 and Table 3.12; Section 5.4). Figure 6.2, which reproduces Figure 5.13, makes it particularly clear that the profit/wage ratio (defined here as the ratio of NNP minus employee compensation over employee compensation) is neither an index of the level nor the trend of the rate of surplus value.

### 6.1.1 *Aggregate money value estimates*

Glyn and Sutcliffe's (1972) study is one of the earliest, and most influential, of this type. The authors argue (p. 54) that the secular post-war decline in the British rate of profit lies at the heart of the stagnation of capital accumulation in Britain. And since the capital/output ratio is roughly stable, the decline in the profit rate can in turn be attributed to a secular fall in the profit share.[4] But a fall in the profit share is "an increase

---

[4] The rate of profit $r = P/K$, where $P$ = aggregate profit and $K$ = aggregate capital advanced. The rate of profit can also be expressed as $r = (P/Y)/(K/Y)$, where $Y$ = aggregate value added, $P/Y$ = the profit share, and $K/Y$ = the capital output ratio.

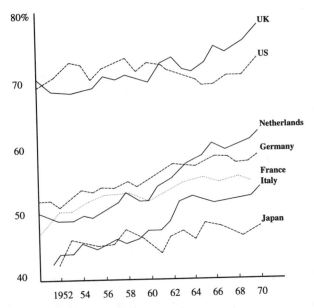

Figure 6.3. Wage shares in advanced capitalist countries, 1950–70.
*Source:* A. Glyn and R. Sutcliffe, *British Capitalism, Workers and the Profit Squeeze,* Harmondsworth: Penguin (1972, p. 76, fig. 7). Reproduced by permission of Penguin Books Ltd.

in labour's share [which is] very roughly the equivalent of a decrease in the rate of exploitation." This means that real wages must have risen faster than labor productivity over extended periods of time. Thus the secular decline in the British rate of profit is ultimately attributed to the fact that "the position of labour as a whole has been improving relative to that of capital" (p. 45). Notice that at the heart of the whole argument is the important association of the rate of exploitation with a NIPA-type measure of the profit/wage ratio.

Glyn and Sutcliffe's primary focus is on Britain, but they also attempt to extend their "labor-squeeze" argument to several other advanced capitalist countries (1972, pp. 73–5). They present data (reproduced in Figure 6.3) on wage shares from 1950 to 1970 for the United Kingdom, the United States, Netherlands, Germany, France, Italy, and Japan.

Given the trends evident in the data, and given the misidentification of the wage share in GNP with the variable capital share in Marxian value added, it is not surprising that the "labor-squeeze" approach gained popularity among Marxists. We will confine our discussion to those who explicitly connect their analysis to Marxian categories. For instance, Boddy and Crotty (1975) transform Glyn and Sutcliffe's secular argument into a cyclical one and apply it to the United States. Basing themselves on chapters of Marx's *Capital* (vol. I), in which all labor is still treated as production labor, they treat the profit share as an index of the rate of exploitation. Cyclical fluctuations in the rate of profit are then explained by fluctuations in the profit share, and hence in the rate of exploitation (Boddy and Crotty 1975, p. 2).[5] Sherman (1986) makes the same association when he states that in "terms of national income accounting, the rate of exploitation is roughly profit/wages" (p. 198). But he takes a more agnostic approach to the determinants of the cyclical fluctuations in the rate of profit, allowing for both "Marxist supply-side" (labor-squeeze) and demand-side (consumption-demand) effects of cyclical variations in the rate of exploitation (p. 192).

Weisskopf (1979) concerns himself with both the cyclical and secular behavior of the rate of profit in the United States since World War II. He explicitly identifies "variable capital with the total wage bill [and] surplus value with the volume of profits,"[6] and net output with the NIPA measure of net output (value added). He also implicitly assumes that all labor is productive, since he defines productivity as real net output per unit of (all) labor (pp. 342–6).[7] Not surprisingly, Weisskopf finds that the "long term decline in the [U.S.] rate of profit from 1949 to 1975 was almost entirely attributable to a rise in the true share of wages, which indicates a rise in the strength of labour" (p. 370). This argument is further developed by Bowles, Gordon, and Weisskopf (1984), who claim that by the late 1960s the rising strength of U.S. workers also took the form of a reduced work effort which served to slow down the rate of growth of productivity (pp. 29–32, 122–49) and further squeeze profits.

### 6.1.2 Aggregate labor value estimates

Okishio (1959) is the first to estimate directly the rate of surplus value in labor value terms. Since he also distinguishes between productive

---

[5] It should be noted that although the Marxian measure of productivity differs markedly from the conventional one in terms of its trend, the (short-run) cyclical patterns of the two are quite similar (Section 5.7, Figures 5.19 and 5.20). Moreover, cyclical fluctuations in productivity are quite modest compared with those in real wages, so that cyclical patterns in the wage share of (all) workers may well mirror corresponding fluctuations in the rate of exploitation. Thus Boddy and Crotty's cyclical results may not be substantially altered when their measure of productivity is replaced by a conventional one. But any attempt to link the short-run cycles to longer-term trends would certainly be affected.

[6] Weisskopf (1979, p. 343) does acknowledge in a footnote that surplus value "is usually defined to correspond to a substantially larger share of national income" than does the NIPA measure of profits, but he ignores this in his data and analysis.

[7] Weisskopf (1979, p. 354) distinguishes between supervisory and nonsupervisory labor, but only because he believes the two types of employment exhibit different cyclical patterns.

Table 6.1. *Wolff's estimates of the money and value rates of surplus value in Puerto Rico*

|  | 1948 | 1963 | Change |
|---|---|---|---|
| S/V (value rate) | 0.9729 | 0.9328 | −4.1% |
| S*/V* ≡ P/W (money rate) | 0.5907 | 0.7529 | +28.5% |
| (S*/V*)/(S/V) | 61% | 81% | |

*Source:* Wolff (1975, p. 940).

and unproductive labor, we will treat his pathbreaking contribution in Section 6.2.3.

Wolff develops labor value estimates by applying the theoretical framework developed by Morishima (1973) to actual input–output tables for Puerto Rico (Wolff 1975, 1977a) and for the United States (Wolff 1979, 1986). This allows him to directly address the question of price–value deviations by comparing his estimates of the money rates of surplus value to the corresponding value rate. In these particular studies, Wolff does not distinguish between productive and unproductive labor.

In his study of Puerto Rico, Wolff explicitly identifies the profit/wage ratio as the equivalent of the money form of the rate of surplus value. However, he arrives at the striking result that (at least for Puerto Rico) the problem of price–value deviations has so great an impact that the money form of the rate of surplus value (the profit/wage ratio in his calculations) is a "poor proxy" for either the level or the trend of the true (labor value) rate of surplus value (Wolff 1975, p. 940). Wolff's data indicate that the money rate of surplus value is only 60%–80% of the value rate. Moreover, the money rate displays a significant rise even as the value rate is actually falling. Table 6.1 reproduces Wolff's estimates for Puerto Rico.

There are two separate issues involved here. First of all, there is the large discrepancy between the money and value measures of the rate of surplus value. This problem apparently arises from the fact that Wolff treats relative wages as indexes of skills (Shaikh 1978b, p. 13). Wolff points out that the discrepancy between his money and labor value measures of the rate of surplus value depend primarily on the ratio of the direct price (price proportional to labor value) of consumption goods to its market price.[8] The

---

[8] Wolff normalizes the sum of direct prices (prices proportional to labor values) TV′ = C′ + V′ + S′ to the sum of market prices TV* = C* + V* + S*. He finds that the market price of constant capital was fairly close to its direct price. Thus

lower this ratio in the workers' consumption goods sector, the lower will be his profit/wage ratio P/W relative to his value rate S/V. Wolff notes that his empirical estimates of this ratio are mostly less than 1.[9] And here it seems very likely that Wolff's procedure leads to biased estimates of this value/price ratio. Estimates of labor values require data on input-output flows and also on labor flows. Ideally, these labor flows should be adjusted for skill differences; only if the differences among sectoral wage rates are due largely to skill differences may one then plausibly substitute relative wage coefficients for labor coefficients. Wolff uses wage coefficients because he is unable to obtain data on labor coefficients (Wolff 1977a, p. 148, n. 9). But for Puerto Rico, the substitution of wage coefficients for skill-adjusted labor coefficients is highly suspect. It is probable that in Puerto Rico (as in most Third World countries) poor people spend most of their income on agricultural products and other staples, and that the workers in the sectors that supply these goods are relatively underpaid (relative to their skill level). Agricultural workers in Puerto Rico are particularly underpaid, averaging between 40% and 60% of the wage of other laborers (Reynolds and Gregory 1965, p. 65, table 2-8). This means that, in a country like Puerto Rico, the substitution of wage coefficients for skill coefficients is likely to seriously underestimate the labor value of workers' consumption goods, thus giving rise to a large discrepancy between the profit/wage ratio and the estimated rate of surplus value. A 20%–30% differential between skill-adjusted wage rates in the two types of sectors would easily account for Wolff's results. Furthermore, to the extent that wages in the consumption-goods sector catch up to the average wage, the gap between the estimated rate of surplus value and the profit/wage ratio would narrow. In itself, such a rise in relative wages would raise the estimate of the labor value of variable capital and hence reduce the growth rate of the value rate of surplus value, all other things being equal. Thus the bias introduced by wage coefficients would also explain the apparent fall in Wolff's estimates of the value rate of surplus value in Table 6.1.

The preceding factors appear to explain why Wolff's estimated rates of surplus value are so much higher than his profit/wage ratios, why this

$V^* + S^* \approx V' + S'$, which implies that $(1 + S^*/V^*) = (1 + S/V) \cdot (V'/V^*)$, where $S'/V' = S/V$ since direct price magnitudes are proportional to labor values. Therefore Wolff's money rate of surplus value differs from his value rate by the ratio of the direct price of workers' consumption $V'$ to its market price $V^*$. But this latter ratio is simply an index of the price–value deviation for consumption goods (Wolff 1977a, pp. 144–5).

[9] Wolff normalizes the sum of prices to equal the sum of values, "values" being defined here as money prices proportional to labor values. Thus the average value/price ratio is 1.

gap appears to narrow over time, and why the estimated value rate of surplus value falls over time. His estimate of the value rate of surplus value is biased upward relative to the level of the profit/wage ratio, but biased downward relative to its trend (to the extent that the gap narrows).

The second problem arises from the fact that Wolff ignores the distinction between productive and unproductive labor. We have seen that even when prices are proportional to values, so that the correct measure of the money rate of surplus value is equal to the corresponding value rate, the profit/wage ratio can be a downward-biased index of both the level and the trend of this true money rate of surplus value. The same reasoning applies to Wolff's value rate (which is his labor equivalent of the profit/wage ratio) vis-à-vis the true value rate (computed using only productive labor). Thus we can say that the level of Wolff's value rate of surplus value is lower than the level of the true value rate (owing to the failure to distinguish between productive and unproductive labor), and that his profit/wage ratio is doubly lower (since its level is downward biased relative to his own measure of the value rate). The impact on trend biases is not so clear, because the two factors seem to operate in opposite directions in this particular study. In any case, Wolff's results must be interpreted in the light of all of these considerations.

The conclusion that Wolff's use of relative wages as indexes of skills is the principal source of the great discrepancy between his value and money estimates is borne out by his subsequent studies on the United States. There, by using labor coefficients directly (Wolff 1979, p. 332, n. 9) without any adjustment for skill levels, he implicitly assumes that the workers in each sector in his input–output tables all have roughly the same mix of skills. This is the opposite extreme from his Puerto Rico study. And here, the results are also quite different: value and money rates of surplus value differ by only 8%–15%, and both display the same general trend (p. 334, table 1). His subsequent article with a different definition of wages yields essentially similar results, although in this case both measures decline (Wolff 1986, p. 94, table 2, cited in Khanjian 1989, p. 119). Finally, Khanjian (1989, table 19) finds that price–value deviations result in variations between value and money rates of surplus value of only 6%–9%. Thus price–value deviations do not seem to pose a significant problem. Of course, all the problems associated with the assumption that all labor is productive still remain.

Wolff's methodology is extended by Sharpe (1982a), and applied to Canada (Sharpe 1982b, pp. 12, 42). Following Mandel's definitions of the basic variables of Marxian economic analysis, Sharpe develops detailed estimates of these variables in both price and value terms. In his various estimates of the value rate of surplus value, he generally assumes that all capitalist wage labor (even in the trade and royalties sectors) is productive. In one set of measures, he even assumes that government administrative labor is productive. Consequently, Sharpe's main estimates of the rate of surplus value are much lower than, and probably grow more slowly than, our equivalent measures.[10]

## 6.2 Studies that do distinguish between productive and unproductive labor

We turn now to those studies that attempt to incorporate the distinction between productive and unproductive labor in their estimates of Marxian categories.

### 6.2.1 *Sectoral money value estimates*

Varga (1928, 1935) provides the earliest set of sectoral estimates of the rate of surplus value. The methodology he developed remains influential to this day. Basing himself on manufacturing census data, he measures variable capital as the wages of production workers, and (the money form of) surplus value as the excess of net value added over variable capital,[11] for seven benchmark years from 1899 to 1931. In a later study (Varga 1968) he also attempts to update these figures to cover the period 1947–58, but these subsequent estimates contain two major calculation errors: for variable capital he mistakenly uses all wages and salaries, rather than the production worker wages he used in earlier years; and for surplus value he mistakenly uses gross value added rather than the excess of gross value added over wage costs (however defined). Although these two errors have offsetting effects on his data, they render his postwar estimates useless.[12] They also invalidate his analysis of the long-term

[10] Sharpe also calculates two alternative measures of the rate of surplus value. As part of his input–output estimate (Sharpe 1982b), he calculates a "narrowly defined" measure of the rate of surplus value which is based on the assumption that surplus value is the same thing as property-type income. This gives an estimate of 29% in 1976, as compared to 109.1% for his main measure and to 188% for Cuneo's estimate of the rate of surplus value in Canadian manufacturing. In an unpublished paper, Sharpe (1982a, pp. 41–5) calculates a NIPA-based constant-dollar estimate which is similar in form to the main estimates of his input–output study. This has a similar trend to his labor value estimates, but an even lower level.

[11] Varga actually calculates surplus value as the difference between the money value of the total product and the sum of materials, depreciation, and wage costs of production. But the difference between the first item and the sum of the next two is simply value added, so his measure of surplus value is net value added minus production wages.

[12] For instance, the census figures for manufacturing in 1947 (U.S. Bureau of the Census 1975, series P6-10, p. 666) list gross value added GVA = 74,291, production

trend of the rate of exploitation in the United States. However, as we shall see, Mandel and Perlo provide the correct figures for the postwar period.

Despite the surprising calculation errors in his later data, Varga's basic approach is very advanced. He not only distinguishes between production and nonproduction workers in manufacturing, but is also careful to note that his estimate of the rate of surplus value "is lower than the actual" rate because it fails to account for surplus value transferred from manufacturing to the trade sector. It is only the lack of adequate data which prevents him from correcting for this effect (Varga 1964, p. 107).

Varga's methodology was adopted by Corey (1934) and Varley (1938), with very similar results (Sharpe 1982a, p. 30). Gillman (1958, pp. 33, 39) takes up the same approach for his primary measures, defining variable capital in manufacturing by the wages of production workers and surplus value as the rest of value added (he measures surplus value both gross and net of depreciation). Gillman provides three sets of estimates of the rate of surplus value extending from 1849 to 1952, although no single set covers the whole period owing to a lack of consistent depreciation estimates for the entire interval.[13] He also looks at the various components of surplus value, such as unproductive expenses and "property-type" income. This aspect of his work is discussed separately in what follows.

Mandel (1975, pp. 174–5) further develops the Varga method. In his theoretical discussion, Mandel makes several important points. He begins by noting the difference in structure between Marxian economic categories and conventional ones. The salaries "of managers, higher employees in industry and the state apparatus" belong in the measure of surplus value (p. 165), as do the taxes paid by capitalist firms (p. 176), while that portion of the business and personal revenue which is the result of the recirculation of primary sector flows is excluded from the measure of the social product because it represents "revenue which has been spent two

worker wages $W_p = 30{,}244$, and total wages and salaries $W = 39{,}696$, all in millions of current dollars. In keeping with his earlier methodology, Varga should have calculated the gross rate of surplus value as $(GVA - W_p)/W_p = 146\%$. Instead, the figure he shows is $GVA/W = 187\%$ (Varga 1964, p. 108). The estimates in the other years for which he makes calculations (1950, 1955, and 1958) are similarly flawed. By the way, it is interesting to note that Varga cites (but does not explain) a "first calculation" by Katz of $S/V = 209\%$ for 1958, which is very close to our own estimate of 200%.

[13] Gillman (1958) estimates the gross rate of realized surplus value in manufacturing from 1849 to 1938 (p. 37), the net rate based on book-value depreciation from 1919 to 1939 (pp. 40, 46, apx. 2), and a more precise net rate based on current-dollar reproduction costs of fixed capital for various benchmark years from 1880 to 1952 (pp. 47–9).

or three times over" (pp. 165, 176, n. 66). These same points figure prominently in our own development of the argument. He also excludes "taxes paid by workers – as distinct from deductions for social security" from variable capital (pp. 176-7). This too would accord with our approach if these taxes are interpreted as net of the corresponding social expenditures on labor (see Section 3.3). But Mandel also argues that the costs of circulation belong "neither to the variable capital paid out each year nor to the annual quantities of surplus-value" (p. 165), and that "services in the real sense of the word – i.e., all except those producing commodity transportation, gas, electricity and water – do not produce commodities, and hence do not create any new value" (p. 176). These last two propositions are diametrically opposed to our own approach. Finally, even though Mandel is careful to state that the "application of Marx's categories to [conventional statistics] must . . . be handled with extreme caution," he nonetheless suggests that "a comparison between the official calculations of the share of the sum of wages and salaries and the share of the mass of profit in the national product certainly provides a reliable indication of the medium-term development of the rate of surplus value, for the necessary correction of these aggregates to align themselves with Marxist categories is unlikely to alter in any decisive way the proportions between them in these periods of time" (p. 166). Sharpe (1982a, p. 5) cites this as evidence that even so knowledgeable a writer as Mandel falls into the error of confusing orthodox categories with Marxian ones. But the matter is not so clear-cut. On one hand, in his empirical work Mandel uses the term "wages and salaries" to mean production worker wages and salaries (a convention that originates in use of the term "wages" to mean "production worker wages" in the Census of Manufactures), and measures "profits" as the excess of value added[14] over production worker wages and salaries. Indeed, Mandel's own empirical methodology is an extension of that in Varga (1928, 1935) and Gillman (1958), in which the distinction between productive and unproductive labor plays a vital role. On the other hand, Mandel also uses (without any methodological objection) the estimates from Vance (1970), which make no particular distinction between productive and unproductive labor.[15] In later texts, though,

---

[14] Since Mandel's empirical estimates focus on manufacturing, the relevant value added is that of this sector. But in his theoretical discussion, the relevant value added would be that of the primary sectors, since he has already excluded the secondary sectors as recirculated primary flows.

[15] Mandel (1975, p. 164) lists estimates by Vance in which the new value added (variable capital plus surplus value) is simply NNP (U.S. Bureau of the Census 1975, series F146). However, the variable capital is larger than even the sum of all private wages and salaries and supplements to income (series F166 and F170).

the importance of this distinction is given great prominence (Mandel 1981, pp. 38–61).

Mandel's own contribution to the empirical discussion is to experiment with the impact of a broader definition of variable capital on Varga's methodology. He defines manufacturing variable capital in two ways (production worker wages and the former plus 50% of the salaries of nonproduction workers), and finds that the broader measure results in a slower but still rising rate of surplus value.[16]

Perlo (1974) further broadens the range of measures of variable capital, defining it as production worker wages in one case and as all wages and salaries in the other.[17] He places the general trend of the gross realized rate of surplus value somewhere in between, probably closer to the first. He also notes that any measure of the realized rate of surplus value in a production sector will understate the level of the true rate because some value is always transferred to the trading sectors (pp. 27–8). Finally, Perlo argues that "monopoly pricing and promonopoly taxation" increasingly benefit capitalists at the expense of workers, so that the realized rate of surplus value probably understates the trend of the true rate. To correct for this bias in the realized rate, he proposes to "calculate the trend in the exploitation of labor by comparing the physical volume of the worker's production with the volume of his consuming power, after allowing for changing retailing prices and tax deductions from his pay" (pp. 29–30). In practice, this means estimating the trend in the true rate of surplus value from the ratio of real take-home pay to labor productivity (p. 30). His "index of worker's share" is therefore much the same as what Aglietta later calls the "real social wage cost."[18] The principal difference between the two is that Aglietta apparently uses pre-tax real wages, whereas Perlo uses post-tax real wages. We may think of these as implicitly representing two alternate positions on the net tax (social wage) paid by workers: if one believes that workers' taxes return to them in the form of social welfare

16  Mandel provides estimates of the realized rate of surplus value in manufacturing gross and net of depreciation, and with and without 50% of salaries. This gives him four alternate measures: gross and net measures with variable capital defined as production worker wages; and gross and net measures with 50% of salaries included in variable capital. The first two grow by roughly 50% over the postwar period, while the latter two grow more slowly (25% for the gross rate and 35% for the net rate). Mandel feels that these latter measures "probably correspond more closely to the actual development" (1975, pp. 174–5).

17  Perlo (1974, pp. 26–7) notes that one should estimate surplus value net of depreciation, but his empirical estimates are confined to gross surplus value.

18  The numerator of both measures is (pre- or post-tax) hourly wages deflated by the consumer price index, and the denominator of both is hourly productivity (Perlo 1974, p. 30; Aglietta 1979, pp. 88–91).

expenditures, then the net tax is essentially small and Aglietta's measure is more accurate; on the other hand, if one believes that workers' taxes are used to subsidize the capitalist class and related state activities, then the net tax is essentially equal to taxes paid, and Perlo's measure is more appropriate. It is interesting to note that, for the United States, our estimates of the social wage indicate that Aglietta's assumption is closer to the mark.[19]

Cuneo (1978, 1982) applies Varga's methodology to the manufacturing industry in Canada from 1917 to 1978. He provides twelve measures in all, of which three are relevant here: $RSV_1$, which is just a Varga-type measure of the gross rate of surplus value for Canadian manufacturing; $RSV_3$, which is the constant-dollar gross rate of surplus value, derived by deflating value added by the Wholesale Price Index and production worker wages by the Consumer Price Index; and $RSV_{12}$, which is the constant-dollar net rate of surplus value derived by subtracting an estimate of depreciation from gross surplus value (Cuneo 1978, p. 290; 1982, pp. 399, 415). He finds that over the postwar period these rates of surplus value rise until the mid-1960s, and then fall afterward (1978, pp. 292–3; 1982, p. 399). Cuneo also provides nine other variants of these rates, but they are all linked to a rather flawed "adjustment" he makes to the basic measure $RSV_1$, for which he was severely criticized by Van Den Berg and Smith (1982) and Emerson and Rowe (1982).[20]

Amsden (1981) applies Varga's methodology to the world economy by estimating realized rates of gross surplus value in manufacturing for a large set of countries[21] for the period 1966–77. Her actual estimates for U.S. manufacturing are the same as in Mandel, Perlo, and Shaikh. She is careful to note that price–value deviations and intersectoral and international transfers of value may make realized sectoral rates of surplus value differ from the true rates in a way that "may vary unsystematically between developed and underdeveloped countries." Nonetheless, she

[19] Shaikh and Tonak (1987, p. 188) find that the net tax stays within ±5% of employee compensation for most of the postwar period in the United States.

[20] For $RSV_2$, Cuneo deflates the production worker wage bill by the consumer price index, but does not deflate value added or surplus value. This is clearly inconsistent. For $RSV_4$–$RSV_{11}$, he reduces the production worker wage bill in year $t$ by the ratio of productive employment in 1949 to that in year $t$. This adjusted measure of variable capital is simply the current wage rate of production workers multiplied by their employment level in 1949. His measures $RSV_4$–$RSV_{11}$ are various gross, net, and constant-dollar versions of the rate of surplus value based on this adjusted measure of production worker employment. The rationale for this is quite obscure (Cuneo 1978, pp. 288, 290; 1982, pp. 397–8, 415).

[21] Amsden (1981, p. 232) notes that "statistics are typically restricted to manufacturing firms above a minimum size," which varies from country to country.

finds that in general the less advanced regions of the capitalist world have much higher rates of (realized) surplus value, largely because the wage gap is so much greater than the corresponding productivity gap (Amsden 1981, pp. 230–3).[22]

Lastly, Shaikh provides a long series on the gross-profit/wage ratio in U.S. manufacturing from 1899 to 1984, à la Varga, as part of his analysis of long waves. He finds that this rate is essentially constant in the pre-Depression period 1899–1929, but rises steadily in the post-WWII period 1947–84. This differential pattern accounts for a somewhat slower fall in the manufacturing rate of profit in the postwar period (Shaikh 1992a).

Almost all of these studies measure the rate of surplus value as the difference between variable capital (defined as the sum of production worker wages and possibly some portion of salaries) and value added. So defined, surplus value is inclusive of the materials and wage costs of unproductive activities, of corporate officers' salaries and bonuses, of indirect business taxes and corporate profit taxes, and of corporate and noncorporate profits. Clearly, only a portion of surplus value takes the form of profits. We have emphasized this point throughout.

Two further sets of sectoral estimates center around the fact that profit is only one component of surplus value. After presenting his initial set of estimates, Gillman (1957) goes on to argue that studies of profitability (such as his) should concentrate on that part of surplus value which is in excess of such expenses as the materials and wage costs of unproductive activities.[23] He calls this portion of surplus value "'net' surplus value

---

22  Amsden finds that the relationship between rates of surplus value and GNP per capita is actually an inverted-∪ shape. At very low levels of development both real wages and productivity are very low, so the rate of surplus value is relatively low. At the intermediate levels represented by newly industrializing and semi-industrialized countries, productivity gains race ahead of wage gains, so that the rate of surplus value is very high. Then, at the level of developed capitalist countries, real wage gains begin to catch up to productivity gains, so that the rate of surplus value is the lowest. Amsden (1981, pp. 237–9) notes that this cross-sectional pattern need not contradict Marx's notion that the average rate of surplus value rises as capitalism develops. But her findings are contradicted by Izumi (1983), who studies the labor value rate of surplus value instead of the realized money rate (as in Amsden). Izumi explains the difference in results by arguing that the transfers of value embodied in realized rates of surplus value make such rates unreliable indicators of the value rate of surplus value. See the discussion of Izumi at the end of Section 6.2.3.

23  Gillman finds that the general Marxian rate of profit, the ratio of surplus value to capital advanced, is roughly constant from 1920 to 1952. But in terms of the portion of surplus value which constitutes property-type income to the capitalist class, the rate of profit declines somewhat (Gillman 1957, p. 97). Of course, this is not because of a rising organic composition but rather because of a rising share of unproductive expenses and taxes. In contrast to this, Shaikh (1992b) finds a

realized," and compares its growth to that of variable capital (pp. 89–91). Whereas surplus value as a whole rises relative to variable capital (i.e., the rate of surplus value rises), the "net" portion declines relative to variable capital because of relatively rising expenses (p. 97). At a later stage, Gillman also excludes indirect business taxes to arrive at the portion of surplus value that represents "property-income" (profits, rents, and interest),[24] which further accelerates the fall in the rate of profit (pp. 101–2).

Gillman's focus on property-type income is perfectly appropriate as long as it is clear that this represents only a portion of total surplus value (which means that its general patterns cannot be analyzed without reference to the whole). And Gillman himself is generally clear about this, despite occasionally confusing terminology such as the term "net rate of surplus value" for what is really a fraction of the rate of surplus value. Unfortunately, such clarity is lacking in the study by the Labor Research Association (1948). In various places in their discussion, they correctly characterize indirect business taxes as "part of surplus value" (p. 22); wages in trade, finance, insurance, real estate, government, and various unproductive services as the share of surplus value going to unproductive workers (who "do not produce surplus value, but only share in that produced elsewhere"; p. 28); and property-type income as "[s]urplus value going to members of the capitalist class" (p. 27). Yet, despite their essentially correct definition of total surplus value, they often refer to the ratio of property-type income to variable capital as "the rate of surplus value." For instance, in their estimate of the "national rate of surplus value" (p. 28), they exclude both indirect business taxes and unproductive wages from the "surplus value" part of this ratio.[25] They repeat this exercise when they turn to the manufacturing sector, further restricting themselves to that part of "surplus value that remains in the industry" (p. 51). This means that they now exclude not only indirect business taxes and unproductive wages, but also rents and interest costs (since these are paid out

sharply rising organic composition, and hence a falling general rate of profit, using the same manufacturing flow data but new data for capital stock and capacity utilization.

[24] Marx focused on the *general* rate of profit, defined as the ratio of surplus value to capital advanced, because he felt that the general dynamics of profitability originated at this level. Such a focus requires one to derive more concrete measures of the rate of profit, such as the ratio of property-type income to capital advanced, in order to locate them in the context of more general trends.

[25] They begin from national income, which is value added minus indirect business taxes, so that the latter is excluded from the start. Then they divide national income into property-type income, wages of workers in productive sectors, and wages of workers in unproductive sectors. The "national rate of surplus value" is defined as the ratio of the first two elements (Labor Research Association 1948, pp. 27–8).

Table 6.2. *Sectoral (manufacturing) estimates of the rate of surplus value, 1899–1984*

| Sources | 1899 | 1900 | 1901 | 1902 | 1903 | 1904 | 1905 | 1906 |
|---|---|---|---|---|---|---|---|---|
| Shaikh | 1.46 | 1.46 | 1.46 | 1.46 | 1.46 | 1.47 | 1.48 | 1.50 |
| Varga | 1.28 | | | | | 1.24 | | |
| Gillman | 1.44 | | | | | 1.47 | | |
| Mandel | | | | | | 1.46 | | |

| Sources | 1917 | 1918 | 1919 | 1920 | 1921 | 1922 | 1923 | 1924 |
|---|---|---|---|---|---|---|---|---|
| Shaikh | 1.47 | 1.47 | 1.47 | 1.39 | 1.32 | 1.37 | 1.42 | 1.49 |
| Varga | | | 1.22 | | 1.06 | | 1.18 | |
| Gillman | | | 1.47 | | 1.32 | | 1.42 | |
| Mandel | | | 1.46 | | | | 1.42 | |

| Sources | 1935 | 1936 | 1937 | 1938 | 1939 | 1940 | 1941 | 1942 |
|---|---|---|---|---|---|---|---|---|
| Shaikh | 1.54 | 1.51 | 1.49 | 1.60 | 1.72 | 1.69 | 1.65 | 1.62 |
| Gillman | 1.54 | | 1.49 | | 1.72 | | | |
| Mandel | 1.53 | | | | 1.82 | | | |
| Perlo | | | | | | | | |

| Sources | 1953 | 1954 | 1955 | 1956 | 1957 | 1958 | 1959 | 1960 |
|---|---|---|---|---|---|---|---|---|
| Shaikh | 1.48 | 1.62 | 1.74 | 1.78 | 1.81 | 1.85 | 1.95 | 1.95 |
| Mandel | | 1.51 | | | | 1.85 | | |
| Perlo | 1.48 | | | | 1.81 | | | 1.95 |

| Source | 1971 | 1972 | 1973 | 1974 | 1975 | 1976 | 1977 | 1978 |
|---|---|---|---|---|---|---|---|---|
| Shaikh | 2.37 | 2.36 | 2.43 | 2.62 | 2.64 | 2.72 | 2.72 | 2.73 |

*Sources:* Shaikh (1992a); Varga (1935; Sharpe 1982a, p. 29); Gillman (1957; Sharpe 1982a, p. 31); Mandel (1975; Sharpe 1982, p. 34); Perlo (1974).

to other sectors) (pp. 47–51). Although they correctly measure the gross rate of surplus value in manufacturing, inclusive of indirect business taxes and unproductive wages (à la Varga),[26] they promptly reduce the measure of gross surplus value by an estimate of "overhead costs" defined as the sum of depreciation, indirect business taxes, rents, interest payments,

[26] Their only departure from Varga comes in their estimate of net surplus value, which they derive by subtracting an estimate of overhead costs from gross surplus value. But this overhead-cost component includes not just depreciation but also "interest, repairs, rent, and taxes" (Labor Research Association 1948, p. 55), so that their measure of net surplus value is considerably understated.

| 1907 | 1908 | 1909 | 1910 | 1911 | 1912 | 1913 | 1914 | 1915 | 1916 |
|------|------|------|------|------|------|------|------|------|------|
| 1.51 | 1.53 | 1.55 | 1.53 | 1.52 | 1.51 | 1.49 | 1.48 | 1.48 | 1.48 |
|      |      | 1.30 |      |      |      |      | 1.24 |      |      |
|      |      | 1.55 |      |      |      |      | 1.48 |      |      |
|      |      |      |      |      |      |      | 1.49 |      |      |

| 1925 | 1926 | 1927 | 1928 | 1929 | 1930 | 1931 | 1932 | 1933 | 1934 |
|------|------|------|------|------|------|------|------|------|------|
| 1.57 | 1.59 | 1.61 | 1.70 | 1.81 | 1.80 | 1.78 | 1.81 | 1.84 | 1.68 |
| 1.28 |      | 1.33 |      | 1.58 |      | 1.47 |      |      |      |
| 1.57 |      | 1.61 |      | 1.81 |      | 1.78 |      | 1.84 |      |
|      |      |      |      | 1.80 |      |      |      |      |      |

| 1943 | 1944 | 1945 | 1946 | 1947 | 1948 | 1949 | 1950 | 1951 | 1952 |
|------|------|------|------|------|------|------|------|------|------|
| 1.58 | 1.55 | 1.52 | 1.49 | 1.46 | 1.47 | 1.49 | 1.59 | 1.51 | 1.49 |
|      |      |      |      | 1.46 |      |      | 1.59 |      |      |
|      |      |      |      | 1.46 |      |      |      |      |      |

| 1961 | 1962 | 1963 | 1964 | 1965 | 1966 | 1967 | 1968 | 1969 | 1970 |
|------|------|------|------|------|------|------|------|------|------|
| 2.00 | 2.03 | 2.09 | 2.13 | 2.18 | 2.21 | 2.22 | 2.26 | 2.26 | 2.28 |
|      |      | 2.09 |      |      | 2.19 |      |      |      |      |
|      |      | 2.07 |      |      |      | 2.21 |      | 2.26 |      |

| 1979 | 1980 | 1981 | 1982 | 1983 | 1984 |
|------|------|------|------|------|------|
| 2.88 | 2.91 | 2.95 | 3.02 | 3.16 | 3.24 |

and all other expenses (pp. 50–1), so as to get back to the portion of surplus value retained in the sector as property-type income.[27] In this way, they reduce the rate of surplus value to a variant of the profit/wage ratio.

This completes our survey of the main sectoral estimates of the rate of surplus value in the United States. Table 6.2 lists these estimates, and

[27] Their treatment of variable capital is also confusing. In their estimate of the national rate of surplus value (Labor Research Association 1948, p. 27), they define variable capital as the wages "paid to those workers in the 'productive' *industries*" (emphasis added). Yet in their estimate of the manufacturing sector, they use the category of "wages" as their measure (p. 54), apparently unaware

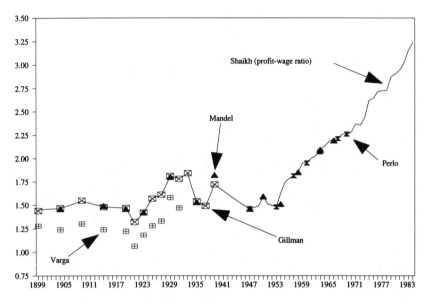

Figure 6.4. Estimates of the rate of surplus value: Manufacturing.
*Source:* Table 6.2.

Figure 6.4 graphs the main ones. The preceding studies have two salient characteristics. First of all, like all sectoral estimates they can only pick up that portion of aggregate surplus value realized in a particular sector (generally manufacturing). At best, this would represent only the realized rate of surplus value, net of any value transferred into or out of it to other sectors. This is why so many authors, from Varga onward, are careful to point out that their sectoral estimates are underrepresentative of the true rate of surplus value. To the extent that these transfers have a trend over time, the resulting estimates will have secular bias.

An entirely separate problem arises from the fact that census data are constructed quite differently from NIPA data. Table 6.3 illustrates the problem for the year 1970 by comparing census and NIPA figures for gross value added and total employee compensation in manufacturing. The census figures for gross value added are typically larger than the corresponding NIPA figures (by 19% for 1970). At the same time, census figures for employee compensation and production worker wages are typically smaller than NIPA-based figures (roughly 20% smaller in 1970). Both these factors serve to make census-based estimates of the sectoral rate of surplus

that this represents only the wages of production workers, not all workers, in this sector (nonproduction workers show up under the category of "payroll").

Table 6.3. *Manufacturing sector, 1970 (billions of current dollars)*

|  | GVA | Employee compensation (EC) | Production worker wages ($W_p$) | Gross rate of SV |
|---|---|---|---|---|
| (1) Census | 300.3 | 141.9 | 91.6 | 228% |
| (2) NIPA/BLS | 252.3 | 181.1[a] | 110.3[b] | 129% |
| (3) Census/NIPA | 1.19 | 0.78 | 0.83 | 1.77 |

[a] NIPA.    [b] BLS.

*Sources:* Row (1): U.S. Bureau of the Census (1975), series P10 (GVA), P7 (EC), and P9 ($W_p$). Row (2): Table E.1 (GVA), Table G.1 (EC), and Table G.2 (V* = $W_p$).

value much higher than NIPA-based sectoral estimates. The discrepancy between the two data sources is well known, and still unresolved.

The sectoral effect and the data-source effect seem to work in opposite directions. Within a common data set, sectoral and aggregate estimates of the rate of surplus value will generally differ, because the former fails to account for value transfers in and out of the sector: value will always be transferred out of the producing sector to the trading sector owing to the difference between producer and purchaser prices, and value may be transferred into or out of the producing sector due to producer price–value deviations induced by the (tendential) equalization of profit rates. To the extent that the latter effect tends to be small, the former will dominate, and sectoral rates of surplus value will tend to be lower than aggregate ones. Comparing NIPA-based aggregate and sectoral rates of surplus value in Figure 6.5 shows this to be the case, although the trends of the two rates are similar. The lower curve in Figure 6.6 makes these notions more precise, by showing that the ratio of the NIPA sectoral to the aggregate rate is roughly 55% and seldom varies by more than ±5%.

The data-source effect works in the opposite direction, because census measures of value added in manufacturing are systematically larger than NIPA ones, as is evident in Figure 6.5.

The net result of these two effects is that census-based sectoral estimates, such as those in Varga and in others who adopt his methodology, tend to have a much sharper upward trend than either the sectoral NIPA-based or aggregate NIPA–IO-based estimates of the rate of surplus value. Figure 6.5 shows that the average level of the census-based estimate over the whole postwar period is roughly equal to that of the average aggregate rate S*/V*, but that the trend of former is much sharper than that of the

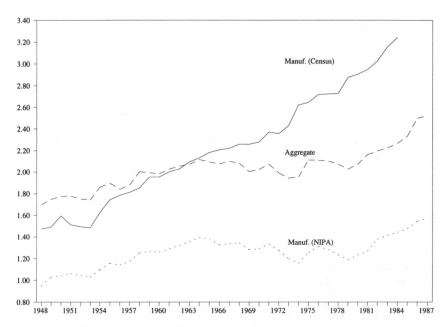

Figure 6.5. Aggregate and sectoral realized rates of surplus value.
*Source:* Table 6.2.

latter. Figure 6.6 shows that the ratio of the former to the latter rises by 66% over the postwar period, from 0.80 in 1948 to 1.33 in 1984.

### 6.2.2 *Aggregate money value estimates*

One of the earliest discussions of the general correspondence between Marxian categories and national economic accounts occurs in the pamphlet by the LRA (Labor Research Association 1948). The bulk of the empirical estimates in this pamphlet are sectoral, which is why it was initially discussed in the previous section. However, it does contain scattered remarks indicating that surplus value consists of indirect taxes, wages of workers in unproductive sectors, and property-type income in all sectors, and that variable capital consists of the wages of workers in the productive sectors (pp. 22, 27–8). This is not exact (among other things, the intermediate inputs of the trading sectors would be left out, the royalties sectors would be double-counted in Marxian value added, and unproductive labor in the productive sectors would be included in variable capital), but it is a start in the right direction. On the basis of their own remarks, the LRA pamphlet should have estimated variable capital as the wages of (all) workers in the productive sectors, and surplus value as the rest of NNP. In fact, however, they do not proceed in this way at all. Instead,

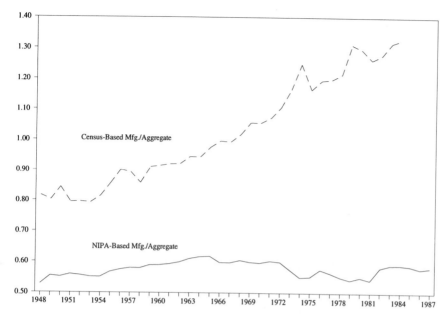

Figure 6.6. Ratios of sectoral rates of surplus value to the aggregate rate. *Source:* Table 6.2.

like Gillman in his second set of estimates, they focus their attention only on that part of surplus value which takes the form of profit-type income. Gillman muddied the waters by labeling this "net surplus value."[28] The LRA pamphlet compounds the confusion, and contradicts its own earlier usage, by simply calling it "surplus value."[29] Its initial potential is thus dissipated by later contradictions and confusions.

A much more consistent treatment appears in Eaton (1966). Eaton's approach is generally quite sophisticated. At a theoretical level, he defines Marxian value added as the value added in productive sectors plus the gross trading margin on this output, and defines variable capital as the wages of workers in the productive sectors (p. 211, including footnote). This is essentially the same as our own revenue-side measures shown in Table 6.4 (to follow).[30] Eaton also points out that variable capital should

---

[28] Gross and net national product are gross and net of depreciation. Gross surplus value is gross of depreciation. It is therefore plausible that net surplus value should be net of depreciation.

[29] They call the ratio of profit-type income to variable capital "the national rate of surplus value" (Labor Research Association 1948, pp. 27–8).

[30] Our measure can be written as $VA^* = (RY_p + VA_p) + GO_t$. If Eaton's measure of productive value added includes rental and finance charges (royalty payments), then his measure is the same as ours.

Table 6.4. *Our basic mapping between Marxian and IO–NIPA categories*

$$TV^* \equiv GO_{pt}$$
$$C^* \equiv M'_p + D_p$$
$$VA^* \equiv TV^* - C^* \equiv VA_{pt} + RY_{pt} + M_{tt}$$
$$V^* \equiv W_p$$
$$S^* \equiv VA^* - V^* = (P_{pt} + RY_{pt}) + IBT_{pt} + (W_{tt} + M_{tt})$$

be corrected for the *net* tax on productive workers, and quotes Callaghan to the effect that the costs of "social services for the workers ... is broadly met from within the working class itself" (Eaton 1963, p. 216). Our own detailed estimates of the net tax lead us to precisely the same conclusion (see Section 5.9). At an empirical level, Eaton restricts the definition of productive sectors to those producing goods only, so that all services are treated as unproductive. In addition, he assumes that productive labor is all labor within productive sectors and that unproductive labor is all labor within unproductive sectors. On this basis, he estimates the rate of surplus value in the United Kingdom to be 186% in 1937.

Mage (1963) raises the discussion of the relation between Marxian categories and national income accounts to an entirely new level. He is the first to really address the issue at a general (as opposed to a sectoral) level, and the first to attempt estimates in both price and labor value quantities – although he fails at the latter. Mage begins with a systematic and wide-ranging presentation of Marx's theory of value, price, surplus value, productive and unproductive labor (in which services are counted as productive), accumulation, effective demand, long-term profitability, and crises (Mage 1963, chaps. I–V). His primary goal in this section is to locate Marx's argument about the long-term tendencies of the rate of surplus value, the organic composition of capital, and the general rate of profit. The rest of his work (chaps. VI–VIII) is devoted to deriving empirical estimates of basic Marxian categories in order to test the empirical validity of Marx's propositions.

Although Mage's approach to the relation between Marxian and orthodox categories is quite sophisticated, it suffers from one major defect. Namely, he never provides a systematic treatment of the overall mapping between the two sets of categories. Instead, he proceeds by estimating separate components of various Marxian categories and then adding them up to arrive at individual desired magnitudes such as variable capital and (his definition of) surplus value. The elements that do not enter his definitions of these measures tend to disappear from view (which cannot happen in our own double-entry IO-based methodology). Nonetheless, one can make the necessary connections between his partial approach and our more general one.

Let us begin with a summary of our own mapping between Marxian categories and those in national income accounts. Leaving aside questions concerning the exact coverage of the trade sector (we include building rentals in the trade sector, whereas Mage implicitly treats all rents as ground rent), we begin from total value as the sum of production and trade sector IO gross outputs ($TV^* \equiv GO_{pt} \equiv GO_p + GO_{tt}$). Constant capital is defined as the sum of depreciation and materials used in the productive sectors ($C^* \equiv M'_p + D_p$). From this we derive Marxian value added as the difference between total value and constant capital ($VA^* \equiv TV^* - C^* \equiv GO_{pt} - M'_p - D_p$), which can also be expressed as the sum of NIPA value added in the trade and production sectors ($VA_{pt} \equiv VA_p + VA_{tt}$), royalties (ground rent and finance charges) in the production and trade sectors ($RY_{pt} \equiv RY_p + RY_{tt}$), and intermediate inputs in the trading sectors ($M_{tt}$). Of this amount, we would count the wages of production workers as variable capital ($V^* \equiv W_p$). Aggregate surplus value is therefore the rest of value added ($S^* \equiv VA^* - V^*$), and this can also be written as the sum of indirect taxes ($IBT_{pt}$), profits ($P_{pt}$), and royalties ($RY_{pt}$) in the production and trade sectors, plus trade-sector intermediate inputs ($M_{tt}$). Table 6.4, which is adapted from Table 3.12, summarizes these relations. Note that the subscript pt refers to the sum of the production and total trade sectors.

Mage proceeds in exactly the opposite direction, building up certain totals from the individual components. Variable capital is defined in essentially the same way as ours, as the "wage received by the productive laborers" in the production and trade sectors (Mage 1963, pp. 164, 188). However, he restricts the definition of surplus value to only the "total of property incomes in the forms of profit, interest and rent" of the production and trade sectors (pp. 79, 164).[31] The lineage of this narrow conception of surplus value can be traced back to Gillman and the Labor Research Association. Gillman treats "property-income" as a portion of surplus value, the Labor Research Association treats it as the only relevant portion, and Mage treats it as the very definition of surplus value.[32] In our

---

[31] Mage correctly restricts himself to flows "originating in the capitalist sector" (1963, p. 164), so as to avoid double counting of revenues. He defines this original source of revenues to be the sum of the production and trade sectors (see Appendix K).

[32] Mage criticizes Gillman for misrepresenting Marx's treatment of the costs of circulation. Since Gillman's treatment appears to be grounded in Marx's own argument, Mage tries to get around this obstacle by arguing that whereas these costs are indeed a deduction from surplus value from "the point of view of the entire

Table 6.5. *Comparison between our mapping and Mage's*

| Shaikh and Tonak | Mage |
|---|---|
| $C^* \equiv M'_p + D_p$ | $C^{*\prime} \equiv (M'_p + D_p) + IBT_{pt} + (W_{tt} + M_{tt})$ |
| $V^* \equiv W_p$ | $V^{*\prime} \equiv W_p$ |
| $S^* \equiv (P_{pt} + RY_{pt}) + IBT_{pt}$ $+ (W_{tt} + M_{tt})$ | $S^{*\prime} \equiv (P_{pt} + RY_{pt})$ |
| $VA^* \equiv W_p + (P_{pt} + RY_{pt}) + IBT_{pt}$ $+ (W_{tt} + M_{tt})$ | $VA^{*\prime} \equiv W_p + (P_{pt} + RY_{pt})$ |
| $(S^*/V^*) \equiv [(P_{pt} + RY_p) + IBT_{pt}$ $+ (W_{tt} + M_{tt})]/W_p$ | $S^{*\prime}/V^{*\prime} \equiv (P_{pt} + RY_{pt})/W_p$ |

terms, Mage's measure of surplus value corresponds to the profits-and-royalties $(P_{pt} + RY_{pt})$ portion of surplus value. This leaves out indirect business taxes $(IBT_{pt})$ of the production and trade sectors as well as the cost of circulation $(W_{tt} + M_{tt})$, both of which Mage is then forced to place in total constant capital: "the appropriate treatment for the outlay on unproductive expense in general . . . is to regard them as part of constant capital" (p. 66). Table 6.5 provides a summary of the comparison between Mage's categories and ours.

Mage's actual empirical estimates are much lower than our theoretical discussion would suggest. Several concrete features of his estimation procedures account for this widened gap. First of all, he excludes agriculture and government enterprises, whereas we include both.[33] Second, as noted earlier, he treats the whole of the (nonimputed) rental sector as a royalties sector, whereas we put a substantial portion of it into total trade. Consequently, even our measure of property-type income will be higher than his.[34] And third, he subtracts estimated taxes on corporate profits and on

capitalist class" (as Marx notes), they are really constant capital from "the standpoint of the process of capitalist production as a whole" (Mage 1963, pp. 61–8). He cites (p. 62) Marx's division of surplus value into profits, rents, and interest, without mentioning that – in the particular discussion cited – Marx is abstracting from unproductive capital.

[33] Mage excludes government enterprises on the ground that they are noncapitalist. Since input–output tables merge government enterprises into industries with similar activities, we perforce count them as part of those industries.

[34] Mage also subtracts the wage equivalent of proprietors and partners (WEQ) from the income of unincorporated enterprises. But we do the same thing, because our measure of total wages is employee compensation *plus* the wage equivalent of proprietors and partners. So, other than the actual estimate of the size of WEQ, this cannot account for the difference between our measures and his.

rental receipts. He even subtracts estimates of the "direct taxes imposed on individual recipients of surplus value" (Mage 1963, p. 166), on the grounds that surplus value should represent only the "net income of the . . . capitalists" (p. 36), "i.e., after-tax net property income" (p. 164).[35] Although he does not make it clear, presumably he would add all of these taxes to constant capital, as he did with indirect business taxes.[36] Not surprisingly, his measure of surplus value is substantially lower than ours.[37]

Mage's actual estimate of variable capital is also quite different from ours. The exclusion of agriculture and government enterprises would make his estimates smaller than ours even if all other things were equal. Moreover, he reduces his measure of variable capital by "the estimated portion of it paid as direct taxes by individual recipients of labor income" (1963, p. 167). This at least has the virtue of consistency, since it parallels his treatment of property-type income. But there is still an inconsistency in his treatment of the unincorporated sector, which further reduces his measure of variable capital: when he calculates the portion of surplus value which corresponds to unincorporated enterprise profits in the production and trade sectors, he does so by subtracting the estimated wage (the wage equivalent WEQ) of proprietors and partners from the total value added of unincorporated enterprises. This removes both the productive wage equivalent (corresponding to the productive portion of the labor of proprietors and partners) and the unproductive wage equivalent. To be consistent, he should have then added the former to variable capital and the latter to total unproductive wages; but he neglects to do either. We, on the other hand, do both.[38] Consequently, his measure of variable capital is somewhat lower than ours.[39]

---

[35] Mandel (1975, p. 176) criticizes Mage for leaving taxes out of his measure of surplus value.

[36] Mage also subtracts corporate officers' salaries from wages and adds them to his estimate of aggregate surplus value. In effect, we do the same thing (see Appendix G), so this does not account for any difference between the two sets of measures.

[37] Mage's measure of capital consumption is also different from ours, since they are derived from different capital stock data.

[38] We start by adding the wage equivalent in each sector to employee compensation in each sector to obtain total wages in each sector. Then one portion of this total is allocated to variable capital, and the rest to unproductive wages. When the former is subtracted from Marxian value added (which includes all wages in the production and trade sectors) to get surplus value, the remainder automatically includes the unproductive wages of the production and trade sectors, including corporate officers' salaries (which NIPA lists under employee compensation).

[39] Because estimates of the ratio of productive to unproductive labor (or wages) in each sector are used to split total wages into variable capital and unproductive wages, differences in estimates of these ratios also contribute to the difference between Mage's figures and ours. But these do not appear to be a significant factor.

Mage complements his money value measures of Marxian categories with a corresponding set of labor value measures. The basic procedure is quite straightforward. By definition, Marxian labor value added is simply the number of hours worked by productive workers ($H_p$). If we can somehow estimate the labor value of productive labor power ($V$) (i.e., of the goods consumed by productive workers), then we can immediately calculate surplus value as $S \equiv H_p - V$. One could then judge how well the labor value measures correspond to the (apparently independent) money value measures.

Since $H_p$ is readily computed from the data already used to make the money value estimates (Mage 1963, pp. 210–11), the only remaining problem is the estimate of $V$. And it is here that Mage adopts an apparently simple and appealing procedure. Since he already has a measure of the money value of variable capital ($V^*$), he converts it into a labor value measure ($V'$) through the estimated labor value of one dollar ($\lambda^*$). By his definition, $V' \equiv \lambda^* \cdot V^*$, and $S' \equiv H_p - V' = H_p - \lambda^* \cdot V^*$ (pp. 196–8). He then presents labor value measures that are very similar to his earlier money value measures (compare charts VI-1, VI-2, and table VI-1 on pp. 172–5 to charts VII-1, VII-2, and table VII-1 on pp. 204–9).

The money value and labor value measures appear to be largely independent of one another, so that their close correspondence seems to imply that price–value deviations are negligible. Although this might indeed be the case, Mage's technique provides no evidence for it at all. To see this, let us define the labor value of one dollar as the ratio of the money value of Marxian value added to the hours of productive labor (which is the labor value of Marxian value added): $\lambda^* \equiv VA^*/H_p$. Then it can be immediately shown that Mage's definitions will yield a "labor value" rate of surplus value which is identical to the corresponding money rate. Recall that Marxian value added $VA^* = V^* + S^*$, while hours of productive labor $H_p = V + S$. Suppose we now define the value of money as $\lambda^* \equiv H_p/VA^*$; then we can multiply the expression for $VA^*$ by $\lambda^*$ to obtain

$$H_p = \lambda^* \cdot V^* + \lambda^* \cdot S^*$$

It is clear that if we further define the "value of labor power" to be $V' = \lambda^* \cdot V^*$, then $S' \equiv H_p - V' = \lambda^* \cdot S^*$, so that $S^*/V^* = S'/V'$. *This is simply an algebraic identity.* Mage seems aware of the tautological nature of his labor value procedure. He argues that the theoretically appropriate measure of $\lambda^*$ would be "the ratio between the *number of hours of productive labor* performed during the year, and the *money value of the net product* of that year." Had he used his own preferred measure, Mage would have ended up with identical rates of surplus value in both value and money terms. But he chose instead to use the ratio of gross labor value added to gross value added, justifying it on the somewhat specious grounds that this "allows direct calculation in labor-units and is therefore preferable in the current context" (1963, p. 197). In fact, his theoretically preferred measure of the value of money is readily calculable from his data, whereas the measure he actually uses requires him to engage in a very roundabout, iterative estimation procedure (pp. 198, 212–14). His justification for all of this makes no sense, save to provide slightly differing estimates in the two sets of measures.

There is another side to this matter. In recent years, several authors (Foley 1982; Lipietz 1982) have tried to turn Mage's algebraic identity into a "new" solution to the transformation problem by simply defining both the value of labor power and the value of money in the appropriate manner. What they neglect to mention are the implications of such a procedure. As just defined, the value of money $\lambda^*$ is the living labor commanded *in exchange* by the net product. This means that the value of labor power $V'$ is the living labor commanded by the money wage bill of productive workers, and that surplus value $S'$ is simply the living labor commanded by the existing mass of profit. Marx argued that price and profits were monetary forms of value and surplus value. The new approach abandons this altogether by defining surplus value to be a form of profit! The whole relation between surplus value and profit is turned on its head. Moreover, this approach does not even have the virtue of being new, since it is really nothing more than Adam Smith's second definition of labor value as the living labor commanded by price. Ricardo and Marx decisively rejected this approach, with good reason.

In summary, Mage pioneers the analysis of the relation between Marxian categories and national income accounts (albeit only on the value, as opposed to the product, side of the accounts). He is theoretically sophisticated, and extraordinarily knowledgeable about empirical issues. He correctly identifies the money form of total value as the sum of the gross output (in the IO sense) of the production and trade sectors. His treatment of variable capital is also a major step forward, since he generalizes Varga's distinction between productive and unproductive labor within manufacturing to all productive sectors. But his text is frustrating because it does not provide any systematic treatment of the relation between Marxian and NIPA categories. Rather than starting with total value or even value added and then working down to surplus value, he proceeds instead by building up the latter from a variety of data sources. Items such as unproductive wages, taxes of various sorts, and the wage equivalent of proprietors and partners tend to get lost in such a process. But perhaps the most important defect of his work is his reduction of surplus value and variable capital to the disposable income of capitalists and workers – that is, to what orthodox economics would call disposable "factor incomes." This is what accounts for his falling rate of surplus value in the postwar period.

The first systematic derivation of the relation between Marxian categories and national income accounts appears in the work of Shaikh (1978b), who begins from the distinction between productive and unproductive labor and builds up to the various forms of the circulation of value. He is also the first to adjust the rate of surplus value for the net tax ("social wage") on labor. The present book is an extension of this earlier work.

Shaikh (1978b) emphasizes the critical importance of having empirical categories that correspond to the theory under consideration (pp. i–iii). He derives the Marxian distinction between productive and unproductive labor from more general considerations (pp. 1–11), and then shows how this fundamental distinction affects the relation between Marxian and orthodox economic categories (pp. 12–31). Beginning with only production activities, he successively introduces trading, rental, financial, and governmental activities. Each stage in the argument is used to further concretize the mapping between Marxian and NIPA categories. His final result is essentially the same as the revenue side of our present approach (p. 30). As Shaikh notes, the total value of the final product appears as the gross product of "the productive sector and trading sector . . . because these are the only two sectors through which the commodity-product itself passes on its way to its realization as money" (p. 31). Constant capital is the intermediate inputs of the productive sector, and variable capital is the wage bill (after net taxes) of productive workers in the productive sector. All of the rest of total value is surplus value (pp. 30–1). Shaikh emphasizes the great conceptual and empirical difference between the resulting "rate of surplus value and . . . its fetishized form, the profit-wage ratio," and points out the implications of this for Glyn and Sutcliffe and others who confuse the two measures. Tables 6.4 and 6.5, which summarize the revenue side of our present approach, can also be viewed as a summary of Shaikh's mapping.

There are some important differences between Shaikh's earlier approach and our current one. Like Mage, he works only on the revenue side, whereas we work within a double-entry framework. Moreover, his empirical database is structured around national income accounts, whereas ours is geared to the far more comprehensive input–output accounting framework. A major advantage of the latter is that it allows us to track the circulation of total value, not just of value added.

In spite of the fact that the basic theory is the same, Shaikh's empirical estimates differ considerably from ours. His measure of surplus value is too low because he is unable to derive an estimate of the input costs of circulation $M'_{tt}$. Shaikh guesses that this factor is probably small, but our

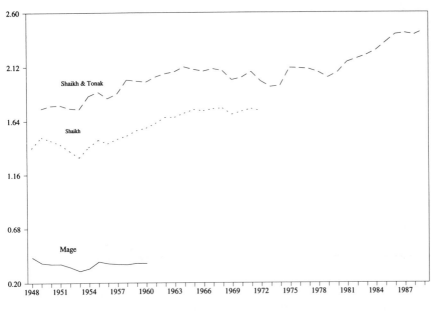

Figure 6.7. Rates of surplus value: Mage, Shaikh, Shaikh and Tonak.
*Sources:* Mage (1963); Shaikh (1978b); Shaikh and Tonak, Table H.1.

data indicates that its inclusion would have raised his estimate of surplus value by over 20% in 1958.[40] Finally, like Mage, Shaikh covers only
the private nonfarm economy (whereas we include both agriculture and
primary-sector government enterprises); restricts the definition of trade
to the wholesale/retail sector (whereas we count building rentals as trading activities); and forgets to put the wage equivalent of proprietors and
partners into total wages after he subtracts it from unincorporated income
to get profits of unincorporated enterprises. All four factors work to reduce his estimate of surplus value to a level considerably below ours.
The second factor (exclusion of agriculture and government enterprises)
and particularly the fourth (exclusion of the wage equivalent from total
wages) also serve to reduce his estimate of variable capital relative to
ours.[41] The net result is that Shaikh's estimates are considerably higher
than Mage's, but still lower than ours; see Figure 6.7.

[40]  From our data, $M'_{tt} = \$31.61$ billion in 1958. Shaikh's estimate of surplus value
(without $M'_{tt}$) is $146.620 billion. Thus his estimate would have been raised by
21.5%, all other things being equal.

[41]  Shaikh's estimates of variable capital are incorrect owing to calculation errors in
the treatment of services. For instance, the correct figures for 1929, 1947, and
1972 in millions of dollars are 21,890, 56,868, and 230,073, respectively.

Aglietta (1979) places the measurement of the rate of surplus value at the heart of his theory. According to him, the "nodal point of [a] theory of capitalist regulation" is that to "study the articulation between the laws of capitalist accumulation and the laws of competition means to elucidate the contradictory process of the generalization of the wage relation" (pp. 17–18). The historical evolution of the rate of surplus value plays a crucial role in this, because "the rate of surplus-value is the pivot of capitalist accumulation" (p. 87).

Although Aglietta does distinguish between productive and unproductive labor (1979, p. 89), he does not carry this over to the measurement of the national product. Like some others in this section, he uses the NIPA measure of value added as a proxy for a corresponding Marxian measure (p. 88). But Aglietta does not attempt to measure the money rate of surplus value directly, because he believes that the impact of price–value deviations is significant enough to make the money rate a biased indicator of the trend of the value rate of surplus value. For this reason, he sets out "to find a more faithful statistical indicator [of the] long run trend" in the value rate of surplus value (p. 88). He concludes that the share of real wages in productivity (the "real social wage cost") is a more appropriate measure of the share of the value of labor power in the value added by living labor, assuming that social productivities (the reciprocals of the unit labor values) of the consumer and producer sectors rise at roughly the same rate in the long run. Our derivation of this relation is in Appendix L. As noted previously, Aglietta's argument is reminiscent of an earlier one by Perlo (1974), who also claims that the trend of the rate of exploitation can be more accurately estimated from the "index of workers' share," which he defines to be the ratio of the real take-home pay of workers to their productivity (Perlo 1974, p. 30).

We have already seen that price–value deviations have only a minor effect on aggregates such as the rate of surplus value, since the money and value rates are quite close and have virtually identical trends (see Section 5.10). Thus Aglietta is wrong in making this particular issue a central concern.[42] Although this does not invalidate his procedure for estimating the long-term trend of the rate of surplus value, it does prevent him from attempting to measure its level.

The theoretical content of Aglietta's technique can be addressed by comparing his real social wage cost (real wage share) $w'$ to the ratio it is presumed to approximate – the share $v'$ of the value of labor power in labor value added. By definition, $v' = V/(V + S) = 1/(1 + e)$, where $e = S/V$.

[42] Aglietta could have measured the money rate of surplus value directly, in order to see if its trend was indeed different from that implied by his real social wage cost indicator.

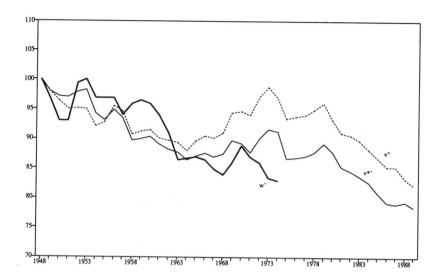

Figure 6.8. Aglietta's real social wage cost versus the unit value of labor power. *Source:* Table L.1.

We will call v' the *unit value of labor power.* Similarly, Aglietta's real social wage cost w' = wr/y, where wr = the real wage rate per unit labor and y = productivity per unit labor. In Appendix L, we show that if the two measures use the same data on real wages and productivity, then

$$v' = (\lambda c/\lambda y)w'$$

where

$\lambda c$ = unit labor value of (workers') consumption goods, and
$\lambda y$ = unit labor value of net output.

Thus, as Aglietta notes, the real social wage index w' will reflect the unit value index v' if $\lambda c/\lambda y$, the ratio of the unit labor values of consumer goods to that of the net product, is stable over time. Although this is a fairly good assumption (Juillard 1992, p. 24, fig. 7), price–value deviations are even more stable, so that Aglietta's roundabout procedure of estimating the trend in the rate of surplus value is not really necessary.

Figure 6.8 compares the index of the unit value of labor power v*' (based on the money rate of surplus value, which we know from Section 5.10 to be a good proxy for the value rate) to two Aglietta-type indexes of the "real social wage cost": v", based on our own data; and w', estimated directly from Aglietta (see Appendix L and Table L.1 for details). Several things stand out in Figure 6.8. One can see that our Aglietta-type measure v″, based on our own data, is indeed a good proxy for the long-term trend of the (true) unit value index v*′. Thus Aglietta is correct in his theoretical claims for such an approximation, even though (as we have argued) the relatively small impact of price–value deviations makes it unnecessary. We also see that Aglietta's own index w′, as derived from his Diagram 1 (Aglietta 1979, p. 91), is a fair proxy for our index v*′: both indicate a rising rate of surplus value (i.e., a falling unit value of labor power) until roughly the mid-1960s, and an apparent change in trend after that. However, it is clear that shorter-run movements are not at all similar. These latter movements are quite important, however, because within his theoretical framework they are supposed to be the "essential determinants of the ups and downs of accumulation" in the "regime of predominantly intensive accumulation" which supposedly characterizes the postwar U.S. economy (p. 203). Given the crucial role played by this index, it is quite surprising that he fails to document the sources and methods involved in its construction. We will not pursue the issue further, except to note that within our approach it is the rate of profit, rather than the rate of surplus value, that drives the long-term patterns of accumulation (see Chapter 7 and Shaikh 1992a).

Gouverneur (1983) presents a rich and subtle treatment of capitalist production and profit. He distinguishes between the production and circulation of use values, between value-producing and surplus-value–producing labors, and between services that are part of commodity production and those that are part of circulation ("commercial and financial business") or social administration ("education, justice, defence, etc."). He is careful to note that unproductive capitalist employees also perform surplus labor (1983, pp. 73–7). Like Eaton, he assumes that the net tax on labor is zero: "we are going to *assume* quite simply that the wage-earner's share in the financing of collective products is *equal* to their share in the consumption of them" (p. 69). At an empirical level, he assumes that the conventional measure of value added represents the Marxian measure of "new revenue created (in monetary terms)," and defines variable capital as the estimated wage bill of productive workers *and* self-employed persons (pp. 93, 243, 246).[43] On this basis, he calculates real (constant-price) rates of "surplus labour" for France, Germany, Belgium, Netherlands, and the United Kingdom. He finds that these rates range from 62% to 98% in

---

[43] Gouverneur calculates the real rate of surplus value $S' = [E/(w/d)] - 1$, where $E$ = net national product per hour of productive labor and $w/d$ = real wage of productive labor. Productive labor is calculated as the hours of all persons (employees and self-employed) in productive and trade sectors (Gouverneur 1983, pp. 92–4, 243–7). The real wage of productive workers is assumed to be equal to the average real wage (p. 250).

1978, and that they generally rise over time. On the whole, his estimates of the rate of surplus value are much smaller than ours would be, largely because his measure of variable capital includes unproductive workers in the productive sectors as well as all workers in the trade sectors. For instance, we calculate the rate of surplus value in the United States in 1978 to be 207% (Table H.1). If we were to instead use Gouverneur's measure of $(NNP - W_p)'/W_p'$, with $W_p' =$ all wages in productive and trading sectors, we would get a rate of surplus value of 81% for the United States – very much the order of magnitude that Gouverneur obtains.[44]

The next set of NIPA-based estimates of the Marxian aggregates comes from Moseley (1982, 1985). Like Shaikh, he is concerned to emphasize the crucial difference between the rate of surplus value and the profit/wage ratio. He notes that his methodology for measuring variable capital "is broadly similar to that in Mage (1963) and Shaikh (1978)" (Moseley 1985, p. 75, n. 1), except that he includes one-half of trade sector wages, and mistakenly includes all agricultural wages and a fraction of the wages of government administrative employees, in variable capital.[45] But like Mage and Shaikh, he too fails to include any portion of the wage equivalent of productive-sector proprietors and partners in variable capital, so that his estimate is about 7% smaller than ours (Moseley 1985, p. 71, table A.1).

Moseley identifies Marxian gross value added with the nonimputed GDP of capitalist businesses. As defined in NIPA, the business sector includes government enterprises (and of course agriculture), but excludes government administration and households and institutions. From this, Moseley further excludes all imputations included in business GDP. By and large this is correct, because it ends up eliminating the fictitious entry for the imputed rental value of owner-occupied housing (the gross housing product) and restores the net interest paid by business to the financial sector (NIPA adds this to intermediate inputs, and subtracts it from value added by creating a matching negative entry for "imputed interest received," as noted in Section 3.2.1 and in Appendix B). But Moseley also subtracts the income of unincorporated enterprises in agriculture,

---

[44] For 1978, NNP = \$2,019.8 billion (Table I.2); $W_p' = $\$1,114.207 billion = all wages (employee compensation plus the wage equivalent of self-employed persons) in the production and wholesale/retail sectors, calculated as total wages minus wages in finance, insurance and real estate, and government administration (Table G.1).

[45] Moseley's estimation of variable capital contains inconsistencies, since he includes all of agricultural wages and part of government wages within productive wages even though his measure of gross value added excludes both agricultural unincorporated enterprises and government administration (Moseley 1985, p. 77: "Variable Capital," n. 11–12; "New Value," n. 1, 10–11). Note that government administration is excluded from the NIPA definition of "business."

construction, and services, presumably on the grounds that they represent noncapitalist flows. This seems improbable to us. Until the invention of the legal form called a "corporation," *all* capitalist enterprises were non-corporate; hence the noncorporate form of these particular enterprises does not render them noncapitalist. Nor is there any compelling reason to believe that most of noncorporate agriculture, construction, and services is nonprofit. In any case, this last set of deductions further reduces Moseley's estimates of net value added by about 6% in 1958.

From the point of view of our present procedure (summarized in Table 6.4), Moseley's procedure leaves out the portion of royalties $RY_{pt}$ which represents ground rent and financial services charges paid by the production and trade sectors,[46] as well as the intermediate inputs $M'_{tt}$ of the trading sectors. On the other hand, it adds in the GDP of the nonimputed royalties sectors (finance, ground rent, and royalties), which partially offsets the first two exclusions. The net effect is that his estimate of Marxian gross value added is some 20% lower than ours in 1958. This is the principal reason for his lower rate of surplus value.

Tonak (1984) focuses on the impact of state taxation and expenditures on the rate of surplus value. As part of his empirical analysis, he extends Shaikh's estimates of the net tax to the whole postwar period in the United States. He also attempts to provide a fairly simple approximation of Marxian value added, from which he subtracts his estimated variable capital to obtain a measure of surplus value. The purpose of this approximation is to trace the impact of the net tax on the U.S. rate of surplus value in the postwar period.

Tonak approximates Marxian gross value added by using the NIPA measure of nonimputed business GDP.[47] This is similar to the approach of Moseley, except that Tonak does not make any further subtractions. Thus in 1958 his measure of value added is about 6% higher than that of Moseley's, though still 12% lower than ours (for the same reasons as in Moseley). As it turns out, his estimate of variable capital is also lower than ours by roughly the same percentage (14%), primarily because (like Mage, Shaikh, and Moseley) he neglects to take account of the productive portion of the wage equivalent.[48] These two underestimates end up

---

[46]  As already noted, Moseley's procedure restores into value added that portion of royalties which represents net interest paid to the financial sector.

[47]  Tonak (1984, p. 110) also makes a small adjustment for surpluses of government-owned liquor stores.

[48]  Tonak defines variable capital as the employee compensation of production workers, estimated as the sum of production worker wages from BLS and the productive fraction of employer contributions to social insurance from NIPA. The estimate of employee compensation is too low, since it should have also included the productive portion of "other labor income." More importantly, Tonak's procedure does not account for the productive portion of the wage equivalent of

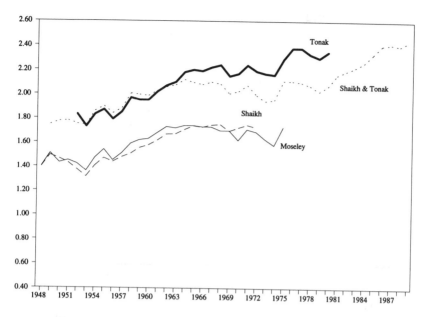

Figure 6.9. Rates of surplus value: Moseley, Shaikh, Tonak, Shaikh and Tonak. *Sources:* Moseley (1985); Shaikh (1978b); Tonak (1984); Shaikh and Tonak, Table H.1.

largely offsetting each other in the determination of the rate of surplus value. Figure 6.9 compares the various estimates to ours, with Shaikh's estimates included as a point of reference for Moseley. It is evident that Moseley's rate of surplus value essentially duplicates the movements in Shaikh's estimates. On the other hand, Tonak's measure approximates ours fairly well up to 1963, but then increasingly overestimates it.

The first systematic investigation of the effects of state taxation and redistribution on the rate of surplus value appears in Shaikh (1978b). He defines the net tax on labor as the difference between actual taxes paid by workers to the state and the social benefit expenditures directed back toward workers by the state. The effective wage of workers is their nominal wage minus any net tax (or plus any "social wage," should the net tax happen to be positive). Because the wages of unproductive workers are part of surplus value, any net tax on their wages amounts to a transfer within surplus value from them to the state. But in the case of productive workers, such a transfer redefines variable capital itself, since the net tax

proprietors and partners, even though his estimate of total labor does include the productive portion of the labor of self-employed persons (Tonak 1984, pp. 161–2, 165–73).

must be subtracted from variable capital and added to surplus value. Shaikh makes detailed estimates of this effect for 1952, 1961, and 1970. Taxes actually paid by workers are assumed to consist of all of social security taxes as well as the estimated labor portion of income taxes and of the small category called "other taxes and nontaxes" (personal property taxes, license and other fees, etc.). The corresponding benefits of workers are estimated as the sum of government expenditures on social security, unemployment benefits, and housing and community development, as well as the workers' share of health, education, utilities, and transportation expenditures. The net tax is calculated as the difference between labor taxes and labor benefits. Shaikh finds that this quantity is positive in all three years sampled. Applying the resulting net tax rate to the wages of productive workers raises his estimated rate of surplus value by 7%–16% (Shaikh 1978b, pp. 35–8).

Tonak (1984) extends this approach to the whole postwar period. Because previously published estimates of the labor proportion of income tax payments were available only for selected years, he develops a good annual proxy for this proportion by taking the share of wages and salaries in personal income.[49] This "labor share" is then used to estimate not only the amounts of income taxes and fees paid by workers, but also the amounts of certain social benefit expenditures (such as health and education) that are deemed to be spent on workers.[50] On the tax side, Tonak corrects for the fact that a portion of property taxes paid by workers shows up under indirect business taxes because NIPA treats homeowners as rental firms renting out their own homes to themselves (a fact we have already encountered in Section 3.1.3), and re-assigns the lottery receipts of the government to the category of workers' taxes (as a kind of voluntary net transfer). On the government expenditure side, he estimates the labor portion of social benefits, both with and without expenditures on public assistance.[51] These factors, plus revisions in the NIPA accounts themselves, account for the differences between Shaikh's and Tonak's estimates of the net tax on labor; but the basic patterns are the same. Tonak too finds that the net tax is generally positive (except in 1975), so that his

---

[49] Tonak shows that his "labor share" is a good proxy for both Kahn's (1966) and Weisskopf's (1984) direct estimates of the portion of income taxes paid by wage and salary earners.

[50] The assumption that expenditures can be allocated to labor in proportion to their share in taxes paid amounts to the assumption that social benefits are accorded to groups in accordance with their "taxable base."

[51] Shaikh omits public assistance on the grounds that it is not a part of labor income of employed workers or their families, and hence does not enter into the net tax on the wages of employed productive workers, i.e. on variable capital (Shaikh 1978b, apx. C.II, p. 60, n. 6).

adjusted rate of surplus value is generally higher than his nominal rate. Our estimates in Section 5.9 are based on Shaikh and Tonak's (forthcoming) extension of these calculations; their effect on the rate of surplus value was shown in Figure 5.24.

Papadimitriou (1988) analyzes the Greek economy from 1958 to 1977, using essentially the same schema as we do; any concrete differences are due to data limitations. Variable capital is defined as the wages of all workers in the production sector, net of estimated corporate officers' salaries (p. 152). Also, the entire real estate sector is treated as a royalties sector, since no consistent evidence could be found on its division between building rents and ground rent (p. 155). Papadimitriou constructs measures of the rate of surplus value, the organic composition of capital, and of the rate of profit. The latter two are adjusted for variations in capacity utilization by means of a Wharton-type measure of the rate of capacity utilization, which he also constructs (p. 157). For the two decades spanned by his data, Papadimitriou finds that the rate of surplus value rises modestly, ranging from 244% in 1958 to a peak of 317% in 1976, and then falls back to 288% in 1977. Over this same interval, however, the organic composition of capital (defined as the ratio of fixed capital to variable capital, divided by the rate of capacity utilization) rises much more sharply, by over 70%. The general rate of profit falls steadily, by roughly 30% overall (p. 153, table 20). Papadimitriou also shows that the rate of surplus value $S^*/V^*$ is about 50% larger, and rises more rapidly, than the broadly defined profit/wage ratio P/W (pp. 170-1). Similarly, the Marxian measure of productivity is almost twice as large as a conventionally defined measure (p. 176); thus, neither conventional measure is a good proxy for its Marxian counterpart. However, he does find that the Marxian measure of GVA* is well approximated by GNP. This implies that, for the Greek economy, the great source of variation between Marxian and orthodox categories arises from the difference between variable capital and all wages.[52]

In an independent study, Tsaliki and Tsoulfidis (1988) provide a similar set of estimates for the Greek economy, also for 1958–73. Working with the 35-sector Greek input output tables in current prices, they estimate the money forms of the rate of surplus value, the value composition of capital, and the rate of profit, all for the nonagricultural economy. They divide the economy into three sectors: nonagricultural production, which includes productive services; circulation, which consists of trade, banking, and housing; and social maintenance, which is public services.

[52] If GVA* $\approx$ GNP, then gross surplus value $S_G^* \approx$ GNP $- V^*$ and $P_G =$ GNP $-$ W, where W = all wages.

Table 6.6. *Rates of surplus value in Greece, selected years*

| | 1958 | 1960 | 1962 | 1964 | 1966 | 1968 | 1970 | 1972 | 1974 | 1976 | 1977 |
|---|---|---|---|---|---|---|---|---|---|---|---|
| Papadimitriou | 2.44 | 2.35 | 2.43 | 2.46 | 2.41 | 2.52 | 2.74 | 2.79 | 2.95 | 3.17 | 2.88 |
| Tsaliki and | | | | | | | | | | | |
| Tsoulfidis | 3.08 | 3.02 | 3.18 | 3.15 | 3.01 | 3.14 | 3.27 | 3.30 | 3.82 | 4.06 | 4.08 |

*Sources:* Papadimitriou (1988, p. 170, table 21); Tsaliki and Tsoulfidis (1988, p. 205, fig. 1).

Variable capital is defined as the wages of nonsupervisory workers in the production sector $(W_p)_p$,[53] and all other wages are unproductive. Surplus value is defined as the sum of produced profit (realized profit plus the change in inventories) in the productive sector, plus the gross output (in the IO sense) of the unproductive sectors. But here they include too much, since only the gross output of the trade sector should be counted (see Section 3.6). For this reason, their estimates of the rate of surplus value are too large, typically about 30% larger than those of Papadimitriou (although the trends of the two are similar). Like Papadimitriou, they adjust their profit rates and value compositions of capital for capacity utilization, which they define as the quadratic trend of real GDP (1988, p. 200, n. 18). In their analysis of the Greek economy, Tsaliki and Tsoulfidis note that it underwent rapid industrialization in the 1960s and 1970s, with correspondingly rapid mechanization of production and high growth rates of capital and investment. But by the late 1970s, these growth rates had collapsed and even turned sharply negative (pp. 189–90). Tsaliki and Tsoulfidis explain this phase change by the rapid mechanization of the economy, which caused the rate of profit to fall, which in turn led to the stagnation of the mass of profit and the collapse of accumulation in the mid-1970s. They find that from 1958 to 1973 the rate of surplus value rises modestly, as do the (utilization-adjusted) wages/capital ratio and the adjusted Marxian and actual rates of profit. But from 1963 to 1977, all these trends are sharply reversed (pp. 205–9, figs. 1–5).

Table 6.6 compares the rate of surplus value estimates of Papadimitriou (1988) and Tsaliki and Tsoulfidis (1988). While the levels are different, the relative movements are quite similar.

### 6.2.3 *Aggregate labor value estimates*

The last set of aggregate estimates in this section is based upon input–output tables. Such tables permit the calculation of both labor value

---

[53] Tsaliki and Tsoulfidis (1988, p. 199) estimate supervisory salaries to be 3% of total wages and salaries.

and money forms of Marxian categories, so that we can directly compare the two. The relations between the two types of calculation were discussed in Section 4.1. It was shown there that if the two sets of calculations are to be *consistent,* in the sense that all money magnitudes would be proportional to the corresponding labor value magnitudes when purchaser prices were proportional to labor values, then the two modes of calculation must be *asymmetric.*

To be more specific, we showed in Section 4.1 that because all commodity bundles in actual input–output tables are valued at producer prices, calculations of unit labor values will actually yield labor-value/producer-price ratios $\lambda_j^*$. Following the procedure developed in Shaikh (1975), these may be calculated as

$$\lambda^* = \mathbf{hp}^* + \lambda^* \cdot \mathbf{app}^*$$

and

$$\lambda^* = \mathbf{hp}^* \cdot (I - \mathbf{app}^*)^{-1},$$

where

$\lambda^* =$ row vector of labor-value/producer-price ratios;
$\lambda_j^* = \lambda_j / p_j$;
$\lambda_j =$ unit labor values; and
$p_j =$ unit producer prices.

In order to derive labor value measures of various commodity bundles, we apply the value/price ratios to the prices (money values) of these same bundles. But since the $\lambda_j^*$s are ratios of labor values to producer prices, we must be careful to apply them only to the producer-price components of these money values. With reference to Figure 4.1, the labor value of productive inputs C is derived by multiplying only the matrix of elements $(\mathbf{M_p})_p$ by the vector of value/producer-price ratios $\lambda^*$, just as the labor value of productive labor power V is derived by multiplying the producer-price component of the consumption basket of production workers $(\mathbf{CONW_p})_p$ by $\lambda^*$. Yet the corresponding money value of constant capital C\*, which is the purchaser price of productive inputs, is equal to their producer price $(\mathbf{M_p})_p$ *plus* the trading margin on these same inputs $(\mathbf{M_p})_t$, while the money form of variable capital V\* is the sum of both the producer-price elements $(\mathbf{CONW_p})_p$ and the corresponding trade margin $(\mathbf{CONW_t})_p$. The asymmetry in the modes of calculation of labor value and money magnitudes is due solely to the fact that input–output tables are cast in terms of producer prices. Their consistency is revealed by the fact that they yield the same result when purchaser prices are proportional to labor values. The revenue side of the money and labor value accounts, shown in Table 4.1 are reproduced here as Table 6.7.

It is a corollary of these results that the procedures which make the calculations of money magnitudes symmetric with labor value ones will yield

Table 6.7. *Money and labor value measure: Revenue side*

| Money value measures | Labor value measures |
|---|---|
| $C^* = M_p = (M_p)_p + (M_t)_p$ | $C = \lambda^* \cdot (M_p)_p$ |
| $VA^* = VA_p + VA_t + RY_p + RY_t + (M_p)_t + (M_t)_t$ | $VA = H_p$ |
| $V^* = W_p = CONW_p = (CONW_p)_p + (CONW_p)_t$ | $V = \lambda^* \cdot (CONW_p)_p$ |
| $S^* = VA - V^*$ | $S = VA - V$ |

incorrect estimates of the former. We shall see that this is precisely the problem with the general methodology proposed by Wolff (1977b, 1987).

The first calculation of the labor value rate of surplus value comes in Okishio's (1959) pathbreaking study for Japan in 1951. Also available in English are subsequent studies by Izumi (1980, 1983) and by Okishio and Nakatani (1985). As noted in the beginning of this chapter, these estimates are part of a long tradition in Japan which began as early as 1924.

Okishio is the first not only to utilize input–output tables, but also to distinguish between productive and unproductive labor (1959, pp. 1–4). His calculations are similar to those we would use, with two notable exceptions. First of all, he treats all services as unproductive, although this may simply be due to the fact that his input–output data combine banking, real estate, and services into one sector (pp. 4, 6). More importantly, his treatment of unproductive activities inflates the measure of productive workers' consumption, which in turn reduces his estimate of the rate of surplus value. Okishio begins by dividing his estimate of an average worker's daily consumption bundle into the commodities $(conw_p)_p$ purchased from productive sectors, and the unproductive expenditures $(conw_p)_u$ comprised of trade margins, rental and royalty payments, and expenditures on services. The correct procedure at this point would have been to multiply the former by $\lambda^*$ to obtain the unit value of labor power $n = V/(V + S) = \lambda^* \cdot (conw_p)_p$, the unit surplus value $(1 - n)$; and the rate of surplus value $e = (1 - n)/n = S/V$. But Okishio argues that – because a portion of the unproductive expenditures goes to support the workers in unproductive industries, whose unproductive expenditures in turn support other unproductive workers, and so on ad infinitum – the total unproductive worker consumption derived from the wages of productive workers should be considered as part of the total consumption of productive workers. Thus he ends up with an expanded measure of the productive consumption vector of productive workers:

$$(\text{conw}_p)'_p = (\text{conw}_p)_p + (\text{conw}_p)'_u = 1.086(\text{conw}_p)_p,$$

where $(\text{conw}_p)'_u = 0.086(\text{conw}_p)_p$.[54]

Okishio's own estimates of the unit value of labor power are $n' = \lambda^* \cdot (\text{conw}_p)'_p = 0.518$, of unit surplus value $(1 - n') = 0.482$, and of the rate of surplus value $e' = (1 - n')/n' = 92.9\%$. He notes that his estimated labor value rate of surplus value "may be considered to be lower than the level which is expected" (1959, p. 8), given the results of previous estimates of the money rate of surplus value. But he argues that the money rates are higher than the value rates because the former reflect large transfers of value from the agricultural sector (pp. 8–9). While this may well be true, his estimate of the value rate is itself biased downward by his treatment of unproductive expenditures. Correcting for this by dividing $n'$ by 1.086 raises the estimated rate of surplus value by about 20%, as shown in Table 6.8 (to follow).

The corrected estimate of $e = 112.8\%$ for 1951 is theoretically and empirically consistent with the subsequent Okishio and Nakatani (1985) estimate of $e = 134.4\%$ in 1980. This latter study also distinguishes between productive and unproductive labor, but counts services as fully productive – probably because the 1980 input–output table does not merge the service sector with the banking and real estate sectors. Productive sectors are defined as all business sectors except trade and finance, insurance, and real estate. Our procedure is quite close to this,[55] except that we count business, legal, household, and miscellaneous professional services as part of the royalties sector. The calculation procedure for unit-value/price ratios, for the value of labor power, and for the rate of surplus value are now identical to the procedures outlined in Section 4.1, with no trace of Okishio's previous treatment of the unproductive expenditures

[54] Let production worker wages $= w_p$. Some of this goes for unproductive expenditures, of which a portion is the equivalent of the wages of the unproductive workers supported out of this revenue. Okishio calculates that 7.9% of $w_p$ goes to directly support unproductive worker wages. Of course, as these workers consume their wages, 7.9% of their wages goes toward unproductive worker wages, etc. Thus the total wage "associated" with productive worker wages $= w_p + (.079)w_p + (.079)(.079)w_p + \cdots = w_p \cdot [1/(1 - .079)] = w_p \cdot (1/.921) = (1.086) \cdot w_p$. Okishio applies the factor 1.086 to the productive components of productive worker consumption to derive his expanded measure of productive worker consumption (Okishio 1959, pp. 6–7, 9–10, table columns 8–9).

[55] Okishio and Nakatani (1985, p. 5) state that unproductive activities are "unnecessary from the technical point of view of the production process." This is an ambiguous statement, due perhaps to the exigencies of translation. Clearly, all nonproduction activities are by definition "technically" unnecessary for production, but this does not imply that they are socially unnecessary. We have tried to emphasize throughout that unproductive activities are not synonymous with unnecessary activities.

of productive workers. Even so, Okishio and Nakatani's estimate of $e = (1 - n)/n = 134.4\%$ in 1980 is substantially lower than Izumi's (1980) estimate of $e = 205\%$ in 1975, which itself is lower than it should be because Izumi overestimates the value of labor power, as we will describe shortly. Okishio and Nakatani (1985, p. 8) once again note that their result is "lower than the expected level," and once again explain this as due to the fact that realized rates of surplus value for manufacturing embody a substantial transfer of value from other sectors. But such a transfer-of-value effect would not explain the discrepancy between their result and that of Izumi, particularly since his measure is for "materials goods producing sectors," in which manufacturing undoubtedly plays a great part. This is an issue that clearly needs further investigation.

Izumi defines productive industries as nonagricultural "materials goods producing sectors" only. Trade, finance and insurance, real estate, communications, and the whole service sector are relegated to the category of "services," all of which are considered unproductive (Izumi 1980, pp. 4–6). Unit labor-value/producer-price ratios are calculated in the manner shown in Section 3.6, and these are applied to the producer-price component of productive worker consumption to derive what we would define as the value of productive labor power V (pp. 9–10). But at this point Izumi (p. 10) stops to ask: "By arguing that the labor of only production workers in the material goods producing sectors creates value, how do we account for the consumption of services by production workers?" His response is to assume that "when production workers consume services, they are, in effect, consuming indirectly the material goods required for the supply of these services" (pp. 10–11). So he adds an estimate of the labor value of the total (direct and indirect) materials requirements $Cm'_u$ of the unproductive (service) sectors[56] to the value of labor power V, yielding an expanded value of labor power $V' = V + Cm'_u$. This is then subtracted from the total hours of productive labor $H_p$ to obtain (reduced) surplus value $S' = H_p - V' = (H_p - V) - Cm'_u = S - Cm'_u$, where $S = $ our definition of surplus value. Note the similarity between the Okishio (1959) and Izumi (1980) treatments of the unproductive expenditures of productive workers: the former adds to productive worker consumption the direct and indirect workers' consumption induced by the unproductive expenditures of production workers, while the latter adds the direct and indirect materials used up in these same unproductive activities. Quite naturally, Izumi also derives estimates of the labor value rate of surplus value which are "consistently lower" than the money rate of surplus value estimated

---

[56] Izumi (1980, pp. 10–12) calculates the direct and indirect materials requirements for the production of materials used by, surplus product used by, and workers' consumption of, the service sector.

Table 6.8. *Estimates of the value rate of surplus value in Japan, selected years*

|                                | 1951  | 1975  | 1980  |
| ------------------------------ | ----- | ----- | ----- |
| Okishio (1959)                 | 0.929 | —     | —     |
| Okishio (corrected)            | 1.128 | —     | —     |
| Izumi (1980, 1983)             | 0.43  | 2.05  | —     |
| Okishio and Nakatani (1985)    | —     | —     | 1.344 |

*Sources:* Okishio (1959, p. 8); Izumi (1980, table 5; 1983, table 1); Okishio and Nakatani (1985, p. 7).

by others at the time (p. 13). He too explains this as arising from transfers of value from agriculture to industry in Japan, which make the realized (money) rate of surplus value in industry much larger than the value rate (1980, p. 13; 1983, p. 13). Izumi (1983) extends his estimates to later years in Japan, as well as to the United States and the Republic of Korea. These later estimates for Japan are somewhat higher and rise rapidly. Table 6.8 compares the estimates of Okishio (1959), Izumi (1980, 1983), and Okishio and Nakatani (1985).

Izumi's discussion is sophisticated and insightful, although we disagree with his treatment of the value of labor power (to which we return shortly). He provides estimates of industry rates of surplus value, and notes that they differ greatly from corresponding profit/wage ratios because the latter reflect transfers of value between industries and between industry and agriculture. This indicates that profit/wage ratios are not reliable indicators of industry rates of exploitation, which invalidates many past studies on the subject (Izumi 1980, pp. 15–21). He also finds that big businesses have higher value rates of surplus value, again in contradiction to studies based on money measures (p. 26).

In a subsequent paper, Izumi extends this same method to a comparison between the rates of surplus value in Japan, the United States, and South Korea (Izumi 1983, p. 10). Here his results are even more at odds with those of other studies, including Amsden's study analyzed earlier in this section, in that he finds value rates to be lowest for South Korea and highest for the United States. This implies that the rate of surplus value rises with the level of development – not only historically, but also cross-sectionally. He explains this by arguing that because previous studies are of money rates of surplus value, they capture not only surplus value produced within the nonagricultural productive sector but also value transferred to that sector. This transfer of surplus value is very large for Japan,

Table 6.9. *Rates of surplus value, Izumi vs. Khanjian*

|  | 1958/1960 | 1963/1965 | 1967 | 1970/1972 | 1975/1977 |
|---|---|---|---|---|---|
| Izumi: South Korea | — | — | — | 0.92 | 1.38 |
| Izumi: Japan | 1.24 | 1.57 | — | 1.70 | 2.05 |
| Izumi: United States | 1.72 | 1.89 | 2.14 | 2.04 | 2.31 |
| Khanjian: United States | 2.64 | 2.64 | 2.88 | 2.87 | 2.91 |
| Izumi/Khanjian | 0.65 | 0.72 | 0.74 | 0.71 | 0.79 |

*Sources:* Izumi (1983, table 1) – for Japan, 1960, 1965, 1970, 1975; for the U.S., 1958, 1961, 1963, 1967, 1972, 1975. Khanjian (1988, table 19) – for the U.S., 1958, 1963, 1967, 1972, 1977.

he argues, coming primarily from Japanese agriculture itself. Hence the finding that the realized rates of surplus value are higher for Japan than for the United States does not necessarily contradict his opposite result for produced rates of surplus value (pp. 14–16). Table 6.9 presents Izumi's estimates of the value rate of surplus value, together with Khanjian's as a reference point for the United States. Note that Izumi's figures for the United States are lower than those of Khanjian by 20%–35% owing to the former's inflation of the measure of the value of labor power (which is discussed further in what follows).

Izumi's inclusion of the value of the unproductive sector's total (direct and indirect) materials requirement $Cm'_u$ within the value of labor power is quite unnecessary. The problem arises because he does not adequately address the content of the category of "services." To the extent that some part of the service sector consists of productive activities, it should be directly included within the productive sector (as we have done). On the other hand, we have shown that unit values calculated from actual input–output tables are really labor-value/producer-price ratios, so that the labor value of a commodity bundle such as the wage basket of workers must be calculated as the product of these value/producer-price ratios and the producer-price component of the commodity bundle. Because such a calculation uses neither the trading margin nor the royalty flows, it seems to exclude unproductive activities simply because they are unproductive. But this is an illusion. Trade margins are excluded because modern input–output tables are constructed in terms of producer prices, which is why the unit-value calculations yield value/producer-price ratios. If these tables were constructed in terms of purchaser prices then they would yield labor-value/purchaser-price ratios, and the corresponding commodity elements in any bundle would also have to be valued at purchaser prices – so that trade margins would now be included. The exclusion of royalties is another matter altogether, since they represent transfers as opposed to purchases. To be consistent with his own sectoral division, Izumi should have used only the producer-price components of the consumption vector.

Izumi's cross-country comparisons are harder to evaluate. His treatment of the value of labor power lowers all of these estimates, but we do not know to what degree this effect operates in Japan and South Korea. He claims that the rate of surplus value is highest in the United States, despite its highest wages and shortest working day, because U.S. average productivity is so much greater. The opposite holds for South Korea, with Japan in the middle (Izumi 1983, p. 14). It is interesting to note that Kalmans (1992, pp. 124–30) also finds that both the money and value rates of surplus value are higher in the United States than in Japan. On the whole, Izumi's study leads him to three conclusions: the rate of exploitation rises over time; it is higher in more advanced capitalist countries; and it grows more rapidly at lower levels of development (p. 19).

Wolff (1977b) provides the first published attempt to construct a general procedure for estimating Marxian categories from input–output tables. He begins with the assumption that all labor is productive, shows how unit labor-value/producer-price ratios may then be calculated, and demonstrates that money and labor value calculations are completely symmetric when all labor is assumed to be productive (pp. 88–9). He then introduces the distinction between productive and unproductive labor, being careful to note that unproductive activities can be quite necessary (p. 97). This leads him to divide the IO tables into productive and unproductive sectors, with the trade sector counted among the latter (pp. 92–4). On this basis, he provides new procedures for the calculation of value/price ratios and labor value magnitudes (pp. 95–6), which are the same as the ones we summarized previously. But in the treatment of money measures, he mistakenly generalizes the previous symmetry between Marxian and IO categories to the situation when some labor is unproductive; this leads him to calculate money magnitudes in an exactly symmetric manner with labor value magnitudes (p. 95).[57] His money measures are therefore inconsistent and incorrect. Khanjian (1988, pp. 122–30) illustrates the problem with a numerical example based on Wolff's procedures. We showed in Section 4.1 that the money rate of surplus value estimated in this manner will typically be larger than the value rate. Indeed, Wolff's estimates of $S^*/V^*$ are generally higher than those of $S/V$ by 4%–8%. Given that the consistent estimates made by Khanjian yield money rates

---

[57] By merging trade with other unproductive sectors, Wolff treats all unproductive flows as types of royalties. It is the absence of a distinct role for trading activities that makes his money accounts symmetric with his labor value accounts; this is also precisely what makes the two inconsistent.

of surplus value that are smaller than the value rates by 7%–9%, we conclude that Wolff's inconsistent procedure creates an upward bias in the estimates of $S^*/V^*$ of about 12%–15% (in years common to both studies).

There are several other features to be noted. Wolff's mapping between Marxian and input–output categories is partial, because it is confined to the use side alone. His estimates of rates of surplus value are somewhat higher than ours, because he subtracts income taxes from his measure of productive worker wages but fails to add in government social benefit expenditures. This reduces his measure of variable capital (1977b, p. 112). He also implicitly treats all income of unincorporated enterprises as property-type income, since he makes no provision for subtracting out the wage equivalent of self-employed persons. Finally, it is striking that Wolff (pp. 87–9, 105, 108–12) repeatedly treats the Marxian measure of the surplus product as synonymous with the Baran–Sweezy concept of "surplus," although he also argues (p. 97) that unproductive activities can be necessary. We will see in Section 6.3 that the two concepts are very different, which becomes quite clear when we compare the respective empirical procedures involved.

Wolff's second attempt comes in his 1987 book, which is a rich and interesting extension of his earlier analysis. It attempts to provide a full double-entry accounting of the relation between Marxian and input–output categories. It shows that U.S. employment and wage bills of unproductive labor rise relative to that of productive labor in the postwar period, and develops a formal two-sector model of their effects on accumulation (1987, pp. x–xi, chaps. 4–5). Productive labor is now distinguished from unproductive labor within the productive sectors (p. 80, n. 19), and only the wages of the former are counted as variable capital. The treatment of taxes on variable capital is also improved, since only the net tax on labor (the difference between taxes paid by labor and social benefit expenditures directed toward labor) is deducted from wages (p. 78). Finally, Wolff distinguishes the rate of exploitation from the rate of surplus value, and introduces a valuable method of calculating the former (p. 84). As in his earlier work, Wolff (1977b, pp. 87–89) identifies the Marxian surplus product with Baran–Sweezy's surplus. But in contradistinction to his earlier position, he now identifies unproductive activities as unnecessary: "the labor power provided by unproductive workers is not essential for the production of any output" (p. 78).

The core of Wolff's book is his double-entry accounting framework. But once again, the framework he presents is symmetric between money and labor value calculations. As in his earlier work, Wolff treats all unproductive activities as part of a general royalties sector (he uses advertising as his illustrative example), which allows him to make the two sets of accounts symmetric – this time on both product and revenue sides (1987, pp. 69–83). Thus his estimates of the money rate of surplus value continue to be inconsistent with his labor value measures. Interestingly enough, even though he devotes a considerable part of his book to the techniques for measuring the rates of exploitation and rates of surplus value, Wolff presents no direct estimates of either (Khanjian 1988, p. 120).[58] However, his estimates of both are implicit in other data that he presents, and we will examine them shortly.

There are two other striking problems with Wolff's measurement of the rate of surplus value. First of all, in his calculation of the net tax on wages, he treats (the producer-price component) of all government expenditures as a benefit to consumers. Expenditures on defense, international affairs, space programs, and so forth are thereby treated as direct consumer benefits (1987, p. 78), which overstates the benefits received by workers. This treatment of government spending is essentially neoclassical, and is greatly at odds with the one we adopt (see Section 5.9). On the other hand, the taxes paid by workers are understated by Wolff because he only counts personal income taxes (net of direct transfers) but not the portion of taxes paid for social security.[59] The end result is that his method overstates the measure of variable capital. Other things being equal, we would expect the estimates of the rate of surplus value in his book to be even lower than those in his 1977 paper. We will see that this is indeed the case.

The second problem arises in Wolff's attempt to distinguish the rate of exploitation from the rate of surplus value. He introduces a valuable method for calculating the average rate of exploitation of all (productive and unproductive) workers (1987, p. 84). Using our notation, let

$H$ = hours of all labor = $H_p + H_u$;

$(\mathbf{conw})_p$ = (column) vector of producer price components of the hourly consumption basket of the average worker;

---

[58] Wolff (1987, p. 133) lists only estimates of "surplus" per worker, which do not provide enough information to calculate his implicit estimates of the money or value rates of surplus value.

[59] Wolff's rationale for leaving in social security taxes is that these taxes function like a pension system and eventually return to working class (1987, p. 62). But he already accounts for the reflux of such payments, since he counts (p. 63) all direct transfers to workers as an addition to wages (actually, as a reduction in net taxes paid). This is inconsistent unless social security taxes are among the taxes deducted from wages.

$$n = \lambda^* \cdot (\mathbf{conw})_p = \text{unit value of labor power (necessary fraction}$$
$$\text{of the average working hour);}$$

$$V_T = n \cdot H = \text{value of all labor power} = V + V_u;$$

and

$$\epsilon = \frac{H - V_T}{V_T} = \frac{1 - n}{n} = \text{the average rate of exploitation,}$$

where
  $V$ = value of productive labor power = $n \cdot H_p$, and
  $V_u$ = value of unproductive labor power = $n \cdot H_u$.

Wolff's measure of the average rate of exploitation $\epsilon$ is the ratio of total surplus labor time $(H - V_T)$ over the value of total labor power $V_T$. This is clearly correct. As shown previously, it depends only on the consumption standards of the average worker for any given vector of value/price ratios. By extension, the rate of exploitation of productive workers would be their surplus labor time $(H_p - V)$ over the value of their labor power $V$. And if, as Wolff assumes, productive workers' consumption standards are the same as those of the average worker,[60] then the rate of exploitation of productive workers would be the same as that of the average worker. But the rate of exploitation of productive workers is the rate of surplus value. So, under Wolff's assumption of equal consumption baskets, the rate of surplus value would equal the average rate of exploitation:

$$e = \frac{H_p - V}{V} = \frac{H_p - (n \cdot H_p)}{n \cdot H_p} = \frac{1 - n}{n}.$$

But Wolff does not define the rate of surplus value in this manner. Instead, he makes a surprising error. He defines surplus value as the excess of all labor time $H$ over only the necessary labor time of productive workers $V$, so that his rate of surplus value becomes (1987, p. 83):

$$e' = \frac{H - V}{V} = \frac{H_p + H_u - V}{V} = \frac{(H_p - V) + H_u}{V} = \frac{S}{V} + \frac{H_u}{V} = e + \frac{H_u}{V}.$$

This measure of the rate of surplus value is peculiar in that the labor time of unproductive labor enters directly into the measure of surplus value. Moreover, all of this unproductive labor time $H_u$ contributes to surplus value, whereas only the excess of productive labor time over the value of productive labor power $V$ enters into surplus value. Thus, in Wolff's formulation, *unproductive labor time is super-productive of surplus value.*

---

[60] Wolff assumes that productive and unproductive workers have the same consumption basket per worker. Compare his formulas for V and V* (Wolff 1987, pp. 82–4).

Note that if unproductive labor time enters into surplus value in this manner, then an increase in the relative level of unproductive employment can raise the rate of surplus value! Indeed, noting that $H = H_p + H_u$ and $V_T/V = H/H_p$, we can rewrite the expression for e' as follows:

$$e' = \frac{H-V}{V} = \frac{H}{V} - 1 = \frac{H}{V_T}\frac{V_T}{V} - 1 = (1+\epsilon)\frac{H}{H_p} - 1 = (1+\epsilon)\frac{H}{H-H_u} - 1$$

$$= \frac{1+\epsilon}{1-H_u/H} - 1.$$

Wolff derives the very same expression for the relation between his measure of the rate of surplus value e' and the average rate of exploitation $\epsilon$, noting in passing that the "rate of surplus value can thus increase from . . . an increase in the ratio of unproductive to productive employment" (1987, p. 85). He does not comment on this rather extraordinary conclusion.

It is possible to extract Wolff's labor value estimates of the average rate of exploitation $\epsilon$, which is really the rate of surplus value e as we would define it (since he calculates $\epsilon$ by assuming that unproductive workers consume the same basket as productive workers). He presents data for $1-n$, from which we can calculate $\epsilon = (1-n)/n$, which is the same as $e = S/V$ as we would define it.[61]

Finally, Khanjian (1989) provides a set of consistent estimates of labor value and money rates of surplus value in the United States, based on the procedures developed in Shaikh (1975). As discussed in Section 4.1, Khanjian's data clearly demonstrate that price–value deviations are small in their effects on the measurement of the rate of surplus value: S/V differs from S*/V* by only 6%–9%, and the trends of the two are virtually identical. This immediately implies that money value estimates of the rate of surplus value are generally excellent proxies for the underlying labor value rates. But Khanjian's numerical estimates are substantially larger than ours, because he makes no adjustment for the wage equivalent of proprietors and partners in the noncorporate sector. Such an adjustment (which we do incorporate) reduces the measure of surplus value and raises the measure of variable capital. This is also why our estimates are lower than those in Wolff, other things being equal.

Table 6.10 compares the implicit estimates of the value rate of surplus value in Wolff (1987) to his own earlier estimates (1977b, p. 103, table 3), to those in Khanjian (1989, table 19), and to our money rate of surplus

---

[61] Wolff's term $S*/N = [N - (N \cdot \lambda_m)]/N$ is what we call $1-n$, since $\lambda_m$ is the unit value of the average labor power. This appears in Wolff (1987, p. 133, table 6.6, line 4).

Table 6.10. *Rates of surplus value, Wolff vs. others*

|                        | 1947 | 1958 | 1963 | 1967 | 1972 | 1977 |
|------------------------|------|------|------|------|------|------|
| Wolff (1987): S/V      | 2.11 | 2.60 | 2.72 | 2.72 | 2.37 | 2.27 |
| Wolff (1977): S/V      | 2.25 | 2.67 | 2.80 | 3.07 | —    | —    |
| Khanjian (1988): S/V   | —    | 2.64 | 2.64 | 2.88 | 2.87 | 2.91 |
| Our estimates: S*/V*   | —    | 2.00 | 2.07 | 2.10 | 1.99 | 2.10 |

*Sources:* For Wolff (1987), $1 - n$ is from table 6.6, line 4, p. 133. For Wolff (1977), $\epsilon = (1 - n)/n$ is from table 3, line 1, p. 103. For Khanjian (1989), S/V is from table 19. For our estimates, S*/V* is from Appendix H.

value (Appendix H). Wolff's later estimates are smaller than his earlier ones, most probably because the later estimates add a significant portion of government expenditures to the measure of variable capital. We noted earlier that Wolff adds too much here, since he counts even defense, international affairs, and the space program among his labor benefits. This is likely to inflate his estimate of V most of all during the Vietnam era, which is probably why his estimate of the rate of surplus value declines between 1967 and 1977. The other measures have already been discussed.

## 6.3 Studies based on the distinction between necessary and unnecessary labor (economic "surplus")

The Marxian distinction between productive and unproductive labor is rooted in the concept of surplus value. Capitalistically employed production labor is productive of surplus value. All other labor is unproductive of surplus value, even though it may be engaged in petty commodity production, in production for direct use, or in various nonproduction activities such as distribution and social maintenance. The dividing line is made at surplus value simply because this is the critical fuel for capitalist accumulation. Profit can also be generated by transfers of value or use value between the circuit of capital and other capitalist and noncapitalist circuits. Nonetheless, the production of surplus value is the primary source of profit in the capitalist mode of production.

We have taken great pains to emphasize that labor which is unproductive of surplus value is not unnecessary labor. Indeed, it is only in neoclassical economics that the concept of production is subsumed under the concept of necessity, with the market as the ultimate arbiter. Since neoclassical approaches deem as "productive" all activity that earns (or could earn) a remuneration on the market, only the nonmarket sphere can possibly harbor "unproductive" (i.e. unnecessary) activities. The state, the household, and the noncapitalist community become prime suspects.

Baran (1957) quite rightly rejects this tradition of market worship. Capitalism creates and sustains many unnecessary activities, he insists, which absorb a significant portion of the economic surplus. Baran (p. 9) defines the surplus as "the difference between society's actual current output and its actual current consumption," but Baran and Sweezy (1966, pp. 9, 112) later refine it to be the difference between "total social output [and] the total socially necessary costs of producing it." Under monopoly capitalism, they argue, surplus tends to grow faster than the demand for it, so that it becomes increasingly necessary to divert the surplus into wasteful sales efforts, state and military expenditures, unnecessary expenditures generated by planned obsolescence, and into external outlets in the Third World (p. 341). In a more positive vein, the economic surplus can be viewed as a potential fund for socially desirable uses. Lippit (1985, p. 10) argues that the economic surplus, which is that part of national output over and above "the essential consumption needs, public as well as private, of all of its citizens," forms a "kind of discretionary fund that the society may choose to utilize in a variety of ways." Stanfield (1973, p. 3) quotes Weisskopf to the effect that the economic surplus is "that part of its productive capacity that a society has some potential freedom to allocate among competing alternatives."

In most discussions of the surplus, the NIPA measure of NNP is taken to be an adequate measure of output. The measure of surplus therefore depends on the definition of the "socially necessary costs" of producing this output. And here the market is no guide, since it clearly sustains hugely wasteful expenditures. Baran and Sweezy therefore turn to some concept of a "rational allocation" of resources as a guide to social necessity. Within this rubric, unproductive labor becomes that labor for which "the demand would be absent in a rationally ordered society" (Baran 1957, pp. 5, 32). Unproductive labor is then socially unnecessary labor.

In the appendix to Baran and Sweezy's book, Phillips provides the first estimates of economic surplus. He defines this as the sum of property income, business waste, and all government expenditures (Baran and Sweezy 1966, pp. 369–70). This is a rather eclectic definition, since the first two items are from the revenue side of NIPA accounts while the third is from the use side. Properly speaking, he should have included government tax revenues rather than government expenditures. Phillips also mentions that the measure of economic surplus also ought to contain an estimate of that portion of "output which is foregone owing to the existence of unemployment" (p. 370), but he does not attempt this himself. In any case, property-type income is defined as the sum of after-tax corporate and noncorporate profits,[62] nonimputed rental payments by business, business net interest payments, and corporate officers' salaries. Business waste is estimated as the sum of costs of sales and distribution, and the costs of finance, real estate, and legal services. Government expenditures are taken directly from national accounts, net of intragovernment transfers (pp. 370–84).

Phillips's economic surplus is essentially the sum of after-tax property-type income, the wage costs of unproductive activities, all taxes, plus the government deficit (since government expenditures equal taxes plus the deficit). In years where the deficit is small, as in the postwar years covered by his data, this is basically the same as (NIPA) value added minus the wages of production workers. Thus Phillips's measure of economic surplus is conceptually similar to that of surplus value. We will see in Figure 6.10 (to follow) that the two are quite close, empirically.

Stanfield (1973) tackles the estimation of the surplus in a much more consistent manner. He approaches it from the use side, as indicated in Table 6.11. He also incorporates Phillips's suggestion that the output foregone due to unemployment ought to be taken into account. Thus he defines potential surplus as potential (full employment) output minus the sum of personal and social essential consumption, whereas actual surplus is actual output minus personal and social essential consumption (Stanfield 1973, pp. 1, 81). He notes that Phillips's estimates are somewhat inconsistent, since they inexplicably "relegate all property incomes and all government expenditures to the economic surplus," thus implicitly assuming that neither supports any necessary expenditures. His own approach assumes that property-type income is partially expended on essential capitalist consumption, just as a part of government expenditure represents essential public consumption (p. 86). By itself, this makes his measure of economic surplus smaller than that of Phillips. On the other hand, his measure of the essential consumption of workers is much smaller than their actual consumption, which tends to expand his measure of economic surplus. We will see that the net effect is to make his measure somewhat smaller than Phillips's.

One of the peculiarities of Stanfield's methodology is that he measures all aggregates in terms of their cost of production, not at their market

---

[62] After-tax noncorporate profits are derived by multiplying unincorporated income by the corporate fraction of after-tax nonlabor income in total income originating in corporations. This estimated after-tax noncorporate nonlabor income is reduced by the net interest payments of unincorporated enterprises (which show up under the net interest component of property-type income) to yield noncorporate profits (Baran and Sweezy 1966, pp. 371–2). Total business profits are then adjusted to take account of what Phillips argues is a systematic overstatement of depreciation charges in official accounts (pp. 372–8).

Table 6.11. *Real surplus value and economic surplus*

| Year | S* | Economic surplus | | (Economic surplus)/S* | |
|------|-----|------------|----------|-----------|----------|
| | | Stanfield[a] | Phillips[b] | Stanfield | Phillips |
| 1948 | 635.62 | 544.09 | 528.23 | 0.86 | 0.83 |
| 1949 | 632.69 | 525.49 | 568.36 | 0.83 | 0.90 |
| 1950 | 691.58 | 589.53 | 591.00 | 0.85 | 0.85 |
| 1951 | 750.05 | 669.72 | 664.79 | 0.89 | 0.89 |
| 1952 | 762.72 | 667.29 | 722.43 | 0.87 | 0.95 |
| 1953 | 789.52 | 696.75 | 747.35 | 0.88 | 0.95 |
| 1954 | 791.38 | 627.16 | 722.24 | 0.79 | 0.91 |
| 1955 | 839.91 | 689.53 | 754.98 | 0.82 | 0.90 |
| 1956 | 842.84 | 689.52 | 765.34 | 0.82 | 0.91 |
| 1957 | 859.38 | 691.01 | 798.93 | 0.80 | 0.93 |
| 1958 | 861.74 | 644.30 | 824.07 | 0.75 | 0.96 |
| 1959 | 914.62 | 708.63 | 869.12 | 0.77 | 0.95 |
| 1960 | 925.67 | 710.76 | 880.34 | 0.77 | 0.95 |
| 1961 | 948.89 | 706.58 | 926.67 | 0.74 | 0.98 |
| 1962 | 1002.00 | 801.31 | 975.53 | 0.80 | 0.97 |
| 1963 | 1040.33 | 808.88 | 1011.50 | 0.78 | 0.97 |
| 1964 | 1106.07 | 871.36 | | 0.79 | |
| 1965 | 1166.70 | 952.87 | | 0.82 | |
| 1966 | 1228.54 | 1060.48 | | 0.86 | |
| 1967 | 1263.85 | 1111.85 | | 0.88 | |
| 1968 | 1307.47 | 1158.84 | | 0.89 | |
| 1969 | 1314.44 | 1189.21 | | 0.90 | |
| 1970 | 1302.53 | 1163.83 | | 0.89 | |

[a] Stanfield's real surplus measure is based on his real actual surplus (1973, p. 81, table 7-6) and the "ratio of surplus elements in market prices to GNP" (called s/p; p. 58, table 5-14). Since his real actual economic surplus was calculated at cost prices, the following formula, after converting 1958 dollars to 1982 dollars, was used in order to translate his surplus figures to the ones in market prices: [surplus in market prices] = [surplus in cost prices] $\times [1/\{1-(s/p)\}]$.
[b] Phillips's real surplus figures are based on his current-dollar estimates (Baran and Sweezy 1966, p. 389, table 22); they are converted to real figures by using GNP deflators (1982 = 100).

prices. This is accomplished by estimating the proportion of "surplus elements" (items that are not costs of production, such as business taxes, profits, net interest, net rents, and the wage costs of nonproduction sectors) in total price, and then using this to restate market-price measures in production-cost terms.[63] For instance, the market price of potential

---

[63] From a Marxian point of view, Stanfield is valuing all commodities at their cost of production $c + v$.

GNP is derived by adjusting actual GNP for fluctuations in capacity utilization, which is then reduced to its production-cost equivalent (1973, pp. 78–81). The market price of total essential consumption is similarly reduced.[64] It consists of the sum of two items: personal essential consumption, defined as the expenditure necessary to maintain the whole population at the "modest but adequate" level represented by the "City Workers' Family Budget" which he takes from the BLS (1973, pp. 13, 27–35); and social essential consumption, defined as the sum of social overhead consumption (government administration, international affairs, civilian safety, sanitation, postal, etc.), some essential fraction of health, education, transportation and public utilities (Stanfield 1973, pp. 39–40), and the replacement-cost depreciation on the capital stock (pp. 22–4, 46).[65]

Stanfield's methodology produces measures of constant-dollar potential and actual economic surplus, valued at production costs. In order to facilitate comparisons, we have restated the constant-dollar actual economic surplus in market prices by reversing Stanfield's own procedure. Table 6.11 and Figures 6.10 and 6.11 compare the economic surplus measures from Phillips and Stanfield with our measure of surplus value, all in constant (1982) dollars. Figure 6.11 compares our real rate of surplus value with what might be called the real rate of economic surplus, defined as the ratio of economic surplus to essential consumption, in Stanfield's data. As anticipated, Phillips's measure of economic surplus is much closer to surplus value than is Stanfield's. Moreover, the Stanfield rate of economic surplus not only is half of the rate of surplus value, but also behaves quite differently over time.

Finally, Erdos (1970) provides an eclectic variation on these themes. His measure is a kind of "political" economic surplus, even though he labels it as (redefined) surplus value. His stated intention is to modernize Marxian categories by making them "correspond as exactly as possible to the empirical facts of our days." But what he actually does is conflate the rate of surplus value with the rate of exploitation, and the concept of exploitation with the concept of oppression. From our point of view, Marxian surplus value is the surplus labor time of productive workers, because only they produce a capitalist surplus product. Some of this goes to support unproductive workers. Both sets of workers are exploited, in the

---

[64] In actual fact, Stanfield (1973) uses different adjustment factors for total output and total essential consumption. Compare his current-dollar GNP and adjusted GNP (table 7-4) with unadjusted and adjusted total essential consumption (tables 5-10 and 5-15).

[65] Stanfield notes that this type of depreciation should apply only to the essential capital stock, but does not attempt to distinguish this portion from total depreciation (1973, p. 24).

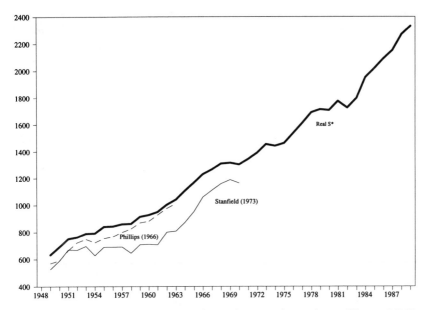

Figure 6.10. Real surplus value and economic surplus (millions of 1982 dollars). *Source:* Table 6.10.

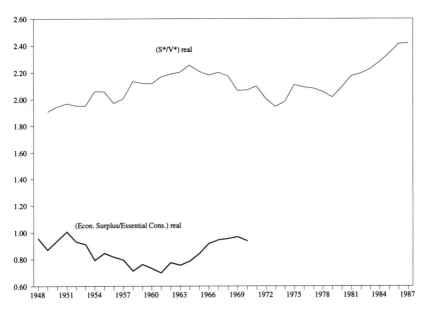

Figure 6.11. Real rates of surplus value and economic surplus. *Sources:* Stanfield (1973); Table 6.10.

specific sense that their surplus labor time is extracted under a system in which they are subordinate to the rule of the capitalist class. The degree of their exploitation is dependent on the rate of surplus labor, not on the uses to which this surplus labor is put by their employers (cf. Shaikh 1986; see also Section 2.2).

Erdos defines socially necessary costs as that part of "new value" which is not used by the oppressing class or the oppressive part of the state apparatus. This covers not only production activities, but also trade and the "socially useful" portion of government activities. The rest of new value is the portion of the product implicated in the oppression of workers (Erdos 1970, pp. 371–3). One can see the family resemblance between this partition and that originally proposed by Baran. At the empirical level, Erdos defines new value as the (NIPA) value added in production and trade, but not in services. Necessary costs are defined as the wages of production and trade workers, net of taxes and transfers, plus one-third of government wages as an estimate of the socially useful portion of government expenditures. The political surplus, which he calls "surplus value," is the rest of new value. So defined, his measure of what might be called the rate of political surplus in the United States is even smaller than Stanfield's rate of economic surplus: 53.1% in 1929, and 46.2% in 1964 (Erdos 1970, p. 384).

It should be evident that the notion of economic surplus is very different from that of surplus value. Surplus value is the excess of the total capitalist product over the actual capitalist costs of its production. It is specific to the capitalist mode of production, and is the foundation for capitalist profitability. It supports investment and capitalist consumption, as well as various forms of social consumption arising from circulation and state activities. Whether or not these activities might be necessary under some "rationally ordered" society, they are largely necessary in capitalist society. The economic surplus, on the other hand, is the difference between the total product and some "normative judgement of what costs are socially necessary" (Bottomore 1983, p. 340). In principle, this is a concept applicable to any mode of production. But this is precisely its weakness, because it abstracts from the historically specific forces that generate not only the output but also the various uses of this output. To treat the economic surplus as a "kind of discretionary fund" which may be "allocated among competing alternatives" (Lippit 1985, p. 10; Stanfield 1973, p. 3) is to imagine that any significant re-allocation can be accomplished without threatening the system which generates this surplus. If it is recognized that a social revolution is required for a new kind of discretionary use, then the surplus itself, not just its current uses, will be significantly altered. Instead of an ahistorical concept such as the economic surplus, we need concepts of the surplus product specific to each mode of production under study. Surplus value is just such a concept for the capitalist mode of production.[66]

---

[66] A concrete social formation will generally encompass some noncapitalist activities. Their products, and any surplus products, must be addressed separately, even if in the end they interact with or enter into the circuit of capital (see Section 2.4).

# 7

## Summary and conclusions

National economic accounts provide the empirical foundation for economic theory and policy. And at the core of all national accounts lie the production accounts, for it is the production of new wealth which has been, at least so far, the real foundation of modern economic success.

The classical economists were deeply concerned with the factors that accounted for the economic success or failure of nations. Their analysis of the structure of production led them to the recognition that not all activities resulted in a product. On the contrary, they classified certain activities – such as wholesale/retail trade, military and police, and administration – as forms of social consumption rather than of production. It followed from this that one had to distinguish between production and nonproduction labor. As we have emphasized throughout, such a distinction does not imply that one of the forms of labor is more necessary, more meritorious, or more politically correct. Nor, in spite of Adam Smith, does it imply that services cannot be production activities. The basic distinction arises from the difference between outcome and output; not all outcomes are outputs. We noted in Chapters 1 and 2 that one way to formalize the difference would be in terms of a vector of characteristics associated with each commodity, some of which would affect its status as an object of social use, and others its status as an object of distribution, et cetera. This would be an adaptation of the approach proposed by Lancaster (1968) within the structure of neoclassical economics. Needless to say, our approach would still differ in substance from a neoclassical one.

To the extent that nonproduction outcomes require the performance of labor and the consumption of use values, they are, like personal consumption itself, forms of social consumption. Marx takes the argument even further. To him, the growth of capitalist economies is fueled by profit. Profit in turn depends on two sources, profit on alienation and surplus value, and the latter is the dominant one in industrial capitalism. For this reason, he refined and made concrete the distinction between production and nonproduction activities. Moreover, within each type of labor, he distinguished sharply between noncapitalist and capitalist activities. It is only capitalist production labor which is surplus-value–producing labor, productive labor for capital. Other labors are then unproductive of surplus value, though they may be productive of value or productive of direct-use value (if they are production labors), or forms of social consumption (if they are nonproduction labors).

## 7.1 Surplus value, profit, and growth

The classical economists recognized that the portion of the net product which is plowed back into production is crucial in determining the rate of growth of the system. It follows that the division of the net product between consumption and investment is of the utmost importance. Once one recognizes that some labor activities are really forms of social consumption, it becomes evident that not all increases in employment have the same effects on growth. Increases in any type of labor give rise to an increased demand for inputs to be used alongside of it and an increased demand for consumption goods to be consumed by it. However, whereas an increase in production labor also gives rise to an increased total product, which recovers not only a portion equivalent to the increased demand for materials and wage goods but also a surplus product over and above that, an increase in nonproduction labor has no such effect.

Malthus saw in this a saving grace. On the assumption that capitalism suffered from a chronic lack of demand, the fact that nonproduction employment generated demand without generating supply implied that an increase in such employment might help "pump up" the system. Both Keynesian and Kaleckian economics picked up this theme, albeit on a different footing (Shaikh 1980). Ricardo, on the other hand, did not subscribe to the notion of a chronic demand deficiency. To him, increases in nonproduction activities tended to diminish the proportion of the surplus product available for investment, and hence to decrease the rate of growth (Coontz 1965, p. 35).

Marx does not fall into either camp. Like Malthus, Keynes, and Kalecki, Marx insists that capitalism is always capable of increasing the level of its output, and hence the mass of surplus value, in the face of an increase in effective demand. But like Ricardo, Marx conducts his analysis in terms of a growing economy. Moreover, within his framework, if the proportion of unproductive employment happens to rise relative to productive employment, then – even though the short-term effect can be stimulatory – the long-term effect on the rate of profit and rate of growth can be deleterious.[1]

The problem can be posed much more precisely by elaborating upon the division of surplus value, and upon the corresponding allocation of the surplus product. To illustrate the issues involved, it is sufficient to consider the simple case in which there are only production, trade, and government activities (as in Section 3.2.B, Table 3.10). Then[2]

$$S^* = P_n + T + E_u = \text{surplus value} \tag{1}$$

and

$$SP^* = I_n + CONC + G + E_u$$
$$= \text{value of surplus product (equal in magnitude to surplus value } S^*),$$

$$\tag{2}$$

where

$P_n$ = profit-type income, net of profit and indirect business taxes;
$T = T_p + IBT$ = profit taxes + indirect business taxes;
$I_n$ = net investment
$CONC$ = capitalist consumption;
$W_t$ = wages of the trade sector = $CONW_t$
= consumption of trade workers;
$M_t$ = materials costs of the trade sector
= materials use in the trade sector;
$E_u = M_t + W_t$ = expenses of the unproductive sector (trade)
= $U_t + CONW_t$ = inputs and wage goods absorbed by the unproductive sector (trade); and
$G$ = government nonproduction use of products and (via government employment) of wage goods.

Equation (1) tells us that aggregate profit on production is that portion of surplus value which remains after taxes and unproductive expenses are deducted, while equation (2) tells us that aggregate investment is that portion of the surplus product which is not absorbed by capitalist personal consumption, government nonproduction activities, and capitalist nonproduction activities.

---

[1] Shaikh (1989) develops a general Marxian model of effective demand in a growth context. He shows that a rise in the exogenously given average propensity to consume c stimulates a jump in the level of production (this is the short-term demand effect of a relative rise in consumption), while it also sets into motion a decline in the growth rate (this is the long-term growth effect of a decline in the savings rate).

[2] From Table 3.8, $S^* = P + IBT + (W_t + M_t)$, where $P$ = profits net of indirect business tax IBT but gross of direct profit taxes. If we define the latter as $T_p$, profits net of that as $P_n$, $T = T_p + IBT$, and $E_u = (W_t + M_t)$, then $S^* = P_n + T_p + E_u$.

If we now divide equation (1) through by the utilized stock of capital $K^* \cdot u$, we find that the NIPA-based capacity utilization–adjusted net rate of profit $r'_n$ equals the similarly adjusted Marxian rate of profit $r^{*'}$ multiplied by the proportion of surplus value not going to business taxes (t) and to unproductive expenses ($e_u$):

$$r'_n = (1 - t - e_u)r^* = (1 - b)r^{*'}, \tag{3}$$

where

$r^{*'} = S^*/(K^* \cdot u)$;
$r'_n = P_n/(K^* \cdot u)$;
$t = T/S^*$;
$e_u = E_u/S^*$; and
$b = t + e_u$.

Marx and the classical economists were concerned with the long-run tendencies of the system under conditions of normal accumulation (i.e., when capacity utilization fluctuated around a normal level).[3] At normal capacity utilization, the Marxian rate of profit is determined by the rate of surplus value and the value composition of capital. Thus the causation in equation (3) runs from $r^{*'}$ to $r'_n$. It follows that the observed net rate of profit $r'_n$ will fall relative to the Marxian general rate $r^{*'}$ when a greater proportion of surplus value is absorbed in business taxes or unproductive expenses. For this reason we label b the *social burden rate*.[4]

If we divide equation (2) through by $K^*$ and note that $SP^* = S^*$, we find that the actual rate of accumulation capital $g_K = I_n/K^*$ equals the Marxian rate of profit multiplied by the product of the social savings rate $s'$ ($= 1 - c'$) and the capacity utilization rate u. Although $g_K$ is a ratio of current-dollar values, it may also be thought of as a ratio of constant-dollar values in which both $I_n$ and $K^*$ are deflated by the same price index. Note that the social consumption rate $c'$ represents the proportion of the surplus product which goes to capitalist personal consumption and unproductive (government- and trade-sector) use. We then find that the observed rate of accumulation will fall relative to the Marxian profit rate when a greater portion of surplus product is absorbed in personal or social consumption. We have:

$$g_K = (1 - c_c - gov - e_u)(S^*/K^*) = (1 - c') \cdot u \cdot r^{*'} = s' \cdot u \cdot r^{*'}, \tag{4}$$

---

[3] The path of accumulation at normal capacity utilization is similar to what Harrod (1939, p. 16) calls the "warranted" path. In Marx, this is perfectly consistent with a persistent level of unemployment (see e.g. Goodwin 1967).

[4] We can also combine equations (1) and (2) to obtain the familiar Kaleckian relation $P_n = CONC + I_n + (G - T)$, in which unproductive expenses $E_u$ appear to have no role. But this is an illusion. The relation of $(P_n + T)$ to $S^*$, and of $(CONC + I_n + G)$ to $SP^*$, is mediated precisely by $E_u$.

where

$$c_c = CONC/S^*;$$
$$gov = G/S^*;$$
$$c' = c_c + gov + e_u; \text{ and}$$
$$s' = 1 - c'.$$

The general rate of profit $r^{*\prime}$ is the common (and principal) determinant of both $r'_n$ and $g_K$. We saw in Section 5.5 that we can decompose its movements into those arising from the rate of surplus value $S^*/V^*$ and the value composition of capital $C^*_f/V^*$ (adjusted for variations in capacity utilization so as to bring out the structural, as opposed to cyclical, pattern). We then found that the data partition into two major phases. From 1948 to 1980, the rate of surplus value rises modestly by roughly 22%, while the adjusted value composition rises by over 77% (and the adjusted materialized composition $C^*_f/(V^* + S^*)$ rises by over 56%). The rising value composition overwhelms the rising rate of surplus value, so that the adjusted Marxian rate of profit falls by almost a third over this period. This is striking empirical support for Marx's theory of falling rate of profit. More detailed analysis is presented in Shaikh (1987, 1992b).

The second period, from 1980 to 1989, spans the Reagan-Bush era, during which the capitalist class and the state collaborated in attacking workers' living standards and labor conditions. The rise in the rate of surplus accelerates in this period, more than doubling its trend rate. Moreover, the growth in the value and materialized compositions decelerate in this period, because the low rate of profit and slow accumulation inhibit the adoption of new, more capital-intensive technologies. The overall effect is to modestly reverse the fall in the general rate of profit, recovering about 8% of its initial value (see Table 5.8 and Figures 5.16 and 5.17).

We saw previously that the ratio of unproductive activities rises sharply over the postwar period (Section 5.3, Figure 5.11). Figure 7.1 shows the corresponding rise of 16% in the social burden rate over the postwar period. Figure 7.2 shows that, as a result, the (net of profit taxes) NIPA-based rate of profit $r'_n$ falls substantially faster than the Marxian rate:[5] while the Marxian rate falls by 25%, the NIPA-based rate falls by 39%.

Figure 7.1 also plots the path of the social consumption rate $c'$, the social savings rate $s' = 1 - c'$, and the adjusted savings rate $s' \cdot u$. We see that $c'$, $s'$, and even $s' \cdot u$ are quite stable over the postwar period. Thus, as Figure 7.2 shows, the actual rate of accumulation follows the path of the

---

[5] From equation (3), $r_n/r^* = P/S^* = (1 - b)$. Because the actual correspondence between surplus value and profit-type income is more complex than that illustrated in equation (1) (see Section 3.6, Table 3.12), the actual data for $P_n$ are derived by subtracting total employee compensation, profit taxes, and indirect business taxes from NNP, as shown in Table H.1.

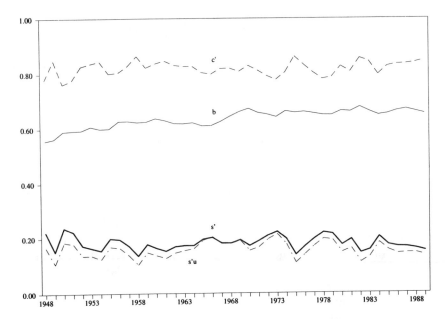

Figure 7.1. Social burden, consumption, and savings rates.
*Note:* b = 1 − (P_n/S*), c′ = 1 − (I_n*/S*), s′ = 1 − c′. *Source:* Table 7.1.

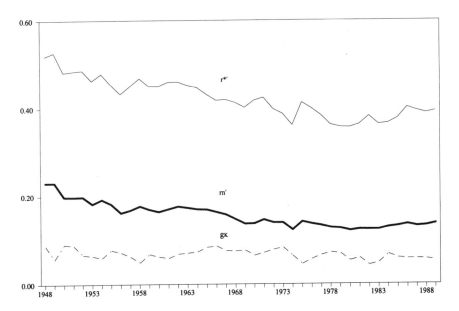

Figure 7.2. Profit and growth rates.
*Note:* r*′ = S*/K*u, r_n′ = P_n/K*u, g_K = I_n*/K*. *Source:* Table 7.1.

Marxian general rate of profit.[6] (Data for Figures 7.1 and 7.2 are from Table 7.1.) This serves to emphasize that the social savings rate s' is dependent not merely on the decisions of firm and households to save, as orthodox theory would have it, but also on the decisions of firms and governments to engage in nonproduction activities.

## 7.2 Marxian and conventional national accounts

The distinction between productive and unproductive labor has other implications as well. We saw in Chapter 2 that the standard of living of workers can be decomposed into a valorized portion, comprised of commodities, and a nonvalorized portion, comprised of direct-use values. Marx focuses on the former, since it is the portion that has to be purchased by workers which in turn regulates the price capitalists must pay for labor power. It is for this reason that Marx defines the value of labor power as the value of the commodities that enter into the workers' standard of living. But the nonvalorized portion of workers' standard of living is the product of some combination of household labor, village labor, and farm labor. And although this portion is of no direct moment to capitalists, since they do not have to pay for it, it can nonetheless be crucial to workers. Thus it is entirely possible for workers to become more expensive to capitalists (if the value of their valorized portion rises) while still becoming poorer overall (if their overall standard of living falls); see Section 2.2.

The classical and Marxian frameworks make a distinction between profit arising from the production of a capitalistic surplus (profit on surplus value) and that arising from transfers of wealth and value (profit on alienation); aggregate profit encompasses both (Section 2.4). A striking example of this is provided in Chapter 3, where it is shown that aggregate profit-type income can exceed aggregate surplus value even within the confines of a single capitalist economy (Section 3.2.2). Something of this sort is also involved in the famous puzzles generated by the so-called transformation problem (Shaikh 1984, 1992). A lesson here is that even unproductive labor may increase aggregate profit (but not aggregate value), to the extent that it is able to effect a transfer into the circuit of capital from a noncapital circuit or noncapitalist sphere of activity.

In all of these instances, the central point has been that it is insufficient to view unproductive labor merely as labor which is unproductive of surplus value. Each type of unproductive labor has its own effects and place in reproduction. Indeed, it is precisely this recognition which orthodox economics turns into a justification for the notion that all necessary labor

---

[6] From equation (4), $g_K/r^* = I/S^* = 1 - c' = s'$.

Table 7.1. *Profit, accumulation, social savings, and burden rates*

| Sources | Variables | 1948 | 1949 | 1950 | 1951 | 1952 | 1953 | 1954 | 1955 | 1956 | 1957 |
|---|---|---|---|---|---|---|---|---|---|---|---|
| Table 5.8 | $b = 1 - (P_n/S^*)$ = social burden rate | 0.56 | 0.56 | 0.59 | 0.59 | 0.59 | 0.61 | 0.60 | 0.60 | 0.63 | 0.63 |
| | $P_n$ = profit-type income net of all taxes | 66.51 | 64.90 | 67.78 | 76.71 | 79.05 | 80.28 | 83.43 | 91.29 | 88.36 | 93.24 |
| | $S^*$ | 149.94 | 148.64 | 165.26 | 188.25 | 194.51 | 204.52 | 208.20 | 228.55 | 236.97 | 250.25 |
| Table D.1 | $c' = 1 - (I^*_n/SP^*)$ = social consumption rate | 0.78 | 0.85 | 0.76 | 0.78 | 0.83 | 0.84 | 0.84 | 0.80 | 0.80 | 0.83 |
| | $I^*_n = IG^* - D'_p - D'_{ry} - D'_{tt}$ = net investment | 33.24 | 22.57 | 39.28 | 41.98 | 33.65 | 33.47 | 32.29 | 45.36 | 46.27 | 42.87 |
| | $SP^*$ | 149.91 | 148.58 | 165.09 | 188.26 | 194.79 | 204.29 | 208.23 | 228.16 | 236.74 | 249.88 |
| | $s' = 1 - c'$ | 0.22 | 0.15 | 0.24 | 0.22 | 0.17 | 0.16 | 0.16 | 0.20 | 0.20 | 0.17 |
| Table 5.8 | $s' \cdot u$ | 0.17 | 0.11 | 0.19 | 0.18 | 0.14 | 0.14 | 0.12 | 0.17 | 0.16 | 0.14 |
| | $u$ = capacity utilization rate | 0.75 | 0.70 | 0.78 | 0.81 | 0.79 | 0.84 | 0.80 | 0.85 | 0.84 | 0.81 |
| | $r^{*\prime}$ = profit rate adjusted for utilization = $r^*/u$ | 0.52 | 0.53 | 0.48 | 0.49 | 0.49 | 0.46 | 0.48 | 0.46 | 0.43 | 0.45 |
| Table 5.8 | $r'_n = r_n/u$ | 0.23 | 0.23 | 0.20 | 0.20 | 0.20 | 0.18 | 0.19 | 0.18 | 0.16 | 0.17 |
| BEA (1987, p. 190) | $g_K = (I^*_n/K^*)$ = rate of accumulation | 0.086 | 0.056 | 0.090 | 0.087 | 0.066 | 0.064 | 0.059 | 0.077 | 0.071 | 0.062 |
| | $K^* = K_{BEA}$ = fixed nonresidential gross private capital (billions of dollars) | 384.30 | 400.20 | 438.70 | 480.80 | 506.20 | 526.60 | 546.20 | 591.20 | 650.30 | 689.70 |

217

Table 7.1 (cont.)

| Variables | 1958 | 1959 | 1960 | 1961 | 1962 | 1963 | 1964 | 1965 | 1966 | 1967 | 1968 | 1969 | 1970 | 1971 | 1972 | 1973 |
|---|---|---|---|---|---|---|---|---|---|---|---|---|---|---|---|---|
| $b$ | 0.62 | 0.62 | 0.64 | 0.63 | 0.62 | 0.62 | 0.62 | 0.61 | 0.61 | 0.63 | 0.64 | 0.66 | 0.67 | 0.66 | 0.65 | 0.64 |
| $P_n$ | 96.54 | 104.46 | 104.04 | 109.64 | 122.08 | 129.08 | 138.11 | 154.28 | 167.85 | 170.38 | 175.58 | 177.83 | 179.61 | 204.43 | 225.26 | 258.07 |
| $S*$ | 256.15 | 278.42 | 286.46 | 296.54 | 320.20 | 337.71 | 364.54 | 395.00 | 430.65 | 454.40 | 493.63 | 523.83 | 547.67 | 596.70 | 645.98 | 719.75 |
| $c'$ | 0.86 | 0.82 | 0.84 | 0.85 | 0.83 | 0.83 | 0.83 | 0.80 | 0.80 | 0.82 | 0.82 | 0.81 | 0.83 | 0.81 | 0.79 | 0.78 |
| $I_n*$ | 34.89 | 49.44 | 46.74 | 45.31 | 54.09 | 58.27 | 63.05 | 77.12 | 86.75 | 82.29 | 89.23 | 100.75 | 93.49 | 112.14 | 134.63 | 160.10 |
| $SP*$ | 256.04 | 278.34 | 285.93 | 295.95 | 319.54 | 337.07 | 364.00 | 394.44 | 430.09 | 453.42 | 493.12 | 523.25 | 546.86 | 596.04 | 645.51 | 719.63 |
| $s'$ | 0.14 | 0.18 | 0.16 | 0.15 | 0.17 | 0.17 | 0.17 | 0.20 | 0.20 | 0.18 | 0.18 | 0.19 | 0.17 | 0.19 | 0.21 | 0.22 |
| $s'\cdot u$ | 0.10 | 0.15 | 0.14 | 0.13 | 0.15 | 0.15 | 0.16 | 0.19 | 0.20 | 0.18 | 0.18 | 0.19 | 0.15 | 0.17 | 0.19 | 0.21 |
| $u$ | 0.77 | 0.84 | 0.84 | 0.83 | 0.87 | 0.90 | 0.93 | 0.98 | 1.01 | 0.99 | 0.99 | 0.99 | 0.90 | 0.88 | 0.93 | 0.96 |
| $r*'$ | 0.47 | 0.45 | 0.45 | 0.46 | 0.46 | 0.45 | 0.45 | 0.43 | 0.42 | 0.42 | 0.41 | 0.40 | 0.42 | 0.42 | 0.40 | 0.39 |
| $r_n'$ | 0.18 | 0.17 | 0.16 | 0.17 | 0.18 | 0.17 | 0.17 | 0.17 | 0.16 | 0.16 | 0.15 | 0.14 | 0.14 | 0.15 | 0.14 | 0.14 |
| $g_K$ | 0.049 | 0.067 | 0.062 | 0.058 | 0.067 | 0.070 | 0.072 | 0.083 | 0.086 | 0.075 | 0.074 | 0.076 | 0.064 | 0.070 | 0.077 | 0.083 |
| $K*$ | 710.90 | 738.00 | 755.70 | 775.40 | 802.30 | 832.00 | 872.30 | 932.30 | 1014.40 | 1093.00 | 1202.50 | 1320.90 | 1453.40 | 1598.90 | 1737.70 | 1940.30 |

| Variables | 1974 | 1975 | 1976 | 1977 | 1978 | 1979 | 1980 | 1981 | 1982 | 1983 | 1984 | 1985 | 1986 | 1987 | 1988 | 1989 |
|---|---|---|---|---|---|---|---|---|---|---|---|---|---|---|---|---|
| b | 0.66 | 0.66 | 0.66 | 0.65 | 0.65 | 0.65 | 0.66 | 0.66 | 0.68 | 0.66 | 0.65 | 0.65 | 0.66 | 0.67 | 0.66 | 0.65 |
| $P_n$ | 263.02 | 297.02 | 329.95 | 373.88 | 429.27 | 474.30 | 493.08 | 566.99 | 556.29 | 631.10 | 739.48 | 783.75 | 808.30 | 847.30 | 932.80 | 1021.30 |
| $S*$ | 778.25 | 867.02 | 968.82 | 1083.13 | 1221.07 | 1346.24 | 1462.70 | 1668.19 | 1724.68 | 1865.80 | 2101.78 | 2258.68 | 2401.11 | 2563.38 | 2752.81 | 2943.35 |
| $c'$ | 0.80 | 0.86 | 0.83 | 0.80 | 0.78 | 0.79 | 0.83 | 0.81 | 0.86 | 0.84 | 0.80 | 0.83 | 0.83 | 0.83 | 0.84 | 0.85 |
| $I_n^*$ | 152.30 | 120.41 | 163.83 | 212.85 | 268.03 | 288.23 | 254.39 | 323.44 | 249.11 | 290.23 | 429.23 | 392.53 | 398.85 | 422.29 | 441.91 | 447.63 |
| $SP*$ | 778.82 | 868.78 | 971.25 | 1086.66 | 1221.76 | 1347.44 | 1463.67 | 1669.40 | 1726.06 | 1867.15 | 2103.70 | 2258.31 | 2389.25 | 2555.52 | 2755.18 | 2945.32 |
| $s'$ | 0.20 | 0.14 | 0.17 | 0.20 | 0.22 | 0.21 | 0.17 | 0.19 | 0.14 | 0.16 | 0.20 | 0.17 | 0.17 | 0.17 | 0.16 | 0.15 |
| $s'\cdot u$ | 0.18 | 0.11 | 0.14 | 0.17 | 0.20 | 0.19 | 0.15 | 0.16 | 0.11 | 0.13 | 0.18 | 0.16 | 0.14 | 0.14 | 0.14 | 0.14 |
| $u$ | 0.90 | 0.79 | 0.83 | 0.87 | 0.89 | 0.89 | 0.85 | 0.84 | 0.77 | 0.84 | 0.89 | 0.89 | 0.85 | 0.87 | 0.90 | 0.89 |
| $r*'$ | 0.36 | 0.41 | 0.40 | 0.38 | 0.36 | 0.36 | 0.36 | 0.36 | 0.38 | 0.36 | 0.37 | 0.38 | 0.40 | 0.39 | 0.39 | 0.39 |
| $r'_n$ | 0.12 | 0.14 | 0.14 | 0.13 | 0.13 | 0.13 | 0.12 | 0.12 | 0.12 | 0.12 | 0.13 | 0.13 | 0.14 | 0.13 | 0.13 | 0.14 |
| $g_K$ | 0.064 | 0.045 | 0.056 | 0.065 | 0.071 | 0.068 | 0.053 | 0.059 | 0.043 | 0.048 | 0.067 | 0.059 | 0.057 | 0.057 | 0.056 | 0.053 |
| $K*$ | 2387.10 | 2661.70 | 2920.80 | 3253.50 | 3774.60 | 4225.20 | 4884.40 | 5503.70 | 5859.20 | 6094.71 | 6432.91 | 6706.44 | 7056.52 | 7459.32 | 7895.58 | 8387.49 |

(necessity being equivalent to marketability) is productive. But here the argument veers too far in the opposite direction, since it obliterates all distinction between capitalist and noncapitalist production, and between production and social consumption (Section 2.3). The whole purpose of this book has been to show that the middle road is truly different, both theoretically and empirically.

The precise mapping between orthodox categories and Marxian ones raises a host of other issues. The primary sectors, production and trade, are directly involved in the production and circulation of the total product. As such, their combined revenue represents the total price of the total product. But the value which is realized in the primary sectors is partially recirculated through a series of transfers between it and various secondary sectors, involving payments of net interest, finance charges, ground rent, fees, royalties, and taxes. The sectors receiving these were grouped into the (private) royalties sector (finance, insurance, ground rent, etc.), and the general government sector (government enterprises are treated as part of other sectors, according to the activity in which they engage).

Since the original sources of the revenues of the secondary sectors are already counted in the revenues of the primary sectors, we cannot count them again in the measure of the total product and its total value. Secondary flows are part of total transactions, but not part of value of the total product. Within IO accounts, this means leaving out the columns and rows of both the (private) royalties sectors and the "government industry" dummy sector. These adjustments ultimately account for the major differences between Marxian and conventional categories.

It should be noted that such exclusions do not mean that we ignore the actual use of the product by the royalties sector or the actual consumption of its workers and capitalists. Royalties payments are deductions from the purchasing power of the primary sector and its associated households; their receipt by the secondary sector enhances purchasing power and that of its associated households. What the former set loses, the latter gains. In this way the redistribution of value brought about through transfers between the primary and secondary sectors leads to a changed use of the product. Thus the product use induced by the royalties sector shows up in the intermediate use of the total product, in the government-use portion of final demand, and in its workers' and capitalists' portion of the personal consumption column of final demand (Section 3.6, Figure 3.11, Table 3.12).

Foreign trade introduces a further instance of transfers of value, since the value realized within the primary sectors reflects not only the value produced within the country but also any (negative or positive) international transfers of value. We must therefore adjust for these transfers in order to recover the magnitude of produced value. Our empirical measures do not include such an adjustment, although we do estimate it to be relatively small for the United States (Section 3.6).

On the whole, royalties flows increase the orthodox measures of gross output and gross product relative to their Marxian counterparts, total value and total product. But the effect on the magnitude of conventional value added and final demand relative to Marxian value added and final product turns out to be theoretically indeterminate. The same can be said for measures of aggregate profit-type income (the sum of profits and royalties) relative to aggregate surplus value (Section 3.2.1; see also Appendix B).

### 7.3 Empirical results

At an empirical level, Marxian total product TP* is roughly 82% of the IO measure of gross product GP, but about 1.5 times larger than the conventional measure of GNP. Marxian gross final product GFP*, on the other hand, is about 15% smaller than GNP. Surplus value S* is almost double the most inclusive measure of profit-type income $P^+$ (defined as NNP minus employee compensation), while productive labor $L_p$ is less than one-half of all employment L. As a result, the rate of surplus value $S^*/V^*$ is typically almost 4 times as large as the ratio of profit-type income to employee compensation $P^+/EC$, while the Marxian measure of productivity $q^*$ (defined as real total product per productive labor hour) is about 3 times as large as the conventional measure (defined as real GDP per labor hour) (Section 5.12, Table 5.14).

Trends over the postwar period also differ. Marxian total product decreases slightly relative to IO gross product, and also declines slightly relative to GNP (except for 1973–77, when the oil-price rise, which shows up in the cost of intermediate inputs, temporarily reverses the trend). Marxian gross final product also declines moderately relative to GNP, as does Marxian net final product relative to NNP (Figure 5.4).

Interestingly, productive employment $L_p$ is stagnant for the first half of the postwar period, and then begins a steady but modest rise in the mid-1960s. But unproductive employment rises sharply throughout, so that the ratio of productive labor to total employment falls by more than 37% while that of unproductive labor to productive labor rises by almost 138% (Table 5.5 and Figures 5.7, 5.9, and 5.11). A similar pattern holds for total wages: the productive worker wage bill $W_p$ (which is the same as variable capital $V^*$) falls relative to total wages W as the unproductive wage bill $W_u$ rises sharply relative to that of productive labor. This tells us that it is the movement in the relative employment levels, not in the relative wage rates, which is crucial. Indeed, the wage rate of unproductive labor actually declines relative to that of productive labor, by about 12%, over the postwar period (Table 5.6 and Figures 5.8–5.11).

The Marxian measure of productivity q* is about three times as large as the conventional measure y, and also rises relative to it for significant periods. From 1972 to 1982, the ratio of the respective numerators of the two measures (i.e. TP*/GDP) rises, in good part because the oil-price rise raises the cost of the intermediate goods that appear in TP* but not in GDP. At the same time, the ratio of productive employment to total employment falls more rapidly than in the previous decade. Thus, even though the growth rate of q* slows down gradually over the whole postwar period, that of y shows a marked change in pattern in the critical period 1972–82, which is then perceived as a pernicious and puzzling "productivity slowdown" (Naples 1987, p. 122). It is interesting to note, however, that the trend (but not the level) of the Marxian measure is very well captured by the approximation y*, defined as Marxian real net final product per productive worker hour (Figures 5.19 and 5.20).

Both surplus value S* and profit-type income P rise strongly over the postwar period, but the former is much larger and rises somewhat faster. On the other hand variable capital V* (the productive worker wage bill) is much smaller and rises much more slowly than total employee compensation EC. Thus the true rate of surplus value is not only almost four times as large as its naive counterpart, the profit/wage ratio P⁺/EC, but also moves very differently: the rate of surplus value rises by almost 50%, while the profit/wage ratio actually falls by almost 27%. The latter gives the impression of a "wage squeeze" on profits; the former shows just the opposite. This serves to emphasize that even the most inclusive measure of the profit/wage ratio is a bad proxy of the rate of surplus value. A similar comment applies for the relation between the Marxian flow measure of constant to variable capital and the conventional IO measure of intermediate input to employee compensation (Section 5.5, Table 5.7, and Figures 5.12–5.15). The ratio of fixed constant capital to variable capital rises by almost 90% over the postwar period, which more than offsets the 50% rise in the rate of surplus value. Consequently, the Marxian rate of profit falls by 24%. The corporate rate of profit falls even faster, by 57%, because a rising portion of surplus value is absorbed in unproductive expenses (so that the portion remaining for profit declines relative to surplus value).

The intervention of the state, via taxes and transfers, requires that we account for a different kind of transfer – out of wages, particularly the wages of productive workers. The nominal wage is altered by (positive or negative transfers) involving net interest, net ground rent, and net taxes (net of social benefit expenditures received). Insofar as these impinge on the wages of production workers, the measure of variable capital changes. Although the calculation of net interest and net ground-rent payments is conceptually straightforward, the estimation of net taxes paid requires a comparison between the gross taxes paid by production workers and the corresponding transfers and other social welfare expenditures (for health, education, roads, parks, etc.) directed back toward them. To the extent that the net transfer is positive, it reduces the measure of variable capital and increases the measures of surplus value and the rate of surplus value.

Although we do not estimate the net interest or ground rent paid by productive workers, we do calculate the net transfer between them and the state. For the United States, the taxes paid turn out to be generally larger than the social benefits received – that is, there is a net tax paid by labor. This implies that true variable capital is somewhat lower, and the true mass and rate of surplus value somewhat higher, than the apparent rates (Section 5.9, Figures 5.23–5.25). Interestingly enough, even though actual government purchases of the total product $G^*$ rise substantially over time, they actually decline relative to the mass of surplus value from 1955 to 1989 (Section 5.8, Table 5.11 and Figure 5.21). Nonetheless, the total government absorption of surplus value $G_T^* = G^* + W_G$ remains fairly stable, relative to surplus value, over this same interval.

All of these mappings were constructed on the assumption that purchasers' prices were proportional to labor values. This allowed us to check that the various elements add up to the correct totals, no matter how complicated the transfers of value involved. It also ensured that any discrepancies that arose between individual Marxian categories and their orthodox counterparts were due solely to conceptual differences, not to any price–value deviations that might exist. In Chapter 4 we extend the analysis to the calculation of actual labor value magnitudes. We show that the correct procedure is consistent, in the sense that it gives the same ratios in value terms and in price terms when unit purchaser prices are equal to unit values (Tables 4.1 and 4.2). This means that in actual input–output tables, where purchaser's prices generally do differ from values, we can then interpret the deviations between value and money ratios as a measure of the aggregate effects of price–value deviations, if the procedure used is consistent in the sense just described.

Using the consistent procedure, Khanjian (1989) shows that value and price rates of surplus value differ by only small amounts (6%–9%), which indicates that the effects of price–value deviations on aggregate measures are quite minor (Section 5.10, Table 5.12, and Figure 5.25). On the other hand, the procedure used by Wolff (1977b, 1987), who also attempts to construct a mapping between input–output accounts and Marxian categories, is inconsistent and is therefore biased (Section 6.2.3). As expected on theoretical grounds, Wolff's estimates of money rates of surplus value are uniformly higher than his labor value estimates by about 4%–8% (Wolff 1977b, p. 103, table 3, lines 1 and 3). On the other hand, Khanjian's estimates indicate that $S^*/V^*$ is uniformly lower than $S/V$ by about 6%–9% (Khanjian 1988, p. 109, table 19). This allows us to estimate that Wolff's inconsistent procedure biases the money rate of surplus value $S^*/V^*$ upward by 12%–15% (the sum of the two sets of differences in years common to both Khanjian and Wolff).

The calculation of labor-value/producer-price ratios also enables us to distinguish the rate of exploitation from the rate of surplus value. The rate of exploitation is the ratio of surplus labor time to necessary labor time. This concept applies to all capitalistically employed wage labor, whether it be productive or unproductive. Necessary labor time is simply the value of the labor power involved – that is, the labor value of the average annual basket of commodities consumed per worker in the activities in question. Surplus labor time is the excess of working time over necessary labor time. For productive workers, their rate of exploitation is also the rate of surplus value, since their surplus labor time results in surplus value. We derive expressions for both ratios, show how they are connected, and derive a simple method of empirically estimating the rate of exploitation of unproductive workers (Section 4.2). At an empirical level, the two rates move in remarkably similar ways, with only small differences in levels: the rate for unproductive labor starts out lower than that of productive labor, principally because of higher wages for the former, but the gap disappears by the mid-1970s. Both rise strongly over time, always staying within 10% of one another (Section 5.6, Figure 5.18).

### 7.4 Comparisons with previous studies

Much of what has been summarized so far has strong implications for previous attempts to measure Marxian categories. We critically review these attempts in Chapter 6, confining our attention to works published in English.

We see, for instance, that the rate of surplus value behaves very differently from a conventional profit/wage ratio, no matter how inclusively the profit measure is defined. For example, during the postwar period the rate of surplus value rises by almost 50%, while the profit/wage ratio actually falls by almost 27%. The impression of a "labor squeeze" given by the latter is therefore false. This result has direct bearing on a good portion of the Marxian literature. In Section 6.1, we critically discuss works by Glyn and Sutcliffe (1972), Boddy and Crotty (1975), Weisskopf (1979), Aglietta (1979), Bowles et al. (1984), and Sherman (1986). All of them interpret some measure of the profit/wage ratio as a proxy for the rate of surplus value, and – upon finding that the latter is falling over the postwar period – mistakenly conclude that it must be the result of a labor force strong enough to squeeze profits by increasing real wages faster than productivity (i.e., by reducing the rate of exploitation of labor), in both the United States and the United Kingdom.

Working within an IO framework, Wolff (1975, 1977a,b, 1979, 1987) and Sharpe (1982b) also treat all labor as productive, thereby implicitly or explicitly associating the rate of surplus value with the profit/wage ratio. Thus, even though neither author draws any labor-squeeze implications from his results, their money and labor value estimates of rates of surplus value suffer from the same basic problems just outlined.[7]

Many authors, though, do utilize the distinction between productive and unproductive labor. But by far the largest portion of these do so only in the context of studying a particular sector – the manufacturing sector (Amsden 1981; Corey 1934; Cuneo 1978, 1982; Gillman 1958; Mandel 1975; Perlo 1974; Sharpe 1982a; Varga 1928, 1935, 1968; Varley 1938). The availability of good long-term data on manufacturing makes it a natural object of study, but it also creates two new problems. First of all, the surplus value realized in the manufacturing sector is much lower than that produced in it, because of value transferred out to the wholesale/retail sector.[8] Thus the NIPA-based realized rate of surplus value in the manufacturing sector is only about 55% of the aggregate rate, although the trends are quite similar. Second, and quite independently, it turns out that there is a substantial difference in estimates derived from census-based manufacturing data and corresponding NIPA-based ones, at least for the United States. This effect works in the opposite direction, and in this case produces a substantial upward bias in trend (Section 6.2.1, Table 6.3, and Figures 6.5 and 6.6). It follows that sectoral realized rates of surplus value do not, in general, provide good proxies for either the sectoral or aggregate produced rates.

Among those who do distinguish between productive and unproductive labor, a second set of authors attempts to estimate aggregate measures directly, either in money form (Eaton 1966; Gouverneur 1983; Labor Research Association 1948; Mage 1963; Moseley 1982, 1985; Papadimitriou 1988; Shaikh 1978b; Tonak 1984; Tsaliki and Tsoulfidis 1988) or in both

---

[7] Wolff's (1975) Puerto Rico study has, in addition, other special problems; see Section 6.1.2.

[8] Value is transferred out by the difference between producers' price and purchasers' price, and may be transferred in or out by deviations between purchasers' price and values. In principle, the overall net transfer could go either way, but in practice price–value deviations are small for any aggregate sector, so that the first set of transfers dominates.

money and value form (Izumi 1980, 1983; Khanjian 1988; Okishio 1959; Okishio and Nakatani 1985; Wolff 1977b, 1987).

Eaton's (1963) sophisticated treatment distinguishes between productive and unproductive sectors, keeps track of the value transferred from the former to the trade sector, and even proposes that variable capital be adjusted for the net tax on labor. Mage (1963) raises the discussion to an entirely new level. He attempts to keep track of total value flows, at least at a conceptual level, by defining it as the sum of the materials costs of the production sectors; variable capital (the wages of production workers within the productive sectors); profits; net rents paid and net interest paid of production and trade sectors; indirect business taxes paid by the production and trade sectors; and the wage and materials costs of unproductive sectors. But since he relegates the latter two items to constant capital, Mage effectively reduces his measure of surplus value to just that part which shows up as profit-type income. This, and other more concrete considerations, lead to a measure of surplus value which is much lower than ours and which, unlike ours, falls over the postwar period.

Shaikh (1978b) provides the first systematic framework for measuring the rate of surplus value in money form. He derives a complete mapping between Marxian and NIPA categories, on the revenue side of the accounts, and shows that the rate of surplus value rises while the profit/wage ratio falls. He also provides the first systematic estimates of the net effects of state taxation and social expenditures on the wage rate and the rate of surplus value. But even though his framework is essentially the same as our present one, his empirical estimates of the rate of surplus are smaller because (in the absence of input–output data) he is unable to estimate the size of the intermediate inputs of the trade sector, and because of several other specific factors. Moseley (1982, 1985) and Tonak (1984) adopt Shaikh's framework, but in an approximate form with some different assumptions. Tonak also extends Shaikh's sample calculations of the net tax on labor to the entire postwar period, by developing a widely adopted "labor-share" method for splitting tax receipts and social benefit expenditures.[9] Our present estimates are based on a further development of Tonak's work by Shaikh and Tonak (1987). Finally, Papadimitriou (1988) and Tsaliki and Tsoulfidis (1988) apply our present schema, subject to data limitations, to the case of Greece, and find that from 1960 to 1977 the rate of surplus value rises (Section 6.2.2).

Aglietta takes a somewhat different tack. Because he (mistakenly) believes that price–value deviations are quite significant in magnitude, he

---

[9] The labor share method is used in studies on Canada, Australia, the United Kingdom, and Sweden; see Shaikh and Tonak (forthcoming).

concludes that the money rate of profit is not likely to be a good indicator of the trend of the value rate. He therefore derives an alternate proxy for this latter rate, in the form of "real social wage cost" of productive labor (the ratio of the real wage of production workers to the real net value added per unit productive labor). Although this method of approximation is a valid one, it is of course dependent on having adequate measures of real production workers' wages and Marxian net product per unit productive labor. The trouble is that Aglietta nowhere explains how he gets his underlying data. We find that, from 1948 to the mid-1960s, his index implies roughly the same long-term trend as our rate of surplus value. But shorter-term movements are not at all similar. These discrepancies are potentially important, because Aglietta places considerable weight on explaining the "ups and downs of accumulation" from the shorter-term movements in the rate of surplus value (Section 6.2.2).

Okishio's (1959) pathbreaking work is the first to utilize input–output tables to estimate the money and value rates of surplus value separately. In this initial study he treats all services as unproductive. He also inflates his measure of productive worker consumption (and hence of variable capital) by including within it some portion of the wages of unproductive workers. Both factors lead to a downward bias in his estimate of the rate of surplus value, relative to our procedures. Izumi (1980) also treats all services as unproductive, and also makes an adjustment like Okishio's to expand the definition of the value of labor power. Okishio and Nakatani (1985) reverse their previous assumptions by treating all services as productive, which gives them a much higher estimate of the rate of surplus value. Izumi (1983), on the other hand, retains his framework and extends it to a comparison of rates of surplus value in Japan, the United States, and South Korea. By comparing his results on the United States to those of Khanjian (1988), we see that his procedure reduces the measured rate of surplus value by 20%–35%, but raises the trend rate slightly. Wolff (1977b, 1987) and Khanjian (1988) have already been discussed (Section 6.2.3).

Finally, there is a set of measures that attempts to quantify "economic surplus." Whereas our measure of capitalist surplus product (SP*) is the excess of the net capitalist product over the actual capitalist costs of its production, the economic surplus is the difference between the total product and some "normative judgement of what costs are socially necessary" (Bottomore 1983, p. 340). Aside from the perennial issue of the appropriate measure of output (all the authors involved seem to treat NIPA net output as the appropriate measure), these two concepts serve different but complementary needs. It is perfectly appropriate within our framework, as we noted in Chapters 1 and 2, to keep track of noncapitalist production and use of wealth. But it is not appropriate, we would argue, to conflate capitalist and noncapitalist surplus products, precisely because the former is the foundation for aggregate profit. Moreover, it seems to us ill-advised to treat economic surplus as a "kind of discretionary fund" to be "allocated among competing alternatives" (Lippit 1985, p. 10; Stanfield 1973, p. 3).

In any case, economic surplus is generally derived by subtracting some measure of essential social consumption from NNP, which assumes that NNP itself is an adequate measure of net product. Phillips (in an appendix to Baran and Sweezy 1966) arrives at the economic surplus by adding together after-tax property-type income, the wage costs of unproductive activities, all taxes, and the government deficit (since government expenditures equal taxes plus the deficit). Because the government deficit is small in the postwar years covered by his data, Phillips's measure amounts to the difference between (NIPA) value added and the wages of production workers, and is therefore similar to that of surplus value. Stanfield (1973) attempts to account for the surplus foregone due to unemployment by defining potential surplus as full-employment output minus the sum of personal and social essential consumption, in contrast to actual surplus based on actual output (pp. 1, 81). On the whole, Phillips's measure of economic surplus is much closer to surplus value than is Stanfield's. Finally, Erdos (1970) provides an eclectic variation on these themes. His measure is a kind of political economic surplus, even though he labels it as (redefined) "surplus value." His stated intention is to modernize Marxian categories by making them "correspond as exactly as possible to the empirical facts of our days." He defines socially necessary costs as that part of "new value" which is not used by the oppressing class or the oppressive part of the state apparatus. At the empirical level, he defines new value as the (NIPA) value added in production and trade. Necessary costs are defined as the wages of production and trade workers, net of taxes and transfers, plus one-third of government wages (an estimate of the socially useful portion of government expenditures). The political surplus, which he calls surplus value, is the rest of new value. So defined, his measure of the rate of political surplus in the United States is even smaller than Stanfield's rate of economic surplus. Overall, measures of real economic surplus are somewhat lower than our corresponding measures of real surplus value, whereas at least Stanfield's measure of the rate of economic surplus is much smaller, and moves differently, from our measure of the rate of surplus value.

### 7.5 Conclusions

The distinction between production and nonproduction activities is a fundamental one, since all branches of economics must at least differentiate between production and personal consumption. But the classical and Marxian traditions also distinguish between production and nonproduction labor, and hence between production and social consumption. And with this distinction comes a substantially different way of accounting for the level and progress of the wealth of nations.

The rise of neoclassical economics all but obliterated these distinctions. Instead, all necessary labor was deemed productive, and the market was enthroned as the ultimate arbiter of social necessity. In spite of its other differences with neoclassical theory, Keynesian economics is part of this official tradition. Soviet-style accounts did little to combat this hegemony; if anything, the physicalist notion embodied in the Soviet-type measure of "national material product" only served to strengthen the grip of the official Western concepts.

But even though it has been virtually banished from orthodox economic theory, the concept of nonproduction labor has remained a part of practical discourse – through the observations and comments of business leaders, government officials, and occasionally even economists, many of whom have pointed to the burden of "unproductive" financial, trading, and guard activities. Moreover, as a purely practical matter, the growth of such activities has been a widely noted feature in all countries of the postwar world.

Within orthodox national accounts, issues of this sort are a matter of detail, because all such activities are forms of national production. But within classical and Marxian frameworks, the consideration of nonproduction labor changes the very nature of the accounts, the picture that we see, and the conclusions that we draw.

In our presentation, we have concentrated on production accounts, since that is where our essential difference with conventional accounts arises. Extending our accounts to encompass other circuits would only further develop this difference, since all such extensions must build on the core provided by the production accounts. We share with most extended accounts the goals of including household and other noncapitalist production activities; of keeping track of financial flows; of linking observed flows and the corresponding stocks; and of accounting for the depletion of resources. But at the same time, the core differences continue to show up even at this level. For instance, unlike orthodox extended accounts, we would not treat household and government durables as capital goods merely because they are durable, and we would not impute a fictitious flow of gross profits. Much less would we apply the same procedure to accumulated "human capital" (see Section 1.3).

Finally, it is important to note that we have emphasized the effects of unproductive activities on profitability and growth because we believe that these interactions are essential to an understanding of the actual workings of the capitalist system. This is not meant to imply that growth is necessarily a good thing. In a world beset with environmental problems and a devastating maldistribution of income, wealth, and resource use, growth (and even maintenance of present levels of production) must be viewed with a jaundiced eye indeed. But capitalism is nonetheless fueled by profitability and driven toward growth. To move beyond these imperatives it is necessary to understand how they operate, in theory and in practice. It is our hope to contribute to this understanding by constructing a framework within which this dynamic, with its attendant contradictions, can be traced and analyzed.

APPENDICES

# A

## Methodology of the input–output database

The primary database from which the condensed tables in Section 5.1 and Appendix C are derived is composed of input–output tables that correspond to the 85-industry IO tables, in that the final versions have 82 rows and 88 columns. All the input–output tables used are originally derived from the benchmark tables produced by the BEA (Bureau of Economic Analysis), which is part of the U.S. Department of Commerce. In an effort to improve the compatibility of the data for different years and from different sources, various adjustments and modifications were carried out on the data series used. Most significantly, Juillard (1988) carried out several adjustments on the input–output tables so as to have as consistent a methodology as possible for all the benchmark years. Several additional adjustments and aggregations were conducted in order to render data sets from different sources more consistent. Among these, the major adjustments were: (1) reversing the methodology of force account construction used with the BEA IO tables; (2) adjusting the BLS (Bureau of Labor Statistics, Department of Labor) capital stock and depreciation matrices for oil and gas exploration costs;[1] and (3) modifying employment and employee compensation data so as to maximize consistency within the adjusted IO tables for all benchmark years.

We wish to thank Michel Juillard and Ara Khanjian for their help with input–output data and methodology, and Paul Cooney for the preparation of the text of Appendix A and the calculation of the U.S. summary input–output tables used in this study.

[1] In the BEA capital stock series, oil and gas exploration costs have been included as part of the capital stock for the petroleum refining industry. Yet these same costs are included as intermediate inputs in the same industry of the BEA IO tables. Hence one must adjust one of the two data sets.

### A.1 Original sources

The Bureau of Economic Analysis of the Department of Commerce has successively published benchmark input–output tables for 1947, 1958, 1963, 1967, 1972, and 1977 (see respectively, BEA 1970, 1965, 1969, 1974, 1979, 1984). Table A.1 lists industries and commodities for the 1972 table. The 1972 BEA table consists of 85 industries with the following six dummy industries: (1) noncomparable imports; (2) scrap; (3) government industry; (4) the rest of the world; (5) the household industry; and (6) inventory valuation adjustment. Additional rows are for value added, which is broken down into three components: (1) employee compensation; (2) indirect business taxes; and (3) property-type income and totals of intermediate inputs and total industry outputs. There are an additional nine columns of final demand listed in Table A.1; the units are millions of 1972 dollars.

Because there were few differences between the list of industries and sectors at the 85-order aggregation level, only the 1972 table is included here. However, there were some changes in industrial classification, in particular for dummy industries, so the lists of industries corresponding to this order for the other five years are included at the end of this appendix (see the BEA publications for individual years). In order to facilitate comparison of the original BEA tables and the present database, a mapping of the sectors from the 1972 85-order table with those of this database is presented in Table A.1.

### A.2 Modifications by Juillard (1988)

The BEA tables vary with respect to the degree of detail of industrial classification and with regard to the treatment of methodological problems such as imports or secondary products. For the most part, any given methodology has been used twice: 1947 and 1958 are more or less comparable, so are 1963 and 1967, and lastly 1972 and 1977. The most serious break with the past occurs with the publication of the 1972 study. Because the methodology employed for the different tables had changed over time, a number of major changes or treatments had to be employed. Juillard carried out this substantial undertaking in order to produce a consistent database. Only the treatment of imports for final use of previous years could not be updated to the new formula (owing to lack of information), so an intermediary solution had to be chosen. The necessary transformations concern (1) industrial classification, (2) secondary products, (3) treatment of imports, and (4) the industry "eating and drinking places." These specific changes are summarized next.

#### A.2.1 *Industrial classification*

The industrial classification used in the input–output tables published by the BEA are based upon, yet distinct from, the Standard Indus-

Table A.1. *Mapping between sectors of the original 1972 85-order table and the final 82 × 88 IO tables*

| Original IO sector | Final tables sector[a] |
|---|---|
| 1 Livestock and products | 1 Agriculture |
| 2 Other agricultural products | 1 Agriculture |
| 3 Forestry and fishery products | 1 Agriculture |
| 4 Agricultural forestry | 1 Agriculture |
| 5 Iron mining | 2 |
| 6 Nonferrous metal mining | 3 |
| 7 Coal mining | 4 |
| 8 Crude petroleum and natural gas | 5 |
| 9 Stone and clay mining | 6 |
| 10 Chemical and fertilizers | 7 |
| 11 New construction | 8 Construction |
| 12 Maintenance and repair construction | 8 Construction |
| 13 Ordnance and accessories | 9 |
| 14 Food and kindred products | 10 |
| 15 Tobacco | 11 |
| 16 Fabrics, yarn, and thread mills | 12 |
| 17 Miscellaneous textile goods and floor coverings | 13 |
| 18 Apparel | 14 |
| 19 Miscellaneous fabricated textile products | 15 |
| 20 Lumber and wood products | 16 |
| 21 Wood containers | 17 |
| 22 Household furniture | 18 |
| 23 Other furniture and fixtures | 19 |
| 24 Paper and allied products | 20 |
| 25 Paperboard containers and boxes | 21 |
| 26 Printing and publishing | 22 |
| 27 Chemicals and allied products | 23 |
| 28 Plastics and synthetic materials | 24 |
| 29 Drugs, cleaning, and toilet preparations | 25 |
| 30 Paints and allied products | 26 |
| 31 Petroleum refining | 27 |
| 32 Rubber and miscellaneous plastic products | 28 |
| 33 Leather tanning and finishing | 29 |
| 34 Footwear and other leather products | 30 |
| 35 Glass and glass products | 31 |
| 36 Stone and clay products | 32 |
| 37 Primary iron and steel manufacturing | 33 |
| 38 Primary nonferrous metals manufacturing | 34 |
| 39 Metal containers | 35 |
| 40 Heating and fabricating metal products | 36 |
| 41 Screw machine products | 37 |
| 42 Other fabricated metal products | 38 |
| 43 Engines and turbines | 39 |
| 44 Farm machinery and equipment | 40 |

Table A.1 *(cont.)*

| Original IO sector | Final tables sector[a] |
|---|---|
| 45  Construction machinery and equipment | 41 |
| 46  Materials handling machinery and equipment | 42 |
| 47  Metalworking machinery and equipment | 43 |
| 48  Special industry machinery and equipment | 44 |
| 49  General industrial machinery and equipment | 45 |
| 50  Miscellaneous machinery | 46 |
| 51  Office and computing machines | 47 |
| 52  Service industry machines | 48 |
| 53  Electric industrial equipment | 49 |
| 54  Household appliances | 50 |
| 55  Electrical wiring and lighting equipment | 51 |
| 56  Radio, TV, and communication equipment | 52 |
| 57  Electronic components and accessories | 53 |
| 58  Miscellaneous electrical machinery | 54 |
| 59  Motor vehicles and equipment | 55 |
| 60  Aircraft and parts | 56 |
| 61  Other transportation equipment | 57 |
| 62  Scientific and controlling instruments | 58 |
| 63  Optical, ophthalmic, and photographic equipment | 59 |
| 64  Miscellaneous manufacturing | 60 |
| 65  Transportation and warehousing | 61 |
| 66  Communications except broadcasting | 62 |
| 67  Radio and TV broadcasting | 63 |
| 68  Public utilities | 64 |
| 69  Wholesale and retail trade | 65 |
| 70  Finance and insurance | 66 |
| 71  Real estate and rental | 67 |
| 72  Hotels and repair places, except auto repair | 68 |
| 73  Business services | 69 |
| 74  Eating and drinking places | 65  Trade |
| 75  Auto repair and services | 70 |
| 76  Amusements | 71 |
| 77  Medical and educational services | 72 |
| 78  Federal government enterprises | 73 |
| 79  State and local government enterprises | 74 |
| 80  Noncomparable imports | 75 |
| 81  Scrap, used, and secondhand goods | 76 |
| 82  Government industry | 77 |
| 83  Rest-of-the-World industry | 78 |
| 84  Household industry | 79 |
| 85  Inventory valuation adjustment | 80 |
| I  Total intermediate inputs | N.I.[b] |
| VA  Value added | 81 |
| EC  Compensation of employees | N.I. |
| IBT  Indirect business taxes | N.I. |

Table A.1 *(cont.)*

| Original IO sector | Final tables sector[a] | |
|---|---|---|
| PTI Property-type income | N.I. | |
| T Total industry output | 82 | |
| *Final demand* (reference is to columns) | | |
| 91 Personal consumption expenditure (PCE) | 81 | |
| 92 Gross private fixed capital formation (INV) | 82 | |
| 93 Change in business inventories (CBI) | 83 | |
| 94 Exports | 84 | |
| 95 Imports | 85 | |
| 96 Federal government, national defense | 86 | Federal government |
| 97 Federal government, nondefense | 86 | Federal government |
| 98 State government, education | 87 | State government |
| 99 State government, other | 87 | State government |
| Total final demand | N.I. | |
| Total commodity output | 88 | Row totals |

[a] Sectoral names are listed only when they differ from the names of the original sector.
[b] N.I. = not included.

trial Classification (SIC) used for the economic census. The degree of detail varies with the different studies: for 1947 and 1958, the productive system is disaggregated into 79 industries, or a 2-digit IO classification; for 1963 and 1967, 368 industries are available, or a 4-digit IO classification; in 1972, the degree of detail reaches 496 industries, or a 6-digit IO classification. Finally, in 1977, 537 industries are available in an updated version of the 6-digit IO classification. The U.S. national accountants tried as much as possible to maintain the consistency of the classification through the years, so that the classification would remain compatible at the higher aggregation levels available for several consecutive years. For this reason, the 2-digit IO classification remained more stable and has integrated the changes in the SIC classification in a consistent way.

However, the list of dummy industries, which are used to describe activities that – for conceptual or statistical reasons – cannot be assigned to any particular industry, has changed between the different studies. For the 1972 table, the dummy industries include: (1) the government industry, which transfers the value added by the employees of the federal, state, or local administration to the final demand; (2) the rest-of-world industry, which accounts for the income of the production factors located abroad; (3) the noncomparable imports industry; (4) the households industry, which accounts for the compensation of household employees;

(5) the inventory valuation industry; and (6) scrap and second-hand goods, which are treated in the 1972 study as the secondary product of several other industries. Before 1972, other secondary products were added to the list of the dummy industries: office supply, business trips, and gifts. For 1958, research and development is also included as a dummy industry. The importance of the differences in the list of dummy industries is limited with regard to activities not present in the later studies as other secondary products. Although based on the SIC, input–output studies incorporate explicit redefinitions whose scope changes for different years. These redefinitions always attempt to yield more homogeneous industries.

### A.2.2 *Secondary products*

The basic statistical unit of the economic census is the *establishment,* generally characterized by a unique location, in contrast to a *company,* which is based on the legal criterion of ownership. The establishment is assigned to the industry corresponding to its primary production. However, the establishment may have several other types of production, which are referred to as secondary products. It is in the interest of IO analysis regarding technology to achieve the greatest possible homogeneity for the definitions of production processes, thus ensuring the greatest stability possible for the technical coefficients. For this reason, national accountants try to reclassify the secondary products in order to obtain more homogeneous production processes. This reclassification of secondary products can be dealt with in three different ways: (1) constant-commodity technology; (2) constant-industry technology; and (3) separation of the input–output table into two tables, Use and Make.

The first case applies when the technology used for production of the secondary product is clearly different from the technology used to produce the primary product. In this case, the activity resulting in the secondary product is simply redefined as belonging to another industry on the assumption of constant-commodity technology; this treatment was used in all six tables. Alternatively, the secondary product may be the object of a fictitious sale – from the industry actually producing it to the one for which this product would be the primary product. This transfer method was used in the 1947, 1958, 1963, and 1967 tables in order to deal with the reclassifications made under the assumption of constant-industry technology. This method has the defect of artificially increasing the share of intermediary products in overall production, with no corresponding justification on technological grounds. The third method, which was used for the tables of 1972 and 1977, corrects this problem by describing industries and commodities separately. This method, which was inspired by the Von Neumann model, requires the separation of the input–output table into two tables. The first table, known as the Use table, describes the use of the different commodities by the different industries and the functions of the final demand; the second, or Make, table displays the production of each commodity by the different branches.

In order to unify the treatment of secondary products in the six tables, this third method was also applied to the earlier tables. These operations were carried out at the highest degree of detail possible: 79 industries for 1947 and 1958, and 368 industries for 1963 and 1967. The first problem involves a number of specific redefinitions: from 1972 on, and contrary to what was done before, the electricity produced and sold by the manufacturing, mining, and railroad sectors is systematically redefined as being produced by the electricity industry. The same is true for the reselling of commodities taking place in the manufacturing sector, which is redefined as occurring in the wholesale trade industry, and for rents and royalties, which are systematically redefined into the real estate industry (BEA 1980, p. 49). In the studies before 1972, these reclassifications were dealt with by using the transfer method, therefore implying the opposite assumption of constant-industry technology.

For published tables that report only the total transfers by industry, magnetic-tape data files are available (distributed by the BEA) that contain the detail of the transfers by commodity and industry. It is therefore possible to use either of the two assumptions of constant technology. It is important to realize that the information in the transfer table is equivalent to that included in the Make table. The transfers indicate the quantity of secondary products produced by each industry. On the other hand, a table without the transfers represents the direct allocation of primary products and their use by the different industries and functions of the final demand; the row totals of this table represent the total production of each commodity. By comparing these totals and the column totals of the transfer table, it is possible to calculate the quantity of each commodity which is produced as the primary product of the corresponding industry. This is accomplished by calculating the differences between the two sets of totals. It is therefore possible to use the transfer table to rebuild Use and Make tables for years prior to 1972, although the manipulation of the two matrices is quite complicated.

By systematically applying the assumption of constant-industry technology to the secondary products described outside the main diagonal of the Make matrix, it is possible to rebuild an input–output table that describes the transactions between industries. Of course, these transactions are made of heterogeneous commodities, since primary and secondary products are mixed together. To obtain such a table, it is enough to pre-multiply the Use table by the column coefficients of the Make table.

However, for such a table there is no ideal solution for the treatment of scrap and second-hand goods, even though the small amounts they represent have little influence on the final results.

If these second-hand products are treated as the other secondary products and so attributed to other industries in the proportion in which they are produced, then they appear as input required by production, and thus any increase in the level of activity of an industry using scrap will generate an increase in the demand for scrap and second-hand goods for the input–output model. On the other hand, because the business sector resells used cars to households and buildings to the government, the gross private investment in the fixed-capital column of an input–output table has a negative amount for scrap and second-hand goods. The mechanical redistribution of this negative amount among the industries producing scrap and second-hand goods results in the appearance of negative amounts in several cells of the investment column, because those industries (such as steel) that are relatively large producers of scrap do not produce investment goods. The advantage of treating scrap and second-hand goods as other secondary products is that it ensures that the balance of accounts for each industry will be maintained. This was the method used for the first five tables: 1947, 1958, 1963, 1967, and 1972.

In order to avoid generating a demand for scrap and second-hand goods, the BEA (1980) recommended an alternative method, which takes scrap and second-hand goods out of the total production of each commodity. This technique has the disadvantage of destroying the equilibrium between resources and uses for each industry, and requires that an implicit adjustment be incorporated into value added. This is the method used for 1977 in this study. It should be stressed again that the amount of scrap and second-hand goods is at most a few percentage points of total production, and that the problem is of a more conceptual nature and less important with respect to its empirical consequences.

### A.2.3 *Imports*

There are two categories of imports, and these are treated differently in the IO tables: comparable imports, for which an equivalent exists domestically; and noncomparable imports, which do not have an equivalent in domestic production. The latter is treated as a dummy industry, entitled *noncomparable imports*. This industry does not have any input, and the corresponding column is therefore empty. The row describes the utilization of noncomparable imports by the different industries and the functions of the final demand. To ensure overall balance of the table and to show the total amount of imports in final demand, the total of the noncomparable imports is entered with a negative sign at the intersection of the noncomparable-imports row and the net-export column (before 1972) or in the imports column (in 1972 and 1977). The noncomparable imports are recorded at the foreign port value, and the transoceanic margins are recorded in the appropriate industries. One should note that if the transport (or other activity recorded as a margin) is accomplished by a foreign carrier, it is a comparable import of services and is dealt with accordingly. The specific treatment for *comparable imports* depends on whether they are (1) intermediate inputs or (2) for final demand.

*Intermediate inputs:* In the BEA tables prior to 1972 (in a manner similar to the treatment of secondary products), comparable imports of intermediary goods are added as inputs to the industry that would produce them in the United States. In the 1972 and 1977 tables, comparable imports of intermediary goods are separately recorded as negative entries in a special column of the final demand reserved for imports. In this case, the imports must be valued in a unit as close as possible to the value of the same commodity on the domestic market; they are therefore recorded at their value at the domestic port of entry, duty included.

The details provided for the tables prior to 1972 are sufficient to present the comparable imports of intermediary goods in the new methodology. Although the details of the operations necessary were not included in the written publication of the BEA, they were available in the magnetic-tape data files. The comparable imports of the earlier tables must be valued at their domestic-entry port value by adding the transoceanic margins to their foreign port value. These amounts are then written with a negative sign in the new column of the final demand reserved for imports. In order to maintain the balance of accounts, the addition of transoceanic margins must be compensated for by subtracting them from the industry that produces the margin services (transportation, wholesale trade, and insurance). Since the imports are recorded with a negative sign in the new presentation, this adjustment is in fact simply an algebraic addition.

*Final demand:* Prior to 1972, the comparable imports of commodities directly used for final demand were directly imputed to the different functions of the final demand in total, and in the same row as the noncomparable imports. In this case also, the imports are recorded at the foreign port value. It was desirable to present the comparable imports of goods allocated to final demand in the new methodology (from 1972 on). Unfortunately, it is not possible to know the detail of the commodity imported directly for final use for the tables prior to 1972. In order to make all six tables consistent, the comparable imports were taken out of final demand for the 1972 and 1977 tables and placed in a separate row, as had been done for the years prior to 1972. Thus, the tables from 1947 to 1967 were kept intact in this regard. The imports used for the final demand in the 1972 study have been identified by comparing a 1972 table presented in the old methodology (BEA 1979) with the new table. For 1977, the comparable imports used directly for the final demand have been estimated on the assumption that the share of the market by imports was constant regardless of the destination of a given commodity – with the exception of export and government use, which have been excluded from the potential users of imports. This choice is justified on the basis of the comparison of the two tables available for 1972.

### A.2.4 *Eating and drinking places*

In the tables from 1947 to 1967, eating and drinking places are included in the retail trade industry; however, they are treated separately in 1972 and 1977 (industry 74). If it were only a disaggregation of the industrial classification then there would be no problem in keeping the consistency between both presentations. However, the trade industry is a margin industry that records only the margin added at the time of the business transaction. When eating and drinking places are treated as trade, the food appears as directly sold by the food industry to the consumer (households or another industry), and only the costs and the value added of preparing the meal are accounted for in the trade industry. In contrast, when eating and drinking places are treated separately, the food appears as input for the eating and drinking places industry, and the output of this industry includes not only the costs and the value added of preparing the meal but also the value of the intermediary goods. Therefore the change in treatment results in an important change in the proportion between input and value added in the input–output tables. In order to correct this inconsistency between the different studies, the elements necessary to separately compute eating and drinking places in the earlier studies have been roughly estimated between 1947 and 1967.

The first step was to determine the total output of eating and drinking places. For 1947 this task was made easier with the information included in the original version of a table published by Leontief (1951) and Evans and Hoffenberg (1952).[2] The original study, although incompatible in its methodology with later studies, treats eating and drinking places separately. For 1958, 1963, and 1967, the figures published by the Economic Growth Project (BLS 1979) were used. The main destination of eating and drinking places' production is of course household consumption. This item is reported in the NIPA (BEA 1986) in table 2.4, line 4. In each year

---

[2] The 1947 table used by us is a revised version prepared by the Office of Business Economics (now the BEA) in order to make it comparable to the later studies (BEA 1970).

the share of household consumption represents between 75% and 80% of the total output of the industry. For other destinations of the product it was not possible to find direct information, so the following estimation method has been used. Starting with the demand structure for eating and drinking places in the 1972 study, an iterative method was employed to ensure that the amount of input shown in each industry is compatible with the tentative level of demand for the eating and drinking places' product.

The input structure is determined in two steps. As mentioned, eating and drinking places are treated in earlier studies as a "margin" industry integrated with trade. It follows that basic inputs are shown directly at their destination and that the margin is shown on the row of the trade industry. For each study, the amount of basic inputs used for private consumption expenditure is shown in a separate table that describes the bridge between the input–output classification and the detailed categories of the final demand (Simon 1965; BEA 1970, 1974).

In particular, these tables display the contribution of each industry for the category of meals and beverages. If we are ready to assume that the method of production for private consumption is the same as for other destinations, we can then determine the amount of inputs used by eating and drinking places. In these tables, the quantity corresponding with trade represents the margin added in the preparation of the meal. If eating and drinking places are represented separately, this margin must be decomposed between material inputs and value added. This is the second step of the transformation. Without additional information, one must assume that this input structure is identical to that for trade. This leads to an unavoidable distortion: oil products are a relatively large input of the trade industry because of the transport also carried by this industry, while this is hardly a characteristic of eating and drinking places.

## A.3 Aggregations and further modifications

### A.3.1 *Main aggregation*

The unpublished tables provided by Juillard for 1963, 1967, 1972, and 1977 had 105 rows and 116 columns, while those for 1947 and 1958 had 90 rows and 99 columns. In order to have all six tables with the same number of rows and columns – that is, $90 \times 98$ (later, $87 \times 98$) – an aggregation was done for the 1963, 1967, 1972, and 1977 tables. There were some differences in the dummy-industry and final-demand columns between the tables of 1947 and 1958 as compared to the later tables. The 1947 and 1958 ($90 \times 99$) matrices had to be made consistent with those of the later years. Table A.2 is a mapping of the correspondence between

Table A.2. *Sectoral correspondence for the different IO tables*[a]

| 1963–77<br>$105 \times 116$ | 1963–77<br>$87 \times 98$ | 1947/58<br>$90 \times 99$ | Final<br>$82 \times 88$ |
|---|---|---|---|
| 1 | 1 | 1 | 1 |
| 2 | 2 | 2 | 1 |
| 3 | 3 | 3 | 1 |
| 4 | 4 | 4 | 1 |
| 5 | 5 | 5 | 2 |
| 6 | 6 | 6 | 3 |
| 7 | 7 | 7 | 4 |
| 8 | 8 | 8 | 5 |
| 9 | 9 | 9 | 6 |
| 10 | 10 | 10 | 7 |
| 11 | 11 | 11 | 8 |
| 12 | 12 | 12 | 8 |
| 13 | 13 | 13 | 9 |
| 14 | 13 | 13 | 9 |
| 15 | 14 | 14 | 10 |
| 16 | 15 | 15 | 11 |
| 17 | 16 | 16 | 12 |
| 18 | 17 | 17 | 13 |
| 19 | 18 | 18 | 14 |
| 20 | 18 | 18 | 14 |
| 21 | 19 | 19 | 15 |
| 22 | 20 | 20 | 16 |
| 23 | 21 | 21 | 17 |
| 24 | 22 | 22 | 18 |
| 25 | 23 | 23 | 19 |
| 26 | 24 | 24 | 20 |
| 27 | 25 | 25 | 21 |
| 28 | 26 | 26 | 22 |
| 29 | 27 | 27 | 23 |
| 30 | 28 | 28 | 24 |
| 31 | 29 | 29 | 25 |
| 32 | 30 | 30 | 26 |
| 33 | 31 | 31 | 27 |
| 34 | 32 | 32 | 28 |
| 35 | 33 | 33 | 29 |
| 36 | 34 | 34 | 30 |
| 37 | 35 | 35 | 31 |
| 38 | 36 | 36 | 32 |
| 39 | 37 | 37 | 33 |
| 40 | 38 | 38 | 34 |
| 41 | 38 | 38 | 34 |
| 42 | 39 | 39 | 35 |
| 43 | 40 | 40 | 36 |

Table A.2 *(cont.)*

| 1963–77<br>$105 \times 116$ | 1963–77<br>$87 \times 98$ | 1947/58<br>$90 \times 99$ | Final<br>$82 \times 88$ |
|---|---|---|---|
| 44 | 41 | 41 | 37 |
| 45 | 42 | 42 | 38 |
| 46 | 43 | 43 | 39 |
| 47 | 44 | 44 | 40 |
| 48 | 45 | 45 | 41 |
| 49 | 46 | 46 | 42 |
| 50 | 47 | 47 | 43 |
| 51 | 48 | 48 | 44 |
| 52 | 49 | 49 | 45 |
| 53 | 50 | 50 | 46 |
| 54 | 51 | 51 | 47 |
| 55 | 52 | 52 | 48 |
| 56 | 53 | 53 | 49 |
| 57 | 54 | 54 | 50 |
| 58 | 55 | 55 | 51 |
| 59 | 56 | 56 | 52 |
| 60 | 57 | 57 | 53 |
| 61 | 58 | 58 | 54 |
| 62 | 59 | 59 | 55 |
| 63 | 60 | 60 | 56 |
| 64 | 61 | 61 | 57 |
| 65 | 62 | 62 | 58 |
| 66 | 63 | 63 | 59 |
| 67 | 64 | 64 | 60 |
| 68 | 65 | 65 | 61 |
| 69 | 65 | 65 | 61 |
| 70 | 65 | 65 | 61 |
| 71 | 65 | 65 | 61 |
| 72 | 65 | 65 | 61 |
| 73 | 65 | 65 | 61 |
| 74 | 65 | 65 | 61 |
| 75 | 67 | 67 | 63 |
| 76 | 66 | 66 | 62 |
| 77 | 68 | 68 | 64 |
| 78 | 69 | 69 | 65 |
| 79 | 74 | 74 | 65 |
| 80 | 69 | 69 | 65 |
| 81 | 70 | 70 | 66 |
| 82 | 70 | 70 | 66 |
| 83 | 70 | 70 | 66 |
| 84 | 71 | 71 | 67 |
| 85 | 71 | 71 | 67 |
| 86 | 72 | 72 | 68 |
| 87 | 72 | 72 | 68 |

Table A.2 *(cont.)*

| 1963–77<br>105 × 116 | 1963–77<br>87 × 98 | 1947/58<br>90 × 99 | Final<br>82 × 88 |
|:---:|:---:|:---:|:---:|
| 88 | 73 | 73 | 69 |
| 89 | 73 | 73 | 69 |
| 90 | 75 | 75 | 70 |
| 91 | 76 | 76 | 71 |
| 92 | 76 | 76 | 71 |
| 93 | 77 | 77 | 72 |
| 94 | 77 | 77 | 72 |
| 95 | 77 | 77 | 72 |
| 96 | 78 | 78 | 73 |
| 97 | 79 | 79 | 74 |
| 98 | 80 | 80 | 75 |
| 99 | 81 | 83 | 76 |
| 100 | 82 | 84 | 77 |
| 101 | 83 | 85 | 78 |
| 102 | 84 | 86 | 79 |
| 103 | 85 | 87 | 80 |
| 104 | 86 | 89 | 81 |
| 105 | 87 | 90 | 82 |
| *Final-demand columns* | | | |
| 104 | 86 | 89 | — |
| 105 | 87 | 92 | 81 |
| 106 | 88 | 93 | 82 |
| 107 | 89 | 94 | 83 |
| 108 | 90 | 95 | 84 |
| 109 | 91 | 96 | 85 |
| 110 | 92 | 97 | 86 |
| 111 | 93 | 97 | 86 |
| 112 | 94 | 98 | 87 |
| 113 | 95 | 98 | 87 |
| 114 | 96 | 98 | 87 |
| 115 | 97 | 98 | 87 |
| 116 | 98 | 99 | 88 |

[a] A listing of the final 82 × 88 IO sectors is provided in Table A.4.

the 105 × 116 sector matrix, the 87 × 98 matrix for the years 1963–77, the 90 × 99 matrix for 1947/1958, and the final 82 × 88 table. For the aggregation of the 1947 and 1958 tables, the procedure was slightly more complicated. In particular, sector 81 (unproductive real estate) had to be combined with sector 71 (productive real estate) so as to have one single sector as in the other tables.

A.3.2 *Force account construction, reverse adjustment*

According to the *Definitions and Conventions of the 1972 Input–Output Study* (BEA 1980):

> The output of the construction industries, whether new or maintenance or repair, includes both construction work performed on a contract basis for an industry or for a final demand sector and work achieved through the utilization of the work force of the industry or the final demand sector (e.g., government). The construction work performed by the work force of the consuming industry or final demand sector is called *force account construction*. The estimate of the value of force account construction for each industry which performs such work is summed by construction type (including maintenance and repair as well as new) and added to the output of the appropriate construction industry. The input side of the force account construction activity is made up of employee compensation and the various materials and services necessary to perform the work. (p. 46)

Thus, in order to reverse this redistribution of construction activity, the individual imputations for each industry had to be transferred back to the original industries, using table C of "imputations" for each individual industry (BEA 1980, pp. 75–7). These were redistributed back to their original rows in two steps. The first step involved only the inner 79 (intermediate portion) of the 85-order industries; the second step was an adjustment for the government final-demand sectors.

The imputations of force account construction (FAC) for the federal and state final-demand columns did not affect the inner $79 \times 79$ matrix, but rather the final demand and value added. The imputations involved for the federal and state final demand were assumed to derive predominantly from the compensation of government employees, and were therefore taken from the government-industry sector. The reasoning behind this is that the majority of this imputation is from wage payments to government employees. Therefore, the difference between the total compensation of general government as listed in NIPA and that listed in the IO tables corresponds to the imputations. These amounts were then transferred from the construction to the government-industry row for the federal and state final-demand columns. In order to have the construction row and column total match, the same amount was removed from the value-added element of construction (11th column) and placed in the value added of government industry (column 82). There is a certain portion of the total imputations that does not correspond to compensation, but since this amount seems to be rather small, there was no point in adopting an unclear, ad hoc procedure to transfer it (see BEA 1980, pp. 46–7).

In order to scale up the FAC vector for 1972 to reflect changes in output, the following formula was used:[3]

[3] The BEA has the actual imputations, but we were not able to obtain them.

$$FACXX = FAC72 \times \frac{QXX}{Q72},$$

where XX denotes a given year. In addition, the value-added elements were similarly scaled up or down in the case of construction, in order to reflect the reverse adjustment.

After aggregating agriculture, construction, and so on, we obtained the $82 \times 88$ tables (see Table A.2). The second step of reverse FAC involved the final-demand government sectors, and was carried out in conjunction with the adjustment (mentioned previously) for the imputed rental. The resulting tables were the final $82 \times 88$ tables.

### A.3.3 *Real estate*

A significant portion of the investment column element of the construction industry row was shifted to the personal consumption expenditure (PCE)-column element of the construction row, since purchases of private homes had been treated as investment in the original IO tables. In those IO tables, the real estate sector has two components: one corresponds to the actual real estate industry; the other is the imputed portion which is based upon owner-occupied dwellings. This imputed portion also can be broken down into two parts; one is fictitious and the other is real. The real portion was shifted to the PCE column because it is composed of actual purchases by private individuals for repair and maintenance of their own homes. At an intermediate stage, the fictitious portion was also included in the table. However, for the final version of the IO tables used for this database, the fictitious portion was removed from the PCE element of the row for real estate and rental, as was the value-added element of the PCE column, thereby eliminating the fictitious element entirely.

### A.3.4 *Final aggregations to produce the $82 \times 88$ IO tables*

As shown in Table A.2, once the $87 \times 98$ tables were obtained, the six government sectors had to be merged into two sectors in order to carry out the second step of the reverse FAC adjustment. This was necessary also in order for the 1947 and 1958 tables to be rendered consistent with the other tables. The resulting tables were then $87 \times 94$. The mapping for this aggregation is shown in Table A.3.

The $87 \times 94$ tables were then used for the first stage of the reverse FAC adjustment. The next required step was the final aggregation to $82 \times 88$. This involved three steps. (1) The first four (agricultural) sectors were merged into one sector – as Ochoa (1984) had done – since there is only one sector for agriculture in the capital stock vector. (2) Likewise, sectors

Table A.3.  *Mapping of government sectors between the*
*87 × 94 and 87 × 98 IO tables*

| 87 × 94 IO table | 87 × 98 IO table |
| --- | --- |
| 92  Federal government | 92  Federal government, defense |
| | 93  Federal government, nondefense |
| 93  State government | 94  State government, education |
| | 95  State government, health |
| | 96  State government, safety |
| | 97  State government, other |
| 94  Row total | 98  Row total |

11 and 12 were also merged for the same reason. (3) Finally, sector 74 (eating and drinking places) was merged into sector 69 (business services, research and development), since the treatment of eating and drinking places changed for tables after 1972. In addition, column 86 was removed from the final-demand matrix because it consisted only of zeros. The resulting 82 × 88 sectoral listing is reproduced here as Table A.4.

A.3.5  *Aggregations from 82 × 88 to 6 × 9 tables*

In order to carry out our calculations, the 82 × 88 tables had to be further aggregated to 6 × 9 tables. The first sector of this final aggregation was that of production: sectors 1–64 were summed together with sectors 68 and 70–75. (The choice of sectors excluded will become clear as the other sectors are described.) The second sector, total trade, consisted of sector 65 (wholesale and retail trade) and a portion of sector 67 (real estate and rental). A certain proportion (g) of the real estate sector (as ground rent) was included in the royalties sector, and the remaining portion $(1 - g)$ was included in the trade sector (as building rent). For the purpose of these tables, we used $g = 0.25$ throughout; a more detailed derivation of g for use with annual data is given in Appendix B. The third sector is that of royalties, which includes sector 66 (finance and insurance), the respective portion (g) of sector 67 (real estate), and sector 69 (business services). The fourth sector is the household industry: sector 79 from the 82 × 88 table. The fifth row is the sum of sectors 80 and 81 (inventory valuation adjustment and value added). The sixth and final row is the totals, which is the same as row 82.

The first four columns of the 6 × 9 table are the same as the first four rows. The fifth column is sector 81 (personal consumption expenditure). The sixth column combined columns 80, 82, and 83: inventory valuation

Table A.4. *Sectoral list for the 82 × 88 IO table*

1 Agriculture
2 Iron mining
3 Nonferrous metal mining
4 Coal mining
5 Crude petroleum and natural gas
6 Stone and clay mining
7 Chemical and fertilizers
8 Construction
9 Ordnance and accessories
10 Food and kindred products
11 Tobacco
12 Fabrics, yarn, and thread mills
13 Miscellaneous textile goods and floor coverings
14 Apparel
15 Miscellaneous fabricated textile products
16 Lumber and wood products
17 Wooden containers
18 Household furniture
19 Other furniture and fixtures
20 Paper and allied products
21 Paperboard, containers, and boxes
22 Printing and publishing
23 Chemicals and allied products
24 Plastic and synthetic materials
25 Drugs, cleaning, and toilet preparations
26 Paints and allied products
27 Petroleum refining
28 Rubber and miscellaneous plastic products
29 Leather tanning
30 Footwear and other leather products
31 Glass and glass products
32 Stone and clay products
33 Primary iron and steel manufacturing
34 Primary nonferrous metals manufacturing
35 Metal containers
36 Heating and fabricating metal products
37 Screw machine products
38 Other fabricated metal products
39 Engines and turbines
40 Farm machinery and equipment
41 Construction machinery and equipment
42 Materials handling equipment
43 Metalworking machinery and equipment
44 Special industry machinery and equipment
45 General industry machinery and equipment
46 Machine shop products
47 Office and computing machines

Table A.4 *(cont.)*

48  Service industry machines
49  Electric transmission equipment
50  Household appliances
51  Electrical wiring and lighting equipment
52  Radio, TV, and communication equipment
53  Electronic components and accessories
54  Miscellaneous electrical machinery
55  Motor vehicles
56  Aircraft and parts
57  Other transportation equipment
58  Professional and scientific instruments
59  Photographic and optical goods
60  Miscellaneous manufacturing
61  Transportation
62  Communications except broadcasting
63  Radio and TV broadcasting
64  Public utilities
65  Wholesale and retail trade
66  Finance and insurance
67  Real estate and rental
68  Hotels and repair places, except auto repair
69  Business services, research and development
70  Auto repair and services
71  Amusements
72  Medical and educational services
73  Federal government
74  State government
75  Noncomparable imports
76  Scrap
77  Government industry
78  Rest-of-the-World industry
79  Household industry
80  Inventory valuation adjustment
81  Value added
82  Column totals

*Final-demand columns*
81  Personal consumption expenditure (PCE)
82  Investment (INV)
83  Change in business inventories (CBI)
84  Exports
85  Imports
86  Federal government
87  State government
88  Row totals

Table A.5. *Sectoral list for the 6 × 9 IO table*

| Row and sector | Sectors from the 82 × 88 table |
| --- | --- |
| 1 Production | Manufacturing (1–64, 68, 70–74) |
| 2 Total trade | Trade (65), part of Real estate (67) |
| 3 Royalties | Finance (66), part of Real estate (67, 69) |
| 4 Household industry | Household industry (79) |
| 5 Value added | IVA (80), Value added (81) |
| 6 Gross output | Column totals (82) |

| Column and sector | Sectors from the 82 × 88 table |
| --- | --- |
| 1 Production | Manufacturing (1–64, 68, 70–74) |
| 2 Total trade | Trade (65), part of Real estate (67) |
| 3 Royalties | Finance (66), part of Real estate (67, 69) |
| 4 Household industry | Household industry (79) |
| 5 Consumption | Personal consumption expenditure (81) |
| 6 Investment | IVA (80), INV (82), CBI (83) |
| 7 Net imports | Exports (84), Imports (85) |
| 8 Government | State government (86), Federal government (87) |
| 9 Gross product | Row totals (88) |

adjustment, investment, and change in business inventories. The seventh column combined columns 84 and 85, exports and imports, and is therefore labeled net imports. The eighth column combined sectors 86 and 87, federal and state government. The last column (as with the last row) is the totals, the same as column 88. For the full list of sectors, see Table A.5.

# B

## Operations on the real estate and finance sectors

*Companion text:* Section 3.1.3; Sections 5.1–5.2

### A. THEORETICAL CONSIDERATIONS

#### B.1 The real estate-and-rentals sector

The real estate-and-rentals sector consists of three basic types of nonproduction activities: fictitious (imputed) rentals of owner-occupied housing; rental and sale of land; and rentals and sales of buildings and equipment.

From our point of view, the imputed portion is quite improper. IO–NIPA accounts treat homeowners who live in their own houses as if they were businesses renting out their homes to themselves. To accommodate such a treatment, they create a set of fictitious rental flows. On the revenue side, home maintenance expenditures of private homeowners are treated as the input costs $M_{ir}$ (ir stands for "imputed rental") of this imputed owner-occupied rental sector, to which is added a wholly fictitious value added $VA_{ir}$ (composed of fictitious wages and profits $W_{ir} + P_{ir}$). On the use side, all the adjustments take place within the consumption column. The home maintenance expenditures from which $M_{ir}$ is derived are shifted from the rows corresponding to the actual commodities purchased (paint, hardware, etc.) to the real estate row, to which is also added a fictitious purchase of real estate services of magnitude $VA_{ir}$ (BEA 1980, p. 47). In actual IO tables, the sum of these fictitious entries virtually doubles the gross output and gross product of the real estate sector.[1]

---

[1] Imputed rentals comprise almost 45% of the whole rental sector's gross output in 1972.

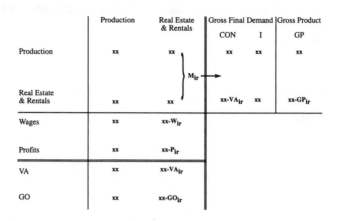

Figure B.1.  Removing imputed rentals.

The whole procedure is meaningless from our point of view. We must therefore exactly *reverse* the imputations just described in order to recapture the actual flows within the real estate-and-rental sector. This requires two operations: In the rental-sector column, we subtract $M_{ir}$ from the intermediate inputs, and $W_{ir}$ and $P_{ir}$ from the corresponding components of value added; in the consumption column, we subtract $VA_{ir} = W_{ir} + P_{ir}$ from the rental row. In principle, we should also now shift $M_{ir}$ from the rental row back to the various other rows that represent the actual commodities used for home maintenance. But since this would change only the distribution of elements in the consumption column, not their total, and since the necessary detailed data are unavailable, we do not undertake this step. Figure B.1 summarizes the process of restoring the rental-sector flows to their actual levels.[2]

Once we have reduced the rental sector to its actual rental flows, we need to separate these flows into revenues derived (1) from the rental and sale of buildings and equipment, and (2) from the rental and sale of land. The former is a trading activity, and must be merged into the trade sector. The latter is a royalty payment, and belongs under private royalties.

Building and equipment rentals are activities in which the use value of a produced good such as a building is sold piecemeal ("rented") over its economic lifetime. As such, it must be merged into the overall trade sector. But in order to do so, its row allocations must be unbundled, in the same way as those of wholesale/retail trade. To recall how this works,

---

[2] Figure B.1 makes it clear that the total M is reduced by $M_{ir}$, and that both VA and FD are reduced by $VA_{ir}$; hence both GO and GP are reduced by $M_{ir} + VA_{ir}$.

| | Production | Bldg. & Eq. Rentals | Gross Final Demand | | Gross Product |
| --- | --- | --- | --- | --- | --- |
| | | | CON | IG | GP |
| Production | -- | -- | -- | 1000 | 1000 |
| Bldg. & Eq. Rentals | 400 | 200 | 1000 | 400 | 2000 |
| Wages | 200 | 400 | | | |
| Profits | 400 | 1400 | | | |
| GVA | 600 | 1800 | | | |
| GO | 1000 | 2000 | | | |

Figure B.2. Rentals in input–output accounts.

first consider the case of a computer retailer. Suppose computer manufacturers sell $1000 worth of computers to retailers, who in turn resell them to businesses, households, or government for a total price of $2000. If we were to record both the sale of the computers to retailers ($1000) and also their subsequent resale by the retailers to their final users ($2000), we would be double counting the same product. Input–output tables get around this difficulty by treating the final sales as if they were composed of two distinct elements: $1000 worth of computers sold directly to businesses,[3] households, and so on; and $1000 worth of trading services sold to the same final users. Only the latter $1000 enters into the input–output measures of the gross output and gross product of the retail sector. This is the so-called unbundling of the $2000 total revenue of the retail sector into its $1000 pass-through costs (costs of goods resold) and its $1000 gross trading margin (which includes operating expenses and gross profits); see Figure 3.6.

The very same treatment should be accorded to building and equipment rentals. But it is not, because input–output and NIPA accounts treat rentals as a production (as opposed to a trading) activity. Consider the case of a computer rental firm. Suppose the computer producer sells the same $1000 worth of computers to a firm which in turn *rents* them out (instead of reselling them, as in the previous example) to final users for rental charges totaling $2000. As shown in Figure B.2, the original sale

---

[3] Sales to business would show up as an entry in the investment column of the computer industry row, since computers are durable capital goods (which is the NIPA definition of fixed capital).

| | Production | Bldg. & Eq. Rentals | Gross Final Demand | | Gross Product |
| --- | --- | --- | --- | --- | --- |
| | | | CON | IG | GP |
| Production | -- | -- | -- | 0=1000-A | 0 |
| Bldg. & Eq. Rentals | 400 | 200 | 1000 | 400 | 2000 |
| Wages | 200 | 400 | | | |
| Profits | 400 | 400=1400-A | | | |
| GVA | 600 | 800 | | | |
| GO | 1000 | 1000 | | | |

Figure B.3. Rentals adjusted for pass-through costs (A = 1000).

of $1000 worth of computers shows up in the production-sector column as the sum of costs (shown here as rental sector inputs of $400) and wages and profits. In the production-sector row, the transaction is recorded in the investment column since rental items are basically durable goods. At the same time, the $2000 revenue of the rental sector would *also* be recorded, as a wholly new total product emanating from this sector. The column of the rental sector would show this amount as the sum of intermediate inputs, wages, and gross profits, the latter encompassing two kinds of depreciation: the depreciation of buildings and equipment used to conduct rental activities; and the amortization A of computers rented out (which we assume to equal $1000).[4] The rental-sector row then shows the sources of rental-sector receipts, which is interpreted here as the distribution of this sector's so-called product to various users. Note that in this treatment the pass-through cost A (the cost of goods resold) has been counted in both gross output (in gross profit of the rental sector) and gross product (in production-sector sales to gross investment $I_G$).[5] It is precisely this cost which we must remove if we wish to make the treatment of computer rentals conform to that of any other trading activity.

[4] If the stock of computers being rented out is constant, then the gross purchases of computers to be rented out ($1000) will just equal the amortization A of computers currently being rented out.

[5] In our theoretical analysis, we generally treat depreciation as part of intermediate inputs. But in Figures B.2–B.4 it is more convenient to adopt the actual input–output convention of leaving depreciation in gross profit on the revenue side and in gross investment on the use side. This makes it easier to explain the actual empirical procedures involved in treating building and equipment rentals as a trading activity.

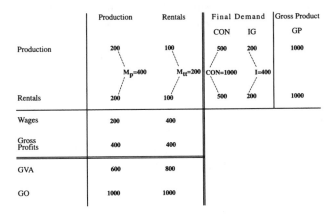

|  | Production | Rentals | Final Demand | | Gross Product |
|---|---|---|---|---|---|
|  |  |  | CON | IG | GP |
| Production | 200 | 100 | 500 | 200 | 1000 |
|  | $M_p=400$ | $M_{tt}=200$ | CON=1000 | I=400 |  |
| Rentals | 200 | 100 | 500 | 200 | 1000 |
| Wages | 200 | 400 |  |  |  |
| Gross Profits | 400 | 400 |  |  |  |
| GVA | 600 | 800 |  |  |  |
| GO | 1000 | 1000 |  |  |  |

Figure B.4. Rentals treated as a trading activity.

To remove the pass-through cost A, we must subtract it from rental-sector gross profits on the revenue side and from gross investment on the use side, as illustrated in Figure B.3. Then the remaining row elements of the rental sector must be unbundled, in this case in the ratio 1:1 (since that is the ratio of pass-through costs A to the gross rental margin). Figure B.4 shows the final result, which is identical to that of any other trading activity (cf. Figure 3.6). This process applies to the building and equipment rental sector as a whole. We will call this the "ABR adjustment," where ABR ≡ amortization of buildings and equipment rented out by the real estate sector to others.[6] It involves two steps:

(1) The annual cost ABR of buildings and equipment rented out to others must be unbundled into production and trade components, and these subtracted from the corresponding rows of the investment column.[7] This reduces aggregate investment, final demand, and gross product by the amount of ABR. At the same time, ABR must be subtracted from the gross value added of the rental sector. This reduces rental-sector value added, aggregate value added, and aggregate gross output by the amount of ABR.

[6] In IO–NIPA accounts, the gross trading margin of the building rental sector includes both the depreciation of plant and equipment used by this sector in conducting business *and* the amortization of buildings rented out by this sector to others. Our ABR adjustment automatically removes the latter, but it takes a separate empirical step to remove the former also. See Section B.3 for details.

[7] In an actual IO table, any purchase of computers will be split into its producer's price and gross trading margin, and these will be recorded in the production and trade rows of the relevant column.

(2) The rental-row elements should be unbundled into their pass-through cost and their rental markups, and the pass-through components shifted back to the production-sector row.

In step (2) it is useful to note that since the unbundling of the rental-row elements (including ABR) merely redistributes given sums between the production and trade rows, it has no effect on the overall sum. This is fortunate, because unbundling is generally not feasible at the IO level owing to a lack of necessary detail. Therefore, in our empirical input–output tables of Section 5.1 and Appendix C, the building-rental component of the total trade sector has been neither adjusted for ABR nor unbundled. However, the ABR adjustment *is* carried out for the final NIPA-based estimates in Section B.3 and Appendix E.

### B.2 The royalties sector

#### B.2.1 *Royalty payments between businesses*

This section details the treatment of royalty payments made by the production and trade sectors to a royalties sector. We begin from our usual numerical example, where a total product of $2000 is sold for $1000 by the producing sector and then resold for $2000 by the trade sector. But now we also suppose that a portion ($250) of what was formerly production and trade profits is paid over in the form of business royalty payments (RY) to a third, royalties-receiving (ry), sector: say, $100 from production ($RY_p = \$100$) and $150 from trade ($RY_t = \$150$).

On the revenue side, this is simply a transfer of $250 of value from the primary sector to the secondary (ry) sector, which in turn splits these receipts into intermediate inputs $M_{ry} = \$50$, wages $W_{ry} = \$100$, and gross profits $P_{ry} = \$100$; see Figure B.5. It also makes it clear that since the royalty payments already appear as payments out of the total revenues of production and trade, we cannot then *also* count them in their re-appearance as the receipts of the royalties sector. This is because the payments are transfers of value rather than purchases of use values.

Figure B.5 can be used to derive the actual use-value flows, with our usual conventions. Total intermediate use M now includes the intermediate inputs $M_{ry}$ of the royalties sector, so that $M = M_p + M_t + M_{ry} = 400 + 200 + 50 = \$650$. Total consumption CON = $1025 is the sum of workers' consumption

$$\begin{aligned}
\text{CONW} &= \text{CONW}_p + \text{CONW}_t + \text{CONW}_{ry} \\
&= W_p + W_t + W_{ry} \\
&= \$200 + \$400 + \$100 = \$700
\end{aligned}$$

and capitalist consumption

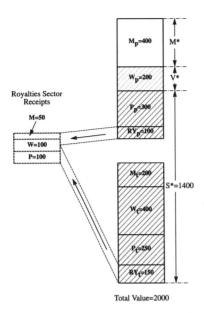

Figure B.5. Division of value: Business royalties payments.

$$CONC = \tfrac{1}{2}P = \tfrac{1}{2}(P_p + P_t + P_{ry})$$
$$= \tfrac{1}{2}(\$300 + \$250 + \$100) = \$325;$$

total intended and unintended investment $I = \tfrac{1}{2}P = \$325$ also. As always, the total use adds up to \$2000. Figure B.6 summarizes these use-value flows.

Our analysis of the effect of business royalty payments on the distribution of value and use value does not depend on whether businesses treat them as costs (e.g., ground rent or banking service charges) or disbursements from value added (e.g., net interest paid to business, households, or government). But this indifference to the form of royalty payments does not carry over to IO tables. In either case, if the production- and trade-sector royalty payments are made to another business sector, the receiving sector will be recorded as a royalties-sector (ry) column in the tables, with a gross output $GO_{ry}$ divided into input costs $M_{ry}$, wages $W_{ry}$, and profits $P_{ry}$.

When the royalty payments are treated as costs, we must also create a new row in which to register these intermediate inputs $RY_p$ and $RY_t$. The row sum of these costs is the gross product $GP_{ry}$ of the royalties sector, which is of course equal to its receipts $GO_{ry}$ (the column sum of its costs

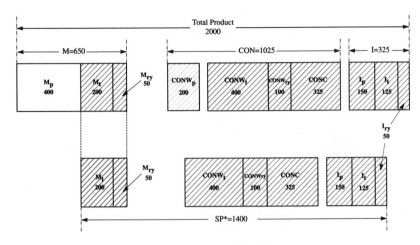

Figure B.6. Use of product: Business royalties payments.

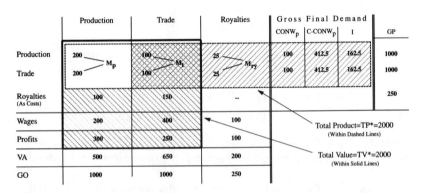

Figure B.7. IO accounts and Marxian categories: Business royalties payments as costs.

and profits). Thus, when royalty payments are recorded as costs, they inflate both total gross product and total gross output by an amount equal to the sum of the royalty payments. As far as input–output accounts are concerned, the treatment is consistent and the tables balance. Figure B.7 illustrates this mapping from the value and use-value flows (see Figures B.5 and B.6) to an input–output table in which the royalty payments are recorded as costs.

The trouble begins when business royalty payments (such as net interest paid) are treated as disbursements from value added. As in the previous case, the receipt by the royalties sector of these payments must be

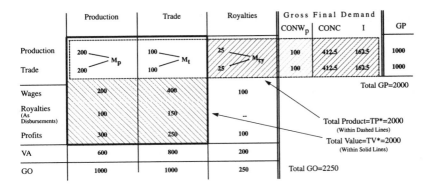

Figure B.8. Partial IO representation of business royalties payments as disbursements from value added.

acknowledged through the creation of a royalties column, with gross output $GO_{ry}$ equal in magnitude to the sum of the royalty payments $RY_p$ and $RY_t$. But now, because the payments themselves are recorded in the value-added row of the productive and trade sectors, there is no corresponding separate royalties row. Thus, whereas total gross output GO has been inflated by $GO_{ry}$, no such addition has been made to total gross product GP. At this point, the tables would not balance. Figure B.8 depicts this unhappy situation.

Within the logic of orthodox economics, in which all sectors are productive, the simplest way out of this dilemma is to define *all* royalty payments made by businesses directly to the royalties sector as costs of "products" purchased from the royalties sector, regardless of whether or not businesses treat them that way. Thus (say) net interest payments made by nonfinancial businesses to the banking sector would be treated in the same way as banking service charges. In the present case, this means shifting $RY_p$ and $RY_t$ out of the value-added row into a newly created royalties row. This is the end result of the procedure followed in input–output accounts.[8] The resulting table is identical to Figure B.7; Table B.1 provides an algebraic summary of the results.

[8] Since royalty payments are transfer payments, it would be much more appropriate to record them in the value-added row of the production and trade columns; net payments would be positive entries and net receipts would be negative entries. This means that the value-added row in the royalties-sector column would contain a negative entry equal in magnitude to the sum of all the royalty payments by the other sectors as well as positive entries for wages and profits. Gross output of this sector would then be zero (which is correct since it is not a production sector) and its total "value added" would be negative by the amount of $M_{ry}$.

Table B.1. *Marxian and IO measures: Business royalties payments*

| Marxian | | Input–output |
|---|---|---|

*A. Revenue side*

$TV^* = GO_p + GO_t = 2000$     $<$     $GO = GO_p + GO_t + GO_{ry} = 2250$
     $= 1000 + 1000$                             $= 1000 + 1000 + 250$

$C^* = M_p = 400$     $<$     $M = (M_p + RY_p) + (M_t + RY_t) + M_{ry}$
                                         $= (400 + 100) + (200 + 150) + 50 = 900$

$VA^* = TV^* - C^* = 1600$     $>$     $VA = GO - M = 1350$
     $= RY_p + VA_p + (GO_t)$                        $= VA_p + VA_t + VA_{ry}$
     $= RY_p + VA_p + (M_t + RY_t + VA_t)$        $= 500 + 650 + 200$
     $= GO_{ry} + M_t + VA_p + VA_t$
     (since $RY_p + RY_t = GO_{ry}$)
     $= VA_p + VA_t + VA_{ry} + M_t + M_{ry}$
     (since $GO_{ry} = M_{ry} + W_{ry} + P_{ry}$)
     $= 500 + 650 + 200 + (200 + 50)$

$V^* = W_p = 200$     $<$     $W = W_p + W_t + W_{ry} = 700$
                                          $= 200 + 400 + 100$

$S^* = VA^* - V^* = 1400$     $>$     $P = P_p + P_t + P_{ry} = 650$
     $= M_t + M_{ry}$                                  $= 300 + 250 + 100$
        $+ VA_p + VA_t + VA_{ry} - W_p$
     $= P_p + P_t + P_{ry}$
        $+ (M_{ry} + W_{ry}) + (M_t + W_t)$
     $= 300 + 250 + 100$
        $+ (50 + 100) + (200 + 400)$

$S^*/V^* = 1400/200 = 700\%$     $\gg$     $P/W = 650/700 = 93\%$
     $= [(M_{ry} + W_{ry})$                       $= P/(W_p + W_t + W_{ry})$
        $+ (M_t + W_t) + P]/W_p$

*B. Use side*

$TP^* = GP_p + GP_t = 2000$     $<$     $GP = GP_p + GP_t + GO_{ry} = 2250$
                                          $= 1000 + 1000 + 250$

$U^* = M_p = 400$     $<$     $M = 900$

$FP^* = TP^* - U^* = 1600$     $>$     $FD = GP - M = 1350$
     $= M_t + M_{ry} + CON + I$                 $= CON + I = 1025 + 325$
     $= 200 + 50 + 1025 + 325$

$NP^* = CONW_p = 200$                (no corresponding category)

$SP^* = FP^* - NP^* = 1400$                (no corresponding category)
     $= M_t + M_{ry} + CON + I - CONW_p$
     $= M_t + M_{ry} + CONW_t + CONW_{ry}$
        $+ CONC + I$
     $= 200 + 50 + 400 + 100 + 325 + 325$

Table B.1 bears out our earlier analysis (Sections 3.1.2 and 3.6) of the general patterns in the mapping between Marxian and IO–NIPA categories. The IO measure of gross output GO = \$2250 now overstates total TV* = \$2000, because the \$250 transferred from the primary sectors to the royalty sector is counted in orthodox economics as a measure of the corresponding amount of *production* by the royalties sector (since orthodox economics treats all sectors as production sectors).[9] Similarly, intermediate inputs M = 900 and total wages W = 700 overstate (respectively) constant capital C* = 400 and variable capital V* = 200, because the conventional measures encompass all labor and all inputs, not only productive ones. On the other hand, total profit P = 650 considerably understates surplus value S* = 1400, because the former reflects only that portion of surplus value which takes the form of aggregate profit, and not the portion absorbed in the costs of unproductive capitalist activities (compare the last expression for S* in Table B.1 with the corresponding expression for P). As a result, the orthodox measure of the profit/wage ratio P/W = 93% greatly understates the rate of surplus value S*/V* = 700% (and hence greatly understates the true rate of exploitation of productive workers).

### B.2.2 *Royalty payments between businesses and households*

In addition to making (net) royalty payments directly to the royalties sector, businesses also make such payments to households. These are recorded as disbursements from value added, since they are not costs of operations. Households in turn make (net) payments to the royalties sector. We will treat these two phases separately.

Ignoring (for the moment) their possible impact on the true wages of productive workers and hence on the magnitude of surplus value, business royalty payments to households merely bring about a different distribution of surplus value and surplus product. Figure B.9 makes it clear that we pick up these royalty payments in the value-added rows of the production and trade sectors. Figure B.10 shows the corresponding use side.

In this particular case, the input–output tables treat the issue in the same way as we do. That is to say, business royalty payments to households are picked up in the value-added rows of the production and trade sectors, and the corresponding distribution of the product shows up in the final-demand columns. Figure B.11 shows the IO–Marxian mapping. The general patterns here are the same as before, with the exception that

---

[9] Royalty payments can indeed be regarded as purchases of "services." But these services serve to redistribute wealth, not to add to it; they are therefore distributive services, not productive ones.

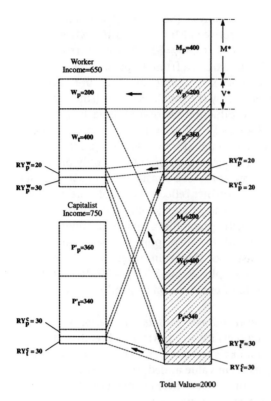

Figure B.9. Revenue side: Business royalties payments to households. *Note:* Both $P'_p$ and $P'_t$ are net of royalties.

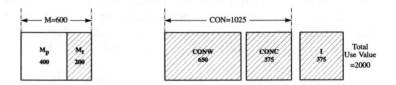

Figure B.10. Use side: Business royalties payments to households.

in this case total gross output $GO = GO_p + GO_t$ equals total value $TV^*$, because there is (as yet) no reflux of revenue to the royalties sector and hence no royalties-sector receipts $GO_{ry}$ to be recorded.

Payments from households to the royalties sector are a bit more complicated. Because business accounts register the *sources* of household income (wages, salaries, royalties paid to households, etc.), they already

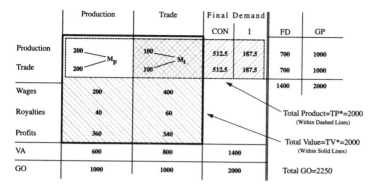

Figure B.11. IO accounts and Marxian categories: Business royalties payments to households.

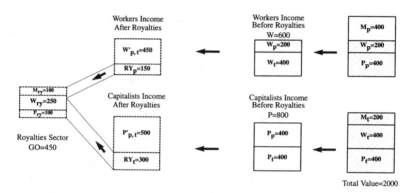

Figure B.12. Revenue side: Household payments to royalties sector.

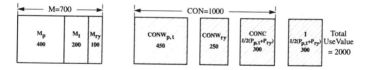

Figure B.13. Use side: Household payments to royalties sector.

include that portion of value which households transfer back to the royalties sector. We therefore cannot also count the total revenue $GO_{ry}$ of the royalties sector, which is merely the receipt of this same transfer. On the use side, these household royalty payments do not appear at all, since they are transfers rather than purchases of the product. Figures B.12 and B.13 illustrate these points.

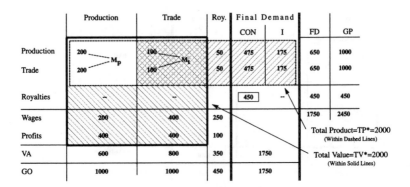

Figure B.14. IO accounts and Marxian categories: Household payments to royalties sector.

In keeping with their theoretical premise that all sectors are production sectors, IO tables treat the payment of royalties by households as purchases of the royalties-sector product (recorded in the royalties row of the consumption column), and treat the receipt of these payments as the measure of the gross output $GO_{ry}$ of the royalties column. From our point of view, this is a spurious inflation of the measures of total gross output and product, because it double counts already recorded revenues. The Marxian measures of total value (outlined in bold lines) and total product (in dashed lines) therefore exclude these elements, as shown in Figure B.14.

Household payments of royalties introduce a new element into our general patterns. When we were dealing only with production and trade, the Marxian measure of value added VA* was larger than the corresponding orthodox measure VA, because VA* included the intermediate input of the trade sector $M_t$ as the part of surplus value absorbed in the costs of trading (see Table 3.6). The consideration of business payments to the royalties sector further strengthened this inequality. The business royalty payments $RY_p + RY_t$ appeared as costs in IO–NIPA accounts, which excluded them from the conventional measures of value added in the production and trade sectors. These same payments re-appear as the receipts (gross output $GO_{ry}$) of the royalties sector, but only a portion $GO_{ry} - M_{ry} = VA_{ry}$ enters into the value added of the royalties sector. $M_{ry}$ therefore disappears from the orthodox measure of aggregate value added. Thus, when we consider business royalty payments in addition to production and trade, VA* exceeds VA by the amount of $M_t$ plus $M_{ry}$ (see Table B.1).

In the case of household royalty payments, a reverse effect operates. Since households are the ones paying the royalties, the payments themselves do not appear as business costs and hence do not reduce the conventional measures of production and trade value added (whose total in this case equals the Marxian measure VA*). But the receipt of these payments is still recorded as the gross output $GO_{ry}$ of the royalties sector, a portion $VA_{ry}$ of which enters into the royalties-sector value added and hence into aggregate value added VA. The net effect of household royalty payments is to increase the conventional measure of aggregate value added relative to its Marxian counterpart, other things being equal. A similar effect will be found for household payments to the government, to the extent that the government in turn transfers some of this revenue back to the royalties sector (through net interest payments, etc.). Thus, *we cannot say a priori which of the two measures will be larger.* Indeed, the empirical evidence indicates that VA exceeds VA*, so that the effect just discussed is apparently strong enough to predominate. Table B.2, based on Figure B.14, illustrates this new type of pattern.

The (direct or government-mediated) reflux of household income into the royalties sector has the further effect of raising aggregate profits relative to surplus value. The reasons are the same as before: Because the household payments are not business costs, they do not reduce the aggregate profits of the production and trade sectors; however, a part of their receipt by the royalties sector shows up as its profits. The net effect is to raise aggregate profits, other things being equal.

## B. EMPIRICAL CONSIDERATIONS

### B.3 Removing imputed rentals

IO–NIPA accounts treat homeowners who live in their own houses as if they were businesses renting out their homes to themselves. Accordingly, they create a set of fictitious rental flows. On the revenue side, a fictitious gross output $GO_{ir}$ (ir stands for "imputed rental") is created by adding together intermediate inputs $M_{ir}$ (which are the estimated home maintenance expenditures of private homeowners) and a wholly fictitious value added $VA_{ir}$. On the use side, a fictitious gross product $GP_{ir} = GO_{ir}$ is added within the cell at the intersection of the real estate row and the personal consumption expenditure (PCE) column (BEA 1980, p. 47, A-22).

We reverse the process just described. This means transferring the intermediate input $M_{ir}$ back into the PCE column, removing $GVA_{ir}$ from the GVA of the real estate-and-rental sector, and removing $GP_{ir} = GO_{ir} = M_{ir} + GVA_{ir}$ from the real estate-and-rental row of the PCE column (see Section A.3.3).

Table B.2. *Marxian and IO measures: Household payments to the royalties sector*

| Marxian | | Input–output |
|---|---|---|
| **A. Revenue side** | | |
| $TV^* = GO_p + GO_t = 2000$ | $<$ | $GO = GO_p + GO_t + GO_{ry} = 2450$ |
| $= 1000 + 1000$ | | $= 1000 + 1000 + 450$ |
| $C^* = M_p = 400$ | $<$ | $M = M_p + M_t + M_{ry} = 700$ |
| | | $= 400 + 200 + 100$ |
| $VA^* = TV^* - C^* = 1600$ | $<$ | $VA = GO - M = 1750$ |
| $= VA_p + VA_t + M_t$ | | $= VA_p + VA_t + VA_{ry}$ |
| $= 600 + 800 + 200$ | | $= 600 + 800 + 350$ |
| $V^* = W_p = 200$ | $<$ | $W = W_p + W_t + W_{ry} = 850$ |
| | | $= 200 + 400 + 250$ |
| $S^* = VA^* - V^* = 1400$ | $>$ | $P = P_p + P_t + P_{ry} = 900$ |
| $= VA_p + VA_t + M_t - W_p$ | | $= 400 + 400 + 100$ |
| $= P_p + P_t + (M_t + W_t)$ | | |
| $= 400 + 400 + (200 + 400)$ | | |
| $S^*/V^* = 1400/200 = 700\%$ | $\gg$ | $P/W = 900/850 = 106\%$ |
| $= [(M_t + W_t) + P]/W_p$ | | $= P/(W_p + W_t + W_{ry})$ |
| **B. Use side** | | |
| $TP^* = GP_p + GP_t = 2000$ | $<$ | $GP = GP_p + GP_t + GO_{ry} = 2450$ |
| | | $= 1000 + 1000 + 450$ |
| $U^* = M_p = 400$ | $<$ | $M = 700$ |
| $FP^* = TP^* - U^* = 1600$ | $<$ | $FD = GP - M = 1750$ |
| $= M_t + M_{ry} + CON^* + I^*$ | | $= CON + I = 1400 + 350$ |
| $= 200 + 100 + 950 + 350$ | | |
| $NP^* = CONW_p = 200$ | | (no corresponding category) |
| $SP^* = FP^* - NP^* = 1400$ | | (no corresponding category) |

## B.4 Splitting nonimputed rentals into $GO_{gr}$ and $GO_{br}$

Once we have recovered the actual rental-sector flows, we need to separate them into revenues $GO_{gr}$ derived from royalties (ground rent, dealers' commissions, and royalty payments) and revenues $GO_{br}$ derived from the rental and sale of buildings and equipment. No direct estimates are available for either component. In a telephone conversation, Mary W. Hook of the BEA has indicated that the rule of thumb in residential real estate is that land accounts for roughly one-third of total revenues. Our calculations yield somewhat smaller estimates, in the range of 25%–30%.

In what follows, we will estimate the royalties portion $GO_{gr}$ in two steps. First, we estimate the sum of dealers' commissions $GO_{r1}$ and direct payments of land rent and royalties $GO_{r2}$. Subtracting this from the total rental sector output $GO_r$ yields an estimate of the combined total of ground and building rents. Of this total, the ground-rent component $GO_{r3}$ is estimated by using the ratio of site price to the sales prices of homes. Total rental-sector royalties $GO_{gr}$ then consist of the sum $GO_{gr1} + GO_{gr2} + GO_{gr3}$, and the ratio of this to total nonimputed rental-sector gross output $GO_r$ gives us the proportion g that we seek. The various steps are detailed next for 1972 (all data are in millions of dollars).

*Sample calculations of $GO_{gr}$ = gross output of the royalties sector:* Let

$$GO_{re} \equiv GO_{gr} + GO_{br} = 99,015$$

> = gross output of the real estate and rental sector (from the 1972 input–output table described in Appendix A);

$$GO_{gr} \equiv GO_{gr1} + GO_{gr2} + GO_{gr3}$$

> = estimated gross output of the ground-rent sector
> = 29,000 (derived in what follows).

(1) $GO_{gr1}$ = dealers' commissions on real estate activities. Total dealers' commissions are available only for 1967, 1972, and 1977.[10] However, the great portion of this total is available for every IO year because it is explicitly listed in the published tables, in the real estate-and-rental row of the investment column (the rest being merged into the real estate intermediate output). For instance, for 1972 total dealers' commissions were $6444.3, of which $4432 are listed in the 1972 IO table (BEA 1979). We therefore use this latter number, since it is available throughout; $GO_{gr1} = 4,432$.

(2) $GO_{gr2}$ = direct payments of royalties and land rent. We begin with the sum of farmland rental and royalty payments (as available directly from NIPA) and rescale it to input–output levels, because the rental-sector value added is different in NIPA and IO tables for a given year (BEA 1986, table 8.06).

| | |
|---|---|
| Farms owned by non-operator landlords[11] | $ 2,300 |
| Royalties | 1,600 |
| $GO'_{gr2}$ (NIPA-based) | 3,900 |
| $(GVA_{re})_{IO}$ (gross value added, real estate, IO) | 76,030 |
| $(GVA_{re})_{NIPA}$ (gross value added, real estate, NIPA) | 59,100 |
| $GO_{gr2} = (GO'_{gr2})[(GVA_{re})_{IO}/(GVA_{re})_{NIPA}]$ | 5,017 |

[10] We thank Nancy Simon of the BEA for making these data available.
[11] This is mostly land rent, according to Mary Hook of the BEA.

(3) $GO_{gr3}$ = land-rent component of total rents paid. There are no direct data for this component. However, we thank Denise McBride of the BEA for referring us to data on the proportion of land costs in residential home sales, as shown in the following tabulation (HUD 1979, p. 133, table 27).

|  | New homes | Existing homes | All homes |
|---|---|---|---|
| Total sale price | 24,788 | 19,769 | 44,557 |
| Total site price | 5,420 | 4,306 | 9,726 |
| Site/sale price | 0.2187 | 0.2178 | 0.2183 |

This proportion $g_3$ – between land costs and total sale price of new and existing homes – can be taken as a proxy for the ratio of land rents to total rents, on the assumption that building and land prices are reflections of their respective rental values; $g_3 = 0.2183$. $GO_{gr3}$ is then calculated as the product of $g_3$ and that portion of total rental-sector revenue not previously captured in $GO_{gr1}$ and $GO_{gr2}$:

$$GO_{gr3} \equiv g_3 \cdot (GO_{gr} - GO_{gr1} - GO_{gr2})$$
$$= 0.218 \cdot (99,015 - 5,017 - 4,432) = 19,551.$$

(4) Combining the estimates for $GO_{gr1}$ and $GO_{gr2}$, we obtain an estimate for $GO_{gr}$ and for our splitting proportion $g \equiv GO_{gr}/GO_{re}$:

$$GO_{gr} \equiv GO_{gr1} + GO_{gr2} + GO_{gr3} = \$29,000;$$

$$g \equiv GO_{gr}/GO_{re} = 0.293$$
$$= \text{estimated land-rent proportion of}$$
$$\text{real estate sector total revenue.}$$

The estimates of g are calculated for all input–output years. Annual values of g are created by interpolating between input–output benchmark estimates, as shown in Appendix D. These are used in Appendix E in the estimation of annual series for primary variables. Table B.3 summarizes the procedure for all IO years.

### B.4 ABR adjustment for building and equipment rentals

The aim of this adjustment is to remove the pass-through cost $ABR \equiv$ amortization of buildings and equipment rented out by the rental sector to others. The calculation of ABR is explained in what follows; its use has already been treated in Section B.1. As noted there, this adjustment is not applied to the input–output tables of Appendix C owing to the lack of necessary detail in the data. However, it is applied to the final

Table B.3. *Calculation of the proportion of ground rent in real estate (g), benchmark years*

| Sources | Variables | 1947 | 1958 | 1963 | 1967 | 1972 | 1977 |
|---|---|---|---|---|---|---|---|
| | g = $GO_{gr}/GO_{re}$ | 0.279 | 0.252 | 0.265 | 0.273 | 0.293 | 0.299 |
| 18 × 21 IO tables | $GO_{re}$ | 16,167 | 33,919 | 45,678 | 64,283 | 99,015 | 166,469 |
| | $GO_{gr} = GO_{gr1} + GO_{gr2} + GO_{gr3}$ | 4,506 | 8,543 | 12,103 | 17,573 | 29,000 | 49,819 |
| IO tables | $GO_{gr1}$ = real estate commissions | 882 | 1,209 | 1,224 | 2,100 | 4,432 | 10,747 |
| | $GO_{gr2}$ = royalties and rents | 2,145 | 2,518 | 2,858 | 3,061 | 5,017 | 9,496 |
| | $\quad = GO'_{gr2} \times (GVA_{IO}/GVA_{NIPA})$ | | | | | | |
| | $GO'_{gr2} = RI_{fl} + RI_{ry}$ | 1,800 | 2,100 | 2,400 | 2,400 | 3,900 | 7,100 |
| 806 8[a] | $RI_{fl}$ = rental income of farm landlords | 1,400 | 1,100 | 1,400 | 1,400 | 2,300 | 2,600 |
| 806 10[a] | $RI_{ry}$ = royalties | 400 | 1,000 | 1,000 | 1,000 | 1,600 | 4,500 |
| 18 × 21 IO tables | $GVA_{IO}$ (real estate) | 13,108 | 26,620 | 35,611 | 49,997 | 76,030 | 125,049 |
| | $GVA_{NIPA}$ | 11,000 | 22,200 | 29,900 | 39,200 | 59,100 | 93,500 |
| | $GO_{gr3} = g_3 \times GO_{re1}$ | 1,479 | 4,816 | 8,021 | 12,412 | 19,551 | 29,576 |
| | $g_3$ = site/sale price | 0.113 | 0.160 | 0.193 | 0.210 | 0.218 | 0.202 |
| HUD (1979, table 27) | New homes, sales price | 9,780 | 14,283 | 15,878 | 18,611 | 24,788 | 36,517 |
| | New homes, site price | 1,092 | 2,223 | 2,978 | 3,777 | 5,420 | 7,335 |
| | Existing homes, sales price | 10,777 | 13,133 | 14,346 | 15,933 | 19,769 | 28,561 |
| | Existing homes, site price | 1,222 | 2,150 | 2,850 | 3,475 | 4,306 | 5,828 |
| | All homes, sales price | 20,557 | 27,416 | 30,224 | 34,544 | 44,557 | 65,078 |
| | All homes, site price | 2,314 | 4,373 | 5,828 | 7,252 | 9,726 | 13,163 |
| | $GO_{re1} = GO_{re} - GO_{gr1} - GO_{gr2}$ | 13,140 | 30,192 | 41,596 | 59,122 | 89,566 | 146,226 |

[a] From NIPA (e.g. BEA 1986), where the first three digits denote the relevant table number and subsequent digits the line numbers within those tables.

Table B.4. *Annual estimates of ABR, 1947–90*

| Variables | 1947 | 1948 | 1949 | 1950 | 1951 | 1952 | 1953 | 1954 | 1955 | 1956 | 1957 | 1958 | 1959 | 1960 | 1961 |
|---|---|---|---|---|---|---|---|---|---|---|---|---|---|---|---|
| DR' | 2,916 | 3,261 | 3,371 | 3,558 | 4,039 | 4,259 | 4,428 | 4,596 | 4,871 | 5,282 | 5,599 | 5,758 | 5,982 | 6,257 | 6,481 |
| DR | 437 | 488 | 480 | 486 | 549 | 566 | 569 | 559 | 574 | 632 | 671 | 673 | 700 | 742 | 789 |
| ABR | 2,479 | 2,774 | 2,891 | 3,073 | 3,490 | 3,693 | 3,859 | 4,037 | 4,297 | 4,650 | 4,928 | 5,085 | 5,282 | 5,515 | 5,692 |

| Variables | 1962 | 1963 | 1964 | 1965 | 1966 | 1967 | 1968 | 1969 | 1970 | 1971 | 1972 | 1973 | 1974 | 1975 | 1976 |
|---|---|---|---|---|---|---|---|---|---|---|---|---|---|---|---|
| DR' | 6,754 | 7,033 | 7,399 | 7,864 | 8,507 | 9,162 | 10,010 | 11,280 | 12,345 | 13,683 | 15,111 | 16,971 | 19,542 | 22,128 | 23,947 |
| DR | 835 | 872 | 896 | 913 | 939 | 972 | 1,012 | 1,066 | 1,113 | 1,140 | 1,151 | 1,193 | 1,348 | 1,478 | 1,547 |
| ABR | 5,919 | 6,161 | 6,504 | 6,951 | 7,568 | 8,190 | 8,998 | 10,214 | 11,232 | 12,543 | 13,960 | 15,778 | 18,194 | 20,651 | 22,400 |

| Variables | 1977 | 1978 | 1979 | 1980 | 1981 | 1982 | 1983 | 1984 | 1985 | 1986 | 1987 | 1988 | 1989 | 1990 |
|---|---|---|---|---|---|---|---|---|---|---|---|---|---|---|
| DR'[a] | 26,637 | 30,250 | 35,281 | 40,842 | 46,255 | 50,436 | 53,059 | 57,455 | 61,320 | — | — | — | — | — |
| DR[b] | 1,711 | 2,007 | 2,408 | 2,903 | — | — | — | — | — | — | — | — | — | — |
| ABR[c] | 24,926 | 28,243 | 32,873 | 37,939 | 29,451 | 31,773 | 34,278 | 36,980 | 39,895 | 43,040 | 46,434 | 50,094 | 54,044 | 58,304 |

[a] DR' values for the period 1986–90 were not available.
[b] DR values for the period 1981–90 were not available.
[c] ABR values for the period 1981–90 were obtained by extrapolating ln ABR.

calculations in Appendix E. The following steps detail the calculation of ABR.

(1) The BEA capital stock data are on an *owner* basis, so that the corresponding total depreciation of the nonimputed real estate sector (DR′) is the depreciation of all building and equipment owned by this sector (i.e., the sum of depreciation DR of stock used by this sector and of amortization ABR of stock rented out to other sectors). We have

$$DR' = DR + ABR,$$

and we calculate DR′ as

DR′ = depreciation of fixed private nonresidential capital
(BEA 1987, p. 97, table A2)

+ depreciation of fixed private residential capital
(BEA 1987, pp. 260–2, table A16),

where the latter depreciation is calculated as total minus federal minus state minus owner-occupied nonfarm minus owner-occupied farm depreciation. For 1972:

$$DR' = 7,796 + (26,007 - 144 - 372 - 17,222 - 954)$$
$$= 15,111.$$

(2) To complete this calculation we need to estimate DR, which is the depreciation of the buildings and equipment used by the real estate sector for its own use. This can be calculated from the BIE capital stock data, which is on a *use* basis, so that its depreciation corresponds to the capital used by each sector (U.S. Bureau of Interindustrial Economics 1983). For 1972, DR = 1,150.

Given DR and DR′, we can calculate ABR (for 1972) as:

$$ABR = DR' - DR = 15,111 - 1,150 = 13,961.$$

Recall that all data are in millions of U.S. dollars.

Table B.4 shows the annual estimates of ABR from 1947 to 1987. Because estimates of DR are available only through 1980, the values of ABR were directly calculated for 1947–80 and extrapolated for 1981–87 via a linear regression on ln ABR versus time ($R^2 = 0.962$).

# C

## Summary input–output tables

*Companion text:* Section 3.6; Section 4.1; Section 5.1

Published input–output tables for the postwar period cover the years 1947, 1958, 1963, 1967, 1972, and 1977. The summary tables that follow (Figures C.2–C.7) were generated from the published tables in the manner described in Appendix A. They are designed to conform to the general theoretical schema developed in the text. Also included is a general table (Figure C.1) with variable names in the relevant cells. All data are in millions of dollars.

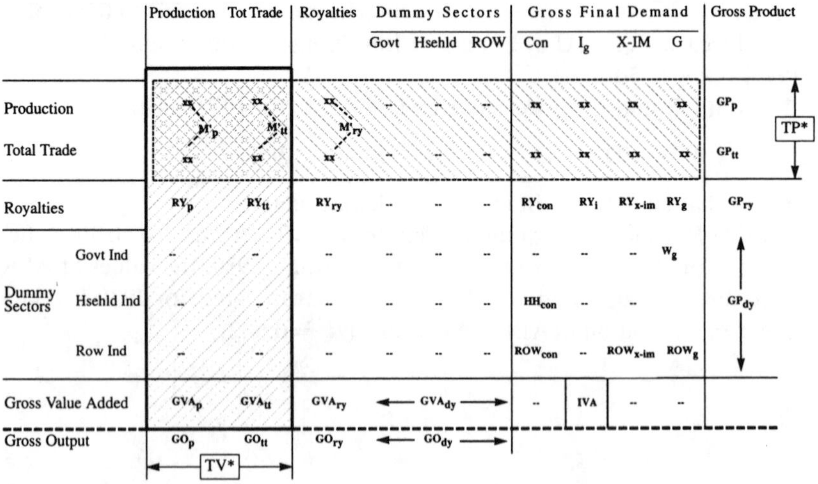

Figure C.1. IO accounts and Marxian categories: Summary mapping.

| 1947 | Production | Tot Trade | Royalties | Dummy Sectors | | | Gross Final Demand | | | | Gross Product |
|---|---|---|---|---|---|---|---|---|---|---|---|
| | | | | Govt | Hshld | ROW | Con | $I_g$ | X-IM | G | |
| Production | 163117.4 | 15491.2 | 3010.7 | -- | -- | -- | 110254.8 | 20943.1 | 8438.4 | 9104.4 | 330360.0 |
| Total Trade | 15705.2 | 4471.3 | 990.5 | -- | -- | -- | 42639.6 | 2569.2 | 1444.6 | 499.8 | 68320.1 |
| Royalties | 6183.3 | 3040.1 | 2726.1 | -- | -- | -- | 5721.4 | 45.7 | 53.3 | 143.5 | 17913.4 |
| Dummy Sectors  Govt Ind | -- | -- | -- | -- | -- | -- | -- | -- | -- | 16220.6 | 16220.6 |
| Dummy Sectors  Hsehld Ind | -- | -- | -- | -- | -- | -- | 2348.0 | -- | -- | | 2348.0 |
| Dummy Sectors  Row Ind | -- | -- | -- | -- | -- | -- | -718.0 | -- | 1592.0 | -50.0 | 824.0 |
| Gross Value Added | 145354.2 | 45317.5 | 17913.4 | 16220.6 | 2348.0 | 824.0 | -- | -1527.9 | -- | -- | 219722.5 |
| Gross Output | 330360.1 | 68320.1 | 17913.4 | 16220.6 | 2348.0 | 824.0 | 160245.9 | 22030.1 | 11528.3 | 25918.2 | 435986.25 |

Figure C.2. 1947 IO table.

| 1958 | Production | Tot Trade | Royalties | Dummy Sectors | | | Gross Final Demand | | | | Gross Product |
|---|---|---|---|---|---|---|---|---|---|---|---|
| | | | | Govt | Hshld | ROW | Con | $I_g$ | X-IM | G | |
| Production | 274137.6 | 24792.1 | 7403.5 | -- | -- | -- | 188816.9 | 36215.0 | -3795.6 | 51134.2 | 578703.7 |
| Total Trade | 32332.9 | 7625.5 | 3273.3 | -- | -- | -- | 69783.2 | 4037.5 | 2216.3 | 1195.7 | 120464.2 |
| Royalties | 16506.2 | 7247.4 | 7785.8 | -- | -- | -- | 14046.9 | 103.7 | 295.6 | 1403.3 | 98497.1 |
| Dummy Sectors  Govt Ind | -- | -- | -- | -- | -- | -- | -- | -- | -- | 40693.8 | 40693.8 |
| Dummy Sectors  Hsehld Ind | -- | -- | -- | -- | -- | -- | 3503.0 | -- | -- | -- | 3503.0 |
| Dummy Sectors  Row Ind | -- | -- | -- | -- | -- | -- | -1152.8 | -- | 3489.8 | -307.0 | 2030.0 |
| Gross Value Added | 255726.9 | 80799.3 | 28566.4 | 40693.8 | 3503.0 | 2030.0 | -- | -622.0 | -- | -- | 410697.5 |
| Gross Output | 578703.7 | 120464.2 | 47029.0 | 40693.8 | 3503.0 | 2030.0 | 274997.2 | 39734.2 | 2206.0 | 93760.1 | 792423.7 |

Figure C.3. 1958 IO table.

| 1963 | Production | Tot Trade | Royalties | Dummy Sectors | | | Gross Final Demand | | | | Gross Product | |
|---|---|---|---|---|---|---|---|---|---|---|---|---|
| | | | | Govt | Hsehld | ROW | Con | $I_g$ | X-IM | G | | |
| Production | 345475.4 | 28535.6 | 10712.1 | -- | -- | -- | 242326.2 | 52613.6 | -2712.7 | 87564.7 | 956648.7 | TP* |
| Total Trade | 38938.8 | 11115.7 | 4148.0 | -- | -- | -- | 89775.2 | 5429.3 | 2851.4 | 2322.9 | 207067.6 | |
| Royalties | 21665.1 | 8203.0 | 10476.8 | -- | -- | -- | 21067.4 | 119.8 | 389.3 | 5009.3 | 98497.1 | |
| Dummy Sectors: Govt Ind | -- | -- | -- | -- | -- | -- | -- | -- | -- | 85083.0 | 85083.0 | |
| Dummy Sectors: Hsehld Ind | -- | -- | -- | -- | -- | -- | 3824.0 | -- | -- | | 4701.0 | |
| Dummy Sectors: Row Ind | -- | -- | -- | -- | -- | -- | -1381.9 | -- | 5284.0 | -860.9 | 4517.0 | |
| Gross Value Added | 332739.7 | 105645.7 | 39965.2 | 57348.8 | 3824.0 | 3259.0 | -- | -1004.0 | -- | -- | 727119.9 | |
| Gross Output | 738819.0 | 153500.1 | 65302.1 | 57348.8 | 3824.0 | 3259.0 | 355610.9 | 57158.7 | 5812.0 | 179119.0 | 1356514.6 | |
| | TV* | | | | | | | | | | | |

Figure C.4. 1963 IO table.

| 1967 | Production | Tot Trade | Royalties | Dummy Sectors | | | Gross Final Demand | | | | Gross Product | |
|---|---|---|---|---|---|---|---|---|---|---|---|---|
| | | | | Govt | Hsehld | ROW | Con | $I_g$ | X-IM | G | | |
| Production | 437069.2 | 38120.3 | 15252.6 | -- | -- | -- | 298998.1 | 87022.4 | -7378.6 | 87564.7 | 956648.7 | TP* |
| Total Trade | 52309.9 | 15497.7 | 6075.7 | -- | -- | -- | 119316.8 | 7230.4 | 4314.2 | 2322.9 | 207067.6 | |
| Royalties | 32979.7 | 12181.8 | 16221.7 | -- | -- | -- | 31125.4 | 208.1 | 771.2 | 5009.3 | 98497.1 | |
| Dummy Sectors: Govt Ind | -- | -- | -- | -- | -- | -- | -- | -- | -- | 85083.0 | 85083.0 | |
| Dummy Sectors: Hsehld Ind | -- | -- | -- | -- | -- | -- | 4701.0 | -- | -- | -- | 4701.0 | |
| Dummy Sectors: Row Ind | -- | -- | -- | -- | -- | -- | -2047.4 | -- | 7425.3 | -860.9 | 4517.0 | |
| Gross Value Added | 434291.1 | 141267.3 | 60946.7 | 85083.0 | 4701.0 | 4517.0 | -- | -3686.0 | -- | -- | 727119.9 | |
| Gross Output | 956649.8 | 207067.1 | 98496.8 | 85083.0 | 4701.0 | 4517.0 | 452094.0 | 90774.9 | 5132.0 | 179119.0 | 1356514.6 | |
| | TV* | | | | | | | | | | | |

Figure C.5. 1967 IO table.

| 1972 | | Production | Tot Trade | Royalties | Dummy Sectors: Govt | Dummy Sectors: Hsehld | Dummy Sectors: ROW | Gross Final Demand: Con | Gross Final Demand: $I_g$ | Gross Final Demand: X-IM | Gross Final Demand: G | Gross Product | |
|---|---|---|---|---|---|---|---|---|---|---|---|---|---|
| Production | | 619148.1 | 54809.2 | 22725.3 | -- | -- | -- | 468702.7 | 127993.8 | -22509.0 | 101767.3 | 1372637.4 | TP* |
| Total Trade | | 78676.1 | 22853.4 | 9696.4 | -- | -- | -- | 181973.3 | 10837.9 | 7046.5 | 2982.2 | 314065.8 | TP* |
| Royalties | | 54094.4 | 17524.9 | 28891.4 | -- | -- | -- | 50171.5 | 249.3 | 1411.4 | 10872.7 | 163215.6 | |
| Dummy Sectors | Govt Ind | -- | -- | -- | -- | -- | -- | -- | -- | -- | 137400.0 | 137400.0 | |
| | Hsehld Ind | -- | -- | -- | -- | -- | -- | 5349.0 | -- | -- | -- | 5349.0 | |
| | Row Ind | -- | -- | -- | -- | -- | -- | -3524.4 | -- | 10645.8 | -203.3 | 6918.1 | |
| Gross Value Added | | 620718.3 | 218878.0 | 101902.4 | 137400.0 | 5349.0 | 6918.1 | -- | -15182.0 | -- | -- | 1075984.7 | |
| Gross Output | | 1372637.9 | 314065.5 | 163215.4 | 137400.0 | 5349.0 | 6918.1 | 702672.1 | 123899.0 | -3405.3 | 252819.0 | 1999585.9 | |
| | | TV* | TV* | | | | | | | | | | |

Figure C.6. 1972 IO table.

| 1977 | | Production | Tot Trade | Royalties | Dummy Sectors: Govt | Dummy Sectors: Hsehld | Dummy Sectors: ROW | Gross Final Demand: Con | Gross Final Demand: $I_g$ | Gross Final Demand: X-IM | Gross Final Demand: G | Gross Product | |
|---|---|---|---|---|---|---|---|---|---|---|---|---|---|
| Production | | 1178165.0 | 97257.3 | 44041.6 | -- | -- | -- | 771824.0 | 216650.2 | -52853.3 | 154507.3 | 2409592.0 | TP* |
| Total Trade | | 130444.1 | 37337.5 | 17270.6 | -- | -- | -- | 288053.6 | 19788.0 | 13640.5 | 2362.0 | 508896.4 | TP* |
| Royalties | | 99881.2 | 29973.2 | 54499.5 | -- | -- | -- | 80449.3 | 521.7 | 3215.9 | 23180.9 | 291721.6 | |
| Dummy Sectors | Govt Ind | -- | -- | -- | -- | -- | -- | -- | -- | -- | 2414655.1 | 241465.1 | |
| | Hsehld Ind | -- | -- | -- | -- | -- | -- | 5930.0 | -- | -- | -- | 5930.0 | |
| | Row Ind | -- | -- | -- | -- | -- | -- | -7233.0 | -- | 32015.6 | -697.8 | 24084.8 | |
| Gross Value Added | | 999264.8 | 345598.3 | 178308.4 | 214465.1 | 5930.0 | 24084.8 | -- | 2021.6 | -- | -- | 1794841.6 | |
| Gross Output | | 2407755.1 | 510166.3 | 294120.0 | 214465.1 | 5930.0 | 24084.8 | 1139023.9 | 238981.5 | -3981.4 | 420817.5 | 3456521.4 | |
| | | TV* | TV* | | | | | | | | | | |

Figure C.7. 1977 IO table.

# D

## Interpolation of key input–output variables

*Companion text:* Section 5.2

The summary input–output tables of Appendix C provide benchmark-year estimates of Marxian variables and their orthodox counterparts. In order to convert these into annual estimates, we use annual NIPA data for value-added and final-demand quantities. But input–output variables such as intermediate inputs M, royalties RY, and rest-of-world flows ROW are unavailable in NIPA. For these variables, we interpolate between input–output benchmark values in the following manner.

(1)  In each input–output year, we calculate the ratio of the component to either its using or receiving industry's gross value added. For material inputs M' (and depreciation D later on), we utilize the using industry's GVA. Thus for $M'_p$ we create the ratio $x_p \equiv (M'_p / GVA_p)_{IO}$, where the subscript IO indicates that both variables are from input–output tables. For royalties RY we use the receiving industry's GVA (i.e. $GVA_{ry}$) as the numeraire, as in $x_i \equiv (RY_i / GVA_{ry})_{IO}$. This is done because some royalties, such as $RY_i$ and $RY_{x-im}$, appear (respectively) as components of the highly unstable final-demand totals I and $X - IM$ (see Figure C.1). Benchmark coefficients created by dividing these royalties by unstable totals are not very useful. The same reasoning applies to the ROW entries in Figure C.1, which are divided by total ROW in order to form coefficients for extrapolation, as in $x_{row_g} \equiv ROW_g / ROW$.

(2)  All coefficients created as described in (1) are linearly interpolated between benchmark (IO) years. The result is an annual series for each coefficient, derived entirely from input–output data.

(3)  The annual observation for each coefficient is multiplied by the NIPA measure of the relevant gross value added (or ROW, in the case of

278

Table D.1. *Interpolation of $M'_p$ between 1963 and 1967*

|  | 1963 | 1964 | 1965 | 1966 | 1967 |
|---|---|---|---|---|---|
| $(M_p)_{IO}$[a] | 384.41 | — | — | — | 489.38 |
| $(GVA_p)_{IO}$[a] | 332.75 | — | — | — | 434.29 |
| $x_p$[b] | 1.155 | 1.148 | 1.141 | 1.134 | 1.127 |
| $(GVA_p)_{NIPA}$[c] | 337.30 | 359.10 | 392.10 | 426.60 | 444.30 |
| $M'_p = x_p \cdot GVA_{NIPA}$ | 389.68 | 412.31 | 447.41 | 483.74 | 500.66 |

[a] Figures C.4 and C.5.
[b] $x_p = (M_p/GVA_p)_{IO}$ for benchmark years 1963 and 1967 (linearly interpolated for 1964–66).
[c] Table E.1.

rest-of-world coefficients) to create a NIPA-based estimate of the original IO variable. Thus

$$(M'_p)_{NIPA} \equiv x_p \cdot (GVA_p)_{NIPA}, \quad (RY_i)_{NIPA} \equiv x_i \cdot (GVA_{ry})_{NIPA}, \quad \text{and}$$
$$(ROW_g)_{NIPA} \equiv x_{row_g} \cdot (ROW)_{NIPA}.$$

The resulting annual estimates are then used in all subsequent calculations. Table D.1 illustrates the procedure for $M'_p$ between the two benchmark years 1963 and 1967.

The interpolation procedure generates annual estimates of the key input–output variables up to 1977, which is the last available input–output table. For 1978–87, we extrapolated all variables except $M'_{ry}$ using the 1977 values of their x-ratios along with relevant GVA's from NIPA. $M'_{ry}$ was estimated as a residual from a formula based on the equality of the identities for the gross output $GO_{ry}$ and gross product $GP_{ry}$ of the royalties sector. This allowed us to preserve the balance of total value and total product even in the extrapolated data. From Figure C.1 we have:

$$GO_{ry} \equiv M'_{ry} + RY_{ry} + GVA_{ry};$$
$$GP_{ry} \equiv RY_p + RY_{tt} + RY_{ry} + RY_{con} + RY_i + RY_{x-im} + RY_g;$$
$$GO_{ry} = GP_{ry}.$$

Therefore,

$$M'_{ry} = (RY_p + RY_{tt} + RY_{con} + RY_i + RY_{x-im} + RY_g) - GVA_{ry}.$$

The results are summarized in Table D.2. Note that

$$GP = M + GFD$$
$$= (M'_p + M'_{tt} + M'_{ry}) + (RY_p + RY_{tt} + RY_{ry}) + GFD.$$

Table D.2. *NIPA-based interpolations of key IO variables (billions of dollars)*[a]

| Variables | 1947 | 1948 | 1949 | 1950 | 1951 | 1952 | 1953 | 1954 | 1955 | 1956 | 1957 | 1958 | 1959 | 1960 | 1961 |
|---|---|---|---|---|---|---|---|---|---|---|---|---|---|---|---|
| $M'_p$ | 173.22 | 198.47 | 189.06 | 212.56 | 244.59 | 254.35 | 268.66 | 261.36 | 287.18 | 303.11 | 314.63 | 308.00 | 334.93 | 343.72 | 347.54 |
| $RY_p$ | 6.53 | 7.51 | 8.21 | 9.06 | 10.10 | 11.20 | 12.52 | 13.57 | 14.73 | 16.19 | 17.61 | 19.04 | 20.80 | 21.89 | 23.03 |
| $M_{tt}$ | 19.92 | 21.68 | 21.36 | 22.74 | 24.73 | 25.42 | 25.97 | 26.38 | 28.43 | 29.84 | 31.18 | 31.61 | 34.00 | 34.61 | 35.24 |
| $RY_{tt}$ | 3.21 | 3.66 | 3.96 | 4.32 | 4.77 | 5.23 | 5.79 | 6.21 | 6.67 | 7.26 | 7.81 | 8.36 | 8.89 | 9.10 | 9.30 |
| $RY_c$ | 6.05 | 6.90 | 7.48 | 8.20 | 9.07 | 9.98 | 11.07 | 11.90 | 12.82 | 13.99 | 15.10 | 16.21 | 18.18 | 19.65 | 21.24 |
| $RY_i$ | 0.05 | 0.05 | 0.06 | 0.06 | 0.07 | 0.08 | 0.08 | 0.09 | 0.10 | 0.10 | 0.11 | 0.12 | 0.13 | 0.13 | 0.13 |
| $RY_G$ | 0.15 | 0.20 | 0.25 | 0.31 | 0.39 | 0.47 | 0.57 | 0.67 | 0.78 | 0.91 | 1.05 | 1.20 | 1.68 | 2.17 | 2.71 |
| $RY_{x-im}$ | 0.06 | 0.07 | 0.09 | 0.10 | 0.12 | 0.15 | 0.17 | 0.20 | 0.23 | 0.26 | 0.30 | 0.34 | 0.37 | 0.39 | 0.41 |
| $D_p$ | 7.93 | 9.42 | 9.29 | 10.81 | 12.85 | 13.80 | 15.04 | 15.08 | 17.07 | 18.54 | 19.79 | 19.92 | 21.44 | 21.78 | 21.80 |
| $D_{tt}$ | 0.98 | 1.12 | 1.16 | 1.30 | 1.48 | 1.60 | 1.71 | 1.81 | 2.04 | 2.23 | 2.42 | 2.56 | 2.78 | 2.86 | 2.95 |
| $D_{ry}$ | 0.43 | 0.49 | 0.52 | 0.57 | 0.62 | 0.68 | 0.75 | 0.79 | 0.84 | 0.91 | 0.97 | 1.03 | 1.12 | 1.17 | 1.22 |
| $ROW_{con}$ | -1.05 | -1.27 | -1.14 | -1.18 | -1.52 | -1.61 | -1.48 | -1.49 | -1.69 | -1.87 | -2.02 | -1.65 | -1.67 | -1.79 | -1.83 |
| $ROW_{x-im}$ | 2.32 | 2.87 | 2.65 | 2.81 | 3.71 | 4.04 | 3.81 | 3.95 | 4.62 | 5.27 | 5.91 | 4.99 | 5.27 | 5.88 | 6.31 |
| $ROW_{x-im}$ | -0.07 | -0.10 | -0.11 | -0.13 | -0.19 | -0.22 | -0.23 | -0.26 | -0.33 | -0.40 | -0.49 | -0.44 | -0.50 | -0.59 | -0.68 |
| $M'_{ry}$ | 4.23 | 4.86 | 5.31 | 5.86 | 6.54 | 7.25 | 8.10 | 8.78 | 9.53 | 10.47 | 11.39 | 12.32 | 13.61 | 14.49 | 15.42 |
| GP | 445.20 | 501.09 | 491.85 | 546.81 | 628.80 | 660.15 | 698.29 | 695.08 | 759.29 | 802.66 | 841.93 | 845.30 | 918.12 | 949.79 | 975.53 |

| Variables | 1962 | 1963 | 1964 | 1965 | 1966 | 1967 | 1968 | 1969 | 1970 | 1971 | 1972 | 1973 | 1974 | 1975 | 1976 |
|---|---|---|---|---|---|---|---|---|---|---|---|---|---|---|---|
| $M'_p$ | 371.40 | 389.68 | 412.31 | 447.41 | 483.74 | 500.66 | 545.14 | 586.54 | 602.47 | 644.70 | 714.33 | 837.40 | 926.56 | 1023.78 | 1187.33 |
| $RY_p$ | 24.07 | 25.31 | 27.39 | 30.07 | 33.60 | 37.18 | 40.60 | 44.93 | 48.35 | 52.92 | 58.15 | 65.08 | 71.71 | 78.69 | 89.45 |
| $M'_{tt}$ | 37.27 | 38.59 | 42.00 | 45.03 | 48.49 | 51.94 | 56.30 | 60.18 | 62.80 | 67.71 | 73.20 | 83.29 | 91.94 | 103.25 | 115.69 |
| $RY_{tt}$ | 9.42 | 9.58 | 10.31 | 11.25 | 12.49 | 13.73 | 14.63 | 15.79 | 16.55 | 17.63 | 18.84 | 20.76 | 22.53 | 24.34 | 27.25 |
| $RY_c$ | 22.80 | 24.61 | 26.44 | 28.81 | 31.95 | 35.09 | 38.19 | 42.11 | 45.17 | 49.26 | 53.94 | 58.71 | 62.90 | 67.10 | 74.14 |
| $RY_t$ | 0.14 | 0.14 | 0.16 | 0.18 | 0.21 | 0.23 | 0.24 | 0.25 | 0.26 | 0.26 | 0.27 | 0.31 | 0.35 | 0.39 | 0.46 |
| $RY_G$ | 3.29 | 3.95 | 4.25 | 4.63 | 5.14 | 5.65 | 6.56 | 7.70 | 8.76 | 10.11 | 11.69 | 13.50 | 15.33 | 17.32 | 20.23 |
| $RY_{x-im}$ | 0.43 | 0.45 | 0.53 | 0.62 | 0.74 | 0.87 | 0.97 | 1.10 | 1.21 | 1.35 | 1.52 | 1.78 | 2.05 | 2.35 | 2.78 |
| $D_p$ | 23.05 | 23.91 | 25.05 | 26.91 | 28.79 | 29.48 | 32.43 | 35.26 | 36.59 | 39.56 | 44.27 | 52.40 | 58.50 | 65.17 | 76.18 |
| $D_{tt}$ | 3.16 | 3.31 | 3.46 | 3.57 | 3.68 | 3.78 | 4.15 | 4.50 | 4.77 | 5.22 | 5.72 | 6.55 | 7.27 | 8.21 | 9.24 |
| $D_{ry}$ | 1.26 | 1.31 | 1.38 | 1.48 | 1.61 | 1.73 | 1.95 | 2.23 | 2.47 | 2.78 | 3.15 | 3.66 | 4.19 | 4.76 | 5.59 |
| $ROW_{con}$ | -2.04 | -2.08 | -2.33 | -2.54 | -2.50 | -2.72 | -3.16 | -3.24 | -3.55 | -4.63 | -5.71 | -7.58 | -8.30 | -6.72 | -7.22 |
| $ROW'_{x-im}$ | 7.38 | 7.94 | 8.79 | 9.47 | 9.17 | 9.86 | 11.04 | 10.89 | 11.54 | 14.51 | 17.23 | 24.25 | 28.37 | 24.73 | 28.93 |
| $ROW_G$ | -0.85 | -0.97 | -1.06 | -1.12 | -1.08 | -1.14 | -1.08 | -0.86 | -0.69 | -0.57 | -0.33 | -0.47 | -0.57 | -0.51 | -0.61 |
| $M'_{ry}$ | 16.32 | 17.36 | 18.52 | 20.03 | 22.06 | 24.05 | 25.88 | 28.21 | 29.91 | 32.23 | 34.86 | 39.21 | 43.41 | 47.86 | 54.66 |
| GP | 1044.76 | 1099.77 | 1173.84 | 1273.88 | 1389.06 | 1462.58 | 1595.80 | 1722.72 | 1800.78 | 1945.90 | 2143.39 | 2440.00 | 2667.47 | 2919.00 | 3305.49 |

Table D.2 *(cont.)*

| Variables | 1977 | 1978 | 1979 | 1980 | 1981 | 1982 | 1983 | 1984 | 1985 | 1986 | 1987 | 1988 | 1989 |
|---|---|---|---|---|---|---|---|---|---|---|---|---|---|
| $M_p^b$ | 1367.27 | 1545.89 | 1710.49 | 1851.27 | 2078.34 | 2114.61 | 2235.61 | 2497.25 | 2618.65 | 2664.48 | 2808.66 | 3122.99 | 3278.25 |
| $RY_p$ | 106.43 | 125.44 | 143.45 | 160.92 | 182.00 | 192.05 | 224.32 | 247.24 | 284.63 | 328.62 | 366.14 | 395.27 | 434.22 |
| $M_{tt}$ | 131.33 | 147.86 | 163.82 | 171.94 | 194.30 | 203.79 | 220.06 | 248.59 | 268.04 | 284.68 | 303.10 | 320.09 | 341.01 |
| $RY_{tt}$ | 31.94 | 37.64 | 43.05 | 48.29 | 54.62 | 57.63 | 67.31 | 74.19 | 85.41 | 98.62 | 109.87 | 118.62 | 130.30 |
| $RY_c$ | 85.72 | 101.03 | 115.54 | 129.62 | 146.59 | 154.68 | 180.68 | 199.14 | 229.25 | 264.69 | 294.91 | 318.37 | 349.74 |
| $RY_i$ | 0.56 | 0.66 | 0.75 | 0.84 | 0.95 | 1.00 | 1.17 | 1.29 | 1.49 | 1.72 | 1.91 | 2.06 | 2.27 |
| $RY_G$ | 24.70 | 29.11 | 33.29 | 37.35 | 42.24 | 44.57 | 52.06 | 57.38 | 66.06 | 76.27 | 84.98 | 91.74 | 100.78 |
| $RY_{x-im}$ | 3.43 | 4.04 | 4.62 | 5.18 | 5.86 | 6.18 | 7.22 | 7.96 | 9.16 | 10.58 | 11.79 | 12.73 | 13.98 |
| $D_p$ | 88.36 | 99.90 | 110.54 | 119.64 | 134.31 | 136.66 | 144.48 | 161.39 | 169.23 | 172.19 | 181.51 | 201.83 | 211.86 |
| $D_{tt}$ | 10.55 | 11.87 | 13.15 | 13.81 | 15.60 | 16.36 | 17.67 | 19.96 | 21.52 | 22.86 | 24.34 | 25.70 | 27.38 |
| $D_{ry}$ | 6.87 | 8.09 | 9.25 | 10.38 | 11.74 | 12.39 | 14.47 | 15.95 | 18.36 | 21.20 | 23.62 | 25.50 | 28.01 |
| $ROW_{con}$ | −7.63 | −9.16 | −13.15 | −14.29 | −15.65 | −15.38 | −14.99 | −14.23 | −12.22 | −10.48 | −8.86 | −10.06 | −11.29 |
| $ROW_{x-im}$ | 33.76 | 40.54 | 58.22 | 63.27 | 69.26 | 68.06 | 66.33 | 63.01 | 54.10 | 46.39 | 39.21 | 44.52 | 49.97 |
| $ROW_G$ | −0.74 | −0.88 | −1.27 | −1.38 | −1.51 | −1.48 | −1.45 | −1.37 | −1.18 | −1.01 | −0.85 | −0.97 | −1.09 |
| $M_{ry}^c$ | 65.33 | 73.99 | 84.61 | 94.92 | 107.35 | 113.28 | 132.31 | 145.83 | 167.88 | 193.83 | 215.96 | 233.15 | 256.12 |
| GP | 3750.53 | 4248.52 | 4731.53 | 5146.84 | 5768.06 | 5951.66 | 6407.16 | 7119.72 | 7594.93 | 7974.71 | 8510.87 | 9198.45 | 9789.83 |

[a] All variables in this table refer to elements of IO tables in Appendix C.
[b] For 1978–89, all variables were extrapolated, as explained in the text.
[c] For 1978–89, $M_{ry}$ is calculated as a residual, as explained in the text.

# E

## Annual estimates of primary variables

*Companion text:* Section 4.2

Our previous IO benchmark estimates in Table 5.2 can be converted into annual series by making use of annually available NIPA data for value-added and final-demand components, and of the interpolated values of key input–output variables (M, RY, ROW) generated in Appendix D. The basic formulas from Section 5.2 are reproduced here.

$$TV^* = GO_p + GO_{tt} = \text{total value,}$$

where

$GO_p = M'_p + RY_p + GVA_p$ and
$GO_{tt} = M'_{tt} + RY_{tt} + NIPA_{tt};$

$$C^*_m = M'_p = \text{materials inputs into production;}$$
$$C^*_d = D_p = \text{depreciation of productive fixed capital;}$$
$$C^* = M'_p + D_p = \text{constant capital used up (flow);}$$
$$GVA^* \equiv TV^* - C^*_m = \text{Marxian gross value added;}$$
$$VA^* \equiv TV^* - C^* = GVA^* - C^*_d = \text{Marxian (net) value added;}$$
$$TP^* = M'_p + M'_{tt} + M'_{ry} + CON^* + I^*_G + (X - IM)^* + G^*;$$
$$CON^* = CON - GVA_{ir} - RY_{con} - HH_{con} - ROW_{con};$$
$$IG^* = I_G - RY_i;\,[1]$$
$$(X - IM)^* = (X - IM) - RY_{x-im} - ROW_{x-im};$$
$$G^* = G - W_G - ROW_G.$$

Table E.1 details annual TV* estimates; Table E.2 describes calculations for annual TP*.

[1] As noted in Section 5.1, the inventory valuation adjustment IVA was merged into value added on the revenue side, and hence into $I^*_G$ on the use side.

Table E.1. *Annual estimates of TV\*, 1948–89 (billions of dollars)*

| | Sources[a] | Variables | 1948 | 1949 |
|---|---|---|---|---|
| 1 | | $TV^* = GO_p + GO_{tt} + S.D.$ | 446.25 | 432.02 |
| 2 | | $GO_p = M'_p + RY'_p + GVA_p$ | 367.68 | 351.67 |
| 3 | Table D.2 | $M'_p \ (= C^*_m)$ | 198.47 | 189.06 |
| 4 | Table D.2 | $RY'_p$ | 7.51 | 8.21 |
| 5 | | $GVA_p = \{GVA_{agr} + GVA_{min} + GVA_{con} + GVA_{man}$ | | |
| | | $\qquad + GVA_{tut} + GVA_{servp} + GVA_{govep}\}$ | 161.70 | 154.40 |
| 6 | 601 4 | $GVA_{agr}$ | 24.00 | 19.50 |
| 7 | 601 7 | $GVA_{min}$ | 9.40 | 8.10 |
| 8 | 601 12 | $GVA_{con}$ | 11.50 | 11.50 |
| 9 | 601 13 | $GVA_{man}$ | 74.70 | 72.20 |
| 10 | 601 37 | $GVA_{tut}$ | 23.70 | 23.90 |
| 11 | | $GVA_{servp}$ | 15.60 | 16.10 |
| 12 | 601 61 | Hotels and other lodging places | 1.60 | 1.70 |
| 13 | 601 62 | Personal services | 3.10 | 3.20 |
| 14 | 601 64 | Auto repair, services, and garages | 1.00 | 0.90 |
| 15 | 601 65 | Miscellaneous repair services | 0.80 | 0.70 |
| 16 | 601 66 | Motion pictures | 1.30 | 1.30 |
| 17 | 601 67 | Amusement and recreation services | 1.30 | 1.30 |
| 18 | 601 68 | Health services | 4.10 | 4.30 |
| 19 | 601 70 | Educational services | 0.90 | 1.00 |
| 20 | 601 71 | Social services and membership organizations | 1.50 | 1.70 |
| 21 | 601 72 | Miscellaneous professional services | 1.10 | 1.10 |
| 22 | | $GVA_{govep} = $ total government enterprises | 2.80 | 3.10 |
| 23 | 601 77 | Government enterprises (federal) | 1.40 | 1.50 |
| 24 | 601 80 | Government enterprises (state and local) | 1.40 | 1.60 |
| 25 | | $GO_{tt} = M'_{tt} + RY'_{tt} + GVA'_{tt}$ | 79.86 | 79.54 |
| 26 | Table D.2 | $M'_{tt}$ | 21.68 | 21.36 |
| 27 | Table D.2 | $RY'_{tt}$ | 3.66 | 3.96 |
| 28 | | $GVA'_{tt} = GVA_{whtr} + GVA_{rettr} + GVA_{br}$ | 54.53 | 54.23 |
| 29 | 601 50 | $GVA_{whtr} = $ wholesale trade | 18.30 | 17.50 |
| 30 | 601 51 | $GVA_{rettr} = $ retail trade | 30.20 | 30.50 |
| 31 | | $GVA_{br} = GVA'_{br} - ABR$ | 6.03 | 6.23 |
| 32 | | $GVA'_{br} = (1 - g) \times GVA_{nir}$ | 8.80 | 9.12 |
| 33 | Table B.5 | $g = (GR/GO)$ | 0.28 | 0.28 |
| 34 | | $GVA_{nir} = $ nonimputed real estate | | |
| | | $\qquad = GVA_{re} - GVA_{ir}$ | 12.20 | 12.60 |
| 35 | 601 58 | $GVA_{re} = $ real estate $= GVA_{ir} + GVA_{nir}$ | 20.60 | 22.00 |
| 36 | | $GVA_{ir} = $ imputed rent $= GHP_{nf} + GHP_f$ | 8.40 | 9.40 |
| 37 | 809 86 | $GHP_{nf} = $ gross housing product (nonfarm) | 7.40 | 8.40 |
| 38 | 809 94 | $GHP_f = $ gross housing product (farm) | 1.00 | 1.00 |
| 39 | Table B.6 | $ABR$ | 2.77 | 2.89 |
| 40 | | $[GVA_{gr} = g \times GVA_{nir}]$ | 3.40 | 3.48 |
| 41 | 601 81 | $S.D. = $ statistical discrepancy | −1.30 | 0.80 |
| 42 | Table D.2 | $D_p \ (= C^*_d)$ | 9.42 | 9.29 |
| 43 | | $C^* = M'_p + D_p$ | 207.89 | 198.36 |
| 44 | | $GVA^* = TV^* - C^*_m$ | 247.78 | 242.95 |
| 45 | | $VA^* = TV^* - C^* = GVA^* - C^*_d$ | 238.35 | 233.66 |

[a] Unless otherwise indicated, all data come from NIPA (e.g. BEA 1986), where the first three digits denote the relevant table number and subsequent digits the line numbers within those tables.

| 1950 | 1951 | 1952 | 1953 | 1954 | 1955 | 1956 | 1957 | 1958 |
|---|---|---|---|---|---|---|---|---|
| 481.79 | 551.61 | 573.67 | 605.61 | 596.59 | 653.31 | 687.44 | 717.68 | 711.79 |
| 395.62 | 455.40 | 474.75 | 502.68 | 490.93 | 539.80 | 570.99 | 594.14 | 584.05 |
| 212.56 | 244.59 | 254.35 | 268.66 | 261.36 | 287.18 | 303.11 | 314.63 | 308.00 |
| 9.06 | 10.10 | 11.20 | 12.52 | 13.57 | 14.73 | 16.19 | 17.61 | 19.04 |
| | | | | | | | | |
| 174.00 | 200.70 | 209.20 | 221.50 | 216.00 | 237.90 | 251.70 | 261.90 | 257.00 |
| 20.80 | 23.90 | 23.20 | 21.40 | 20.80 | 20.00 | 19.80 | 19.60 | 22.10 |
| 9.30 | 10.20 | 10.20 | 10.70 | 11.00 | 12.50 | 13.60 | 13.70 | 12.60 |
| 13.20 | 15.60 | 16.90 | 17.50 | 17.70 | 19.10 | 21.30 | 22.20 | 21.80 |
| 84.00 | 99.00 | 103.30 | 112.50 | 106.70 | 121.30 | 127.20 | 131.80 | 124.30 |
| 26.60 | 30.20 | 32.20 | 34.20 | 33.80 | 36.80 | 39.60 | 41.70 | 41.90 |
| 17.10 | 18.40 | 19.30 | 20.80 | 21.70 | 24.00 | 26.10 | 28.10 | 29.50 |
| 1.70 | 1.80 | 1.90 | 2.00 | 2.10 | 2.20 | 2.30 | 2.50 | 2.50 |
| 3.40 | 3.60 | 3.70 | 3.90 | 4.00 | 4.20 | 4.60 | 4.90 | 5.00 |
| 1.00 | 1.10 | 1.20 | 1.30 | 1.40 | 1.60 | 1.90 | 2.10 | 2.20 |
| 0.80 | 0.90 | 0.90 | 1.00 | 1.00 | 1.00 | 1.20 | 1.30 | 1.20 |
| 1.30 | 1.30 | 1.20 | 1.20 | 1.30 | 1.30 | 1.30 | 1.20 | 1.10 |
| 1.30 | 1.30 | 1.40 | 1.60 | 1.60 | 1.70 | 1.90 | 2.00 | 2.10 |
| 4.70 | 5.20 | 5.70 | 6.20 | 6.40 | 7.70 | 8.20 | 9.00 | 9.90 |
| 1.00 | 1.10 | 1.10 | 1.20 | 1.30 | 1.40 | 1.60 | 1.70 | 1.90 |
| 1.90 | 2.10 | 2.20 | 2.40 | 2.60 | 2.90 | 3.10 | 3.40 | 3.60 |
| 1.20 | 1.50 | 1.80 | 2.00 | 2.10 | 2.40 | 2.90 | 3.40 | 3.50 |
| 3.00 | 3.40 | 4.10 | 4.40 | 4.30 | 4.20 | 4.10 | 4.80 | 4.80 |
| 1.30 | 1.50 | 2.00 | 2.10 | 1.90 | 1.50 | 1.20 | 1.80 | 1.70 |
| 1.70 | 1.90 | 2.10 | 2.30 | 2.40 | 2.70 | 2.90 | 3.00 | 3.10 |
| 85.37 | 93.52 | 97.12 | 100.33 | 102.96 | 111.71 | 118.34 | 124.74 | 127.84 |
| 22.74 | 24.73 | 25.42 | 25.97 | 26.38 | 28.43 | 29.84 | 31.18 | 31.61 |
| 4.32 | 4.77 | 5.23 | 5.79 | 6.21 | 6.67 | 7.26 | 7.81 | 8.36 |
| 58.30 | 64.02 | 66.46 | 68.57 | 70.37 | 76.61 | 81.24 | 85.75 | 87.87 |
| 19.70 | 22.40 | 22.60 | 23.10 | 23.40 | 26.50 | 28.80 | 30.30 | 30.90 |
| 31.80 | 34.40 | 36.30 | 37.30 | 38.20 | 40.60 | 42.50 | 44.70 | 45.50 |
| 6.80 | 7.22 | 7.56 | 8.17 | 8.77 | 9.51 | 9.94 | 10.75 | 11.47 |
| 9.88 | 10.71 | 11.26 | 12.03 | 12.80 | 13.81 | 14.59 | 15.68 | 16.55 |
| 0.27 | 0.27 | 0.27 | 0.27 | 0.26 | 0.26 | 0.26 | 0.26 | 0.25 |
| | | | | | | | | |
| 13.60 | 14.70 | 15.40 | 16.40 | 17.40 | 18.70 | 19.70 | 21.10 | 22.20 |
| 24.30 | 26.90 | 29.40 | 32.30 | 35.10 | 38.10 | 40.70 | 44.00 | 47.10 |
| 10.70 | 12.20 | 14.00 | 15.90 | 17.70 | 19.40 | 21.00 | 22.90 | 24.90 |
| 9.60 | 11.00 | 12.80 | 14.70 | 16.50 | 18.10 | 19.80 | 21.60 | 23.50 |
| 1.10 | 1.20 | 1.20 | 1.20 | 1.20 | 1.30 | 1.20 | 1.30 | 1.40 |
| 3.07 | 3.49 | 3.69 | 3.86 | 4.04 | 4.30 | 4.65 | 4.93 | 5.09 |
| 3.72 | 3.99 | 4.14 | 4.37 | 4.60 | 4.89 | 5.11 | 5.42 | 5.65 |
| 0.80 | 2.70 | 1.80 | 2.60 | 2.70 | 1.80 | $-1.90$ | $-1.20$ | $-0.10$ |
| 10.81 | 12.85 | 13.80 | 15.04 | 15.08 | 17.07 | 18.54 | 19.79 | 19.92 |
| 223.37 | 257.45 | 268.15 | 283.70 | 276.44 | 304.24 | 321.64 | 334.42 | 327.92 |
| 269.23 | 307.02 | 319.32 | 336.95 | 335.23 | 366.14 | 384.33 | 403.05 | 403.79 |
| 258.42 | 294.17 | 305.52 | 321.91 | 320.15 | 349.07 | 365.79 | 383.25 | 383.87 |

*(more)*

Table E.1 *(cont.)*

|    | 1959 | 1960 | 1961 | 1962 | 1963 | 1964 | 1965 | 1966 |
|----|------|------|------|------|------|------|------|------|
| 1  | 774.37 | 796.20 | 812.01 | 870.18 | 914.05 | 973.89 | 1057.74 | 1150.25 |
| 2  | 637.23 | 656.61 | 666.98 | 714.58 | 752.28 | 798.80 | 869.58 | 943.94 |
| 3  | 334.93 | 343.72 | 347.54 | 371.40 | 389.68 | 412.31 | 447.41 | 483.74 |
| 4  | 20.80 | 21.89 | 23.03 | 24.07 | 25.31 | 27.39 | 30.07 | 33.60 |
| 5  | 281.50 | 291.00 | 296.40 | 319.10 | 337.30 | 359.10 | 392.10 | 426.60 |
| 6  | 20.40 | 21.70 | 21.80 | 22.30 | 22.30 | 21.40 | 24.20 | 25.30 |
| 7  | 12.50 | 12.80 | 12.90 | 13.10 | 13.40 | 13.80 | 14.00 | 14.60 |
| 8  | 23.70 | 24.30 | 25.30 | 27.10 | 28.90 | 31.60 | 34.70 | 37.90 |
| 9  | 141.80 | 144.40 | 145.00 | 158.60 | 168.10 | 180.20 | 198.40 | 217.40 |
| 10 | 45.10 | 47.30 | 48.90 | 51.90 | 54.80 | 58.30 | 62.60 | 67.40 |
| 11 | 32.10 | 34.30 | 36.50 | 39.40 | 42.20 | 45.70 | 49.30 | 54.30 |
| 12 | 2.70 | 2.80 | 2.90 | 3.10 | 3.40 | 3.50 | 3.90 | 4.40 |
| 13 | 5.20 | 5.40 | 5.70 | 6.00 | 6.30 | 6.80 | 7.10 | 7.80 |
| 14 | 2.40 | 2.70 | 2.80 | 3.20 | 3.40 | 3.80 | 4.00 | 4.30 |
| 15 | 1.20 | 1.30 | 1.40 | 1.40 | 1.60 | 1.70 | 1.80 | 2.00 |
| 16 | 1.10 | 1.10 | 1.20 | 1.20 | 1.30 | 1.40 | 1.60 | 1.70 |
| 17 | 2.40 | 2.70 | 2.80 | 3.00 | 3.20 | 3.40 | 3.60 | 3.70 |
| 18 | 11.00 | 11.50 | 12.20 | 13.30 | 14.20 | 15.70 | 17.00 | 18.90 |
| 19 | 2.00 | 2.20 | 2.50 | 2.80 | 3.10 | 3.40 | 3.80 | 4.30 |
| 20 | 4.10 | 4.60 | 5.00 | 5.40 | 5.70 | 6.00 | 6.50 | 7.20 |
| 21 | 3.80 | 4.00 | 4.30 | 4.70 | 5.00 | 5.60 | 6.10 | 7.00 |
| 22 | 5.90 | 6.20 | 6.00 | 6.70 | 7.60 | 8.10 | 8.90 | 9.70 |
| 23 | 2.30 | 2.20 | 1.90 | 2.20 | 2.70 | 2.90 | 3.40 | 3.90 |
| 24 | 3.60 | 4.00 | 4.10 | 4.50 | 4.90 | 5.20 | 5.50 | 5.80 |
| 25 | 138.64 | 142.39 | 146.23 | 155.60 | 162.37 | 176.50 | 189.36 | 204.21 |
| 26 | 34.00 | 34.61 | 35.24 | 37.27 | 38.59 | 42.00 | 45.03 | 48.49 |
| 27 | 8.89 | 9.10 | 9.30 | 9.42 | 9.58 | 10.31 | 11.25 | 12.49 |
| 28 | 95.75 | 98.67 | 101.70 | 108.91 | 114.19 | 124.19 | 133.09 | 143.23 |
| 29 | 34.00 | 35.10 | 36.10 | 38.50 | 40.20 | 43.40 | 46.80 | 51.20 |
| 30 | 49.30 | 50.60 | 51.90 | 55.60 | 58.10 | 63.70 | 68.10 | 73.00 |
| 31 | 12.45 | 12.97 | 13.70 | 14.81 | 15.89 | 17.09 | 18.19 | 19.03 |
| 32 | 17.73 | 18.49 | 19.39 | 20.73 | 22.06 | 23.59 | 25.14 | 26.60 |
| 33 | 0.25 | 0.25 | 0.26 | 0.26 | 0.26 | 0.26 | 0.27 | 0.27 |
| 34 | 23.70 | 24.80 | 26.10 | 28.00 | 29.90 | 32.10 | 34.30 | 36.40 |
| 35 | 50.70 | 54.10 | 57.40 | 61.70 | 65.60 | 69.80 | 74.50 | 79.40 |
| 36 | 27.00 | 29.30 | 31.30 | 33.70 | 35.70 | 37.70 | 40.20 | 43.00 |
| 37 | 25.60 | 27.80 | 29.80 | 32.20 | 34.10 | 36.10 | 38.50 | 41.20 |
| 38 | 1.40 | 1.50 | 1.50 | 1.50 | 1.60 | 1.60 | 1.70 | 1.80 |
| 39 | 5.28 | 5.52 | 5.69 | 5.92 | 6.16 | 6.50 | 6.95 | 7.57 |
| 40 | 5.97 | 6.31 | 6.71 | 7.27 | 7.84 | 8.51 | 9.16 | 9.80 |
| 41 | −1.50 | −2.80 | −1.20 | 0.00 | −0.60 | −1.40 | −1.20 | 2.10 |
| 42 | 21.44 | 21.78 | 21.80 | 23.05 | 23.91 | 25.05 | 26.91 | 28.79 |
| 43 | 356.38 | 365.51 | 369.34 | 394.45 | 413.59 | 437.36 | 474.32 | 512.53 |
| 44 | 439.44 | 452.48 | 464.47 | 498.78 | 524.38 | 561.59 | 610.33 | 666.51 |
| 45 | 417.99 | 430.69 | 442.67 | 475.73 | 500.46 | 536.54 | 583.42 | 637.72 |

| 1967 | 1968 | 1969 | 1970 | 1971 | 1972 | 1973 | 1974 |
|---|---|---|---|---|---|---|---|
| 1200.79 | 1307.97 | 1406.84 | 1457.17 | 1568.48 | 1728.88 | 1980.04 | 2161.80 |
| 982.14 | 1069.74 | 1152.47 | 1186.22 | 1270.83 | 1407.88 | 1623.58 | 1771.47 |
| 500.66 | 545.14 | 586.54 | 602.47 | 644.70 | 714.33 | 837.40 | 926.56 |
| 37.18 | 40.60 | 44.93 | 48.35 | 52.92 | 58.15 | 65.08 | 71.71 |
| 444.30 | 484.00 | 521.00 | 535.40 | 573.20 | 635.40 | 721.10 | 773.20 |
| 24.90 | 25.70 | 28.60 | 29.90 | 32.20 | 37.40 | 56.20 | 55.00 |
| 15.20 | 16.20 | 17.10 | 18.70 | 18.80 | 20.20 | 23.40 | 36.90 |
| 39.70 | 43.50 | 48.70 | 51.40 | 56.50 | 63.00 | 70.40 | 74.50 |
| 222.90 | 243.60 | 257.10 | 252.30 | 265.70 | 292.50 | 326.40 | 338.50 |
| 70.70 | 76.40 | 82.60 | 88.40 | 97.10 | 108.00 | 118.70 | 129.10 |
| 59.90 | 65.90 | 73.40 | 80.20 | 87.30 | 96.80 | 107.90 | 118.90 |
| 4.90 | 5.30 | 5.80 | 6.30 | 6.80 | 7.60 | 8.40 | 9.00 |
| 8.30 | 8.70 | 9.00 | 9.30 | 9.40 | 9.80 | 10.30 | 10.90 |
| 4.70 | 5.20 | 5.90 | 6.30 | 7.20 | 8.10 | 9.40 | 10.20 |
| 2.10 | 2.30 | 2.60 | 2.70 | 2.90 | 3.30 | 3.70 | 4.40 |
| 1.80 | 2.10 | 2.00 | 2.30 | 2.20 | 2.40 | 2.70 | 2.80 |
| 3.90 | 4.20 | 4.40 | 4.80 | 5.10 | 5.50 | 6.40 | 6.90 |
| 21.60 | 24.30 | 27.80 | 31.40 | 34.70 | 39.10 | 43.90 | 49.90 |
| 4.80 | 5.40 | 6.30 | 7.10 | 8.00 | 9.20 | 10.00 | 10.60 |
| 7.80 | 8.40 | 9.60 | 10.00 | 11.00 | 11.80 | 13.10 | 14.20 |
| 7.80 | 8.40 | 9.50 | 10.30 | 11.20 | 12.80 | 15.00 | 16.70 |
| 11.00 | 12.70 | 13.50 | 14.50 | 15.60 | 17.50 | 18.10 | 20.30 |
| 5.00 | 6.20 | 6.50 | 6.80 | 7.40 | 8.60 | 8.20 | 9.90 |
| 6.00 | 6.50 | 7.00 | 7.70 | 8.20 | 8.90 | 9.90 | 10.40 |
| 219.05 | 239.33 | 258.27 | 272.04 | 295.85 | 322.60 | 360.75 | 392.03 |
| 51.94 | 56.30 | 60.18 | 62.80 | 67.71 | 73.20 | 83.29 | 91.94 |
| 13.73 | 14.63 | 15.79 | 16.55 | 17.63 | 18.84 | 20.76 | 22.53 |
| 153.38 | 168.39 | 182.30 | 192.69 | 210.51 | 230.56 | 256.70 | 277.57 |
| 54.50 | 60.00 | 64.80 | 68.20 | 74.00 | 83.10 | 93.60 | 107.30 |
| 78.50 | 86.80 | 94.40 | 100.50 | 109.80 | 119.40 | 132.00 | 138.70 |
| 20.38 | 21.59 | 23.10 | 23.99 | 26.71 | 28.06 | 31.10 | 31.57 |
| 28.57 | 30.59 | 33.32 | 35.22 | 39.25 | 42.02 | 46.88 | 49.76 |
| 0.27 | 0.27 | 0.28 | 0.28 | 0.29 | 0.29 | 0.29 | 0.29 |
| 39.20 | 42.10 | 46.10 | 49.00 | 54.90 | 59.10 | 66.30 | 70.50 |
| 84.90 | 90.70 | 98.70 | 105.40 | 116.70 | 126.10 | 139.50 | 151.10 |
| 45.70 | 48.60 | 52.60 | 56.40 | 61.80 | 67.00 | 73.20 | 80.60 |
| 43.90 | 46.60 | 50.50 | 54.10 | 59.40 | 64.40 | 70.30 | 77.20 |
| 1.80 | 2.00 | 2.10 | 2.30 | 2.40 | 2.60 | 2.90 | 3.40 |
| 8.19 | 9.00 | 10.21 | 11.23 | 12.54 | 13.96 | 15.78 | 18.19 |
| 10.63 | 11.51 | 12.78 | 13.78 | 15.65 | 17.08 | 19.42 | 20.74 |
| −0.40 | −1.10 | −3.90 | −1.10 | 1.80 | −1.60 | −4.30 | −1.70 |
| 29.48 | 32.43 | 35.26 | 36.59 | 39.56 | 44.27 | 52.40 | 58.50 |
| 530.13 | 577.57 | 621.80 | 639.06 | 684.26 | 758.60 | 889.80 | 985.05 |
| 700.13 | 762.83 | 820.30 | 854.70 | 923.78 | 1014.55 | 1142.64 | 1235.25 |
| 670.66 | 730.40 | 785.04 | 818.11 | 884.22 | 970.28 | 1090.24 | 1176.75 |

*(more)*

Table E.1 *(cont.)*

|    | 1975    | 1976    | 1977    | 1978    | 1979    | 1980    | 1981    | 1982    |
|----|---------|---------|---------|---------|---------|---------|---------|---------|
| 1  | 2366.72 | 2691.95 | 3054.58 | 3456.06 | 3832.06 | 4140.14 | 4653.19 | 4762.47 |
| 2  | 1931.16 | 2209.88 | 2517.80 | 2851.83 | 3160.15 | 3425.89 | 3847.44 | 3921.46 |
| 3  | 1023.78 | 1187.33 | 1367.27 | 1545.89 | 1710.49 | 1851.27 | 2078.34 | 2114.61 |
| 4  | 78.69   | 89.45   | 106.43  | 125.44  | 143.45  | 160.92  | 182.00  | 192.05  |
| 5  | 828.70  | 933.10  | 1044.10 | 1180.50 | 1306.20 | 1413.70 | 1587.10 | 1614.80 |
| 6  | 56.30   | 55.70   | 58.90   | 70.10   | 83.10   | 77.20   | 92.00   | 89.60   |
| 7  | 41.30   | 46.00   | 50.20   | 56.50   | 72.70   | 107.30  | 143.70  | 132.10  |
| 8  | 76.50   | 86.20   | 97.90   | 115.60  | 131.40  | 137.70  | 138.40  | 140.90  |
| 9  | 357.30  | 409.30  | 465.30  | 518.80  | 561.80  | 581.00  | 643.10  | 634.60  |
| 10 | 141.70  | 160.40  | 178.90  | 201.00  | 216.10  | 240.80  | 269.60  | 288.40  |
| 11 | 133.20  | 149.70  | 166.00  | 188.70  | 209.10  | 235.80  | 262.30  | 289.10  |
| 12 | 10.10   | 11.50   | 12.70   | 15.40   | 17.40   | 18.90   | 20.40   | 21.70   |
| 13 | 11.40   | 12.80   | 14.20   | 15.90   | 17.00   | 18.80   | 19.50   | 21.30   |
| 14 | 11.20   | 12.90   | 14.80   | 17.50   | 19.60   | 21.10   | 23.10   | 23.50   |
| 15 | 4.60    | 5.10    | 5.90    | 6.90    | 7.60    | 9.20    | 9.20    | 9.60    |
| 16 | 3.10    | 3.80    | 4.20    | 5.60    | 5.00    | 5.00    | 5.50    | 6.30    |
| 17 | 7.70    | 8.60    | 9.80    | 10.40   | 11.50   | 12.40   | 14.00   | 15.10   |
| 18 | 57.80   | 66.20   | 73.60   | 82.60   | 93.10   | 108.10  | 124.70  | 142.00  |
| 19 | 11.40   | 11.70   | 12.10   | 13.10   | 14.40   | 16.00   | 17.50   | 19.10   |
| 20 | 15.90   | 17.10   | 18.70   | 21.30   | 23.50   | 26.30   | 28.40   | 30.50   |
| 21 | 18.80   | 20.30   | 23.80   | 27.80   | 33.90   | 39.60   | 47.50   | 45.70   |
| 22 | 22.40   | 25.80   | 26.90   | 29.80   | 32.00   | 33.90   | 38.00   | 40.10   |
| 23 | 11.00   | 13.80   | 14.20   | 15.90   | 17.60   | 18.60   | 21.90   | 22.20   |
| 24 | 11.40   | 12.00   | 12.70   | 13.90   | 14.40   | 15.30   | 16.10   | 17.90   |
| 25 | 433.06  | 478.48  | 536.78  | 606.13  | 672.91  | 709.35  | 801.65  | 841.12  |
| 26 | 103.25  | 115.69  | 131.33  | 147.87  | 163.83  | 171.94  | 194.31  | 203.79  |
| 27 | 24.34   | 27.25   | 31.94   | 37.64   | 43.05   | 48.29   | 54.62   | 57.63   |
| 28 | 305.47  | 335.53  | 373.51  | 420.63  | 466.03  | 489.11  | 552.73  | 579.70  |
| 29 | 117.50  | 125.50  | 139.80  | 157.90  | 179.50  | 193.90  | 214.00  | 219.00  |
| 30 | 156.20  | 174.20  | 193.00  | 215.50  | 236.30  | 245.00  | 269.10  | 287.50  |
| 31 | 31.77   | 35.83   | 40.71   | 47.23   | 50.23   | 50.21   | 69.63   | 73.20   |
| 32 | 52.42   | 58.23   | 65.64   | 75.47   | 83.11   | 88.15   | 99.08   | 104.97  |
| 33 | 0.30    | 0.30    | 0.30    | 0.30    | 0.30    | 0.30    | 0.30    | 0.30    |
| 34 | 74.40   | 82.80   | 93.50   | 107.70  | 118.60  | 125.80  | 141.40  | 149.80  |
| 35 | 161.80  | 178.50  | 198.70  | 228.00  | 254.70  | 281.50  | 318.70  | 342.70  |
| 36 | 87.40   | 95.70   | 105.20  | 120.30  | 136.10  | 155.70  | 177.30  | 192.90  |
| 37 | 83.60   | 91.30   | 100.20  | 114.80  | 129.60  | 148.10  | 168.10  | 183.60  |
| 38 | 3.80    | 4.40    | 5.00    | 5.50    | 6.50    | 7.60    | 9.20    | 9.30    |
| 39 | 20.65   | 22.40   | 24.93   | 28.24   | 32.87   | 37.94   | 29.45   | 31.77   |
| 40 | 21.98   | 24.57   | 27.86   | 32.23   | 35.49   | 37.65   | 42.32   | 44.83   |
| 41 | 2.50    | 3.60    | 0.00    | −1.90   | −1.00   | 4.90    | 4.10    | −0.10   |
| 42 | 65.17   | 76.18   | 88.36   | 99.90   | 110.54  | 119.64  | 134.31  | 136.66  |
| 43 | 1088.95 | 1263.51 | 1455.63 | 1645.79 | 1821.04 | 1970.91 | 2212.65 | 2251.27 |
| 44 | 1342.95 | 1504.62 | 1687.31 | 1910.17 | 2121.56 | 2288.87 | 2574.85 | 2647.86 |
| 45 | 1277.77 | 1428.45 | 1598.95 | 1810.27 | 2011.02 | 2169.23 | 2440.54 | 2511.20 |

| 1983 | 1984 | 1985 | 1986 | 1987 | 1988 | 1989 |
|------|------|------|------|------|------|------|
| 5085.62 | 5689.10 | 6014.56 | 6236.33 | 6614.45 | 7223.85 | 7639.86 |
| 4167.12 | 4653.80 | 4901.13 | 5067.02 | 5378.21 | 5903.11 | 6215.87 |
| 2235.61 | 2497.25 | 2618.65 | 2664.48 | 2808.66 | 3122.99 | 3278.25 |
| 224.31 | 247.24 | 285.00 | 328.55 | 365.80 | 395.27 | 434.22 |
| 1707.20 | 1909.30 | 1997.48 | 2073.99 | 2203.75 | 2384.84 | 2503.40 |
| 74.30 | 92.90 | 92.01 | 93.60 | 100.67 | 104.26 | 113.48 |
| 118.40 | 119.40 | 114.17 | 74.29 | 76.84 | 80.02 | 80.25 |
| 149.60 | 171.50 | 186.57 | 203.80 | 219.17 | 237.40 | 247.72 |
| 683.20 | 771.90 | 789.54 | 832.42 | 875.54 | 940.66 | 966.00 |
| 320.00 | 354.40 | 374.10 | 393.50 | 408.20 | 444.30 | 460.90 |
| 317.60 | 347.30 | 383.30 | 416.38 | 460.74 | 510.82 | 557.24 |
| 24.30 | 27.00 | 30.36 | 32.43 | 36.01 | 41.25 | 44.47 |
| 23.10 | 25.00 | 29.70 | 31.88 | 33.99 | 38.50 | 42.99 |
| 26.10 | 29.20 | 33.21 | 36.28 | 38.13 | 40.50 | 43.59 |
| 10.80 | 12.80 | 12.44 | 13.69 | 13.84 | 15.59 | 16.94 |
| 6.60 | 7.30 | 9.02 | 10.48 | 12.51 | 13.53 | 14.72 |
| 16.80 | 17.80 | 19.91 | 22.08 | 24.82 | 27.40 | 29.75 |
| 156.10 | 169.00 | 184.56 | 200.30 | 226.14 | 250.30 | 273.31 |
| 21.00 | 23.50 | 25.75 | 27.57 | 29.50 | 32.49 | 35.53 |
| 32.80 | 35.70 | 38.35 | 41.67 | 45.81 | 51.24 | 55.95 |
| 49.90 | 56.90 | 63.62 | 74.43 | 83.60 | 93.92 | 104.92 |
| 44.10 | 51.90 | 57.80 | 60.00 | 62.60 | 67.40 | 77.80 |
| 23.60 | 27.90 | 30.80 | 30.30 | 30.30 | 32.70 | 39.70 |
| 20.50 | 24.00 | 27.00 | 29.70 | 32.30 | 34.70 | 38.10 |
| 913.30 | 1029.90 | 1118.18 | 1171.11 | 1246.83 | 1348.98 | 1441.03 |
| 220.06 | 248.59 | 268.62 | 279.00 | 295.80 | 320.09 | 341.01 |
| 67.31 | 74.19 | 85.53 | 98.59 | 109.77 | 118.62 | 130.30 |
| 625.92 | 707.12 | 764.03 | 793.51 | 841.25 | 910.28 | 969.72 |
| 226.50 | 263.10 | 280.84 | 282.05 | 294.77 | 317.38 | 339.47 |
| 316.40 | 350.80 | 377.40 | 400.54 | 426.36 | 459.95 | 485.98 |
| 83.02 | 93.22 | 105.78 | 110.93 | 120.12 | 132.96 | 144.28 |
| 117.30 | 130.20 | 145.68 | 153.97 | 166.56 | 183.05 | 198.32 |
| 0.30 | 0.30 | 0.30 | 0.30 | 0.30 | 0.30 | 0.30 |
| 167.40 | 185.80 | 207.90 | 219.73 | 237.69 | 261.23 | 283.02 |
| 374.20 | 409.10 | 449.00 | 478.63 | 517.29 | 561.63 | 607.12 |
| 206.80 | 223.30 | 241.10 | 258.90 | 279.60 | 300.40 | 324.10 |
| 198.00 | 214.50 | 233.20 | 251.70 | 272.10 | 292.80 | 316.30 |
| 8.80 | 8.80 | 7.90 | 7.20 | 7.50 | 7.60 | 7.80 |
| 34.28 | 36.98 | 39.90 | 43.04 | 46.43 | 50.09 | 54.04 |
| 50.10 | 55.60 | 62.22 | 65.76 | 71.13 | 78.18 | 84.70 |
| 5.20 | 5.40 | −4.75 | −1.80 | −10.59 | −28.25 | −17.05 |
| 144.48 | 161.39 | 169.23 | 172.19 | 181.51 | 201.83 | 211.86 |
| 2380.09 | 2658.64 | 2787.88 | 2836.67 | 2990.17 | 3324.82 | 3490.11 |
| 2850.01 | 3191.85 | 3395.91 | 3571.85 | 3805.79 | 4100.86 | 4361.61 |
| 2705.53 | 3030.46 | 3226.68 | 3399.66 | 3624.28 | 3899.03 | 4149.75 |

*Glossary of variables in Table E.1*

| | |
|---|---|
| ABR | Amortization of buildings and equipment rented out by the rental sector to others |
| $C^*$ | Constant capital used up (flow) |
| $D_p \, (= C_d^*)$ | Depreciation of productive fixed capital |
| $g$ | Estimated proportion of land rent in the total revenue of the real estate sector |
| $GHP_f$ | Gross housing product (imputed, farm) |
| $GHP_{nf}$ | Gross housing product (imputed, nonfarm) |
| $GO_p$ | Gross output of productive sectors |
| $GO_{tt}$ | Gross output of trade sector |
| $GVA'_{br}$ | Gross value added (or GNP, gross national product) of rental sector |
| $GVA^*$ | Marxian gross value added |
| $GVA_{agr}$ | Gross value added (or GNP) by agriculture, forestry, and fisheries |
| $GVA_{br}$ | Gross value added (or GNP) of rental sector (net of ABR) |
| $GVA_{con}$ | Gross value added (or GNP) by construction |
| $GVA_{govep}$ | Gross value added (or GNP) by government enterprises (federal, state, local) |
| $GVA_{gr}$ | Ground rent (nonimputed) |
| $GVA_{ir}$ | Gross housing product (imputed, farm and nonfarm) |
| $GVA_{man}$ | Gross value added (or GNP) by manufacturing |
| $GVA_{min}$ | Gross value added (or GNP) by mining |
| $GVA_{nir}$ | Gross value added (or GNP) of rental sector (nonimputed) |
| $GVA_p$ | Gross value added (or GNP) by productive sectors |
| $GVA_{re}$ | Gross value added (or GNP) of real estate-and-rental sector (imputed and nonimputed) |
| $GVA_{rettr}$ | Gross value added (or GNP) by retail trade |
| $GVA_{servp}$ | Gross value added (or GNP) by productive subsectors of services |
| $GVA'_{tt}$ | Gross value added (or GNP) by trade sector (wholesale and retail) |
| $GVA_{tut}$ | Gross value added (or GNP) by transportation and public utilities |
| $GVA_{whtr}$ | Gross value added (or GNP) by wholesale trade |
| $M'_p \, (= C_m^*)$ | Materials inputs into production |
| $M'_{tt}$ | Intermediate inputs of trade sector |
| $RY'_p$ | Royalties of productive sectors |
| $RY'_{tt}$ | Royalties of trade sector |
| S.D. | Statistical discrepancy |
| $TV^*$ | Total value |
| $VA^*$ | Marxian net value added |

Table E.2. *Procedure for calculating TP\*, 1948–89 (billions of dollars)*

| Sources[a] | Variables | 1948 | 1949 | 1950 | 1951 | 1952 | 1953 | 1954 | 1955 | 1956 | 1957 | 1958 | 1959 | 1960 | 1961 |
|---|---|---|---|---|---|---|---|---|---|---|---|---|---|---|---|
| | TP* | 446.21 | 431.96 | 481.62 | 551.62 | 573.95 | 605.37 | 596.63 | 652.91 | 687.21 | 717.30 | 711.67 | 774.29 | 795.67 | 811.42 |
| Table D.2 | $M'_p$ (=$C^*_m$) | 198.47 | 189.06 | 212.56 | 244.59 | 254.35 | 268.66 | 261.36 | 287.18 | 303.11 | 314.63 | 308.00 | 334.93 | 343.72 | 347.54 |
| Table D.2 | $M_{tt}$ | 21.68 | 21.36 | 22.74 | 24.73 | 25.42 | 25.97 | 26.38 | 28.43 | 29.84 | 31.18 | 31.61 | 34.00 | 34.61 | 35.24 |
| Table D.2 | $M'_{ry}$ | 4.86 | 5.31 | 5.86 | 6.54 | 7.25 | 8.10 | 8.78 | 9.53 | 10.47 | 11.39 | 12.32 | 13.61 | 14.49 | 15.42 |
| | GFP=TP*−$C^*_m$ | 247.74 | 242.90 | 269.06 | 307.03 | 319.61 | 336.71 | 335.26 | 365.74 | 384.10 | 402.67 | 403.67 | 439.36 | 451.95 | 463.88 |
| | CON* | 158.46 | 160.16 | 171.79 | 185.65 | 194.14 | 204.41 | 209.09 | 224.27 | 234.18 | 246.03 | 251.64 | 269.19 | 279.74 | 286.69 |
| 101 2 | CON | 174.90 | 173.80 | 192.10 | 208.10 | 219.10 | 232.60 | 239.80 | 257.90 | 270.60 | 285.30 | 294.60 | 316.30 | 330.70 | 341.10 |
| Table E.1 | $GVA_{tr}$ | 8.40 | 9.40 | 10.70 | 12.20 | 14.00 | 15.90 | 17.70 | 19.40 | 21.00 | 22.90 | 24.90 | 27.00 | 29.30 | 31.30 |
| Table D.2 | $RY_{con}$ | 6.90 | 7.48 | 8.20 | 9.07 | 9.98 | 11.07 | 11.90 | 12.82 | 13.99 | 15.10 | 16.21 | 18.18 | 19.65 | 21.24 |
| 601 73 | $HH_{con}$ | 2.40 | 2.40 | 2.60 | 2.70 | 2.60 | 2.70 | 2.60 | 3.10 | 3.30 | 3.30 | 3.50 | 3.60 | 3.80 | 3.70 |
| Table D.2 | $ROW_{con}$ | −1.27 | −1.14 | −1.18 | −1.52 | −1.61 | −1.48 | −1.49 | −1.69 | −1.87 | −2.02 | −1.65 | −1.67 | −1.79 | −1.83 |
| | IG* | 44.27 | 33.55 | 51.96 | 56.94 | 49.73 | 50.96 | 49.97 | 65.31 | 67.95 | 66.06 | 58.40 | 74.79 | 72.55 | 71.27 |
| 101 6 | IG | 47.10 | 36.50 | 55.10 | 60.50 | 53.50 | 54.90 | 54.10 | 69.70 | 72.70 | 71.10 | 63.60 | 80.20 | 78.20 | 77.10 |
| Table D.2 | $RY_f$ | 0.05 | 0.06 | 0.06 | 0.07 | 0.08 | 0.08 | 0.09 | 0.10 | 0.10 | 0.11 | 0.12 | 0.13 | 0.13 | 0.13 |
| Table E.1 | −ABR | 2.77 | 2.89 | 3.07 | 3.49 | 3.69 | 3.86 | 4.04 | 4.30 | 4.65 | 4.93 | 5.09 | 5.28 | 5.52 | 5.69 |
| | (X−IM)* | 4.06 | 3.76 | −0.71 | 0.67 | −0.98 | −2.69 | −1.55 | −1.85 | −0.24 | 1.09 | −2.03 | −4.14 | −0.37 | 0.48 |
| 101 15 | X−IM | 7.00 | 6.50 | 2.20 | 4.50 | 3.20 | 1.30 | 2.60 | 3.00 | 5.30 | 7.30 | 3.30 | 1.50 | 5.90 | 7.20 |
| Table D.2 | $RY_{x-im}$ | 0.07 | 0.09 | 0.10 | 0.12 | 0.15 | 0.17 | 0.20 | 0.23 | 0.26 | 0.30 | 0.34 | 0.37 | 0.39 | 0.41 |
| Table D.2 | $ROW_{x-im}$ | 2.87 | 2.65 | 2.81 | 3.71 | 4.04 | 3.81 | 3.95 | 4.62 | 5.27 | 5.91 | 4.99 | 5.27 | 5.88 | 6.31 |
| | G* | 14.40 | 18.76 | 17.42 | 32.50 | 44.06 | 49.96 | 42.59 | 40.05 | 41.89 | 46.93 | 51.73 | 51.92 | 50.93 | 54.77 |
| 301 7 | G | 32.60 | 39.00 | 38.80 | 60.40 | 75.80 | 82.70 | 76.00 | 75.30 | 79.60 | 87.30 | 95.40 | 97.90 | 100.60 | 108.40 |
| Table D.2 | $RY_G$ | 0.20 | 0.25 | 0.31 | 0.39 | 0.47 | 0.57 | 0.67 | 0.78 | 0.91 | 1.05 | 1.20 | 1.68 | 2.17 | 2.71 |
| 301 8 | $W_G$ | 18.10 | 20.10 | 21.20 | 27.70 | 31.50 | 32.40 | 33.00 | 34.80 | 37.20 | 39.80 | 42.90 | 44.80 | 48.10 | 51.60 |
| Table D.2 | $ROW_g$ | −0.10 | −0.11 | −0.13 | −0.19 | −0.22 | −0.23 | −0.26 | −0.33 | −0.40 | −0.49 | −0.44 | −0.50 | −0.59 | −0.68 |
| Table E.1 | $C^*_d$ | 9.42 | 9.29 | 10.81 | 12.85 | 13.80 | 15.04 | 15.08 | 17.07 | 18.54 | 19.79 | 19.92 | 21.44 | 21.78 | 21.80 |
| | FP*=GFP*−$C^*_d$ | 238.32 | 233.60 | 258.25 | 294.18 | 305.81 | 321.68 | 320.18 | 348.67 | 365.56 | 382.88 | 383.75 | 417.91 | 430.16 | 442.08 |

Table E.2 *(cont.)*

| Sources[a] | Variables | 1962 | 1963 | 1964 | 1965 | 1966 | 1967 | 1968 | 1969 | 1970 | 1971 | 1972 | 1973 | 1974 | 1975 |
|---|---|---|---|---|---|---|---|---|---|---|---|---|---|---|---|
| | TP* | 869.52 | 913.42 | 973.35 | 1057.19 | 1149.69 | 1199.81 | 1307.46 | 1406.26 | 1456.35 | 1567.82 | 1728.41 | 1979.91 | 2162.38 | 2368.48 |
| Table D.2 | $M'_p$ (=$C^*_m$) | 371.40 | 389.68 | 412.31 | 447.41 | 483.74 | 500.66 | 545.14 | 586.54 | 602.47 | 644.70 | 714.33 | 837.40 | 926.56 | 1023.78 |
| Table D.2 | $M'_t$ | 37.27 | 38.59 | 42.00 | 45.03 | 48.49 | 51.94 | 56.30 | 60.18 | 62.80 | 67.71 | 73.20 | 83.29 | 91.94 | 103.25 |
| Table D.2 | $M'_{ry}$ | 16.32 | 17.36 | 18.52 | 20.03 | 22.06 | 24.05 | 25.88 | 28.21 | 29.91 | 32.23 | 34.86 | 39.21 | 43.41 | 47.86 |
| | GFP*=TP*−$C^*_m$ | 498.12 | 523.74 | 561.05 | 609.78 | 665.94 | 699.15 | 762.32 | 819.72 | 853.88 | 923.12 | 1014.08 | 1142.52 | 1235.82 | 1344.71 |
| 101 2 | CON* | 303.64 | 319.67 | 343.59 | 370.24 | 400.85 | 421.33 | 464.47 | 502.02 | 537.49 | 580.57 | 637.77 | 708.07 | 776.70 | 860.42 |
| | CON | 361.90 | 381.70 | 409.30 | 440.70 | 477.30 | 503.60 | 552.50 | 597.90 | 640.00 | 691.60 | 757.60 | 837.20 | 916.50 | 1012.80 |
| Table E.1 | $GVA_{lr}$ | 33.70 | 35.70 | 37.70 | 40.20 | 43.00 | 45.70 | 48.60 | 52.60 | 56.40 | 61.80 | 67.00 | 73.20 | 80.60 | 87.40 |
| Table D.2 | $RY_{con}$ | 22.80 | 24.61 | 26.44 | 28.81 | 31.95 | 35.09 | 38.19 | 42.11 | 45.17 | 49.26 | 53.94 | 58.71 | 62.90 | 67.10 |
| 601 73 | $HH_{con}$ | 3.80 | 3.80 | 3.90 | 4.00 | 4.00 | 4.20 | 4.40 | 4.40 | 4.50 | 4.60 | 4.60 | 4.80 | 4.60 | 4.60 |
| Table D.2 | $ROW_{con}$ | −2.04 | −2.08 | −2.33 | −2.54 | −2.50 | −2.72 | −3.16 | −3.24 | −3.55 | −4.63 | −5.71 | −7.58 | −8.30 | −6.72 |
| | IG* | 81.54 | 86.80 | 92.94 | 109.07 | 120.83 | 117.28 | 127.76 | 142.73 | 137.31 | 159.69 | 187.77 | 222.71 | 222.26 | 198.56 |
| 101 6 | IG | 87.60 | 93.10 | 99.60 | 116.20 | 128.60 | 125.70 | 137.00 | 153.20 | 148.80 | 172.50 | 202.00 | 238.80 | 240.80 | 219.60 |
| Table D.2 | $RY_t$ | 0.14 | 0.14 | 0.16 | 0.18 | 0.21 | 0.23 | 0.24 | 0.25 | 0.26 | 0.26 | 0.27 | 0.31 | 0.35 | 0.39 |
| Table E.1 | ABR | 5.92 | 6.16 | 6.50 | 6.95 | 7.57 | 8.19 | 9.00 | 10.21 | 11.23 | 12.54 | 13.96 | 15.78 | 18.19 | 20.65 |
| | (X−IM)* | −0.92 | −0.20 | 1.59 | −0.39 | −2.41 | −3.33 | −6.51 | −6.39 | −4.25 | −9.56 | −15.55 | −9.23 | −14.12 | 4.02 |
| 101 15 | X−IM | 6.90 | 8.20 | 10.90 | 9.70 | 7.50 | 7.40 | 5.50 | 5.60 | 8.50 | 6.30 | 3.20 | 16.80 | 16.30 | 31.10 |
| Table D.2 | $RY_{x-im}$ | 0.43 | 0.45 | 0.53 | 0.62 | 0.74 | 0.87 | 0.97 | 1.10 | 1.21 | 1.35 | 1.52 | 1.78 | 2.05 | 2.35 |
| Table D.2 | $ROW_{x-im}$ | 7.38 | 7.94 | 8.79 | 9.47 | 9.17 | 9.86 | 11.04 | 10.89 | 11.54 | 14.51 | 17.23 | 24.25 | 23.87 | 24.73 |
| | G* | 60.26 | 61.52 | 62.41 | 65.80 | 76.14 | 87.90 | 94.42 | 92.96 | 90.63 | 92.46 | 96.04 | 98.47 | 115.63 | 130.59 |
| 301 7 | G | 118.10 | 123.80 | 130.00 | 138.60 | 158.60 | 179.80 | 197.70 | 207.30 | 218.20 | 232.30 | 250.00 | 266.50 | 299.10 | 335.10 |
| Table D.2 | $RY_G$ | 3.29 | 3.95 | 4.25 | 4.63 | 5.14 | 5.65 | 6.56 | 7.70 | 8.76 | 10.11 | 11.69 | 13.50 | 15.33 | 17.32 |
| 301 8 | $W_G$ | 55.40 | 59.30 | 64.40 | 69.30 | 78.40 | 87.40 | 97.80 | 107.50 | 119.50 | 130.30 | 142.60 | 155.00 | 168.70 | 187.70 |
| Table D.2 | $ROW_g$ | −0.85 | −0.97 | −1.06 | −1.12 | −1.08 | −1.14 | −1.08 | −0.86 | −0.69 | −0.57 | −0.33 | −0.47 | −0.57 | −0.51 |
| Table E.1 | $C^*_d$ | 23.05 | 23.91 | 25.05 | 26.91 | 28.79 | 29.48 | 32.43 | 35.26 | 36.59 | 39.56 | 44.27 | 52.40 | 58.50 | 65.17 |
| | FP*=GFP*−$C^*_d$ | 475.07 | 499.83 | 536.00 | 582.87 | 637.16 | 669.68 | 729.89 | 784.46 | 817.30 | 883.56 | 969.81 | 1090.12 | 1177.33 | 1279.53 |

| Sources[a] | Variables | 1976 | 1977 | 1978 | 1979 | 1980 | 1981 | 1982 | 1983 | 1984 | 1985 | 1986 | 1987 | 1988 | 1989 |
|---|---|---|---|---|---|---|---|---|---|---|---|---|---|---|---|
| | TP* | 2694.39 | 3058.10 | 3456.76 | 3833.25 | 4141.10 | 4654.40 | 4763.86 | 5086.97 | 5691.02 | 6014.18 | 6224.47 | 6606.59 | 7226.22 | 7641.82 |
| Table D.2 | $M'_p (=C^*_m)$ | 1187.33 | 1367.27 | 1545.89 | 1710.49 | 1851.27 | 2078.34 | 2114.61 | 2235.61 | 2497.25 | 2618.65 | 2664.48 | 2808.66 | 3122.99 | 3278.25 |
| Table D.2 | $M'_{tr}$ | 115.69 | 131.33 | 147.87 | 163.83 | 171.94 | 194.31 | 203.79 | 220.06 | 248.59 | 268.62 | 279.00 | 295.80 | 320.09 | 341.01 |
| Table D.2 | $M'_{ry}$ | 54.66 | 65.33 | 73.99 | 84.61 | 94.92 | 107.35 | 113.28 | 132.31 | 145.83 | 168.11 | 193.79 | 215.76 | 233.15 | 256.12 |
| | GFP=TP*−$C^*_m$ | 1507.06 | 1690.83 | 1910.87 | 2122.76 | 2289.84 | 2576.06 | 2649.25 | 2851.36 | 3193.77 | 3395.53 | 3559.99 | 3797.93 | 4103.23 | 4363.57 |
| 101 2 | CON* | 961.28 | 1068.01 | 1185.13 | 1321.81 | 1454.98 | 1599.86 | 1710.89 | 1853.81 | 2013.39 | 2161.53 | 2275.73 | 2434.73 | 2619.76 | 2777.29 |
| | CON | 1129.30 | 1257.20 | 1403.50 | 1566.80 | 1732.60 | 1915.10 | 2050.70 | 2234.50 | 2430.50 | 2629.00 | 2797.40 | 3009.40 | 3238.20 | 3450.10 |
| Table E.1 | $GVA_{tr}$ | 95.70 | 105.20 | 120.30 | 136.10 | 155.70 | 177.30 | 192.90 | 206.80 | 223.30 | 241.10 | 258.90 | 279.60 | 300.40 | 324.10 |
| Table D.2 | $RY_{con}$ | 74.14 | 85.72 | 101.03 | 115.54 | 129.62 | 146.59 | 154.68 | 180.67 | 199.14 | 229.56 | 264.63 | 294.63 | 318.37 | 349.74 |
| 601 73 | $HH_{con}$ | 5.40 | 5.90 | 6.20 | 6.50 | 6.60 | 7.00 | 7.60 | 8.20 | 8.90 | 9.03 | 9.08 | 9.13 | 9.72 | 10.25 |
| Table D.2 | $ROW_{con}$ | −7.22 | −7.63 | −9.16 | −13.15 | −14.29 | −15.65 | −15.38 | −14.99 | −14.23 | −12.22 | −10.93 | −8.69 | −10.06 | −11.29 |
| | IG* | 254.84 | 318.62 | 387.90 | 421.18 | 398.22 | 485.10 | 414.52 | 466.85 | 626.53 | 601.72 | 614.64 | 651.16 | 694.94 | 714.89 |
| 101 6 | IG | 277.70 | 344.10 | 416.80 | 454.80 | 437.00 | 515.50 | 447.30 | 502.30 | 664.80 | 643.10 | 659.40 | 699.50 | 747.10 | 771.20 |
| Table D.2 | $RY_i$ | 0.46 | 0.56 | 0.66 | 0.75 | 0.84 | 0.95 | 1.00 | 1.17 | 1.29 | 1.49 | 1.72 | 1.91 | 2.06 | 2.27 |
| Table E.1 | ABR | 22.40 | 24.93 | 28.24 | 32.87 | 37.94 | 29.45 | 31.77 | 34.28 | 36.98 | 39.90 | 43.04 | 46.43 | 50.09 | 54.04 |
| | (X−IM)* | −12.91 | −35.29 | −40.48 | −44.04 | −36.36 | −41.22 | −47.94 | −79.65 | −129.87 | −141.28 | −156.38 | −164.96 | −131.34 | −110.05 |
| 101 15 | X−IM | 18.80 | 1.90 | 4.10 | 18.80 | 32.10 | 33.90 | 26.30 | −6.10 | −58.90 | −78.00 | −97.40 | −114.70 | −74.10 | −46.10 |
| Table D.2 | $RY_{x-im}$ | 2.78 | 3.43 | 4.04 | 4.62 | 5.18 | 5.86 | 6.18 | 7.22 | 7.96 | 9.18 | 10.58 | 11.78 | 12.73 | 13.98 |
| Table D.2 | $ROW_{x-im}$ | 28.93 | 33.76 | 40.54 | 58.22 | 63.27 | 69.26 | 68.06 | 66.33 | 63.01 | 54.10 | 48.40 | 38.48 | 44.52 | 49.97 |
| | G* | 133.49 | 142.84 | 156.47 | 175.38 | 206.13 | 230.67 | 254.71 | 257.99 | 289.29 | 336.83 | 353.20 | 365.44 | 366.63 | 384.31 |
| 301 7 | G | 356.90 | 387.30 | 425.20 | 467.80 | 530.40 | 588.10 | 641.70 | 675.00 | 735.90 | 820.80 | 872.20 | 921.40 | 962.50 | 1025.60 |
| Table D.2 | $RY_G$ | 20.23 | 24.70 | 29.11 | 33.29 | 37.35 | 42.24 | 44.57 | 52.06 | 57.38 | 66.15 | 76.25 | 84.90 | 91.74 | 100.78 |
| 301 8 | $W_G$ | 203.80 | 220.50 | 240.50 | 260.40 | 288.30 | 316.70 | 343.90 | 366.40 | 390.60 | 419.00 | 443.80 | 471.90 | 505.10 | 541.60 |
| Table D.2 | $ROW_g$ | −0.61 | −0.74 | −0.88 | −1.27 | −1.38 | −1.51 | −1.48 | −1.45 | −1.37 | −1.18 | −1.05 | −0.84 | −0.97 | −1.09 |
| Table E.1 | $C^*_d$ | 76.18 | 88.36 | 99.90 | 110.54 | 119.64 | 134.31 | 136.66 | 144.48 | 161.39 | 169.23 | 172.19 | 181.51 | 201.83 | 211.86 |
| | FP*=GFP*−$C^*_d$ | 1430.88 | 1602.47 | 1810.97 | 2012.22 | 2170.20 | 2441.75 | 2512.59 | 2706.88 | 3032.38 | 3226.30 | 3387.80 | 3616.42 | 3901.40 | 4151.71 |

[a] Unless otherwise indicated, all data come from NIPA (e.g. BEA 1986), where the first three digits denote the relevant table number and subsequent digits the line numbers within those tables.

*Glossary of variables in Table E.2*

| | |
|---|---|
| ABR | Amortization of buildings and equipment rented out by the rental sector to others |
| CON | Personal consumption expenditures |
| CON* | Marxian final personal consumption expenditures |
| $C_d^*$ | Depreciation of productive fixed capital |
| FP* | Marxian final product |
| G | Government purchases of goods and services |
| G* | Marxian government purchases of goods and services |
| GFP* | Marxian gross final product |
| $GVA_{ir}$ | Gross housing product (imputed, farm and nonfarm) |
| $HH_{con}$ | Consumer payments to household sector |
| IG | Gross private domestic investment |
| IG* | Marxian gross private domestic investment |
| $M_p'$ $(= C_m^*)$ | Materials inputs into production |
| $M_{ry}'$ | Intermediate inputs of royalties sector |
| $M_{tt}'$ | Intermediate inputs of trade sector |
| $ROW_{x-im}$ | Trade sector's payments to rest-of-world sector |
| $ROW_{con}$ | Consumer payments to rest-of-world sector |
| $ROW_g$ | Government payments to rest-of-world sector |
| $RY_{x-im}$ | Trade sector's payments to royalties sector |
| $RY_{con}$ | Consumer payments to royalties sector |
| $RY_g$ | Government payments to royalties sector |
| $RY_i$ | Business payments to royalties sector |
| TP* | Marxian total product |
| $W_g$ | Government compensation of employees |
| X − IM | Net export of goods and services |
| (X − IM)* | Marxian net export of goods and services |

# F

## Productive and unproductive labor

Our primary database for employment comes from NIPA. For total employment L we use persons engaged in production (PEP), since this includes both employees and self-employed persons. We use BLS data to calculate the ratios of production labor to total labor in each production sector, which are then applied to relevant NIPA employment totals in order to split them into comparable components.

Productive labor is the production labor employed in capitalist production sectors: agriculture, mining, construction, transportation and public utilities, manufacturing, and productive services (defined as all services except business services, legal services, and private households; see Table E.1 for a full listing of productive services). It excludes nonproduction labor (sales etc.) employed in the production sectors, as well as all labor in nonproduction sectors such as trade or finance. Total productive labor is the sum of the production workers in each production sector. Total unproductive labor is the sum of nonproduction workers in the production sectors and all workers in the nonproduction sectors.

Total employment in production nonservice sectors is directly available from NIPA. But since we only count a portion of the service sector as productive, we estimate the employment in productive services by calculating the ratio of productive service sectors' GNP to total services' GNP and applying that ratio to the total employment in services (Tables E.1 and F.1). Listing the production sectors as $j = 1, ..., k$ and the nonproduction sectors as $j = k+1, ..., n$, we have:

$L_j$ = total employment in the $j$th sector (from NIPA)

= persons engaged in production (PE:)

= full-time equivalent employees (FEE)

+ self-employed persons (SEP);

$$L = \sum L_j = \text{total labor};$$

$(L_p/L)'_j = $ ratio of production/total workers in the $j$th production sector, $j = 1, ..., k$ (BLS);

$$(L_p)_j = (L_p/L)'_j \cdot (L_j)$$
= estimated production worker employment in the $j$th production sector, $j = 1, ..., k$;

$L_p = \sum(L_p)_j = $ total productive labor;

$L_u = L - L_p = $ total unproductive labor.

Table F.1 summarizes productive and unproductive labor for the years 1948–89.

*Glossary of variables in Table F.1*

| | |
|---|---|
| g | Estimated proportion of land rent in the total revenue of the real estate sector |
| $(GNP_{pr})_{serv}$ | Total GNP produced by productive services |
| $GNP_{serv}$ | Total GNP produced by all services |
| L | Total employment in all sectors |
| $L_{agr}$ | Total employment in agriculture, forestry, and fisheries |
| $L_{br}$ | Total employment in the building rental sector |
| $L_{con}$ | Total employment in construction |
| $L_d$ | Total employment in dummy sectors (government – federal, state, and local) |
| $L_{fi}$ | Total employment in finance and insurance |
| $L_{fire}$ | Total employment in finance, insurance, and real estate |
| $L_{gefed}$ | Total employment in government enterprises (federal) |
| $L_{gesl}$ | Total employment in government enterprises (state and local) |
| $L_{getotal}$ | Total employment in government enterprises (federal, state, and local) |
| $L_{govntfed}$ | Total employment in government (federal) |
| $L_{govntsl}$ | Total employment in government (state and local) |
| $L_{gr}$ | Total employment in the ground-rent sector |
| $L_{man}$ | Total employment in manufacturing |
| $L_{min}$ | Total employment in mining |
| $L_p$ | Estimated total productive labor in all sectors |
| $(L_p)_{agr}$ | Estimated total productive labor in agriculture, forestry, and fisheries |
| $(L_p)_{con}$ | Estimated total productive labor in construction |
| $(L_p)_{gefed}$ | Estimated total productive labor in government enterprises (federal) |
| $(L_p)_{gesl}$ | Estimated total productive labor in government enterprises (state and local) |
| $(L_p)_{getotal}$ | Estimated total productive labor in government enterprises (federal, state, and local) |

| | |
|---|---|
| $(L_p)_{man}$ | Estimated total productive labor in manufacturing |
| $(L_p)_{min}$ | Estimated total productive labor in mining |
| $(L_p)_{serv}$ | Estimated total productive labor in productive subsectors of services |
| $(L_p)_{tut}$ | Estimated total productive labor in transportation and public utilities |
| $(L_p'')_{serv}$ | Total production workers in all services (BLS) |
| $(L_p')_{con}$ | Total production workers in construction (BLS) |
| $(L_p')_{man}$ | Total production workers in manufacturing (BLS) |
| $(L_p')_{min}$ | Total production workers in mining (BLS) |
| $(L_p')_{serv}$ | Estimated total productive labor in all services |
| $(L_p')_{tut}$ | Total production workers in transportation and public utilities (BLS) |
| $L_p/L$ | Ratio of productive to total labor |
| $L_p/L_u$ | Ratio of productive to unproductive labor |
| $L_r$ | Total employment in royalties sectors |
| $L_{re}$ | Total employment in real estate |
| $L_{rettr}$ | Total employment in retail trade |
| $L_{serv}$ | Total employment in all services |
| $L_{tut}$ | Total employment in transportation and public utilities |
| $L_u$ | Estimated total unproductive labor in all sectors |
| $(L_u)_{agr}$ | Estimated total unproductive labor in agriculture, forestry, and fisheries |
| $(L_u)_{con}$ | Estimated total unproductive labor in construction |
| $(L_u)_{getotal}$ | Estimated total unproductive labor in government enterprises (federal, state, and local) |
| $(L_u)_{man}$ | Estimated total unproductive labor in manufacturing |
| $(L_u)_{min}$ | Estimated total unproductive labor in mining |
| $(L_u)_{serv}$ | Estimated total unproductive labor in all services |
| $(L_u)_{tut}$ | Estimated total unproductive labor in transportation and public utilities |
| $L_{whtr}$ | Total employment in wholesale trade |
| $L_{serv}''$ | Total workers in all services (BLS) |
| $L_{con}'$ | Total workers in construction (BLS) |
| $L_{man}'$ | Total workers in manufacturing (BLS) |
| $L_{min}'$ | Total workers in mining (BLS) |
| $L_{tut}'$ | Total workers in transportation and public utilities (BLS) |
| $(GNP_{pr}/GNP)_{serv}$ | Ratio of GNP produced by productive subsectors of services to GNP produced by all services |
| $(L_p/L)_{nongovtot}$ | Ratio of production to total workers in all nongovernmental sectors (BLS) |
| $(L_p/L)_{serv}''$ | Ratio of production to total workers in all services (BLS) |
| $(L_p/L)_{con}'$ | Ratio of production to total workers in construction (BLS) |
| $(L_p/L)_{man}'$ | Ratio of production to total workers in manufacturing (BLS) |
| $(L_p/L)_{min}'$ | Ratio of production to total workers in mining (BLS) |
| $(L_p/L)_{tut}'$ | Ratio of production to total workers in transportation and public utilities (BLS) |

Table F.1. *Productive and unproductive labor, 1948–89*

| Sources[a] | Sectors | Units | 1948 | 1949 | 1950 | 1951 | 1952 | 1953 | 1954 | 1955 | 1956 | 1957 | 1958 | 1959 | 1960 | 1961 |
|---|---|---|---|---|---|---|---|---|---|---|---|---|---|---|---|---|
| | PRODUCTION $L_p$ | thousands | 32,994 | 31,201 | 32,226 | 33,123 | 32,768 | 33,043 | 31,230 | 31,714 | 31,864 | 31,433 | 29,349 | 30,020 | 30,047 | 29,363 |
| | Manufacturing | | | | | | | | | | | | | | | |
| 610B 13 | $L_{man}$ | thousands | 15,961 | 14,777 | 15,508 | 16,665 | 16,904 | 17,652 | 16,378 | 16,852 | 17,121 | 17,077 | 15,606 | 16,371 | 16,498 | 16,075 |
| SEHE[b] | $(L_p)_{man}$ | thousands | 12,910 | 11,790 | 12,523 | 13,368 | 13,359 | 14,055 | 12,817 | 13,288 | 13,436 | 13,189 | 11,997 | 12,603 | 12,586 | 12,083 |
| SEHE | $L_{man}$ | thousands | 15,582 | 14,441 | 15,241 | 16,393 | 16,632 | 17,594 | 16,314 | 16,882 | 17,243 | 17,174 | 15,945 | 16,675 | 16,796 | 16,236 |
| | $(L_p/L)_{man}$ | | 0.829 | 0.816 | 0.822 | 0.815 | 0.803 | 0.799 | 0.786 | 0.787 | 0.779 | 0.768 | 0.752 | 0.756 | 0.749 | 0.740 |
| | $(L_p)_{man}=(L_p/L)_{man}\times L_{man}$ | thousands | 13,224 | 12,064 | 12,742 | 13,590 | 13,571 | 14,101 | 12,867 | 13,264 | 13,341 | 13,115 | 11,742 | 12,373 | 12,363 | 11,897 |
| | $(L_u)_{man}=L_{man}-(L_p)_{man}$ | thousands | 2,737 | 2,713 | 2,766 | 3,075 | 3,327 | 3,551 | 3,511 | 3,588 | 3,780 | 3,962 | 3,864 | 3,998 | 4,135 | 4,178 |
| | Mining | | | | | | | | | | | | | | | |
| 610B 7 | $L_{min}$ | thousands | 1,028 | 956 | 957 | 972 | 949 | 908 | 833 | 835 | 873 | 869 | 775 | 742 | 721 | 685 |
| SEHE | $(L_p)_{min}$ | thousands | 906 | 839 | 816 | 840 | 801 | 765 | 686 | 680 | 702 | 695 | 611 | 590 | 570 | 532 |
| SEHE | $L_{min}$ | thousands | 994 | 930 | 901 | 929 | 898 | 866 | 791 | 792 | 822 | 828 | 751 | 732 | 712 | 672 |
| | $(L_p/L)_{min}$ | | 0.911 | 0.902 | 0.906 | 0.904 | 0.892 | 0.883 | 0.867 | 0.859 | 0.854 | 0.839 | 0.814 | 0.806 | 0.801 | 0.792 |
| | $(L_p)_{min}=(L_p/L)_{min}\times L_{min}$ | thousands | 937 | 862 | 867 | 879 | 846 | 802 | 722 | 717 | 746 | 729 | 631 | 598 | 577 | 542 |
| | $(L_u)_{min}=L_{min}-(L_p)_{min}$ | thousands | 91 | 94 | 90 | 93 | 103 | 106 | 111 | 118 | 127 | 140 | 144 | 144 | 144 | 143 |
| | Construction | | | | | | | | | | | | | | | |
| 610B 12 | $L_{con}$ | thousands | 3,305 | 3,155 | 3,415 | 3,628 | 3,601 | 3,528 | 3,394 | 3,463 | 3,580 | 3,525 | 3,397 | 3,533 | 3,491 | 3,461 |
| SEHE | $(L_p)_{con}$ | thousands | 1,954 | 1,949 | 2,101 | 2,343 | 2,360 | 2,341 | 2,316 | 2,477 | 2,653 | 2,577 | 2,420 | 2,577 | 2,497 | 2,426 |
| SEHE | $L_{con}$ | thousands | 2,198 | 2,194 | 2,364 | 2,637 | 2,668 | 2,659 | 2,646 | 2,839 | 3,039 | 2,962 | 2,817 | 3,004 | 2,926 | 2,859 |
| | $(L_p/L)_{con}$ | | 0.889 | 0.888 | 0.889 | 0.889 | 0.885 | 0.880 | 0.875 | 0.872 | 0.873 | 0.870 | 0.859 | 0.858 | 0.853 | 0.849 |
| | $(L_p)_{con}=(L_p/L)_{con}\times L_{con}$ | thousands | 2,938 | 2,803 | 3,035 | 3,224 | 3,185 | 3,106 | 2,971 | 3,021 | 3,125 | 3,067 | 2,918 | 3,031 | 2,979 | 2,937 |
| | $(L_u)_{con}=L_{con}-(L_p)_{con}$ | thousands | 367 | 352 | 380 | 404 | 416 | 422 | 423 | 442 | 455 | 458 | 479 | 502 | 512 | 524 |
| | Transportation and public utilities | | | | | | | | | | | | | | | |
| 610B 37 | $L_{tut}$ | thousands | 4,318 | 4,135 | 4,172 | 4,377 | 4,390 | 4,438 | 4,226 | 4,283 | 4,389 | 4,377 | 4,099 | 4,083 | 4,100 | 3,993 |
| SEHE[c] | $(L_p)_{tut}$ | thousands | 3,964 | 3,761 | 3,791 | 3,954 | 3,947 | 3,971 | 3,753 | 3,799 | 3,874 | 3,845 | 3,577 | 3,604 | 3,580 | 3,469 |
| SEHE | $L_{tut}$ | thousands | 4,189 | 4,001 | 4,034 | 4,226 | 4,248 | 4,290 | 4,084 | 4,141 | 4,244 | 4,241 | 3,978 | 4,011 | 4,004 | 3,903 |
| | $(L_p/L)_{tut}$ | | 0.946 | 0.940 | 0.940 | 0.936 | 0.929 | 0.926 | 0.919 | 0.917 | 0.913 | 0.907 | 0.899 | 0.899 | 0.894 | 0.889 |
| | $(L_p)_{tut}=(L_p/L)_{tut}\times L_{tut}$ | thousands | 4,086 | 3,887 | 3,921 | 4,095 | 4,079 | 4,108 | 3,883 | 3,929 | 4,006 | 3,968 | 3,686 | 3,669 | 3,666 | 3,549 |
| | $(L_u)_{tut}=L_{tut}-(L_p)_{tut}$ | thousands | 232 | 248 | 251 | 282 | 311 | 330 | 343 | 354 | 383 | 409 | 413 | 414 | 434 | 444 |
| | Services[d] | | | | | | | | | | | | | | | |
| 610B 60 | $L_{serv}$ | thousands | 7,707 | 7,688 | 7,911 | 8,033 | 8,006 | 8,097 | 8,019 | 8,382 | 8,720 | 9,006 | 9,158 | 9,430 | 9,817 | 10,005 |
| SEHE[c] | $(L_p)_{serv}$ | thousands | 4,858 | 4,903 | 4,998 | 5,169 | 5,293 | 5,419 | 5,556 | 5,805 | 6,027 | 6,228 | 6,289 | 6,567 | 6,825 | 7,041 |
| SEHE | $L_{serv}$ | thousands | 5,181 | 5,240 | 5,357 | 5,547 | 5,699 | 5,835 | 5,969 | 6,240 | 6,497 | 6,708 | 6,765 | 7,087 | 7,378 | 7,620 |
| | $(L_p/L)_{serv}$ | | 0.938 | 0.936 | 0.933 | 0.932 | 0.929 | 0.929 | 0.931 | 0.930 | 0.928 | 0.928 | 0.930 | 0.927 | 0.925 | 0.924 |
| | $(L_p)_{serv}=(L_p/L)_{serv}\times L_{serv}$ | thousands | 7,227 | 7,194 | 7,381 | 7,486 | 7,436 | 7,520 | 7,464 | 7,798 | 8,089 | 8,362 | 8,514 | 8,738 | 9,081 | 9,245 |
| | $GNP_{pr\ serv}$[d] | billions of \$ | 15.6 | 16.1 | 17.1 | 18.4 | 19.3 | 20.8 | 21.7 | 24.0 | 26.1 | 28.1 | 29.5 | 32.1 | 34.3 | 36.5 |
| 601 60 | $GNP_{serv}$ | billions of \$ | 21.9 | 22.6 | 24.2 | 26.4 | 28.1 | 30.2 | 31.6 | 35.1 | 38.7 | 41.7 | 44.0 | 48.3 | 51.4 | 54.9 |
| | $(GNP_{pr}/GNP)_{serv}$ | | 0.712 | 0.712 | 0.707 | 0.697 | 0.687 | 0.689 | 0.687 | 0.684 | 0.674 | 0.674 | 0.670 | 0.665 | 0.667 | 0.665 |
| | $(L_p)_{serv}=(GNP_{pr}/GNP)_{serv}\times(L_p)_{serv}$ | thousands | 5,148 | 5,125 | 5,215 | 5,217 | 5,107 | 5,179 | 5,126 | 5,332 | 5,455 | 5,635 | 5,708 | 5,807 | 6,060 | 6,146 |
| | $(L_u)_{serv}=L_{serv}-(L_p)_{serv}$ | thousands | 2,559 | 2,563 | 2,696 | 2,816 | 2,899 | 2,918 | 2,893 | 3,050 | 3,265 | 3,371 | 3,450 | 3,623 | 3,757 | 3,859 |

298

| Code | Variable | Unit | | | | | | | | | | | | | | |
|---|---|---|---|---|---|---|---|---|---|---|---|---|---|---|---|---|
| | Agriculture$^e$ | | | | | | | | | | | | | | | |
| 610B 4 | $L_{agr}$ | thousands | 6,625 | 6,440 | 6,402 | 6,022 | 5,879 | 5,696 | 5,713 | 5,525 | 5,251 | 5,010 | 4,848 | 4,704 | 4,531 | 4,442 |
| | $(L_p/L)_{min}$ | | 0.911 | 0.902 | 0.906 | 0.904 | 0.892 | 0.883 | 0.867 | 0.859 | 0.854 | 0.839 | 0.814 | 0.806 | 0.801 | 0.792 |
| | $(L_p)_{agr} = (L_p/L)_{min} \times L_{agr}$ | thousands | 6,038 | 5,810 | 5,798 | 5,445 | 5,244 | 5,032 | 4,955 | 4,744 | 4,484 | 4,205 | 3,944 | 3,791 | 3,627 | 3,517 |
| | $(L_u)_{agr} = L_{agr} - (L_p)_{agr}$ | thousands | 587 | 630 | 604 | 577 | 635 | 664 | 758 | 781 | 767 | 805 | 904 | 913 | 904 | 925 |
| | Government enterprises/ | | | | | | | | | | | | | | | |
| | Federal | | | | | | | | | | | | | | | |
| 610B 81 | $L_{gefed}$ | thousands | 538 | 570 | 553 | 578 | 620 | 599 | 599 | 597 | 603 | 622 | 633 | 645 | 664 | 680 |
| | $(L_p/L)_{nongovtot}$ | | 0.831 | 0.822 | 0.823 | 0.817 | 0.806 | 0.802 | 0.792 | 0.788 | 0.780 | 0.771 | 0.756 | 0.753 | 0.748 | 0.739 |
| | $(L_p)_{gefed} = (L_p/L)_{nongovtot} \times L_{gefed}$ | thousands | 447 | 469 | 455 | 472 | 500 | 480 | 474 | 471 | 470 | 479 | 478 | 486 | 496 | 503 |
| | State and local | | | | | | | | | | | | | | | |
| 610B 86 | $L_{gesl}$ | thousands | 211 | 221 | 234 | 246 | 284 | 292 | 293 | 300 | 302 | 305 | 320 | 352 | 372 | 368 |
| | $(L_p/L)_{nongovtot}$ | | 0.831 | 0.822 | 0.823 | 0.817 | 0.806 | 0.802 | 0.792 | 0.788 | 0.780 | 0.771 | 0.756 | 0.753 | 0.748 | 0.739 |
| | $(L_p)_{gesl} = (L_p/L)_{nongovtot} \times L_{gesl}$ | thousands | 175 | 182 | 193 | 201 | 229 | 234 | 232 | 236 | 236 | 235 | 242 | 265 | 278 | 272 |
| | $(L_p)_{getoal} = (L_p)_{gefed} + (L_p)_{gesl}$ | thousands | 623 | 650 | 648 | 674 | 729 | 714 | 706 | 707 | 706 | 714 | 720 | 751 | 774 | 775 |
| | $L_{getoal} = L_{gefed} + L_{gesl}$ | thousands | 749 | 791 | 787 | 824 | 904 | 891 | 892 | 897 | 905 | 927 | 953 | 997 | 1,036 | 1,048 |
| | $(L_u)_{getoal} = L_{getoal} - (L_p)_{getoal}$ | thousands | 126 | 141 | 139 | 150 | 175 | 177 | 186 | 190 | 199 | 213 | 233 | 246 | 262 | 273 |
| 610B 50 | TOTAL TRADE $L_{tt} = L_{whtr} + L_{rettr}$ | thousands | 10,690 | 10,622 | 10,789 | 11,282 | 11,465 | 11,586 | 11,471 | 11,757 | 12,127 | 12,185 | 12,070 | 12,262 | 12,496 | 12,353 |
| | Wholesale trade $L_{whtr} = (L_u)_{whtr}$ | thousands | 2,839 | 2,783 | 2,818 | 2,980 | 3,056 | 3,103 | 3,092 | 3,164 | 3,307 | 3,318 | 3,295 | 3,351 | 3,421 | 3,419 |
| 610B 51 | Retail trade $L_{rettr} = (L_u)_{rettr}$ | thousands | 7,851 | 7,839 | 7,971 | 8,302 | 8,409 | 8,483 | 8,379 | 8,593 | 8,820 | 8,867 | 8,775 | 8,911 | 9,075 | 8,934 |
| | Building rent $L_{br} = L_{re} - L_{gr}$ | thousands | 435 | 415 | 424 | 437 | 443 | 453 | 466 | 476 | 479 | 463 | 456 | 460 | 458 | 448 |
| | ROYALTIES $L_r = L_{fi} + L_{gr}$ | thousands | 1,420 | 1,453 | 1,517 | 1,608 | 1,698 | 1,794 | 1,883 | 1,957 | 2,046 | 2,131 | 2,172 | 2,208 | 2,296 | 2,336 |
| | Finance and insurance | | | | | | | | | | | | | | | |
| 610B 52 | $L_{fi} = L_{fire} - L_{re}$ | thousands | 1,252 | 1,294 | 1,357 | 1,445 | 1,535 | 1,630 | 1,716 | 1,788 | 1,879 | 1,971 | 2,017 | 2,053 | 2,139 | 2,181 |
| | $L_{fire} = (L_u)_{fire}$ | thousands | 1,855 | 1,868 | 1,941 | 2,045 | 2,141 | 2,247 | 2,349 | 2,433 | 2,525 | 2,594 | 2,628 | 2,668 | 2,754 | 2,784 |
| 610B 58 | $L_{re}$ = total real estate | thousands | 603 | 574 | 584 | 600 | 606 | 617 | 633 | 645 | 646 | 623 | 611 | 615 | 615 | 603 |
| | Ground rent | | | | | | | | | | | | | | | |
| Table B.5 | $L_{gr} = L_{re} \times g$ | thousands | 168 | 159 | 160 | 163 | 163 | 164 | 167 | 169 | 167 | 160 | 155 | 155 | 157 | 155 |
| | g | | 0.28 | 0.28 | 0.27 | 0.27 | 0.27 | 0.27 | 0.26 | 0.26 | 0.26 | 0.26 | 0.25 | 0.25 | 0.25 | 0.26 |
| | DUMMY $L_d = L_{govinfed} + L_{govtnsl}$ | thousands | 6,063 | 6,487 | 6,718 | 8,518 | 9,218 | 9,204 | 9,049 | 8,939 | 9,031 | 9,209 | 9,231 | 9,309 | 9,545 | 9,894 |
| | Government | | | | | | | | | | | | | | | |
| 610B 78 | Federal = $L_{govinfed}$ | thousands | 2,922 | 3,114 | 3,230 | 4,957 | 5,555 | 5,390 | 5,070 | 4,796 | 4,667 | 4,641 | 4,429 | 4,365 | 4,391 | 4,477 |
| 610B 83 | State and local = $L_{govtnsl}$ | thousands | 3,141 | 3,373 | 3,488 | 3,561 | 3,663 | 3,814 | 3,979 | 4,143 | 4,364 | 4,568 | 4,802 | 4,944 | 5,154 | 5,417 |
| | TOTALS | | | | | | | | | | | | | | | |
| | L | thousands | 58,301 | 56,919 | 58,600 | 62,366 | 63,457 | 64,247 | 62,324 | 63,366 | 64,522 | 64,779 | 62,765 | 64,099 | 64,989 | 64,740 |
| | $L_p$ | thousands | 32,994 | 31,201 | 32,226 | 33,123 | 32,768 | 33,043 | 31,230 | 31,714 | 31,864 | 31,433 | 29,349 | 30,020 | 30,047 | 29,363 |
| | $L_u = L - L_p$ | thousands | 25,307 | 25,718 | 26,374 | 29,243 | 30,689 | 31,204 | 31,094 | 31,652 | 32,658 | 33,346 | 33,416 | 34,079 | 34,942 | 35,377 |
| | $L_p/L$ | | 0.566 | 0.548 | 0.550 | 0.531 | 0.516 | 0.514 | 0.501 | 0.500 | 0.494 | 0.485 | 0.468 | 0.468 | 0.462 | 0.454 |
| | $L_p/L_u$ | | 1.304 | 1.213 | 1.222 | 1.133 | 1.068 | 1.059 | 1.004 | 1.002 | 0.976 | 0.943 | 0.878 | 0.881 | 0.860 | 0.830 |

# Table F.1 (cont.)

| Sources[a] | Sectors | Units | 1962 | 1963 | 1964 | 1965 | 1966 | 1967 | 1968 | 1969 | 1970 | 1971 | 1972 | 1973 | 1974 | 1975 |
|---|---|---|---|---|---|---|---|---|---|---|---|---|---|---|---|---|
| | PRODUCTION $L_p$ | thousands | 29,937 | 30,013 | 30,280 | 31,365 | 32,566 | 32,856 | 33,445 | 34,125 | 33,247 | 32,727 | 33,896 | 35,462 | 35,657 | 33,615 |
| | Manufacturing | | | | | | | | | | | | | | | |
| 610B 13 | $L_{man}$ | thousands | 16,658 | 16,776 | 17,006 | 17,902 | 19,112 | 19,335 | 19,642 | 20,057 | 19,177 | 18,336 | 18,819 | 19,871 | 19,804 | 18,062 |
| SEHE[b] | $(L_p)_{man}$ | thousands | 12,488 | 12,555 | 12,781 | 13,434 | 14,296 | 14,308 | 14,514 | 14,767 | 14,044 | 13,544 | 14,045 | 14,834 | 14,638 | 13,043 |
| SEHE | $L_{man}$ | thousands | 16,853 | 16,995 | 17,274 | 18,062 | 19,214 | 19,447 | 19,781 | 20,167 | 19,367 | 18,623 | 19,151 | 20,154 | 20,077 | 18,323 |
| | $(L_p/L)_{man}$ | | 0.741 | 0.739 | 0.740 | 0.744 | 0.744 | 0.736 | 0.734 | 0.732 | 0.725 | 0.727 | 0.733 | 0.736 | 0.729 | 0.712 |
| | $(L_p)_{man}=(L_p/L)_{man}\times L_{man}$ | thousands | 12,344 | 12,393 | 12,583 | 13,315 | 14,220 | 14,226 | 14,412 | 14,686 | 13,906 | 13,335 | 13,802 | 14,626 | 14,439 | 12,857 |
| | $(L_u)_{man}=L_{man}-(L_p)_{man}$ | thousands | 4,314 | 4,383 | 4,423 | 4,587 | 4,892 | 5,109 | 5,230 | 5,371 | 5,271 | 5,001 | 5,017 | 5,245 | 5,365 | 5,205 |
| | Mining | | | | | | | | | | | | | | | |
| 610B 7 | $L_{min}$ | thousands | 666 | 647 | 642 | 644 | 640 | 624 | 618 | 626 | 629 | 617 | 625 | 641 | 701 | 755 |
| SEHE | $(L_p)_{min}$ | thousands | 512 | 498 | 497 | 494 | 487 | 469 | 461 | 472 | 473 | 455 | 475 | 486 | 530 | 571 |
| SEHE | $L_{min}$ | thousands | 650 | 635 | 634 | 632 | 627 | 613 | 606 | 619 | 623 | 609 | 628 | 642 | 697 | 752 |
| | $(L_p/L)_{min}$ | | 0.788 | 0.784 | 0.784 | 0.782 | 0.777 | 0.765 | 0.761 | 0.763 | 0.759 | 0.747 | 0.756 | 0.757 | 0.760 | 0.759 |
| | $(L_p)_{min}=(L_p/L)_{min}\times L_{min}$ | thousands | 525 | 507 | 503 | 503 | 497 | 477 | 470 | 477 | 478 | 461 | 473 | 485 | 533 | 573 |
| | $(L_u)_{min}=L_{min}-(L_p)_{min}$ | thousands | 141 | 140 | 139 | 141 | 143 | 147 | 148 | 149 | 151 | 156 | 152 | 156 | 168 | 182 |
| | Construction | | | | | | | | | | | | | | | |
| 610B 12 | $L_{con}$ | thousands | 3,541 | 3,619 | 3,728 | 3,903 | 3,985 | 3,965 | 4,084 | 4,256 | 4,179 | 4,261 | 4,499 | 4,835 | 4,816 | 4,296 |
| SEHE | $(L_p)_{con}$ | thousands | 2,500 | 2,562 | 2,637 | 2,749 | 2,818 | 2,741 | 2,822 | 3,012 | 2,990 | 3,071 | 3,257 | 3,405 | 3,294 | 2,808 |
| SEHE | $L_{con}$ | thousands | 2,948 | 3,010 | 3,097 | 3,232 | 3,317 | 3,248 | 3,350 | 3,575 | 3,588 | 3,704 | 3,889 | 4,097 | 4,020 | 3,525 |
| | $(L_p/L)_{con}$ | | 0.848 | 0.851 | 0.851 | 0.851 | 0.850 | 0.844 | 0.842 | 0.843 | 0.833 | 0.829 | 0.837 | 0.831 | 0.819 | 0.797 |
| | $(L_p)_{con}=(L_p/L)_{con}\times L_{con}$ | thousands | 3,003 | 3,080 | 3,174 | 3,320 | 3,386 | 3,346 | 3,440 | 3,586 | 3,483 | 3,533 | 3,768 | 4,018 | 3,946 | 3,422 |
| | $(L_u)_{con}=L_{con}-(L_p)_{con}$ | thousands | 538 | 539 | 554 | 583 | 599 | 619 | 644 | 670 | 697 | 728 | 731 | 817 | 870 | 874 |
| | Transportation and public utilities | | | | | | | | | | | | | | | |
| 610B 37 | $L_{tut}$ | thousands | 3,989 | 3,976 | 4,008 | 4,108 | 4,240 | 4,330 | 4,394 | 4,488 | 4,530 | 4,498 | 4,546 | 4,670 | 4,744 | 4,584 |
| SEHE[c] | $(L_p)_{tut}$ | thousands | 3,465 | 3,451 | 3,490 | 3,561 | 3,638 | 3,718 | 3,757 | 3,863 | 3,914 | 3,872 | 3,943 | 4,034 | 4,079 | 3,894 |
| SEHE | $L_{tut}$ | thousands | 3,906 | 3,903 | 3,951 | 4,036 | 4,158 | 4,268 | 4,318 | 4,442 | 4,515 | 4,476 | 4,541 | 4,656 | 4,725 | 4,542 |
| | $(L_p/L)_{tut}$ | | 0.887 | 0.884 | 0.883 | 0.882 | 0.875 | 0.871 | 0.870 | 0.870 | 0.867 | 0.865 | 0.868 | 0.866 | 0.863 | 0.857 |
| | $(L_p)_{tut}=(L_p/L)_{tut}\times L_{tut}$ | thousands | 3,539 | 3,516 | 3,540 | 3,625 | 3,710 | 3,772 | 3,823 | 3,903 | 3,927 | 3,891 | 3,947 | 4,046 | 4,095 | 3,930 |
| | $(L_u)_{tut}=L_{tut}-(L_p)_{tut}$ | thousands | 450 | 460 | 468 | 483 | 530 | 558 | 571 | 585 | 603 | 607 | 599 | 624 | 649 | 654 |
| | Services[d] | | | | | | | | | | | | | | | |
| 610B 60 | $L_{serv}$ | thousands | 10,310 | 10,597 | 10,920 | 11,306 | 11,874 | 12,443 | 12,821 | 13,313 | 13,380 | 13,577 | 14,200 | 14,879 | 15,313 | 15,650 |
| SEHE[c] | $(L_p)_{serv}$ | thousands | 7,369 | 7,631 | 7,939 | 8,295 | 8,749 | 9,246 | 9,727 | 10,205 | 10,481 | 10,655 | 11,059 | 11,606 | 12,100 | 12,479 |
| SEHE | $L_{serv}$ | thousands | 7,982 | 8,277 | 8,660 | 9,036 | 9,498 | 10,045 | 10,567 | 11,169 | 11,548 | 11,797 | 12,276 | 12,857 | 13,441 | 13,892 |
| | $(L_p/L)_{serv}$ | | 0.923 | 0.922 | 0.917 | 0.918 | 0.921 | 0.920 | 0.921 | 0.914 | 0.908 | 0.903 | 0.901 | 0.903 | 0.900 | 0.898 |
| | $(L_p)_{serv}=(L_p/L)_{serv}\times L_{serv}$ | thousands | 9,518 | 9,770 | 10,011 | 10,379 | 10,938 | 11,453 | 11,802 | 12,164 | 12,144 | 12,263 | 12,792 | 13,431 | 13,785 | 14,058 |
| | $(GNP_{pr})_{serv}$[d] | billions of \$ | 39.4 | 42.2 | 45.7 | 49.3 | 54.3 | 59.9 | 65.9 | 73.4 | 80.2 | 87.3 | 96.8 | 107.9 | 118.9 | 133.2 |
| 601 60 | $GNP_{serv}$ | billions of \$ | 59.2 | 63.3 | 69.0 | 74.6 | 82.5 | 90.6 | 99.1 | 110.5 | 121.2 | 130.2 | 144.6 | 163.2 | 179.4 | 199.8 |
| | $(GNP_{pr}/GNP)_{serv}$ | | 0.666 | 0.667 | 0.662 | 0.661 | 0.658 | 0.661 | 0.665 | 0.664 | 0.667 | 0.671 | 0.669 | 0.661 | 0.663 | 0.667 |
| | $(L_p)_{serv}=(GNP_{pr}/GNP)_{serv}\times(L_p)_{serv}$ | thousands | 6,335 | 6,513 | 6,630 | 6,859 | 7,199 | 7,572 | 7,848 | 8,080 | 8,103 | 8,222 | 8,564 | 8,880 | 9,136 | 9,372 |
| | $(L_u)_{serv}=L_{serv}-(L_p)_{serv}$ | thousands | 3,975 | 4,084 | 4,290 | 4,447 | 4,675 | 4,871 | 4,973 | 5,233 | 5,277 | 5,355 | 5,636 | 5,999 | 6,177 | 6,278 |

| Code | | thousands | | | | | | | | | | | | | | |
|---|---|---|---|---|---|---|---|---|---|---|---|---|---|---|---|---|
| | **Agriculture**[e] | | | | | | | | | | | | | | | |
| 610B 4 | $L_{agr}$ | thousands | 4,310 | 4,079 | 3,862 | 3,713 | 3,432 | 3,338 | 3,303 | 3,193 | 3,118 | 3,065 | 3,116 | 3,181 | 3,255 | 3,191 |
| | $(L_p/L)_{min}$ | | 0.788 | 0.784 | 0.784 | 0.782 | 0.777 | 0.765 | 0.761 | 0.763 | 0.759 | 0.747 | 0.756 | 0.757 | 0.760 | 0.759 |
| | $(L_p)_{agr}=(L_p/L)_{min}\times L_{agr}$ | thousands | 3,395 | 3,199 | 3,027 | 2,902 | 2,666 | 2,554 | 2,513 | 2,435 | 2,367 | 2,290 | 2,357 | 2,408 | 2,475 | 2,423 |
| | $(L_u)_{agr}=L_{agr}-(L_p)_{agr}$ | thousands | 915 | 880 | 835 | 811 | 766 | 784 | 790 | 758 | 751 | 775 | 759 | 773 | 780 | 768 |
| | **Government enterprises**[f] | | | | | | | | | | | | | | | |
| | *Federal* | | | | | | | | | | | | | | | |
| 610B 81 | $L_{gefed}$ | thousands | 691 | 694 | 700 | 718 | 785 | 824 | 835 | 848 | 866 | 870 | 843 | 838 | 854 | 838 |
| | $(L_p/L)_{nongovtot}$ | | 0.738 | 0.736 | 0.733 | 0.734 | 0.732 | 0.725 | 0.725 | 0.722 | 0.717 | 0.715 | 0.718 | 0.717 | 0.712 | 0.700 |
| | $(L_p)_{gefed}=(L_p/L)_{nongovtot}\times L_{gefed}$ | thousands | 510 | 511 | 513 | 527 | 575 | 598 | 605 | 612 | 621 | 622 | 606 | 601 | 608 | 587 |
| | *State and local* | | | | | | | | | | | | | | | |
| 610B 86 | $L_{gesl}$ | thousands | 389 | 399 | 420 | 428 | 429 | 429 | 461 | 479 | 507 | 521 | 530 | 555 | 596 | 644 |
| | $(L_p/L)_{nongovtot}$ | | 0.738 | 0.736 | 0.733 | 0.734 | 0.732 | 0.725 | 0.725 | 0.722 | 0.717 | 0.715 | 0.718 | 0.717 | 0.712 | 0.700 |
| | $(L_p)_{gesl}=(L_p/L)_{nongovtot}\times L_{gesl}$ | thousands | 287 | 294 | 308 | 314 | 314 | 311 | 334 | 346 | 363 | 373 | 381 | 398 | 424 | 451 |
| | $(L_p)_{getotal}=(L_p)_{gefed}+(L_p)_{gesl}$ | thousands | 797 | 804 | 821 | 841 | 888 | 909 | 939 | 958 | 984 | 995 | 986 | 999 | 1,032 | 1,037 |
| | $L_{getotal}=L_{gefed}+L_{gesl}$ | thousands | 1,080 | 1,093 | 1,120 | 1,146 | 1,214 | 1,253 | 1,296 | 1,327 | 1,373 | 1,391 | 1,373 | 1,393 | 1,450 | 1,482 |
| | $(L_u)_{getotal}=L_{getotal}-(L_p)_{getotal}$ | thousands | 283 | 289 | 299 | 305 | 326 | 344 | 357 | 369 | 389 | 396 | 387 | 394 | 418 | 445 |
| 610B 50 | TOTAL TRADE $L_{rti}=L_{whtr}+L_{rettr}$ | thousands | 12,433 | 12,499 | 12,849 | 13,213 | 13,615 | 13,822 | 14,179 | 14,637 | 14,889 | 15,158 | 15,488 | 16,209 | 16,565 | 16,500 |
| 610B 51 | Wholesale trade $L_{whtr}=(L_u)_{whtr}$ | thousands | 3,448 | 3,480 | 3,555 | 3,648 | 3,782 | 3,849 | 3,920 | 4,041 | 4,123 | 4,154 | 4,252 | 4,492 | 4,617 | 4,521 |
| | Retail trade $L_{rettr}=(L_u)_{rettr}$ | thousands | 8,985 | 9,019 | 9,294 | 9,565 | 9,833 | 9,973 | 10,259 | 10,596 | 10,766 | 11,004 | 11,236 | 11,717 | 11,948 | 11,979 |
| | Building rent $L_{bbr}=L_{re}-L_{gr}$ | thousands | 456 | 464 | 465 | 478 | 490 | 503 | 523 | 539 | 559 | 596 | 619 | 680 | 697 | 695 |
| | ROYALTIES $L_{rt}=L_{\beta}+L_{gr}$ | thousands | 2,380 | 2,445 | 2,504 | 2,597 | 2,676 | 2,829 | 2,970 | 3,114 | 3,190 | 3,240 | 3,340 | 3,522 | 3,637 | 3,710 |
| | **Finance and insurance** | | | | | | | | | | | | | | | |
| 610B 52 | $L_{\beta}=L_{fire}-L_{re}$ | thousands | 2,220 | 2,280 | 2,337 | 2,423 | 2,496 | 2,642 | 2,773 | 2,907 | 2,972 | 3,003 | 3,089 | 3,240 | 3,347 | 3,418 |
| 610B 58 | $L_{fire}=(L_u)_{fire}$ | thousands | 2,836 | 2,909 | 2,969 | 3,075 | 3,166 | 3,332 | 3,493 | 3,653 | 3,749 | 3,836 | 3,959 | 4,202 | 4,334 | 4,405 |
| | $L_{re}=$ total real estate | thousands | 616 | 629 | 632 | 652 | 670 | 690 | 720 | 746 | 777 | 833 | 870 | 962 | 987 | 987 |
| | **Ground rent** | | | | | | | | | | | | | | | |
| Table B.5 | $L_{gr}=L_{re}\times g$ | thousands | 160 | 165 | 167 | 174 | 180 | 187 | 197 | 207 | 218 | 237 | 251 | 282 | 290 | 292 |
| | $g$ | | 0.26 | 0.26 | 0.26 | 0.27 | 0.27 | 0.27 | 0.27 | 0.28 | 0.28 | 0.29 | 0.29 | 0.29 | 0.29 | 0.30 |
| | DUMMY $L_d=L_{govmfed}+L_{govmsl}$ | thousands | 10,268 | 10,460 | 10,770 | 11,118 | 12,023 | 12,695 | 13,099 | 13,325 | 13,251 | 13,198 | 13,231 | 13,418 | 13,630 | 13,902 |
| | **Government** | | | | | | | | | | | | | | | |
| 610B 78 | Federal$=L_{govmfed}$ | thousands | 4,718 | 4,657 | 4,660 | 4,671 | 5,203 | 5,626 | 5,696 | 5,636 | 5,228 | 4,845 | 4,501 | 4,356 | 4,307 | 4,278 |
| 610B 83 | State and local$=L_{govmsl}$ | thousands | 5,550 | 5,803 | 6,110 | 6,447 | 6,820 | 7,069 | 7,403 | 7,689 | 8,023 | 8,353 | 8,730 | 9,062 | 9,323 | 9,624 |
| | **TOTALS** | | | | | | | | | | | | | | | |
| | $L$ | thousands | 66,091 | 66,655 | 67,874 | 70,128 | 73,301 | 75,137 | 76,929 | 78,875 | 78,275 | 77,937 | 79,856 | 83,299 | 84,612 | 82,827 |
| | $L_p$ | thousands | 29,937 | 30,013 | 30,280 | 31,365 | 32,566 | 32,856 | 33,445 | 34,125 | 33,247 | 32,727 | 33,896 | 35,462 | 35,657 | 33,615 |
| | $L_u=L-L_p$ | thousands | 36,154 | 36,642 | 37,594 | 38,763 | 40,735 | 42,281 | 43,484 | 44,750 | 45,028 | 45,210 | 45,960 | 47,837 | 48,955 | 49,212 |
| | $L_p/L$ | | 0.453 | 0.450 | 0.446 | 0.447 | 0.444 | 0.437 | 0.435 | 0.433 | 0.425 | 0.420 | 0.424 | 0.426 | 0.421 | 0.406 |
| | $L_p/L_u$ | | 0.828 | 0.819 | 0.805 | 0.809 | 0.799 | 0.777 | 0.769 | 0.763 | 0.738 | 0.724 | 0.738 | 0.741 | 0.728 | 0.683 |

Table F.1 *(cont.)*

| Sources[a] | Sectors | Units | 1976 | 1977 | 1978 | 1979 | 1980 | 1981 | 1982 | 1983 | 1984 | 1985 | 1986 | 1987 | 1988 | 1989 |
|---|---|---|---|---|---|---|---|---|---|---|---|---|---|---|---|---|
| | **PRODUCTION $L_p$** | | | | | | | | | | | | | | | | |
| | **Manufacturing** | | | | | | | | | | | | | | | | |
| | | thousands | 34,677 | 35,798 | 37,610 | 38,598 | 37,863 | 37,738 | 36,203 | 36,088 | 37,872 | 38,229 | 38,312 | 39,344 | 40,538 | 41,148 |
| 610B 13 | $L_{man}$ | thousands | 18,839 | 19,557 | 20,417 | 20,949 | 20,167 | 20,096 | 18,607 | 18,316 | 19,255 | 19,124 | 18,876 | 18,969 | 19,361 | 19,418 |
| SEHE[b] | $(L_p)_{man}$ | thousands | 13,638 | 14,135 | 14,734 | 15,068 | 14,214 | 14,020 | 12,742 | 12,530 | 13,285 | 13,092 | 12,877 | 12,995 | 13,221 | 13,257 |
| SEHE | $L_{man}$ | thousands | 18,997 | 19,628 | 20,505 | 21,040 | 20,285 | 20,170 | 18,781 | 18,434 | 19,378 | 19,260 | 18,965 | 19,065 | 19,350 | 19,426 |
| | $(L_p/L)_{man}$ | | 0.718 | 0.720 | 0.719 | 0.716 | 0.701 | 0.695 | 0.678 | 0.680 | 0.686 | 0.680 | 0.679 | 0.682 | 0.683 | 0.682 |
| | $(L_p)_{man}=(L_p/L)_{man} \times L_{man}$ | thousands | 13,525 | 14,084 | 14,671 | 15,003 | 14,131 | 13,969 | 12,624 | 12,450 | 13,201 | 13,000 | 12,817 | 12,930 | 13,229 | 13,252 |
| | $(L_u)_{man}=L_{man}-(L_p)_{man}$ | thousands | 5,314 | 5,473 | 5,746 | 5,946 | 6,036 | 6,127 | 5,983 | 5,866 | 6,054 | 6,124 | 6,039 | 6,132 | 6,166 | 6,166 |
| | **Mining** | | | | | | | | | | | | | | | | |
| 610B 7 | $L_{min}$ | thousands | 791 | 831 | 885 | 957 | 1,049 | 1,161 | 1,134 | 960 | 975 | 925 | 782 | 722 | 733 | 699 |
| SEHE | $(L_p)_{min}$ | thousands | 592 | 618 | 638 | 719 | 762 | 841 | 821 | 673 | 686 | 658 | 545 | 515 | 512 | 499 |
| SEHE | $L_{min}$ | thousands | 779 | 813 | 851 | 958 | 1,027 | 1,139 | 1,128 | 952 | 966 | 927 | 777 | 721 | 713 | 700 |
| | $(L_p/L)_{min}$ | | 0.760 | 0.760 | 0.750 | 0.751 | 0.742 | 0.738 | 0.728 | 0.707 | 0.710 | 0.710 | 0.701 | 0.714 | 0.718 | 0.713 |
| | $(L_p)_{min}=(L_p/L)_{min} \times L_{min}$ | thousands | 601 | 632 | 663 | 718 | 778 | 857 | 825 | 679 | 692 | 657 | 549 | 516 | 526 | 498 |
| | $(L_u)_{min}=L_{min}-(L_p)_{min}$ | thousands | 190 | 199 | 222 | 239 | 271 | 304 | 309 | 281 | 283 | 268 | 233 | 206 | 207 | 201 |
| | **Construction** | | | | | | | | | | | | | | | | |
| 610B 12 | $L_{con}$ | thousands | 4,400 | 4,735 | 5,305 | 5,607 | 5,392 | 5,209 | 4,862 | 4,956 | 5,499 | 5,831 | 6,043 | 6,167 | 6,377 | 6,442 |
| SEHE | $(L_p)_{con}$ | thousands | 2,814 | 3,021 | 3,354 | 3,565 | 3,421 | 3,261 | 2,998 | 3,033 | 3,406 | 3,659 | 3,775 | 3,902 | 3,990 | 4,049 |
| SEHE | $L_{con}$ | thousands | 3,576 | 3,851 | 4,229 | 4,463 | 4,346 | 4,188 | 3,905 | 3,948 | 4,383 | 4,673 | 4,816 | 4,998 | 5,110 | 5,200 |
| | $(L_p/L)_{con}$ | | 0.787 | 0.784 | 0.793 | 0.799 | 0.787 | 0.779 | 0.768 | 0.768 | 0.777 | 0.783 | 0.784 | 0.781 | 0.781 | 0.779 |
| | $(L_p)_{con}=(L_p/L)_{con} \times L_{con}$ | thousands | 3,462 | 3,714 | 4,207 | 4,479 | 4,244 | 4,056 | 3,733 | 3,807 | 4,273 | 4,566 | 4,737 | 4,815 | 4,979 | 5,016 |
| | $(L_u)_{con}=L_{con}-(L_p)_{con}$ | thousands | 938 | 1,021 | 1,098 | 1,128 | 1,148 | 1,153 | 1,129 | 1,149 | 1,226 | 1,265 | 1,306 | 1,352 | 1,398 | 1,426 |
| | **Transportation and public utilities** | | | | | | | | | | | | | | | | |
| 610B 37 | $L_{ut}$ | thousands | 4,594 | 4,717 | 4,945 | 5,166 | 5,162 | 5,218 | 5,136 | 5,077 | 5,248 | 5,306 | 5,337 | 5,464 | 5,615 | 5,689 |
| SEHE[c] | $(L_p)_{ut}$ | thousands | 3,918 | 4,008 | 4,142 | 4,299 | 4,293 | 4,283 | 4,190 | 4,074 | 4,261 | 4,339 | 4,345 | 4,464 | 4,574 | 4,694 |
| SEHE | $L_{ut}$ | thousands | 4,582 | 4,713 | 4,923 | 5,136 | 5,146 | 5,165 | 5,082 | 4,954 | 5,129 | 5,238 | 5,255 | 5,385 | 5,527 | 5,648 |
| | $(L_p/L)_{ut}$ | | 0.855 | 0.850 | 0.841 | 0.837 | 0.834 | 0.829 | 0.824 | 0.822 | 0.831 | 0.828 | 0.827 | 0.829 | 0.828 | 0.831 |
| | $(L_p)_{ut}=(L_p/L)_{ut} \times L_{ut}$ | thousands | 3,928 | 4,011 | 4,161 | 4,324 | 4,306 | 4,327 | 4,235 | 4,175 | 4,360 | 4,395 | 4,413 | 4,529 | 4,647 | 4,728 |
| | $(L_u)_{ut}=L_{ut}-(L_p)_{ut}$ | thousands | 666 | 706 | 784 | 842 | 856 | 891 | 901 | 902 | 888 | 911 | 924 | 935 | 968 | 961 |
| | **Services[d]** | | | | | | | | | | | | | | | | |
| 610B 60 | $L_{serv}$ | thousands | 16,252 | 17,035 | 18,022 | 18,849 | 19,526 | 20,230 | 20,729 | 21,571 | 22,895 | 23,929 | 24,787 | 26,146 | 27,394 | 28,614 |
| SEHE[c] | $(L_p^*)_{serv}$ | thousands | 13,043 | 13,683 | 14,476 | 15,193 | 15,921 | 16,565 | 16,880 | 17,455 | 18,382 | 19,368 | 20,248 | 21,198 | 22,467 | 23,695 |
| SEHE | $L_{serv}$ | thousands | 14,551 | 15,303 | 16,252 | 17,112 | 17,890 | 18,619 | 19,036 | 19,694 | 20,761 | 22,000 | 23,053 | 24,196 | 25,669 | 27,096 |
| | $L_p/L_{serv}$ | | 0.896 | 0.894 | 0.891 | 0.888 | 0.890 | 0.890 | 0.887 | 0.886 | 0.885 | 0.880 | 0.878 | 0.876 | 0.875 | 0.874 |
| | $(L_p^*)_{serv}=(L_p/L)_{serv} \times L_{serv}$ | thousands | 14,568 | 15,232 | 16,053 | 16,735 | 17,377 | 17,998 | 18,381 | 19,119 | 20,271 | 21,066 | 21,771 | 22,906 | 23,977 | 25,022 |
| | $(GNP_{pr})_{serv}^{d}$ | billions of $ | 149.7 | 166.0 | 188.7 | 209.1 | 235.8 | 262.3 | 289.1 | 317.6 | 347.3 | 383.3 | 416.4 | 460.7 | 510.8 | 557.2 |
| 601 60 | $GNP_{serv}$ | billions of $ | 224.9 | 253.4 | 289.1 | 328.7 | 374.0 | 422.6 | 463.6 | 515.5 | 580.2 | 648.1 | 716.3 | 793.5 | 885.2 | 970.5 |
| | $(GNP_{pr}/GNP)_{serv}$ | | 0.666 | 0.655 | 0.653 | 0.636 | 0.630 | 0.621 | 0.624 | 0.616 | 0.599 | 0.591 | 0.581 | 0.581 | 0.577 | 0.574 |
| | $(L_p)_{serv}=(GNP_{pr}/GNP)_{serv} \times (L_p)_{serv}$ | thousands | 9,697 | 9,978 | 10,478 | 10,646 | 10,956 | 11,171 | 11,463 | 11,779 | 12,134 | 12,459 | 12,655 | 13,300 | 13,386 | 14,367 |
| | $(L_u)_{serv}=L_{serv}-(L_p)_{serv}$ | thousands | 6,555 | 7,057 | 7,544 | 8,203 | 8,570 | 9,059 | 9,266 | 9,792 | 10,761 | 11,470 | 12,132 | 12,846 | 13,558 | 14,247 |

| Line | Variable | Units | | | | | | | | | | | | | | |
|---|---|---|---|---|---|---|---|---|---|---|---|---|---|---|---|---|
| 610B 4 | **Agriculture[a]** | | | | | | | | | | | | | | | |
| | $L_{agr}$ | thousands | 3,210 | 3,105 | 3,187 | 3,161 | 3,212 | 3,122 | 3,157 | 3,074 | 3,052 | 2,953 | 2,964 | 3,038 | 3,068 | 3,042 |
| | $(L_p/L)_{min}$ | | 0.760 | 0.760 | 0.750 | 0.751 | 0.742 | 0.738 | 0.728 | 0.707 | 0.710 | 0.710 | 0.701 | 0.714 | 0.718 | 0.713 |
| | $(L_p)_{agr}=(L_p/L)_{min} \times L_{agr}$ | thousands | 2,439 | 2,360 | 2,389 | 2,372 | 2,383 | 2,305 | 2,298 | 2,173 | 2,167 | 2,096 | 2,079 | 2,170 | 2,216 | 2,169 |
| | $(L_u)_{agr}=L_{agr}-(L_p)_{agr}$ | thousands | 771 | 745 | 798 | 789 | 829 | 817 | 859 | 901 | 885 | 857 | 885 | 868 | 870 | 873 |
| | **Government enterprises[f]** | | | | | | | | | | | | | | | |
| | **Federal** | | | | | | | | | | | | | | | |
| 610B 81 | $L_{gefed}$ | thousands | 819 | 813 | 821 | 838 | 846 | 852 | 836 | 834 | 854 | 860 | 856 | 881 | 905 | 917 |
| | $(L_p/L)_{nongovtot}$ | | 0.700 | 0.696 | 0.693 | 0.686 | 0.675 | 0.667 | 0.656 | 0.650 | 0.647 | 0.640 | 0.634 | 0.632 | 0.630 | 0.626 |
| | $(L_p)_{gefed}=(L_p/L)_{nongovtot} \times L_{gefed}$ | thousands | 573 | 566 | 569 | 575 | 571 | 568 | 548 | 542 | 553 | 551 | 542 | 557 | 570 | 574 |
| | **State and local** | | | | | | | | | | | | | | | |
| 610B 86 | $L_{gesl}$ | thousands | 645 | 650 | 680 | 700 | 730 | 727 | 728 | 743 | 760 | 791 | 822 | 833 | 848 | 868 |
| | $(L_p/L)_{nongovtot}$ | | 0.700 | 0.695 | 0.693 | 0.686 | 0.675 | 0.667 | 0.656 | 0.650 | 0.647 | 0.640 | 0.634 | 0.632 | 0.630 | 0.626 |
| | $(L_p)_{gesl}=(L_p/L)_{nongovtot} \times L_{gesl}$ | thousands | 451 | 452 | 471 | 481 | 493 | 485 | 478 | 483 | 492 | 506 | 521 | 527 | 534 | 544 |
| | $(L_p)_{getotal}=(L_p)_{gefed}+(L_p)_{gesl}$ | thousands | 1,025 | 1,018 | 1,040 | 1,056 | 1,064 | 1,053 | 1,026 | 1,025 | 1,044 | 1,057 | 1,063 | 1,084 | 1,105 | 1,118 |
| | $L_{getotal}=L_{gefed}+L_{gesl}$ | thousands | 1,464 | 1,463 | 1,501 | 1,538 | 1,576 | 1,579 | 1,564 | 1,577 | 1,614 | 1,651 | 1,678 | 1,714 | 1,753 | 1,785 |
| | $(L_u)_{getotal}=L_{getotal}-(L_p)_{getotal}$ | thousands | 439 | 445 | 461 | 482 | 512 | 526 | 538 | 552 | 570 | 594 | 615 | 630 | 648 | 667 |
| | TOTAL TRADE $L_{tt}=L_{whtr}+L_{rettr}$ | thousands | 17,097 | 17,840 | 18,812 | 19,425 | 19,395 | 19,604 | 19,419 | 19,815 | 21,038 | 21,747 | 22,215 | 22,943 | 23,558 | 24,375 |
| 610B 50 | Wholesale trade $L_{whtr}=(L_u)_{whtr}$ | thousands | 4,690 | 4,832 | 5,072 | 5,339 | 5,396 | 5,522 | 5,409 | 5,409 | 5,697 | 5,697 | 5,834 | 5,991 | 6,149 | 6,399 |
| 610B 51 | Retail trade $L_{rettr}=(L_u)_{rettr}$ | thousands | 12,407 | 13,008 | 13,740 | 14,086 | 13,999 | 14,082 | 14,010 | 14,406 | 15,341 | 15,943 | 16,381 | 16,952 | 17,409 | 17,976 |
| | Building rent $L_{br}=L_{re}-L_{gr}$ | thousands | 718 | 757 | 822 | 885 | 901 | 882 | 892 | 942 | 986 | 1,029 | 1,057 | 1,111 | 1,157 | 1,168 |
| | ROYALTIES $L_t=L_{fi}+L_{gr}$ | thousands | 3,789 | 3,951 | 4,196 | 4,420 | 4,580 | 4,740 | 4,833 | 4,967 | 5,151 | 5,334 | 5,609 | 5,849 | 5,925 | 5,955 |
| | **Finance and insurance** | | | | | | | | | | | | | | | |
| 610B 52 | $L_{fi}=L_{fire}-L_{re}$ | thousands | 3,486 | 3,629 | 3,845 | 4,042 | 4,195 | 4,363 | 4,452 | 4,565 | 4,730 | 4,894 | 5,157 | 5,374 | 5,431 | 5,456 |
| 610B 58 | $L_{fire}=(L_u)_{fire}$ | thousands | 4,507 | 4,708 | 5,018 | 5,305 | 5,481 | 5,622 | 5,725 | 5,909 | 6,137 | 6,363 | 6,666 | 6,690 | 7,082 | 7,123 |
| | $L_{re}=$ total real estate | thousands | 1,021 | 1,079 | 1,173 | 1,263 | 1,286 | 1,259 | 1,273 | 1,344 | 1,407 | 1,469 | 1,509 | 1,586 | 1,651 | 1,667 |
| | **Ground rent** | | | | | | | | | | | | | | | |
| Table B.5 | $L_{gr}=L_{re} \times g$ | thousands | 303 | 322 | 351 | 378 | 385 | 377 | 381 | 402 | 421 | 440 | 452 | 475 | 494 | 499 |
| | $g$ | | 0.30 | 0.30 | 0.30 | 0.30 | 0.30 | 0.30 | 0.30 | 0.30 | 0.30 | 0.30 | 0.30 | 0.30 | 0.30 | 0.30 |
| | DUMMY $L_d=L_{govinfed}+L_{govnsl}$ | thousands | 13,997 | 14,125 | 14,447 | 14,568 | 14,774 | 14,741 | 14,657 | 14,697 | 14,894 | 15,202 | 15,483 | 15,768 | 16,003 | 16,324 |
| | **Government** | | | | | | | | | | | | | | | |
| 610B 78 | Federal$=L_{govinfed}$ | thousands | 4,248 | 4,234 | 4,244 | 4,211 | 4,268 | 4,285 | 4,307 | 4,340 | 4,395 | 4,438 | 4,440 | 4,483 | 4,483 | 4,504 |
| 610B 83 | State and local$=L_{govnsl}$ | thousands | 9,749 | 9,891 | 10,203 | 10,357 | 10,506 | 10,456 | 10,350 | 10,357 | 10,499 | 10,764 | 11,043 | 11,285 | 11,520 | 11,820 |
| | **TOTALS** | | | | | | | | | | | | | | | |
| | $L$ | thousands | 85,151 | 88,116 | 92,539 | 95,525 | 95,734 | 96,582 | 94,990 | 95,952 | 100,607 | 103,031 | 104,831 | 107,891 | 110,962 | 113,511 |
| | $L_p$ | thousands | 34,677 | 35,798 | 37,610 | 38,598 | 37,863 | 37,738 | 36,203 | 36,088 | 37,872 | 38,229 | 38,312 | 39,344 | 40,538 | 41,148 |
| | $L_u=L-L_p$ | thousands | 50,474 | 52,318 | 54,929 | 56,927 | 57,871 | 58,844 | 58,787 | 59,864 | 62,735 | 64,802 | 66,519 | 68,547 | 70,424 | 72,363 |
| | $L_p/L$ | | 0.407 | 0.406 | 0.406 | 0.404 | 0.396 | 0.391 | 0.381 | 0.376 | 0.376 | 0.376 | 0.365 | 0.365 | 0.365 | 0.363 |
| | $L_p/L_u$ | | 0.687 | 0.684 | 0.685 | 0.678 | 0.654 | 0.641 | 0.616 | 0.603 | 0.604 | 0.590 | 0.576 | 0.574 | 0.576 | 0.569 |

[a] Unless otherwise indicated, all data come from NIPA (e.g. BEA 1986), where the first three digits (and following letter, if any) denote the relevant table number and subsequent digits the line numbers within those tables.

[b] Supplement to Employment, Hours, and Earnings, United States, 1909–84 (BLS 1989). SEHE and its subsequent editions are the main source of $L'_p$ and $L'$ of all sectors except agriculture, services, and government enterprises.

[c] For the period 1948–63, the data on $L'_p$ and $L'$ of transportation and services were not available in SEHE. Hence, for the period in question the data were obtained by extrapolation.

[d] To determine the share of production workers in the productive subsectors of services (BEA 1986, table 610B, lines 61, 62, 64–68, 70–73), we used the GNP share of those subsectors as a proxy.

[e] For the ratio of production to total workers in agriculture, we used the mining sector's ratio, owing to the lack of appropriate data.

[f] For the ratio of production to total workers in the government enterprises, we used the average ratio based on private sectors.

303

# G

## Wages and variable capital

Our primary database for wages comes from NIPA. We use employee compensation (EC) because it includes wages and salaries of employees as well as employer contributions to social security. This is the appropriate base for estimates of variable capital, since it represents the total cost of labor power to the capitalist.

A combination of BLS and NIPA data is used to estimate the wage per production worker. This is then applied to the estimate of the number of productive workers from Appendix F to derive the total wage bill of productive labor (variable capital). The wage bill of unproductive workers is derived as the difference between total NIPA wages and total variable capital. The basic steps involved will now be outlined.

Starting with the NIPA measure of employee compensation EC, we make two adjustments. First, because EC covers only employees whereas our measure of total employment L includes both employees and self-employed persons, we need to make some estimate of the *wage equivalent* of self-employed persons. Second, we must split the resulting measure of total wages into wages of productive and unproductive workers. Let

$EC_j$ = total employee compensation in the $j$th sector (NIPA);

$FEE_j$ = total full-time equivalent employees in the $j$th sector (NIPA);

$ec_j \equiv (EC/FEE)_j$ = employee compensation per full-time equivalent employee;

$W_j \equiv ec_j \cdot L_j$ = estimated total wage

= employee compensation and wage equivalent of self-employed persons in the $j$th sector;

$W = \sum W_j$ = aggregate total wage (including wage equivalent).

304

See Table G.1.

Having expanded our measure of wages to encompass the wage equivalent of self-employed persons, we turn to its division into the wages of productive and unproductive workers.[1] The first step is to derive an estimate of the unit employee compensation of productive workers ($ec_p$). We have:

$(w_p)'_j$ = unit wage of production workers in the $j$th production sector, $j = 1, ..., k$ (from BLS);

$x_j \equiv (EC/WS)_j$ = ratio of employee compensation to wages and salaries in the $j$th production sector, $j = 1, ..., k$ (from NIPA);

$(ec_p)_j \equiv (w_p)'_j \cdot (x_j)$ = estimated employee compensation of production workers in the $j$th production sector.

For services, long-term data on $w_p$ and $x$ were unavailable, so we assumed productive workers in services had the same wage as the average service worker: $(ec_p)_{serv} = ec_{serv}$.

Given $W$ and the various $(ec_p)_j$ just derived, together with the data from Appendix F on the numbers of productive and unproductive workers ($L_p, L_u$), we can derive the wage bill of productive workers ($W_p \equiv ec_p \cdot L_p$) as well as the wage bill and wage rate of unproductive workers ($W_u = W - W_p$, $ec_u = W_u/L_u$).[2] We have:

$V_j \equiv (ec_p)_j \cdot (L_p)_j \equiv (W_p)_j$ = variable capital in the $j$th production sector;

$V^* \equiv W_p = \Sigma(W_p)_j$ = total variable capital;

$W_u \equiv W - V^*$ = total wages of unproductive workers in all sectors;

$ec_p \equiv W_p/L_p$ = average wage of productive workers;

$ec_u \equiv W_u/L_u$ = average wage of unproductive workers.

See Table G.2.

Finally, there are two implicit aspects of our procedure upon which we can cast some empirical light; both relate to our use of employee compensation as the base for wages and salaries. Employee compensation includes corporate officers' salaries (COS). These should be excluded from variable capital because they actually represent income of capitalists, not wages of workers (Mage 1963, pp. 188–9). Indeed, our method effectively

[1] If we could safely assume that production and nonproduction workers have the same wage, then we could use the ratio $L_p/L$ to split total wages $W$. But we shall see that $w_p$ is not the same as $w_u$, which is why we adopt our own procedure.

[2] The BLS does not publish data on the wage rates of nonproduction workers.

## Table G.1. Total wage (W), 1948–89

| Sources[a] | Sectors | Units | 1948 | 1949 | 1950 | 1951 | 1952 | 1953 | 1954 | 1955 | 1956 | 1957 | 1958 | 1959 | 1960 | 1961 |
|---|---|---|---|---|---|---|---|---|---|---|---|---|---|---|---|---|
| | **PRODUCTION** | | | | | | | | | | | | | | | |
| | **Manufacturing** | | | | | | | | | | | | | | | |
| 604B 13 | $EC_{man}$ | millions of $ | 49,454 | 47,059 | 53,628 | 63,691 | 68,876 | 76,433 | 72,922 | 80,050 | 86,504 | 90,270 | 86,489 | 95,841 | 99,478 | 99,678 |
| 607B 13 | $FEE_{man}$ | thousands | 15,521 | 14,368 | 15,110 | 16,252 | 16,482 | 17,241 | 15,999 | 16,490 | 16,774 | 16,745 | 15,291 | 16,060 | 16,189 | 15,772 |
| | $ec_{man}=(EC/FEE)_{man}$ | dollars | 3,186 | 3,275 | 3,549 | 3,919 | 4,179 | 4,433 | 4,558 | 4,854 | 5,157 | 5,391 | 5,656 | 5,968 | 6,145 | 6,320 |
| 610B 13 | $L_{man}$ | thousands | 15,961 | 14,777 | 15,508 | 16,665 | 16,904 | 17,652 | 16,378 | 16,852 | 17,121 | 17,077 | 15,606 | 16,371 | 16,498 | 16,075 |
| | $W_{man}=ec_{man}\times L_{man}$ | millions of $ | 50,856 | 48,399 | 55,041 | 65,310 | 70,639 | 78,255 | 74,649 | 81,807 | 88,293 | 92,060 | 88,271 | 97,697 | 101,377 | 101,593 |
| | **Mining** | | | | | | | | | | | | | | | |
| 604B 7 | $EC_{min}$ | millions of $ | 3,597 | 3,182 | 3,503 | 3,990 | 4,059 | 4,183 | 3,843 | 4,161 | 4,674 | 4,830 | 4,322 | 4,419 | 4,444 | 4,371 |
| 607B 7 | $FEE_{min}$ | thousands | 993 | 923 | 924 | 937 | 914 | 872 | 794 | 798 | 837 | 833 | 742 | 710 | 692 | 657 |
| | $ec_{min}=(EC/FEE)_{min}$ | dollars | 3,622 | 3,447 | 3,791 | 4,258 | 4,441 | 4,797 | 4,840 | 5,214 | 5,584 | 5,798 | 5,825 | 6,224 | 6,422 | 6,653 |
| 610B 7 | $L_{min}$ | thousands | 1,028 | 956 | 957 | 972 | 949 | 908 | 833 | 835 | 873 | 869 | 775 | 742 | 721 | 685 |
| | $W_{min}=ec_{min}\times L_{min}$ | millions of $ | 3,724 | 3,296 | 3,628 | 4,139 | 4,214 | 4,356 | 4,032 | 4,354 | 4,875 | 5,039 | 4,514 | 4,618 | 4,630 | 4,557 |
| | **Construction** | | | | | | | | | | | | | | | |
| 604B 12 | $EC_{con}$ | millions of $ | 7,662 | 7,490 | 8,624 | 10,665 | 11,597 | 12,194 | 12,452 | 13,408 | 14,919 | 15,342 | 15,152 | 16,623 | 17,246 | 17,716 |
| 607B 12 | $FEE_{con}$ | thousands | 2,321 | 2,194 | 2,411 | 2,668 | 2,683 | 2,643 | 2,611 | 2,734 | 2,853 | 2,801 | 2,705 | 2,838 | 2,805 | 2,777 |
| | $ec_{con}=(EC/FEE)_{con}$ | dollars | 3,301 | 3,414 | 3,577 | 3,997 | 4,322 | 4,614 | 4,769 | 4,904 | 5,229 | 5,477 | 5,601 | 5,857 | 6,148 | 6,380 |
| 610B 12 | $L_{con}$ | thousands | 3,305 | 3,155 | 3,415 | 3,628 | 3,601 | 3,528 | 3,394 | 3,463 | 3,580 | 3,525 | 3,397 | 3,533 | 3,491 | 3,461 |
| | $W_{con}=ec_{con}\times L_{con}$ | millions of $ | 10,910 | 10,771 | 12,215 | 14,502 | 15,565 | 16,277 | 16,186 | 16,983 | 18,721 | 19,308 | 19,028 | 20,694 | 21,464 | 22,080 |
| | **Transportation and public utilities** | | | | | | | | | | | | | | | |
| 604B 37 | $EC_{tut}$ | millions of $ | 14,498 | 14,333 | 15,141 | 17,185 | 18,260 | 19,364 | 19,084 | 20,285 | 21,994 | 23,145 | 22,719 | 24,187 | 25,149 | 25,375 |
| 607B 37 | $FEE_{tut}$ | thousands | 4,121 | 3,939 | 3,972 | 4,170 | 4,182 | 4,228 | 4,025 | 4,087 | 4,195 | 4,182 | 3,908 | 3,897 | 3,914 | 3,808 |
| | $ec_{tut}=(EC/FEE)_{tut}$ | dollars | 3,518 | 3,639 | 3,812 | 4,121 | 4,366 | 4,580 | 4,741 | 4,963 | 5,243 | 5,534 | 5,813 | 6,207 | 6,425 | 6,664 |
| 610B 37 | $L_{tut}$ | thousands | 4,318 | 4,135 | 4,172 | 4,377 | 4,390 | 4,438 | 4,226 | 4,283 | 4,389 | 4,377 | 4,099 | 4,083 | 4,100 | 3,993 |
| | $W_{tut}=ec_{tut}\times L_{tut}$ | millions of $ | 15,191 | 15,046 | 15,903 | 18,038 | 19,168 | 20,326 | 20,037 | 21,258 | 23,011 | 24,224 | 23,829 | 25,341 | 26,344 | 26,608 |
| | **Services** | | | | | | | | | | | | | | | |
| 604B 60 | $EC_{serv}$ | millions of $ | 13,153 | 13,573 | 14,458 | 15,800 | 16,906 | 18,161 | 18,899 | 20,770 | 22,844 | 24,650 | 26,112 | 28,460 | 31,016 | 32,979 |
| 607B 60 | $FEE_{serv}$ | thousands | 6,177 | 6,157 | 6,372 | 6,483 | 6,434 | 6,513 | 6,437 | 6,801 | 7,097 | 7,323 | 7,452 | 7,694 | 8,005 | 8,133 |
| | $ec_{serv}=(EC/FEE)_{serv}$ | dollars | 2,129 | 2,204 | 2,269 | 2,437 | 2,628 | 2,788 | 2,936 | 3,054 | 3,219 | 3,366 | 3,504 | 3,699 | 3,875 | 4,055 |
| 610B 60 | $L_{serv}$ | thousands | 7,707 | 7,688 | 7,911 | 8,033 | 8,006 | 8,097 | 8,019 | 8,382 | 8,720 | 9,006 | 9,158 | 9,430 | 9,817 | 10,005 |
| | $W_{serv}=ec_{serv}\times L_{serv}$ | millions of $ | 16,411 | 16,948 | 17,950 | 19,578 | 21,037 | 22,578 | 23,544 | 25,598 | 28,068 | 30,315 | 32,090 | 34,881 | 38,037 | 40,570 |
| | **Agriculture** | | | | | | | | | | | | | | | |
| 604B 4 | $EC_{agr}$ | millions of $ | 3,319 | 3,143 | 3,184 | 3,340 | 3,314 | 3,210 | 3,097 | 3,087 | 3,129 | 3,235 | 3,431 | 3,517 | 3,694 | 3,889 |
| 607B 4 | $FEE_{agr}$ | thousands | 2,072 | 2,000 | 2,067 | 1,999 | 1,933 | 1,882 | 1,902 | 1,847 | 1,769 | 1,747 | 1,780 | 1,771 | 1,755 | 1,763 |
| | $ec_{agr}=(EC/FEE)_{agr}$ | dollars | 1,602 | 1,572 | 1,540 | 1,671 | 1,714 | 1,706 | 1,628 | 1,671 | 1,769 | 1,852 | 1,928 | 1,986 | 2,105 | 2,206 |
| 610B 4 | $L_{agr}$ | thousands | 6,625 | 6,440 | 6,402 | 6,022 | 5,879 | 5,696 | 5,713 | 5,525 | 5,251 | 5,010 | 4,848 | 4,704 | 4,531 | 4,442 |
| | $W_{agr}=ec_{agr}\times L_{agr}$ | millions of $ | 10,612 | 10,120 | 9,862 | 10,062 | 10,079 | 9,715 | 9,302 | 9,234 | 9,288 | 9,277 | 9,345 | 9,342 | 9,537 | 9,799 |
| | **Government enterprises**[b] | | | | | | | | | | | | | | | |
| 604B 81 | $EC_{gefed}$ | millions of $ | 1,676 | 1,857 | 1,935 | 2,140 | 2,433 | 2,366 | 2,367 | 2,535 | 2,689 | 2,859 | 3,187 | 3,276 | 3,555 | 3,790 |
| 604B 86 | $EC_{gesl}$ | millions of $ | 640 | 707 | 760 | 859 | 1,056 | 1,138 | 1,187 | 1,274 | 1,310 | 1,368 | 1,494 | 1,750 | 1,934 | 1,962 |
| | $W_{genreal}=EC_{gefed}+EC_{gesl}$ | millions of $ | 2,316 | 2,564 | 2,695 | 2,999 | 3,489 | 3,504 | 3,554 | 3,809 | 3,999 | 4,227 | 4,681 | 5,026 | 5,489 | 5,752 |

**TOTAL TRADE**

**Wholesale trade**

| Code | Variable | Unit | | | | | | | | | | | | | | |
|---|---|---|---|---|---|---|---|---|---|---|---|---|---|---|---|---|
| 604B 50 | $EC_{whtr}$ | millions of $ | 9,568 | 9,431 | 10,086 | 11,354 | 11,936 | 12,665 | 13,029 | 13,919 | 15,448 | 16,327 | 16,789 | 18,074 | 19,172 | 19,781 |
| 607B 50 | $FEE_{whtr}$ | thousands | 2,586 | 2,528 | 2,559 | 2,715 | 2,784 | 2,830 | 2,821 | 2,891 | 3,031 | 3,041 | 3,017 | 3,069 | 3,132 | 3,130 |
| | $ec_{whtr} = (EC/FEE)_{whtr}$ | dollars | 3,700 | 3,731 | 3,941 | 4,182 | 4,287 | 4,475 | 4,619 | 4,815 | 5,097 | 5,369 | 5,565 | 5,889 | 6,121 | 6,320 |
| 610B 50 | $L_{whtr}$ | thousands | 2,839 | 2,783 | 2,818 | 2,980 | 3,056 | 3,103 | 3,092 | 3,164 | 3,307 | 3,318 | 3,295 | 3,351 | 3,421 | 3,419 |
| | $W_{whtr} = ec_{whtr} \times L_{whtr}$ | millions of $ | 10,504 | 10,382 | 11,107 | 12,462 | 13,102 | 13,887 | 14,281 | 15,233 | 16,855 | 17,814 | 18,336 | 19,735 | 20,941 | 21,607 |

**Retail trade**

| Code | Variable | Unit | | | | | | | | | | | | | | |
|---|---|---|---|---|---|---|---|---|---|---|---|---|---|---|---|---|
| 604B 51 | $EC_{rettr}$ | millions of $ | 15,170 | 15,596 | 16,751 | 18,175 | 19,176 | 20,434 | 20,929 | 22,392 | 23,908 | 25,129 | 25,561 | 27,626 | 29,553 | 30,102 |
| 607B 51 | $FEE_{rettr}$ | thousands | 5,852 | 5,805 | 5,942 | 6,275 | 6,384 | 6,482 | 6,405 | 6,570 | 6,781 | 6,811 | 6,698 | 6,900 | 7,100 | 7,040 |
| | $ec_{rettr} = (EC/FEE)_{rettr}$ | dollars | 2,592 | 2,687 | 2,819 | 2,896 | 3,004 | 3,152 | 3,268 | 3,408 | 3,526 | 3,689 | 3,816 | 4,004 | 4,162 | 4,276 |
| 610B 51 | $L_{rettr}$ | thousands | 7,851 | 7,839 | 7,971 | 8,302 | 8,409 | 8,483 | 8,379 | 8,593 | 8,820 | 8,867 | 8,775 | 8,911 | 9,075 | 8,934 |
| | $W_{rettr} = ec_{rettr} \times L_{rettr}$ | millions of $ | 20,352 | 21,061 | 22,471 | 24,406 | 25,259 | 26,742 | 27,379 | 29,287 | 31,097 | 32,715 | 33,487 | 35,678 | 37,774 | 38,200 |

**Building rental**

| Code | Variable | Unit | | | | | | | | | | | | | | |
|---|---|---|---|---|---|---|---|---|---|---|---|---|---|---|---|---|
| | $W_{br} = W_{re} - W_{gr}$ | millions of $ | 1,083 | 1,039 | 1,136 | 1,238 | 1,298 | 1,401 | 1,534 | 1,655 | 1,771 | 1,782 | 1,777 | 1,908 | 1,937 | 2,002 |

**ROYALTIES**

**Finance and insurance**

| Code | Variable | Unit | | | | | | | | | | | | | | |
|---|---|---|---|---|---|---|---|---|---|---|---|---|---|---|---|---|
| 604B 52 | $EC_{fi} = EC_{fire} - EC_{re}$ | millions of $ | 4,033 | 4,325 | 4,778 | 5,312 | 5,847 | 6,440 | 7,030 | 7,606 | 8,331 | 9,056 | 9,840 | 10,713 | 11,491 | 12,394 |
| | $EC_{fire}$ | millions of $ | 5,186 | 5,448 | 6,029 | 6,640 | 7,207 | 7,870 | 8,571 | 9,309 | 10,178 | 10,896 | 11,669 | 12,704 | 13,519 | 14,486 |
| 607B 52 | $FEE_{fi} = FEE_{fire} - FEE_{re}$ | thousands | 1,172 | 1,214 | 1,275 | 1,357 | 1,438 | 1,524 | 1,592 | 1,673 | 1,769 | 1,861 | 1,908 | 1,946 | 2,031 | 2,073 |
| | $FEE_{fire}$ | dollars | 1,635 | 1,663 | 1,742 | 1,826 | 1,902 | 1,986 | 2,060 | 2,163 | 2,268 | 2,339 | 2,377 | 2,426 | 2,511 | 2,541 |
| | $ec_{fi} = (EC/FEE)_{fi}$ | thousands | 3,441 | 3,563 | 3,747 | 3,915 | 4,066 | 4,226 | 4,416 | 4,546 | 4,709 | 4,866 | 5,157 | 5,505 | 5,658 | 5,979 |
| 610B 52 | $L_{fi} = L_{fire} - L_{re}$ | thousands | 1,252 | 1,294 | 1,357 | 1,445 | 1,535 | 1,630 | 1,716 | 1,788 | 1,879 | 1,971 | 2,017 | 2,053 | 2,139 | 2,181 |
| | $L_{fire}$ | thousands | 1,855 | 1,868 | 1,941 | 2,045 | 2,141 | 2,247 | 2,349 | 2,433 | 2,525 | 2,594 | 2,628 | 2,754 | 2,784 | |
| | $W_{fi} = ec_{fi} \times L_{fi}$ | millions of $ | 4,308 | 4,610 | 5,085 | 5,656 | 6,241 | 6,888 | 7,578 | 8,129 | 8,849 | 9,591 | 10,402 | 11,302 | 12,102 | 13,040 |

**Ground rent**

| Code | Variable | Unit | | | | | | | | | | | | | | |
|---|---|---|---|---|---|---|---|---|---|---|---|---|---|---|---|---|
| 604B 58 | $EC_{re}$ | millions of $ | 1,153 | 1,123 | 1,251 | 1,328 | 1,360 | 1,430 | 1,541 | 1,703 | 1,847 | 1,840 | 1,829 | 1,991 | 2,028 | 2,092 |
| 607B 58 | $FEE_{re}$ | thousands | 463 | 449 | 467 | 469 | 464 | 462 | 468 | 490 | 499 | 478 | 469 | 480 | 480 | 468 |
| 610B 58 | $ec_{re} = (EC/FEE)_{re}$ | dollars | 2,490 | 2,501 | 2,679 | 2,832 | 2,931 | 3,095 | 3,293 | 3,476 | 3,701 | 3,849 | 3,900 | 4,148 | 4,225 | 4,470 |
| | $L_{re}$ | thousands | 603 | 574 | 584 | 600 | 606 | 617 | 633 | 645 | 646 | 623 | 611 | 615 | 615 | 603 |
| | $W_{re} = ec_{re} \times L_{re}$ | millions of $ | 1,502 | 1,436 | 1,564 | 1,699 | 1,776 | 1,910 | 2,084 | 2,242 | 2,391 | 2,398 | 2,383 | 2,551 | 2,598 | 2,695 |
| Table B.5 | $g$ | | 0.28 | 0.28 | 0.27 | 0.27 | 0.27 | 0.26 | 0.26 | 0.26 | 0.26 | 0.26 | 0.25 | 0.25 | 0.25 | 0.26 |
| | $W_{gr} = W_{re} \times g$ | millions of $ | 419 | 397 | 428 | 461 | 478 | 509 | 550 | 587 | 620 | 616 | 606 | 642 | 661 | 693 |

**DUMMY**

**Government**[b]

| Code | Variable | Unit | | | | | | | | | | | | | | |
|---|---|---|---|---|---|---|---|---|---|---|---|---|---|---|---|---|
| 604B 78 | $EC_{govfed}$ | millions of $ | 9,556 | 10,679 | 11,095 | 16,582 | 19,275 | 19,075 | 18,346 | 18,958 | 19,604 | 20,227 | 21,325 | 21,714 | 22,588 | 23,640 |
| 604B 83 | $EC_{govsl}$ | millions of $ | 8,521 | 9,442 | 10,145 | 11,159 | 12,252 | 13,334 | 14,698 | 15,838 | 17,620 | 19,556 | 21,578 | 23,133 | 25,470 | 27,934 |
| | $W_{govtot} = EC_{govfed} + EC_{govsl}$ | millions of $ | 18,077 | 20,121 | 21,240 | 27,741 | 31,527 | 32,409 | 33,044 | 34,796 | 37,224 | 39,783 | 42,903 | 44,847 | 48,058 | 51,574 |
| | $W = $ Total EC and WEQ | millions of $ | 164,763 | 164,753 | 178,761 | 206,232 | 222,097 | 236,846 | 235,670 | 252,731 | 272,671 | 286,751 | 289,269 | 311,712 | 328,351 | 338,075 |

Table G.1 *(cont.)*

| Sources[a] | Sectors | Units | 1962 | 1963 | 1964 | 1965 | 1966 | 1967 | 1968 | 1969 | 1970 | 1971 | 1972 | 1973 | 1974 | 1975 |
|---|---|---|---|---|---|---|---|---|---|---|---|---|---|---|---|---|
| | **PRODUCTION** | | | | | | | | | | | | | | | |
| | *Manufacturing* | | | | | | | | | | | | | | | |
| 604B 13 | $EC_{man}$ | millions of $ | 107,928 | 112,503 | 119,955 | 129,484 | 144,515 | 151,429 | 165,427 | 179,756 | 181,135 | 185,224 | 203,876 | 230,716 | 250,654 | 252,540 |
| 607B 13 | $FEE_{man}$ | thousands | 16,360 | 16,484 | 16,722 | 17,624 | 18,852 | 19,068 | 19,386 | 19,789 | 18,906 | 18,087 | 18,571 | 19,605 | 19,538 | 17,783 |
| | $ec_{man}=(EC/FEE)_{man}$ | dollars | 6,597 | 6,825 | 7,173 | 7,347 | 7,666 | 7,942 | 8,533 | 9,084 | 9,581 | 10,241 | 10,978 | 11,768 | 12,829 | 14,201 |
| 610B 13 | $L_{man}$ | thousands | 16,658 | 16,776 | 17,006 | 17,902 | 19,112 | 19,335 | 19,642 | 20,057 | 19,177 | 18,336 | 18,819 | 19,871 | 19,804 | 18,062 |
| | $W_{man}=ec_{man}\times L_{man}$ | millions of $ | 109,894 | 114,496 | 121,992 | 131,526 | 146,508 | 153,549 | 167,612 | 182,190 | 183,731 | 187,774 | 206,599 | 233,846 | 254,067 | 256,502 |
| | *Mining* | | | | | | | | | | | | | | | |
| 604B 7 | $EC_{min}$ | millions of $ | 4,429 | 4,462 | 4,652 | 4,859 | 5,135 | 5,303 | 5,569 | 6,176 | 6,704 | 6,982 | 7,715 | 8,595 | 10,457 | 12,923 |
| 607B 7 | $FEE_{min}$ | thousands | 640 | 623 | 619 | 624 | 621 | 604 | 599 | 611 | 615 | 602 | 612 | 626 | 685 | 739 |
| | $ec_{min}=(EC/FEE)_{min}$ | dollars | 6,920 | 7,162 | 7,515 | 7,787 | 8,269 | 8,780 | 9,297 | 10,108 | 10,901 | 11,598 | 12,606 | 13,730 | 15,266 | 17,487 |
| 610B 7 | $L_{min}$ | thousands | 666 | 647 | 642 | 644 | 640 | 624 | 618 | 626 | 629 | 617 | 625 | 641 | 701 | 755 |
| | $W_{min}=ec_{min}\times L_{min}$ | millions of $ | 4,609 | 4,634 | 4,825 | 5,015 | 5,292 | 5,479 | 5,746 | 6,328 | 6,857 | 7,156 | 7,879 | 8,801 | 10,701 | 13,203 |
| | *Construction* | | | | | | | | | | | | | | | |
| 604B 12 | $EC_{con}$ | millions of $ | 18,969 | 20,279 | 22,116 | 24,167 | 26,675 | 27,800 | 31,136 | 35,165 | 37,469 | 40,748 | 44,474 | 50,560 | 53,985 | 52,860 |
| 607B 12 | $FEE_{con}$ | thousands | 2,855 | 2,939 | 3,049 | 3,221 | 3,327 | 3,301 | 3,418 | 3,562 | 3,481 | 3,538 | 3,739 | 4,011 | 3,928 | 3,442 |
| | $ec_{con}=(EC/FEE)_{con}$ | dollars | 6,644 | 6,900 | 7,254 | 7,503 | 8,018 | 8,422 | 9,109 | 9,872 | 10,764 | 11,517 | 11,895 | 12,605 | 13,744 | 15,357 |
| 610B 12 | $L_{con}$ | thousands | 3,541 | 3,619 | 3,728 | 3,903 | 3,985 | 3,965 | 4,084 | 4,256 | 4,179 | 4,261 | 4,499 | 4,835 | 4,816 | 4,296 |
| | $W_{con}=ec_{con}\times L_{con}$ | millions of $ | 23,527 | 24,971 | 27,041 | 29,284 | 31,951 | 33,392 | 37,203 | 42,016 | 44,982 | 49,075 | 53,514 | 60,947 | 66,189 | 65,975 |
| | *Transportation and public utilities* | | | | | | | | | | | | | | | |
| 604B 37 | $EC_{tut}$ | millions of $ | 26,477 | 27,436 | 29,221 | 31,123 | 33,700 | 35,886 | 39,060 | 42,759 | 46,998 | 50,999 | 56,429 | 63,088 | 68,928 | 72,913 |
| 607B 37 | $FEE_{tut}$ | thousands | 3,807 | 3,795 | 3,827 | 3,926 | 4,063 | 4,145 | 4,209 | 4,303 | 4,341 | 4,296 | 4,339 | 4,475 | 4,524 | 4,357 |
| | $ec_{tut}=(EC/FEE)_{tut}$ | dollars | 6,955 | 7,230 | 7,635 | 7,927 | 8,294 | 8,658 | 9,280 | 9,937 | 10,827 | 11,871 | 13,005 | 14,098 | 15,236 | 16,735 |
| 610B 37 | $L_{tut}$ | thousands | 3,989 | 3,976 | 4,008 | 4,108 | 4,240 | 4,330 | 4,394 | 4,488 | 4,530 | 4,498 | 4,546 | 4,670 | 4,744 | 4,584 |
| | $W_{tut}=ec_{tut}\times L_{tut}$ | millions of $ | 27,743 | 28,745 | 30,603 | 32,566 | 35,168 | 37,488 | 40,777 | 44,597 | 49,044 | 53,397 | 59,121 | 65,837 | 72,280 | 76,712 |
| | *Services* | | | | | | | | | | | | | | | |
| 604B 60 | $EC_{serv}$ | millions of $ | 35,689 | 38,231 | 41,455 | 45,089 | 50,208 | 55,551 | 61,806 | 70,360 | 77,669 | 84,743 | 95,046 | 107,839 | 120,642 | 133,805 |
| 607B 60 | $FEE_{serv}$ | thousands | 8,398 | 8,639 | 8,923 | 9,317 | 9,822 | 10,369 | 10,741 | 11,136 | 11,247 | 11,428 | 12,003 | 12,680 | 13,045 | 13,351 |
| | $ec_{serv}=(EC/FEE)_{serv}$ | dollars | 4,250 | 4,425 | 4,646 | 4,839 | 5,112 | 5,357 | 5,754 | 6,318 | 6,906 | 7,415 | 7,919 | 8,505 | 9,248 | 10,022 |
| 610B 60 | $L_{serv}$ | thousands | 10,310 | 10,597 | 10,920 | 11,306 | 11,874 | 12,443 | 12,821 | 13,313 | 13,380 | 13,577 | 14,200 | 14,879 | 15,313 | 15,650 |
| | $W_{serv}=ec_{serv}\times L_{serv}$ | millions of $ | 43,814 | 46,896 | 50,733 | 54,715 | 60,697 | 66,662 | 73,775 | 84,115 | 92,399 | 100,679 | 112,443 | 126,541 | 141,617 | 156,846 |
| | *Agriculture* | | | | | | | | | | | | | | | |
| 604B 4 | $EC_{agr}$ | millions of $ | 4,057 | 4,202 | 4,327 | 4,529 | 4,685 | 4,772 | 5,049 | 5,455 | 5,764 | 5,900 | 6,260 | 7,466 | 8,611 | 9,213 |
| 607B 4 | $FEE_{agr}$ | thousands | 1,723 | 1,677 | 1,552 | 1,476 | 1,382 | 1,314 | 1,298 | 1,274 | 1,280 | 1,276 | 1,293 | 1,368 | 1,458 | 1,440 |
| | $ec_{agr}=(EC/FEE)_{agr}$ | dollars | 2,355 | 2,506 | 2,788 | 3,068 | 3,390 | 3,632 | 3,890 | 4,282 | 4,503 | 4,624 | 4,841 | 5,458 | 5,906 | 6,398 |
| 610B 4 | $L_{agr}$ | thousands | 4,310 | 4,079 | 3,862 | 3,713 | 3,432 | 3,338 | 3,303 | 3,193 | 3,118 | 3,065 | 3,116 | 3,181 | 3,255 | 3,191 |
| | $W_{agr}=ec_{agr}\times L_{agr}$ | millions of $ | 10,148 | 10,221 | 10,767 | 11,393 | 11,635 | 12,122 | 12,848 | 13,672 | 14,041 | 14,172 | 15,086 | 17,361 | 19,224 | 20,416 |
| | *Government enterprises*[b] | | | | | | | | | | | | | | | |
| 604B 81 | $EC_{gefed}$ | millions of $ | 3,968 | 4,311 | 4,586 | 4,914 | 5,401 | 5,791 | 6,459 | 7,076 | 8,377 | 8,829 | 9,590 | 10,424 | 11,824 | 12,976 |
| 604B 86 | $EC_{gesl}$ | millions of $ | 2,192 | 2,325 | 2,574 | 2,777 | 3,000 | 3,227 | 3,658 | 4,094 | 4,597 | 5,140 | 5,606 | 6,433 | 7,352 | 8,502 |
| | $W_{getotal}=EC_{gefed}+EC_{gesl}$ | millions of $ | 6,160 | 6,636 | 7,160 | 7,691 | 8,401 | 9,018 | 10,117 | 11,170 | 12,974 | 13,969 | 15,196 | 16,857 | 19,176 | 21,478 |

## TOTAL TRADE

### Wholesale trade

| Code | Variable | Units | | | | | | | | | | | | | | | |
|---|---|---|---|---|---|---|---|---|---|---|---|---|---|---|---|---|---|
| 604B 50 | $EC_{whtr}$ | millions of \$ | 20,875 | 21,988 | 23,496 | 25,264 | 27,838 | 29,849 | 32,479 | 35,887 | 38,904 | 41,460 | 45,629 | 51,587 | 57,902 | 61,390 |
| 607B 50 | $FEE_{whtr}$ | thousands | 3,161 | 3,193 | 3,268 | 3,372 | 3,501 | 3,585 | 3,668 | 3,782 | 3,864 | 3,891 | 4,005 | 4,230 | 4,342 | 4,260 |
| | $ec_{whtr} = (EC/FEE)_{whtr}$ | dollars | 6,604 | 6,886 | 7,190 | 7,492 | 7,951 | 8,326 | 8,855 | 9,489 | 10,068 | 10,655 | 11,393 | 12,196 | 13,335 | 14,411 |
| 610B 50 | $L_{whtr}$ | thousands | 3,448 | 3,480 | 3,555 | 3,648 | 3,782 | 3,849 | 3,920 | 4,041 | 4,123 | 4,154 | 4,252 | 4,492 | 4,617 | 4,521 |
| | $W_{whtr} = ec_{whtr} \times L_{whtr}$ | millions of \$ | 22,770 | 23,964 | 25,559 | 27,332 | 30,072 | 32,047 | 34,710 | 38,345 | 41,512 | 44,262 | 48,443 | 54,782 | 61,569 | 65,151 |

### Retail trade

| Code | Variable | Units | | | | | | | | | | | | | | | |
|---|---|---|---|---|---|---|---|---|---|---|---|---|---|---|---|---|---|
| 604B 51 | $EC_{retr}$ | millions of \$ | 32,175 | 34,182 | 36,702 | 39,500 | 42,879 | 45,966 | 50,765 | 55,927 | 60,250 | 65,040 | 71,250 | 79,097 | 86,228 | 93,007 |
| 607B 51 | $FEE_{retr}$ | thousands | 7,198 | 7,364 | 7,643 | 7,941 | 8,301 | 8,541 | 8,867 | 9,180 | 9,329 | 9,524 | 9,764 | 10,281 | 10,465 | 10,501 |
| | $ec_{retr} = (EC/FEE)_{retr}$ | dollars | 4,470 | 4,642 | 4,802 | 4,974 | 5,166 | 5,382 | 5,725 | 6,092 | 6,458 | 6,829 | 7,297 | 7,694 | 8,240 | 8,857 |
| 610B 51 | $L_{retr}$ | thousands | 8,985 | 9,019 | 9,294 | 9,565 | 9,833 | 9,973 | 10,259 | 10,596 | 10,766 | 11,004 | 11,236 | 11,717 | 11,948 | 11,979 |
| | $W_{retr} = ec_{retr} \times L_{retr}$ | millions of \$ | 40,163 | 41,864 | 44,630 | 47,578 | 50,793 | 53,673 | 58,734 | 64,554 | 69,531 | 75,147 | 81,991 | 90,145 | 98,447 | 106,098 |

### Building rental

| Code | Variable | Units | | | | | | | | | | | | | | | |
|---|---|---|---|---|---|---|---|---|---|---|---|---|---|---|---|---|---|
| | $W_{br} = W_{re} - W_{gr}$ | millions of \$ | 2,114 | 2,246 | 2,365 | 2,501 | 2,691 | 2,819 | 3,196 | 3,587 | 4,044 | 4,616 | 5,254 | 6,173 | 6,611 | 6,824 |

## ROYALTIES

### Finance and insurance

| Code | Variable | Units | | | | | | | | | | | | | | | |
|---|---|---|---|---|---|---|---|---|---|---|---|---|---|---|---|---|---|
| | $EC_{fi} = EC_{fire} - EC_{re}$ | millions of \$ | 13,095 | 13,953 | 15,034 | 16,130 | 17,546 | 19,457 | 22,011 | 24,198 | 26,368 | 28,794 | 31,803 | 34,942 | 38,628 | 43,349 |
| 604B 52 | $EC_{fire}$ | millions of \$ | 15,320 | 16,339 | 17,569 | 18,851 | 20,497 | 22,535 | 25,530 | 28,210 | 30,922 | 33,956 | 37,774 | 41,993 | 46,020 | 50,934 |
| | $FEE_{fi} = FEE_{fire} - FEE_{re}$ | thousands | 2,112 | 2,173 | 2,231 | 2,317 | 2,387 | 2,525 | 2,657 | 2,784 | 2,862 | 2,898 | 2,989 | 3,119 | 3,241 | 3,291 |
| 607B 52 | $FEE_{re}$ | thousands | 2,592 | 2,666 | 2,729 | 2,837 | 2,924 | 3,074 | 3,233 | 3,387 | 3,491 | 3,564 | 3,692 | 3,896 | 4,020 | 4,064 |
| | $ec_{fi} = (EC/FEE)_{fi}$ | dollars | 6,200 | 6,421 | 6,739 | 6,962 | 7,351 | 7,706 | 8,284 | 8,692 | 9,213 | 9,936 | 10,640 | 11,203 | 11,919 | 13,172 |
| | $L_{fi} = L_{fire} - L_{re}$ | thousands | 2,220 | 2,280 | 2,337 | 2,423 | 2,496 | 2,642 | 2,773 | 2,907 | 2,972 | 3,003 | 3,089 | 3,240 | 3,347 | 3,418 |
| 610B 52 | $L_{fire}$ | thousands | 2,836 | 2,909 | 2,969 | 3,075 | 3,166 | 3,332 | 3,493 | 3,653 | 3,749 | 3,836 | 3,959 | 4,202 | 4,334 | 4,405 |
| | $W_{fi} = ec_{fi} \times L_{fi}$ | millions of \$ | 13,765 | 14,640 | 15,748 | 16,868 | 18,347 | 20,359 | 22,972 | 25,267 | 27,381 | 29,837 | 32,867 | 36,298 | 39,891 | 45,022 |

### Ground rent

| Code | Variable | Units | | | | | | | | | | | | | | | |
|---|---|---|---|---|---|---|---|---|---|---|---|---|---|---|---|---|---|
| 604B 58 | $EC_{re}$ | millions of \$ | 2,225 | 2,386 | 2,535 | 2,721 | 2,951 | 3,078 | 3,519 | 4,012 | 4,554 | 5,162 | 5,971 | 7,051 | 7,392 | 7,585 |
| 607B 58 | $FEE_{re}$ | thousands | 480 | 493 | 498 | 520 | 537 | 549 | 576 | 603 | 629 | 666 | 703 | 777 | 779 | 773 |
| | $ec_{re} = (EC/FEE)_{re}$ | dollars | 4,635 | 4,840 | 5,090 | 5,233 | 5,495 | 5,607 | 6,109 | 6,653 | 7,240 | 7,751 | 8,494 | 9,075 | 9,489 | 9,812 |
| 610B 58 | $L_{re}$ | thousands | 616 | 629 | 632 | 652 | 670 | 690 | 720 | 746 | 777 | 833 | 870 | 962 | 987 | 987 |
| | $W_{re} = ec_{re} \times L_{re}$ | millions of \$ | 2,855 | 3,044 | 3,217 | 3,412 | 3,682 | 3,869 | 4,399 | 4,963 | 5,626 | 6,456 | 7,389 | 8,730 | 9,366 | 9,685 |
| Table B.5 | $g$ | | 0.26 | 0.26 | 0.26 | 0.27 | 0.27 | 0.27 | 0.27 | 0.28 | 0.28 | 0.29 | 0.29 | 0.29 | 0.29 | 0.30 |
| | $W_{gr} = W_{re} \times g$ | millions of \$ | 742 | 799 | 852 | 911 | 991 | 1,049 | 1,202 | 1,376 | 1,582 | 1,841 | 2,135 | 2,557 | 2,755 | 2,861 |

## DUMMY

### Government[b]

| Code | Variable | Units | | | | | | | | | | | | | | | |
|---|---|---|---|---|---|---|---|---|---|---|---|---|---|---|---|---|---|
| 604B 78 | $EC_{govfed}$ | millions of \$ | 25,194 | 26,464 | 28,513 | 29,962 | 34,279 | 37,847 | 41,871 | 44,880 | 48,407 | 51,067 | 54,858 | 57,108 | 61,052 | 66,542 |
| 604B 83 | $EC_{govsl}$ | millions of \$ | 30,243 | 32,857 | 35,873 | 39,294 | 44,115 | 49,530 | 55,898 | 62,601 | 71,067 | 79,255 | 87,732 | 97,933 | 107,647 | 121,109 |
| | $W_{govso} = EC_{govfed} + EC_{govsl}$ | millions of \$ | 55,437 | 59,321 | 64,386 | 69,256 | 78,394 | 87,377 | 97,769 | 107,481 | 119,474 | 130,322 | 142,590 | 155,041 | 168,699 | 187,651 |
| | $W = $ Total EC and WEQ | millions of \$ | 360,886 | 379,432 | 406,662 | 436,635 | 480,940 | 515,034 | 566,661 | 624,698 | 667,551 | 712,247 | 783,118 | 875,185 | 961,227 | 1,024,738 |

| Sources[a] | Sectors | Units | 1976 | 1977 | 1978 | 1979 | 1980 | 1981 | 1982 | 1983 | 1984 | 1985 | 1986 | 1987 | 1988 | 1989 |
|---|---|---|---|---|---|---|---|---|---|---|---|---|---|---|---|---|
| | **PRODUCTION** | | | | | | | | | | | | | | | |
| | *Manufacturing* | | | | | | | | | | | | | | | |
| 604B 13 | $EC_{man}$ | millions of \$ | 286,704 | 324,274 | 366,271 | 409,736 | 436,141 | 475,363 | 473,056 | 490,606 | 540,658 | 563,178 | 579,190 | 598,082 | 639,252 | 662,166 |
| 607B 13 | $FEE_{man}$ | thousands | 18,546 | 19,245 | 20,087 | 20,603 | 19,804 | 19,730 | 18,249 | 17,941 | 18,891 | 18,773 | 18,492 | 18,601 | 18,963 | 19,009 |
| | $ec_{man}=(EC/FEE)_{man}$ | dollars | 15,459 | 16,850 | 18,234 | 19,887 | 22,023 | 24,093 | 25,922 | 27,346 | 28,620 | 29,999 | 31,321 | 32,153 | 33,710 | 34,834 |
| 610B 13 | $L_{man}$ | thousands | 18,839 | 19,557 | 20,417 | 20,949 | 20,167 | 20,096 | 18,607 | 18,316 | 19,255 | 19,124 | 18,876 | 18,969 | 19,361 | 19,418 |
| | $W_{man}=ec_{man}\times L_{man}$ | millions of \$ | 291,234 | 329,531 | 372,288 | 416,617 | 444,135 | 484,181 | 482,336 | 500,861 | 551,076 | 573,708 | 591,217 | 609,914 | 652,669 | 676,413 |
| | *Mining* | | | | | | | | | | | | | | | |
| 604B 7 | $EC_{min}$ | millions of \$ | 14,606 | 16,923 | 19,832 | 23,725 | 28,773 | 35,830 | 37,454 | 33,107 | 35,280 | 34,722 | 30,273 | 28,442 | 29,741 | 29,625 |
| 607B 7 | $FEE_{min}$ | thousands | 767 | 811 | 864 | 936 | 1,021 | 1,135 | 1,100 | 931 | 950 | 905 | 756 | 695 | 704 | 674 |
| | $ec_{min}=(EC/FEE)_{min}$ | dollars | 19,043 | 20,867 | 22,954 | 25,347 | 28,181 | 31,568 | 34,049 | 35,561 | 37,137 | 38,367 | 40,044 | 40,924 | 42,246 | 43,954 |
| 610B 7 | $L_{min}$ | thousands | 791 | 831 | 885 | 957 | 1,049 | 1,161 | 1,134 | 960 | 975 | 925 | 782 | 722 | 733 | 699 |
| | $W_{min}=ec_{min}\times L_{min}$ | millions of \$ | 15,063 | 17,340 | 20,314 | 24,257 | 29,562 | 36,651 | 38,612 | 34,138 | 36,208 | 35,489 | 31,314 | 29,547 | 30,966 | 30,724 |
| | *Construction* | | | | | | | | | | | | | | | |
| 604B 12 | $EC_{con}$ | millions of \$ | 57,883 | 64,701 | 76,048 | 88,107 | 92,672 | 97,859 | 97,703 | 100,483 | 113,899 | 124,640 | 134,046 | 142,441 | 154,775 | 161,982 |
| 607B 12 | $FEE_{con}$ | thousands | 3,510 | 3,772 | 4,198 | 4,440 | 4,206 | 4,043 | 3,731 | 3,785 | 4,251 | 4,519 | 4,673 | 4,780 | 4,950 | 5,009 |
| | $ec_{con}=(EC/FEE)_{con}$ | dollars | 16,491 | 17,153 | 18,115 | 19,844 | 22,033 | 24,205 | 26,187 | 26,548 | 26,793 | 27,581 | 28,685 | 29,799 | 31,268 | 32,338 |
| 610B 12 | $L_{con}$ | thousands | 4,400 | 4,735 | 5,305 | 5,607 | 5,392 | 5,209 | 4,862 | 4,956 | 5,499 | 5,831 | 6,043 | 6,167 | 6,377 | 6,442 |
| | $W_{con}=ec_{con}\times L_{con}$ | millions of \$ | 72,560 | 81,219 | 96,102 | 111,265 | 118,803 | 126,082 | 127,320 | 131,573 | 147,337 | 160,827 | 173,345 | 183,773 | 199,394 | 208,323 |
| | *Transportation and public utilities* | | | | | | | | | | | | | | | |
| 604B 37 | $EC_{tut}$ | millions of \$ | 81,837 | 91,240 | 103,523 | 116,839 | 128,129 | 140,836 | 149,692 | 155,354 | 165,408 | 172,747 | 179,268 | 188,987 | 200,169 | 209,597 |
| 607B 37 | $FEE_{tut}$ | thousands | 4,373 | 4,495 | 4,697 | 4,888 | 4,880 | 4,920 | 4,828 | 4,752 | 4,927 | 4,988 | 5,018 | 5,128 | 5,271 | 5,366 |
| | $ec_{tut}=(EC/FEE)_{tut}$ | dollars | 18,714 | 20,298 | 22,040 | 23,903 | 26,256 | 28,625 | 31,005 | 32,692 | 33,572 | 34,633 | 35,725 | 36,854 | 37,976 | 39,060 |
| 610B 37 | $L_{tut}$ | thousands | 4,594 | 4,717 | 4,945 | 5,166 | 5,162 | 5,218 | 5,136 | 5,077 | 5,248 | 5,306 | 5,337 | 5,464 | 5,615 | 5,689 |
| | $W_{tut}=ec_{tut}\times L_{tut}$ | millions of \$ | 85,973 | 95,746 | 108,989 | 123,484 | 135,533 | 149,366 | 159,242 | 165,979 | 176,185 | 183,760 | 190,664 | 201,370 | 213,233 | 222,213 |
| | *Services* | | | | | | | | | | | | | | | |
| 604B 60 | $EC_{serv}$ | millions of \$ | 149,827 | 168,205 | 193,987 | 223,146 | 255,867 | 292,584 | 326,023 | 359,056 | 398,998 | 437,917 | 478,570 | 536,093 | 595,234 | 651,980 |
| 607B 60 | $FEE_{serv}$ | thousands | 13,906 | 14,541 | 15,473 | 16,210 | 16,794 | 17,376 | 17,704 | 18,348 | 19,517 | 20,468 | 21,371 | 22,537 | 23,544 | 24,715 |
| | $ec_{serv}=(EC/FEE)_{serv}$ | dollars | 10,774 | 11,568 | 12,537 | 13,766 | 15,236 | 16,838 | 18,415 | 19,569 | 20,444 | 21,395 | 22,393 | 23,787 | 25,282 | 26,380 |
| 610B 60 | $L_{serv}$ | thousands | 16,252 | 17,035 | 18,022 | 18,849 | 19,526 | 20,230 | 20,729 | 21,571 | 22,895 | 23,929 | 24,787 | 26,146 | 27,394 | 28,614 |
| | $W_{serv}=ec_{serv}\times L_{serv}$ | millions of \$ | 175,103 | 197,055 | 225,944 | 259,474 | 297,491 | 340,641 | 381,279 | 422,128 | 468,057 | 511,596 | 555,066 | 621,941 | 692,569 | 754,835 |
| | *Agriculture* | | | | | | | | | | | | | | | |
| 604B 4 | $EC_{agr}$ | millions of \$ | 10,505 | 11,246 | 12,525 | 13,973 | 15,049 | 15,507 | 16,993 | 17,183 | 18,034 | 18,710 | 19,511 | 21,398 | 23,050 | 24,192 |
| 607B 4 | $FEE_{agr}$ | thousands | 1,532 | 1,490 | 1,525 | 1,524 | 1,530 | 1,444 | 1,480 | 1,477 | 1,466 | 1,458 | 1,476 | 1,561 | 1,648 | 1,608 |
| | $ec_{agr}=(EC/FEE)_{agr}$ | dollars | 6,857 | 7,548 | 8,213 | 9,169 | 9,836 | 10,739 | 11,482 | 11,634 | 12,302 | 12,833 | 13,219 | 13,708 | 13,987 | 15,045 |
| 610B 4 | $L_{agr}$ | thousands | 3,210 | 3,105 | 3,187 | 3,161 | 3,212 | 3,122 | 3,157 | 3,074 | 3,052 | 2,953 | 2,964 | 3,038 | 3,086 | 3,042 |
| | $W_{agr}=ec_{agr}\times L_{agr}$ | millions of \$ | 22,011 | 23,435 | 26,175 | 28,982 | 31,593 | 33,527 | 36,248 | 35,762 | 37,544 | 37,895 | 39,181 | 41,645 | 43,163 | 45,766 |
| | *Government enterprises[b]* | | | | | | | | | | | | | | | |
| 604B 81 | $EC_{gefed}$ | millions of \$ | 14,057 | 14,918 | 16,079 | 17,600 | 19,749 | 22,434 | 23,106 | 24,783 | 26,894 | 28,776 | 29,306 | 32,012 | 35,098 | 36,617 |
| 604B 86 | $EC_{gesl}$ | millions of \$ | 9,194 | 9,829 | 10,946 | 12,104 | 13,787 | 15,190 | 16,520 | 17,789 | 19,166 | 21,118 | 23,089 | 24,312 | 25,954 | 27,849 |
| | $W_{gesoal}=EC_{gefed}+EC_{gesl}$ | millions of \$ | 23,251 | 24,747 | 27,025 | 29,704 | 33,536 | 37,624 | 39,626 | 42,572 | 46,060 | 49,894 | 52,395 | 56,324 | 61,052 | 64,466 |

**TOTAL TRADE**

**Wholesale trade**

| Line | Variable | Units | | | | | | | | | | | | | | |
|---|---|---|--:|--:|--:|--:|--:|--:|--:|--:|--:|--:|--:|--:|--:|--:|
| 604B 50 | $EC_{whtr}$ | millions of $ | 68,356 | 75,909 | 86,563 | 99,078 | 110,193 | 121,780 | 128,304 | 133,066 | 148,526 | 158,577 | 167,056 | 178,193 | 195,486 | 209,774 |
| 607B 50 | $FEE_{whtr}$ | thousands | 4,408 | 4,574 | 4,824 | 5,059 | 5,102 | 5,225 | 5,125 | 5,089 | 5,371 | 5,496 | 5,537 | 5,676 | 5,812 | 6,050 |
| | $ec_{whtr}=(EC/FEE)_{whtr}$ | dollars | 15,507 | 16,596 | 17,944 | 19,585 | 21,598 | 23,307 | 25,035 | 26,148 | 27,653 | 28,853 | 30,171 | 31,394 | 33,635 | 34,673 |
| 610B 50 | $L_{whtr}$ | thousands | 4,690 | 4,832 | 5,072 | 5,339 | 5,396 | 5,522 | 5,409 | 5,409 | 5,697 | 5,804 | 5,834 | 5,991 | 6,149 | 6,399 |
| | $W_{whtr}=ec_{whtr}\times L_{whtr}$ | millions of $ | 72,729 | 80,191 | 91,013 | 104,562 | 116,543 | 128,702 | 135,414 | 141,433 | 157,541 | 167,464 | 176,017 | 188,082 | 206,821 | 221,875 |

**Retail trade**

| Line | Variable | Units | | | | | | | | | | | | | | |
|---|---|---|--:|--:|--:|--:|--:|--:|--:|--:|--:|--:|--:|--:|--:|--:|
| 604B 51 | $EC_{rettr}$ | millions of $ | 104,145 | 115,071 | 129,900 | 143,479 | 154,515 | 166,758 | 175,649 | 189,867 | 209,716 | 225,689 | 242,066 | 258,442 | 277,714 | 293,387 |
| 607B 51 | $FEE_{rettr}$ | thousands | 10,975 | 11,481 | 12,195 | 12,489 | 12,371 | 12,470 | 12,400 | 12,722 | 13,729 | 14,444 | 14,869 | 15,403 | 15,911 | 16,428 |
| | $ec_{rettr}=(EC/FEE)_{rettr}$ | dollars | 9,489 | 10,023 | 10,652 | 11,488 | 12,490 | 12,373 | 14,165 | 14,866 | 15,275 | 15,625 | 16,280 | 16,779 | 17,454 | 17,859 |
| 610B 51 | $L_{rettr}$ | thousands | 12,407 | 13,008 | 13,740 | 14,086 | 13,999 | 14,082 | 14,010 | 14,406 | 15,341 | 15,943 | 16,381 | 16,952 | 17,409 | 17,976 |
| | $W_{rettr}=ec_{rettr}\times L_{rettr}$ | millions of $ | 117,734 | 130,376 | 146,357 | 161,826 | 174,849 | 188,315 | 198,455 | 214,158 | 234,340 | 249,111 | 266,681 | 284,432 | 303,861 | 321,033 |

**Building rental**

| Line | Variable | Units | | | | | | | | | | | | | | |
|---|---|---|--:|--:|--:|--:|--:|--:|--:|--:|--:|--:|--:|--:|--:|--:|
| | $W_{br}=W_{re}-W_{gr}$ | millions of $ | 7,634 | 8,809 | 10,616 | 12,736 | 14,045 | 14,950 | 16,080 | 18,353 | 21,067 | 23,542 | 25,506 | 28,485 | 32,136 | 33,283 |

**ROYALTIES**

**Finance and insurance**

| Line | Variable | Units | | | | | | | | | | | | | | |
|---|---|---|--:|--:|--:|--:|--:|--:|--:|--:|--:|--:|--:|--:|--:|--:|
| 604B 52 | $EC_{fi}=EC_{fire}-EC_{re}$ | millions of $ | 48,361 | 53,983 | 61,399 | 69,687 | 80,259 | 90,236 | 101,325 | 113,703 | 123,984 | 137,267 | 157,281 | 175,194 | 188,986 | 194,587 |
| | $EC_{fire}$ | millions of $ | 56,951 | 63,857 | 73,101 | 83,222 | 95,180 | 106,576 | 118,707 | 133,071 | 146,443 | 162,480 | 185,182 | 205,979 | 223,446 | 230,329 |
| 607B 52 | $FEE_{fi}=FEE_{fire}-FEE_{re}$ | thousands | 3,370 | 3,512 | 3,704 | 3,901 | 4,048 | 4,189 | 4,252 | 4,363 | 4,522 | 4,683 | 4,937 | 5,145 | 5,201 | 5,231 |
| | $FEE_{fire}$ | thousands | 4,178 | 4,361 | 4,610 | 4,854 | 5,018 | 5,166 | 5,229 | 5,370 | 5,587 | 5,800 | 6,109 | 6,362 | 6,458 | 6,502 |
| | $ec_{fi}=(EC/FEE)_{fi}$ | dollars | 14,350 | 15,371 | 16,576 | 17,864 | 19,827 | 21,541 | 23,830 | 26,061 | 27,418 | 29,312 | 31,858 | 34,051 | 36,336 | 37,199 |
| | $L_{fi}=L_{fire}-L_{re}$ | thousands | 3,486 | 3,629 | 3,845 | 4,042 | 4,195 | 4,363 | 4,452 | 4,565 | 4,730 | 4,894 | 5,157 | 5,374 | 5,431 | 5,456 |
| 610B 52 | $L_{fire}$ | thousands | 4,507 | 4,708 | 5,018 | 5,305 | 5,481 | 5,622 | 5,725 | 5,909 | 6,137 | 6,363 | 6,666 | 6,960 | 7,082 | 7,123 |
| | $W_{fi}=ec_{fi}\times L_{fi}$ | millions of $ | 50,026 | 55,781 | 63,736 | 72,206 | 83,174 | 93,984 | 106,091 | 118,967 | 129,687 | 143,452 | 164,290 | 182,992 | 197,343 | 202,957 |

**Ground rent**

| Line | Variable | Units | | | | | | | | | | | | | | |
|---|---|---|--:|--:|--:|--:|--:|--:|--:|--:|--:|--:|--:|--:|--:|--:|
| 604B 58 | $EC_{re}$ | millions of $ | 8,590 | 9,874 | 11,702 | 13,535 | 14,921 | 16,340 | 17,382 | 19,368 | 22,459 | 25,213 | 27,901 | 30,785 | 34,460 | 35,742 |
| 607B 58 | $FEE_{re}$ | thousands | 808 | 849 | 906 | 953 | 970 | 977 | 977 | 1,007 | 1,065 | 1,111 | 1,172 | 1,217 | 1,257 | 1,271 |
| | $ec_{re}=(EC/FEE)_{re}$ | dollars | 10,631 | 11,630 | 12,916 | 14,203 | 15,382 | 16,725 | 17,791 | 19,233 | 21,088 | 22,572 | 23,806 | 25,296 | 27,414 | 28,121 |
| 610B 58 | $L_{re}$ | thousands | 1,021 | 1,079 | 1,173 | 1,263 | 1,286 | 1,259 | 1,273 | 1,344 | 1,407 | 1,469 | 1,509 | 1,586 | 1,651 | 1,667 |
| | $W_{re}=ec_{re}\times L_{re}$ | millions of $ | 10,854 | 12,549 | 15,151 | 17,938 | 19,782 | 21,056 | 22,648 | 25,850 | 29,671 | 33,158 | 35,924 | 40,119 | 45,261 | 46,878 |
| Table B.5 | $g$ | | 0.30 | 0.30 | 0.30 | 0.29 | 0.29 | 0.29 | 0.29 | 0.29 | 0.29 | 0.29 | 0.29 | 0.29 | 0.29 | 0.29 |
| | $W_{gr}=W_{re}\times g$ | millions of $ | 3,221 | 3,739 | 4,534 | 5,202 | 5,737 | 6,106 | 6,568 | 7,496 | 8,605 | 9,616 | 10,418 | 11,635 | 13,126 | 13,595 |

**DUMMY**

**Government[b]**

| Line | Variable | Units | | | | | | | | | | | | | | |
|---|---|---|--:|--:|--:|--:|--:|--:|--:|--:|--:|--:|--:|--:|--:|--:|
| 604B 78 | $EC_{govfed}$ | millions of $ | 70,871 | 75,528 | 81,685 | 86,918 | 96,099 | 107,424 | 117,022 | 124,695 | 132,005 | 140,223 | 143,539 | 150,869 | 159,313 | 168,550 |
| 604B 83 | $EC_{govsl}$ | millions of $ | 132,947 | 144,970 | 158,857 | 173,526 | 192,154 | 209,314 | 226,877 | 241,695 | 258,885 | 278,752 | 300,260 | 322,081 | 346,466 | 373,005 |
| | $W_{govtot}=EC_{govfed}+EC_{govsl}$ | millions of $ | 203,818 | 220,498 | 240,542 | 260,444 | 288,253 | 316,738 | 343,899 | 366,390 | 390,890 | 418,975 | 443,799 | 472,950 | 505,779 | 541,555 |
| | $W=$ Total EC and WEQ | millions of $ | 1,140,356 | 1,268,469 | 1,433,637 | 1,610,759 | 1,773,254 | 1,956,867 | 2,071,620 | 2,199,810 | 2,404,596 | 2,565,699 | 2,719,892 | 2,913,089 | 3,152,110 | 3,337,038 |

[a] Unless otherwise indicated, all data come from NIPA (e.g. BEA 1986), where the first three digits (and following letter, if any) denote the relevant table number and subsequent digits the line numbers within those tables.

[b] There are no self-employed persons in government, so the total wage of this sector is total employee compensation.

*Glossary of variables in Table G.1*

| | |
|---|---|
| $EC_{agr}$ | Total employee compensation in agriculture, forestry, and fisheries |
| $ec_{agr}$ | Employee compensation per full-time equivalent employee (FEE) in agriculture, forestry, and fisheries |
| $EC_{con}$ | Total employee compensation in construction |
| $ec_{con}$ | Employee compensation per FEE in construction |
| $EC_{fire}$ | Total employee compensation in finance, insurance, and real estate |
| $EC_{fi}$ | Total employee compensation in finance and insurance |
| $ec_{fi}$ | Employee compensation per FEE in finance and insurance |
| $EC_{gefed}$ | Total employee compensation in government enterprises (federal) |
| $EC_{gesl}$ | Total employee compensation in government enterprises (state and local) |
| $EC_{govfed}$ | Total employee compensation in government (federal) |
| $EC_{govsl}$ | Total employee compensation in government (state and local) |
| $EC_{man}$ | Total employee compensation in manufacturing |
| $ec_{man}$ | Employee compensation per FEE in manufacturing |
| $EC_{min}$ | Total employee compensation in mining |
| $ec_{min}$ | Employee compensation per FEE in mining |
| $EC_{re}$ | Total employee compensation in real estate |
| $EC_{rettr}$ | Total employee compensation in retail trade |
| $ec_{rettr}$ | Employee compensation per FEE in retail trade |
| $ec_{re}$ | Employee compensation per FEE in real estate |
| $EC_{serv}$ | Total employee compensation in services |
| $ec_{serv}$ | Employee compensation per FEE in services |
| $EC_{tut}$ | Total employee compensation in transportation and public utilities |
| $ec_{tut}$ | Employee compensation per FEE in transportation and public utilities |
| $EC_{whtr}$ | Total employee compensation in wholesale trade |
| $ec_{whtr}$ | Employee compensation per FEE in wholesale trade |
| $FEE_{agr}$ | Total full-time equivalent employees in agriculture, forestry, and fisheries |
| $FEE_{con}$ | Total full-time equivalent employees in construction |
| $FEE_{fire}$ | Total full-time equivalent employees in finance, insurance, and real estate |
| $FEE_{fi}$ | Total full-time equivalent employees in finance and insurance |
| $FEE_{man}$ | Total full-time equivalent employees in manufacturing |
| $FEE_{min}$ | Total full-time equivalent employees in mining |
| $FEE_{re}$ | Total full-time equivalent employees in real estate |
| $FEE_{rettr}$ | Total full-time equivalent employees in retail trade |
| $FEE_{serv}$ | Total full-time equivalent employees in services |
| $FEE_{tut}$ | Total full-time equivalent employees in transportation and public utilities |
| $FEE_{whtr}$ | Total full-time equivalent employees in wholesale trade |

| | |
|---|---|
| g | Estimated proportion of land rent in the total revenue of the real estate sector |
| $L_{agr}$ | Total employment in agriculture, forestry, and fisheries |
| $L_{con}$ | Total employment in construction |
| $L_{fire}$ | Total employment in finance, insurance, and real estate |
| $L_{fi}$ | Total employment in finance and insurance |
| $L_{man}$ | Total employment in manufacturing |
| $L_{min}$ | Total employment in mining |
| $L_{re}$ | Total employment in real estate |
| $L_{rettr}$ | Total employment in retail trade |
| $L_{serv}$ | Total employment in services |
| $L_{tut}$ | Total employment in transportation and public utilities |
| $L_{whtr}$ | Total employment in wholesale trade |
| W | Total employee compensation (including wage equivalent and COS, corporate officers' salaries) in all sectors |
| $W_{agr}$ | Total employee compensation (including wage equivalent and COS) in agriculture, forestry, and fisheries |
| $W_{br}$ | Total employee compensation (including wage equivalent and COS) in building rental |
| $W_{con}$ | Total employee compensation (including wage equivalent and COS) in construction |
| $W_{fi}$ | Total employee compensation (including wage equivalent and COS) in finance and insurance |
| $W_{getotal}$ | Total employee compensation in government enterprises (federal, state, and local) |
| $W_{govtot}$ | Total employee compensation in government (federal, state, and local) |
| $W_{gr}$ | Total employee compensation (including wage equivalent and COS) in ground rent |
| $W_{man}$ | Total employee compensation (including wage equivalent and COS) in manufacturing |
| $W_{min}$ | Total employee compensation (including wage equivalent and COS) in mining |
| $W_{rettr}$ | Total employee compensation (including wage equivalent and COS) in retail trade |
| $W_{re}$ | Total employee compensation (including wage equivalent and COS) in real estate |
| $W_{serv}$ | Total employee compensation (including wage equivalent and COS) in services |
| $W_{tut}$ | Total employee compensation (including wage equivalent and COS) in transportation and public utilities |
| $W_{whtr}$ | Total employee compensation (including wage equivalent and COS) in wholesale trade |

## Table G.2. Total variable capital and total wages of unproductive workers, 1948–89

| Sources[a] | Sectors | Units | 1948 | 1949 | 1950 | 1951 | 1952 | 1953 | 1954 | 1955 | 1956 | 1957 | 1958 | 1959 | 1960 | 1961 |
|---|---|---|---|---|---|---|---|---|---|---|---|---|---|---|---|---|
| | PRODUCTION = $W_p$ = V* | millions of $ | 88,410 | 85,021 | 93,161 | 105,912 | 111,013 | 117,388 | 111,952 | 120,518 | 128,824 | 132,999 | 127,717 | 139,570 | 144,230 | 146,130 |
| | Manufacturing | | | | | | | | | | | | | | | |
| SEHE | | | | | | | | | | | | | | | | |
| 604B 13 | $EC_{man}$ | $/worker/week | 53.08 | 53.80 | 58.28 | 63.34 | 66.75 | 70.47 | 70.49 | 75.30 | 78.78 | 81.19 | 82.32 | 88.29 | 89.72 | 92.34 |
| 605B 13 | $WS_{man}$ | millions of $ | 49,454 | 47,059 | 53,628 | 63,691 | 68,876 | 76,433 | 72,922 | 80,050 | 86,504 | 90,270 | 86,489 | 95,841 | 99,478 | 99,678 |
| | $WS_{man}$ | millions of $ | 47,145 | 44,638 | 50,316 | 59,357 | 64,182 | 71,253 | 67,574 | 73,889 | 79,489 | 82,515 | 78,719 | 86,937 | 89,776 | 89,912 |
| | $x_{man} = (EC/WS)_{man}$ | | 1.049 | 1.054 | 1.066 | 1.073 | 1.073 | 1.073 | 1.079 | 1.083 | 1.088 | 1.094 | 1.099 | 1.102 | 1.108 | 1.109 |
| Table F.1 | $(L_p)_{man}$ | thousands | 13,224 | 12,064 | 12,742 | 13,590 | 13,577 | 14,101 | 12,867 | 13,264 | 13,341 | 13,115 | 11,742 | 12,373 | 12,363 | 11,897 |
| | $(ec_p)_{man} = (w_p)_{man} \times x_{man} \times 52$ | $/worker/year | 2,895 | 2,949 | 3,230 | 3,534 | 3,725 | 3,931 | 3,956 | 4,242 | 4,458 | 4,619 | 4,703 | 5,061 | 5,170 | 5,323 |
| | $V_{man} = (ec_p)_{man} \times (L_p)_{man} = (W_p)_{man}$ | millions | 38,288 | 35,582 | 41,158 | 48,029 | 50,574 | 55,430 | 50,898 | 56,269 | 59,475 | 60,572 | 55,224 | 62,625 | 63,911 | 63,332 |
| | Mining | | | | | | | | | | | | | | | |
| SEHE | $(w_p)_{min}$ | $/worker/week | 65.52 | 62.33 | 67.16 | 74.11 | 77.59 | 83.03 | 82.60 | 89.54 | 95.06 | 98.25 | 96.08 | 103.68 | 105.04 | 106.92 |
| 604B 7 | $EC_{min}$ | millions of $ | 3,597 | 3,182 | 3,503 | 3,990 | 4,059 | 4,183 | 3,843 | 4,161 | 4,674 | 4,361 | 4,322 | 4,419 | 4,444 | 4,371 |
| 605B 7 | $WS_{min}$ | millions of $ | 3,372 | 2,967 | 3,202 | 3,644 | 3,717 | 3,814 | 3,495 | 3,767 | 4,213 | 4,361 | 3,897 | 3,957 | 3,962 | 3,876 |
| | $x_{min} = (EC/WS)_{min}$ | | 1.067 | 1.072 | 1.094 | 1.095 | 1.092 | 1.097 | 1.100 | 1.105 | 1.109 | 1.108 | 1.109 | 1.117 | 1.122 | 1.128 |
| Table F.1 | $(L_p)_{min}$ | thousands | 937 | 862 | 867 | 879 | 846 | 802 | 722 | 717 | 746 | 729 | 631 | 598 | 577 | 542 |
| | $(ec_p)_{min} = (w_p)_{min} \times x_{min} \times 52$ | $/worker/year | 3,634 | 3,476 | 3,821 | 4,220 | 4,406 | 4,735 | 4,723 | 5,143 | 5,484 | 5,658 | 5,541 | 6,021 | 6,127 | 6,270 |
| | $V_{min} = (ec_p)_{min} \times (L_p)_{min} = (W_p)_{min}$ | millions | 3,405 | 2,998 | 3,311 | 3,709 | 3,730 | 3,798 | 3,412 | 3,687 | 4,089 | 4,127 | 3,494 | 3,601 | 3,536 | 3,400 |
| | Construction | | | | | | | | | | | | | | | |
| SEHE | $(w_p)_{con}$ | $/worker/week | 65.23 | 67.56 | 69.68 | 76.96 | 82.86 | 86.41 | 88.54 | 90.90 | 96.38 | 100.21 | 103.78 | 108.41 | 112.67 | 118.08 |
| 604B 12 | $EC_{con}$ | millions of $ | 7,662 | 7,490 | 8,624 | 10,665 | 11,597 | 12,194 | 12,452 | 13,408 | 14,919 | 15,342 | 15,152 | 16,623 | 17,246 | 17,716 |
| 605B 12 | $WS_{con}$ | millions of $ | 7,252 | 7,085 | 8,143 | 10,069 | 10,962 | 11,507 | 11,707 | 12,596 | 14,019 | 14,341 | 14,349 | 15,603 | 16,129 | 16,491 |
| | $x_{con} = (EC/WS)_{con}$ | | 1.057 | 1.057 | 1.059 | 1.059 | 1.058 | 1.060 | 1.064 | 1.064 | 1.064 | 1.070 | 1.056 | 1.065 | 1.069 | 1.074 |
| Table F.1 | $(L_p)_{con}$ | thousands | 2,938 | 2,803 | 3,035 | 3,224 | 3,185 | 3,106 | 2,971 | 3,021 | 3,125 | 3,067 | 2,918 | 3,031 | 2,979 | 2,937 |
| | $(ec_p)_{con} = (w_p)_{con} \times x_{con} \times 52$ | $/worker/year | 3,584 | 3,714 | 3,837 | 4,239 | 4,558 | 4,762 | 4,897 | 5,032 | 5,334 | 5,578 | 5,699 | 6,006 | 6,265 | 6,596 |
| | $V_{con} = (ec_p)_{con} \times (L_p)_{con} = (W_p)_{con}$ | millions | 10,259 | 10,409 | 11,647 | 13,664 | 14,520 | 14,790 | 14,548 | 15,202 | 16,669 | 17,107 | 16,630 | 18,203 | 18,663 | 19,372 |
| | Transportation and public utilities | | | | | | | | | | | | | | | |
| SEHE | $(w_p)_{tut}$ (railroads wages) | $/worker/week | 60.11 | 62.36 | 64.14 | 70.93 | 74.30 | 76.33 | 78.74 | 82.12 | 88.40 | 94.24 | 101.50 | 106.43 | 108.84 | 112.94 |
| 604B 37 | $EC_{tut}$ | millions of $ | 14,498 | 14,333 | 15,141 | 17,185 | 18,260 | 19,364 | 19,084 | 20,285 | 21,994 | 23,145 | 22,719 | 24,187 | 25,149 | 25,375 |
| 605B 37 | $WS_{tut}$ | millions of $ | 13,587 | 13,385 | 14,081 | 15,977 | 16,961 | 18,004 | 17,679 | 18,757 | 20,274 | 21,248 | 20,820 | 21,976 | 22,783 | 22,903 |
| | $x_{tut} = (EC/WS)_{tut}$ | | 1.067 | 1.071 | 1.075 | 1.076 | 1.077 | 1.076 | 1.079 | 1.081 | 1.085 | 1.089 | 1.091 | 1.101 | 1.104 | 1.108 |
| Table F.1 | $(L_p)_{tut}$ | thousands | 3,335 | 3,472 | 3,586 | 3,967 | 4,160 | 4,269 | 4,420 | 4,618 | 4,987 | 5,338 | 5,759 | 6,091 | 6,247 | 6,507 |
| | $(ec_p)_{tut} = (w_p)_{tut} \times x_{tut} \times 52$ | $/worker/year | 4,086 | 3,887 | 3,921 | 4,095 | 4,079 | 4,108 | 3,883 | 3,929 | 4,006 | 3,968 | 3,686 | 3,669 | 3,666 | 3,549 |
| | $V_{tut} = (ec_p)_{tut} \times (L_p)_{tut} = (W_p)_{tut}$ | millions | 13,628 | 13,497 | 14,061 | 16,247 | 16,966 | 17,537 | 17,165 | 18,146 | 19,979 | 21,183 | 21,228 | 22,347 | 22,902 | 23,092 |
| | Services | | | | | | | | | | | | | | | |
| Table G.1 | $(w_p)_{serv} = ((EC/FEE)_{serv} = (ec_p)_{serv}$ | $/worker/year | 2,129 | 2,204 | 2,269 | 2,437 | 2,628 | 2,788 | 2,936 | 3,054 | 3,219 | 3,366 | 3,504 | 3,699 | 3,875 | 4,055 |
| 607B 60 | $FEE_{serv}$ | thousands | 6,177 | 6,157 | 6,372 | 6,483 | 6,434 | 6,513 | 6,437 | 6,801 | 7,097 | 7,323 | 7,452 | 7,694 | 8,005 | 8,133 |
| 604B 60 | $EC_{serv}$ | millions of $ | 13,153 | 13,573 | 14,458 | 15,800 | 16,906 | 18,161 | 18,899 | 20,770 | 22,844 | 24,650 | 26,112 | 28,460 | 31,016 | 32,979 |
| Table F.1 | $(L_p)_{serv}$ | thousands | 5,148 | 5,125 | 5,215 | 5,217 | 5,107 | 5,179 | 5,126 | 5,332 | 5,455 | 5,635 | 5,708 | 5,807 | 6,060 | 6,146 |
| | $V_{serv} = (ec_p)_{serv} \times (L_p)_{serv} = (W_p)_{serv}$ | millions of $ | 10,961 | 11,297 | 11,834 | 12,715 | 13,419 | 14,442 | 15,049 | 16,283 | 17,560 | 18,966 | 20,001 | 21,481 | 23,480 | 24,923 |

| Ref | Variable | Units | | | | | | | | | | | | | | |
|---|---|---|---|---|---|---|---|---|---|---|---|---|---|---|---|---|
| | **Agriculture** | | | | | | | | | | | | | | | |
| Table G.1 | $(w_p)_{agr} = (EC/FEE)_{agr} = (ec_p)_{agr}$ | $/worker/year | 1,602 | 1,572 | 1,540 | 1,671 | 1,714 | 1,706 | 1,628 | 1,671 | 1,769 | 1,852 | 1,928 | 1,986 | 2,105 | 2,206 |
| 607B 4 | $FEE_{agr}$ | thousands | 2,072 | 2,000 | 2,067 | 1,999 | 1,933 | 1,882 | 1,902 | 1,847 | 1,769 | 1,747 | 1,780 | 1,771 | 1,755 | 1,763 |
| 604B 4 | $EC_{agr}$ | millions of $ | 3,319 | 3,143 | 3,184 | 3,340 | 3,314 | 3,210 | 3,097 | 3,087 | 3,129 | 3,235 | 3,431 | 3,517 | 3,694 | 3,889 |
| Table G.1 | $(L_p)_{agr}$ | thousands | 6,038 | 5,810 | 5,798 | 5,445 | 5,244 | 5,032 | 4,955 | 4,744 | 4,484 | 4,205 | 3,944 | 3,791 | 3,627 | 3,517 |
| | $V_{agr} = (ec_p)_{agr} \times (L_p)_{agr} = (W_p)_{agr}$ | millions of $ | 9,673 | 9,130 | 8,931 | 9,098 | 8,990 | 8,582 | 8,068 | 7,928 | 7,932 | 7,787 | 7,603 | 7,529 | 7,635 | 7,757 |
| | **Government enterprises** | | | | | | | | | | | | | | | |
| 607B 81 | $w_{ge} = (EC/FEE)_{ge} = (ec_p)_{ge}$ | $/worker/year | 3,092 | 3,241 | 3,424 | 3,640 | 3,860 | 3,933 | 3,984 | 4,246 | 4,419 | 4,560 | 4,912 | 5,041 | 5,298 | 5,489 |
| 607B 86 | $FEE_{gefed}$ | thousands | 538 | 570 | 553 | 578 | 620 | 599 | 599 | 597 | 603 | 622 | 633 | 645 | 664 | 680 |
| | $FEE_{gesl}$ | thousands | 211 | 221 | 234 | 246 | 284 | 292 | 293 | 300 | 302 | 305 | 320 | 352 | 372 | 368 |
| | $FEE_{getoal}$ | thousands | 749 | 791 | 787 | 824 | 904 | 891 | 892 | 897 | 905 | 927 | 953 | 997 | 1,036 | 1,048 |
| 604B 81 | $EC_{fed}$ | millions of $ | 1,676 | 1,857 | 1,935 | 2,140 | 2,433 | 2,366 | 2,367 | 2,535 | 2,689 | 2,859 | 3,187 | 3,276 | 3,555 | 3,790 |
| 604B 86 | $EC_{sl}$ | millions of $ | 640 | 707 | 760 | 859 | 1,056 | 1,138 | 1,187 | 1,274 | 1,310 | 1,368 | 1,494 | 1,750 | 1,934 | 1,962 |
| | $EC_{getoal}$ | millions of $ | 2,316 | 2,564 | 2,695 | 2,999 | 3,489 | 3,504 | 3,554 | 3,809 | 3,999 | 4,227 | 4,681 | 5,026 | 5,489 | 5,752 |
| Table F.1 | $(L_p)_{gefed} = (L_p/L)_{nongovtox} \times L_{gefed}$ | thousands | 447 | 469 | 455 | 472 | 500 | 480 | 474 | 471 | 470 | 479 | 478 | 486 | 496 | 503 |
| Table F.1 | $(L_p)_{gesl} = (L_p/L)_{nongovtox} \times L_{gesl}$ | thousands | 175 | 182 | 193 | 201 | 229 | 234 | 232 | 236 | 236 | 235 | 242 | 265 | 278 | 272 |
| Table F.1 | $(L_p)_{getoal} = (L_p)_{gefed} + (L_p)_{gesl}$ | thousands | 623 | 650 | 648 | 674 | 729 | 714 | 706 | 707 | 706 | 714 | 720 | 751 | 774 | 775 |
| | $V_{ge} = (ec_p)_{ge} \times (L_p)_{getoal}$ | millions of $ | 1,925 | 2,108 | 2,218 | 2,451 | 2,814 | 2,810 | 2,813 | 3,002 | 3,120 | 3,257 | 3,538 | 3,785 | 4,103 | 4,253 |
| | TOTAL TRADE = $W_{tt}$ | millions of $ | 31,939 | 32,482 | 34,714 | 37,746 | 39,659 | 42,029 | 43,194 | 46,175 | 49,723 | 52,311 | 53,600 | 57,321 | 60,652 | 61,810 |
| | **Wholesale trade** | | | | | | | | | | | | | | | |
| Table G.1 | $W_{whtr}$ | millions of $ | 10,504 | 10,382 | 11,107 | 12,462 | 13,102 | 13,887 | 14,281 | 15,233 | 16,855 | 17,814 | 18,336 | 19,735 | 20,941 | 21,607 |
| | **Retail trade** | | | | | | | | | | | | | | | |
| Table G.1 | $W_{retr}$ | millions of $ | 20,352 | 21,061 | 22,471 | 24,046 | 25,259 | 26,742 | 27,379 | 29,287 | 31,097 | 32,715 | 33,487 | 35,678 | 37,774 | 38,200 |
| | **Building rental** | | | | | | | | | | | | | | | |
| Table G.1 | $W_{br} = W_{re} - W_{gr}$ | millions of $ | 1,083 | 1,039 | 1,136 | 1,238 | 1,298 | 1,401 | 1,534 | 1,655 | 1,771 | 1,782 | 1,777 | 1,908 | 1,937 | 2,002 |
| | ROYALTIES = $W_r$ | millions of $ | 5,810 | 6,046 | 6,650 | 7,355 | 8,018 | 8,798 | 9,662 | 10,371 | 11,240 | 11,989 | 12,785 | 13,853 | 14,700 | 15,735 |
| | **Finance and insurance** | | | | | | | | | | | | | | | |
| Table G.1 | $W_{fi}$ | millions of $ | 4,308 | 4,610 | 5,085 | 5,656 | 6,241 | 6,888 | 7,578 | 8,129 | 8,849 | 9,591 | 10,402 | 11,302 | 12,102 | 13,040 |
| | **Ground rent** | | | | | | | | | | | | | | | |
| Table G.1 | $W_{re}$ | millions of $ | 1,502 | 1,436 | 1,564 | 1,699 | 1,776 | 1,910 | 2,084 | 2,242 | 2,391 | 2,398 | 2,383 | 2,551 | 2,598 | 2,695 |
| | DUMMY = $W_d$ | millions of $ | 18,077 | 20,121 | 21,240 | 27,741 | 31,527 | 32,409 | 33,044 | 34,796 | 37,224 | 39,783 | 42,903 | 44,847 | 48,058 | 51,574 |
| | **Government** | | | | | | | | | | | | | | | |
| Table G.1 | $W_{govtot}$ | millions of $ | 18,077 | 20,121 | 21,240 | 27,741 | 31,527 | 32,409 | 33,044 | 34,796 | 37,224 | 39,783 | 42,903 | 44,847 | 48,058 | 51,574 |
| Table G.1 | W = Total EC and WEQ | millions of $ | 164,763 | 164,753 | 178,761 | 206,232 | 222,097 | 236,846 | 235,670 | 252,731 | 272,671 | 286,751 | 289,269 | 311,712 | 328,351 | 338,075 |
| | Total variable capital = $V^* = W_p$ | millions of $ | 88,410 | 85,021 | 93,161 | 105,912 | 111,013 | 117,388 | 111,952 | 120,518 | 128,824 | 132,999 | 127,717 | 139,570 | 144,230 | 146,130 |
| | $W_u = W - V^*$ | millions of $ | 76,353 | 79,732 | 85,601 | 100,320 | 111,084 | 119,458 | 123,719 | 132,213 | 143,847 | 153,752 | 161,552 | 172,141 | 184,120 | 191,945 |
| | $(W_u)_{lu} = W_u - (W_r)_{lu}$ | millions of $ | 20,527 | 21,083 | 22,997 | 27,477 | 31,880 | 36,222 | 37,819 | 40,871 | 45,660 | 49,668 | 52,264 | 56,120 | 60,710 | 62,826 |
| | $(W_u)_{lu} = W_u + W_r + W_d$ | millions of $ | 55,826 | 58,649 | 62,603 | 72,842 | 79,204 | 83,236 | 85,900 | 91,342 | 98,187 | 104,084 | 109,288 | 116,021 | 123,410 | 129,120 |
| | $ec_p = V^*/L_p = W_p/L_p$ | $/prod. worker | 2,680 | 2,725 | 2,891 | 3,198 | 3,388 | 3,553 | 3,585 | 3,800 | 4,043 | 4,231 | 4,352 | 4,649 | 4,800 | 4,977 |
| | $ec_u = W_u/L_u$ | $/unpr. worker | 3,017 | 3,100 | 3,246 | 3,431 | 3,620 | 3,828 | 3,979 | 4,177 | 4,405 | 4,611 | 4,835 | 5,051 | 5,269 | 5,426 |

315

# Table G.2 (cont.)

**PRODUCTION = $W_p$ = V***

| Sources[a] | Sectors | Units | 1962 | 1963 | 1964 | 1965 | 1966 | 1967 | 1968 | 1969 | 1970 | 1971 | 1972 | 1973 | 1974 | 1975 |
|---|---|---|---|---|---|---|---|---|---|---|---|---|---|---|---|---|
| | **Manufacturing** | | | | | | | | | | | | | | | |
| SEHE | $(W_p)_{man}$ | \$/worker/week | 95.56 | 99.23 | 102.97 | 107.53 | 112.19 | 114.49 | 122.51 | 129.51 | 133.33 | 142.44 | 154.21 | 166.46 | 176.80 | 198.79 |
| 604B 13 | $EC_{man}$ | millions of \$ | 107,928 | 112,503 | 119,955 | 129,484 | 144,515 | 151,429 | 165,427 | 179,756 | 181,135 | 185,224 | 203,876 | 230,716 | 250,654 | 252,540 |
| 605B 13 | $WS_{man}$ | millions of \$ | 96,793 | 100,740 | 107,298 | 115,678 | 128,206 | 134,313 | 146,047 | 157,718 | 158,392 | 160,665 | 175,488 | 196,573 | 211,844 | 211,607 |
| | $x_{man} = (EC/WS)_{man}$ | | 1.115 | 1.117 | 1.118 | 1.119 | 1.127 | 1.127 | 1.133 | 1.140 | 1.144 | 1.153 | 1.162 | 1.174 | 1.183 | 1.193 |
| Table F.1 | $(L_p)_{man}$ | thousands | 12,344 | 12,393 | 12,583 | 13,315 | 14,220 | 14,226 | 14,412 | 14,686 | 13,906 | 13,335 | 13,802 | 14,626 | 14,439 | 12,857 |
| | $(ec_p)_{man} = (w_p)_{man} \times x_{man} \times 52$ | \$/worker/year | 5,541 | 5,762 | 5,986 | 6,259 | 6,576 | 6,712 | 7,216 | 7,676 | 7,929 | 8,539 | 9,316 | 10,159 | 10,878 | 12,337 |
| | $V_{man} = (ec_p)_{man} \times (L_p)_{man} = (W_p)_{man}$ | millions | 68,392 | 71,415 | 75,321 | 83,337 | 93,511 | 95,484 | 103,995 | 112,726 | 110,258 | 113,871 | 128,576 | 148,588 | 157,065 | 158,615 |
| | **Mining** | | | | | | | | | | | | | | | |
| SEHE | $(W_p)_{min}$ | \$/worker/week | 110.70 | 114.40 | 117.74 | 123.52 | 130.24 | 135.89 | 142.71 | 154.80 | 164.40 | 172.14 | 189.14 | 201.40 | 219.14 | 249.31 |
| 604B 7 | $EC_{min}$ | millions of \$ | 4,429 | 4,462 | 4,652 | 4,859 | 5,135 | 5,303 | 5,569 | 6,176 | 6,704 | 6,982 | 7,715 | 8,595 | 10,457 | 12,923 |
| 605B 7 | $WS_{min}$ | millions of \$ | 3,901 | 3,940 | 4,100 | 4,308 | 4,504 | 4,634 | 4,862 | 5,376 | 5,816 | 6,043 | 6,647 | 7,325 | 8,871 | 10,884 |
| | $x_{min} = (EC/WS)_{min}$ | | 1.135 | 1.132 | 1.135 | 1.128 | 1.140 | 1.144 | 1.145 | 1.149 | 1.153 | 1.155 | 1.161 | 1.173 | 1.179 | 1.187 |
| Table F.1 | $(L_p)_{min}$ | thousands | 525 | 507 | 503 | 503 | 497 | 477 | 470 | 477 | 478 | 461 | 473 | 485 | 533 | 573 |
| | $(ec_p)_{min} = (w_p)_{min} \times x_{min} \times 52$ | \$/worker/year | 6,536 | 6,737 | 6,947 | 7,245 | 7,721 | 8,086 | 8,500 | 9,247 | 9,854 | 10,342 | 11,416 | 12,289 | 13,433 | 15,393 |
| | $V_{min} = (ec_p)_{min} \times (L_p)_{min} = (W_p)_{min}$ | millions | 3,429 | 3,418 | 3,496 | 3,647 | 3,838 | 3,861 | 3,996 | 4,414 | 4,706 | 4,768 | 5,396 | 5,963 | 7,160 | 8,824 |
| | **Construction** | | | | | | | | | | | | | | | |
| SEHE | $(W_p)_{con}$ | \$/worker/week | 122.47 | 127.19 | 132.06 | 138.38 | 146.26 | 154.95 | 164.49 | 181.54 | 195.45 | 211.67 | 221.19 | 235.89 | 249.25 | 264.08 |
| 604B 12 | $EC_{con}$ | millions of \$ | 18,969 | 20,279 | 22,116 | 24,167 | 26,675 | 27,800 | 31,136 | 35,165 | 37,469 | 40,748 | 44,474 | 50,560 | 53,985 | 52,860 |
| 605B 12 | $WS_{con}$ | millions of \$ | 17,627 | 18,704 | 20,455 | 22,294 | 24,496 | 25,543 | 28,479 | 32,231 | 34,147 | 37,052 | 40,182 | 45,126 | 47,892 | 46,285 |
| | $x_{con} = (EC/WS)_{con}$ | | 1.076 | 1.084 | 1.081 | 1.084 | 1.089 | 1.088 | 1.093 | 1.091 | 1.097 | 1.100 | 1.107 | 1.120 | 1.127 | 1.142 |
| Table F.1 | $(L_p)_{con}$ | thousands | 3,003 | 3,080 | 3,174 | 3,320 | 3,386 | 3,346 | 3,440 | 3,586 | 3,483 | 3,533 | 3,768 | 4,018 | 3,946 | 3,422 |
| | $(ec_p)_{con} = (w_p)_{con} \times x_{con} \times 52$ | \$/worker/year | 6,853 | 7,171 | 7,425 | 7,800 | 8,282 | 8,769 | 9,351 | 10,299 | 11,152 | 12,105 | 12,730 | 13,743 | 14,610 | 15,683 |
| | $V_{con} = (ec_p)_{con} \times (L_p)_{con} = (W_p)_{con}$ | millions | 20,580 | 22,089 | 23,568 | 25,895 | 28,039 | 29,343 | 32,172 | 36,931 | 38,837 | 42,764 | 47,967 | 55,226 | 57,654 | 53,670 |
| | **Transportation and public utilities** | | | | | | | | | | | | | | | |
| SEHE | $(W_p)_{tut}$ | \$/worker/week | 115.87 | 118.40 | 121.80 | 130.80 | 135.65 | 139.97 | 151.02 | 162.66 | 171.94 | 188.35 | 214.67 | 240.30 | 249.92 | 261.97 |
| 604B 37 | $EC_{tut}$ | millions of \$ | 26,477 | 27,436 | 29,221 | 31,123 | 33,700 | 35,886 | 39,060 | 42,759 | 46,998 | 50,999 | 56,429 | 63,088 | 68,928 | 72,913 |
| 605B 37 | $WS_{tut}$ (railroads wages) | millions of \$ | 23,846 | 24,627 | 26,087 | 27,598 | 29,697 | 31,594 | 34,148 | 37,540 | 40,527 | 43,607 | 47,611 | 53,192 | 57,447 | 59,892 |
| | $x_{tut} = (EC/WS)_{tut}$ | | 1.110 | 1.114 | 1.120 | 1.128 | 1.135 | 1.136 | 1.144 | 1.139 | 1.160 | 1.170 | 1.185 | 1.186 | 1.200 | 1.217 |
| Table F.1 | $(L_p)_{tut}$ | thousands | 6,690 | 6,859 | 7,094 | 7,670 | 8,005 | 8,267 | 8,983 | 9,634 | 10,368 | 11,454 | 13,230 | 14,820 | 15,593 | 16,584 |
| | $(ec_p)_{tut} = (w_p)_{tut} \times x_{tut} \times 52$ | \$/worker/year | 3,539 | 3,516 | 3,540 | 3,625 | 3,710 | 3,772 | 3,823 | 3,903 | 3,927 | 3,891 | 3,947 | 4,046 | 4,095 | 3,930 |
| | $V_{tut} = (ec_p)_{tut} \times (L_p)_{tut} = (W_p)_{tut}$ | millions | 23,674 | 24,113 | 25,117 | 27,801 | 29,695 | 31,184 | 34,342 | 37,602 | 40,717 | 44,570 | 52,225 | 59,965 | 63,860 | 65,176 |
| | **Services** | | | | | | | | | | | | | | | |
| Table G.1 | $(w_p)_{serv} = (EC/FEE)_{serv} = (ec_p)_{serv}$ | \$/worker/year | 4,250 | 4,425 | 4,646 | 4,839 | 5,112 | 5,357 | 5,754 | 6,318 | 6,906 | 7,415 | 7,919 | 8,505 | 9,248 | 10,022 |
| 607B 60 | $FEE_{serv}$ | thousands | 8,398 | 8,639 | 8,923 | 9,317 | 9,822 | 10,369 | 10,741 | 11,136 | 11,247 | 11,428 | 12,003 | 12,680 | 13,045 | 13,351 |
| 604B 60 | $EC_{serv}$ | millions of \$ | 35,689 | 38,231 | 41,455 | 45,089 | 50,208 | 55,551 | 61,806 | 70,360 | 77,669 | 84,743 | 95,046 | 107,839 | 120,642 | 133,805 |
| Table F.1 | $(L_p)_{serv}$ | thousands | 6,335 | 6,513 | 6,630 | 6,859 | 7,199 | 7,572 | 7,848 | 8,080 | 8,103 | 8,222 | 8,564 | 8,880 | 9,136 | 9,372 |
| | $V_{serv} = (ec_p)_{serv} \times (L_p)_{serv} = (W_p)_{serv}$ | millions of \$ | 26,921 | 28,824 | 30,804 | 33,193 | 36,800 | 40,568 | 45,159 | 51,051 | 55,954 | 60,971 | 67,811 | 75,522 | 84,494 | 93,928 |

| Table ref | Variable / equation | Units | | | | | | | | | | | | | | |
|---|---|---|---|---|---|---|---|---|---|---|---|---|---|---|---|---|
| **Agriculture** | | | | | | | | | | | | | | | | |
| Table G.1 | $(w_p)_{agr} = (EC/FEE)_{agr} = (ec_p)_{agr}$ | $/worker/year | 2,355 | 2,506 | 2,788 | 3,068 | 3,390 | 3,632 | 3,890 | 4,282 | 4,503 | 4,624 | 4,841 | 5,458 | 5,906 | 6,398 |
| 607B 4 | $FEE_{agr}$ | thousands | 1,723 | 1,677 | 1,552 | 1,476 | 1,382 | 1,314 | 1,298 | 1,274 | 1,280 | 1,276 | 1,293 | 1,368 | 1,458 | 1,440 |
| 604 4 | $EC_{agr}$ | millions of $ | 4,057 | 4,202 | 4,327 | 4,529 | 4,685 | 4,772 | 5,049 | 5,455 | 5,764 | 5,900 | 6,260 | 7,466 | 8,611 | 9,213 |
| Table G.1 | $(L_p)_{agr}$ | thousands | 3,395 | 3,199 | 3,027 | 2,902 | 2,666 | 2,554 | 2,513 | 2,435 | 2,367 | 2,290 | 2,357 | 2,408 | 2,475 | 2,423 |
| | $V_{agr} = (ec_p)_{agr} \times (L_p)_{agr} = (w_p)_{agr}$ | millions of $ | 7,994 | 8,016 | 8,441 | 8,905 | 9,037 | 9,275 | 9,774 | 10,425 | 10,660 | 10,588 | 11,411 | 13,142 | 14,618 | 15,502 |
| **Government enterprises** | | | | | | | | | | | | | | | | |
| | $w_{ge} = (EC/FEE)_{ge} = (ec_p)_{ge}$ | $/worker/year | 5,704 | 6,071 | 6,393 | 6,711 | 6,920 | 7,197 | 7,806 | 8,417 | 9,449 | 10,042 | 11,068 | 12,101 | 13,225 | 14,493 |
| 607B 81 | $FEE_{gefed}$ | thousands | 691 | 694 | 700 | 718 | 785 | 824 | 835 | 848 | 866 | 870 | 843 | 838 | 854 | 838 |
| 607B 86 | $FEE_{gesl}$ | thousands | 389 | 399 | 420 | 428 | 429 | 429 | 461 | 479 | 507 | 521 | 530 | 555 | 596 | 644 |
| | $FEE_{geoal}$ | thousands | 1,080 | 1,093 | 1,120 | 1,146 | 1,214 | 1,253 | 1,296 | 1,327 | 1,373 | 1,391 | 1,373 | 1,393 | 1,450 | 1,482 |
| 604B 81 | $EC_{fed}$ | millions of $ | 3,968 | 4,311 | 4,586 | 4,914 | 5,401 | 5,791 | 6,459 | 7,076 | 8,377 | 8,829 | 9,590 | 10,424 | 11,824 | 12,976 |
| 604B 86 | $EC_{sl}$ | millions of $ | 2,192 | 2,325 | 2,574 | 2,777 | 3,000 | 3,227 | 3,658 | 4,094 | 4,597 | 5,140 | 5,606 | 6,433 | 7,352 | 8,502 |
| | $EC_{geoal}$ | millions of $ | 6,160 | 6,636 | 7,160 | 7,691 | 8,401 | 9,018 | 10,117 | 11,170 | 12,974 | 13,969 | 15,196 | 16,857 | 19,176 | 21,478 |
| Table F.1 | $(L_p)_{gefed} = (L_p/L_n)_{nongovot} \times L_{gefed}$ | thousands | 510 | 511 | 513 | 527 | 575 | 598 | 605 | 612 | 621 | 622 | 606 | 601 | 608 | 587 |
| Table F.1 | $(L_p)_{gesl} = (L_p/L_n)_{nongovot} \times L_{gesl}$ | thousands | 287 | 294 | 308 | 314 | 314 | 311 | 334 | 346 | 363 | 373 | 381 | 398 | 424 | 451 |
| Table F.1 | $(L_p)_{geoal} = (L_p)_{gefed} + (L_p)_{gesl}$ | thousands | 797 | 804 | 821 | 841 | 888 | 909 | 939 | 958 | 984 | 995 | 986 | 999 | 1,032 | 1,037 |
| | $V_{ge} = (ec_p)_{ge} \times (L_p)_{geoal}$ | millions of $ | 4,547 | 4,883 | 5,251 | 5,646 | 6,148 | 6,543 | 7,331 | 8,066 | 9,299 | 9,994 | 10,918 | 12,084 | 13,653 | 15,035 |
| **TOTAL TRADE = $W_{tt}$** | | millions of $ | 65,047 | 68,074 | 72,554 | 77,411 | 83,556 | 88,539 | 96,641 | 106,485 | 115,086 | 124,025 | 135,689 | 151,100 | 166,627 | 178,072 |
| **Wholesale trade** | | | | | | | | | | | | | | | | |
| Table G.1 | $W_{whtr}$ | millions of $ | 22,770 | 23,964 | 25,559 | 27,332 | 30,072 | 32,047 | 34,710 | 38,345 | 41,512 | 44,262 | 48,443 | 54,782 | 61,569 | 65,151 |
| **Retail trade** | | | | | | | | | | | | | | | | |
| Table G.1 | $W_{rettr}$ | millions of $ | 40,163 | 41,864 | 44,630 | 47,578 | 50,793 | 53,673 | 58,734 | 64,554 | 69,531 | 75,147 | 81,991 | 90,145 | 98,447 | 106,098 |
| **Building rental** | | | | | | | | | | | | | | | | |
| Table G.1 | $W_{br} = W_{re} - W_{gr}$ | millions of $ | 2,114 | 2,246 | 2,365 | 2,501 | 2,691 | 2,819 | 3,196 | 3,587 | 4,044 | 4,616 | 5,254 | 6,173 | 6,611 | 6,824 |
| **ROYALTIES = $W_r$** | | | | | | | | | | | | | | | | |
| Table G.1 | | millions of $ | 16,620 | 17,684 | 18,965 | 20,280 | 22,029 | 24,227 | 27,371 | 30,231 | 33,007 | 36,294 | 40,256 | 45,027 | 49,257 | 54,707 |
| **Finance and insurance** | | | | | | | | | | | | | | | | |
| | $W_{fi}$ | millions of $ | 13,765 | 14,640 | 15,748 | 16,868 | 18,347 | 20,359 | 22,972 | 25,267 | 27,381 | 29,837 | 32,867 | 36,298 | 39,891 | 45,022 |
| **Ground rent** | | | | | | | | | | | | | | | | |
| Table G.1 | $W_{re}$ | millions of $ | 2,855 | 3,044 | 3,217 | 3,412 | 3,682 | 3,869 | 4,399 | 4,963 | 5,626 | 6,456 | 7,389 | 8,730 | 9,366 | 9,685 |
| **DUMMY = $W_d$** | | | | | | | | | | | | | | | | |
| Table G.1 | $W_{re}$ | millions of $ | 55,437 | 59,321 | 64,386 | 69,256 | 78,394 | 87,377 | 97,769 | 107,481 | 119,474 | 130,322 | 142,590 | 155,041 | 168,699 | 187,651 |
| **Government** | | | | | | | | | | | | | | | | |
| | $W_{govot}$ | millions of $ | 55,437 | 59,321 | 64,386 | 69,256 | 78,394 | 87,377 | 97,769 | 107,481 | 119,474 | 130,322 | 142,590 | 155,041 | 168,699 | 187,651 |
| **W = Total EC and WEQ** | | | | | | | | | | | | | | | | |
| Table G.1 | $W$ | millions of $ | 360,886 | 379,432 | 406,662 | 436,635 | 480,940 | 515,034 | 566,661 | 624,698 | 667,551 | 712,247 | 783,118 | 875,185 | 961,227 | 1,024,738 |
| | Total variable capital = $V^* = W_p$ | millions of $ | 155,536 | 162,758 | 171,998 | 188,426 | 207,068 | 216,257 | 236,769 | 261,216 | 270,432 | 287,525 | 324,303 | 370,490 | 398,505 | 410,750 |
| | $W_u = W - V^*$ | millions of $ | 205,350 | 216,673 | 234,665 | 248,210 | 273,872 | 298,777 | 329,892 | 363,482 | 397,120 | 424,721 | 458,815 | 504,695 | 562,722 | 613,988 |
| | $(W_u)_p = W_u - (W_u)_u$ | millions of $ | 68,245 | 71,594 | 78,759 | 81,264 | 89,893 | 98,634 | 108,112 | 119,285 | 129,553 | 140,280 | 153,527 | 178,138 | 193,558 |  |
| | $(W_u)_u = W_{ui} + W_r + W_d$ | millions of $ | 137,104 | 145,079 | 155,906 | 166,946 | 183,979 | 200,143 | 221,781 | 244,197 | 267,567 | 290,641 | 318,535 | 351,168 | 384,583 | 420,430 |
| | $ec_p = V^*/L_p = W_p/L_p$ | $/prod. worker | 5,196 | 5,423 | 5,680 | 6,007 | 6,359 | 6,582 | 7,079 | 7,655 | 8,134 | 8,785 | 9,568 | 10,447 | 11,176 | 12,219 |
| | $ec_u = W_u/L_u$ | $/unpr. worker | 5,680 | 5,913 | 6,242 | 6,403 | 6,723 | 7,067 | 7,587 | 8,123 | 8,819 | 9,394 | 9,983 | 10,550 | 11,495 | 12,476 |

# Table G.2 (cont.)

| Sources[a] | Sectors | Units | 1976 | 1977 | 1978 | 1979 | 1980 | 1981 | 1982 | 1983 | 1984 | 1985 | 1986 | 1987 | 1988 | 1989 |
|---|---|---|---|---|---|---|---|---|---|---|---|---|---|---|---|---|
| | PRODUCTION = $W_p = V^*$ | millions of $ | 459,625 | 515,814 | 589,202 | 664,783 | 706,526 | 772,351 | 786,528 | 839,732 | 928,680 | 967,993 | 998,546 | 1,060,901 | 1,146,222 | 1,206,396 |
| | **Manufacturing** | | | | | | | | | | | | | | | |
| SEHE | $(w_p)_{man}$ | $/worker/week | 209.32 | 228.90 | 249.27 | 268.94 | 288.62 | 318.00 | 330.26 | 354.08 | 374.03 | 386.37 | 396.01 | 406.31 | 418.81 | 430.09 |
| 604B 13 | $EC_{man}$ | millions of $ | 286,704 | 324,274 | 366,271 | 409,736 | 436,141 | 475,363 | 473,056 | 490,606 | 540,658 | 563,178 | 579,190 | 598,082 | 639,252 | 662,166 |
| 605B 13 | $WS_{man}$ | millions of $ | 238,046 | 266,707 | 300,093 | 334,840 | 355,570 | 386,660 | 384,038 | 397,391 | 439,105 | 460,857 | 473,218 | 490,292 | 524,004 | 541,838 |
| Table F.1 | $x_{man} = (EC/WS)_{man}$ | | 1.204 | 1.216 | 1.221 | 1.224 | 1.227 | 1.229 | 1.232 | 1.235 | 1.231 | 1.222 | 1.224 | 1.220 | 1.220 | 1.222 |
| | $(L_p)_{man}$ | thousands | 13,525 | 14,084 | 14,671 | 15,003 | 14,131 | 13,969 | 12,624 | 12,450 | 13,201 | 13,000 | 12,817 | 12,930 | 13,229 | 13,252 |
| | $(ec_p)_{man} = (w_p)_{man} \times x_{man} \times 52$ | $/worker/year | 13,110 | 14,472 | 15,820 | 17,113 | 18,409 | 20,329 | 21,154 | 22,731 | 23,948 | 24,552 | 25,204 | 25,773 | 26,568 | 27,331 |
| | $V_{man} = (ec_p)_{man} \times (L_p)_{man} = (W_p)_{man}$ | millions | 177,301 | 203,821 | 232,099 | 256,743 | 260,144 | 283,974 | 267,050 | 282,997 | 316,126 | 319,165 | 323,029 | 333,235 | 351,454 | 362,182 |
| | **Mining** | | | | | | | | | | | | | | | |
| SEHE | $(w_p)_{min}$ | $/worker/week | 273.90 | 301.20 | 332.88 | 365.07 | 397.06 | 438.75 | 459.88 | 479.40 | 503.58 | 519.93 | 525.81 | 530.85 | 541.44 | 569.75 |
| 604B 7 | $EC_{min}$ | millions of $ | 14,606 | 16,923 | 19,832 | 23,725 | 28,773 | 35,830 | 37,454 | 33,107 | 35,280 | 34,722 | 30,273 | 28,442 | 29,741 | 29,625 |
| 605B 7 | $WS_{min}$ | millions of $ | 12,243 | 14,076 | 16,476 | 19,673 | 23,897 | 29,832 | 31,217 | 27,563 | 29,238 | 28,992 | 25,190 | 23,578 | 24,615 | 24,461 |
| Table F.1 | $x_{min} = (EC/WS)_{min}$ | | 1.193 | 1.202 | 1.204 | 1.206 | 1.204 | 1.201 | 1.200 | 1.201 | 1.207 | 1.198 | 1.202 | 1.206 | 1.208 | 1.211 |
| | $(L_p)_{min}$ | thousands | 601 | 632 | 663 | 718 | 778 | 857 | 825 | 679 | 692 | 657 | 549 | 516 | 526 | 498 |
| | $(ec_p)_{min} = (w_p)_{min} \times x_{min} \times 52$ | $/worker/year | 16,992 | 18,830 | 20,836 | 22,894 | 24,860 | 27,402 | 28,692 | 29,943 | 31,598 | 32,380 | 32,859 | 33,299 | 34,018 | 35,882 |
| | $V_{min} = (ec_p)_{min} \times (L_p)_{min} = (W_p)_{min}$ | millions | 10,214 | 11,895 | 13,824 | 16,443 | 19,349 | 23,490 | 23,681 | 20,321 | 21,878 | 21,260 | 18,024 | 17,173 | 17,906 | 17,879 |
| | **Construction** | | | | | | | | | | | | | | | |
| SEHE | $(w_p)_{con}$ | $/worker/week | 283.73 | 296.65 | 318.69 | 342.99 | 367.78 | 399.26 | 426.82 | 442.97 | 458.51 | 464.46 | 466.75 | 479.68 | 495.73 | 512.41 |
| 604B 12 | $EC_{con}$ | millions of $ | 57,883 | 64,701 | 76,048 | 88,107 | 92,672 | 97,859 | 97,703 | 100,485 | 113,899 | 124,640 | 134,046 | 142,441 | 154,775 | 161,982 |
| 605B 12 | $WS_{con}$ | millions of $ | 49,988 | 55,219 | 64,626 | 74,526 | 78,111 | 82,297 | 81,588 | 83,151 | 93,781 | 102,890 | 110,230 | 117,536 | 127,859 | 133,477 |
| Table F.1 | $x_{con} = (EC/WS)_{con}$ | | 1.158 | 1.172 | 1.177 | 1.182 | 1.186 | 1.189 | 1.198 | 1.208 | 1.215 | 1.211 | 1.212 | 1.211 | 1.211 | 1.214 |
| | $(L_p)_{con}$ | thousands | 3,462 | 3,714 | 4,207 | 4,479 | 4,244 | 4,056 | 3,733 | 3,807 | 4,273 | 4,566 | 4,737 | 4,815 | 4,979 | 5,016 |
| | $(ec_p)_{con} = (w_p)_{con} \times x_{con} \times 52$ | $/worker/year | 17,084 | 18,075 | 19,501 | 21,086 | 22,690 | 24,687 | 26,578 | 27,836 | 28,957 | 29,257 | 29,515 | 30,229 | 31,205 | 32,336 |
| | $V_{con} = (ec_p)_{con} \times (L_p)_{con} = (W_p)_{con}$ | millions | 59,153 | 67,138 | 82,047 | 94,439 | 96,303 | 100,132 | 99,210 | 105,983 | 123,741 | 133,581 | 139,806 | 145,541 | 155,377 | 162,198 |
| | **Transportation and public utilities** | | | | | | | | | | | | | | | |
| SEHE | $(w_p)_{tut}$ (railroads wages) | $/worker/week | 300.66 | 321.47 | 343.92 | 392.47 | 426.56 | 457.95 | 484.15 | 541.85 | 573.19 | 594.70 | 608.38 | 627.33 | 673.50 | 693.00 |
| 604B 37 | $EC_{tut}$ | millions of $ | 81,837 | 91,240 | 103,523 | 116,839 | 128,129 | 140,836 | 149,692 | 155,354 | 165,408 | 172,747 | 179,268 | 188,987 | 200,169 | 209,597 |
| 605B 37 | $WS_{tut}$ | millions of $ | 66,585 | 74,158 | 84,168 | 95,063 | 103,958 | 114,431 | 119,874 | 124,344 | 132,306 | 139,275 | 144,153 | 152,399 | 161,047 | 168,356 |
| Table F.1 | $x_{tut} = (EC/WS)_{tut}$ | | 1.229 | 1.230 | 1.230 | 1.229 | 1.233 | 1.231 | 1.249 | 1.249 | 1.250 | 1.240 | 1.244 | 1.240 | 1.243 | 1.245 |
| | $(ec_p)_{tut} = (w_p)_{tut} \times x_{tut} \times 52$ | $/worker/year | 19,216 | 20,567 | 21,996 | 25,083 | 27,338 | 29,308 | 31,438 | 35,203 | 37,263 | 38,356 | 39,342 | 40,453 | 43,530 | 44,863 |
| | $(L_p)_{tut}$ | thousands | 3,928 | 4,011 | 4,161 | 4,324 | 4,306 | 4,327 | 4,235 | 4,175 | 4,360 | 4,395 | 4,413 | 4,529 | 4,647 | 4,728 |
| | $V_{tut} = (ec_p)_{tut} \times (L_p)_{tut} = (W_p)_{tut}$ | millions | 75,484 | 82,503 | 91,516 | 108,463 | 117,729 | 126,816 | 133,125 | 146,978 | 162,462 | 168,589 | 173,609 | 183,231 | 202,275 | 212,118 |
| | **Services** | | | | | | | | | | | | | | | |
| Table G.1 | $(w_p)_{serv} = (EC/FEE)_{serv} = (ec_p)_{serv}$ | $/worker/year | 10,774 | 11,568 | 12,537 | 13,766 | 15,236 | 16,838 | 18,415 | 19,569 | 20,444 | 21,395 | 22,393 | 23,787 | 25,282 | 26,380 |
| 607B 60 | $FEE_{serv}$ | thousands | 13,906 | 14,541 | 15,473 | 16,210 | 16,794 | 17,376 | 17,704 | 18,348 | 19,517 | 20,468 | 21,371 | 22,537 | 23,544 | 24,715 |
| 604B 60 | $EC_{serv}$ | millions of $ | 149,827 | 168,205 | 193,987 | 223,146 | 255,867 | 292,584 | 326,023 | 359,056 | 398,998 | 437,917 | 478,570 | 536,093 | 595,234 | 651,980 |
| | $(L_p)_{serv}$ | thousands | 9,697 | 9,978 | 10,478 | 10,646 | 10,956 | 11,171 | 11,463 | 11,779 | 12,134 | 12,459 | 12,655 | 13,000 | 13,836 | 14,367 |
| Table F.1 | $V_{serv} = (ec_p)_{serv} \times (L_p)_{serv} = (W_p)_{serv}$ | millions of $ | 104,475 | 115,423 | 131,361 | 146,552 | 166,919 | 188,105 | 211,085 | 230,506 | 248,067 | 266,560 | 283,399 | 316,381 | 349,802 | 379,012 |

| | | | | | | | | | | | | | | | | |
|---|---|---|---|---|---|---|---|---|---|---|---|---|---|---|---|---|
| | Agriculture | | | | | | | | | | | | | | | |
| Table G.1 | $(w_p)_{agr}=(EC/FEE)_{agr}=(ec_p)_{agr}$ | $/worker/year | 6,857 | 7,548 | 8,213 | 9,169 | 9,836 | 10,739 | 11,482 | 11,634 | 12,302 | 12,833 | 13,219 | 13,708 | 13,987 | 15,045 |
| 607B 4 | $FEE_{agr}$ | thousands | 1,532 | 1,490 | 1,525 | 1,524 | 1,530 | 1,444 | 1,480 | 1,477 | 1,466 | 1,458 | 1,476 | 1,561 | 1,648 | 1,608 |
| 604B 4 | $EC_{agr}$ | millions of $ | 10,505 | 11,246 | 12,525 | 13,973 | 15,049 | 15,507 | 16,993 | 17,183 | 18,034 | 18,710 | 19,511 | 21,398 | 23,050 | 24,192 |
| Table G.1 | $(L_p)_{agr}$ | thousands | 2,439 | 2,360 | 2,389 | 2,372 | 2,383 | 2,305 | 2,298 | 2,173 | 2,167 | 2,096 | 2,079 | 2,170 | 2,216 | 2,169 |
| | $V_{agr}=(ec_p)_{agr}\times(L_p)_{agr}=(W_p)_{agr}$ | millions of $ | 16,727 | 17,814 | 19,624 | 21,752 | 23,441 | 24,755 | 26,383 | 25,281 | 26,662 | 26,898 | 27,482 | 29,746 | 30,995 | 32,625 |
| | Government enterprises | | | | | | | | | | | | | | | |
| | $w_{ge}=(EC/FEE)_{ge}=(ec_p)_{ge}$ | $/worker/year | 15,882 | 16,915 | 18,005 | 19,313 | 21,279 | 23,828 | 25,336 | 26,996 | 28,485 | 30,220 | 31,225 | 32,842 | 34,768 | 36,115 |
| 607B 81 | $FEE_{gefed}$ | thousands | 819 | 813 | 821 | 838 | 846 | 852 | 836 | 834 | 857 | 860 | 856 | 882 | 908 | 917 |
| 607B 86 | $FEE_{gesl}$ | thousands | 645 | 650 | 680 | 700 | 730 | 727 | 728 | 743 | 760 | 791 | 822 | 833 | 848 | 868 |
| | $FEE_{getotal}$ | thousands | 1,464 | 1,463 | 1,501 | 1,538 | 1,576 | 1,579 | 1,564 | 1,577 | 1,617 | 1,651 | 1,678 | 1,715 | 1,756 | 1,785 |
| 604B 81 | $EC_{fed}$ | millions of $ | 14,057 | 14,918 | 16,079 | 17,600 | 19,749 | 22,434 | 23,106 | 24,783 | 26,894 | 28,776 | 29,306 | 32,012 | 35,098 | 36,617 |
| 6048 86 | $EC_{sl}$ | millions of $ | 9,194 | 9,829 | 10,946 | 12,104 | 13,787 | 15,190 | 16,520 | 17,789 | 19,166 | 21,118 | 23,089 | 24,312 | 25,954 | 27,849 |
| | $EC_{getotal}$ | millions of $ | 23,251 | 24,747 | 27,025 | 29,704 | 33,536 | 37,624 | 39,626 | 42,572 | 46,060 | 49,894 | 52,395 | 56,324 | 61,052 | 64,466 |
| Table F.1 | $(L_p)_{gefed}=(L_p/L)_{nongovtot}\times L_{gefed}$ | thousands | 573 | 566 | 569 | 575 | 571 | 568 | 548 | 542 | 553 | 551 | 542 | 557 | 570 | 574 |
| Table F.1 | $(L_p)_{gesl}=(L_p/L)_{nongovtot}\times L_{gesl}$ | thousands | 451 | 452 | 471 | 481 | 493 | 485 | 478 | 483 | 492 | 506 | 521 | 527 | 534 | 544 |
| Table F.1 | $(L_p)_{getotal}=(L_p)_{gefed}+(L_p)_{gesl}$ | thousands | 1,025 | 1,018 | 1,040 | 1,056 | 1,064 | 1,053 | 1,026 | 1,025 | 1,044 | 1,057 | 1,063 | 1,084 | 1,105 | 1,118 |
| | $V_{ge}=(ec_p)_{ge}\times(L_p)_{getotal}$ | millions of $ | 16,272 | 17,221 | 18,731 | 20,391 | 22,641 | 25,079 | 25,994 | 27,666 | 29,744 | 31,940 | 33,198 | 35,595 | 38,413 | 40,382 |
| | TOTAL TRADE $=W_{tt}$ | millions of $ | 198,096 | 219,376 | 247,987 | 279,124 | 305,437 | 331,967 | 349,949 | 373,944 | 412,947 | 440,117 | 468,204 | 500,999 | 542,817 | 576,191 |
| | Wholesale trade | | | | | | | | | | | | | | | |
| Table G.1 | $W_{whtr}$ | millions of $ | 72,729 | 80,191 | 91,013 | 104,562 | 116,543 | 128,702 | 135,414 | 141,433 | 157,541 | 167,464 | 176,017 | 188,082 | 206,821 | 221,875 |
| | Retail trade | | | | | | | | | | | | | | | |
| Table G.1 | $W_{rettr}$ | millions of $ | 117,734 | 130,376 | 146,357 | 161,826 | 174,849 | 188,315 | 198,455 | 214,158 | 234,340 | 249,111 | 266,681 | 284,432 | 303,861 | 321,033 |
| | Building rental | | | | | | | | | | | | | | | |
| Table G.1 | $W_{br}=W_{re}-W_{gr}$ | millions of $ | 7,634 | 8,809 | 10,616 | 12,736 | 14,045 | 14,950 | 16,080 | 18,353 | 21,067 | 23,542 | 25,506 | 28,485 | 32,136 | 33,283 |
| | ROYALTIES $=W_r$ | millions of $ | 60,880 | 68,330 | 78,887 | 90,144 | 102,955 | 115,041 | 128,739 | 144,817 | 159,358 | 176,610 | 200,213 | 223,111 | 242,605 | 249,835 |
| | Finance and insurance | | | | | | | | | | | | | | | |
| Table G.1 | $W_{fi}$ | millions of $ | 50,026 | 55,781 | 63,736 | 72,206 | 83,174 | 93,984 | 106,091 | 118,967 | 129,687 | 143,452 | 164,290 | 182,992 | 197,343 | 202,957 |
| | Ground rent | | | | | | | | | | | | | | | |
| Table G.1 | $W_{re}$ | millions of $ | 10,854 | 12,549 | 15,151 | 17,938 | 19,782 | 21,056 | 22,648 | 25,850 | 29,671 | 33,158 | 35,924 | 40,119 | 45,261 | 46,878 |
| | DUMMY $=W_d$ | millions of $ | 203,818 | 220,498 | 240,542 | 260,444 | 288,253 | 316,738 | 343,899 | 366,390 | 390,890 | 418,975 | 443,799 | 472,950 | 505,779 | 541,555 |
| | Government | | | | | | | | | | | | | | | |
| Table G.1 | $W_{govtot}$ | millions of $ | 203,818 | 220,498 | 240,542 | 260,444 | 288,253 | 316,738 | 343,899 | 366,390 | 390,890 | 418,975 | 443,799 | 472,950 | 505,779 | 541,555 |
| Table G.1 | $W=$ Total EC and WEQ | millions of $ | 1,140,356 | 1,268,469 | 1,433,637 | 1,610,759 | 1,773,254 | 1,956,867 | 2,071,620 | 2,199,810 | 2,404,596 | 2,565,699 | 2,719,892 | 2,913,089 | 3,152,110 | 3,337,038 |
| | Total variable capital $=V^*=W_p$ | millions of $ | 459,625 | 515,814 | 589,202 | 664,783 | 706,526 | 772,351 | 786,528 | 839,732 | 928,680 | 967,993 | 998,546 | 1,060,901 | 1,146,222 | 1,206,396 |
| | $W_u=W-V^*$ | millions of $ | 680,731 | 752,654 | 844,434 | 945,976 | 1,066,728 | 1,184,516 | 1,285,092 | 1,360,078 | 1,475,916 | 1,597,705 | 1,721,347 | 1,852,188 | 2,005,888 | 2,130,642 |
| | $(W_u)_p=W_u-(W_u)_u$ | millions of $ | 217,936 | 244,450 | 277,019 | 316,265 | 370,083 | 420,770 | 462,505 | 474,927 | 512,720 | 562,003 | 609,131 | 655,128 | 714,688 | 763,061 |
| | $(W_u)_u=W_{tt}+W_r+W_d$ | millions of $ | 462,795 | 508,204 | 567,416 | 629,711 | 696,645 | 763,746 | 822,587 | 885,151 | 963,196 | 1,035,702 | 1,112,216 | 1,197,060 | 1,291,201 | 1,367,581 |
| | $ec_p=V^*/L_p=W_p/L_p$ | $/prod. worker | 13,254 | 14,409 | 15,666 | 17,223 | 18,660 | 20,466 | 21,726 | 23,269 | 24,522 | 25,321 | 26,063 | 26,965 | 28,275 | 29,318 |
| | $ec_u=W_u/L_u$ | $/unpr. worker | 13,487 | 14,386 | 15,373 | 16,617 | 18,433 | 20,130 | 21,860 | 22,719 | 23,526 | 24,655 | 25,878 | 27,021 | 28,483 | 29,444 |

[a] SEHE denotes Supplement to Employment, Hours, and Earnings, United States, 1909–84 (BLS 1989). Unless otherwise indicated, all data come from NIPA (e.g. BEA 1986), where the first (two or) three digits (and following letter, if any) denote the relevant table number and subsequent digits the line numbers within those tables.

*Glossary of variables in Table G.2*

| | |
|---|---|
| $EC_{agr}$ | Total employee compensation in agriculture, forestry, and fisheries |
| $EC_{con}$ | Total employee compensation in construction |
| $EC_{fed}$ | Total employee compensation in government enterprises (federal) |
| $EC_{getotal}$ | Total employee compensation in government enterprises (federal, state, and local) |
| $EC_{man}$ | Total employee compensation in manufacturing |
| $EC_{min}$ | Total employee compensation in mining |
| $ec_p$ | Average annual wage of productive workers |
| $(ec_p)_{con}$ | Estimated annual per-worker employee compensation in construction |
| $(ec_p)_{man}$ | Estimated annual per-worker employee compensation in manufacturing |
| $(ec_p)_{min}$ | Estimated annual per-worker employee compensation in mining |
| $(ec_p)_{tut}$ | Estimated annual per-worker employee compensation in transportation and public utilities |
| $EC_{serv}$ | Total employee compensation in services |
| $EC_{sl}$ | Total employee compensation in government enterprises (state and local) |
| $EC_{tut}$ | Total employee compensation in transportation and public utilities |
| $ec_u$ | Average annual wage of unproductive workers |
| $FEE_{agr}$ | Total full-time equivalent employees in agriculture, forestry, and fisheries |
| $FEE_{gefed}$ | Total full-time equivalent employees in government enterprises (federal) |
| $FEE_{gesl}$ | Total full-time equivalent employees in government enterprises (state and local) |
| $FEE_{getotal}$ | Total full-time equivalent employees in government enterprises (federal, state, and local) |
| $FEE_{serv}$ | Total full-time equivalent employees in services |
| $(L_p)_{agr}$ | Estimated total productive labor in agriculture, forestry, and fisheries |
| $(L_p)_{con}$ | Estimated total productive labor in construction |
| $(L_p)_{gefed}$ | Estimated total productive labor in government enterprises (federal) |
| $(L_p)_{gesl}$ | Estimated total productive labor in government enterprises (state and local) |
| $(L_p)_{getotal}$ | Estimated total productive labor in government enterprises (federal, state, and local) |
| $(L_p)_{man}$ | Estimated total productive labor in manufacturing |
| $(L_p)_{min}$ | Estimated total productive labor in mining |

| $(L_p)_{serv}$ | Estimated total productive labor in productive services |
|---|---|
| $(L_p)_{tut}$ | Estimated total productive labor in transportation and public utilities |
| $V_{agr}, (W_p)_{agr}$ | Variable capital in agriculture, forestry, and fisheries |
| $V_{con}, (W_p)_{con}$ | Variable capital in construction |
| $V_{ge}$ | Variable capital in government enterprises |
| $V_{man}, (W_p)_{man}$ | Variable capital in manufacturing |
| $V_{min}, (W_p)_{min}$ | Variable capital in mining |
| $V_{serv}$ | Variable capital in services |
| $V_{tut}, (W_p)_{tut}$ | Variable capital in transportation and public utilities |
| $V^*, W_p$ | Variable capital |
| $W$ | Estimated total wage: employee compensation, wage equivalent of self-employed persons, and corporate officers' salaries |
| $W_{br}$ | Total employee compensation in building rental sector |
| $W_d$ | Total employee compensation in dummy sectors |
| $W_{fi}$ | Total employee compensation in finance and insurance |
| $w_{ge}$ | Unit wage of production workers in government enterprises |

does just that. We calculate variable capital as the product of production worker wages $w_p$, the ratio x of employee compensation to wages and salaries, and the number $L_p$ of production workers. In this calculation, corporate officers' salaries play an insignificant role – only through their very slight effect on the compensation/wage ratio x. In effect, the slightly higher compensation/salary ratio $x'$ of corporate officers is weighted by their very small share in total wages and salaries (4.2% in manufacturing for 1968; U.S. Internal Revenue Service, *Statistics of Income*), so that the ratio x is virtually unaffected when we deduct corporate officers' compensation and salaries from the numerator and denominator, respectively (the difference is 0.7% in manufacturing for 1968). Thus our estimate of $V^*$, and hence of $S^*/V^*$, is essentially the same as if we had first deducted corporate officers' salaries from employee compensation and from wages and salaries.

However, the same is not true for our total measure of wages W, because this directly contains corporate officers' salaries. Therefore, our measure of unproductive wages $W_u \equiv W - V^*$ is larger by the amount of COS. As long as we recognize that $W_u$ is the sum of unproductive worker wages and corporate salaries, this poses no serious problem.

The use of EC as our base also requires that we estimate the unit employee compensation of production workers $ec_p$ by enhancing the BLS data on their unit wage by an estimate of the ratio x (of employee compensation EC to wages and salaries WS) for production workers in each sector. For this ratio x, we use the ratio of EC to WS of all workers in each sector, implicitly assuming that this ratio is roughly the same for both production and nonproduction workers. Employee compensation being the sum of supplements and wages and salaries, this assumption can be checked by calculating the ratio of supplements to wages for production and nonproduction workers (these data are available only for the period 1966–77). From the *Handbook of Labor Statistics* (BLS 1980, tables 132 and 133) we find that for 1968 there are only small differences between production and nonproduction workers with respect to the ratios of supplements to wages and salaries:

|  | Non-office[3] workers | All workers | Ratio of non-office to all |
|---|---|---|---|
| Manufacturing | 0.131 | 0.126 | 1.039 |
| Nonmanufacturing | 0.114 | 0.107 | 1.061 |

[3] For manufacturing, "non-office" is equivalent to production workers. See BLS (1980, p. 318, table 132, n. 5).

# H

## Surplus value and profit

The estimates of value added and final product in Appendix E and of variable capital in Appendix G allow us to calculate surplus value and surplus product. By definition:

$$S^* = VA^* - V^* = \text{surplus value (in money form)};$$

$$S^*/V^* = \text{rate of surplus value};$$

$$NP^* = \text{necessary product (consumption of productive workers)}$$
$$= V^*;$$

and

$$SP^* = FP^* - NP^* = \text{surplus product}.$$

The Marxian measures may be compared to naive estimates $P^+$ and $P^+/EC$.

$$P^+ = VA - EC = \text{profit-type income (gross of all business taxes)},$$

where
$VA = FD = NNP = \text{net national product (NIPA) and}$
$EC = \text{total wages.}$
Hence

$$P^+/EC = \text{profit-type income/wage ratio}.$$

We may also define more restricted measures of profit, such as $P \equiv P^+ - IBT$ (where $IBT = $ indirect business taxes) and $P_n = P^+ - IBT - $ corporate income tax $= $ profit, net of all business taxes.

Table H.1 details surplus value and profit for the period 1948–89.

Table H.1. *Surplus value and profit, 1948–89 (billions of dollars)*

| Sources | Variables | 1948 | 1949 | 1950 | 1951 | 1952 | 1953 | 1954 | 1955 | 1956 | 1957 | 1958 |
|---|---|---|---|---|---|---|---|---|---|---|---|---|
| | $S^*=VA^*-V^*$ | 149.94 | 148.64 | 165.26 | 188.25 | 194.51 | 204.52 | 208.20 | 228.55 | 236.97 | 250.25 | 256.15 |
| Table E.1 | $VA^*$ | 238.35 | 233.66 | 258.42 | 294.17 | 305.52 | 321.91 | 320.15 | 349.07 | 365.79 | 383.25 | 383.87 |
| Table G.2 | $V^*$ | 88.41 | 85.02 | 93.16 | 105.91 | 111.01 | 117.39 | 111.95 | 120.52 | 128.82 | 133.00 | 127.72 |
| | $S^*/V^*$ | 1.70 | 1.75 | 1.77 | 1.78 | 1.75 | 1.74 | 1.86 | 1.90 | 1.84 | 1.88 | 2.01 |
| | $SP^*=FP^*-NP^*$ | 149.91 | 148.58 | 165.09 | 188.26 | 194.79 | 204.29 | 208.23 | 228.16 | 236.74 | 249.88 | 256.04 |
| | $FP^*=GFP^*-D_p$ | 238.32 | 233.60 | 258.25 | 294.18 | 305.81 | 321.68 | 320.18 | 348.67 | 365.56 | 382.88 | 383.75 |
| | $GFP^*=TP^*-M'_p$ | 247.74 | 242.90 | 269.06 | 307.03 | 319.61 | 336.71 | 335.26 | 365.74 | 384.10 | 402.67 | 403.67 |
| Table E.2 | $TP^*$ | 446.21 | 431.96 | 481.62 | 551.62 | 573.95 | 605.37 | 596.63 | 652.91 | 687.21 | 717.30 | 711.67 |
| Table E.1 | $M'_p$ | 198.47 | 189.06 | 212.56 | 244.59 | 254.35 | 268.66 | 261.36 | 287.18 | 303.11 | 314.63 | 308.00 |
| Table E.2 | $D_p$ | 9.42 | 9.29 | 10.81 | 12.85 | 13.80 | 15.04 | 15.08 | 17.07 | 18.54 | 19.79 | 19.92 |
| Table G.2 | $NP^*=V^*$ | 88.41 | 85.02 | 93.16 | 105.91 | 111.01 | 117.39 | 111.95 | 120.52 | 128.82 | 133.00 | 127.72 |
| | $P^*=VA-EC$ | 99.11 | 96.40 | 109.18 | 124.61 | 126.15 | 130.28 | 130.63 | 145.59 | 145.36 | 152.14 | 154.24 |
| 112 1[a] | $VA=FD=NNP$ | 241.20 | 238.40 | 264.60 | 306.20 | 322.50 | 340.70 | 340.00 | 371.50 | 390.10 | 409.90 | 414.00 |
| 604B 1[a] | $EC$ | 142.09 | 142.00 | 155.42 | 181.60 | 196.35 | 210.42 | 209.37 | 225.92 | 244.74 | 257.76 | 259.76 |
| | $P^*/EC$ | 0.70 | 0.68 | 0.70 | 0.69 | 0.64 | 0.62 | 0.62 | 0.64 | 0.59 | 0.59 | 0.59 |
| | $P_n=(P^*)-IBT$ −corporate income tax | 66.51 | 64.90 | 67.78 | 76.71 | 79.05 | 80.28 | 83.43 | 91.29 | 88.36 | 93.24 | 96.54 |
| B-79[b] | $IBT=$indirect business tax | 20.20 | 21.30 | 23.50 | 25.30 | 27.70 | 29.70 | 29.60 | 32.30 | 35.00 | 37.50 | 38.70 |
| B-80, B-82[c] | Corporate income tax | 12.40 | 10.20 | 17.90 | 22.60 | 19.40 | 20.30 | 17.60 | 22.00 | 22.00 | 21.40 | 19.00 |
| | $P=(P^*)-IBT$ | 78.91 | 75.10 | 85.68 | 99.31 | 98.45 | 100.58 | 101.03 | 113.29 | 110.36 | 114.64 | 115.54 |

| Sources | Variables | 1959 | 1960 | 1961 | 1962 | 1963 | 1964 | 1965 | 1966 | 1967 | 1968 | 1969 |
|---|---|---|---|---|---|---|---|---|---|---|---|---|
| | $S^* = VA^* - V^*$ | 278.42 | 286.46 | 296.54 | 320.20 | 337.71 | 364.54 | 395.00 | 430.65 | 454.40 | 493.63 | 523.83 |
| Table E.1 | $VA^*$ | 417.99 | 430.69 | 442.67 | 475.73 | 500.46 | 536.54 | 583.42 | 637.72 | 670.66 | 730.40 | 785.04 |
| Table G.2 | $V^*$ | 139.57 | 144.23 | 146.13 | 155.54 | 162.76 | 172.00 | 188.43 | 207.07 | 216.26 | 236.77 | 261.22 |
| | $S^*/V^*$ | 1.99 | 1.99 | 2.03 | 2.06 | 2.07 | 2.12 | 2.10 | 2.08 | 2.10 | 2.08 | 2.01 |
| | $SP^* = FP^* - NP^*$ | 278.34 | 285.93 | 295.95 | 319.54 | 337.07 | 364.00 | 394.44 | 430.09 | 453.42 | 493.12 | 523.25 |
| | $FP^* = GFP^* - D_p$ | 417.91 | 430.16 | 442.08 | 475.07 | 499.83 | 536.00 | 582.87 | 637.16 | 669.68 | 729.89 | 784.46 |
| | $GFP^* = TP^* - M'_p$ | 439.36 | 451.95 | 463.88 | 498.12 | 523.74 | 561.05 | 609.78 | 665.94 | 699.15 | 762.32 | 819.72 |
| Table E.2 | $TP^*$ | 774.29 | 795.67 | 811.42 | 869.52 | 913.42 | 973.35 | 1057.19 | 1149.69 | 1199.81 | 1307.46 | 1406.26 |
| Table E.1 | $M'_p$ | 334.93 | 343.72 | 347.54 | 371.40 | 389.68 | 412.31 | 447.41 | 483.74 | 500.66 | 545.14 | 586.54 |
| Table E.2 | $D_p$ | 21.44 | 21.78 | 21.80 | 23.05 | 23.91 | 25.05 | 26.91 | 28.79 | 29.48 | 32.43 | 35.26 |
| Table G.2 | $NP^* = V^*$ | 139.57 | 144.23 | 146.13 | 155.54 | 162.76 | 172.00 | 188.43 | 207.07 | 216.26 | 236.77 | 261.22 |
| | $P^+ = VA - EC$ | 169.96 | 172.24 | 180.54 | 197.78 | 209.98 | 224.91 | 247.88 | 266.95 | 273.48 | 293.98 | 304.13 |
| 112 1[a] | $VA = FD = NNP$ | 451.20 | 468.90 | 486.10 | 525.20 | 555.50 | 595.90 | 647.70 | 709.90 | 749.00 | 818.70 | 882.50 |
| 604B 1[a] | $EC$ | 281.24 | 296.66 | 305.56 | 327.42 | 345.52 | 370.99 | 399.82 | 442.95 | 475.52 | 524.72 | 578.37 |
| | $P^+/EC$ | 0.60 | 0.58 | 0.59 | 0.60 | 0.61 | 0.61 | 0.62 | 0.60 | 0.58 | 0.56 | 0.53 |
| | $P_n = (P^+) - IBT$ | 104.46 | 104.04 | 109.64 | 122.08 | 129.08 | 138.11 | 154.28 | 167.85 | 170.38 | 175.58 | 177.83 |
| | − corporate income tax | | | | | | | | | | | |
| B-79[b] | $IBT =$ indirect business tax | 41.90 | 45.50 | 48.10 | 51.70 | 54.70 | 58.80 | 62.70 | 65.40 | 70.40 | 79.00 | 86.60 |
| B-80, B-82[c] | Corporate income tax | 23.60 | 22.70 | 22.80 | 24.00 | 26.20 | 28.00 | 30.90 | 33.70 | 32.70 | 39.40 | 39.70 |
| | $P = (P^+) - IBT$ | 128.06 | 126.74 | 132.44 | 146.08 | 155.28 | 166.11 | 185.18 | 201.55 | 203.08 | 214.98 | 217.53 |

Table H.1 *(cont.)*

| Sources | Variables | 1970 | 1971 | 1972 | 1973 | 1974 | 1975 | 1976 | 1977 | 1978 | 1979 | 1980 |
|---|---|---|---|---|---|---|---|---|---|---|---|---|
| | $S^* = VA^* - V^*$ | 547.67 | 596.70 | 645.98 | 719.75 | 778.25 | 867.02 | 968.82 | 1083.13 | 1221.07 | 1346.24 | 1462.70 |
| Table E.1 | $VA^*$ | 818.11 | 884.22 | 970.28 | 1090.24 | 1176.75 | 1277.77 | 1428.45 | 1598.95 | 1810.27 | 2011.02 | 2169.23 |
| Table G.2 | $V^*$ | 270.43 | 287.53 | 324.30 | 370.49 | 398.50 | 410.75 | 459.63 | 515.81 | 589.20 | 664.78 | 706.53 |
| | $S^*/V^*$ | 2.03 | 2.08 | 1.99 | 1.94 | 1.95 | 2.11 | 2.11 | 2.10 | 2.07 | 2.03 | 2.07 |
| | $SP^* = FP^* - NP^*$ | 546.86 | 596.04 | 645.51 | 719.63 | 778.82 | 868.78 | 971.25 | 1086.66 | 1221.76 | 1347.44 | 1463.67 |
| | $FP^* = GFP^* - D_p$ | 817.30 | 883.56 | 969.81 | 1090.12 | 1177.33 | 1279.53 | 1430.88 | 1602.47 | 1810.97 | 2012.22 | 2170.20 |
| | $GFP^* = TP^* - M'_p$ | 853.88 | 923.12 | 1014.08 | 1142.52 | 1235.82 | 1344.71 | 1507.06 | 1690.83 | 1910.87 | 2122.76 | 2289.84 |
| Table E.2 | $TP^*$ | 1456.35 | 1567.82 | 1728.41 | 1979.91 | 2162.38 | 2368.48 | 2694.39 | 3058.10 | 3456.76 | 3833.25 | 4141.10 |
| Table E.1 | $M'_p$ | 602.47 | 644.70 | 714.33 | 837.40 | 926.56 | 1023.78 | 1187.33 | 1367.27 | 1545.89 | 1710.49 | 1851.27 |
| Table E.2 | $D_p$ | 36.59 | 39.56 | 44.27 | 52.40 | 58.50 | 65.17 | 76.18 | 88.36 | 99.90 | 110.54 | 119.64 |
| Table G.2 | $NP^* = V^*$ | 270.43 | 287.53 | 324.30 | 370.49 | 398.50 | 410.75 | 459.63 | 515.81 | 589.20 | 664.78 | 706.53 |
| | $P^* = VA - EC$ | 308.31 | 345.73 | 378.56 | 428.37 | 444.12 | 487.92 | 545.75 | 612.38 | 690.57 | 751.00 | 789.88 |
| 112 1[a] | $VA = FD = NNP$ | 926.60 | 1005.10 | 1104.80 | 1241.20 | 1335.40 | 1436.60 | 1603.60 | 1789.00 | 2019.80 | 2242.40 | 2428.10 |
| 604B 1[a] | $EC$ | 618.29 | 659.37 | 726.24 | 812.83 | 891.29 | 948.68 | 1057.85 | 1176.62 | 1329.23 | 1491.40 | 1638.22 |
| | $P^*/EC$ | 0.50 | 0.52 | 0.52 | 0.53 | 0.50 | 0.51 | 0.52 | 0.52 | 0.52 | 0.50 | 0.48 |
| | $P_n = (P^*) - IBT$ <br> − corporate income tax | 179.61 | 204.43 | 225.26 | 258.07 | 263.02 | 297.02 | 329.95 | 373.88 | 429.27 | 474.30 | 493.08 |
| B-79[b] | $IBT$ = indirect business tax | 94.30 | 103.60 | 111.40 | 121.00 | 129.30 | 140.00 | 151.60 | 165.50 | 177.80 | 188.70 | 212.00 |
| B-80, B-82[c] | Corporate income tax | 34.40 | 37.70 | 41.90 | 49.30 | 51.80 | 50.90 | 64.20 | 73.00 | 83.50 | 88.00 | 84.80 |
| | $P = (P^*) - IBT$ | 214.01 | 242.13 | 267.16 | 307.37 | 314.82 | 347.92 | 394.15 | 446.88 | 512.77 | 562.30 | 577.88 |

| Sources | Variables | 1981 | 1982 | 1983 | 1984 | 1985 | 1986 | 1987 | 1988 | 1989 |
|---|---|---|---|---|---|---|---|---|---|---|
| | $S^* = VA^* - V^*$ | 1668.19 | 1724.68 | 1865.80 | 2101.78 | 2258.68 | 2401.11 | 2563.38 | 2752.81 | 2943.35 |
| Table E.1 | $VA^*$ | 2440.54 | 2511.20 | 2705.53 | 3030.46 | 3226.68 | 3399.66 | 3624.28 | 3899.03 | 4149.75 |
| Table G.2 | $V^*$ | 772.35 | 786.53 | 839.73 | 928.68 | 967.99 | 998.55 | 1060.90 | 1146.22 | 1206.40 |
| | $S^*/V^*$ | 2.16 | 2.19 | 2.22 | 2.26 | 2.33 | 2.40 | 2.42 | 2.40 | 2.44 |
| | $SP^* = FP^* - NP^*$ | 1669.40 | 1726.06 | 1867.15 | 2103.70 | 2258.31 | 2389.25 | 2555.52 | 2755.18 | 2945.32 |
| | $FP^* = GFP^* - D_p$ | 2441.75 | 2512.59 | 2706.88 | 3032.38 | 3226.30 | 3387.80 | 3616.42 | 3901.40 | 4151.71 |
| | $GFP^* = TP^* - M'_p$ | 2576.06 | 2649.25 | 2851.36 | 3193.77 | 3395.53 | 3559.99 | 3797.93 | 4103.23 | 4363.57 |
| Table E.2 | $TP^*$ | 4654.40 | 4763.86 | 5086.97 | 5691.02 | 6014.18 | 6224.47 | 6606.59 | 7226.22 | 7641.82 |
| Table E.1 | $M'_p$ | 2078.34 | 2114.61 | 2235.61 | 2497.25 | 2618.65 | 2664.48 | 2808.66 | 3122.99 | 3278.25 |
| Table E.2 | $D_p$ | 134.31 | 136.66 | 144.48 | 161.39 | 169.23 | 172.19 | 181.51 | 201.83 | 211.86 |
| Table G.2 | $NP^* = V^*$ | 772.35 | 786.53 | 839.73 | 928.68 | 967.99 | 998.55 | 1060.90 | 1146.22 | 1206.40 |
| | $P^+ = VA - EC$ | 897.39 | 875.79 | 988.40 | 1142.88 | 1210.05 | 1260.05 | 1339.20 | 1454.30 | 1567.40 |
| 112 1[a] | $VA = FD = NNP$ | 2704.80 | 2782.80 | 3009.10 | 3356.60 | 3577.60 | 3771.50 | 4028.60 | 4359.40 | 4646.40 |
| 604B 1[a] | $EC$ | 1807.41 | 1907.01 | 2020.70 | 2213.93 | 2367.55 | 2511.40 | 2689.40 | 2905.10 | 3079.00 |
| | $P^+/EC$ | 0.50 | 0.46 | 0.49 | 0.52 | 0.51 | 0.50 | 0.50 | 0.50 | 0.51 |
| | $P_n = (P^+) - IBT$ −corporate income tax | 566.99 | 556.29 | 631.10 | 739.48 | 783.75 | 808.30 | 847.30 | 932.80 | 1021.30 |
| B-79[b] | $IBT =$ indirect business tax | 249.30 | 256.40 | 280.10 | 309.50 | 329.90 | 345.50 | 365.00 | 385.30 | 411.00 |
| B-80, B-82[c] | Corporate income tax | 81.10 | 63.10 | 77.20 | 93.90 | 96.40 | 106.30 | 126.90 | 136.20 | 135.10 |
| | $P = (P^+) - IBT$ | 648.09 | 619.39 | 708.30 | 833.38 | 880.15 | 914.60 | 974.20 | 1069.00 | 1156.40 |

[a] From NIPA (e.g. BEA 1986), where the first three digits (and following letter, if any) denote the relevant table number and subsequent digits the line numbers within those tables.

[b] Table from CEA (1991). For 1948–58, CEA (1971, table C-66) and CEA (1983, table B-77) were used.

327

*Glossary of variables in Table H.1*

| | |
|---|---|
| Dp | Depreciation of productive fixed capital |
| EC | Employee compensation |
| FD = NNP | Final demand = net national product (NIPA) |
| FP* | Marxian final product |
| GFP* | Marxian gross final product |
| $M'_p$ | Materials inputs into production |
| NP* = V* | Necessary product (consumption of productive workers) |
| $P^+$ | Property-type income (gross of all business taxes) |
| P | Property-type income (net of indirect business taxes) |
| $P_n$ | Property-type income (net of all business taxes) |
| S* | Surplus value (in money form) |
| S*/V* | Rate of surplus value |
| SP* | Surplus product |
| TP* | Marxian total product |
| V* | Variable capital (in money form) |
| VA | Net national product (NIPA) |
| VA* | Marxian net value added |

# I

## Rates of exploitation of productive and unproductive workers

Our calculations are based upon the formula for relative rates of exploitation, derived in Section 4.2:

$$\frac{(1+e_u)}{(1+e_p)} \approx \frac{h_u/h_p}{ec_u/ec_p},$$

where

$e_u, e_p$ = rates of exploitation of productive and unproductive workers;
$h_u, h_p$ = hours per unproductive and productive worker; and
$ec_u, ec_p$ = employee compensation per unproductive and productive worker.

Since the rate of exploitation of productive workers is simply the rate of surplus value, we substitute $S^*/V^*$ for $e_p$ and derive $e_u$:

$$e_u = \frac{h_u/h_p}{ec_u/ec_p} \cdot [1+S^*/V^*] - 1.$$

Individual steps in the calculation are shown next. Table I.1 gives the annual results and sources for the variables.

(1) The first step is to calculate the average hours of production workers $h_p$:

$$H_p'' = h_p'' \cdot L_p'' = \text{total hours of production and nonsupervisory workers in the private nonagricultural sector,}$$

where

$h_p''$ = average hours per production and nonsupervisory worker in the private nonagricultural sector, and
$L_p''$ = number of production and nonsupervisory workers in the private nonagricultural sector.

Table I.1. *Rates of exploitation of unproductive workers, 1948–89*

| | Sources | Variables | Units | 1948 | 1949 | 1950 | 1951 | 1952 | 1953 | 1954 |
|---|---|---|---|---|---|---|---|---|---|---|
| 1 | | $H_p^s = h_p^s \times L_p^s$ | thousand weekly hours | 1,379,560.00 | 1,306,464.60 | 1,367,090.20 | 1,445,377.50 | 1,462,055.70 | 1,492,682.40 | 1,418,391.60 |
| 2 | CEA, B-44 | $h_p^s$ | weekly hours | 40.00 | 39.40 | 39.80 | 39.90 | 39.90 | 39.60 | 39.10 |
| 3 | C-2$^a$ | $L_p^s$ | thousands | 34,489.00 | 33,159.00 | 34,349.00 | 36,225.00 | 36,643.00 | 37,694.00 | 36,276.00 |
| 4 | | $H_p' = H_p^s - (H_p)_t - (H_p)_{fire}$ | thousand weekly hours | 974,250.00 | 901,024.50 | 954,038.70 | 1,016,042.60 | 1,025,118.30 | 1,051,364.00 | 976,936.40 |
| 5 | | $(H_p)_t = (h_p)_t \times (L_p)_t$ | thousand weekly hours | 348,611.60 | 348,097.50 | 354,051.00 | 368,185.50 | 373,320.00 | 375,645.00 | 373,512.00 |
| 6 | BLS$^b$ | $(h_p)_t$ | weekly hours | 40.40 | 40.50 | 40.50 | 40.50 | 40.00 | 39.50 | 39.50 |
| 7 | BLS$^b$ | $(L_p)_t$ | thousands | 8,629.00 | 8,595.00 | 8,742.00 | 9,091.00 | 9,333.00 | 9,510.00 | 9,456.00 |
| 8 | | $(H_p)_{fire} = (h_p)_{fire} \times (L_p)_{fire}$ | thousand weekly hours | 56,698.40 | 57,342.60 | 59,000.50 | 61,149.40 | 63,617.40 | 65,673.40 | 67,943.20 |
| 9 | C-2, C-3$^a$ | $(h_p)_{fire}$ | weekly hours | 37.90 | 37.80 | 37.70 | 37.70 | 37.80 | 37.70 | 37.60 |
| 10 | C-2, C-3$^a$ | $(L_p)_{fire}$ | thousands | 1,496.00 | 1,517.00 | 1,565.00 | 1,622.00 | 1,683.00 | 1,742.00 | 1,807.00 |
| 11 | | $L_p' = L_p^s - (L_p)_t - (L_p)_{fire}$ | thousands | 24,364.00 | 23,047.00 | 24,042.00 | 25,512.00 | 25,627.00 | 26,442.00 | 25,013.00 |
| 12 | | $H_p = (H_p'/L_p') \times 52$ | hours/prod. worker/year | 2,079.34 | 2,032.94 | 2,063.47 | 2,070.96 | 2,080.08 | 2,067.58 | 2,030.97 |
| 13 | | $h_u = ht(L/L_u) - h_p(L_p/L_u)$ | hours/unpr. worker/year | 2,042.53 | 2,057.29 | 2,059.45 | 2,059.37 | 2,045.62 | 2,039.86 | 2,050.29 |
| 14 | Table J.1 | $h$ | hours/FEE/year | 2,063.36 | 2,043.94 | 2,061.66 | 2,065.52 | 2,063.42 | 2,054.12 | 2,040.61 |
| 15 | Table F.1 | $L$ | thousands | 58,301.00 | 56,919.00 | 58,600.00 | 62,366.00 | 63,457.00 | 64,247.00 | 62,324.00 |
| 16 | Table F.1 | $L_p$ | thousands | 32,993.91 | 31,201.36 | 32,226.07 | 33,123.36 | 32,768.23 | 33,042.76 | 31,230.31 |
| 17 | | $L_u = L - L_p$ | thousands | 25,307.09 | 25,717.64 | 26,373.93 | 29,242.64 | 30,688.77 | 31,204.24 | 31,093.69 |
| 18 | | $h_u/h_p$ | | 0.98 | 1.01 | 1.00 | 0.99 | 0.98 | 0.99 | 1.01 |
| 19 | Table G.2 | $ec_u$ | $/unpr. worker | 3,017.07 | 3,100.28 | 3,245.65 | 3,430.59 | 3,619.70 | 3,828.25 | 3,978.90 |
| 20 | Table G.2 | $ec_p$ | $/prod. worker/year | 2,679.59 | 2,724.93 | 2,890.85 | 3,197.52 | 3,387.82 | 3,552.62 | 3,584.71 |
| 21 | | $ec_u/ec_p$ | | 1.13 | 1.14 | 1.12 | 1.07 | 1.07 | 1.08 | 1.11 |
| 22 | | $(1+e_u)/(1+e_p) = (h_u/h_p)/(ec_u/ec_p)$ | | 0.87 | 0.89 | 0.89 | 0.93 | 0.92 | 0.92 | 0.91 |
| 23 | Table H.1 | $S^*/V^*$ | | 1.70 | 1.75 | 1.77 | 1.78 | 1.75 | 1.74 | 1.86 |
| 24 | | $e_u = [(1+e_u)/(1+e_p)] \times (1+S^*/V^*) - 1$ | | 1.35 | 1.44 | 1.47 | 1.57 | 1.53 | 1.51 | 1.60 |
| 25 | | $e_u/e_p$ | | 0.80 | 0.83 | 0.83 | 0.89 | 0.88 | 0.87 | 0.86 |

| | 1955 | 1956 | 1957 | 1958 | 1959 | 1960 | 1961 | 1962 | 1963 | 1964 | 1965 | 1966 |
|---|---|---|---|---|---|---|---|---|---|---|---|---|
| 1 | 1,485,000.00 | 1,512,853.50 | 1,489,299.20 | 1,409,408.00 | 1,485,120.00 | 1,486,717.60 | 1,466,375.40 | 1,508,487.30 | 1,534,656.40 | 1,569,672.00 | 1,640,386.40 | 1,708,011.40 |
| 2 | 39.60 | 39.30 | 38.80 | 38.50 | 39.00 | 38.60 | 38.60 | 38.70 | 38.80 | 38.70 | 38.80 | 38.60 |
| 3 | 37,500.00 | 38,495.00 | 38,384.00 | 36,608.00 | 38,080.00 | 38,516.00 | 37,989.00 | 38,979.00 | 39,553.00 | 40,560.00 | 42,278.00 | 44,249.00 |
| 4 | 1,032,778.60 | 1,052,112.30 | 1,031,952.50 | 958,322.50 | 1,015,936.60 | 1,008,764.60 | 993,639.10 | 1,027,767.20 | 1,046,407.90 | 1,070,193.80 | 1,123,356.20 | 1,178,402.80 |
| 5 | 381,195.00 | 388,380.30 | 384,020.10 | 375,809.60 | 391,375.60 | 398,159.00 | 391,962.20 | 397,280.00 | 402,336.00 | 411,935.10 | 428,196.60 | 438,522.00 |
| 6 | 39.40 | 39.10 | 38.70 | 38.60 | 38.80 | 38.60 | 38.30 | 38.20 | 38.10 | 37.90 | 37.70 | 37.10 |
| 7 | 9,675.00 | 9,933.00 | 9,923.00 | 9,736.00 | 10,087.00 | 10,315.00 | 10,234.00 | 10,400.00 | 10,560.00 | 10,869.00 | 11,358.00 | 11,820.00 |
| 8 | 71,026.40 | 72,360.90 | 73,326.60 | 75,275.90 | 77,807.80 | 79,794.00 | 80,774.10 | 83,440.10 | 85,912.50 | 87,543.10 | 88,833.60 | 91,086.60 |
| 9 | 37.60 | 36.90 | 36.70 | 37.10 | 37.30 | 37.20 | 36.90 | 37.30 | 37.50 | 37.30 | 37.20 | 37.30 |
| 10 | 1,889.00 | 1,961.00 | 1,998.00 | 2,029.00 | 2,086.00 | 2,145.00 | 2,189.00 | 2,237.00 | 2,291.00 | 2,347.00 | 2,388.00 | 2,442.00 |
| 11 | 25,936.00 | 26,601.00 | 26,463.00 | 24,843.00 | 25,907.00 | 26,056.00 | 25,566.00 | 26,342.00 | 26,702.00 | 27,344.00 | 28,532.00 | 29,987.00 |
| 12 | 2,070.65 | 2,056.68 | 2,027.79 | 2,005.91 | 2,039.17 | 2,013.19 | 2,021.01 | 2,028.85 | 2,037.80 | 2,035.18 | 2,047.33 | 2,043.45 |
| 13 | 2,049.77 | 2,052.51 | 2,038.20 | 2,059.53 | 2,056.04 | 2,059.73 | 2,055.10 | 2,057.79 | 2,054.85 | 2,058.45 | 2,038.63 | 2,022.79 |
| 14 | 2,060.22 | 2,054.57 | 2,033.15 | 2,034.46 | 2,048.14 | 2,038.21 | 2,039.64 | 2,044.68 | 2,047.17 | 2,048.07 | 2,042.52 | 2,031.97 |
| 15 | 63,366.00 | 64,522.00 | 64,779.00 | 62,765.00 | 64,099.00 | 64,989.00 | 64,740.00 | 66,091.00 | 66,655.00 | 67,874.00 | 70,128.00 | 73,301.00 |
| 16 | 31,714.45 | 31,864.18 | 31,433.17 | 29,348.97 | 30,020.46 | 30,046.71 | 29,363.23 | 29,936.58 | 30,013.06 | 30,279.87 | 31,365.18 | 32,565.57 |
| 17 | 31,651.55 | 32,657.82 | 33,345.83 | 33,416.03 | 34,078.54 | 34,942.29 | 35,376.77 | 36,154.42 | 36,641.94 | 37,594.13 | 38,762.82 | 40,735.43 |
| 18 | 0.99 | 1.00 | 1.01 | 1.03 | 1.01 | 1.02 | 1.01 | 1.01 | 1.01 | 1.01 | 1.00 | 0.99 |
| 19 | 4,177.14 | 4,404.69 | 4,610.83 | 4,834.57 | 5,051.31 | 5,269.27 | 5,425.74 | 5,679.79 | 5,913.26 | 6,242.06 | 6,403.30 | 6,723.18 |
| 20 | 3,800.09 | 4,042.90 | 4,231.17 | 4,351.67 | 4,649.18 | 4,800.21 | 4,976.64 | 5,195.52 | 5,422.92 | 5,680.27 | 6,007.47 | 6,358.51 |
| 21 | 1.10 | 1.09 | 1.09 | 1.11 | 1.09 | 1.10 | 1.09 | 1.09 | 1.09 | 1.10 | 1.07 | 1.06 |
| 22 | 0.90 | 0.92 | 0.92 | 0.92 | 0.93 | 0.93 | 0.93 | 0.93 | 0.93 | 0.92 | 0.93 | 0.94 |
| 23 | 1.90 | 1.84 | 1.88 | 2.01 | 1.99 | 1.99 | 2.03 | 2.06 | 2.07 | 2.12 | 2.10 | 2.08 |
| 24 | 1.61 | 1.60 | 1.66 | 1.78 | 1.78 | 1.78 | 1.83 | 1.84 | 1.84 | 1.87 | 1.89 | 1.88 |
| 25 | 0.85 | 0.87 | 0.88 | 0.89 | 0.89 | 0.90 | 0.90 | 0.89 | 0.89 | 0.88 | 0.90 | 0.91 |

Table I.1 *(cont.)*

| | 1967 | 1968 | 1969 | 1970 | 1971 | 1972 | 1973 | 1974 | 1975 | 1976 | 1977 | 1978 |
|---|---|---|---|---|---|---|---|---|---|---|---|---|
| 1 | 1,715,206.00 | 1,756,679.40 | 1,817,441.60 | 1,786,587.60 | 1,776,661.20 | 1,847,669.00 | 1,926,216.90 | 1,927,528.50 | 1,840,775.10 | 1,909,581.70 | 1,986,444.00 | 2,081,984.80 |
| 2 | 38.00 | 37.80 | 37.70 | 37.10 | 36.90 | 37.00 | 36.90 | 36.90 | 36.10 | 36.10 | 36.00 | 35.80 |
| 3 | 45,137.00 | 46,473.00 | 48,208.00 | 48,156.00 | 48,148.00 | 49,937.00 | 52,201.00 | 52,809.00 | 50,991.00 | 52,897.00 | 55,179.00 | 58,156.00 |
| 4 | 1,177,566.00 | 1,205,826.20 | 1,246,217.10 | 1,208,790.80 | 1,191,280.50 | 1,243,679.10 | 1,302,849.30 | 1,297,908.70 | 1,215,680.90 | 1,264,165.20 | 1,319,470.40 | 1,384,694.50 |
| 5 | 443,628.60 | 452,766.20 | 467,455.80 | 472,137.50 | 477,886.50 | 493,311.50 | 509,139.00 | 512,965.80 | 509,279.70 | 527,371.30 | 543,322.80 | 566,505.10 |
| 6 | 36.60 | 36.10 | 35.70 | 35.30 | 35.10 | 34.90 | 34.60 | 34.20 | 33.70 | 33.70 | 33.30 | 32.90 |
| 7 | 12,121.00 | 12,542.00 | 13,094.00 | 13,375.00 | 13,615.00 | 14,135.00 | 14,715.00 | 14,999.00 | 15,023.00 | 15,649.00 | 16,316.00 | 17,219.00 |
| 8 | 94,011.40 | 98,087.00 | 103,768.70 | 105,659.30 | 107,494.20 | 110,678.40 | 114,228.60 | 116,654.00 | 115,814.50 | 118,045.20 | 123,650.80 | 130,785.20 |
| 9 | 37.10 | 37.00 | 37.10 | 36.70 | 36.60 | 36.60 | 36.60 | 36.60 | 36.50 | 36.40 | 36.40 | 36.40 |
| 10 | 2,534.00 | 2,651.00 | 2,797.00 | 2,879.00 | 2,937.00 | 3,024.00 | 3,121.00 | 3,196.00 | 3,173.00 | 3,243.00 | 3,397.00 | 3,593.00 |
| 11 | 30,482.00 | 31,280.00 | 32,317.00 | 31,902.00 | 31,596.00 | 32,778.00 | 34,365.00 | 34,614.00 | 32,795.00 | 34,005.00 | 35,466.00 | 37,344.00 |
| 12 | 2,008.84 | 2,004.57 | 2,005.24 | 1,970.32 | 1,960.58 | 1,973.01 | 1,971.43 | 1,949.83 | 1,927.59 | 1,933.14 | 1,934.60 | 1,928.13 |
| 13 | 2,002.36 | 1,983.89 | 1,986.12 | 1,981.37 | 1,985.51 | 1,985.96 | 1,975.28 | 1,946.57 | 1,946.89 | 1,935.51 | 1,930.12 | 1,917.76 |
| 14 | 2,005.20 | 1,992.88 | 1,994.39 | 1,976.68 | 1,975.04 | 1,980.46 | 1,973.64 | 1,947.94 | 1,939.06 | 1,934.54 | 1,931.94 | 1,921.97 |
| 15 | 75,137.00 | 76,929.00 | 78,875.00 | 78,275.00 | 77,937.00 | 79,856.00 | 83,299.00 | 84,612.00 | 82,827.00 | 85,151.00 | 88,116.00 | 92,539.00 |
| 16 | 32,856.32 | 33,445.35 | 34,125.42 | 33,247.21 | 32,727.42 | 33,896.34 | 35,462.13 | 35,657.47 | 33,615.19 | 34,677.07 | 35,797.86 | 37,609.57 |
| 17 | 42,280.68 | 43,483.65 | 44,749.58 | 45,027.79 | 45,209.58 | 45,959.66 | 47,836.87 | 48,954.53 | 49,211.81 | 50,473.93 | 52,318.14 | 54,929.43 |
| 18 | 1.00 | 0.99 | 0.99 | 1.01 | 1.01 | 1.01 | 1.00 | 1.00 | 1.00 | 1.00 | 1.00 | 0.99 |
| 19 | 7,066.52 | 7,586.58 | 8,122.58 | 8,819.44 | 9,394.50 | 9,982.99 | 10,550.34 | 11,494.79 | 12,476.44 | 13,486.78 | 14,386.11 | 15,373.08 |
| 20 | 6,581.91 | 7,079.28 | 7,654.58 | 8,133.96 | 8,785.45 | 9,567.50 | 10,447.47 | 11,175.92 | 12,219.18 | 13,254.44 | 14,409.09 | 15,666.28 |
| 21 | 1.07 | 1.07 | 1.06 | 1.08 | 1.07 | 1.04 | 1.01 | 1.03 | 1.02 | 1.02 | 1.00 | 0.98 |
| 22 | 0.93 | 0.92 | 0.93 | 0.93 | 0.95 | 0.96 | 0.99 | 0.97 | 0.99 | 0.98 | 1.00 | 1.01 |
| 23 | 2.10 | 2.08 | 2.01 | 2.03 | 2.08 | 1.99 | 1.94 | 1.95 | 2.11 | 2.11 | 2.10 | 2.07 |
| 24 | 1.88 | 1.85 | 1.81 | 1.81 | 1.91 | 1.89 | 1.92 | 1.87 | 2.08 | 2.06 | 2.10 | 2.11 |
| 25 | 0.89 | 0.89 | 0.90 | 0.89 | 0.92 | 0.95 | 0.99 | 0.96 | 0.98 | 0.98 | 1.00 | 1.02 |

| | 1979 | 1980 | 1981 | 1982 | 1983 | 1984 | 1985 | 1986 | 1987 | 1988 | 1989 |
|---|---|---|---|---|---|---|---|---|---|---|---|
| 1 | 2,155,101.90 | 2,134,132.10 | 2,144,630.40 | 2,068,929.60 | 2,102,450.00 | 2,232,172.80 | 2,289,579.60 | 2,332,261.20 | 2,401,026.00 | 2,476,990.10 | 2,542,200.40 |
| 2 | 35.70 | 35.30 | 35.20 | 34.80 | 35.00 | 35.20 | 34.90 | 34.80 | 34.80 | 34.70 | 34.60 |
| 3 | 60,367.00 | 60,457.00 | 60,927.00 | 59,452.00 | 60,070.00 | 63,414.00 | 65,604.00 | 67,019.00 | 68,995.00 | 71,383.00 | 73,474.00 |
| 4 | 1,439,825.90 | 1,418,935.10 | 1,422,306.90 | 1,355,041.00 | 1,374,959.60 | 1,466,338.30 | 1,497,183.40 | 1,520,133.90 | 1,568,326.20 | 1,621,733.70 | 1,674,382.70 |
| 5 | 578,584.80 | 573,546.40 | 578,247.60 | 568,681.30 | 579,936.60 | 613,086.10 | 632,299.50 | 642,220.80 | 658,725.60 | 677,824.50 | 694,431.00 |
| 6 | 32.60 | 32.20 | 32.20 | 31.90 | 31.80 | 31.90 | 31.50 | 31.20 | 31.20 | 31.10 | 31.00 |
| 7 | 17,748.00 | 17,812.00 | 17,958.00 | 17,827.00 | 18,237.00 | 19,219.00 | 20,073.00 | 20,584.00 | 21,113.00 | 21,795.00 | 22,401.00 |
| 8 | 136,691.20 | 141,650.60 | 145,163.70 | 144,582.80 | 147,261.60 | 154,358.50 | 160,706.00 | 169,078.00 | 174,530.40 | 173,217.50 | 174,346.00 |
| 9 | 36.20 | 36.20 | 36.30 | 36.20 | 36.20 | 36.50 | 36.40 | 36.40 | 36.30 | 35.90 | 35.80 |
| 10 | 3,776.00 | 3,913.00 | 3,999.00 | 3,994.00 | 4,068.00 | 4,229.00 | 4,415.00 | 4,645.00 | 4,808.00 | 4,825.00 | 4,870.00 |
| 11 | 38,843.00 | 38,732.00 | 38,970.00 | 37,631.00 | 37,765.00 | 39,966.00 | 41,116.00 | 41,790.00 | 43,074.00 | 44,763.00 | 46,203.00 |
| 12 | 1,927.53 | 1,905.00 | 1,897.87 | 1,872.45 | 1,893.23 | 1,907.86 | 1,893.51 | 1,891.53 | 1,893.32 | 1,883.93 | 1,884.46 |
| 13 | 1,910.36 | 1,900.67 | 1,890.02 | 1,909.21 | 1,910.08 | 1,904.83 | 1,893.96 | 1,866.49 | 1,860.33 | 1,870.20 | 1,858.90 |
| 14 | 1,917.30 | 1,902.38 | 1,893.09 | 1,895.20 | 1,903.75 | 1,905.97 | 1,893.79 | 1,875.64 | 1,872.36 | 1,875.22 | 1,868.16 |
| 15 | 95,525.00 | 95,734.00 | 96,582.00 | 94,990.00 | 95,952.00 | 100,607.00 | 103,031.00 | 104,831.00 | 107,891.00 | 110,962.00 | 113,511.00 |
| 16 | 38,598.17 | 37,863.38 | 37,737.65 | 36,202.80 | 36,087.93 | 37,871.95 | 38,229.04 | 38,312.30 | 39,343.69 | 40,538.03 | 41,148.07 |
| 17 | 56,926.83 | 57,870.62 | 58,844.35 | 58,787.20 | 59,864.07 | 62,735.05 | 64,801.96 | 66,518.70 | 68,547.31 | 70,423.97 | 72,362.93 |
| 18 | 0.99 | 1.00 | 1.02 | 1.02 | 1.01 | 1.00 | 1.00 | 0.99 | 0.98 | 0.99 | 0.99 |
| 19 | 16,617.40 | 18,432.98 | 20,129.64 | 21,860.07 | 22,719.44 | 23,536.17 | 24,655.20 | 25,877.64 | 27,020.58 | 28,483.03 | 29,443.84 |
| 20 | 17,223.18 | 18,659.88 | 20,466.34 | 21,725.60 | 23,269.07 | 24,521.58 | 25,320.89 | 26,063.32 | 26,964.96 | 28,275.23 | 29,318.41 |
| 21 | 0.96 | 0.99 | 0.98 | 1.01 | 0.98 | 0.96 | 0.97 | 0.99 | 1.00 | 1.01 | 1.00 |
| 22 | 1.03 | 1.01 | 1.01 | 1.01 | 1.03 | 1.04 | 1.03 | 0.99 | 0.98 | 0.99 | 0.98 |
| 23 | 2.03 | 2.07 | 2.16 | 2.19 | 2.22 | 2.26 | 2.33 | 2.40 | 2.42 | 2.40 | 2.44 |
| 24 | 2.11 | 2.10 | 2.20 | 2.24 | 2.33 | 2.40 | 2.42 | 2.38 | 2.35 | 2.35 | 2.38 |
| 25 | 1.04 | 1.01 | 1.02 | 1.02 | 1.05 | 1.06 | 1.04 | 0.99 | 0.97 | 0.98 | 0.97 |

[a] Table number from BLS (1991a).
[b] BLS (1991b, vol. I., p. 730).

333

*Glossary of variables in Table I.1*

| | |
|---|---|
| $ec_p$ | Employee compensation per productive worker |
| $ec_u$ | Employee compensation per unproductive worker |
| $e_p$ | Rate of exploitation of productive workers |
| $e_u$ | Rate of exploitation of unproductive workers |
| $h$ | Average hours worked per full-time equivalent employee in domestic industries |
| $h_p$ | Average productive worker hours |
| $H'_p$ | Production worker hours in the roughly productive sectors |
| $H''_p$ | Total hours of production and nonsupervisory workers in the private nonagricultural sector |
| $h''_p$ | Average hours of production and nonsupervisory workers in the private nonagricultural sector |
| $(H_p)_{fire}$ | Total "production" worker hours in finance, insurance, and real estate |
| $(h_p)_{fire}$ | Hours per "production" worker in finance, insurance, and real estate |
| $(H_p)_t$ | Total "production" worker hours in trade |
| $(h_p)_t$ | Hours per "production" worker in trade |
| $h_u$ | Average unproductive worker hours |
| $L$ | Total employment |
| $L_p$ | Total productive employment |
| $L'_p$ | Number of production workers in the roughly productive sectors |
| $L''_p$ | Number of production and nonsupervisory workers in the private nonagricultural sector |
| $(L_p)_{fire}$ | Number of "production" workers in finance, insurance, and real estate |
| $(L_p)_t$ | Number of "production" workers in trade |
| $L_u$ | Total unproductive employment |

(2) The private nonagricultural sector includes unproductive sectors such as trade, finance, and real estate. Hence we need to adjust total hours for this, in order to better approximate hours per productive worker $h_p$. We calculate as follows:

$$(H_p)_t = (h_p)_t \cdot (L_p)_t = \text{total "production" worker hours in trade;}$$

$$(H_p)_{fire} = (h_p)_{fire} \cdot (L_p)_{fire} = \text{total "production" worker hours in finance, insurance, and real estate;}$$

$$H'_p = H''_p - (H_p)_t - (H_p)_{fire} = \text{production worker hours in the roughly productive sectors;}$$

$$L'_p = L''_p - (L_p)_t - (L_p)_{fire} = \text{number of production workers in the roughly productive sectors;}$$

$$h_p = H'_p / L'_p = \text{average productive worker hours.}$$

(3) Total productive worker hours can now be calculated as the product of average hours $h_p$ (just calculated) and our previously calculated total productive employment $L_p$ (which includes self-employed persons) from Table F.1:

$$H_p = h_p \cdot L_p.$$

(4) Finally, we can estimate average hours $h_u$ of unproductive workers by noting that total hours of all workers $H = H_u + H_p = h_u \cdot L_u + h_p \cdot L_p$, that total employment $L = L_u + L_p$, and that average hours worked $h = H/L$, so that

$$h_u = h \cdot (L/L_u) - h_p \cdot (L_p/L_u).$$

# J

## Measures of productivity

The Marxian measure of productivity q* is the primary one. It is derived by deflating our measure of total product TP* by the GNP price deflator py (in 1982 dollars), and then dividing by hours of productive labor $H_p$ to obtain hourly productivity. Because orthodox measures of productivity are based on value added rather than total product, we also calculate a quasi-Marxian measure y*, which is real Marxian value added per productive worker hour. This differs greatly in level from q*, but has essentially the same trend, because the proportion C*/TP* of circulating constant capital to total product is extremely stable (see Section 5.2, Figure 5.6, and Appendix E). These Marxian productivity measures are listed in Table J.1.

Orthodox measures of productivity vary considerably. The most common one is real GDP per employee hour, which we call y. Also available is the BLS measure $y_1$ of real GDP originating in the nonfarm business sector by their estimate of hours of persons engaged in production (employees plus self-employed persons) in this same sector. Since the BLS measure is only available in index-number form, we calculate an equivalent measure of productivity $y_2$ in the nonfarm business sector, as the ratio of real GDP to total hours of all persons engaged. The total-hours measure H2 is in turn calculated by multiplying the average hours per full-time equivalent employee in domestic industries (from NIPA) by estimated nonfarm total employment (based on our employment data in Table F.1).

Table J.1 presents the calculations of Marxian and orthodox measures of productivity, along with associated measures of hours worked.

## Glossary of variables in Table J.1

| | |
|---|---|
| FEE | Total full-time equivalent employees in domestic industries |
| GDP | Total GDP |
| GDP2 | Nonfarm private business GDP |
| GDP2r | Nonfarm private business GDP in 1982 dollars |
| GDPr | Total GDP in 1982 dollars |
| GFPr | Marxian gross final product in 1982 dollars |
| GFP* | Marxian gross final product |
| h | Average annual full-time equivalent employee hours in domestic industries |
| H1 | Total hours worked in domestic industries |
| H2 | Total hours worked in nonfarm private businesses by workers and the self-employed |
| $H_p$ | Total hours worked by productive workers |
| $h_p$ | Average annual productive worker hours |
| L | Total employment |
| L' | Total nonfarm, nongovernment employment |
| $L_{farm}$ | Total employment in farms |
| $L_{govnt}$ | Total employment in government |
| $L_p$ | Total productive employment |
| py | Implicit price deflator for GNP (1982 = 100) |
| q* | Marxian measure of productivity: total real product per productive worker hour |
| TPr | Total product in 1982 dollars |
| TP* | Marxian total product |
| y* | Quasi-Marxian measure of productivity: real Marxian value added per productive worker hour |
| y | Orthodox measure of productivity: GDP per full- and part-time workers' hours |
| $y_1$ | BLS measure of productivity (1948 = 100): nonfarm private business product per person engaged in production |
| $y_2$ | Orthodox measure of productivity: nonfarm real GDP per hour of persons engaged in production |

## Table J.1. *Productivity of labor, 1948–89*

| | Sources[a] | Variables | Units | 1948 | 1949 |
|---|---|---|---|---|---|
| 1 | | $q^* = TPr/H_p$ | 1982 \$/hr by prod. workers | 27.56 | 28.98 |
| 2 | | $q^*$ (index numbers, 1948 = 100) | | 100.00 | 105.15 |
| 3 | | $TPr = TP^*/py$ | billions of 1982 \$ | 1,890.71 | 1,838.13 |
| 4 | Table E.2 | $TP^*$ | billions of \$ | 446.21 | 431.96 |
| 5 | 704 1 | py (price deflator for GNP) | | 23.6 | 23.5 |
| 6 | see line 23 | $H_p$ | millions | 68,605.51 | 63,430.64 |
| 7 | | $y^* = GFPr/H_p$ | 1982 \$/hr by prod. workers | 15.30 | 16.30 |
| 8 | | $y^*$ (index numbers, 1948 = 100) | | 100.00 | 106.50 |
| 9 | | $GFPr = GFP^*/py$ | billions of 1982 \$ | 1,049.74 | 1,033.61 |
| 10 | Table H.1 | $GFP^*$ | billions of \$ | 247.7 | 242.9 |
| 11 | see line 23 | $H_p$ | millions | 68,605.51 | 63,430.64 |
| 12 | | $y = GDPr/H1$ | 1982 \$/hr pt & ft workers | 11.11 | 11.51 |
| 13 | | $y$ (index numbers, 1948 = 100) | | 100.00 | 103.61 |
| 14 | | $GDPr = GDP/py$ | billions of 1982 \$ | 1,102.12 | 1,102.13 |
| 15 | 107 2 | GDP | billions of \$ | 260.10 | 259.00 |
| 16 | see line 28 | $H1 =$ total hrs. in domestic industries | millions | 99,227 | 95,769 |
| 17 | B-46[b] | $y_1$ (BLS; 1948 = 100) | GDP in 1982 \$/hr by PEP | 100.0 | 101.7 |
| 18 | | $y_2 = GDP2r/H2$ (nonfarm prv. bus.) | 1982 \$/hr by workers & SEP | 9.59 | 10.03 |
| 19 | | $y_2$ (index numbers, 1948 = 100) | | 100.00 | 104.57 |
| 20 | | $GDP2r = GDP2/py$ | billions of 1982 \$ | 908.47 | 907.66 |
| 21 | 107 4 | GDP2 (nonfarm prv. bus.) | billions of \$ | 214.40 | 213.30 |
| 22 | see line 26 | $H2 =$ total hrs. in prv. non-agr. | millions | 94,683 | 90,467 |
| | | Derivation of hours worked | | | |
| 23 | | $H_p = h_p \times L_p$ | millions | 68,605.51 | 63,430.64 |
| 24 | Table I.1 | $h_p$ | hours/prod. worker/year | 2,079.34 | 2,032.94 |
| 25 | Table F.1 | $L_p$ | thousands | 32,993.91 | 31,201.36 |
| 26 | | $H2 = h \times L'$ | millions | 94,683.48 | 90,467.01 |
| 27 | | $h = H1/FEE$ domestic industries | hours/worker/year | 2,063.36 | 2,043.94 |
| 28 | 611 2 | $H1 =$ total hrs. in domestic industries | millions | 99,227 | 95,769 |
| 29 | 607B 2 | FEE domestic industries | thousands | 48,090.00 | 46,855.00 |
| 30 | | $L' = L - L_{govnt} - L_{farm}$ | thousands | 45,888.00 | 44,261.00 |
| 31 | Table F.1 | $L$ | thousands | 58,301 | 56,919 |
| 32 | Table F.1 | $L_{govnt}$ | thousands | 6,063.00 | 6,487.00 |
| 33 | 610B 5 | $L_{farm}$ | thousands | 6,350.00 | 6,171.00 |

[a] Unless otherwise indicated, all data come from NIPA (e.g. BEA 1986), where the first three digits (and following letter, if any) denote the relevant table number and subsequent digits the line numbers within those tables.
[b] Table number from CEA (1989).

| 1950 | 1951 | 1952 | 1953 | 1954 | 1955 | 1956 | 1957 | 1958 |
|---|---|---|---|---|---|---|---|---|
| 30.30 | 32.04 | 33.02 | 34.21 | 35.77 | 36.55 | 37.32 | 38.67 | 40.70 |
| 109.96 | 116.25 | 119.82 | 124.14 | 129.78 | 132.63 | 135.41 | 140.32 | 147.69 |
| 2,015.13 | 2,197.70 | 2,250.80 | 2,337.35 | 2,268.55 | 2,400.42 | 2,445.57 | 2,464.96 | 2,396.20 |
| 481.62 | 551.62 | 573.95 | 605.37 | 596.63 | 652.91 | 687.21 | 717.30 | 711.67 |
| 23.9 | 25.1 | 25.5 | 25.9 | 26.3 | 27.2 | 28.1 | 29.1 | 29.7 |
| 66,497.62 | 68,597.01 | 68,160.46 | 68,318.52 | 63,427.87 | 65,669.66 | 65,534.53 | 63,740.01 | 58,871.32 |
| 16.93 | 17.83 | 18.39 | 19.03 | 20.10 | 20.48 | 20.86 | 21.71 | 23.09 |
| 110.64 | 116.54 | 120.18 | 124.36 | 131.35 | 133.82 | 136.32 | 141.88 | 150.88 |
| 1,125.76 | 1,223.22 | 1,253.36 | 1,300.05 | 1,274.76 | 1,344.63 | 1,366.90 | 1,383.76 | 1,359.16 |
| 269.1 | 307.0 | 319.6 | 336.7 | 335.3 | 365.7 | 384.1 | 402.7 | 403.7 |
| 66,497.62 | 68,597.01 | 68,160.46 | 68,318.52 | 63,427.87 | 65,669.66 | 65,534.53 | 63,740.01 | 58,871.32 |
| 11.98 | 12.14 | 12.34 | 12.68 | 13.02 | 13.27 | 13.26 | 13.52 | 13.87 |
| 107.82 | 109.27 | 111.08 | 114.16 | 117.22 | 119.51 | 119.39 | 121.72 | 124.89 |
| 1,200.00 | 1,320.32 | 1,370.20 | 1,426.64 | 1,407.98 | 1,482.72 | 1,513.17 | 1,538.14 | 1,528.28 |
| 286.80 | 331.40 | 349.40 | 369.50 | 370.30 | 403.30 | 425.20 | 447.60 | 453.90 |
| 100,205 | 108,785 | 111,053 | 112,508 | 108,142 | 111,699 | 114,113 | 113,771 | 110,174 |
| 108.2 | 111.4 | 114.1 | 116.5 | 118.3 | 121.7 | 122.4 | 124.7 | 127.6 |
| 10.57 | 10.87 | 11.20 | 11.60 | 11.95 | 12.29 | 12.39 | 12.63 | 12.81 |
| 110.16 | 113.27 | 116.71 | 120.92 | 124.50 | 128.06 | 129.12 | 131.65 | 133.47 |
| 997.07 | 1,080.08 | 1,124.31 | 1,183.01 | 1,166.54 | 1,245.22 | 1,286.12 | 1,305.84 | 1,275.76 |
| 238.30 | 271.10 | 286.70 | 306.40 | 306.80 | 338.70 | 361.40 | 380.00 | 378.90 |
| 94,331 | 99,379 | 100,404 | 101,968 | 97,653 | 101,342 | 103,815 | 103,378 | 99,621 |
| 66,497.62 | 68,597.01 | 68,160.46 | 68,318.52 | 63,427.87 | 65,669.66 | 65,534.53 | 63,740.01 | 58,871.32 |
| 2,063.47 | 2,070.96 | 2,080.08 | 2,067.58 | 2,030.97 | 2,070.65 | 2,056.68 | 2,027.79 | 2,005.91 |
| 32,226.07 | 33,123.36 | 32,768.23 | 33,042.76 | 31,230.31 | 31,714.45 | 31,864.18 | 31,433.17 | 29,348.97 |
| 94,331.33 | 99,378.60 | 100,403.71 | 101,968.33 | 97,653.28 | 101,342.27 | 103,815.48 | 103,377.54 | 99,621.27 |
| 2,061.66 | 2,065.52 | 2,063.42 | 2,054.12 | 2,040.61 | 2,060.22 | 2,054.57 | 2,033.15 | 2,034.46 |
| 100,205 | 108,785 | 111,053 | 112,508 | 108,142 | 111,699 | 114,113 | 113,771 | 110,174 |
| 48,604.00 | 52,667.00 | 53,820.00 | 54,772.00 | 52,995.00 | 54,217.00 | 55,541.00 | 55,958.00 | 54,154.00 |
| 45,755.00 | 48,113.00 | 48,659.00 | 49,641.00 | 47,855.00 | 49,190.00 | 50,529.00 | 50,846.00 | 48,967.00 |
| 58,600 | 62,366 | 63,457 | 64,247 | 62,324 | 63,366 | 64,522 | 64,779 | 62,765 |
| 6,718.00 | 8,518.00 | 9,218.00 | 9,204.00 | 9,049.00 | 8,939.00 | 9,031.00 | 9,209.00 | 9,231.00 |
| 6,127.00 | 5,735.00 | 5,580.00 | 5,402.00 | 5,420.00 | 5,237.00 | 4,962.00 | 4,724.00 | 4,567.00 |

*(more)*

Table J.1 *(cont.)*

| | 1959 | 1960 | 1961 | 1962 | 1963 | 1964 | 1965 | 1966 |
|---|---|---|---|---|---|---|---|---|
| 1 | 41.61 | 42.57 | 43.82 | 44.88 | 46.09 | 48.01 | 48.71 | 49.36 |
| 2 | 150.97 | 154.46 | 159.02 | 162.84 | 167.26 | 174.20 | 176.74 | 179.11 |
| 3 | 2,547.01 | 2,574.98 | 2,600.71 | 2,725.78 | 2,819.18 | 2,958.52 | 3,127.77 | 3,284.82 |
| 4 | 774.29 | 795.67 | 811.42 | 869.52 | 913.42 | 973.35 | 1,057.19 | 1,149.69 |
| 5 | 30.4 | 30.9 | 31.2 | 31.9 | 32.4 | 32.9 | 33.8 | 35.0 |
| 6 | 61,216.73 | 60,489.83 | 59,343.48 | 60,736.75 | 61,160.48 | 61,625.11 | 64,214.98 | 66,546.13 |
| 7 | 23.61 | 24.18 | 25.05 | 25.71 | 26.43 | 27.67 | 28.09 | 28.59 |
| 8 | 154.30 | 158.02 | 163.74 | 168.02 | 172.73 | 180.85 | 183.61 | 186.86 |
| 9 | 1,445.26 | 1,462.61 | 1,486.80 | 1,561.50 | 1,616.48 | 1,705.31 | 1,804.07 | 1,902.69 |
| 10 | 439.4 | 451.9 | 463.9 | 498.1 | 523.7 | 561.0 | 609.8 | 665.9 |
| 11 | 61,216.73 | 60,489.83 | 59,343.48 | 60,736.75 | 61,160.48 | 61,625.11 | 64,214.98 | 66,546.13 |
| 12 | 14.21 | 14.34 | 14.72 | 15.05 | 15.40 | 15.88 | 16.18 | 16.32 |
| 13 | 127.97 | 129.07 | 132.57 | 135.49 | 138.66 | 142.98 | 145.68 | 146.94 |
| 14 | 1,620.72 | 1,656.31 | 1,698.72 | 1,787.15 | 1,858.02 | 1,958.66 | 2,068.93 | 2,189.71 |
| 15 | 492.70 | 511.80 | 530.00 | 570.10 | 602.00 | 644.40 | 699.30 | 766.40 |
| 16 | 114,022 | 115,534 | 115,368 | 118,759 | 120,646 | 123,339 | 127,866 | 134,171 |
| 17 | 131.7 | 133.1 | 137.5 | 141.8 | 147.0 | 152.9 | 156.7 | 160.3 |
| 18 | 13.33 | 13.41 | 13.79 | 14.16 | 14.56 | 15.08 | 15.36 | 15.51 |
| 19 | 138.89 | 139.75 | 143.74 | 147.60 | 151.70 | 157.12 | 160.07 | 161.63 |
| 20 | 1,374.67 | 1,399.35 | 1,426.28 | 1,500.63 | 1,562.35 | 1,654.10 | 1,745.56 | 1,834.00 |
| 21 | 417.90 | 432.40 | 445.00 | 478.70 | 506.20 | 544.20 | 590.00 | 641.90 |
| 22 | 103,153 | 104,358 | 103,414 | 105,959 | 107,339 | 109,719 | 113,654 | 118,263 |
| 23 | 61,216.73 | 60,489.83 | 59,343.48 | 60,736.75 | 61,160.48 | 61,625.11 | 64,214.98 | 66,546.13 |
| 24 | 2,039.17 | 2,013.19 | 2,021.01 | 2,028.85 | 2,037.80 | 2,035.18 | 2,047.33 | 2,043.45 |
| 25 | 30,020.46 | 30,046.71 | 29,363.23 | 29,936.58 | 30,013.06 | 30,279.87 | 31,365.18 | 32,565.57 |
| 26 | 103,152.52 | 104,358.48 | 103,413.69 | 105,959.31 | 107,339.38 | 109,719.32 | 113,654.13 | 118,262.70 |
| 27 | 2,048.14 | 2,038.21 | 2,039.64 | 2,044.68 | 2,047.17 | 2,048.07 | 2,042.52 | 2,031.97 |
| 28 | 114,022 | 115,534 | 115,368 | 118,759 | 120,646 | 123,339 | 127,866 | 134,171 |
| 29 | 55,671.00 | 56,684.00 | 56,563.00 | 58,082.00 | 58,933.00 | 60,222.00 | 62,602.00 | 66,030.00 |
| 30 | 50,364.00 | 51,201.00 | 50,702.00 | 51,822.00 | 52,433.00 | 53,572.00 | 55,644.00 | 58,201.00 |
| 31 | 64,099 | 64,989 | 64,740 | 66,091 | 66,655 | 67,874 | 70,128 | 73,301 |
| 32 | 9,309.00 | 9,545.00 | 9,894.00 | 10,268.00 | 10,460.00 | 10,770.00 | 11,118.00 | 12,023.00 |
| 33 | 4,426.00 | 4,243.00 | 4,144.00 | 4,001.00 | 3,762.00 | 3,532.00 | 3,366.00 | 3,077.00 |

| 1967 | 1968 | 1969 | 1970 | 1971 | 1972 | 1973 | 1974 | 1975 |
|---|---|---|---|---|---|---|---|---|
| 50.64 | 51.73 | 51.63 | 52.93 | 55.03 | 55.58 | 57.21 | 57.60 | 61.64 |
| 183.73 | 187.70 | 187.36 | 192.07 | 199.69 | 201.67 | 207.60 | 208.99 | 223.67 |
| 3,342.09 | 3,468.05 | 3,533.32 | 3,467.51 | 3,531.12 | 3,717.01 | 3,999.83 | 4,004.40 | 3,994.07 |
| 1,199.81 | 1,307.46 | 1,406.26 | 1,456.35 | 1,567.82 | 1,728.41 | 1,979.91 | 2,162.38 | 2,368.48 |
| 35.9 | 37.7 | 39.8 | 42.0 | 44.4 | 46.5 | 49.5 | 54.0 | 59.3 |
| 66,003.05 | 67,043.56 | 68,429.60 | 65,507.62 | 64,164.82 | 66,877.80 | 69,911.08 | 69,525.84 | 64,796.39 |
| 29.51 | 30.16 | 30.10 | 31.04 | 32.40 | 32.61 | 33.01 | 32.92 | 35.00 |
| 192.84 | 197.11 | 196.71 | 202.83 | 211.76 | 213.12 | 215.77 | 215.13 | 228.72 |
| 1,947.50 | 2,022.06 | 2,059.60 | 2,033.06 | 2,079.09 | 2,180.82 | 2,308.11 | 2,288.56 | 2,267.64 |
| 699.2 | 762.3 | 819.7 | 853.9 | 923.1 | 1,014.1 | 1,142.5 | 1,235.8 | 1,344.7 |
| 66,003.05 | 67,043.56 | 68,429.60 | 65,507.62 | 64,164.82 | 66,877.80 | 69,911.08 | 69,525.84 | 64,796.39 |
| 16.57 | 16.89 | 16.82 | 17.06 | 17.61 | 17.97 | 18.09 | 17.92 | 18.25 |
| 149.16 | 152.06 | 151.46 | 153.61 | 158.57 | 161.76 | 162.90 | 161.37 | 164.34 |
| 2,257.38 | 2,349.87 | 2,404.77 | 2,400.48 | 2,462.61 | 2,584.09 | 2,713.33 | 2,691.30 | 2,665.94 |
| 810.40 | 885.90 | 957.10 | 1,008.20 | 1,093.40 | 1,201.60 | 1,343.30 | 1,453.30 | 1,580.90 |
| 136,251 | 139,131 | 142,950 | 140,696 | 139,823 | 143,825 | 149,963 | 150,157 | 146,052 |
| 164.3 | 169.2 | 168.6 | 169.4 | 174.5 | 179.8 | 183.7 | 180.2 | 183.5 |
| 15.83 | 16.18 | 16.04 | 16.07 | 16.49 | 16.80 | 16.74 | 16.58 | 16.93 |
| 165.01 | 168.65 | 167.19 | 167.50 | 171.86 | 175.06 | 174.46 | 172.85 | 176.40 |
| 1,888.02 | 1,963.93 | 2,007.29 | 1,978.81 | 2,021.40 | 2,126.67 | 2,218.99 | 2,203.52 | 2,172.68 |
| 677.80 | 740.40 | 798.90 | 831.10 | 897.50 | 988.90 | 1,098.40 | 1,189.90 | 1,288.40 |
| 119,247 | 121,368 | 125,128 | 123,129 | 122,585 | 126,613 | 132,559 | 132,867 | 128,370 |
| 66,003.05 | 67,043.56 | 68,429.60 | 65,507.62 | 64,164.82 | 66,877.80 | 69,911.08 | 69,525.84 | 64,976.39 |
| 2,008.84 | 2,004.57 | 2,005.24 | 1,970.32 | 1,960.58 | 1,973.01 | 1,971.43 | 1,949.83 | 1,927.59 |
| 32,856.32 | 33,445.35 | 34,125.42 | 33,247.21 | 32,727.42 | 33,896.34 | 35,462.13 | 35,657.47 | 33,615.19 |
| 119,246.95 | 121,368.45 | 125,128.12 | 123,129.26 | 122,584.85 | 126,612.82 | 132,559.45 | 132,867.08 | 128,369.70 |
| 2,005.20 | 1,992.88 | 1,994.39 | 1,976.68 | 1,975.04 | 1,980.46 | 1,973.64 | 1,947.94 | 1,939.06 |
| 136,251 | 139,131 | 142,950 | 140,696 | 139,823 | 143,825 | 149,963 | 150,157 | 146,052 |
| 67,949.00 | 69,814.00 | 71,676.00 | 71,178.00 | 70,795.00 | 72,622.00 | 75,983.00 | 77,085.00 | 75,321.00 |
| 59,469.00 | 60,901.00 | 62,740.00 | 62,291.00 | 62,067.00 | 63,931.00 | 67,165.00 | 68,209.00 | 66,202.00 |
| 75,137 | 76,929 | 78,875 | 78,275 | 77,937 | 79,856 | 83,299 | 84,612 | 82,827 |
| 12,695.00 | 13,099.00 | 13,325.00 | 13,251.00 | 13,198.00 | 13,231.00 | 13,418.00 | 13,630.00 | 13,902.00 |
| 2,973.00 | 2,929.00 | 2,810.00 | 2,733.00 | 2,672.00 | 2,694.00 | 2,716.00 | 2,773.00 | 2,723.00 |

*(more)*

Table J.1 *(cont.)*

| | 1976 | 1977 | 1978 | 1979 | 1980 | 1981 | 1982 | 1983 |
|---|---|---|---|---|---|---|---|---|
| 1 | 63.70 | 65.61 | 66.02 | 65.55 | 66.99 | 69.13 | 70.28 | 71.66 |
| 2 | 231.13 | 238.08 | 239.57 | 237.85 | 243.08 | 250.86 | 255.00 | 260.02 |
| 3 | 4,270.03 | 4,543.98 | 4,787.75 | 4,876.91 | 4,832.09 | 4,951.49 | 4,763.86 | 4,896.03 |
| 4 | 2,694.39 | 3,058.10 | 3,456.76 | 3,833.25 | 4,141.10 | 4,654.40 | 4,763.86 | 5,086.97 |
| 5 | 63.1 | 67.3 | 72.2 | 78.6 | 85.7 | 94.0 | 100.0 | 103.9 |
| 6 | 67,035.79 | 69,254.48 | 72,516.17 | 74,399.03 | 72,129.89 | 71,621.12 | 67,787.90 | 68,322.81 |
| 7 | 35.63 | 36.28 | 36.50 | 36.30 | 37.04 | 38.26 | 39.08 | 40.17 |
| 8 | 232.85 | 237.09 | 238.53 | 237.24 | 242.09 | 250.07 | 255.42 | 262.51 |
| 9 | 2,388.36 | 2,512.38 | 2,646.64 | 2,700.71 | 2,671.92 | 2,740.49 | 2,649.25 | 2,744.33 |
| 10 | 1,507.1 | 1,690.8 | 1,910.9 | 2,122.8 | 2,289.8 | 2,576.1 | 2,649.3 | 2,851.4 |
| 11 | 67,035.79 | 69,254.48 | 72,516.17 | 74,399.03 | 72,129.89 | 71,621.12 | 67,787.90 | 68,322.81 |
| 12 | 18.58 | 18.81 | 18.94 | 18.77 | 18.91 | 19.20 | 19.10 | 19.56 |
| 13 | 167.32 | 169.34 | 170.55 | 169.02 | 170.24 | 172.85 | 171.93 | 176.10 |
| 14 | 2,791.92 | 2,919.91 | 3,073.68 | 3,135.37 | 3,132.32 | 3,192.02 | 3,114.80 | 3,229.84 |
| 15 | 1,761.70 | 1,965.10 | 2,219.20 | 2,464.40 | 2,684.40 | 3,000.50 | 3,114.80 | 3,355.80 |
| 16 | 150,229 | 155,247 | 162,255 | 167,014 | 165,652 | 166,268 | 163,114 | 165,129 |
| 17 | 188.4 | 191.8 | 193.5 | 190.5 | 189.9 | 191.8 | 190.1 | 195.6 |
| 18 | 17.34 | 17.57 | 17.65 | 17.38 | 17.49 | 17.68 | 17.48 | 17.94 |
| 19 | 180.70 | 183.17 | 183.98 | 181.10 | 182.27 | 184.27 | 182.17 | 187.00 |
| 20 | 2,295.88 | 2,424.67 | 2,562.47 | 2,613.87 | 2,609.57 | 2,658.51 | 2,581.30 | 2,696.82 |
| 21 | 1,448.70 | 1,631.80 | 1,850.10 | 2,054.50 | 2,236.40 | 2,499.00 | 2,581.30 | 2,802.00 |
| 22 | 132,420 | 137,962 | 145,157 | 150,427 | 149,213 | 150,362 | 147,680 | 150,308 |
| 23 | 67,035.79 | 69,254.48 | 72,516.17 | 74,399.03 | 72,129.89 | 71,621.12 | 67,787.90 | 68,322.81 |
| 24 | 1,933.14 | 1,928.13 | 1,928.13 | 1,905.00 | 1,905.00 | 1,897.87 | 1,872.45 | 1,893.23 |
| 25 | 34,677.07 | 35,797.86 | 37,609.57 | 38,598.17 | 37,863.38 | 37,737.65 | 36,202.80 | 36,087.93 |
| 26 | 132,419.58 | 137,961.91 | 145,157.12 | 150,427.45 | 149,213.50 | 150,362.28 | 147,679.51 | 150,308.34 |
| 27 | 1,934.54 | 1,931.94 | 1,921.97 | 1,917.30 | 1,902.38 | 1,893.09 | 1,895.20 | 1,903.75 |
| 28 | 150,229 | 155,247 | 162,255 | 167,014 | 165,652 | 166,268 | 163,114 | 165,129 |
| 29 | 77,656.00 | 80,358.00 | 84,421.00 | 87,109.00 | 87,076.00 | 87,829.00 | 86,067.00 | 86,739.00 |
| 30 | 68,450.00 | 71,411.00 | 75,525.00 | 78,458.00 | 78,435.00 | 79,427.00 | 77,923.00 | 78,954.00 |
| 31 | 85,151 | 88,116 | 92,539 | 95,525 | 95,734 | 96,582 | 94,990 | 95,952 |
| 32 | 13,997.00 | 14,125.00 | 14,447.00 | 14,568.00 | 14,774.00 | 14,741.00 | 14,657.00 | 14,697.00 |
| 33 | 2,704.00 | 2,580.00 | 2,567.00 | 2,499.00 | 2,525.00 | 2,414.00 | 2,410.00 | 2,301.00 |

| 1984 | 1985 | 1986 | 1987 | 1988 | 1989 |
|---|---|---|---|---|---|
| 73.13 | 74.25 | 74.75 | 74.47 | 78.01 | 78.03 |
| 265.37 | 269.41 | 271.25 | 270.21 | 283.05 | 283.13 |
| 5,284.14 | 5,374.60 | 5,417.29 | 5,547.09 | 5,957.31 | 6,050.53 |
| 5,691.02 | 6,014.18 | 6,224.47 | 6,606.59 | 7,226.22 | 7,641.82 |
| 107.7 | 111.9 | 114.9 | 119.1 | 121.3 | 126.3 |
| 72,254.44 | 72,387.05 | 72,468.79 | 74,490.29 | 76,370.62 | 77,542.07 |
| 41.04 | 41.92 | 42.75 | 42.81 | 44.29 | 44.56 |
| 268.23 | 273.96 | 279.42 | 279.78 | 289.48 | 291.19 |
| 2,965.43 | 3,034.44 | 3,098.34 | 3,188.86 | 3,382.71 | 3,454.93 |
| 3,193.8 | 3,395.5 | 3,560.0 | 3,797.9 | 4,103.2 | 4,363.6 |
| 72,254.44 | 72,387.05 | 72,468.79 | 74,490.29 | 76,370.62 | 77,542.07 |
| 19.90 | 20.01 | 20.45 | 20.54 | 21.07 | 21.15 |
| 179.14 | 180.19 | 184.08 | 184.95 | 189.67 | 190.41 |
| 3,458.50 | 3,551.56 | 3,660.05 | 3,775.82 | 3,990.27 | 4,088.04 |
| 3,724.80 | 3,974.20 | 4,205.40 | 4,497.00 | 4,840.20 | 5,163.20 |
| 173,815 | 177,456 | 179,011 | 183,804 | 189,408 | 193,299 |
| 199.8 | 202.5 | 206.7 | 208.7 | 213.9 | 212.4 |
| 18.20 | 18.40 | 19.62 | 19.64 | 19.37 | 19.33 |
| 189.72 | 191.73 | 204.44 | 204.71 | 201.84 | 201.47 |
| 2,896.10 | 2,987.31 | 3,212.45 | 3,314.44 | 3,376.17 | 3,441.49 |
| 3,119.10 | 3,342.80 | 3,691.10 | 3,947.50 | 4,095.30 | 4,346.60 |
| 159,095 | 162,383 | 163,771 | 168,743 | 174,335 | 178,029 |
| 72,254.44 | 72,387.05 | 72,468.79 | 74,490.29 | 76,370.62 | 77,542.07 |
| 1,907.86 | 1,893.51 | 1,891.53 | 1,893.32 | 1,883.93 | 1,884.46 |
| 37,871.95 | 38,229.04 | 38,312.30 | 39,343.69 | 40,538.03 | 41,148.07 |
| 159,095.19 | 162,383.30 | 163,771.43 | 168,742.73 | 174,335.02 | 178,028.62 |
| 1,905.97 | 1,893.79 | 1,875.64 | 1,872.36 | 1,875.22 | 1,868.16 |
| 173,815 | 177,456 | 179,011 | 183,804 | 189,408 | 193,299 |
| 91,195.00 | 93,704.00 | 95,440.00 | 98,167.00 | 101,006.00 | 103,470.00 |
| 83,472.00 | 85,745.00 | 87,315.00 | 90,123.00 | 92,968.00 | 95,296.00 |
| 100,607 | 103,031 | 104,831 | 107,891 | 110,962 | 113,511 |
| 14,894.00 | 15,202.00 | 15,483.00 | 15,768.00 | 16,003.00 | 16,324.00 |
| 2,241.00 | 2,084.00 | 2,033.00 | 2,000.00 | 1,991.00 | 1,891.00 |

# K

## Government absorption of surplus value

A useful supplementary measure concerns the relation between total surplus value and the portion absorbed by government purchases of commodities and of (administrative) labor power. Government purchases of commodities directly absorb a portion of the surplus product, and government administrative employment indirectly absorbs another portion through the consumption expenditures of government workers (see Section 3.2.B). Thus, total government expenditure $G_T^* \equiv G^* + W_G$ is a measure of the total absorption of the surplus product by unproductive government expenditures. Table K.1 shows $G_T^*$ and $G_T^*/SP^*$ for the postwar period (where $SP^* =$ Marxian surplus product).

Table K.1. *Government absorption of surplus value, 1948–89 (billions of dollars)*

| Sources | Variables | 1948 | 1949 | 1950 | 1951 | 1952 | 1953 | 1954 | 1955 | 1956 | 1957 | 1958 | 1959 | 1960 | 1961 |
|---|---|---|---|---|---|---|---|---|---|---|---|---|---|---|---|
| | $G^*_T = G^* + WG$ | 32.50 | 38.86 | 38.62 | 60.20 | 75.56 | 82.36 | 75.59 | 74.85 | 79.09 | 86.73 | 94.63 | 96.72 | 99.03 | 106.37 |
| Table E.2 | $G^*$ | 14.40 | 18.76 | 17.42 | 32.50 | 44.06 | 49.96 | 42.59 | 40.05 | 41.89 | 46.93 | 51.73 | 51.92 | 50.93 | 54.77 |
| Table E.2 | WG | 18.10 | 20.10 | 21.20 | 27.70 | 31.50 | 32.40 | 33.00 | 34.80 | 37.20 | 39.80 | 42.90 | 44.80 | 48.10 | 51.60 |
| Table H.1 | SP* | 149.91 | 148.58 | 165.09 | 188.26 | 194.79 | 204.29 | 208.23 | 228.16 | 236.74 | 249.88 | 256.04 | 278.34 | 285.93 | 295.95 |
| | $G^*_T/SP^*$ | 0.22 | 0.26 | 0.23 | 0.32 | 0.39 | 0.40 | 0.36 | 0.33 | 0.33 | 0.35 | 0.37 | 0.35 | 0.35 | 0.36 |

| Sources | Variables | 1962 | 1963 | 1964 | 1965 | 1966 | 1967 | 1968 | 1969 | 1970 | 1971 | 1972 | 1973 | 1974 | 1975 |
|---|---|---|---|---|---|---|---|---|---|---|---|---|---|---|---|
| | $G^*_T = G^* + WG$ | 115.66 | 120.82 | 126.81 | 135.10 | 154.54 | 175.30 | 192.22 | 200.46 | 210.13 | 222.76 | 238.64 | 253.47 | 284.33 | 318.29 |
| Table E.2 | $G^*$ | 60.26 | 61.52 | 62.41 | 65.80 | 76.14 | 87.90 | 94.42 | 92.96 | 90.63 | 92.46 | 96.04 | 98.47 | 115.63 | 130.59 |
| Table E.2 | WG | 55.40 | 59.30 | 64.40 | 69.30 | 78.40 | 87.40 | 97.80 | 107.50 | 119.50 | 130.30 | 142.60 | 155.00 | 168.70 | 187.70 |
| Table H.1 | SP* | 319.54 | 337.07 | 364.00 | 394.44 | 430.09 | 453.42 | 493.12 | 523.25 | 546.86 | 596.04 | 645.51 | 719.63 | 778.82 | 868.78 |
| | $G^*_T/SP^*$ | 0.36 | 0.36 | 0.35 | 0.34 | 0.36 | 0.39 | 0.39 | 0.38 | 0.38 | 0.37 | 0.37 | 0.35 | 0.37 | 0.37 |

| Sources | Variables | 1976 | 1977 | 1978 | 1979 | 1980 | 1981 | 1982 | 1983 | 1984 | 1985 | 1986 | 1987 | 1988 | 1989 |
|---|---|---|---|---|---|---|---|---|---|---|---|---|---|---|---|
| | $G^*_T = G^* + WG$ | 337.29 | 363.34 | 396.97 | 435.78 | 494.43 | 547.37 | 598.61 | 624.39 | 679.89 | 755.83 | 797.00 | 837.34 | 871.73 | 925.91 |
| Table E.2 | $G^*$ | 133.49 | 142.84 | 156.47 | 175.38 | 206.13 | 230.67 | 254.71 | 257.99 | 289.29 | 336.83 | 353.20 | 365.44 | 366.63 | 384.31 |
| Table E.2 | WG | 203.80 | 220.50 | 240.50 | 260.40 | 288.30 | 316.70 | 343.90 | 366.40 | 390.60 | 419.00 | 443.80 | 471.90 | 505.10 | 541.60 |
| Table H.1 | SP* | 971.25 | 1086.66 | 1221.76 | 1347.44 | 1463.67 | 1669.40 | 1726.06 | 1867.15 | 2103.70 | 2258.31 | 2389.25 | 2555.52 | 2755.18 | 2945.32 |
| | $G^*_T/SP^*$ | 0.35 | 0.33 | 0.32 | 0.32 | 0.34 | 0.33 | 0.35 | 0.33 | 0.32 | 0.33 | 0.33 | 0.33 | 0.32 | 0.31 |

# L

## Aglietta's index of the rate of surplus value

Aglietta distinguishes between productive and unproductive labor. However, he believes that price–value deviations make the money form of the rate of surplus value a biased indicator of the trend of the value rate of surplus value. For this reason, he sets out "to find a more faithful statistical indicator [of the] long run trend" in the rate of surplus value (Aglietta 1979, p. 88). He concludes that the share of real wages in productivity is a more appropriate measure of the share of the value of labor power in labor value added, assuming that social productivities (the reciprocals of the unit labor values) of the consumer and producer sectors rise at roughly the same rate in the long run. To see this, we will derive his results in a somewhat different way. Using our own notation, the share of production worker wages in current-dollar value added can be written as

$$v^{*\prime} = W_p/VA = (w \cdot H_p)/(py \cdot VAr) = (pc \cdot wr)/(py \cdot y) = (pc/py) \cdot (wr/y),$$

where

$VA \equiv$ current-dollar (NIPA) net output (value added);
$VAr \equiv$ constant-dollar (NIPA) net output (value added);
$H_p \equiv$ total hours of productive labor;
$w =$ nominal wage rate of production workers;
$pc \equiv$ price index of consumer goods;
$wr \equiv$ hourly real wage of production workers $= w/pc$;
$py \equiv$ price index for net output; and
$y \equiv$ real (constant-dollar) net output per labor hour $= VAr/H_p$.

By way of contrast, the constant-dollar wage share, which Aglietta (1979, p. 89) calls the "real social wage cost," is

$$w' \equiv (W_p/pc)/(VA/py) = wr/yr.$$

Finally, since the aggregate value of labor power is the value of the real wage of an hour of productive labor ($\lambda c \cdot wr$) multiplied by the hours

346

worked by productive labor $H_p$, and since the value added by living (productive) labor $(V + S)$ is also the labor value of real net output $(\lambda y \cdot VAr)$, we can express the value ratio $V/(V + S)$ as

$$v' \equiv V/(V + S) = (\lambda c \cdot wr \cdot H_p)/(\lambda y \cdot VAr)$$
$$= (\lambda c/\lambda y)(wr/y) = (\lambda c/\lambda y)w',$$

where

$\lambda c \equiv$ unit labor value of (workers') consumption goods, and
$\lambda y \equiv$ unit labor value of net output.

We can now see three things. First, the trend of the current-dollar production wage share $v^{*\prime}$ will reflect that of the value share $v'$ if departmental price–value deviations $(pc/\lambda c$ and $py/\lambda c)$ are small or at least move in similar ways over time. Our direct comparison of money and value rates of surplus value (Section 5.10) indicates that this is indeed the case, so Aglietta is wrong to place so much emphasis on price–value deviations.

Second, an Aglietta-type index $w'$ will reflect the equivalent Marxian value ratio $v'$ if $(\lambda c/\lambda y)$, the ratio of the unit labor values of consumer goods to that of the net product, is stable over the long run.[1] These unit values, being quantities of direct and indirect labor required per unit product, can be thought of as reciprocals of the social productivity of labor. Thus, as Aglietta notes, the condition for $w'$ to reflect the trend of $v'$ is that the social productivity of labor in the sectors producing consumption goods and the net product improve at roughly the same rate. Juillard (1992) has indeed found this to be true: in his estimates, the ratio of the unit labor values of the consumer and producer sectors in the U.S.

---

[1] Aglietta defines $m_t$ as the current-dollar value added per hour of labor, which in our notation can be written as $m_t = (Y/L)_t = [(py \cdot Yr)/(\lambda y \cdot Yr)]_t = (py/\lambda y)_t$, since the money value of net output is its price index multiplied by its real level, and the labor value of net output (which is equal to the total amount of living labor time L) is its unit value index multiplied by its real level. He also defines $\mathbf{m}_t$ as the ratio of the money wage bill to the value of labor power, which we can write as $\mathbf{m}_t = (W/V)_t = [(pc \cdot CRw)/(\lambda c \cdot CRw)]_t = (pc/\lambda c)_t$, where CRw is the total real consumption of workers (this assumes workers consume their wages). Then the ratio $\mathbf{m}_t/m_t = (pc/\lambda c)_t/(py/\lambda y)_t =$ the ratio of the price–value deviations of consumer goods and net product, respectively, at time t. Aglietta (1979, p. 89) calls the index number $(\mathbf{m}_t/m_t)/(\mathbf{m}_0/m_0)$ "the index of the share of wages at a constant rate of surplus value," and argues that the condition for his assumed correlation between the variable capital share $v' \equiv V/(V + S)$ and the real wage share ("the real social wage cost") is "that the index of the share of wages at a constant rate of surplus value can be represented by the index of consumer prices [relative to net output prices]" (p. 89). From our expression for the ratio $\mathbf{m}_t/m_t$, it is evident that this condition holds only if the index number of relative unit values of consumer goods and net output is roughly constant over the long run. This is precisely the condition derived here.

economy never varies by more than 3% over the entire postwar period from 1948 to 1980 – except for a four-year interval from 1955 to 1958, when it rises by a total of 10% (Juillard 1992, p. 24, fig. 7).

Finally, the index w′ will reflect the trend in the Marxian money value index of exploitation v*′ if pc/py is stable over time. A sufficient (but not a necessary) condition for this is that the two previously described relations – between v*′ and v′ and between v′ and w′ – hold.

For empirical purposes, we construct an exploitation index v*′ and Aglietta-type measures of the "real social wage cost" v″, both based on the sketchy citations of his data sources. Because we were unable to adequately approximate it with any existing series from the sources he cites, we chose to estimate Aglietta's real social wage cost w′ directly from his own Diagram 1 (Aglietta 1979, p. 91). See Table L.1 for further details.

*Glossary of variables in Table L.1*

| | |
|---|---|
| $ec_p$ | Employee compensation per production worker |
| $ec_{pr}$ | Real employee compensation per production worker |
| $ec'_{pr}$ | Real hourly employee compensation per production worker |
| $h_p$ | Average hours of productive labor |
| pc | Price deflator for personal consumption |
| S* | Surplus value (in money form) |
| V* | Variable capital (in money form) |
| v*′ | Exploitation index (productive wage bill/value added) |
| v″ | Aglietta-type "real social wage cost" |
| w′ | Aglietta's own "real social wage cost" |
| y* | Marxian real net final product per productive worker hour |

# Table L.1. Aglietta's index of S*/V*, 1948–89

| Sources | Variables | Units | 1948 | 1949 | 1950 | 1951 | 1952 | 1953 | 1954 | 1955 | 1956 | 1957 | 1958 |
|---|---|---|---|---|---|---|---|---|---|---|---|---|---|
| | $v^* = V^*/(V^*+S^*)$[a] | index numbers[a] | 100.00 | 98.10 | 97.19 | 97.07 | 97.96 | 98.31 | 94.28 | 93.08 | 94.95 | 93.56 | 89.70 |
| | $v^* = V^*/(V^*+S^*)$ | | 0.37 | 0.36 | 0.36 | 0.36 | 0.36 | 0.36 | 0.35 | 0.35 | 0.35 | 0.35 | 0.33 |
| Table H.1 | $V^*$ | billions of $ | 88.41 | 85.02 | 93.16 | 105.91 | 111.01 | 117.39 | 111.95 | 120.52 | 128.82 | 133.00 | 127.72 |
| Table H.1 | $S^*$ | billions of $ | 149.94 | 148.64 | 165.26 | 188.25 | 194.51 | 204.52 | 208.20 | 228.55 | 236.97 | 250.25 | 256.15 |
| | $v'' = ec'_{pr}/y^*$ | index numbers[a] | 100.00 | 98.05 | 96.38 | 95.04 | 95.17 | 95.01 | 92.09 | 92.71 | 95.54 | 94.61 | 90.74 |
| | $v'' = ec_{pr}/y^*$ | | 0.33 | 0.32 | 0.32 | 0.31 | 0.31 | 0.31 | 0.30 | 0.30 | 0.31 | 0.31 | 0.30 |
| Table J.1 | $y^*$ | index numbers[a] | 100.00 | 106.50 | 110.64 | 116.54 | 120.18 | 124.36 | 131.35 | 133.82 | 136.32 | 141.88 | 150.88 |
| | $ec'_{pr} = ec_{pr}/h_p$ | 1982 $/hour | 5.01 | 5.24 | 5.35 | 5.55 | 5.73 | 5.93 | 6.07 | 6.22 | 6.53 | 6.73 | 6.87 |
| | $ec_{pr} = ec_p/pc$ | 1982 $/prod. worker | 10,426.40 | 10,644.25 | 11,033.78 | 11,501.86 | 11,928.96 | 12,250.43 | 12,318.59 | 12,881.65 | 13,431.57 | 13,648.93 | 13,771.11 |
| Table G.2 | $ec_p$ | $/prod. worker | 2,679.59 | 2,724.93 | 2,890.85 | 3,197.02 | 3,387.82 | 3,552.62 | 3,584.71 | 3,800.09 | 4,042.90 | 4,231.17 | 4,351.61 |
| 704 2[b] | pc (price deflator) | | 25.70 | 25.60 | 26.20 | 27.80 | 28.40 | 29.00 | 29.10 | 29.50 | 30.10 | 31.00 | 31.60 |
| Table I.1 | $h_p$ | hours/prod. worker/year | 2,079.34 | 2,032.94 | 2,063.47 | 2,070.96 | 2,080.08 | 2,067.58 | 2,030.97 | 2,070.65 | 2,056.68 | 2,027.79 | 2,005.91 |
| | $w'$ | index numbers[a] | 100.00 | 96.97 | 92.93 | 92.93 | 99.49 | 96.97 | 96.97 | 96.97 | 96.97 | 93.94 | 95.96 |
| Aglietta | $w'^c$ | | 99.00 | 96.00 | 92.00 | 92.00 | 98.50 | 99.00 | 96.00 | 96.00 | 96.00 | 93.00 | 95.00 |

| Sources | Variables | Units | 1959 | 1960 | 1961 | 1962 | 1963 | 1964 | 1965 | 1966 | 1967 | 1968 | 1969 |
|---|---|---|---|---|---|---|---|---|---|---|---|---|---|
| | $v^* = V^*/(V^*+S^*)$ | index numbers[a] | 90.02 | 90.28 | 89.00 | 88.14 | 87.68 | 86.43 | 87.07 | 87.54 | 86.93 | 87.39 | 89.71 |
| | $v^* = V^*/(V^*+S^*)$ | | 0.33 | 0.33 | 0.33 | 0.33 | 0.33 | 0.32 | 0.32 | 0.32 | 0.32 | 0.32 | 0.33 |
| Table H.1 | $V^*$ | billions of $ | 139.57 | 144.23 | 146.13 | 155.54 | 162.76 | 172.00 | 188.43 | 207.07 | 216.26 | 236.77 | 261.22 |
| Table H.1 | $S^*$ | billions of $ | 278.42 | 286.46 | 296.54 | 320.20 | 337.71 | 364.54 | 395.00 | 430.65 | 454.40 | 493.63 | 523.83 |
| | $v'' = ec'_{pr}/y^*$ | index numbers[a] | 91.23 | 91.46 | 90.07 | 89.66 | 89.32 | 87.94 | 89.53 | 90.49 | 90.12 | 90.92 | 94.39 |
| | $v'' = ec_{pr}/y^*$ | | 0.30 | 0.30 | 0.30 | 0.29 | 0.29 | 0.29 | 0.29 | 0.30 | 0.30 | 0.30 | 0.31 |
| Table J.1 | $y^*$ | index numbers[a] | 154.30 | 158.02 | 163.74 | 168.02 | 172.73 | 180.85 | 183.61 | 186.86 | 192.84 | 197.11 | 196.71 |
| | $ec'_{pr} = ec_{pr}/h_p$ | 1982 $/hour | 7.06 | 7.25 | 7.39 | 7.55 | 7.74 | 7.97 | 8.24 | 8.48 | 8.71 | 8.99 | 9.31 |
| | $ec_{pr} = ec_p/pc$ | 1982 $/prod. worker | 14,393.74 | 14,590.29 | 14,944.85 | 15,326.01 | 15,764.30 | 16,229.34 | 16,874.93 | 17,325.63 | 17,505.07 | 18,013.43 | 18,669.72 |
| Table G.2 | $ec_p$ | $/prod. worker | 4,649.18 | 4,800.21 | 4,976.64 | 5,195.52 | 5,422.92 | 5,680.27 | 6,007.47 | 6,358.51 | 6,581.91 | 7,079.28 | 7,654.58 |
| 704 2[b] | pc (price deflator) | | 32.30 | 32.90 | 33.30 | 33.90 | 34.40 | 35.00 | 35.60 | 36.70 | 37.60 | 39.30 | 41.00 |
| Table I.1 | $h_p$ | hours/prod. worker/year | 2,039.17 | 2,013.19 | 2,021.01 | 2,028.85 | 2,037.80 | 2,035.18 | 2,047.33 | 2,043.45 | 2,008.84 | 2,004.57 | 2,005.24 |
| | $w'$ | index numbers[a] | 96.46 | 95.96 | 93.94 | 90.91 | 86.36 | 86.67 | 86.87 | 86.36 | 84.85 | 83.84 | 85.86 |
| Aglietta | $w'^c$ | | 95.50 | 95.00 | 93.00 | 90.00 | 85.50 | 85.80 | 86.00 | 85.50 | 84.00 | 83.00 | 85.00 |

Table L.1 (cont.)

| Sources | Variables | Units | 1970 | 1971 | 1972 | 1973 | 1974 | 1975 | 1976 | 1977 | 1978 | 1979 | 1980 |
|---|---|---|---|---|---|---|---|---|---|---|---|---|---|
| | $v^* = V^*/(V^*+S^*)$ | index numbers[a] | 89.12 | 87.67 | 90.11 | 91.62 | 91.30 | 86.67 | 86.75 | 86.97 | 87.75 | 89.12 | 87.81 |
| | $v^{*\prime} = V^*/(V^*+S^*)$ | | 0.33 | 0.33 | 0.33 | 0.34 | 0.34 | 0.32 | 0.32 | 0.32 | 0.33 | 0.33 | 0.33 |
| Table H.1 | $V^*$ | billions of $ | 270.43 | 287.53 | 324.30 | 370.49 | 398.50 | 410.75 | 459.63 | 515.81 | 589.20 | 664.78 | 706.53 |
| Table H.1 | $S^*$ | billions of $ | 547.67 | 596.70 | 645.98 | 719.75 | 778.25 | 867.02 | 968.82 | 1,083.13 | 1,221.07 | 1,346.24 | 1,462.70 |
| | $v^{*\prime\prime} = ec'_{pr}/y^*$ | index numbers[a] | 94.62 | 93.99 | 97.17 | 98.75 | 96.96 | 93.81 | 93.81 | 93.93 | 94.88 | 96.05 | 93.18 |
| | $v^{*\prime\prime} = ec''_{pr}/y^*$ | | 0.31 | 0.31 | 0.32 | 0.32 | 0.32 | 0.31 | 0.31 | 0.31 | 0.31 | 0.31 | 0.31 |
| Table I.1 | $y^*$ | 1982 $/hour | 202.83 | 211.76 | 213.12 | 215.77 | 215.13 | 228.72 | 232.85 | 237.09 | 238.53 | 237.24 | 242.09 |
| | $ec'_{pr} = ec_{pr}/h_p$ | 1982 $/hour | 9.62 | 9.98 | 10.38 | 10.68 | 10.46 | 10.71 | 10.95 | 11.17 | 11.35 | 11.43 | 11.31 |
| Table G.2 | $ec_{pr} = ec_p/pc$ | 1982 $/prod. worker | 18,960.29 | 19,566.71 | 20,487.16 | 21,063.45 | 20,394.01 | 20,640.50 | 21,173.22 | 21,602.83 | 21,880.28 | 22,024.52 | 21,547.20 |
| 704 2[b] | $ec_p$ | $/prod. worker | 8,133.96 | 8,785.45 | 9,567.50 | 10,447.47 | 11,175.92 | 12,219.18 | 13,254.44 | 14,409.09 | 15,666.28 | 17,223.18 | 18,659.88 |
| Table I.1 | pc (price deflator) | hours/prod. worker/year | 42.90 | 44.90 | 46.70 | 49.60 | 54.80 | 59.20 | 62.60 | 66.70 | 71.60 | 78.20 | 86.60 |
| | $h_p$ | | 1,970.32 | 1,960.58 | 1,973.01 | 1,971.43 | 1,949.83 | 1,927.59 | 1,933.14 | 1,934.60 | 1,928.13 | 1,927.53 | 1,905.00 |
| Aglietta | $w'$ | index numbers[a] | 88.89 | 86.87 | 85.86 | 83.33 | 82.83 | | | | | | |
| | $w''^c$ | | 88.00 | 86.00 | 85.00 | 82.50 | 82.00 | | | | | | |

| Sources | Variables | Units | 1981 | 1982 | 1983 | 1984 | 1985 | 1986 | 1987 | 1988 | 1989 |
|---|---|---|---|---|---|---|---|---|---|---|---|
| | $v^* = V^*/(V^*+S^*)$ | index numbers[a] | 85.32 | 84.44 | 83.68 | 82.62 | 80.88 | 79.19 | 78.92 | 79.26 | 78.38 |
| | $v^{*\prime} = V^*/(V^*+S^*)$ | | 0.32 | 0.31 | 0.31 | 0.31 | 0.30 | 0.29 | 0.29 | 0.29 | 0.29 |
| Table H.1 | $V^*$ | billions of $ | 772.35 | 786.53 | 839.73 | 928.68 | 967.99 | 998.55 | 1,060.90 | 1,146.22 | 1,206.40 |
| Table H.1 | $S^*$ | billions of $ | 1,668.19 | 1,724.68 | 1,865.80 | 2,101.78 | 2,258.68 | 2,401.11 | 2,563.38 | 2,752.81 | 2,943.35 |
| | $v^{*\prime\prime} = ec'_{pr}/y^*$ | index numbers[a] | 90.91 | 90.60 | 89.69 | 88.16 | 86.76 | 85.30 | 85.24 | 83.25 | 82.03 |
| | $v^{*\prime\prime} = ec''_{pr}/y^*$ | | 0.30 | 0.30 | 0.29 | 0.29 | 0.28 | 0.28 | 0.28 | 0.27 | 0.27 |
| Table I.1 | $y^*$ | 1982 $/hour | 250.07 | 255.42 | 262.51 | 268.23 | 273.96 | 279.42 | 279.78 | 289.48 | 291.19 |
| | $ec'_{pr} = ec_{pr}/h_p$ | 1982 $/hour | 11.40 | 11.60 | 11.81 | 11.86 | 11.92 | 11.95 | 11.96 | 12.08 | 11.98 |
| Table G.2 | $ec_{pr} = ec_p/pc$ | 1982 $/prod. worker | 21,634.60 | 21,725.60 | 22,352.61 | 22,621.38 | 22,567.64 | 22,604.79 | 22,640.60 | 22,765.88 | 22,569.98 |
| 704 2[b] | $ec_p$ | $/prod. worker | 20,466.34 | 21,725.60 | 23,269.07 | 24,521.58 | 25,320.89 | 26,063.32 | 26,964.96 | 28,275.23 | 29,318.41 |
| Table I.1 | pc (price deflator) | hours/prod. worker/year | 94.60 | 100.00 | 104.10 | 108.40 | 112.20 | 115.30 | 119.10 | 124.20 | 129.90 |
| | $h_p$ | | 1,897.87 | 1,872.45 | 1,893.23 | 1,907.86 | 1,893.51 | 1,891.53 | 1,893.32 | 1,883.93 | 1,884.46 |

[a] 1948=100.
[b] Data in this row come from NIPA (e.g. BEA 1986), line 2 of table 704.
[c] Aglietta's (1979, p. 91) social wage cost estimates.

# M

## Mage and NIPA measures of the capitalist sector gross product

Mage (1963) bases his calculations on "the aggregate non-farm private business economy," which is whole domestic economy minus: general government, government enterprises, and private households and nonprofit institutions (p. 161); finance, insurance, and real estate (pp. 165, 181); and professional services (pp. 165, 183). What remains is mining, construction, manufacturing, transportation, communication, utilities, productive services, and wholesale/retail trade, which is simply his *definition* of capitalist production and trade (i.e. primary) sectors. His own method of deriving this estimate of the primary-sector gross product is to build it up by separately estimating its various components from a variety of data sources (Mage 1963, chap. VI and apx. to chap. VI). But it could have been derived far more easily in a direct manner.[1]

We begin by deriving the NIPA estimate of GDP in the primary sectors, and then compare it to Mage's own capitalist-sector gross product, as shown in Table M.1.[2]

Mage's estimate is somewhat larger than the direct NIPA equivalent. To see why, it is useful to break down Mage's measure into categories comparable to those of NIPA–IO GDP; see Table M.2. The sole conceptual difference between Mage's measure and the equivalent NIPA one arises from the items under the heading of net interest and net rent. As

---

[1] We use data on gross product by sector, which were unavailable in Mage's time (and have been discontinued in recent times). But Mage could have combined existing data on national income by sector with corresponding data on indirect business taxes by sector (which he himself uses: Mage 1963, p. 271, table D-III, footnote for column g).

[2] Table M.1 incorporates data from BEA (1976), which was used because it contains a table of gross product by sector (table 6.1) that does not appear in subsequent NIPA summaries.

Table M.1. *NIPA-based GDP in production and trade sectors, 1958 (billions of dollars)*

---

GDP(PT) = [(GDP nonfarm business) − (finance, insurance, real estate)
       − (government enterprise) − (professional services)][a]
    = 370.7 − 61.2 − 5.0 − 6.6 = 297.9

GVA (Mage) = 305.4[b]

---

[a] BEA 1976, table 6.1: line 181 minus line 135 minus line 173 minus professional services. Mage's category of professional services is meant to represent noncapitalist professional services, which is why he only deducts it in his estimates of the unincorporated sector (Mage 1963, p. 183). We estimate this as the sum of the unincorporated income of medical and legal services – table 6.14 (BEA 1976): line 17 plus line 18 equals $6,556 million.
[b] Mage (1963, p. 271): table D-III, column h (gross product).

Table M.2. *Components of Mage's gross product and NIPA GDP*

| GDP (NIPA–IO)[a] | Gross product (Mage)[b] |
| --- | --- |
| Indirect business taxes | Indirect business taxes |
| Employee compensation | Employee compensation |
| Corporate profits | Corporate profits |
| Income of unincorporated enterprises | Income of unincorporated enterprises |
| Net interest | Net interest paid |
| — | Net rents |
| Capital consumption allowances | Capital consumption allowances |

---

[a] The entries under the NIPA–IO measure of GDP are quite straightforward except for net interest and the absence of net rent. For nonfinancial sectors, net interest is only actual net interest paid minus net interest paid to the financial sector. For nonrental sectors, net rents paid are treated as part of the costs of operation (intermediate inputs) rather than value added; see Section B.1 for further details.
[b] Mage (1963, pp. 270–1, table D-III). Indirect business taxes and employee compensation appear directly in this table. The elements in columns b–e in Mage's table add up to the remaining five elements listed under Mage's gross product above. "Other gross surplus value" in column b of Mage's table D-III represents gross surplus value minus corporate officers' salaries (which appear under employee compensation), which can also be expressed as the sum of: corporate profits net of profits taxes; profit of unincorporated enterprises, defined as their total income minus the wage equivalent for proprietors and partners; total (corporate and noncorporate) net interest paid; total net rents paid net of real estate taxes; and total capital consumption allowances (Mage 1963, pp. 180–8). When we add to this the elements in column c (wage equivalent), d (corporate tax liability), and e (real estate taxes), we obtain the last five elements listed in Table M.2.

noted in Table M.2, the NIPA category of net interest in nonfinancial sectors is actual total net interest paid minus net interest paid to the financial sectors (the latter being treated as imputed interest received). One can therefore recover total net interest paid, as Mage (1963, pp. 182–4) did

Table M.3. *NIPA equivalent of Mage's nonfarm gross value added, 1958 (billions of dollars)*

GDP(PT)' = NIPA equivalent of Mage's gross value added
= GDP(PT) + imputed interest received[a] + net rents paid[b]
= 297.9 + 2.5 + 6.9 = 307.3
GVA (Mage) = 305.4

[a] BEA (1976): table 8.2, lines 39 and 41.
[b] Mage (1963): [p. 252, table B-IV, column d (after-tax corporate net rents paid)] + [p. 255, table B-V, column d (after-tax noncorporate net rents paid)] + [p. 271, table D-III, column e (real estate tax)].

from Internal Revenue Service data,[3] simply by adding the imputed interest received by the production and trade sectors (which is listed in separate NIPA tables) back into NIPA net interest. The problem of net rents paid is somewhat more complicated, since these are treated as part of the costs of operation (intermediate inputs) rather than value added, so that they appear only in input–output tables. For this category, we use Mage's own estimates. Table M.3 illustrates the steps in the calculation of the NIPA equivalent of Mage's capitalist sector gross product in 1958, and compares the final estimate with Mage's own (laboriously built-up) total.

Although our procedure is considerably simpler, it produces virtually the same result as Mage's. The difference between the two estimates is less than six-tenths of one percent. Table M.4 breaks down our NIPA-based estimate into three broad elements: indirect business taxes, employee compensation, and gross profit-type income (defined as NIPA profit-type return, net interest plus imputed interest received, and capitalist consumption allowances), and compares these components to the corresponding ones in Mage.

It is apparent that differences between individual components are somewhat greater than between totals, though no individual component differs by more than 6%–7%. Both indirect business taxes and employee compensation are larger in Mage than in our NIPA-based estimates, while profit-type income is correspondingly smaller. But this seems to be due to revisions within the NIPA data itself, since the figures in Mage are from earlier publications than the ones we use: Mage (1963, p. 176) takes his data from a 1962 publication.

[3] Mage also uses IRS data to estimate actual net rent paid. But this is already included in NIPA gross value added. Furthermore, as we are concerned only with the GVA of the production and trade sectors, no adjustment is needed for imputed rentals since these appear only in the revenue of the rental sector.

Table M.4. *Components of NIPA-equivalent and Mage's capitalist sector nonfarm gross product, 1958 (billions of dollars)*

|  | NIPA-equivalent[a] | Mage[b] |
|---|---|---|
| Indirect business taxes | 29.2 | 31.2 |
| Employee compensation | 181.2 | 183.1 |
| Gross property-type income | 96.9 | 91.1 |
| Capitalist gross product | 307.3 | 305.5 |

[a] Each component represents (nonfarm business) minus (finance, insurance, and real estate) minus (government enterprise) minus (professional services). The latter was estimated by taking a proportion x of the relevant component of the GDP of total services, where x is the ratio of noncapitalist professional services income to the GDP of all services; from Table M.1 and NIPA table 6.1, line 153 (BEA 1976), respectively, $x = 6.6/42.3$. Thus, the indirect business tax was derived from table 6.1 (BEA 1976) as line 185 minus line 139 minus line 179 minus $x \cdot$ (line 157); employee compensation was defined as line 182 minus line 136 minus line 174 minus $x \cdot$ (line 154). Gross property-type income was the remainder of the adjusted GDP(PT)' estimated in Table M.3.
[b] Gross property-type income based on Mage's data is defined here as the sum of other gross surplus value, proprietor wage equivalent, profit tax liability, and real estate tax (Mage 1963, pp. 270–1, table D-III). See also Table M.5.

Finally, for the sake of completeness, it is worth summarizing the relation between the category we call gross property-type income and what Mage defines as gross surplus value. Table M.5 compares the two, using Mage's own figures for 1958.

Table M.5.  *Relation between gross property-type income and Mage's gross surplus value, 1958 (millions of dollars)*

| | |
|---|---:|
| Gross property-type income: | 90,993[a] |
| Other gross surplus value: | 50,086 |
| Proprietor wage equivalent: | 23,729 |
| Profit tax liability: | 15,513 |
| Real estate tax: | 1,665 |
| Other gross surplus value: | 50,086[b] |
| Corporate gross surplus value: | 53,001 |
| Noncorporate gross surplus value: | 7,460 |
| *less* Corporate officers' salaries: | −10,375 |
| Mage's gross surplus value: | 60,461 |
| Gross property-type income: | 90,993 |
| *less* Proprietor wage equivalent: | −23,729 |
| *less* Profit tax liability: | −15,513 |
| *less* Real estate tax: | −1,665 |
| *plus* Corporate officers' salaries: | +10,375 |

[a] Mage (1963): pp. 270–1, table D-III, columns b–e.
[b] Mage (1963): table B-IV, column g; table B-V, column g; table B-IV, column b.

# N

## The net transfer between workers and the state, and its impact on the rate of surplus value

In order to measure the net impact of state expenditures and taxes on the rate of surplus standard of living of wage and salary earners, we need to examine the net transfer between these wage and salary earners and the state. This net transfer is defined as benefits received by workers minus taxes paid. In this appendix we briefly outline the methods of allocating various government expenditures and taxes to labor, and then report estimates of the net transfer for the period 1952–85. Because the net transfer is negative over most of this period, it actually represents a *net tax on workers*. What follows is a brief summary of the methodology in Shaikh and Tonak (1987).

In determining the portion of state expenditures directed toward workers, we begin by classifying them into three major groups. The first group consists of items such as labor training and services, housing and community services, income support, social security, and welfare (except for the small items called military disability and military retirement, which we treat as a cost of war). These services are assumed to be received entirely by workers either in money or in commodity form. The second group includes such conventional categories as education, health and hospitals, recreational and cultural activities, energy, natural resources, transportation, and postal services; these are treated as social consumption in general, and the workers' share in them is estimated by multiplying the group total by the share of total labor income in personal income. The last group comprises two kinds of expenditures. (a) Central executive, legislative and judicial activities, international affairs, space, national defense, civilian safety, veteran benefits, and agriculture; these are the expenses of reproducing and maintaining the system itself, what Marx calls the *faux frais* of capitalist society (Marx 1977, p. 446). (b) Economic development, regulation and services, net interest, and others and unallocables; this set represents expenditures directed mainly toward small businesses, related administrative activities, and interest payments to the highest income brackets. We therefore exclude both (a) and (b) from labor income and consumption.

Our point of departure on the tax side is total employee compensation. This is the total cost incurred by capitalists for the purchase of labor power; it includes wages and also such benefits as employer contributions for social insurance and other labor income. Two main groups of taxes flow out of this total. Employee compensation is the cost to capitalists of hiring workers. But the income received by workers is less than this because a certain portion, labeled employee and employer contributions, is deducted for social security.[1] Accordingly, our first group of taxes consists of the portion of employee compensation which goes toward social security taxes; the second group consists of personal income taxes, motor vehicle licenses, property taxes (primarily on homes), and other taxes and nontaxes (a very small category which includes passport fees, fines, etc.). Since these are levied on both earned and unearned incomes, the portion emanating from labor is estimated by using the share of total labor income in personal income.

To summarize, social welfare expenditures directed toward workers are the sum of all government expenditures on labor training and services, housing and community services, income support, social security and welfare (except for military disability and retirement), and the bulk of education, health and hospitals, recreational and cultural activities, energy, natural resources, transportation, and postal service expenditures. Similarly, taxes levied directly on workers' compensation include all social security contributions as well as the bulk of personal income taxes, motor vehicle licenses, property taxes, and other taxes and nontaxes.[2] The *net transfer* is then the difference between social welfare expenditures directed toward the working class and taxes taken out of the flow of employee compensation. Table N.1 illustrates the calculations for 1964. Table N.2 presents the whole series from 1952 to 1985, with rates calculated relative to total employee compensation EC.

[1] An additional very small category was added here. It consists of net government receipts from lotteries, etc., which we treat as a kind of direct tax. It is actually listed as a net expenditure in government accounts, but since it is consistently negative we treat it as a positive net tax (Tonak 1987).

[2] We leave out the group of taxes comprising corporate profit taxes, indirect business taxes, and estate and gift taxes (which only apply to the highest income levels), because they are generally not levied on workers.

Table N.1. *Estimation of the net transfer for the United States, 1964*

|  | Total | Labor |
|---|---|---|
| *Social welfare expenditures[a]* | | |
| Group I | | |
|     Income support, social security, welfare | 29.9 | 29.9 |
|     Housing and commu .y services | 2.8 | 2.8 |
|     Labor training and services | 0.7 | 0.7 |
| Group II[b] | | |
|     Education | 27.6 | 20.1 |
|     Health and hospitals | 6.4 | 4.7 |
|     Recreational and cultural activities | 1.2 | 0.9 |
|     Energy | 1.0 | 0.7 |
|     Natural resources | 2.0 | 1.5 |
|     Postal service | 0.8 | 0.6 |
|     Transportation | 13.1 | 6.7 |
| B1 = Total benefits and income received by labor | | 68.0 |
| *Taxes[c]* | | |
| Group I | | |
|     Contributions for social insurance | 30.1 | 30.1 |
| Group II[d] | | |
|     Personal income taxes (federal and state) | 50.0 | 36.4 |
|     Other taxes and nontaxes | 3.8 | 2.8 |
|     Motor vehicle taxes and licenses | 1.1 | 0.8 |
|     Personal property taxes | 8.4 | 6.1 |
| T1 = Total taxes paid by labor | | 76.2 |
| *Net transfer:* | $68.0 - 76.2 = -8.1$ | |

*Note:* All figures are rounded.

[a] The data for social welfare expenditures are directly available in BEA (1981, pp. 151, 159).

[b] To obtain the portions of these expenditures directed toward labor, all items in this group are multiplied by the "labor share" (0.727 for 1964); transportation is also adjusted by the gas share of passenger cars (Tonak 1984, chap. IV, apx. II).

[c] The data for the taxes are directly available in BEA (1981, pp. 121, 123, 129, 134).

[d] To obtain the portions of these taxes paid by labor, all items in this group are multiplied by the "labor share" (0.727 for 1964), except for property taxes. For property taxes we consider only the part paid by homeowners, which in turn is adjusted by using the "labor share" (Tonak 1984, chap. IV, apx. I).

Table N.2. Benefit, tax, net transfer rates, and adjusted and unadjusted rates of surplus value, 1952–89

| Sources[a] | Variables | 1952 | 1953 | 1954 | 1955 | 1956 | 1957 | 1958 | 1959 | 1960 | 1961 | 1962 | 1963 | 1964 |
|---|---|---|---|---|---|---|---|---|---|---|---|---|---|---|
| S & T | Benefit rate (B1/EC) | 0.11 | 0.11 | 0.13 | 0.13 | 0.13 | 0.14 | 0.17 | 0.16 | 0.17 | 0.18 | 0.18 | 0.18 | 0.19 |
| S & T | Tax rate (T1/EC) | 0.18 | 0.17 | 0.17 | 0.17 | 0.18 | 0.19 | 0.19 | 0.19 | 0.21 | 0.21 | 0.21 | 0.22 | 0.21 |
| S & T | Net transfer rate (Ntrrate) | −0.07 | −0.06 | −0.04 | −0.05 | −0.05 | −0.04 | −0.02 | −0.03 | −0.04 | −0.02 | −0.03 | −0.04 | −0.02 |
| Table G.2 | $V^*$ | 111.01 | 117.39 | 111.95 | 120.52 | 128.82 | 133.00 | 127.72 | 139.57 | 144.23 | 146.13 | 155.54 | 162.76 | 172.00 |
| | $NtrV^* =$ Net transfer out of $V^* = (Ntrrate)V^*$ | −7.55 | −7.38 | −4.72 | −5.69 | −6.30 | −5.90 | −2.55 | −4.37 | −5.74 | −3.58 | −4.75 | −5.91 | −3.76 |
| Table H.1 | $S^*$ | 194.51 | 204.52 | 208.20 | 228.55 | 236.97 | 250.25 | 256.15 | 278.42 | 286.46 | 296.54 | 320.20 | 337.71 | 364.54 |
| Table H.1 | $S^*/V^*$ | 1.75 | 1.74 | 1.86 | 1.90 | 1.84 | 1.88 | 2.01 | 1.99 | 1.99 | 2.03 | 2.06 | 2.07 | 2.12 |
| | $(S^{**}/V^{**}) = (S^* − NtrV^*)/(V^* + NtrV^*)$ | 1.95 | 1.93 | 1.99 | 2.04 | 1.99 | 2.02 | 2.07 | 2.09 | 2.11 | 2.11 | 2.16 | 2.19 | 2.19 |

| Sources[a] | Variables | 1965 | 1966 | 1967 | 1968 | 1969 | 1970 | 1971 | 1972 | 1973 | 1974 | 1975 | 1976 | 1977 |
|---|---|---|---|---|---|---|---|---|---|---|---|---|---|---|
| S & T | Benefit rate (B1/EC) | 0.19 | 0.20 | 0.21 | 0.22 | 0.22 | 0.24 | 0.25 | 0.26 | 0.26 | 0.27 | 0.31 | 0.30 | 0.29 |
| S & T | Tax rate (T1/EC) | 0.21 | 0.23 | 0.24 | 0.25 | 0.26 | 0.25 | 0.25 | 0.27 | 0.27 | 0.28 | 0.27 | 0.28 | 0.28 |
| S & T | Net transfer rate (Ntrrate) | −0.02 | −0.03 | −0.02 | −0.03 | −0.05 | −0.02 | 0.01 | −0.01 | −0.01 | −0.01 | 0.04 | 0.02 | 0.01 |
| Table G.2 | $V^*$ | 188.43 | 207.07 | 216.26 | 236.77 | 261.22 | 270.43 | 287.53 | 324.30 | 370.49 | 398.50 | 410.75 | 459.63 | 515.81 |
| | $NtrV^* =$ Net transfer out of $V^* = (Ntrrate)V^*$ | −3.46 | −6.34 | −5.12 | −7.26 | −12.24 | −4.82 | 1.48 | −3.55 | −5.20 | −2.30 | 15.77 | 9.28 | 3.64 |
| Table H.1 | $S^*$ | 395.00 | 430.65 | 454.40 | 493.63 | 523.83 | 547.67 | 596.70 | 645.98 | 719.75 | 778.25 | 867.02 | 968.82 | 1083.13 |
| Table H.1 | $S^*/V^*$ | 2.10 | 2.08 | 2.10 | 2.08 | 2.01 | 2.03 | 2.08 | 1.99 | 1.94 | 1.95 | 2.11 | 2.11 | 2.10 |
| | $(S^{**}/V^{**}) = (S^* − NtrV^*)/(V^* + NtrV^*)$ | 2.15 | 2.18 | 2.18 | 2.18 | 2.15 | 2.08 | 2.06 | 2.02 | 1.98 | 1.97 | 2.00 | 2.05 | 2.08 |

| Sources[a] | Variables | 1978 | 1979 | 1980 | 1981 | 1982 | 1983 | 1984 | 1985 | 1986 | 1987 | 1988 | 1989 |
|---|---|---|---|---|---|---|---|---|---|---|---|---|---|
| S & T | Benefit rate (B1/EC) | 0.28 | 0.28 | 0.29 | 0.30 | 0.30 | 0.30 | 0.29 | 0.29 | 0.29 | 0.28 | 0.28 | 0.29 |
| S & T | Tax rate (T1/EC) | 0.29 | 0.30 | 0.30 | 0.31 | 0.31 | 0.31 | 0.31 | 0.31 | 0.31 | 0.32 | 0.31 | 0.32 |
| S & T | Net transfer rate (Ntrrate) | −0.01 | −0.02 | 0.00 | −0.01 | −0.01 | 0.00 | −0.02 | −0.03 | −0.02 | −0.03 | −0.03 | −0.04 |
| Table G.2 | $V^*$ | 589.20 | 664.78 | 706.53 | 772.35 | 786.53 | 839.73 | 928.68 | 967.99 | 998.55 | 1060.90 | 1146.22 | 1206.40 |
| | $NtrV^* =$ Net transfer out of $V^* = (Ntrrate)V^*$ | −3.06 | −11.10 | −1.82 | −10.52 | −6.01 | −2.49 | −18.23 | −24.26 | −24.91 | −35.25 | −39.01 | −65.77 |
| Table H.1 | $S^*$ | 1221.07 | 1346.24 | 1462.70 | 1668.19 | 1724.68 | 1865.80 | 2101.78 | 2258.68 | 2401.11 | 2563.38 | 2752.81 | 2943.35 |
| Table H.1 | $S^*/V^*$ | 2.07 | 2.03 | 2.07 | 2.16 | 2.19 | 2.22 | 2.26 | 2.33 | 2.40 | 2.42 | 2.40 | 2.44 |
| | $(S^{**}/V^{**}) = (S^* − NtrV^*)/(V^* + NtrV^*)$ | 2.09 | 2.08 | 2.08 | 2.20 | 2.22 | 2.23 | 2.33 | 2.42 | 2.49 | 2.53 | 2.52 | 2.58 |

[a] S & T denotes Shaikh and Tonak (forthcoming).

# REFERENCES

Aglietta, M. 1979. *A Theory of Capitalist Regulation: The U.S. Experience* (trans. D. Fernbach). London: New Left Books.

Amsden, A. 1981. "An International Comparison of the Rate of Surplus Value in Manufacturing Industry," *Cambridge Journal of Economics* 5: 229–49.

Bach, G. L. 1966. *Economics: An Introduction to Analysis and Policy.* New York: Prentice-Hall.

Baran, P. A. 1957. *The Political Economy of Growth.* New York: Monthly Review Press.

Baran, P. A., and Sweezy, P. M. 1966. *Monopoly Capital.* New York: Monthly Review Press.

BEA. *See* U.S. Department of Commerce, Bureau of Economic Analysis.

BIE. *See* U.S. Bureau of Interindustrial Economics.

Beckerman, W. 1968. *An Introduction to National Income Analysis.* London: Weidenfeld and Nicolson.

BLS. *See* U.S. Department of Labor, Bureau of Labor Statistics.

Boddy, R., and Crotty, J. 1975. "Class Conflict and Macro-Policy: The Political Business Cycle," *Review of Radical Political Economics* 7: 1–19.

Bottomore, T. (ed.) 1983. *A Dictionary of Marxist Thought.* Oxford: Basil Blackwell.

Bowles, S., and Gintis, H. 1982. "The Crisis of Liberal Democratic Capitalism: The Case of the United States," *Politics and Society* 11: 51–93.

Bowles, S., Gordon, D. M., and Weisskopf, T. E. 1984. *Beyond the Wasteland.* New York: Anchor Press.

Carson, C. S. 1984. "The Underground Economy: An Introduction," *Survey of Current Business* 64: 21–37.

Carson, C. S., and Honsa, J. 1990. "The United Nations System of National Accounts: An Introduction," *Survey of Current Business* 70: 20–30.

Carson, C. S., and Jaszi, G. 1982. "Comments," *Survey of Current Business* 62: 57–9.

CEA. *See* Council of Economic Advisers.

Chernomas, R. 1991. "Is Unproductive Labor a (Missing) Link in the Mainstream Economic Analysis of Growth Stagnation?" Unpublished manuscript, Department of Economics, University of Manitoba, Winnipeg.

Coontz, S. 1965. *Productive Labor and Effective Demand.* London: Routledge and Kegan Paul.

Corey, L. 1934. *The Decline of American Capitalism*. Salem, NH: Ayer (reprinted in 1972).

Council of Economic Advisers (CEA). Various years. *Economic Report of the President*. Washington, DC: Government Printing Office.

Cuneo, C. J. 1978. "Class Exploitation in Canada," *Canadian Review of Sociology and Anthropology* 15: 284–300.

   1982. "Class Struggle and Measurement of the Rate of Surplus Value," *Canadian Review of Sociology and Anthropology* 19: 377–424.

Denison, E. F. 1982. "Integrated Economic Accounts for the United States, 1947–1980: Comment," *Survey of Current Business* 62: 59–65.

Eaton, J. 1966. *Political Economy: A Marxist Textbook*. New York: International.

Eisner, R. 1985. "The Total Incomes System of Accounts," *Survey of Current Business* 65: 24–48.

   1988. "Extended Accounts for National Income and Product," *Journal of Economic Literature* 26: 1611–84.

Emerson, R. J., and Rowe, P. N. 1982. "Professor Cuneo's Analysis of Class Exploitation in Canada," *Canadian Review of Sociology and Anthropology* 19: 279–88.

Erdos, T. 1970. "Surplus Value and Its Rate in Contemporary Capitalism," *Acta Oeconomica* 5: 371–88.

Evans, W. D., and Hoffenberg, M. 1952. "Interindustry Relations Study for 1947," *Review of Economics and Statistics* 34: 97–142.

Farnham, A. 1989. "What Milken Means," *Fortune* (24 April), pp. 16–17.

Foley, D. 1982. "The Value of Money, the Value of Labor Power, and the Marxian Transformation Problem," *Review of Radical Political Economics* 14: 37–46.

Foss, M. F. 1984. *Changing Utilization of Fixed Capital: An Element in Long Term Growth*. Washington, DC: American Enterprise Institute for Public Policy Research.

Gillman, J. 1958. *The Falling Rate of Profit, Marx's Law and Its Significance to Twentieth Century Capitalism*. New York: Cameron Associates.

Glyn, A., and Sutcliffe, R. 1972. *British Capitalism, Workers and the Profits Squeeze*. Harmondsworth: Penguin.

Goldsmith, R. W. 1968. "National Wealth," in *International Encyclopedia of the Social Sciences*. New York: Macmillan.

Goodwin, R. M. 1967. "A Growth Cycle," in C. H. Feinstein (ed.), *Socialism, Capitalism and Economic Growth*. London: Cambridge University Press.

Gough, I. 1972. "Productive and Unproductive Labour in Marx," *New Left Review* 12: 47–72.

Gouverneur, J. 1983. *Contemporary Capitalism and Marxist Economics*. Oxford: M. Robertson.

Harrod, R. F. 1939. "An Essay in Dynamic Theory," *Economic Journal* 49: 14–33.

Hicks, U. 1946. "The Terminology of Tax Analysis," *Economic Journal* 56: 38–50.

HUD. *See* U.S. Department of Housing and Urban Development.

Hunt, E. K. 1979. "The Categories of Productive and Unproductive Labour in Marxist Economic Theory," *Science and Society* 43: 303–25.

Izumi, H. No date. "A Survey of Estimations of the Rate of Surplus Value in Japan," unpublished manuscript.

   1980. (trans.) "Estimation of Surplus Value Using Labor Values," *Keizai* 193.

   1983. (trans.) "International Comparisons of the Rate of Surplus Value Using Labor Values," *Keizai* 227.

Jorgenson, D. W., and Fraumeni, B. M. 1987. "The Accumulation of Human and Non-Human Capital, 1948–1984," unpublished manuscript, Department of Economics, Harvard University, Cambridge, MA.

Juillard, M. 1988. "Un Schema de Reproduction pour l'Economie des Etats-Unis: 1948–1980. Tentative de Modelisation et de Quantification," Ph.D. dissertation, Universite de Geneve, Geneve.

1992. "The Regime of Intensive Accumulation of the Post-War: The Case of France and the U.S.," in D. Papadimitriou (ed.), *Profits, Deficits and Instability*. New York: St. Martin's.

Kahn, H. C. 1968. *Employee Compensation Under the Income Tax*. New York: National Bureau of Economic Research.

Kalmans, R. 1992. "The Political Economy of Exploitation: A Comparative Study of the Rate of Surplus Value in Japan and the United States, 1958–1980," Ph.D. dissertation, Department of Economics, New School for Social Research, New York.

Kendrick, J. W. 1970. "The Historical Development of National Income Accounts," *History of Political Economy* 11: 284–315.

Khanjian, A. 1989. "Measuring and Comparing the Price and Value Rates of Surplus Value in the U.S., 1958–1977," Ph.D. dissertation, Department of Economics, New School for Social Research, New York.

Labor Research Association. 1948. *Trends in American Capitalism: Profit and Living Standards*. New York: International.

Lancaster, K. J. 1968. *Mathematical Economics*. London: Macmillan.

Leontief, W. 1951. *The Structure of the American Economy: 1919–1939*. New York: Oxford University Press.

Lipietz, A. 1982. "The So-Called 'Transformation Problem' Revisited," *Journal of Economic Theory* 26: 59–88.

Lippit, V. 1985. "The Concept of the Surplus in Economic Development," *Review of Radical Political Economics* 17: 1–19.

Mage, S. H. 1963. "The Law of the Falling Tendency of the Rate of Profit: Its Place in the Marxian Theoretical System and Relevance to the United States," Ph.D. dissertation, Department of Economics, Columbia University, New York.

Mandel, E. 1975. *Late Capitalism*. London: New Left Books.

1976. "Introduction," in K. Marx, *Capital,* vol. 1, New York: Vintage.

1981. "Introduction," in K. Marx, *Capital,* vol. 2. New York: Vintage.

Marx, K. 1963. *Theories of Surplus-Value,* Part I. Moscow: Progress Publishers.

1967a. *Capital,* vol. 1. New York: International.

1967b. *Capital,* vol. 3. New York: International.

1977. *Capital,* vol. 1 (trans. B. Fowkes). New York: Vintage.

Miller, J. 1989. "Social Wage or Social Profit," *Review of Radical Political Economics* 21: 82–90.

Morishima, M. 1973. *Marx's Economics*. Cambridge: Cambridge University Press.

Moseley, F. B. 1982. "The Rate of Surplus-Value in the United States: 1947–1977," Ph.D. dissertation, University of Massachusetts, Amherst.

1985. "The Rate of Surplus Value in the Postwar U.S. Economy: A Critique of Weisskopf's Estimates," *Cambridge Journal of Economics* 9: 57–79.

Naples, M. 1987. "Cyclical and Secular Productivity Slowdown," in R. Cherry et al., *The Imperiled Economy. Book I: Macroeconomics from a Left Perspective*. New York: Union for Radical Political Economics.

Nordhaus, W., and Tobin, J. 1972. *Economic Growth*. New York: National Bureau of Economic Research.

Ochoa, E. 1984. "Labor Values and Prices of Production: An Interindustry Study of the U.S. Economy, 1947–1972," Ph.D. dissertation, Department of Economics, New School for Social Research, New York.

1988. "Values, Prices and Wage-Profit Curves in the U.S. Economy," *Cambridge Journal of Economics* 13: 413-30.

O'Connor, J. 1975. "Productive and Unproductive Labor," *Politics and Society* 5: 297-336.

Okishio, N. 1959. "Measurement of the Rate of Surplus Value," *Histotsubasbi University Institute of Economic Research* 10: 1-9.

Okishio, N., and Nakatani, T. 1985. "A Measurement of the Rate of Surplus Value in Japan: The 1980 Case," *Kobe University Economic Review* 31: 1-13.

Papadimitriou, D. 1988. "The Structure of the Greek Economy, 1958-1977: An Empirical Analysis of Marxian Economics," Ph.D. dissertation, Department of Economics, New School for Social Research, New York.

Perlo, V. 1974. *The Unstable Economy: Booms and Recessions in the United States since 1945.* New York: International.

Petrovic, P. 1987. "The Deviation of Production Prices from Labor Values: Some Methodology and Empirical Evidence," *Cambridge Journal of Economics* 11: 197-210.

Phillips, J. D. 1966. "Appendix: Estimating the Economic Surplus," in Baran and Sweezy (1966).

Poulantzas, N. 1975. *Classes in Contemporary Capitalism.* London: New Left Books.

Repetto, R., McGrath, W., Wells, M., Beer, C., and Rossini, F. 1989. *Wasting Assets: Natural Resources in National Income Accounts.* Washington, DC: World Resources Institute.

Reynolds, L. G., and Gregory, P. 1965. *Wages, Productivity, and Industrialization in Puerto Rico.* Homewood, IL: Irwin.

Ricardo, D. 1951. *Notes on Malthus,* vol. II of P. Sraffa (ed.), *The Works and Correspondence of David Ricardo.* Cambridge: Cambridge University Press.

Ruggles, N. D. 1982. "Integrated Economic Accounts for the United States, 1947-1980," *Survey of Current Business* 62: 1-53.

1987. "Social Accounting," in J. Eatwell, M. Milgate, and P. Newman (eds)., *The New Palgrave: A Dictionary of Economics.* London: Macmillan.

Sanger, D. E. 1992. "Japan's Premier Joins Critics of Americans' Work Habits," *New York Times* (4 February), pp. A1, A6.

Scott, M. 1990. "Extended Accounts for National Income and Product: A Comment," *Journal of Economic Literature* 28: 1172-86.

Shaikh, A. 1975. "IO Accounts and Marxian Categories," unpublished manuscript, Department of Economics, New School for Social Research, New York.

1978a. "An Introduction to the History of Crisis Theories," in *U.S. Capitalism in Crisis,* Union for Radical Political Economics. New York: Monthly Review Press, pp. 219-41.

1978b. "National Income Accounts and Marxian Categories," unpublished manuscript, Department of Economics, Graduate Faculty, New School for Social Research, New York.

1980a. "On the Laws of International Exchange," in E. J. Nell (ed.), *Growth, Profits, and Property: Essays in the Revival of Political Economy.* New York: Cambridge University Press.

1980b. "Production and Non-Production Labor: Theoretical and Empirical Implications," working paper, Lehrman Institute, New York.

1984. "The Transformation from Marx to Sraffa," in E. Mandel and A. Freeman (eds.), *Ricardo, Marx, Sraffa.* London: Verso.

1986. "Surplus Value," in J. Eatwell, M. Milgate, and P. Newman (eds.), *The New Palgrave: A Dictionary of Economic Theory and Doctrine.* London: Macmillan.

1987. "The Falling Rate of Profit and the Economic Crisis in the U.S.," in R. Cherry et al. (eds.), *The Imperiled Economy,* Book I. New York: Union for Radical Political Economics.

1989. "Accumulation, Finance and Effective Demand in Marx, Keynes, and Kalecki," in W. Semmler (ed.), *Financial Dynamics and Business Cycles: New Perspectives.* Armonk, NY: M. E. Sharpe.

1992a. "A Comment on 'The Value Controversy Reconsidered' by Itoh," in B. Roberts and S. Feiner (eds.), *Radical Economics.* Boston: Kluwer.

1992b. "The Falling Rate of Profit, and Long Waves in Accumulation: Theory and Evidence," in A. Kleinknecht et al. (eds.), *New Findings in Long Wave Research.* London: MacMillan.

Shaikh, A., and Tonak, E. A. 1987. "The Welfare State and Myth of the Social Wage," in R. Cherry et al. (eds.), *The Imperiled Economy,* Book I. New York: Union for Radical Political Economics.

Forthcoming. "The Social Wage in the United States," in A. Shaikh and I. Bakker (eds.), *The Welfare State and the Social Wage: An International Study.*

Sharpe, A. 1982a. "A Survey of Empirical Marxian Economics," unpublished manuscript, Ottawa.

1982b. "The Structure of the Canadian Economy, 1961–76: A Marxian Input–Output Analysis," Ph.D. dissertation, Economics Department, McGill University, Montreal.

Sherman, H. J. 1986. "Changes in the Character of the U.S. Business Cycle," *Review of Radical Political Economics* 18: 190–204.

Simon, N. 1965. "Personal Consumption Expenditures in the 1958 Input–Output Study," *Survey of Current Business* 45: 7–20.

Stanfield, R. A. 1973. *The Economic Surplus and Neo-Marxism.* Lexington, MA: D. C. Heath.

Studenski, P. 1958. *The Income of Nations.* New York University Press.

Summers, L. H., and Summers, V. P. 1989. "When Financial Markets Work too Well: A Cautious Case for a Securities Transactions Tax," *Journal of Financial Services Research* 3: 261–86.

Thurow, L. C. 1980. *The Zero Sum Society.* New York: Basic Books.

1992. *Head to Head: The Coming Economic Battle among Japan, Europe, and America.* New York: Morrow.

Tice, H. S., and Moczar, L. J. 1986. "Foreign Transactions in the National Income and Product Accounts: An Overview," *Survey of Current Business* 66: 1–18.

Tonak, E. Ahmet. 1984. "A Conceptualization of State Revenues and Expenditures: U.S., 1952–1980," Ph.D. dissertation, Department of Economics, New School for Social Research, New York.

1987. "The U.S. Welfare State and the Working Class: 1952–80," *Review of Radical Political Economics* 19: 47–72.

Tsaliki, P., and Tsoulfidis, L. 1988. "Capital Accumulation and the Rate of Profit in Postwar Greek Economy," *Journal of Modern Hellenism* 5: 189–209.

Uchitelle, L. 1989. "A Sharp Rise of Private Guards," *New York Times* 14 October, pp. 33, 37.

United Nations. 1991. *National Accounts Statistics: Main Aggregates and Detailed Tables, 1989,* Part I. New York: United Nations.

U.S. Bureau of the Census. 1975. *Historical Statistics of the United States: Colonial Times to 1970.* Washington, DC: Government Printing Office.

U.S. Bureau of Interindustrial Economics (BIE). 1983. BIE Capital Stock Database (magnetic tape). Washington, DC.

U.S. Department of Commerce, Bureau of Economic Analysis (BEA). 1965. "The Transactions Table of the 1958 Input–Output Study and Revised Direct and Total Requirements Data," *Survey of Current Business* 45: 33–49.

1969. "Input–Output Structure of the U.S. Economy: 1963," *Survey of Current Business* 49: 30–5.

1970. "Input–Output Structure of the U.S. Economy: 1947," mimeo, March.

1971. "Personal Consumption Expenditures in the 1963 Input–Output Study," *Survey of Current Business* 51: 34–8.

1974. "The Input–Output Structure of the U.S. Economy: 1967," *Survey of Current Business* 54: 38–43.

1976. "The National Income and Product Accounts of the U.S., 1929–1974, Statistical Tables," *Survey of Current Business* 56.

1979. "Dollar Value Tables for the 1972 Input–Output Study," *Survey of Current Business* 59: 51–72.

1980. "Definitions and Conventions of the 1972 Input–Output Study," by P. M. Ritz. BEA Staff Paper no. 34. Washington, DC: Government Printing Office.

1981. *The National Income and Product Accounts of the United States, 1929–76: Statistical Tables.* Washington, DC: Government Printing Office.

1984. "The Input–Output Structure of the U.S. Economy, 1977," *Survey of Current Business* 64: 42–84.

1986. *The National Income and Product Accounts for the United States, 1929–1982: Statistical Tables.* Washington, DC: Government Printing Office.

1987. *Fixed Reproducible Tangible Wealth, 1929–85.* Washington, DC: Government Printing Office.

U.S. Department of Housing and Urban Development (HUD). 1979. *Statistical Yearbook.* Washington, DC: Government Printing Office.

U.S. Department of Labor, Bureau of Labor Statistics (BLS). 1979. *Time Series Data for Input–Output Industries: Output, Price, and Employment,* Bulletin 2018. Washington, DC: Government Printing Office.

1980. *Handbook of Labor Statistics,* Bulletin 2070. Washington, DC: Government Printing Office.

1989. *Supplement to Employment, Hours, and Earnings, U.S., 1909–1984.* Washington, DC: Government Printing Office.

1991a. *Employment and Training Report of the President.* Washington, DC: Government Printing Office.

1991b. *Employment and Earnings, United States, 1909–90,* Bulletin 1312-12. Washington, DC: Government Printing Office.

U.S. Internal Revenue Service, *Statistics of Income* (annual).

Van Den Berg, A., and Smith, M. R. 1982. "On 'Class Exploitation' in Canada," *Canadian Review of Sociology and Anthropology* 19: 264–78.

Varga, E. 1928. *The Decline of Capitalism: The Economics of the Decline of Capitalism After Stabilization.* London: Communist Party of Great Britain.

1935. *The Great Crisis and Its Political Consequences, 1928–34.* New York: International (reprinted by Howard Fertig, New York, 1974).

1964. *Politico-Economic Problems of Capitalism.* Moscow: Progress Publishers.

Vance, T. N. 1970. *The Permanent War Economy.* Berkeley: Independent Socialist Press.

Varley, D. 1938. "On the Computation of the Rate of Surplus Value," *Science and Society* 2: 393–6.

Weisskopf, T. 1979. "Marxian Crisis Theory and the Rate of Profit in the Postwar U.S.," *Cambridge Journal of Economics* 3: 341–78.

1984. "An Estimation of Federal Income Taxes Paid by Labor," private correspondence with E. A. Tonak, 13 February.

Wolff, E. N. 1975. "The Rate of Surplus Value in Puerto Rico," *Journal of Political Economy* 83: 935–49.

1977a. "Capitalist Development, Surplus Value and Reproduction: An Empirical Examination of Puerto Rico," in J. Schwartz (ed.), *The Subtle Anatomy of Capitalism.* Santa Monica, CA: Goodyear.

1977b. "Unproductive Labor and the Rate of Surplus Value in the United States, 1947–67," in P. Zarembka (ed.), *Research in Political Economy,* vol. I. Greenwich, CT: JAI Press, pp. 87–115.

1979. "The Rate of Surplus Value, the Organic Composition, and the General Rate of Profit in the U.S. Economy, 1947–67," *American Economic Review* 69: 329–41.

1986. "The Productivity Slowdown and the Fall in the U.S. Rate of Profit, 1947–1976," *Review of Radical Political Economics* 18: 87–109.

1987. *Growth, Accumulation and Unproductive Activity; An Analysis of the Postwar U.S. Economy.* New York: Cambridge University Press.

Wright, E. O. 1978. *Class, Crisis and the State.* London: New Left Books.

Young, A. H., and Tice, H. S. 1985. "An Introduction to National Economic Accounting," *Survey of Current Business* 65: 59–76.

# AUTHOR INDEX

369

# SUBJECT INDEX

ABR (amortization of building and
equipment rentals), *see* rentals, building
and equipment
accumulation: actual rate of, 214–16;
capital, 213–14; long-term patterns of,
184
advertising, 26–7
agriculture enterprises, 176, 177, 181
alienation: *see* profit on alienation
amortization of building and equipment
rentals: *see* rentals, building and
equipment
annual series, 92–108

balance sheets, national, 6, 8
BEA: *see* Bureau of Economic Analysis
benchmark tables: *see* Bureau of Economic
Analysis, input–output tables
benefits, workers', 188
BIE: *see* Bureau of Interindustrial
Economics
BLS: *see* Bureau of Labor Statistics
Britain, 155–6
building and equipment rentals: *see* rentals,
building and equipment
Bureau of Economic Analysis, 9; capital
stock data, 273; capital stock series,
233n; input–output tables, 91–2, 233, 234;
on scrap and second-hand goods
industry, 240
Bureau of Interindustrial Economics, 273
Bureau of Labor Statistics, 108, 206, 295;
on production and nonproduction
workers, 108; on real gross domestic
product, 336; on wages, 112–13, 304, 321
business: payments to government, 60, 62;
profit-type income, 62; profits, 57–8;

rental payments, 146; and royalties,
258–67; taxes, 167, 353; value added, 62;
waste, 204
business sector: consumer stocks and,
13–14; defined in NIPA, 185; government
stocks and, 13–14
businesses, unincorporated, 13

capacity utilization, 122–4; classical
economics and, 213; defined, 190;
warranted path and, 213n; Wharton-type
measure of, 189
capital: accumulation, 213–14; business,
13–14; circuits of, 56, 59; expenditures, 9;
human, 13; intangible, 13; labor and, 30,
31, 152; organic composition of, 189;
research and development as, 14; stock,
13–14, 233n, 273; transfer-in of, 59; value
composition of, 122, 150, 214; *see also*
constant capital; variable capital
capitalism: consumption under, 43, 46;
demand and, 211; growth under, 229–30;
labor under, 29–31, 49, 129, 160–1, 202;
monopoly, 203; noncapitalist activities
and, 211; production under, 184; profit
under, 184; profitability under, 229–30;
surplus value under, 29–31; transactions,
8; unincorporated enterprises and, 186;
user values under, 34; workers' standard
of living under, 216
census data, 170–2, 225
circulation sector, 189
citizen wage: *see* social wage
classical economics, 210, 211; capacity
utilization in, 213; labor in, 33, 229;
production in, 3, 5, 18, 25; profit in,
210–11; surplus value in, 210–11

371